# CHARLES DIXON

## 1872 – 1934

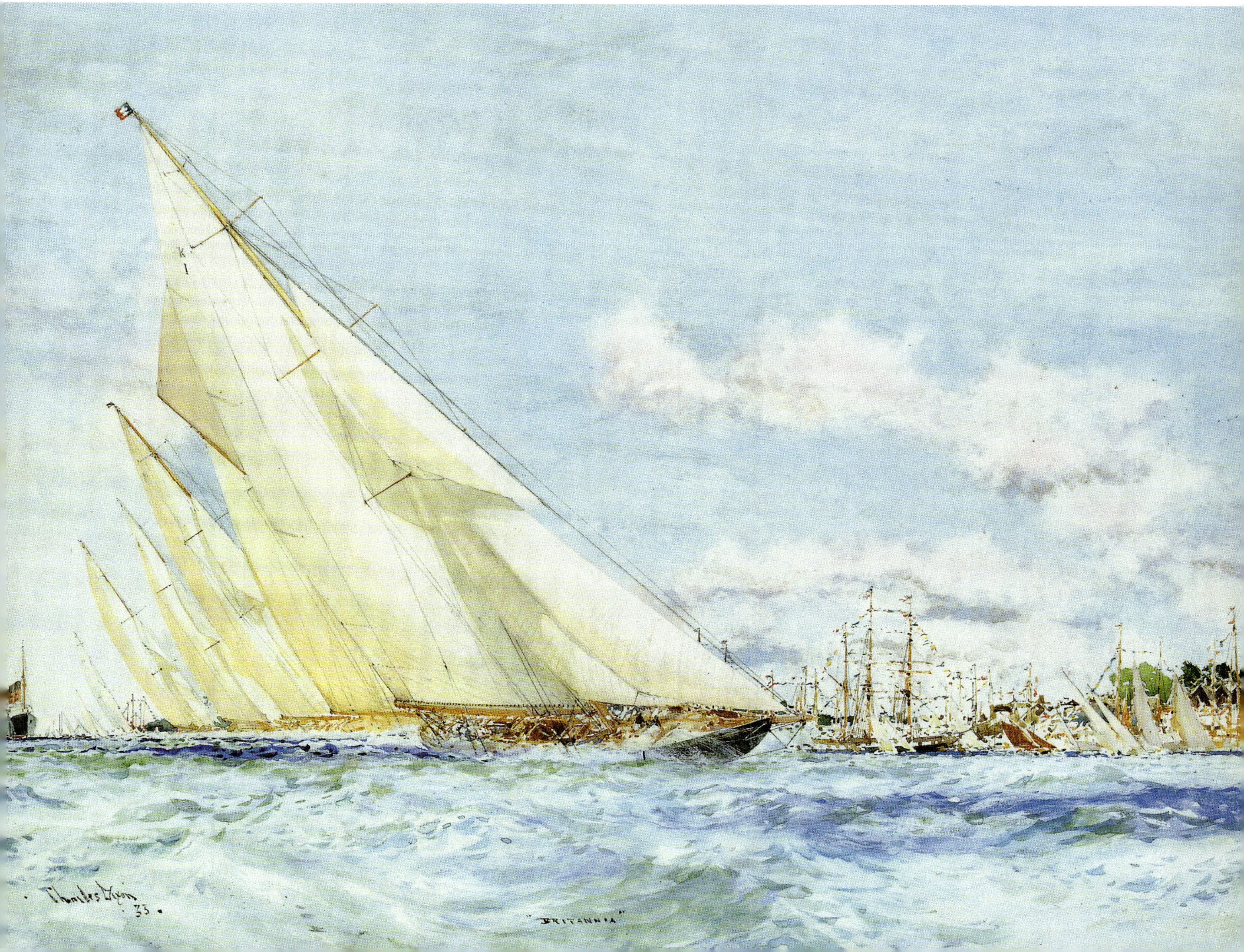

*Previous page:*
*The Royal Yacht* Britannia *Winning at Cowes, 1933*
*Charles Dixon, Watercolour, signed and dated '33 and inscribed* 'Britannia'
N.R. Omell Gallery

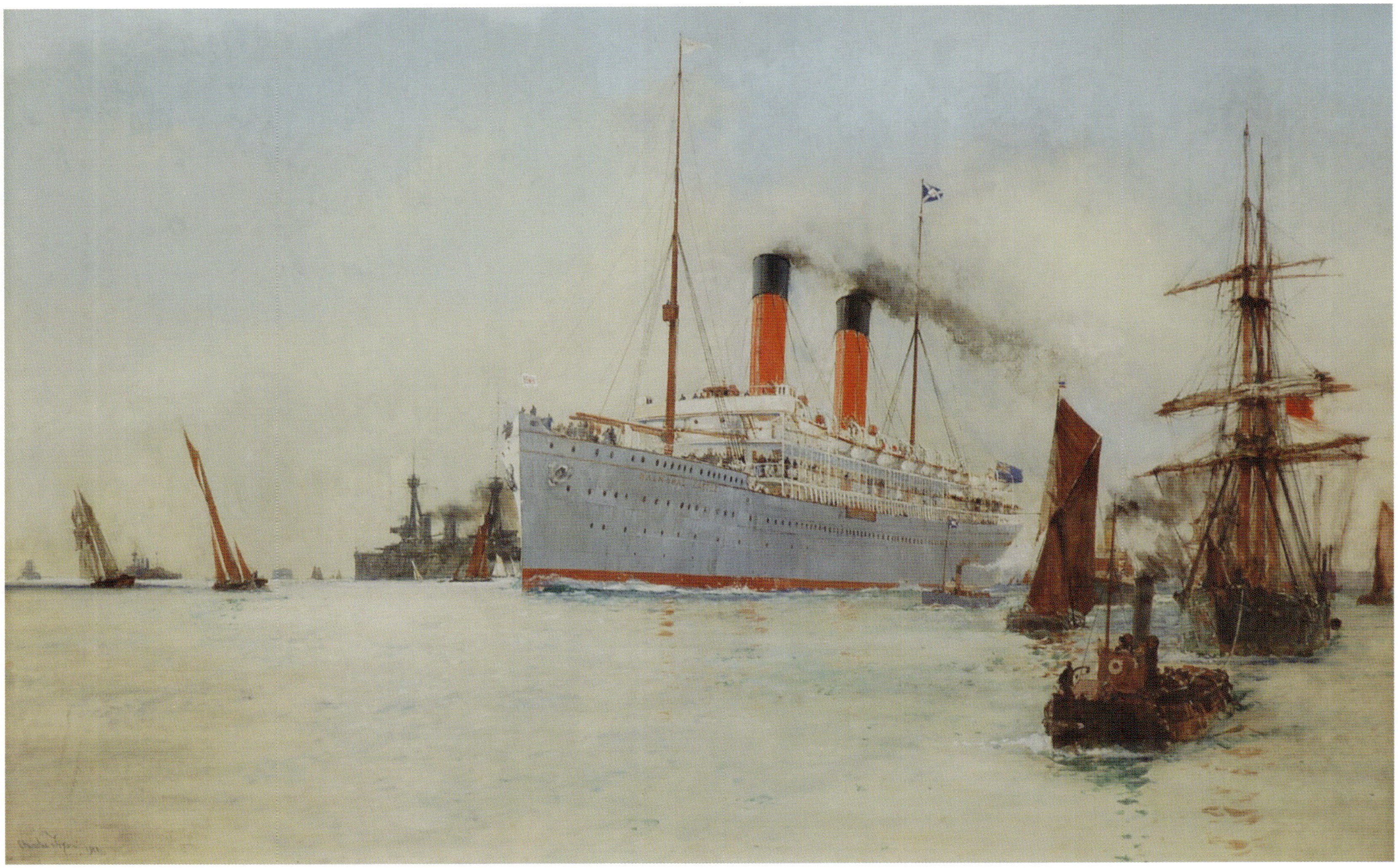

*The Balmoral Castle coming up the Solent*
*Charles Dixon, Watercolour, signed and dated 1910, 27¾x43¼"*
Private Collection

# Charles Dixon

*And the Golden Age of Marine Painting*

STUART BOYD

HALSTAR

*In memory of*
*Vivian Davies*
*(1929 – 2004)*

First published in Great Britain in 2009



British Library Cataloguing-in-Publication Data
A CIP record for this title is available from the British Library

ISBN 978 1 906690 15 1

**HALSTAR**
Halsgrove House,
Ryelands Industrial Estate,
Bagley Road, Wellington, Somerset TA21 9PZ
Tel: 01823 653777 Fax: 01823 216796
email: sales@halsgrove.com

An imprint of Halstar Ltd, part of the Halsgrove group of companies
Information on all Halsgrove titles is available at: www.halsgrove.com

Printed and bound in India on behalf of JFDi Print Services Ltd

# *Contents*

# Acknowledgements

In writing this biography I have been extremely fortunate to receive help from many quarters but first wish to acknowledge the interest and encouragement from members of Charles Dixon's family, especially his granddaughter, Elizabeth Dixon and great nephew, Phillip Dixon, who I suspect may have, from time to time, given up any prospect of seeing it come to fruition.

The enjoyment of a book on marine art will undoubtedly depend largely on the quality and diversity of the illustrations selected. These have come from many sources but I am particularly indebted to the N R Omell and Royal Exchange Art Galleries, London, for their generous permission to use images taken from catalogues of their annual exhibitions of marine paintings over many years.

I would also like to record my deep appreciation for the assistance received from the following galleries, auction house, collectors of Dixon's work and others who have kindly given their time and provided material in various forms: Polly Adam, Lucien Arkas, Katy Ball (Portsmouth AG), Baron Fine Art, Martin Barraclough, Chris Beetles Ltd, Bourne Gallery, Richard Cosby (Maritime Prints and Originals), Susie Cox (P&O), Robert Crewdson, Christopher Deakes, Dr & Mrs D. Dixon, Laura Edmundson (Sotheby's), John Francis, Kevin Fuller, Haynes Fine Art, Charlotte Henwood (MOD Art Collection), David Humphreys, Robert Hunter, David Hutchings, Alistair Laird (Bonhams), John Morton Lee, Lincoln Joyce Fine Art, Philip Mitchell, Richard Martin Gallery, Michael Naxton, Guy Powell, James Taylor, Bill Wallace, Philip Whittall, Tom Williams.

Finally I would like to express my thanks to Geoff Hunt for writing the Foreword, sincere thanks to Simon Butler, the Publisher for his unstinting patience; his staff at Halsgrove for putting it all together, and my wife, Lesley, for her endless help and support throughout.

# *Foreword*

Those of us who paint shipping subjects in this later, meaner age, must suppress a pang of envy when contemplating the maritime world inhabited by Charles Dixon and his friends, a world so rich both in subject matter and material rewards.

The period spanning Queen Victoria's Golden Jubilee in 1887 to the outbreak of war in 1939 contained some of the greatest glories of Britain's seagoing heritage. The Royal Navy was at its biggest and most powerful; British shipbuilding and shipping companies seemed to provide and man much of the world's merchant shipping; and it was also the age of the great transatlantic ocean liners, culminating in 30-knot giants such as the *Queen Mary*. Under sail, the ubiquitous Thames barges still hauled cargoes alongside the last great square-rigged windjammers, while the rich took their sailing pleasures aboard yachts such as the J class, unprecedented for their speed, size and beauty. And it was the age in which the enthusiasm for maritime heritage led to the preservation of both HMS *Victory* and the *Cutty Sark*. All this attracted the attention of artists working in their different fields. Conrad and Forester wrote novels and Masefield wrote poetry about seafaring, and Elgar set it to music. And naturally there were marine painters, a minor galaxy of them, led by bright stars such as W L Wyllie, Norman Wilkinson, Charles Pears and Charles Dixon himself. These painters had an immense range of subjects to choose from, they were well supported by the patronage of shipping companies and they responded with a remarkable flowering of British marine art.

Somewhere late in this period, in 1939, the Society of Marine Artists was founded (with exactly unfortunate timing, it set its inaugural exhibition for September of that year; it would be seven years before that exhibition could take place). Of course, it was born out of the plenty of Britain's shipping wealth and grandeur, yet with great foresight the Society's founding fathers laid down that it should concern itself not just with ships and shipping, but with all matters marine and maritime, thus giving their successors the freedom to rejoice in whatever aspect of mankind's relationship with the ocean they wished; in a phrase, to celebrate the sea. Dixon did not live to see the creation of this Society, but as one of the leading marine painters of his day, a man clearly wholly engaged with his art in all its aspects, he would no doubt have been a founding member and one of its principal figures. He and his contemporaries have left us with the great strength of their art, a new chapter in the long heritage of British marine painting, and the foundation of the Royal Society of Marine Artists. Stuart Boyd has done us a great service by bringing their world to life with this excellent account not only of Dixon himself, but very many of his fellow artists. It deserves a place on the bookshelf of anyone who is seriously interested in British marine painting.

***Geoff Hunt***
***Past President***
***The Royal Society of Marine Artists***

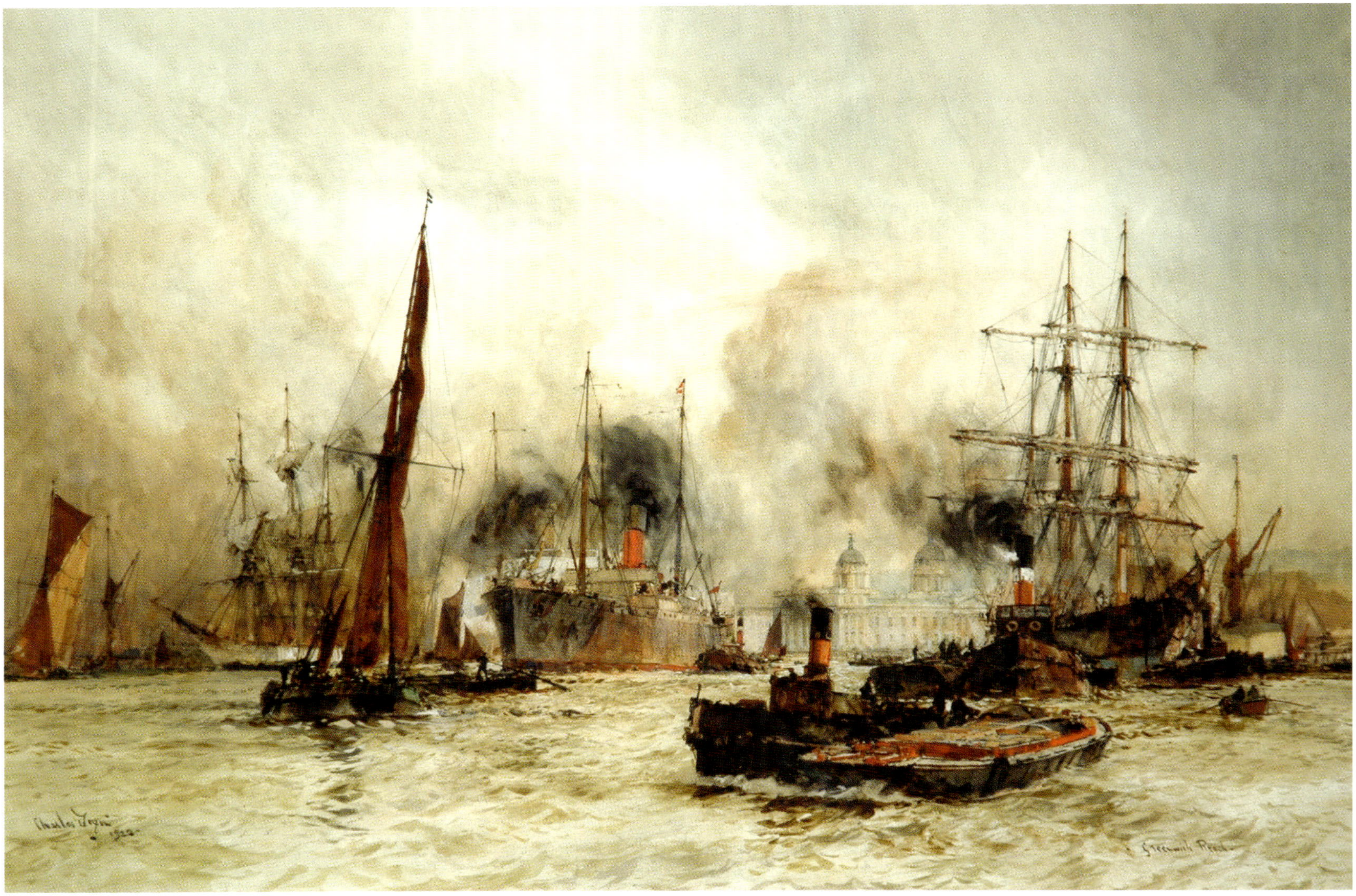

*The Thames Above Greenwich*
*Charles Dixon, Watercolour, Signed*
LINCOLN JOYCE FINE ART

# Introduction

It is well known that Britain's growth to power and influence has been largely shaped by the momentous part that the sea has played in the life and history of this country, and that the peoples of the British Isles have for centuries been dependent upon their maritime capabilities goes without saying. To our forbears the sea was a dominant principle and the British have every reason to be thankful to their ancestors for their courage and sense of adventure. Trade, Empire and prosperity followed in the wake of seamen who set out into the unknown, the formidable strength of our fleets at the heart of much British success in the sphere of commerce, war and diplomacy. Given the extent therefore to which the events of our illustrious maritime past have had such an important influence on our national destiny, it seems axiomatic that for over five centuries there has been a specialist vein of nautical paintings, drawings and engraving running through British art that has been concerned with recording Britain's maritime heritage with its infinite range of subjects for the artist's attention. This was summed up by A L Baldry, in his book *British Marine Painting*, published in 1919, when he wrote "no record of British scenery would be complete, and no appeal to British sentiment would be effective, if our artists ignored the wide variety of subjects the sea offers them, for the sea is with us a tradition, and the love of the sea is one of the strongest of our national interests".

By way of highlighting the work of some of the many artists whose contribution to the genre has greatly enriched British marine painting over the centuries, a number of monographs and specialist studies have been written concerning some of Britain's finest marine painters, notably Charles Brooking (1723-1759), Nicholas Pocock (1740-1821), George Chambers (1803-1840), John Wilson Carmichael (1800-1868), Edward William Cooke (1811-1880) and, of course, towering above them all J M W Turner (1775-1851), the greatest English painter of the sea – all of whom consolidated the British tradition of marine painting in the first half of the nineteenth century. They were followed by later exponents such as Charles Napier Hemy (1841-1917), renowned for his brilliant oils of coastal and fishing scenes, W L Wyllie (1851-1931), Jack Spurling (1871-1933), Charles Pears (1873-1953), Arthur Briscoe (1873-1943), whose work provides such telling images of the human element at work 'before the mast', Norman Wilkinson (1878-1971) and Montague Dawson (1895-1943); marine artists whose paintings have been used as important pictorial adjuncts to our maritime history by recording the story of commercial sail in the final magnificent stage of its evolution, and the progress of steam which finally supplanted it.

The twilight of the Victorian era and the gradual transition from sail to steam propulsion provided these specialist marine painters with a unique opportunity to capture on canvas and paper a romantic epoch in British maritime history, when England's position as a great Naval and mercantile power had reached its pinnacle. One artist who was to seize this opportunity to the full was Charles Edward Dixon RI, (1872-1934), now recognised as one of Britain's most gifted marine painters of the late nineteenth and early twentieth centuries. During his lifetime Dixon painted a vast array of maritime subjects, including dramatic First World War naval battles, fleet reviews, historic reconstructions of scenes dating back to the fifteenth century, regattas, the great clipper ships, lifeboat manoeuvres in stormy seas, America's Cup yacht races, graceful liners, and as a skilled illustrator pictorial reports of events current to the age in which he lived, such as Queen Victoria's funeral; yet his greatest contribution has been the colourful and atmospheric record of shipping on the Thames. At the beginning of the twentieth century, dockland London was the largest port in the world and virtually choked with traffic from around the globe when topsail schooners and Thames sailing barges mingled with steam tugs and dirty British coasters. His output was extensive and remarkable for its mastery of watercolour and it is now extremely rare for a sale of marine paintings held at any of the leading London auction houses to take place without the artist's work represented, his nostalgic views of the London river in strong demand by collectors as they vie with each other to capture a glimpse of an era, now sadly gone forever.

In his book *Nineteenth Century British Marine Painting*, Denys Brooke Hart is fulsome in his praise of Dixon's art, describing him as a 'standard bearer of British marine painting'. Notwithstanding this eulogy, after his death in 1934, Dixon's work had become overlooked and it was not until almost 40 years later when two exhibitions of his paintings were held in London in 1973, one at the National Maritime Museum, Greenwich and another at the Hampton Hill Gallery, that a revival of interest occurred, thereby helping to re-establish his status. Throughout his lifetime Dixon exhibited 52 pictures at the Royal Academy, remarkably the first when he was aged 16, and 170 at the Royal Institute of Painters in Watercolours, and examples of his work may be found in the Royal Collection, in National and many provincial municipal galleries in the United Kingdom and also in public collections in North America, Australia, New Zealand and Canada. However, despite such a rich legacy, very little biographical information has been available to shed light on the artist's life and this book is an attempt to redress the balance by bringing him into greater prominence and enabling those with an interest in this specialist genre to become better acquainted with the range and versatility of his art which, stylistically, comes at the end of the Romantic tradition of British Marine Painting. Moreover, this is not solely a monograph on Charles Dixon, but includes cameos of a number of contemporaries, some lesser known, but whose lives, like his, were inextricably bound to the sea and ships and to whose pictures collectors respond so spontaneously.

# CHAPTER ONE
# Early Promise

Charles Dixon was born on 8 December 1872 in the Thameside village of Streatley, in the Royal County of Berkshire, although his birthplace is recorded incorrectly in reference books as Goring, its Oxfordshire neighbour on the opposite bank of the river. Given its proximity to the upper Thames, it seems entirely fitting that Charles' birthplace should provide him with such an auspicious start, for this was the river that imbued him with such immense inspiration throughout his life as a painter. Born into an artistic family, Charles was the third eldest of four sons of the history and genre painter, Alfred Dixon (1842-1919) and his wife, Mary Jane. Judging by Alfred Dixon's various exhibition addresses, it seems that he and his family had lived a somewhat transient existence before taking up residence in Streatley, a move probably initiated by Alfred since its rural beauty, along with that of other Thameside towns such as Goring and Sonning, had long attracted many renowned painters of the nineteenth century, including Miles Birkett Foster (1825-1899), noted for his classical evocations of the English countryside.

An entry in the electoral register for 1873 records Alfred Dixon living at Coombe Cottage, Streatley, yet it is not known how long the family had lived in the Thames Valley before moving to London. Such an itinerant lifestyle on the part of Alfred Dixon was no doubt something of an occupational necessity with exhibition and studio addresses as far afield as Llandovery and Sunderland, but it may also account for the paucity of information about Charles' early life, where he went to school and whether he received any formal art education. However, what is certain is that although born in the shires, the young Charles Dixon grew up in the heart of London for, after Streatley and by 1881, the family were living in premises in Abbey Road, Fulham in the Borough of Chelsea, where Charles, or Charlie as he was known, produced small sketchbooks in which he illustrated his real and also imagined stories with small, incisive and charming pen and ink drawings. Executed with remarkable flair, these quite sophisticated efforts for a nine year old, with their excellent tonal quality, gave notice of the extent to which from childhood he had developed a fine taste for drawing, an ability, no doubt, nurtured by his father, who was probably his primary source of instruction and is said to have advised his son 'to work from nature'. The sketchbooks, which are dated 1881, are now preserved in the National Maritime Museum, Greenwich and reveal not only early evidence of Charles' artistic endowment, but also provide a glimmer of insight into the domestic, social and artistic life of a Victorian middle class family. This is achieved by the quite beguiling little tales which accompany the sketches and point to a happy childhood and lively sense of fun on the part of the young Dixon. Like many professional artists of the day (as indeed now) Alfred Dixon's financial fortunes were prone to fluctuate and this somewhat parlous existence is well depicted in 'Worries and Troubles of an Artist' – one of a number of highly perceptive and comically poignant drawings by Charles, showing his father's effort to make ends meet. In another he captures the sheer joy on hearing that Alfred's painting 'A Stowaway' had been sold and payment of £250 received!

Alfred Dixon, or 'AD' as he was known, was born in Middlesex in 1842 and is recorded as a London painter of domestic and other figure subjects. A traditional historical painter, he also painted flowers. Oil

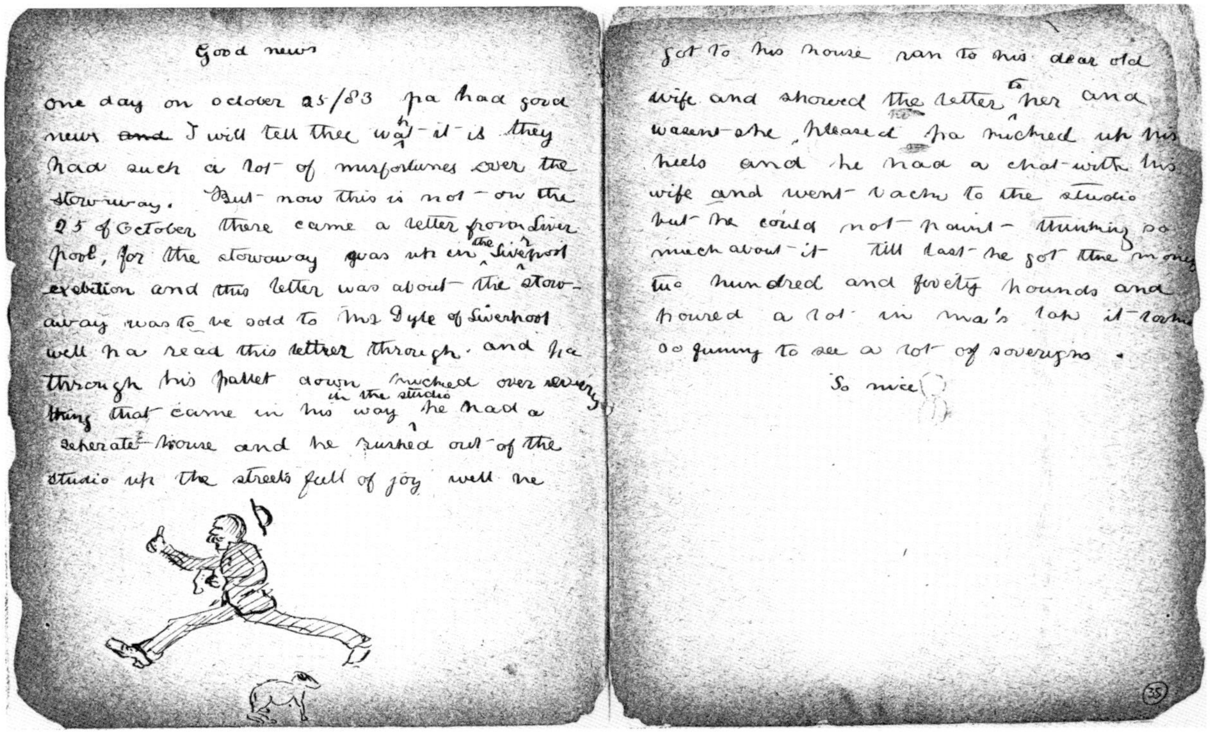

Good news

one day on october 25/83 pa had good news ~~and~~ I will tell thee what it is they had such a lot of misfortunes over the stowaway. But now this is not - on the 25 of October there came a letter from Liverpool, for the stowaway was up in the Liverpool exebition and this letter was about the stowaway was to be sold to Mr Dyle of Liverpool well pa read this letter through. and pa through his pallet down knocked over every thing that came in his way in the studio he had a seperate house and he rushed out of the studio up the streets full of joy well he got to his house ran to his dear old wife and showed the letter to her and wasent she pleased pa kicked up his heels and he had a chat with his wife and went back to the studio but he could not paint - thinking so much about it till last he got the money two hundred and forty pounds and poured a lot in ma's lap it looked so funny to see a lot of soverigns.

So nice

*Worries and troubles of an artist*
*Charles Dixon, Pen & Ink illustration from notebook c.1881*
National Maritime Museum

seems to have been his preferred medium. His work would have appealed to the Victorians' taste for rather sorrowful themes, with a number of his titles having a social realist flavour such as 'Forsaken', a scene in a women's workhouse which is in the collection of Sunderland Art Gallery, and the moribund 'Bereaved' – Seaham Colliery, 1880, showing women waiting at the pithead after an accident. Another oil painting by Alfred in the Sunderland Art Gallery collection is a portrait of Thomas Dixon, apparently a notable figure and benefactor in Sunderland in the late nineteenth century and this, coupled with references to Sunderland in Charles' sketchbooks, suggest that there were family connections in the North East and that they may have spent time accompanying Alfred on painting trips there. Between 1870 and 1891, Alfred Dixon exhibited 18 pictures at the Royal Academy and at the Royal Institute of Painters in Oils. He also exhibited with the Royal Society of British Artists, at the Suffolk Street Gallery and at a number of provincial venues, including Liverpool, Sunderland, Newcastle and Manchester and it was at the Walker Gallery, Liverpool that he exhibited 'A Stowaway' in which Charles, aged about ten or eleven, was used as the subject. Clearly the picture tells its own story and was painted by Alfred with his usual veracity. Unfortunately, the oil painting, which was formerly in the collection of the Walker Gallery and purchased directly from Alfred Dixon by the museum in 1883, was destroyed during the Liverpool blitz of 1941.

Bordeaux
*Charles Dixon, Pen & Ink illustration from notebook c.1881*
National Maritime Museum

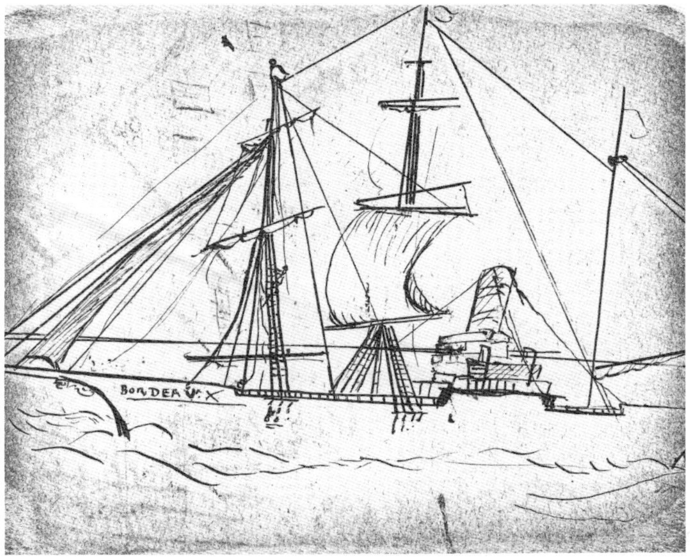


By all accounts Alfred Dixon was a strong and quite dominant character who took a keen parental interest in his son's grounding as an artist, a development that was to flourish and bring early success. This occurred in 1889, when, at the age of 16, Charles had two watercolours 'Off Custom House Quay' and 'The Thames from Cherry Garden Pier' hung at the Royal Academy, their titles reflecting what

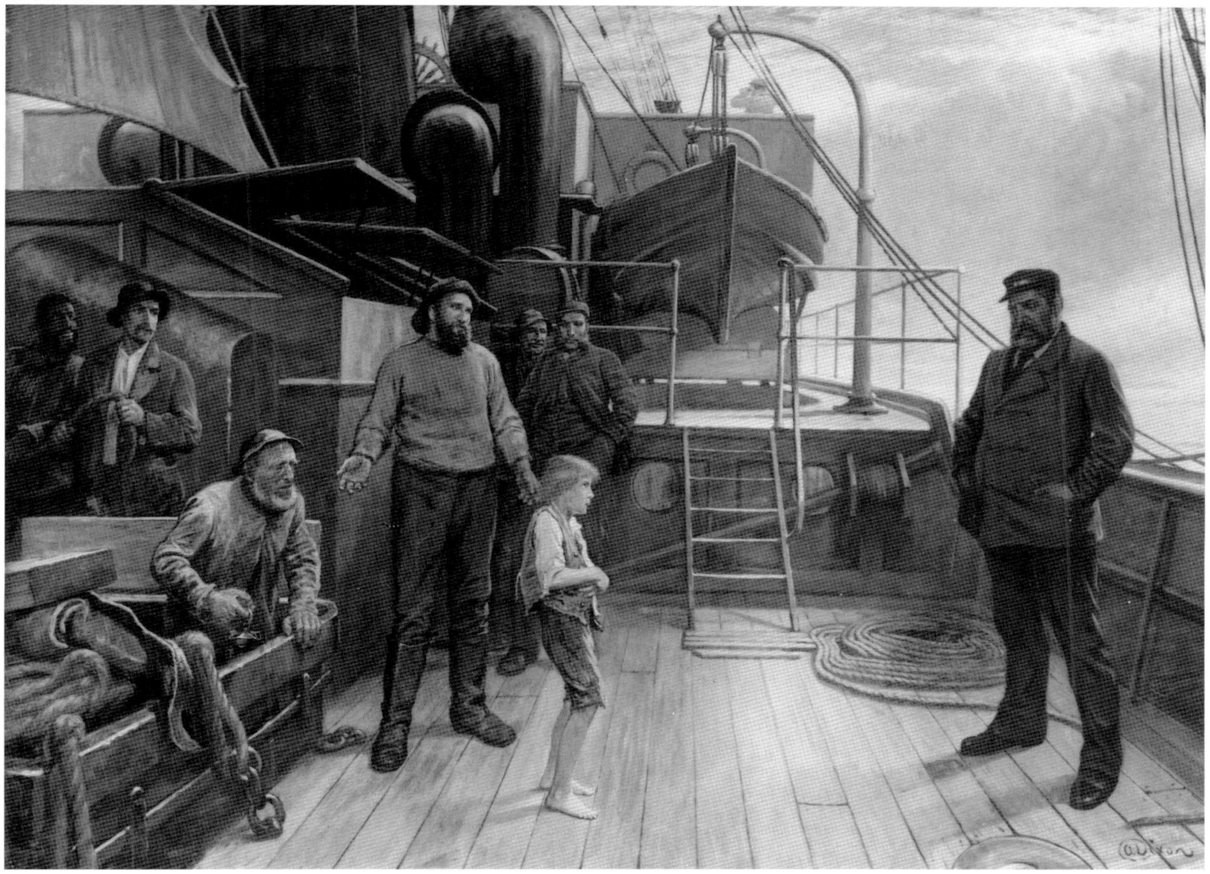

*The Stowaway*
*Alfred Dixon, Oil on canvas*
WALKER ART GALLERY, LIVERPOOL

was to become his enduring predilection with the London river so that, by the end of his life, his name had become permanently associated with it. Such a prodigious achievement was remarkable and unsurpassed even by eminent practitioners such as William Lionel Wyllie, now widely regarded as one of the greatest marine painters bridging the nineteenth and twentieth centuries who, like Dixon, had long recognised the magical fascination of the Thames below Tower Bridge, and for whom the great river had become a major preoccupation.

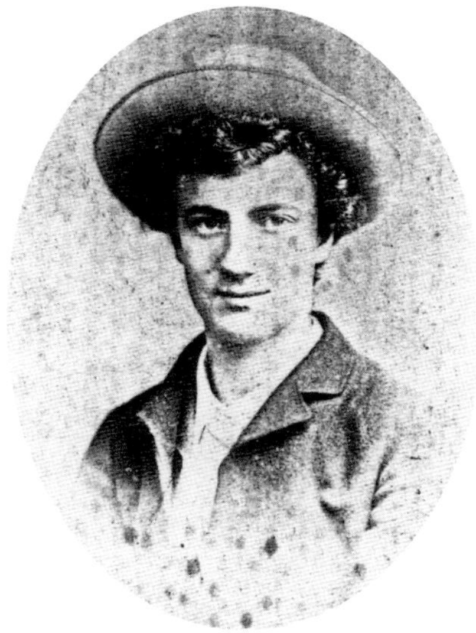

*Photo of Charles Dixon*
*c.1890*

By coincidence, the occasion in 1889 when Charles exhibited his first pictures at the Royal Academy was the year that Alfred's large oil 'In the Camp of the Enemy', a scene during the American Civil War, had also been accepted, an achievement no doubt eclipsed by the precocious success of his teenage son. During his lifetime Charles Dixon's love of all things maritime remained undiminished, for all but two of his 52 exhibits at the Royal Academy were marine subjects. Yet, unlike many specialist artists whose skill as professional marine painters had been honed from practical experience at sea or as a shipwright in the dockyard, he came from an artistic rather than a nautical background, although his obituary makes reference to him "having at times made trips on tramp steamers". It is interesting therefore to speculate as to the factors that may have evoked such a strong passion for matters nautical. Was it due to living so close to the busy, thriving and active river Thames after the family moved to London which gave him the opportunity to observe the ships and river craft on the then busiest waterway in the world, or perhaps that, combined with the influence of W L Wyllie? Certainly they would have met around the time when Dixon made his mark at the Royal Academy in 1889 for his studio address that year is listed

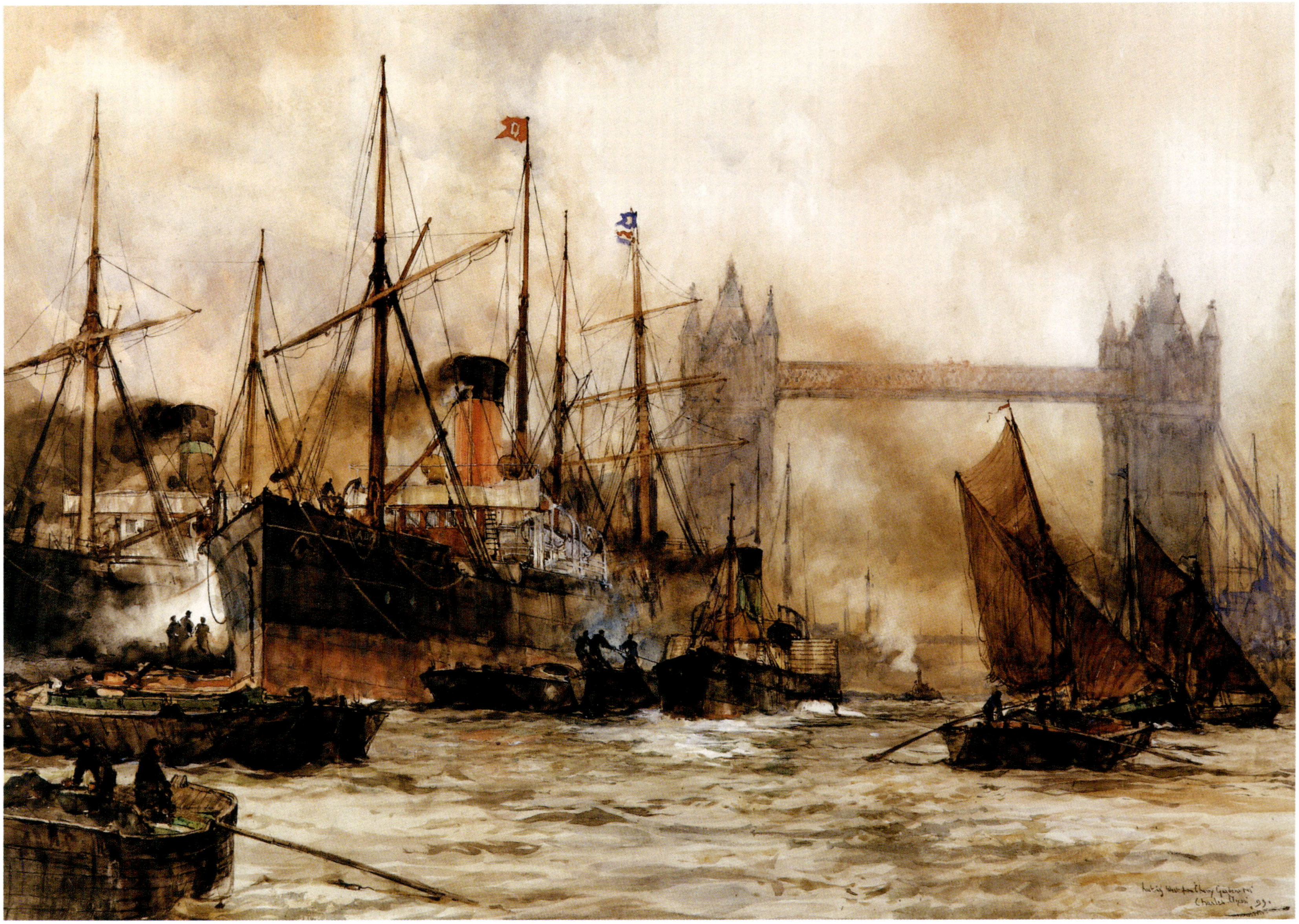

*The Pool of London – Looking West from Cherry Garden Pier*
*Charles Dixon, Watercolour, Signed*
BOURNE GALLERY

as 3 St John's Wood Studio, the same given for Wyllie and apparently the only one he ever rented in London. St John's Wood was at that time a fashionable artists' colony.

In piecing together Dixon's early career, it seems unlikely that the remarkable adolescent talent which had found its way through the portals of the Royal Academy would not have come to the attention of prospective employers keen to harness the skills of the young tyro and the years up to the end of the nineteenth century saw his career develop and flourish. This was particularly evident around 1900 when marine painting, as practised by Dixon, W L Wyllie and their followers, inclined increasingly towards illustration, a tendency confirmed by the requirements of the Great War. It seems, therefore, Dixon, along with many of his contemporaries in the field of marine art who wished to turn their hand to illustration, was working simultaneously for many of the various weekly papers of the day, such as *The Graphic*, *The Sphere* and *The Illustrated London News*. The latter was founded in 1842 and became the first journal to present news and pictures together as a regular policy. Costing sixpence, it was first published on 14 May 1842 and appeared every Saturday. Its 16 pages included pictures of the war in Afghanistan, a train crash in France, a steam boat explosion in Canada, and a fancy dress ball at Buckingham Palace. Thus topical news of a pictorial nature became its forte, its staff of artists roaming the world looking for exciting material and in turn sending back a stream of sketches of battles, natural wonders and catastrophes. *The Illustrated London News* was unchallenged in England until 1869 which saw the arrival of *The Graphic*, a new illustrated weekly and in 1900 *The Sphere*. The work of an illustrator engaged by these publications required a sharp eye for detail, a decisive sense of dramatic composition and, above all, a sense of occasion, and it seems that on all counts Dixon fully met the criteria. Unfortunately the offices of the *ILN* were bombed during the Second World War, when all staff records and editorial notes were destroyed and, although impossible to pinpoint Dixon's employment dates with that magazine.

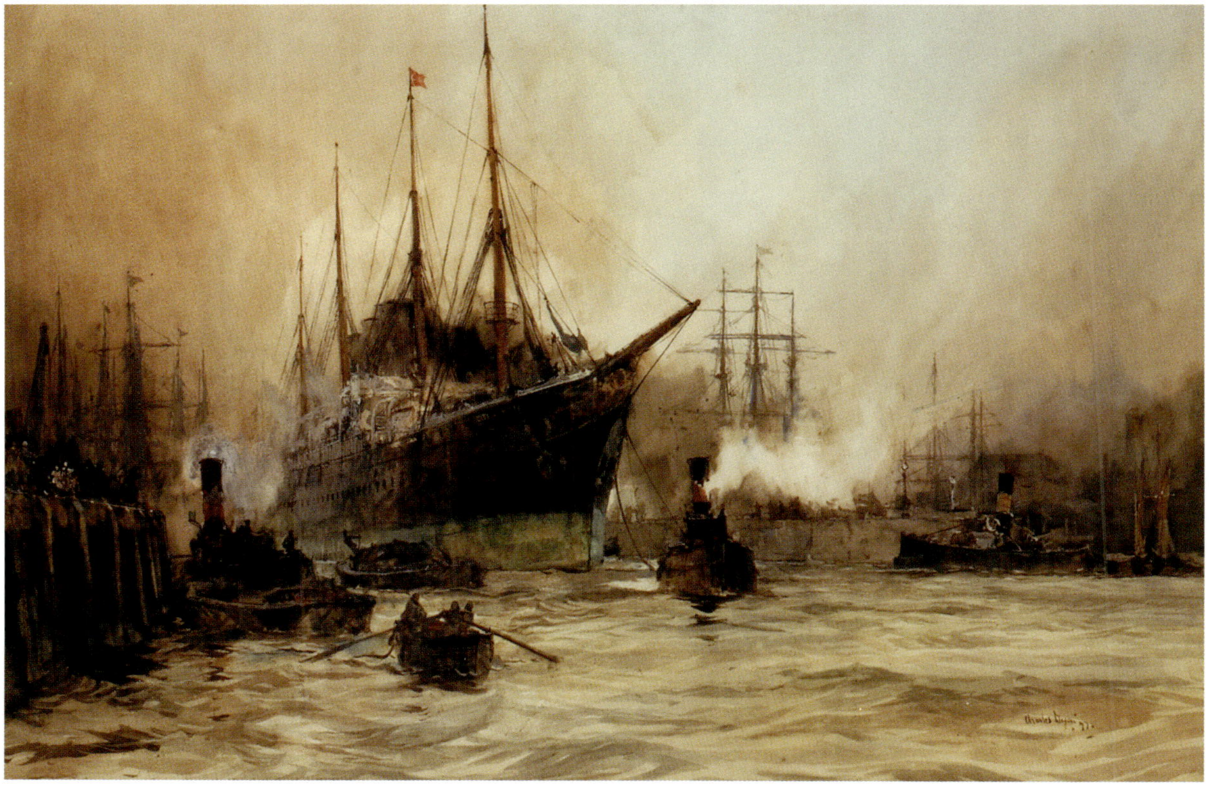

*The Anchor Line Steamship*
City of Rome *Slipping her Moorings*
*Charles Dixon, Watercolour, 18x30",*
*Signed and dated '97*
HAYNES FINE ART

He drew for *The Graphic,* for whom he did the bulk of his illustrative work, from at least 1899 and was a prolific contributor, his vigorous style responding well to the public's demand for dramatic factual images of events happening at home and around the world, such as the death of Queen Victoria, the Anglo Boer Wars, developments in the Naval arms race between the major powers before the First World War and the war itself.

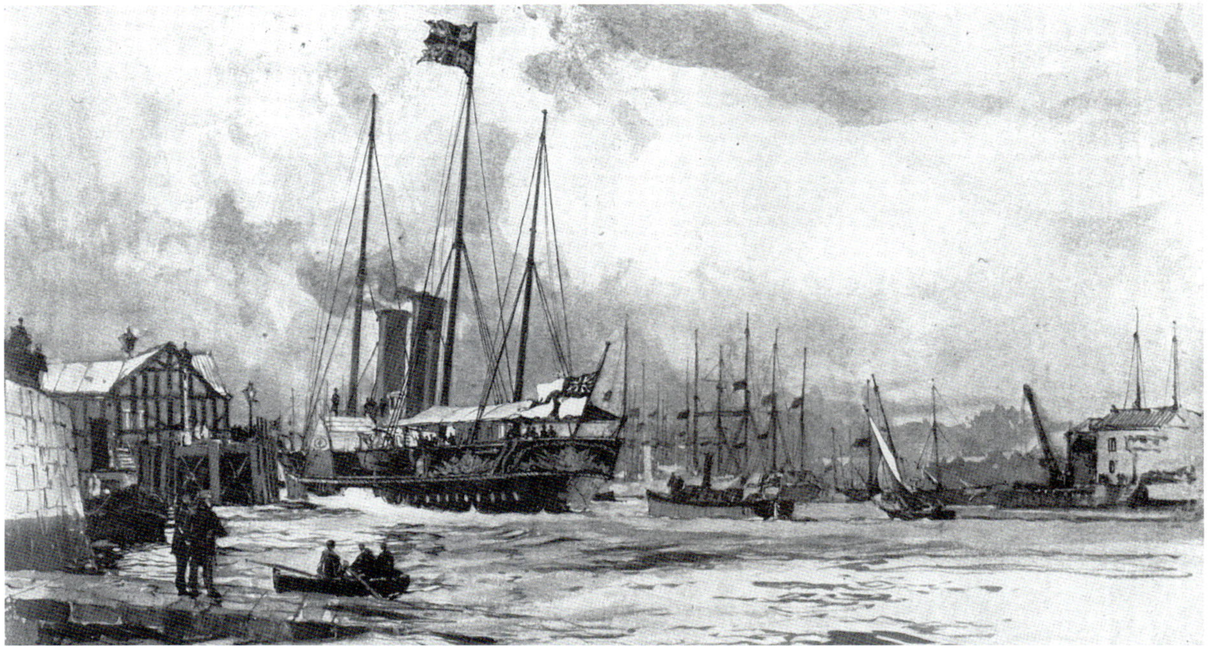

*The Arrrival of the Crown Prince of Prussia at Cowes (probably for the funeral of Queen Victoria)*
*Charles Dixon, Illustration for* The Graphic, *2 February, 1901*

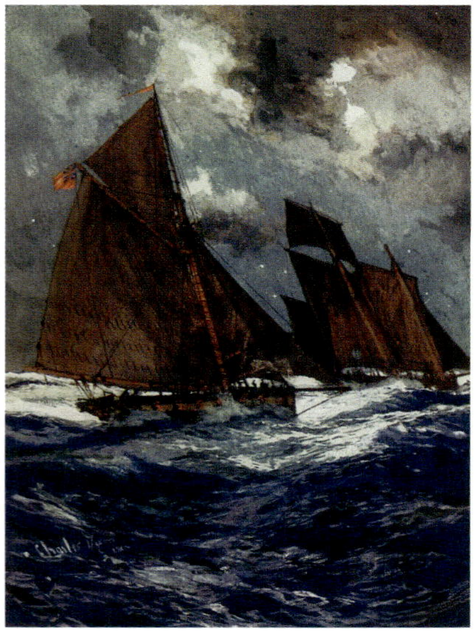

*Revenue Cruiser Chasing Smuggling Lugger*
*Charles Dixon, Illustration for* Kings Cutters and Smugglers 1700–1855, *by E Keeble Chatterton*

This, of course, was long before the days of highly sophisticated photo-journalism as we now know it and editors then relied on freelance illustrators, like Dixon, to record visual scenes of the conflict and other important episodes occurring throughout the Empire with their imaginative and spontaneous compositions. Colour was not used in magazines at that time, which meant that the illustrations (more commonly referred to as wash drawings) were produced in monochrome, using either a black-and-white or a brown-and-white base, so the artist had to rely completely on tone to convey the drama and excitement of an event, a wonderful discipline to which Dixon was well suited. This can be seen in a centrefold he did for *The Graphic* on 1 July 1911. As an illustrator Dixon brought to bear all his best skill as a draughtsman and many of his illustrations for *The Graphic* provided important documentary records of significant maritime events and rank amongst some of the best of his art. Apart from providing material for these prestigious magazines, he also worked for several prominent nautical publications of the day producing cover illustrations for magazines such as *Yachting Monthly*, launched in 1906. A deep interest in history meant that he also loved to paint historical sea pieces of bygone days, some of which provided the colour plates in books by F Keble Chatterton such as *Kings Cutters and Smugglers* and *The Fore and Aft Rig*. Others include *The Sea – Its History and Romance* by Frank C Bowen, which was written in four volumes and traces the history of the sea and ships through the ages, particularly the part played by the Anglo Saxons. This abiding fascination with Britain's maritime past is also reflected in the titles of many of his paintings exhibited at the RI and RA, such as 'Oak, Hemp and Powder: Trafalgar 1905' and the last picture he exhibited at the Academy. In reconstructing these famous historical events, Dixon would have relied to a large extent on his collection of ship models, an invaluable prop and source of

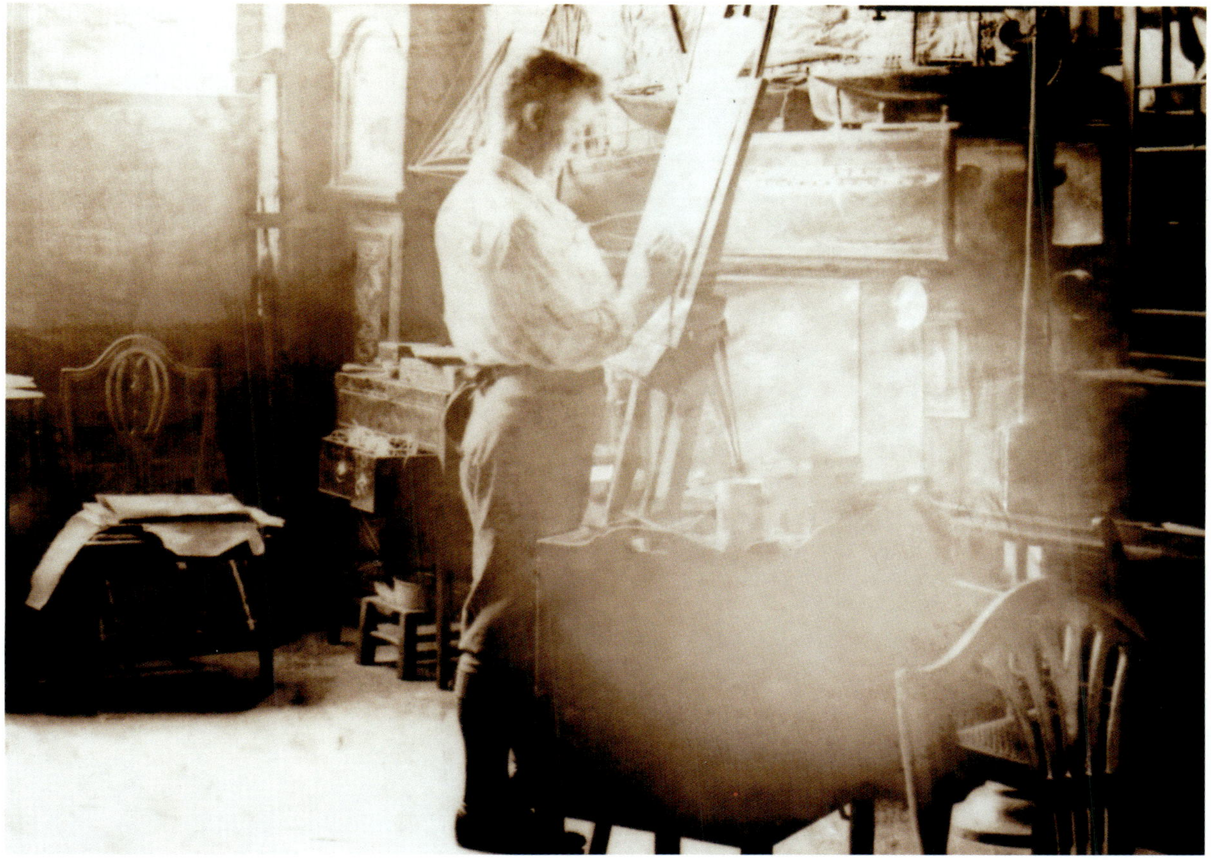

*Photograph of Charles Dixon at his easel*

reference for the marine artists striving for accuracy in depicting a piece of machinery as complicated as a fully-rigged ship.

Although Dixon's historical pieces are beautifully composed and show great authority, it was, however, the contemporary scene and commercial work in the field of advertising that enabled him to express his talent to the full. As the nineteenth century turned into the twentieth century, the passenger steam ship had become established as the leading form of transport and, by 1900, across the north Atlantic alone over 30 shipping companies were running regular passenger services, linking the Old World with the New. During what became a rapidly developing period of intercontinental travel, when ocean liners became the aristocrats of the maritime world, firms such as White Star, Cunard, Canadian Pacific, Holland America and P&O were looking to marine artists such as Dixon to promote their businesses by commissioning them to produce artwork in the form of large arresting colourful posters, a far cry from the sophisticated media advertising of today. The advent of colour lithography, a process resulting in vibrant colours, and its increasing use from the 1870s, revolutionised advertising design. Before that posters were mainly typographical in form. Now it was possible to have text and images wholly integrated and, by the end of the nineteenth century, the quantity of advertising material on display to promote holidays and travel was enormous. Fierce competition was the keynote behind the greatly increased provision for passenger traffic, and economic survival dictated that the facilities be fully utilised. This meant capturing and manipulating public imagination on a large scale in an attempt to create an outlet to justify excessive supply. As far as the sea-going passenger was concerned, posters

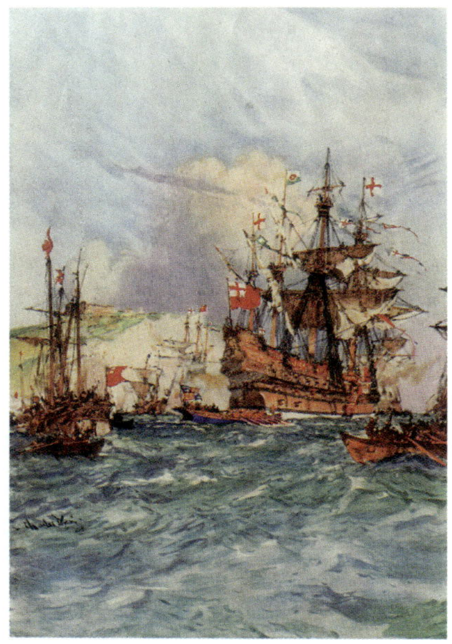

*The* Great Harry, *1520*
*Charles Dixon, Illustration for*
The Sea- Its History and Romance, *by F. Bowen*

were designed to be targeted at the increasing number of wealthy individuals who might be tempted to take advantage of the expensive opulence provided by the transatlantic liners and of course generated further scope for the marine artist. As a consequence, there emerged a somewhat specialised school of poster painters which included artists of the calibre of Dixon, Norman Wilkinson, Charles Pears and the superb Odin Rosenvinge (1880-1959), an outstanding draughtsman who also worked for many leading shipping lines, and a great admirer of Dixon. Although W L Wyllie's vast repertoire also included poster and postcard work, his output in both artforms was nowhere near as prolific as Dixon, Pears and Rosenvinge, yet in 1835 he did produce the first shipping poster in Britain designed by a recognised artist. Painted for P&O, it showed one of their vessels off the Eddystone.

Poster painting also became the domain of many other established marine artists such as Charles Turner (1883-1965), who produced work for Cunard, Arthur Burgess (1879-1957) for Orient, and Maurice Randall (1865-1950) who had sailed briefly as an Officer with the Union Castle Line and for whom he

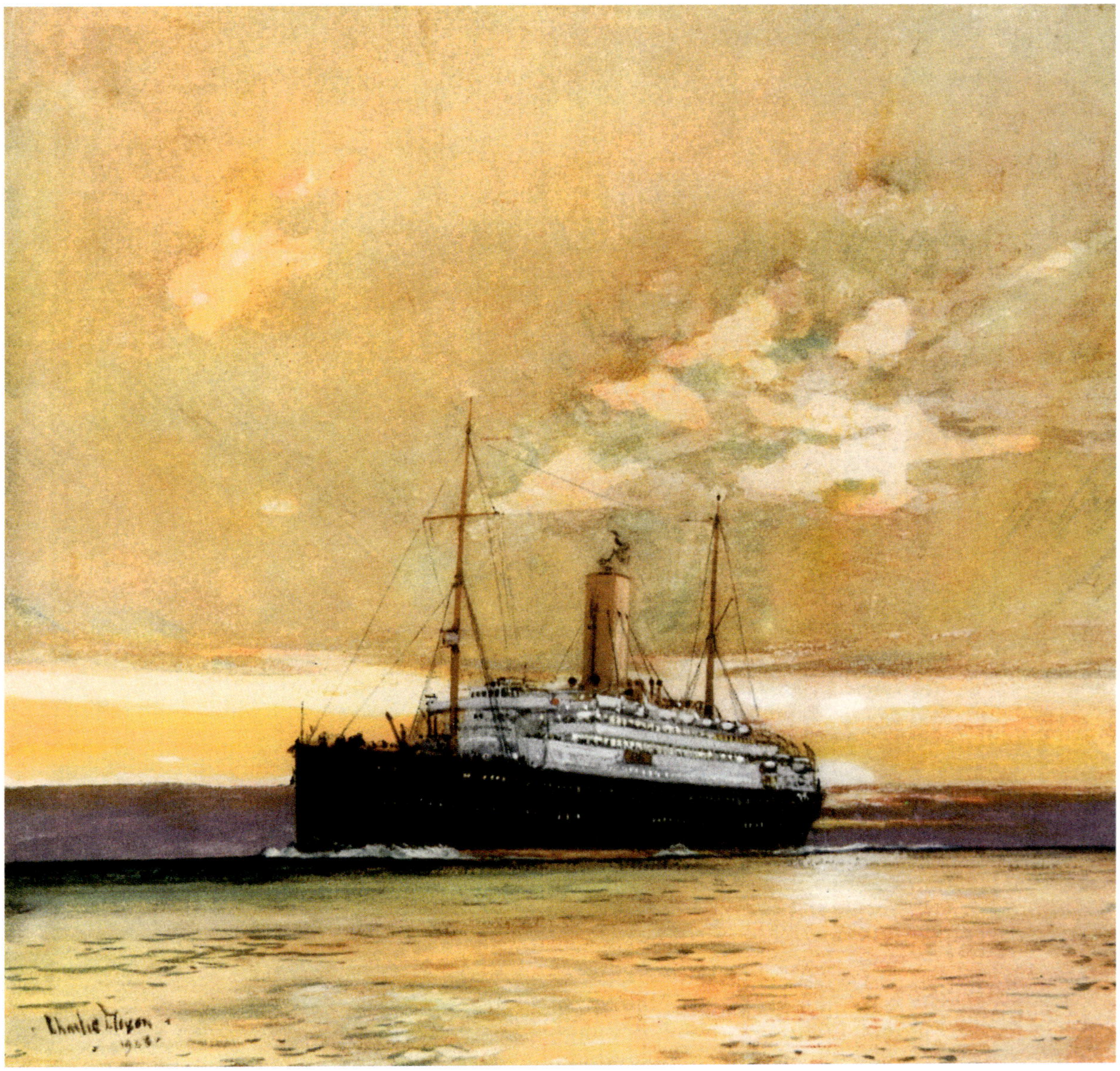

*The* Arcadian
*Charles Dixon, Poster for the Royal Mail Steam Packet Company*

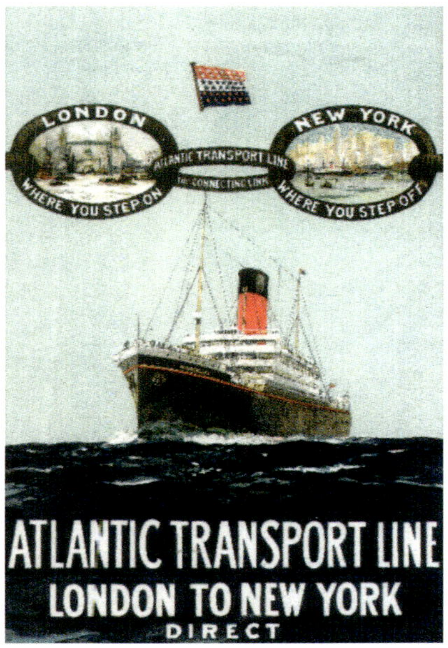


*Atlantic Transport Line, London to New York Direct*
*Charles Dixon, Poster*

painted throughout his career; these were but a few of the many excellent artists whose talents were utilised in this way. By all accounts this was a highly competitive field since it was not uncommon for there to be over thirty tenders for one poster contract and so artists needed to demonstrate all their versatility in adapting to what was basically a more graphic or design-orientated approach to their work. Throughout his career, Dixon produced posters for a large number of shipping firms such as Cunard, the Royal Mail Steam Packet Company, the Atlantic Transport Line, and Canadian Pacific. But it was P&O with whom he had one of his longest associations, his watercolour studies of distant and exotic cruise destinations regularly appearing on the front cover of the Nautical Magazine *Blue Peter*.

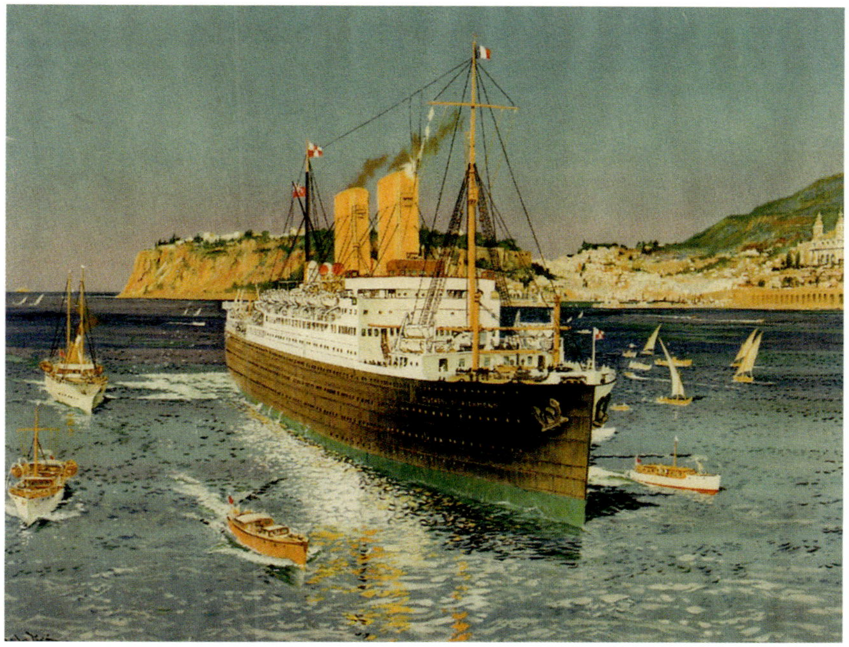

Duchess of the Atlantic, *1929*
*Charles Dixon, Poster, 39x29¼", for Canadian Pacific*
BONHAMS & BUTTERFIELDS

A slice of social history comes alive in the posters: they tell us very clearly how the shipping (and railway) companies tried to attract potential passengers. By 1910, for example, P&O was advertising pleasure cruises of two or three weeks to the Azores in Spring, the Norwegian Fjords and the Baltic in Summer, and Dalmatia, Venice, Greece and Constantinople in the Autumn. The type of poster work that Dixon was producing for P&O and many other lines was, however, not confined to the shipping companies, but extended to organisations such as the Empire Marketing Board, established in 1926 to promote the goods being produced by the British Empire. Many of the posters designed and painted for this organisation, which amount to over a thousand different images and often unpublished, are held by the Public Record Office in Kew, London, as part of its extensive archive of Victorian and Edwardian advertising material. The archive includes well-crafted examples by Dixon, Norman Wilkinson and Charles Pears, whose work features prominently in the collection, as does the work by highly talented Kenneth Shoesmith (1896-1939), all of whom through their bold and vibrant colours and attractive compositions managed to imbue their work with more imagination and a greater sense of atmosphere than a photograph might allow.

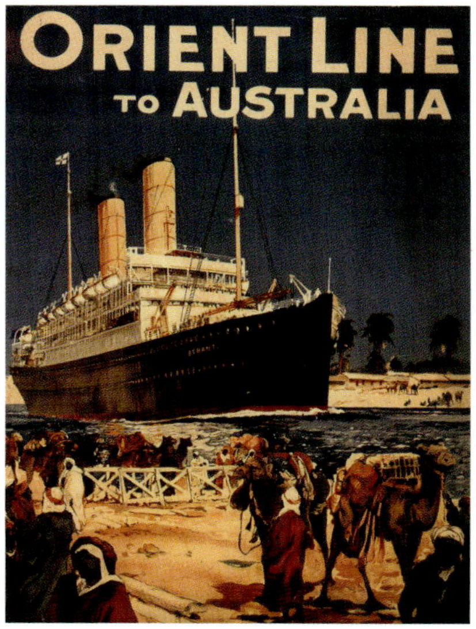


*Orient Line to Australia*
*Charles Dixon, Poster for P&O*

An additional means of advertising for the shipping companies was the postcard, which began to appear in Britain towards the end of the 1890s, with all manner of companies issuing cards that showed their ships, from the big lines to small coastal firms. The material for artistic, as opposed to photographic postcards came from three main sources: advertising posters, paintings commissioned by companies for their boardrooms, or ships and work specially created for postcards. Dixon produced work for all the major British lines and also some foreign ones and was one of many good artists much in demand to paint studies of the companies' ships, which were then reproduced in large quantities in postcard form and given to passengers. These colourful artist impressions of a big liner at speed, or lying serenely at anchor in some far-flung sunny port, were infinitely more attractive than a dull monochrome card and some excellent work was produced. The number of paintings that Dixon and others were turning out for reproduction as posters and postcards by the shipping firms was quite phenomenal, and, in most cases, of high quality; such as the card he painted for Cunard showing one of its liners in North River, New York. Since it was founded in 1840, Cunard has become synonymous with transatlantic travel and sailing from Britain to America was, and in many ways still is, the quintessential voyage. Throughout

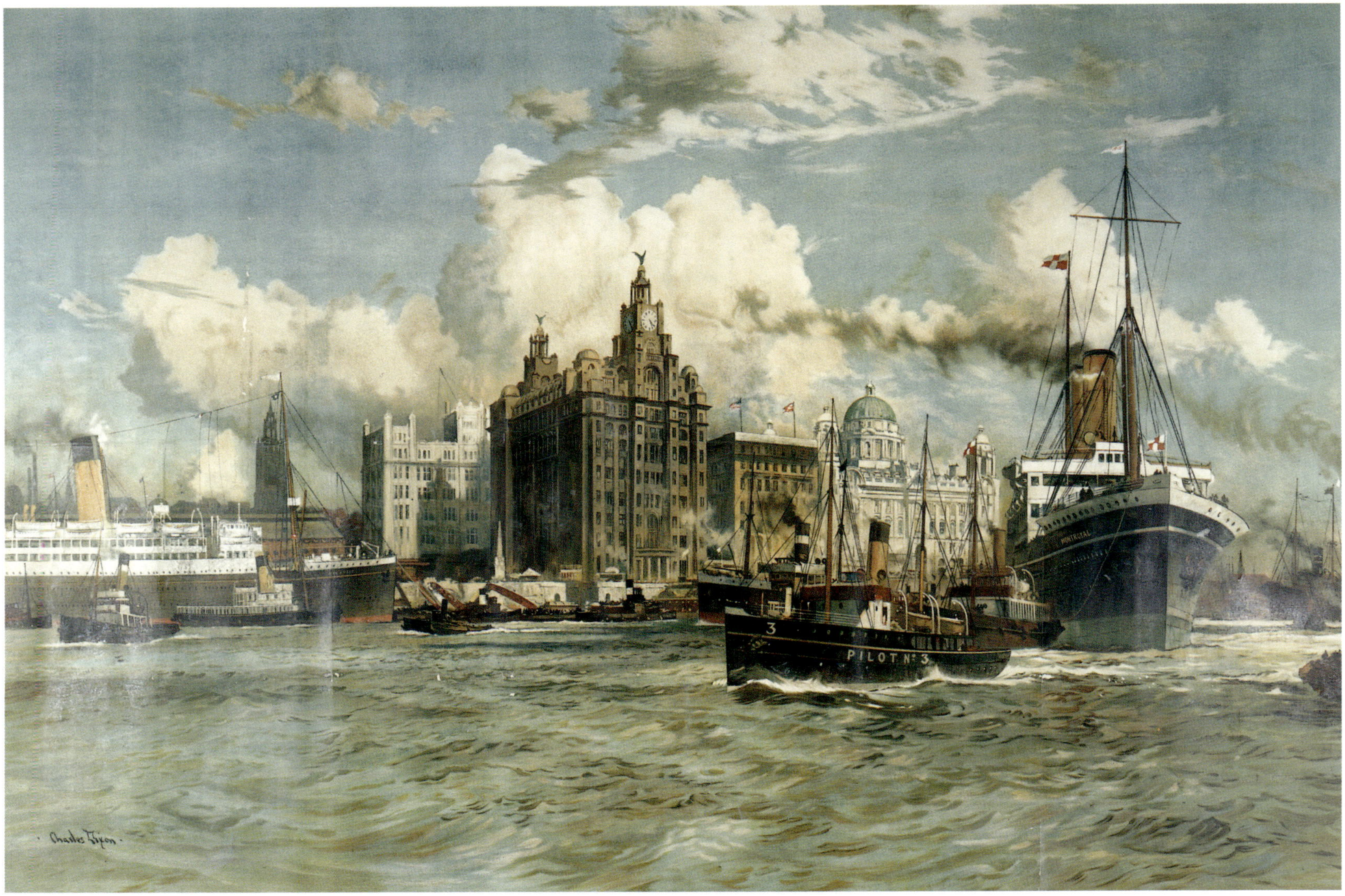


*The River Mersey: The Western Gate of Empire*
*Charles Dixon, Poster for the Empire Marketing Board*
THE NATIONAL ARCHIVES KEW, LONDON

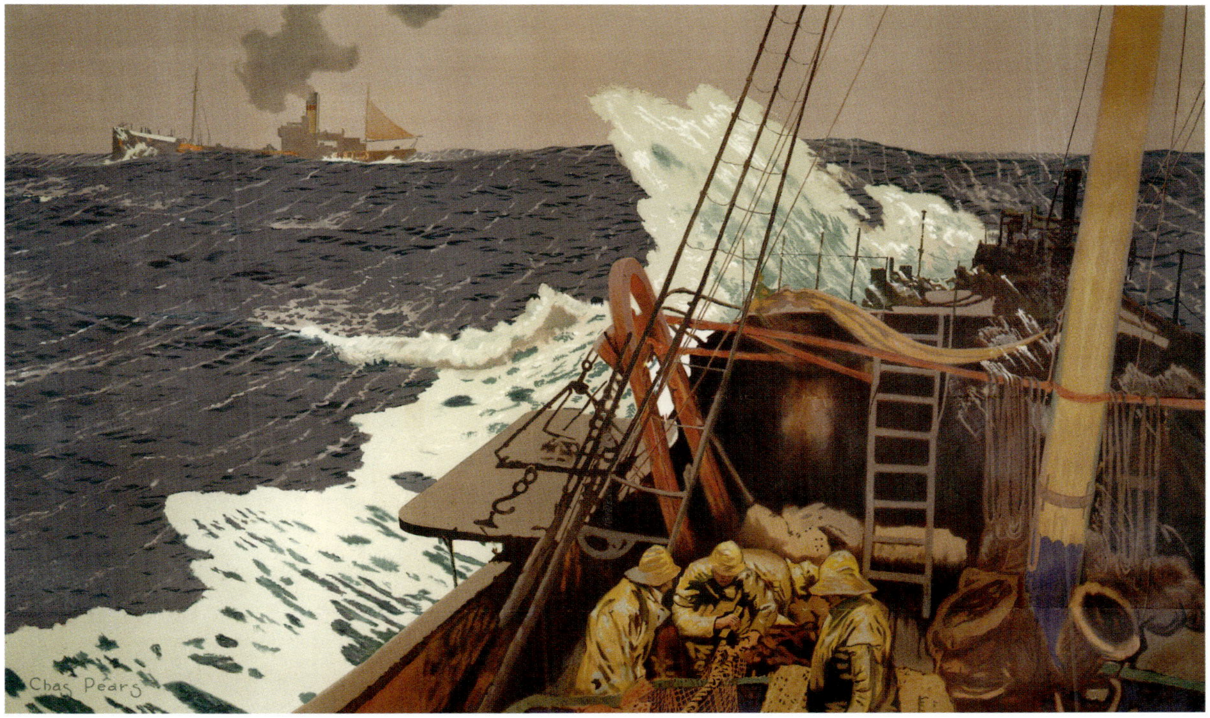


*There's all the Health of the Fish in the Sea*
*Charles Pears, Poster for the Empire Marketing Board*
THE NATIONAL ARCHIVES KEW, LONDON

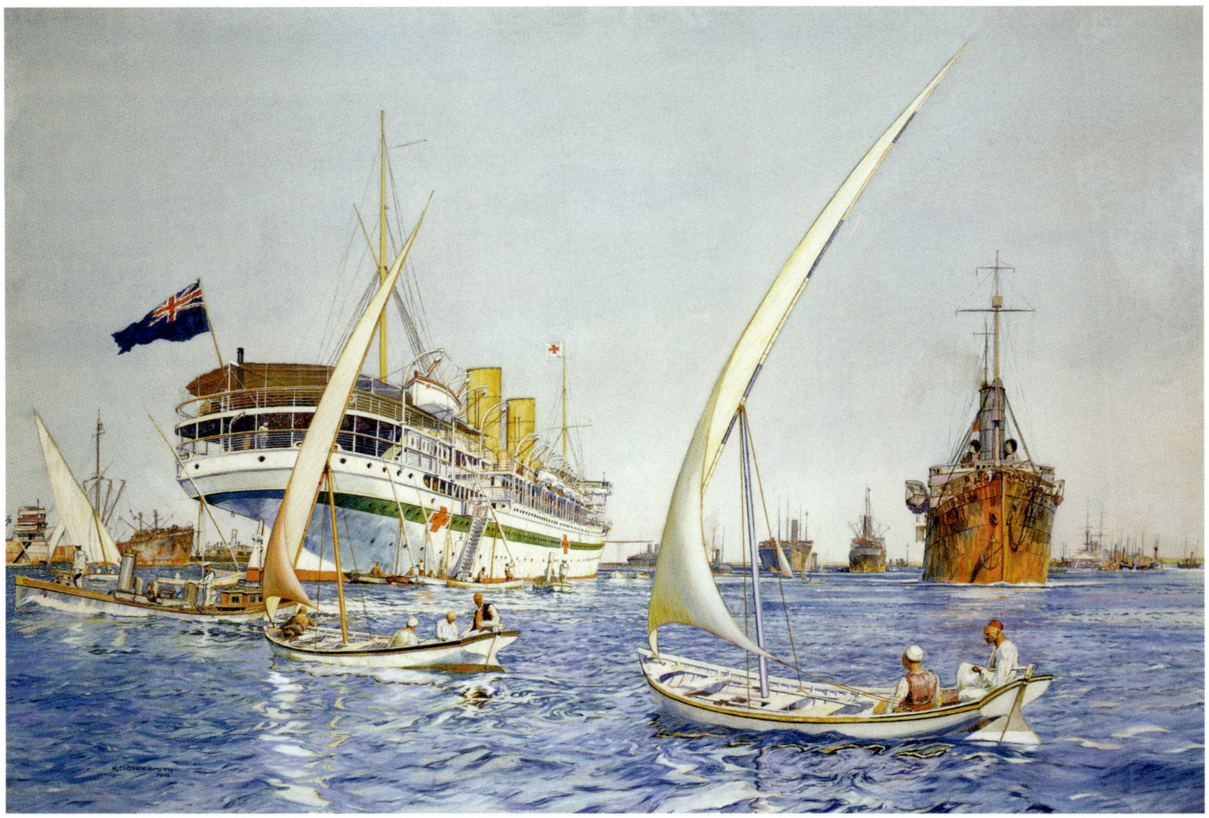

*The P&O Hospital Ship*
Egypt *at Alexandria, 1918*
*Kenneth D. Shoesmith, Watercolour,*
*Signed and Dated 1918*
N.R. OMELL GALLERY

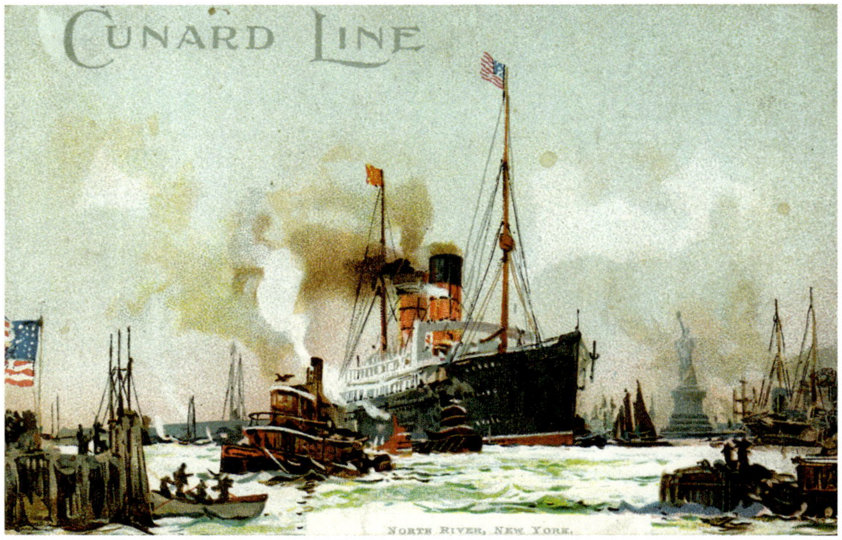


*Cunarder Entering North River, New York*
*Charles Dixon, Postcard for Cunard Line*

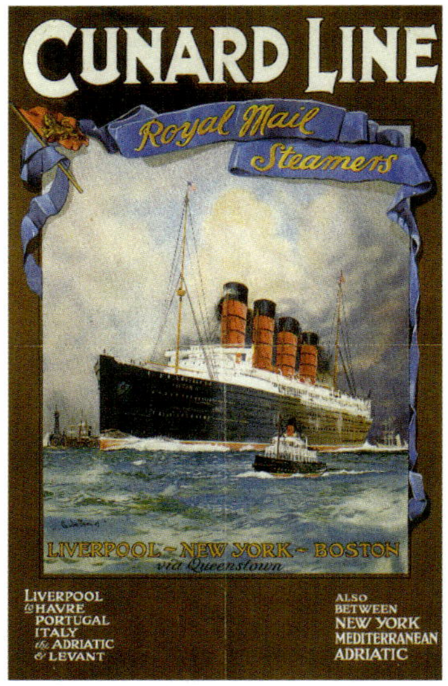


*The Royal Mail Steamer* Lusitania, *1907*
*Charles Dixon, Poster for Royal Mail Steamships*

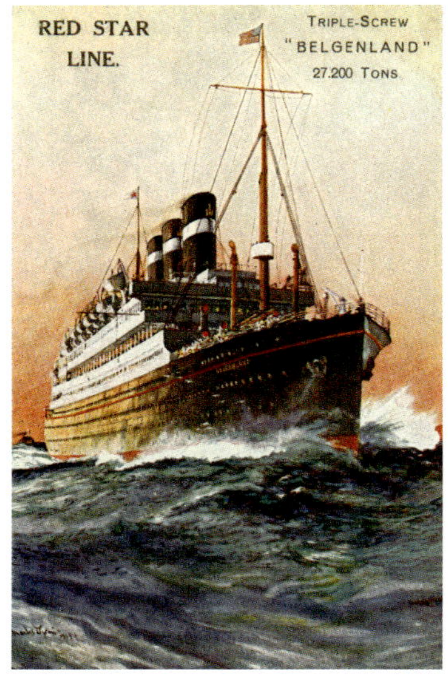


*Triple-Screw* Belgenland, *27,000 tons*
*Charles Dixon, Postcard for Red Star Line*

the company's long and distinguished history, for many travellers 'going Cunard' was the ultimate cachet, epitomised in the poster illustration by Dixon, which shows the *Lusitania* leaving her home port of Liverpool bound for New York at a time when the line reigned supreme on the transatlantic run. When the poster was produced in 1907, the *Lusitania* and her sister ship, the *Mauretania*, were the largest and fastest vessels in the world (the *Lusitania* the first liner to exceed 30,000 tons). Indeed, on three occasions, the *Lusitania* won the coveted blue riband as the fastest transatlantic liner – an achievement that clearly Cunard were keen for Dixon to acknowledge in his illustration!

Although he worked as a postcard artist for many other shipping firms besides Cunard, such as the White Star, P&O, Union Castle, Canadian Pacific, Holland America, British India and also Red Star, some of Dixon's best efforts were for the Royal Mail Company who, in 1904, commissioned him to produce a set of six postcards. It seems that the series, of which one, 'Rio de Janeiro' was very favourably reported on by *Picture Postcard Gazette* and was a milestone in British shipping postcards, for it not only added a valuable dimension to presentation in suggesting possible destinations to the viewer, but also helped to allay any lingering scepticism on the part of the passenger lines as to the promotional impact that might be achieved by using top artists. Indeed according to Christopher Deakes' excellent book *A Postcard History of the Passenger Liner*, Dixon's postcards of the liner '*Cymric* at Boston' is from arguably the best set of cards painted for White Star – North Atlantic. *Cymric* was sunk in 1916 when carrying valuable plant from the US and there followed a public outcry since it was felt she should have sailed in convoy

*Rio de Janeiro*
*Charles Dixon, Postcard for Royal Mail Line*

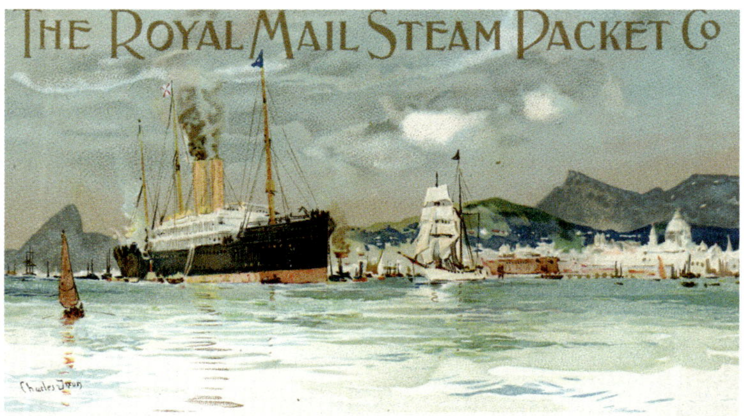


For about a hundred years the postcards revealed the wealth of artistic talent that had applied itself to depicting the passenger liner of the time. Perhaps inevitably, given the domination of its merchant fleets over other countries, most artists were British, but many of these mini-masterpieces were

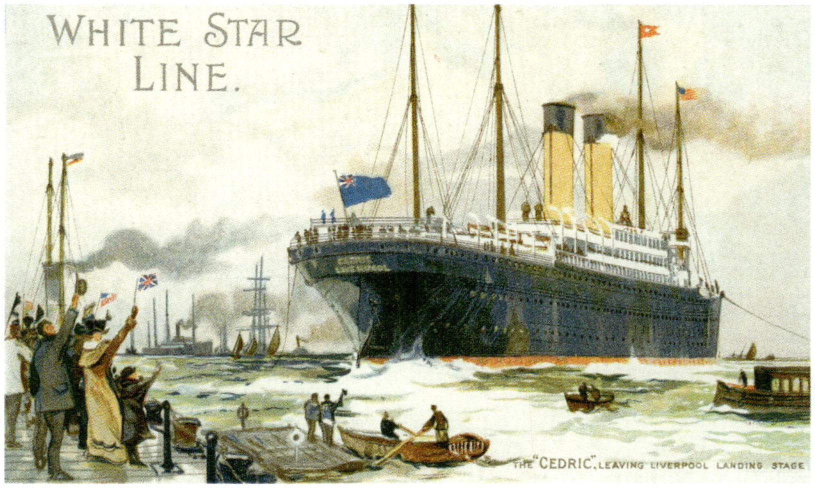


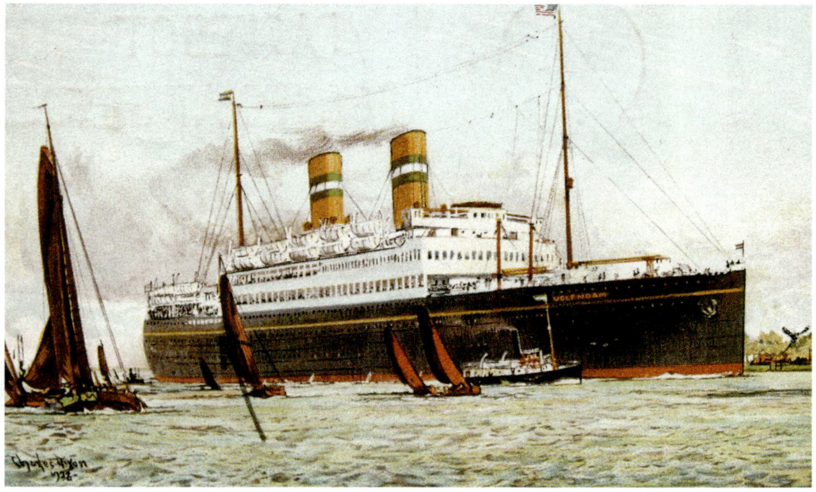

contributed by painters of other nations, particularly Germany. The range of ability and interpretation of all these poster and postcard artists was vast, but what they have in common is that through their work, they have been able to tell an evocative story of the vanished world of elegant ships and leisurely travel, expressed succinctly by one contented lady passenger on the card of SS *Omrah*, sent in 1907 to her aunt in Chelsea – "having glorious weather, getting on splendidly". Sadly the great liners of the most romantic age of sea travel are now nostalgic memories. If the marine artists who painted them were able to see their counterparts of the twenty-first century, they would surely be impressed by the sheer size of today's liners but repelled by the bland artificiality in present-day ship construction compared to the elegant, magnificent vessels they portrayed a century ago.

Dixon's advertising work, however, was far from limited to the shipping firms for, as a popular artist, his work found favour with a diverse range of businesses keen to use his skills as an illustrator, such as OXO, extolling the benefits of their famous beverage, and Fry's Chocolate for whom he painted a set of four watercolours of famous London landmarks. These were commissioned by Waddington's, the print makers, for Fry's, who intended them to be used as reproductions on their chocolate boxes. It seems that the subjects for his commercial work were of almost unlimited scope and in 'Outward Bound' he provided the cover for a set of sheet music.

Above Left:
Cedric
*Charles Dixon, Postcard for White Star Line*

Above:
Vollendam
*Charles Dixon, Postcard for Holland America Line*

Below Left:
Cymric
*Charles Dixon, Postcard for White Star Line*

Below:
*SS* Omrah
*Charles Dixon, Postcard for Orient-Royal Mail Line*

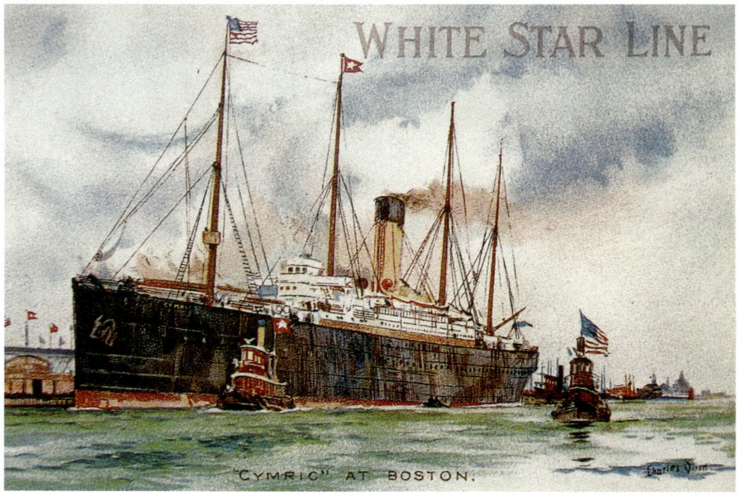


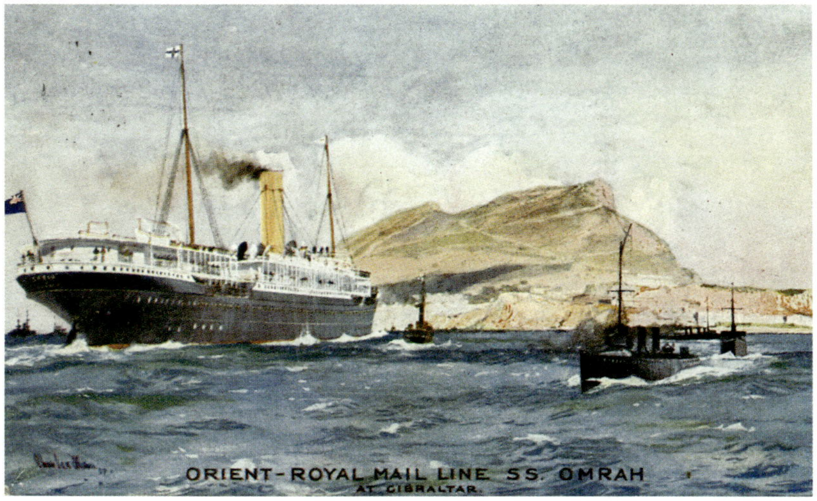

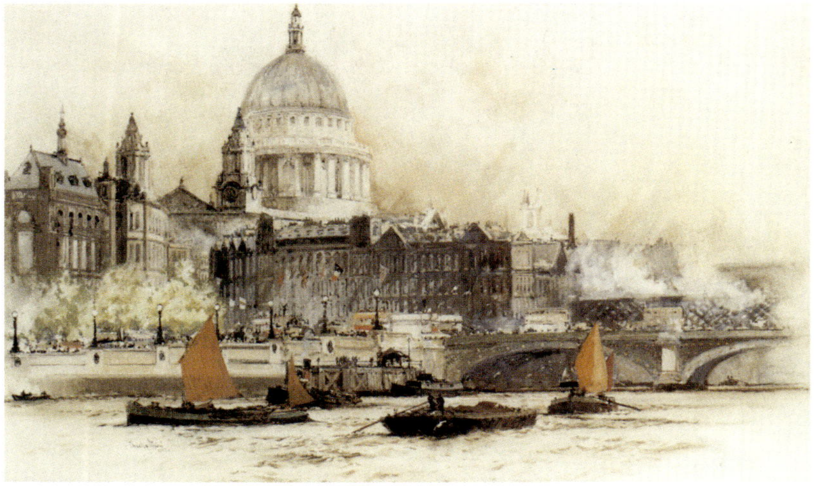

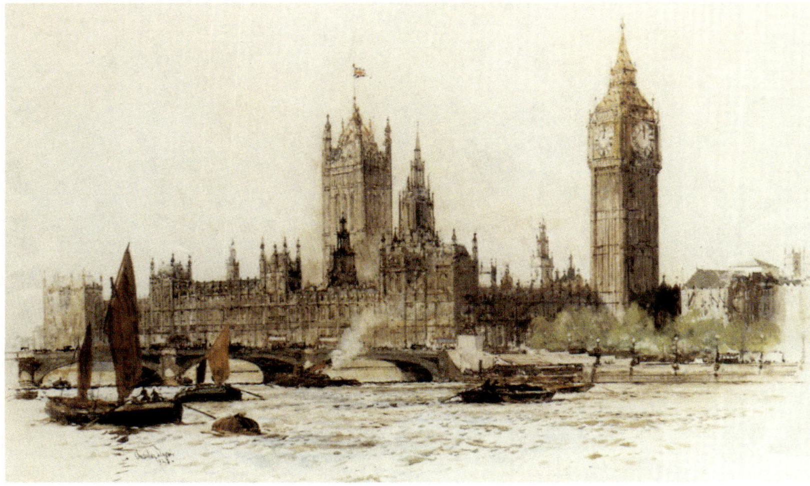

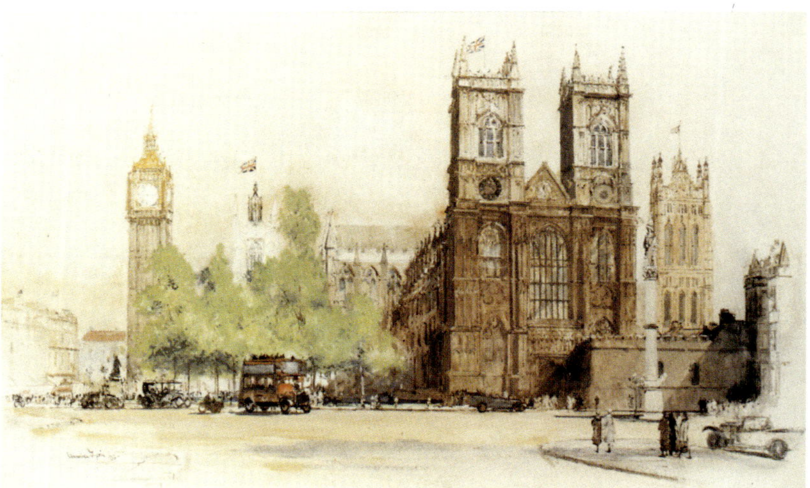

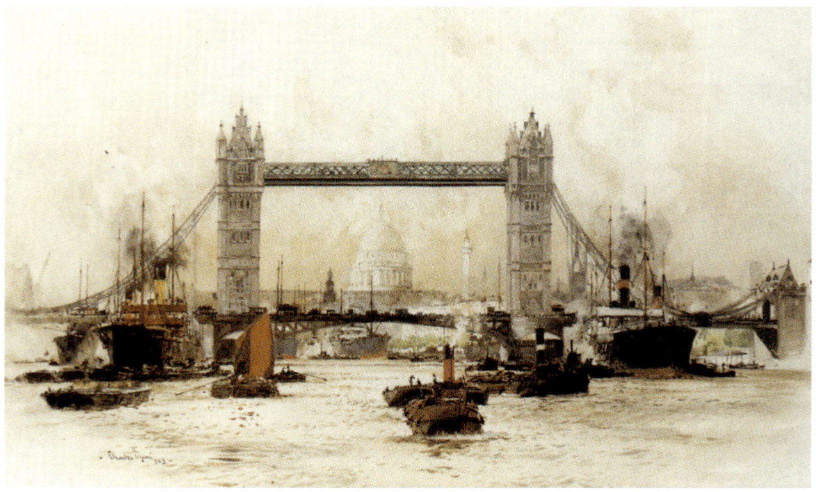

*Set of four London views*
*Charles Dixon, Illustrations for Fry's Chocolate*
BRISTOL AUCTION ROOMS

which is fluid and somewhat ethereal, ideal and arguably the best for creating a sense of movement and for application in the specialist field of marine art. Dixon's technique was clever, confident and deceptive and conveys a feeling of a great wealth of unlaboured detail. Basically, this involved putting large areas of subdued colouring on to wet paper, on top of these shadows outline detail is laid, often in body-colour, but the pictures themselves are far less meticulous on inspection than is first implied; the use of body-colour leaving an impression of weight one sometimes sees in small oils. The use of white highlights and other details in body-colouring means that it is quite easy to see when the thinner washes of colour behind have faded or the paper discoloured. Dixon strove to capture a light in his Thames scenes that is often so brown, or ochre, that it seems the original paper yellowed with age. Unfortunately, due to this, his watercolours are particularly susceptible to fading if exposed to light because of the thinness of the translucent washes, most notably in the areas of sky and sea and which is apparent in 'Off Gravesend'.

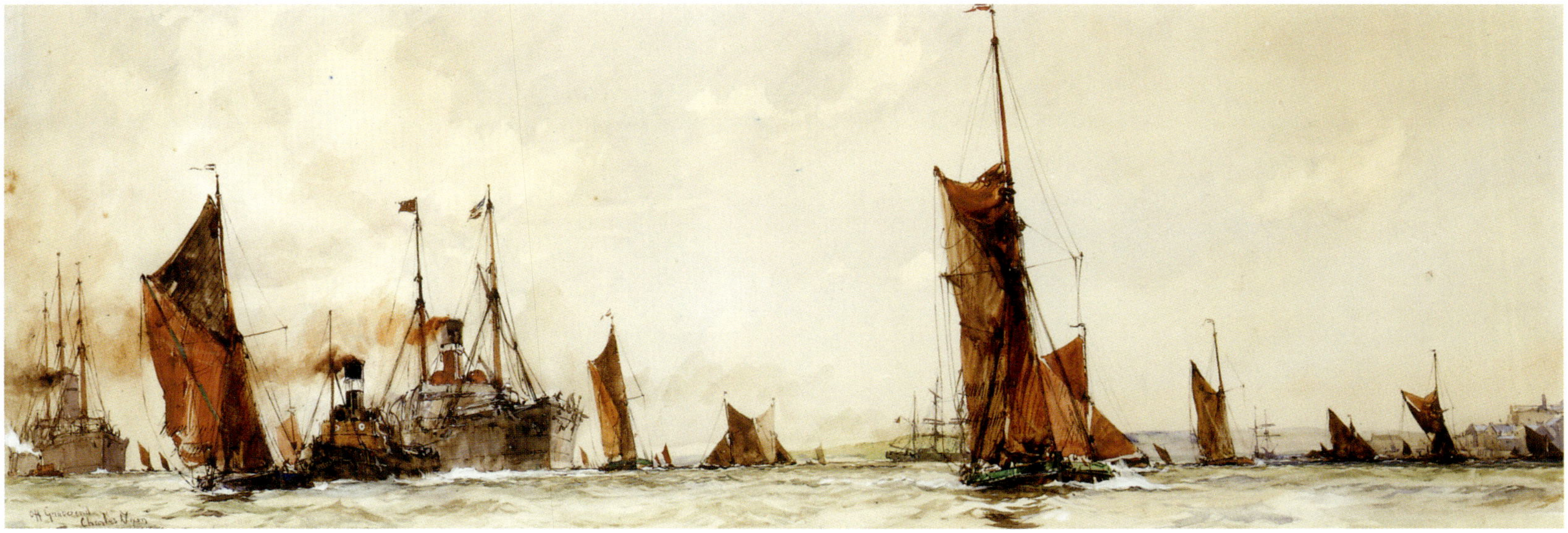

*Off Gravesend*
*Charles Dixon, Watercolour, 11x30", Signed and dated '03*
HAYNES FINE ART

Any discussion of Charles Dixon's artistic merit more often than not will invite comparison with that of W L Wyllie, some twenty years older and, as the dominating force in British marine painting of the time, Dixon would have assimilated much in developing his own graphic skills, although there is no evidence to suggest that he received lessons. Certainly Dixon lacked Wyllie's broader based training, but his work does bear some resemblance, yet shows a strength and individuality of its own, his somewhat earthy palette contrasting with Wyllie's lighter and usually more restrained approach to the use of colour. Moreover, it is readily apparent that Dixon's palette was not confined to the sombre tones he used to convey the smoke-laden and murky atmosphere of the great shipping lanes of the Thames and elsewhere for, as one critic wrote, 'the brilliant colours which characterise his work are very much his own and appear to have escaped the flattery of imitation'. However, in 1934, the art critic of *The Times*, when alluding to the artist's tendency to give full reign to heightened colouring, was less complimentary when he wrote 'his colour on occasion was inclined to be unpleasantly hot', clearly a reference to Dixon's vivid evocations of sea and sunlight, giving the impression that his yachts in the Solent could easily be mistaken for sailing in the Mediterranean. This criticism of Dixon's colour sense came at the end of his life, yet it seems unlikely that even had it been voiced so publicly earlier in his career, it would have been

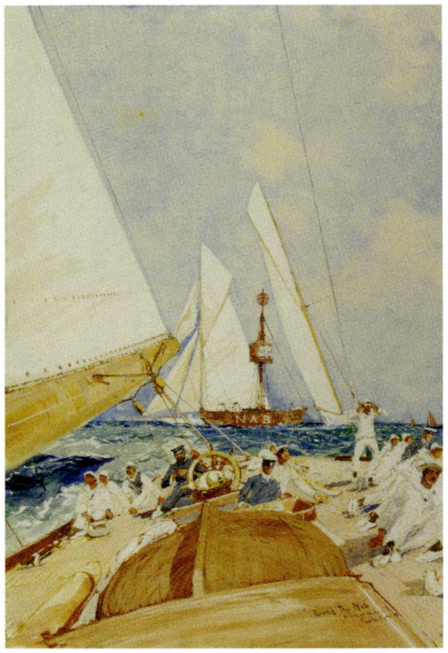

*Round the Nab on Shamrock*
*Charles Dixon, Watercolour,*
*19x13", Signed and insribed*
Culture and Sport Glasgow (Museums)

heeded; Dixon no doubt claiming that the over-intensity of colouring to which his detractors had objected was, in fact, the quality which gave his watercolours their strength, dash and vigour and that he was able to employ the boldest resources of his palette without becoming implausible in his rendering of the actual scene. Apart from his vivid blues, he was also particularly fond of green and would find any opportunity to include a green funnel or a hull in a composition such as 'Barque being towed through Greenwich Reach', a particularly interesting subject, since there were only a few sailing ship owners who painted their ships green. Unlike W L Wyllie, Norman Wilkinson, Frank Mason and Arthur Briscoe, Dixon's repertoire did not include etching, although certainly he was able to convey much of the etcher's and advertiser's economy in his work, for when his watercolours are illustrated in black and white in magazines, catalogues and books, it is a tribute to their sophisticated tonality that they often look like charcoal drawings, for Dixon, by achieving a degree of contrast and depth in his images, successfully avoided the rather flat effect noticeable in the illustrative work of some of his contemporaries. Apart from the early years of his artistic development, when there is evidence of looser brushwork in his watercolours, such as 'The Working Thames', 1889, Dixon's style remained virtually unchanged throughout, always displaying the unmistakeable appearance of being a product of an artist well acquainted with boats, ships and tides and whose considerable experience as a yachtsman gave inspiration and freshness to his work. His unique style appealed not only to patrons but also to fellow artists such as Frank Saltfleet (1860-1937) and William G Whittington, who exhibited between 1904 and 1914, at first glance their watercolours bearing a distinct similarity to Dixon's Thames subjects.

Dixon invariably adopted an extended horizontal format for his watercolours, enabling him to provide a panoramic view of his Thames scenes with a typical image size of approximately 10" x 30" and usually signed 'Charles Dixon', although it is not uncommon to find some of his early pictures signed 'Charlie

*A Barque towing through Greenwich Reach*
*Charles Dixon, Watercolour,*
*20x29", Signed and dated 1896*
Royal Exchange Art Gallery

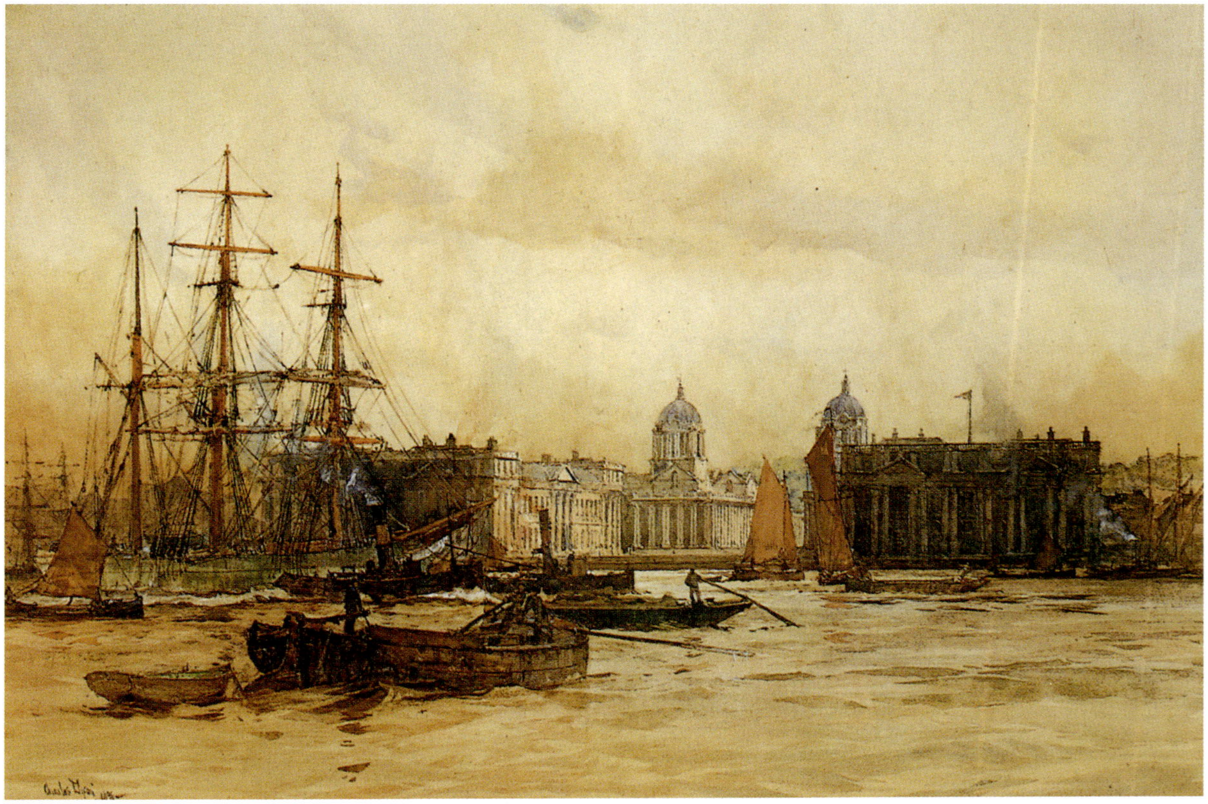

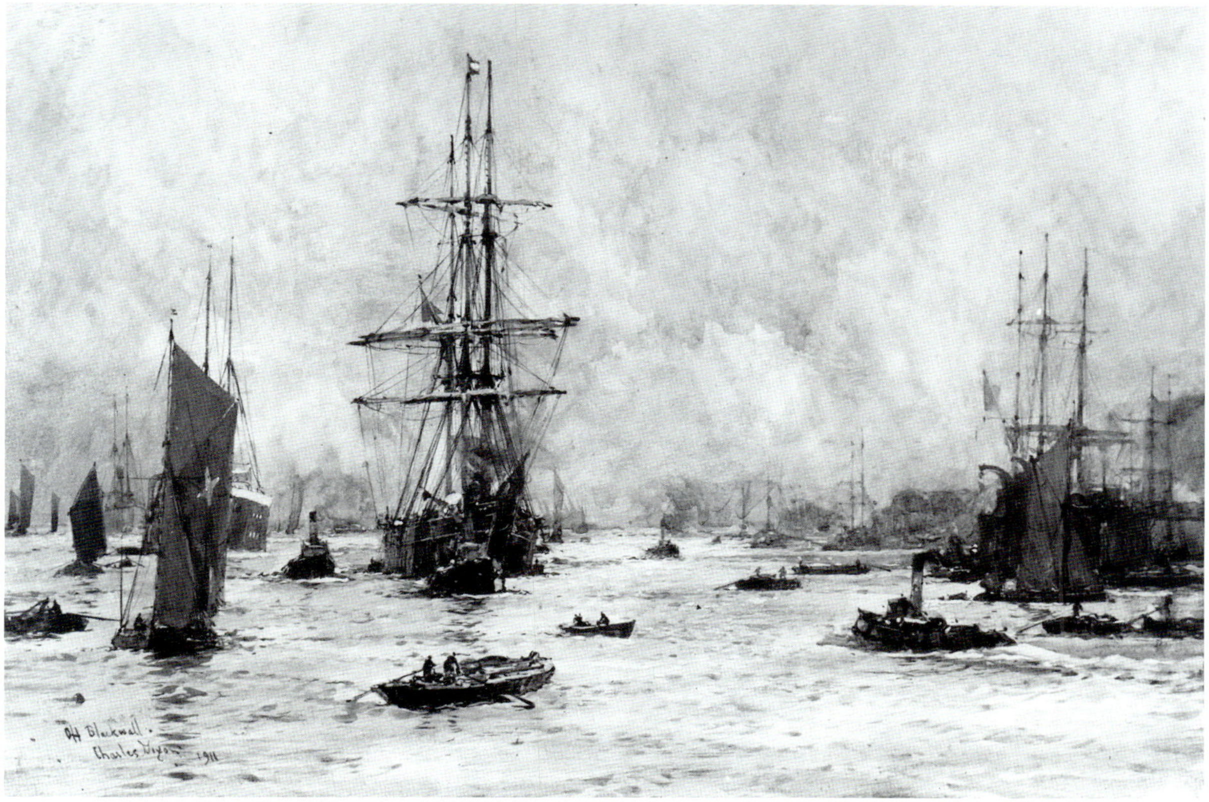

*Off Blackwall*
*Charles Dixon, Watercolour,*
*7x12", Signed, inscribed and dated 1911*
VICTORIA AND ALBERT MUSEUM

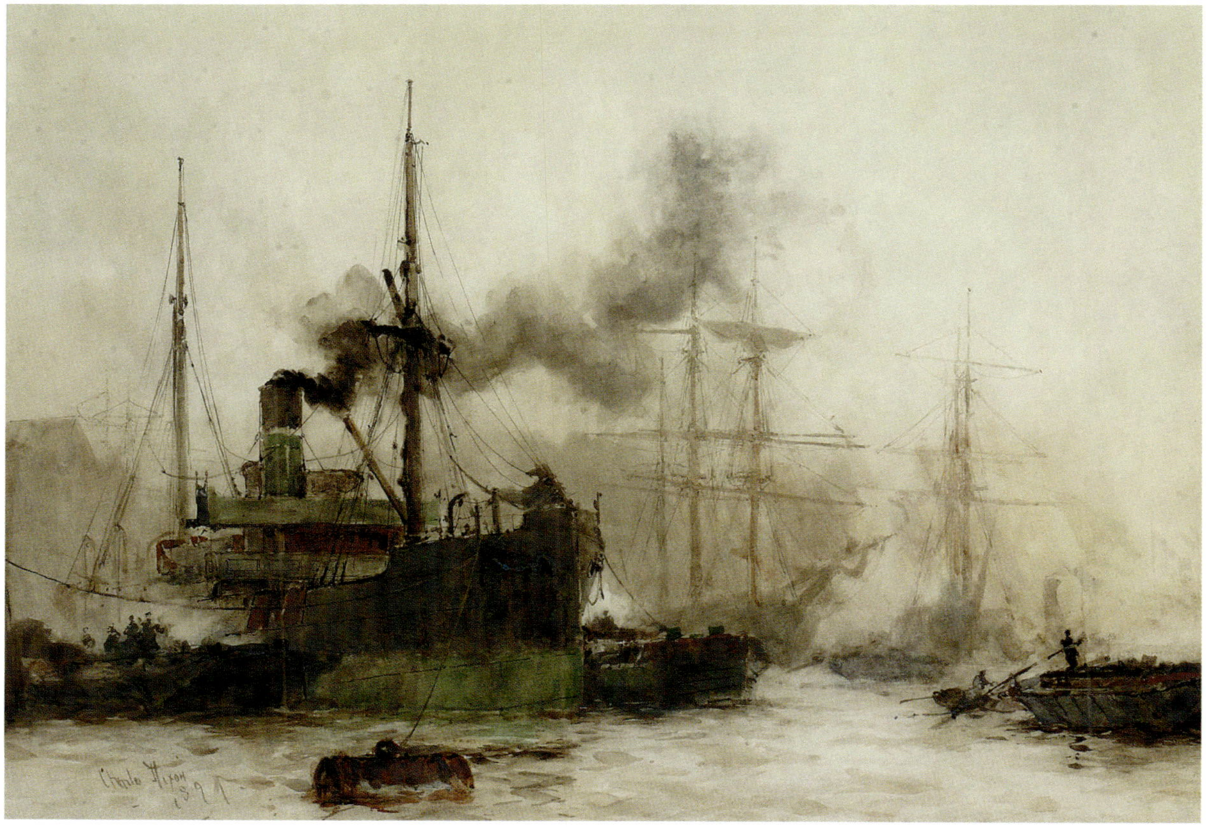

*The Working Thames*
*Charles Dixon, Watercolour,*
*Signed and dated 1889*
PRIVATE COLLECTION

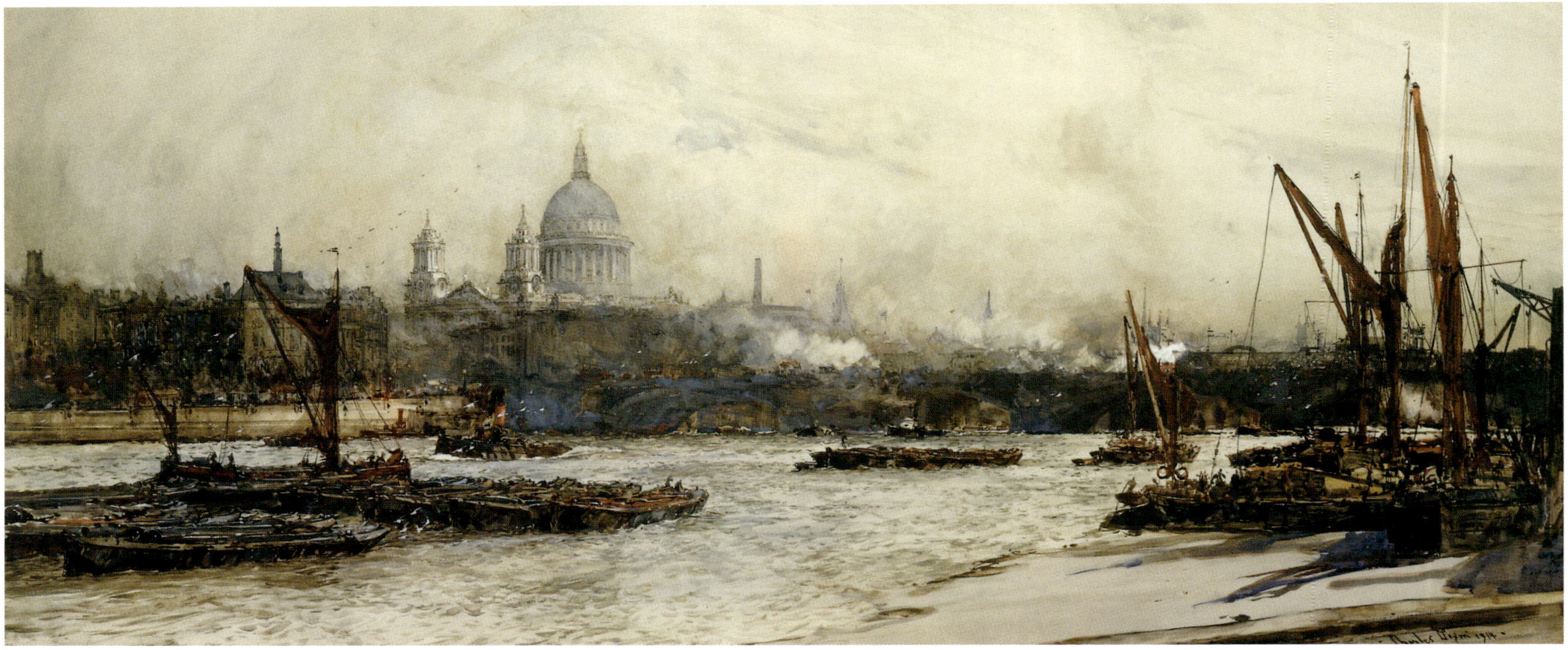

*St Paul's*
*Charles Dixon, Watercolour, Signed*
CHRIS BEETLES LTD

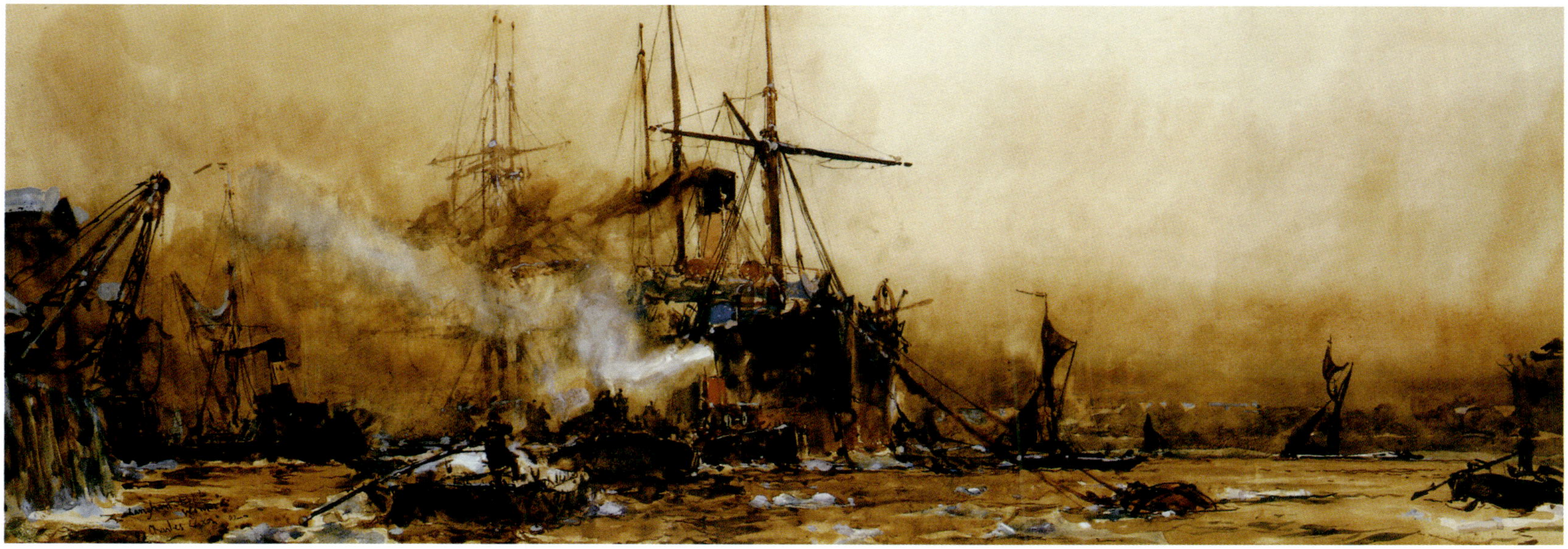

Dixon'. Sometimes his watercolours bear the inscription 'Langham sketch' described in the *Art Journal* 1895 as the 'Father of Sketching Clubs' or 'London sketch', and recall Dixon's membership of both institutions. Founded in 1838 and 1895 respectively, they were said to exist 'for work and entertainment' and all the leading illustrative artists of the day were members. Before admission to the Langham, a very searching test was applied for a 'time drawing' had to be presented. Each club had basically the same objectives, meeting every Friday evening during the winter months to complete a two-hour sketch from one or two given subjects. These were then fixed around the walls and received much criticism. This was followed by supper, usually of the boiled beef and carrots variety and later impromptu entertainment by members. The atmosphere at these weekly gatherings is best summed up in a history of the London Sketch – 'There is no end to the versatility of these clever companionable bohemians who, on smoking nights, combine much strenuous work with a good deal of play where, in the thick of the smoke, members let themselves go with no uncertainty'. These highly popular soirées would certainly have appealed to Dixon who by his 'clubbable' nature would have enjoyed the regular gatherings of like-minded artists. Moreover, they provided a method of working which tested the artists' retentive powers and Dixon's capacity to paint watercolours, particularly large ones, very quickly, was well suited to the weekly challenge. Inevitably the quality of work produced at these sessions varied from week to week but most was said to have been of a very high standard, particularly given the time constraints, as can be seen in the 11″ x 30″ watercolour Dixon produced at the club in 1902, inscribed Langham sketch 'Winter'. Quite often he would personalise the product of one of his Langham sessions to a friend such as 'On the London Road', in this case to a Mr Scott, who was the lucky recipient of a watercolour of a wooden-wall sailing ship being towed up Limehouses Reach and which Dixon had inscribed 'To Gilbert W Scott, with best wishes, Charles Dixon'. After joining the London Sketch Club in 1903, Dixon was elected its President for 1911–12, an honour bestowed upon him at a period leading up to the First World War, when the club was regarded as being at its most prestigious with only a certain number of artists admitted. Dixon also belonged to the Savages, which, despite its name, was generally perceived as a more dignified club, and according to the rules of the day 'was instituted for the association of gentlemen concerned professionally with literature, art, science, drama or music'. During Dixon's membership two particularly memorable events took place, the first on 6 July 1901 when he was present at a farewell

*Winter*
*Charles Dixon, Watercolour, 11x30″*
*Signed and inscribed 'Langham sketch, winter'*
HAYNES FINE ART

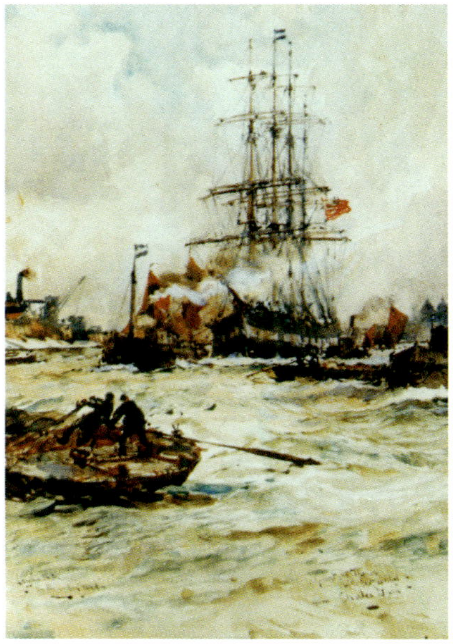

*On the London Road*
*Charles Dixon, Watercolour, 13½x9½″*
*Signed and inscribed 'On the London Road', Gilbert W Scott with best wishes from Charles Dixon*
PRIVATE COLLECTION

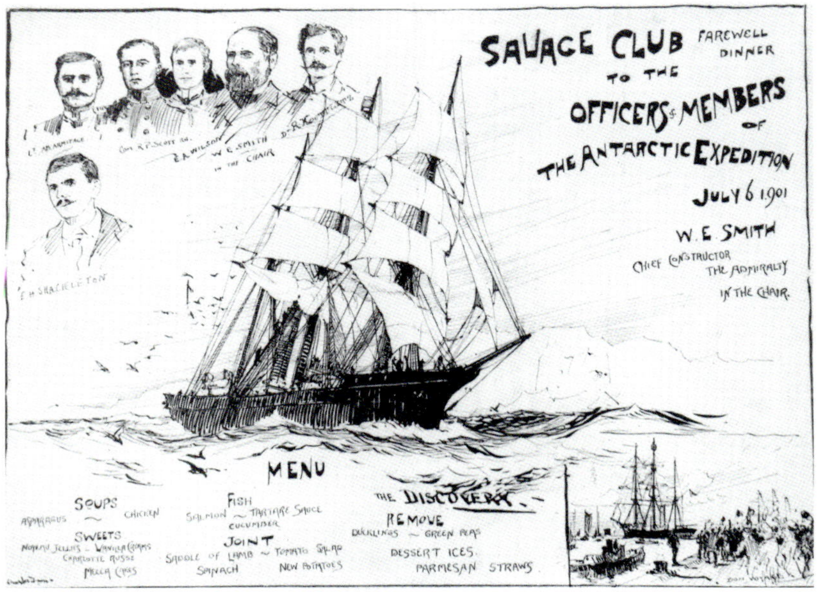


*Savage Club Farewwll Dinner*
*Menu card by Charles Dixon,*
*'To the officers and Members of the Antarctic Expedition 6 July 1901'*

dinner hosted by the club for Sir Ernest Shackleton and the officers and members of the Antarctic expedition, an occasion when Dixon was charged with designing the menu card. Certainly the Edwardians loved to enjoy themselves and be entertained and, on 20 February 1909, Dixon was present at an even more auspicious event when the club held a special dinner during which His Royal Highness, the Prince of Wales 'took the Chair' and is said to have delighted everyone with his charm of manner. Another marine painter and 'Brother Savage' was Thomas Bush Hardy (1842-1897), whose pictures achieved solid success with late Victorian audiences and remain very popular today. Hardy was the most prolific marine artist of his generation and, although described in the history of the club as 'the eminent watercolour artist whose facility in sketching was probably greater than that of any other man of his time', the quality of his work fluctuated to the extent that in his obituary in *The Times*, the critic commented 'his genuine artistic gift would have led him far if he had cared to subject to the discipline of study and labour'. This was more likely an oblique reference to the time Hardy spent flaunting his extrovert personality around the club and, no doubt, his alleged partiality to an over indulgence of alcohol.

Although there were a number of art clubs and professional societies to which the marine artist could belong, it seems hard to believe it was not until 1939 that such a great maritime nation as Britain celebrated the formation of a society devoted solely to marine painting, the situation eventually being

*Dutch Coast: Katwijk*
*Thomas Bush Hardy, Watercolour, Signed*
BOURNE GALLERY

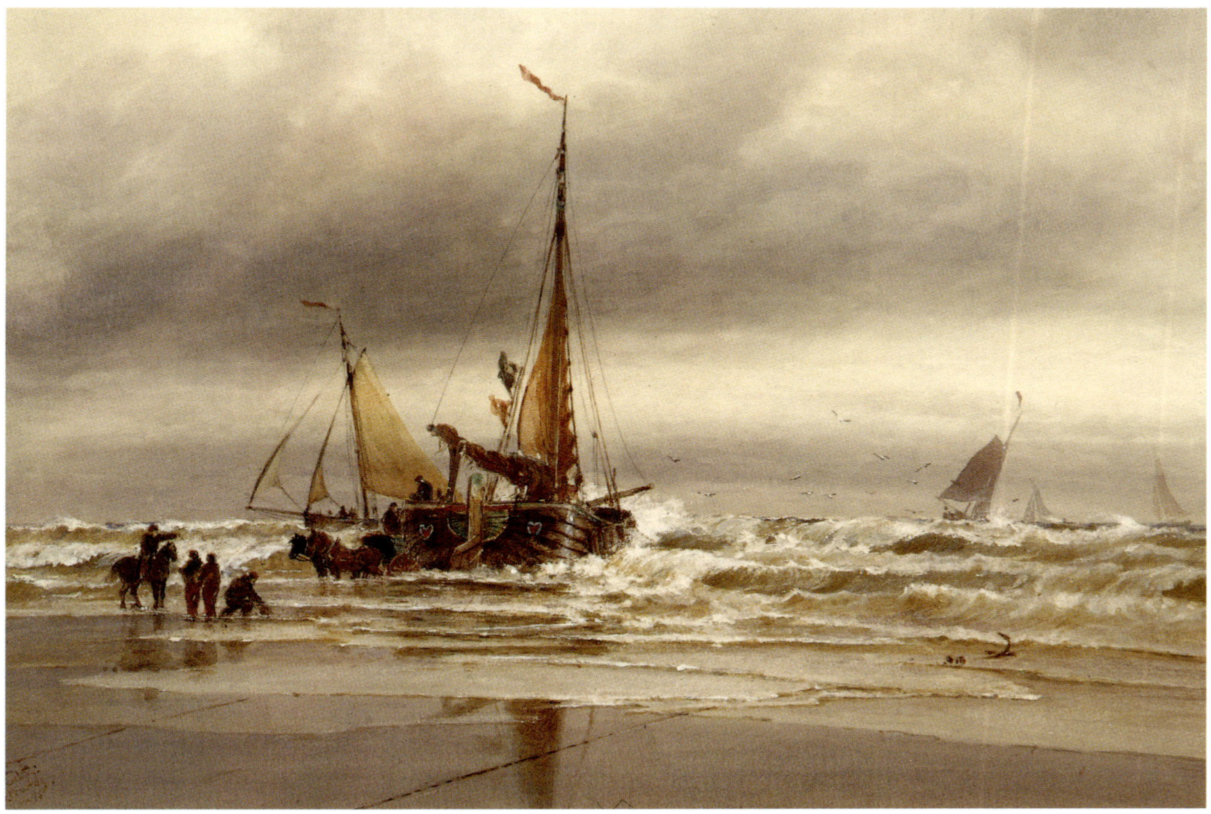

rectified with the founding of the Society of Marine Artists (SMA). The SMA was the result of the endeavours of people like Charles Pears, N Wilkinson, A Burgess, H Wyllie and A Briscoe, its aim to educate and serve a large and appreciative audience by making a special place for the genre among the country's cultural institutions. In 1966 its efforts were recognised through the granting of the title 'Royal Society of Marine Artists' and its annual exhibition is always eagerly awaited by knowledgeable and enthusiastic collectors. Always keen to advance the cause of British marine art, it seems inconceivable, therefore that, had he lived longer, Dixon would not have thrown his weight behind such a formidable coalescence.

Throughout his life Dixon's work centred on what he understood best, the marine view, yet, apart from responding to commissions on a wide range of nautical subjects, he was equally at ease painting scenes beyond his usual purview, in which the architectural landscape stretching alongside the banks of the river rather than the vessels in it becomes the main focus of his work. In 'The Houses of Parliament' we see a fine example of Dixon's draughtsmanship in which the architectural detail of the Palace of Westminster and strong and confident handling of watercolour is used to portray one of the greatest perpendicular Gothic revival buildings in existence. Although London and the South coast of England provided the settings for most of Dixon's work, his UK subjects were drawn from a much wider geographical span and ranged from the Firth of Clyde and the Mersey to the Gower Coast in South Wales. It seems he also spent time in East Anglia from where he painted 'The Herring Harvest, Lowestoft', 'A Byway in Norfolk' and 'Entering Lowestoft Harbour', several titles he exhibited at the RI. It was the East coast that also provided the location for the large oil depicting Coxswain Henry Blogg driving the Cromer lifeboat on to the Barge, *Sepoy* in December 1933 and rescuing her two-man crew. A

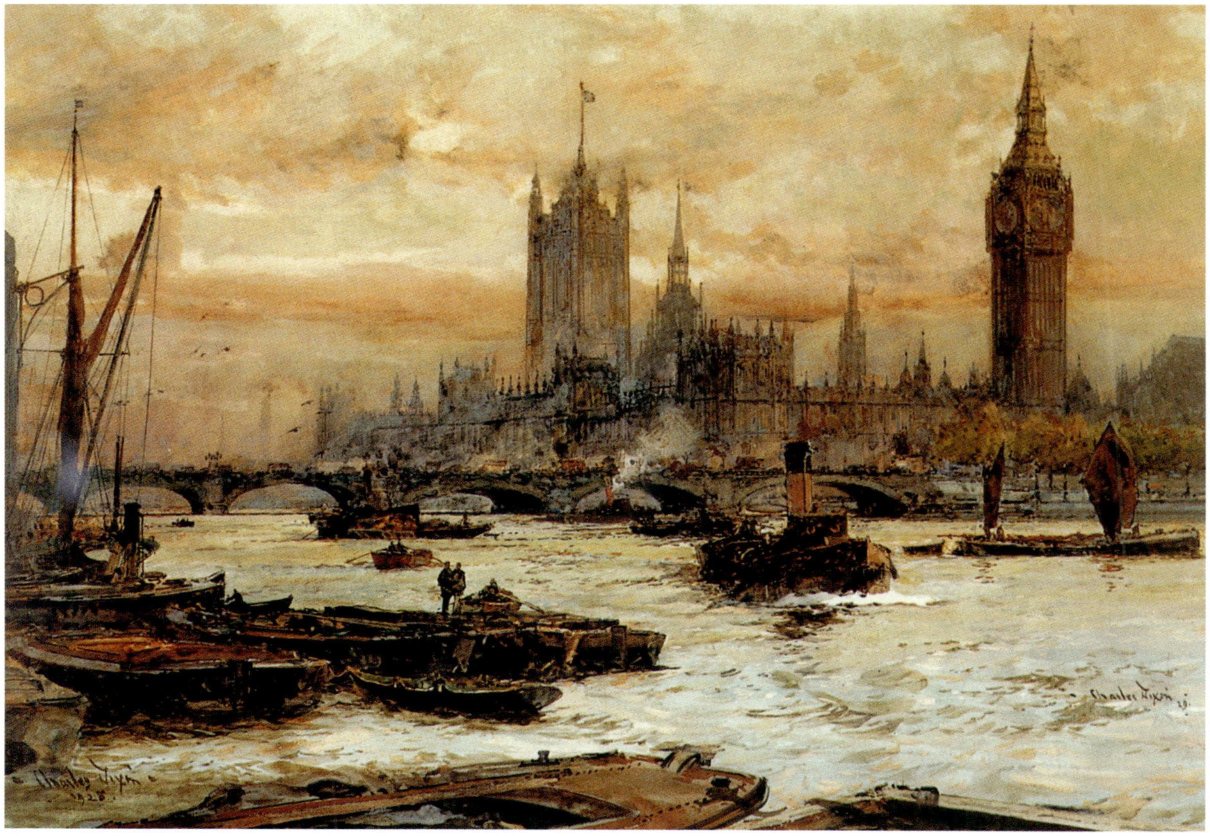

*The Houses of Parliament*
*Charles Dixon, Watercolour, 14x20¼"*
*Signed and dated 1928*
HAYNES FINE ART

*In Swansea Bay*
*Charles Dixon, Watercolour, Signed*
Maritime Prints and Originals

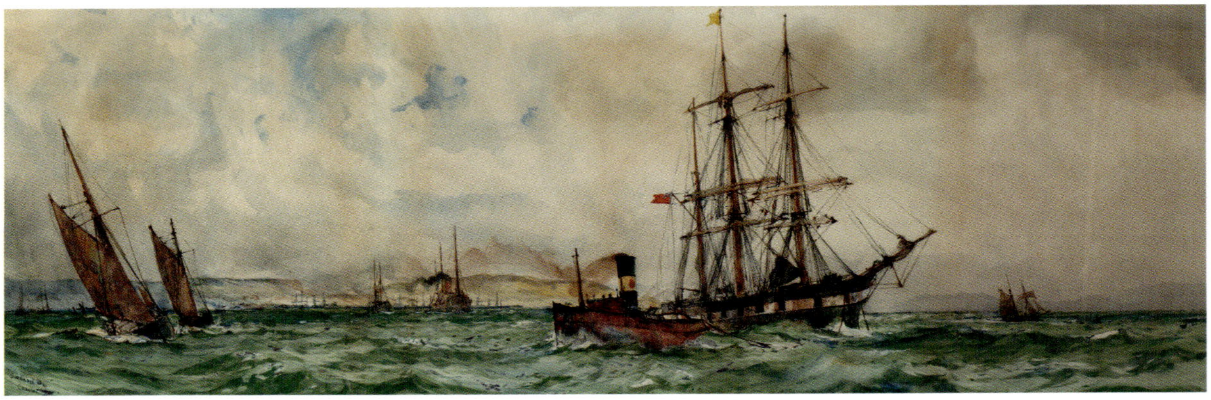

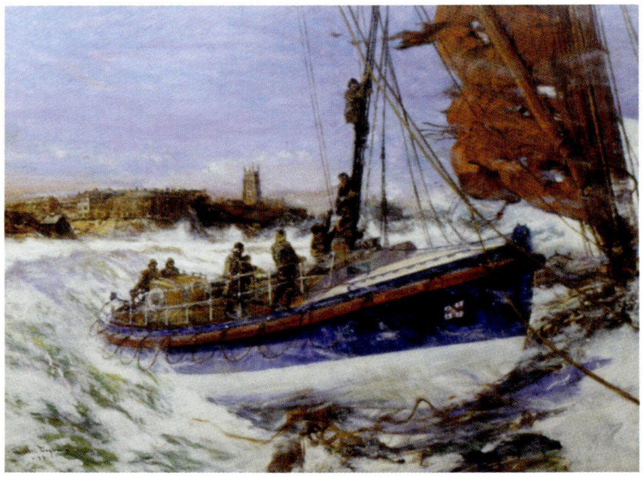

*The Coxswain driving the Cromer Lifeboat on to the Deck of the Barge,* Sepoy
*Charles Dixon, Oil on Canvas, Signed, 30"x40"*
RNLI Collection

painting which is in the collection of the Royal National Lifeboat Institution and used on a number of occasions as the cover for their Christmas cards.

Of all England's varied coastline, the South West stands out for its rugged beauty where Devon and Cornwall come down to the water's edge. From the intimacy of verdant little creeks in Devon to the vast rolling perspectives of Falmouth harbour, there is a variety in this coast hard to find elsewhere in Britain which has long attracted painters of harbour, coast and sea, yet strangely an area which Dixon seems to have forsaken.

Apart from London, Itchenor and Portsmouth, it was Southampton which, in the heyday of its long maritime history, also provided the perfect venue for Dixon; for it was here that he was able to picture the great transatlantic liners such as White Star's RMS *Olympic*, seen here leaving Southampton in 1910, and also her sister ship *Britannic*. This is a particularly interesting piece of artistic licence by Dixon for he shows *Britannic* in her 'civilian' form as a cruise ship, although in reality she never looked like this since, before her completion as a liner, she was requisitioned and converted for use as a hospital ship, in which role she was sunk by a mine in 1916. As regards the imaginary location of the vessel, the busy seaway with tugs, paddle steamer and yachts is probably a representation of the Solent, as Southampton was her intended home port. In 1934 Dixon was once again in Southampton to sketch what would have been one of the last drawings he did for *The Illustrated London News*, showing the world's largest liner *Majestic*, also of the White Star line, when on 19 January she entered the King George V graving dock, the largest in the world and the first time the dock had been put into commercial use. The White Star line is, of course, famous for one ship above all others – the *Titanic*, and it was to Northern Ireland that Dixon travelled to paint possibly the most evocative of his watercolours 'The Titanic Fitting Out'. This almost black and white picture of the ship was painted by Dixon at the Harland and Wolff shipyard, Belfast in March 1912, the month before embarking on her fateful voyage and, until recently, was believed to be the only contemporary painting of the White Star liner taken from life. It seems prophetic that the scene was painted at night, illuminated only faintly by electric light. This was probably how the ship looked as she lay dead in the water, slowing filling by the bows after a giant iceberg had cut through her double bottom. The painting is very dark and filled with menace and the very antithesis to the more sparkling brightness found in Dixon's work. This is a unique

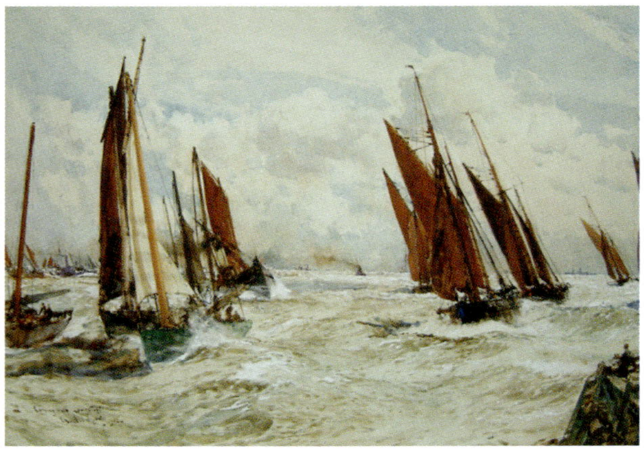

*Entering Lowestoft Harbour*
*Charles Dixon, Watercolour, 14½x20½", Signed and dated 1914*
Private Collection

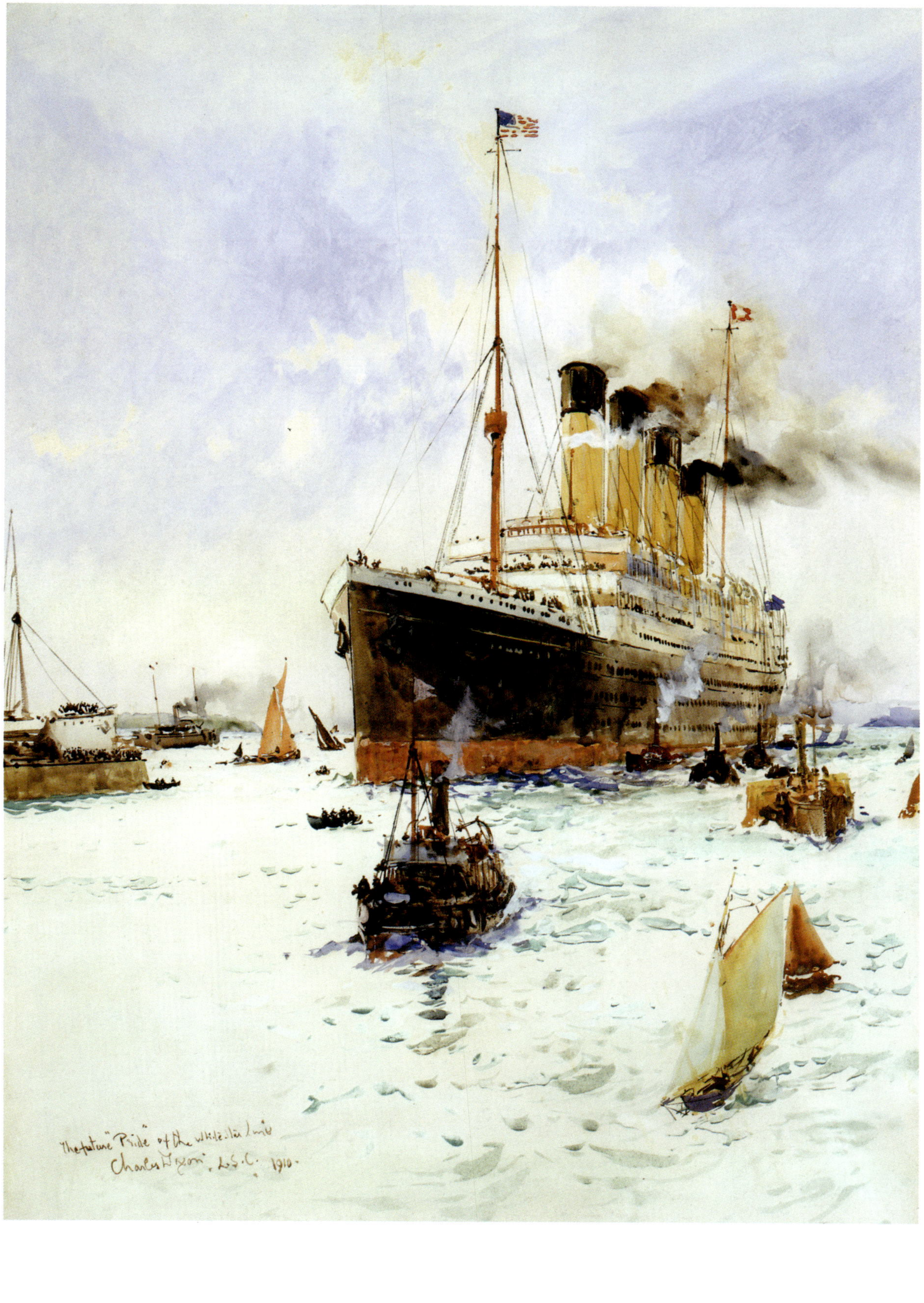


*RMS* Olympic *leaving Southampton*
*Charles Dixon, Watercolour,*
*25¾x19", Signed, inscribed and dated 1910*
N.R. OMELL GALLERY

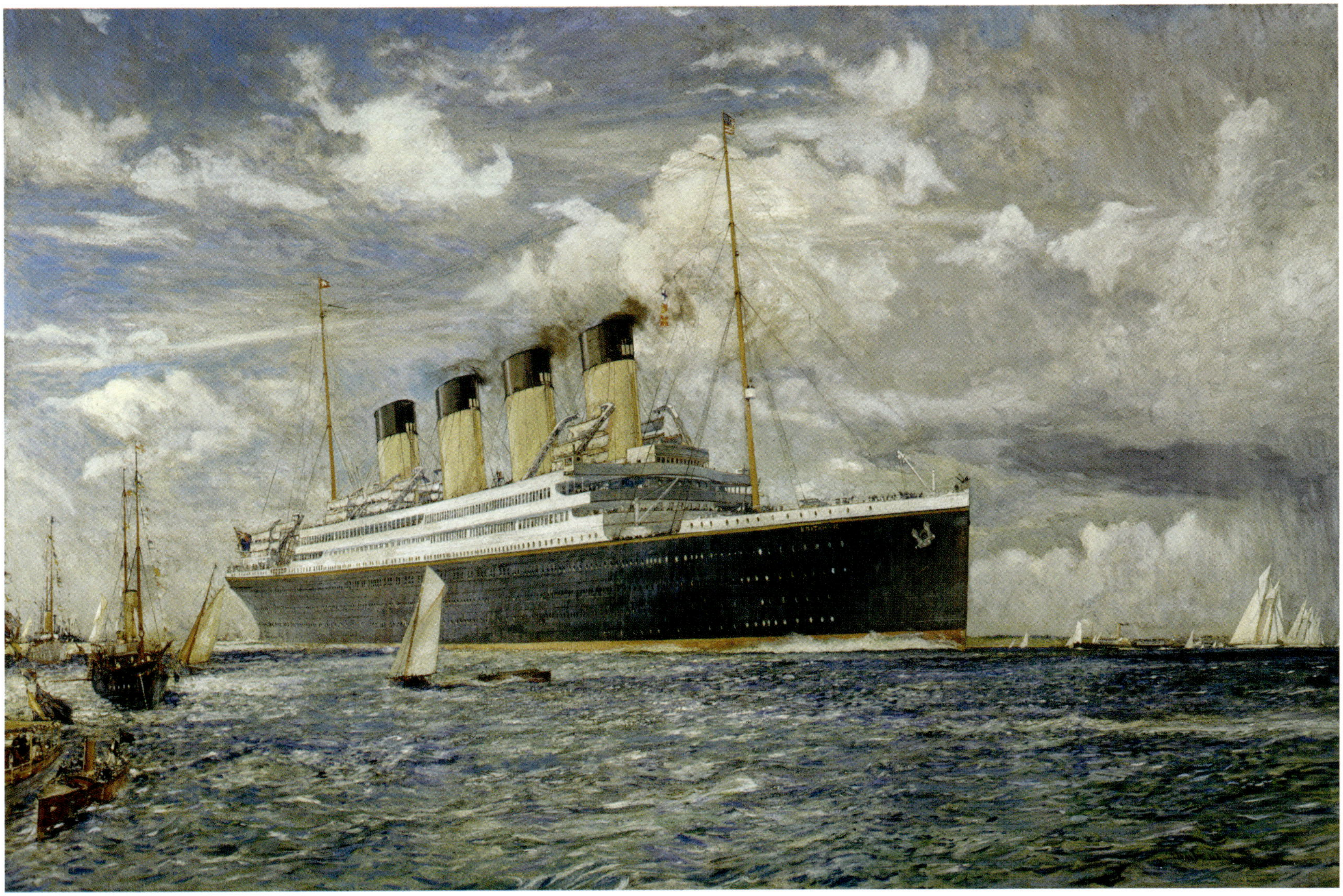

Britannic

*Charles Dixon, Oil on Canvas, 40x60", Signed*

ULSTER FOLK AND TRANSPORT MUSEUM

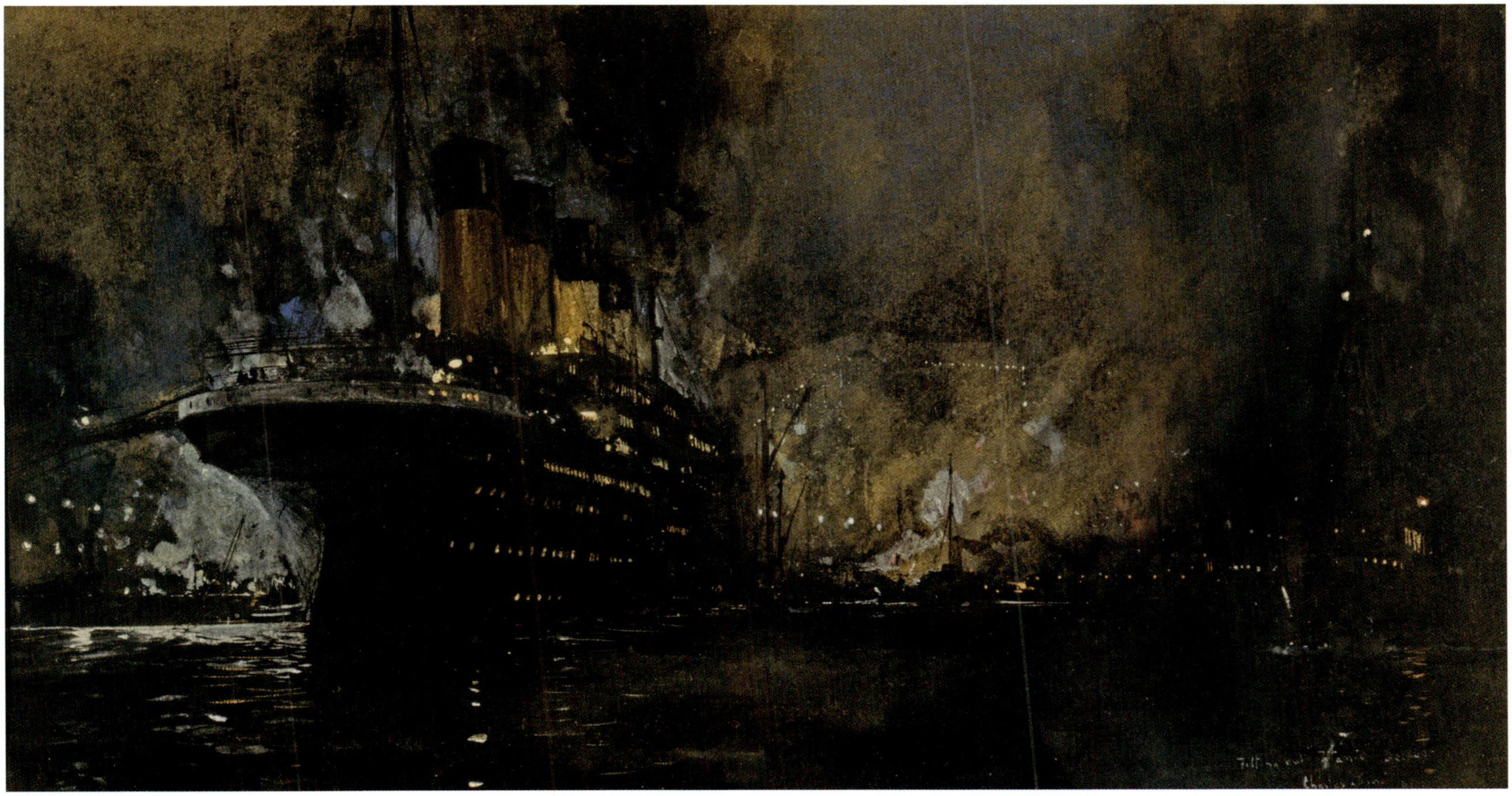

*The* Titanic *Fitting Out, Harland and Wolff Shipyard, Belfast, March 1912*
*Charles Dixon, Watercolour, 8x15¼", Signed*
Ulster Folk and Transport Museum

interpretation of a ship preparing for what was supposed to be her joyous entry into service, but in retrospect no optimism is expressed in this haunting image, only the loneliness of a sad prophecy.

RMS *Titanic*, pride of the White Star line and the largest vessel in the world, sank in the North Atlantic at twenty minutes to two o'clock in the morning of 15 April 1912 with the loss of 1523 lives. Within hours, as reports of the tragedy began to fill the front pages of newspapers across the Globe, the ship herself had assumed that mantle of immortality which, having already lasted what soon will be a century, shows no sign of abating. Furthermore, the sequence of human error, technical miscalculation and sheer bad luck culminating in her loss is better known than those surrounding any other comparable disaster in maritime history. Despite all this familiarity, however, the sinking of the *Titanic* still exerts an endless fascination and even now, these many years after she foundered, the public at large remains as obsessed with her fate as those who were alive when it occurred, and it seems that this poignant tale of man's frailty beside the forces of nature will probably endure for as long as there are ships on the sea. Although Dixon's watercolour of *Titanic* being fitted out at Belfast was thought to have been the only contemporary portrait of the ship painted from life, a previously unknown watercolour, image size 6.75 x 9 inches, by him showing *Titanic* leaving Southampton on 10th April 1912 came to light at Christie's sale of marine paintings in London in May 2007. This was obviously a major discovery for those who remain fascinated by the ship, a fascination reflected by the fact that someone was prepared to pay £16,000 for what, in essence, represents a somewhat run-of-the-mill ship portrait of the kind routinely executed by the artist and thought to have been commissioned by *The Graphic*.

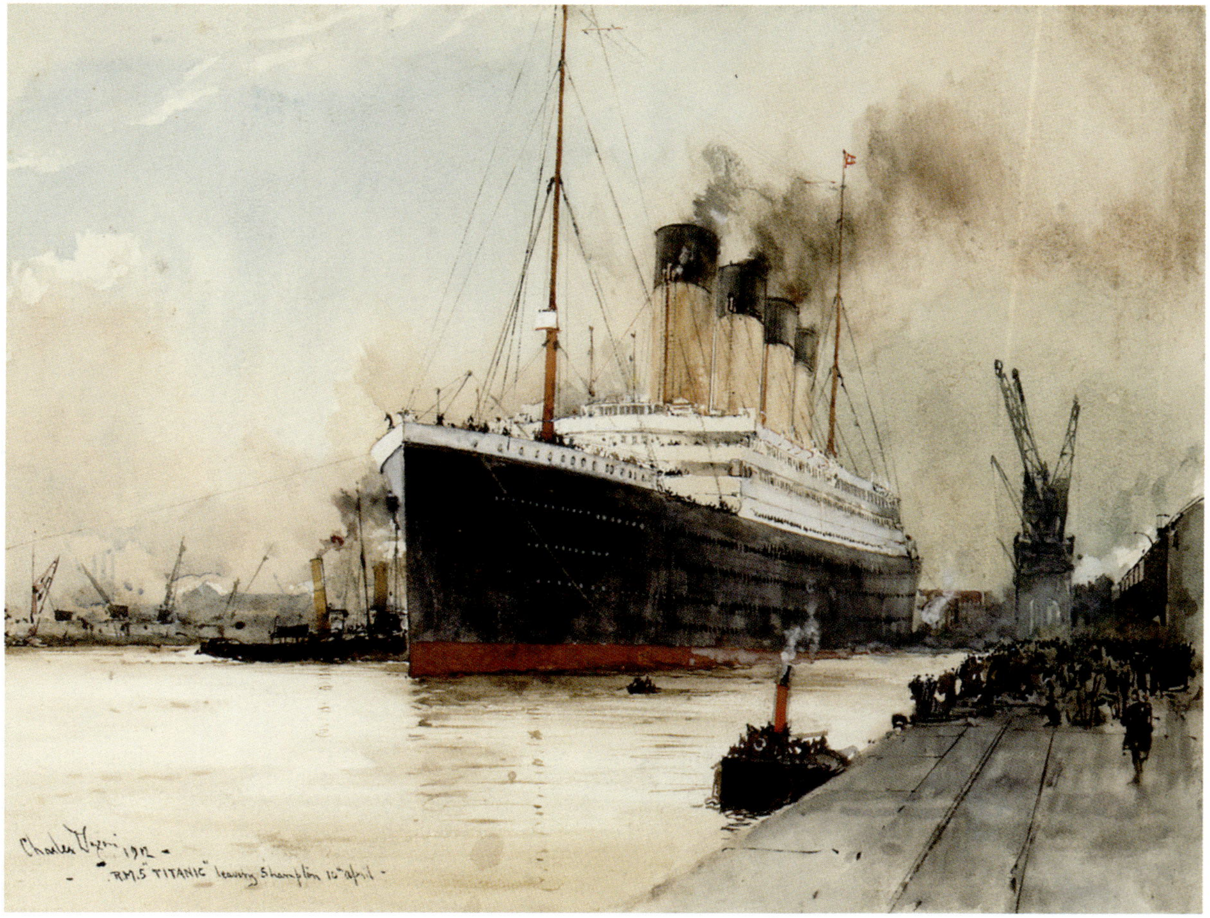


*RMS* Titanic *Clearing the Dockside at Southampton, 10 April 1912*
*Charles Dixon, Watercolour, 6¾x9", Signed, inscribed and dated 1912*
CHRISTIES IMAGES LTD

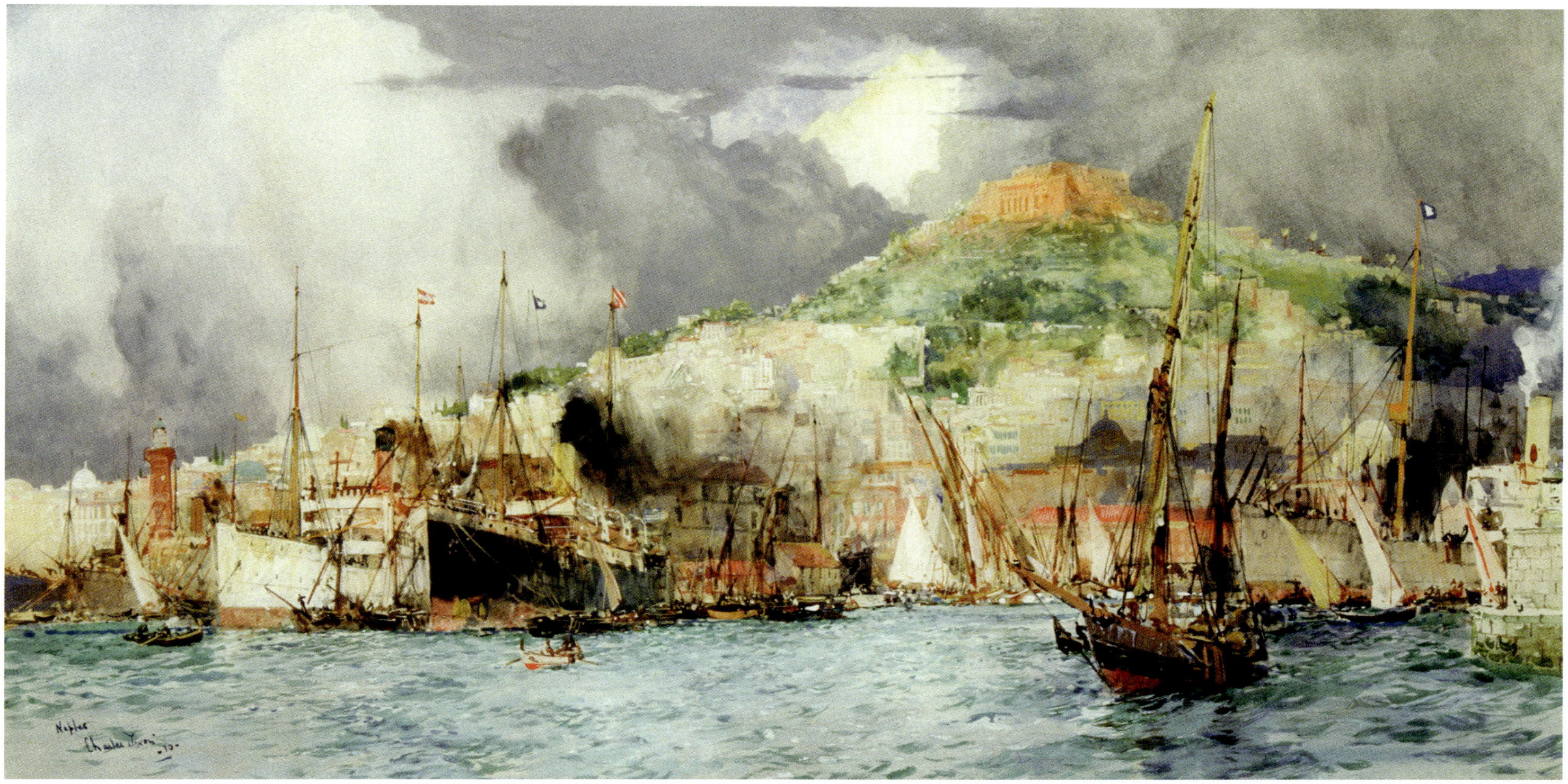

*Shipping in Naples*
*Charles Dixon, Watercolour, Signed*
PRIVATE COLLECTION/BRIDGEMAN ART LIBRARY

In sharp contrast to the smoke and grime of Dixon's dockland scenes are the watercolours he painted of warm and sunny locations such as Greece, Egypt, Italy, Gibraltar and the South of France, places that were to provide ideal subjects for the radiant colours so typical of his palette. Given his excellent draughtsmanship and fine colour sense, it would be natural to deduce that with titles such as 'The Steps of the Acropolis, 1909', 'The Propylaea, Athens', 'Off Gibraltar' 'Shipping in Naples' and 'Feluccas on the Nile, 1910' that these were the products of much overseas travel. Indeed, in his book *Nineteenth Century Marine Watercolours*, Adrian Vincent underscores the notion of Dixon having spent much time abroad, referring to him as 'a soldier who travelled in South Africa, the Middle East and North Africa'. This reference, however, is erroneous, for here Dixon has been confused with a namesake, Charles M Dixon (Fl 1890-1906), who painted landscapes and figures. The question often posed, therefore, is to what extent did C E Dixon actually visit many of the destinations that were such a regular feature of his watercolours, particularly those used for shipping posters and postcards, or did he rely largely on supposition supported by extant material? In some cases artists travelled as guests of the cruise lines to paint scenes of life on board and picture their vessels in a setting that would promote the companies' business. One example was W L Wyllie, who travelled with P&O, another Norman Wilkinson, whose art had appeared on Allan Line cards in 1903 and who offered to paint some posters for Booth Line in exchange for a round trip to South America. There is, however, no record of Dixon having received similar treatment from the companies he painted for, more likely opportunities for distant travel being facilitated through a thirty-year friendship with his famous patron, Sir Thomas Lipton, who, between 1899 and 1930, he accompanied on each of his five challenges for the America's Cup. During his lifetime, apart from his racing yachts, each named *Shamrock*, Lipton owned two steam-driven vessels, *Erin* and

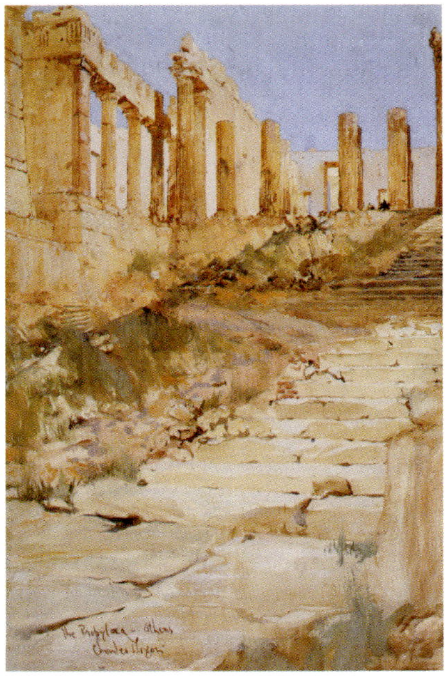

*The Propylaea, Athens*
*Charles Dixon, Watercolour, Signed and inscribed*
CHRIS BEETLES LTD

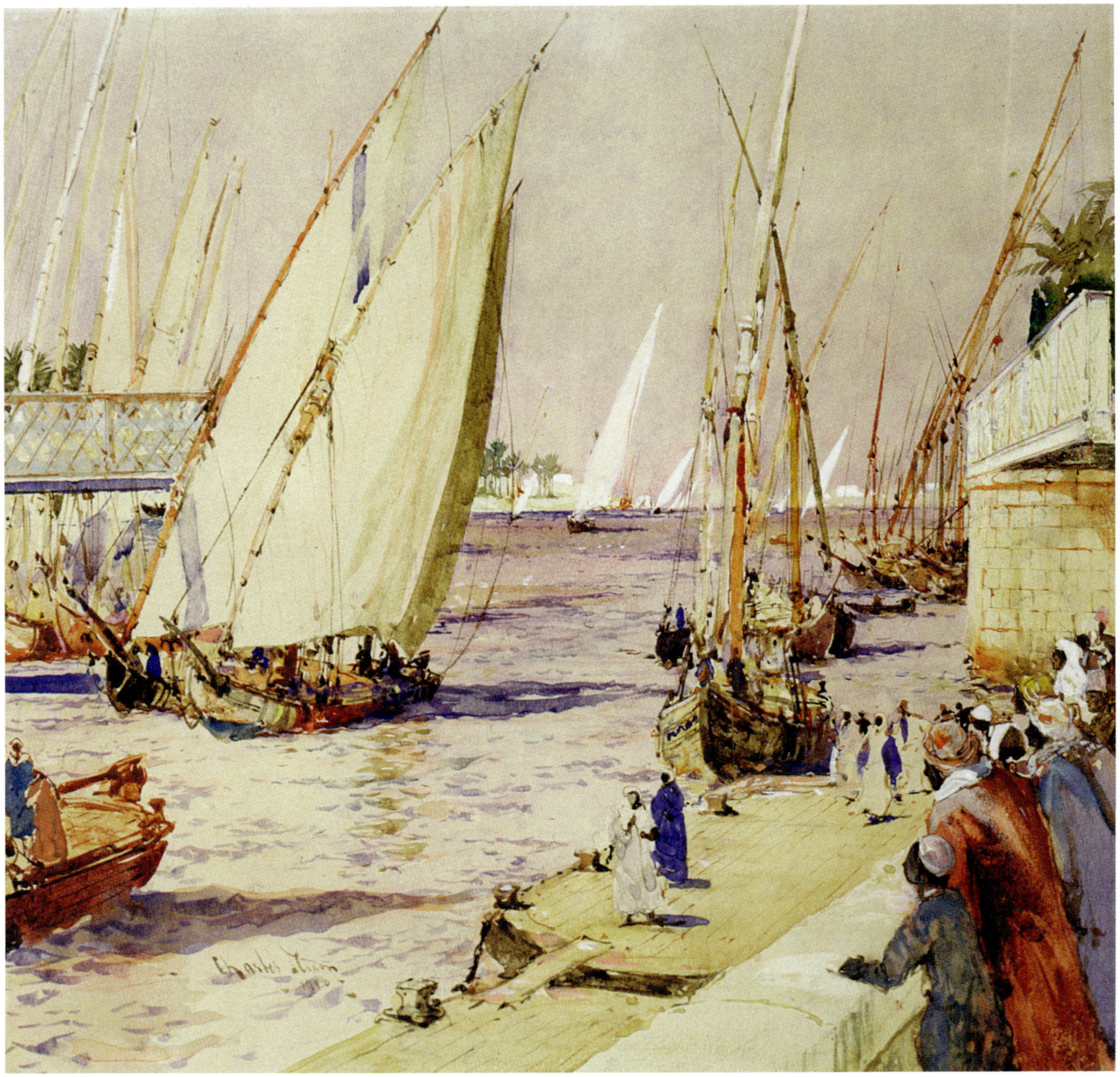

*Feluccas on the Trading Route*
*Charles Dixon, Pen, Brown Ink and Watercolour, 9½x9½", Signed and dated 1910*
BRIDGEMAN ART LIBRARY

*Erin II*, each fitted out with all the comforts of a luxury home and not only provided Lipton with the ideal vantage point to watch his five *Shamrocks* compete, but also ensured the perfect floating base to entertain in the lavish style befitting a multi-millionaire. Both yachts were to feature quite often in Dixon's paintings of the America's Cup races, but also at anchor in more leisurely destinations. *Erin* is seen here lying off Jamaica, perhaps a relaxing distraction for Lipton after the hurly burly of New York and the disappointment of another defeat for *Shamrock*. Lipton's determination to bring home the Cup meant that Dixon was able to enjoy the opportunity to stray outside European waters and his paintings of the America's Cup races provide a tangible record of his visits to the United States. Clearly he was fascinated by the thriving activity of the New York waterfront and North River. Indeed, in 1893, his entries at the Royal Academy, 'Liberty – New York Harbour' and 'New York', at the Royal Institute of Painters in Watercolours, suggest that as a young man of twenty-one, he had already crossed the Atlantic, one of many excursions he made there throughout his life.

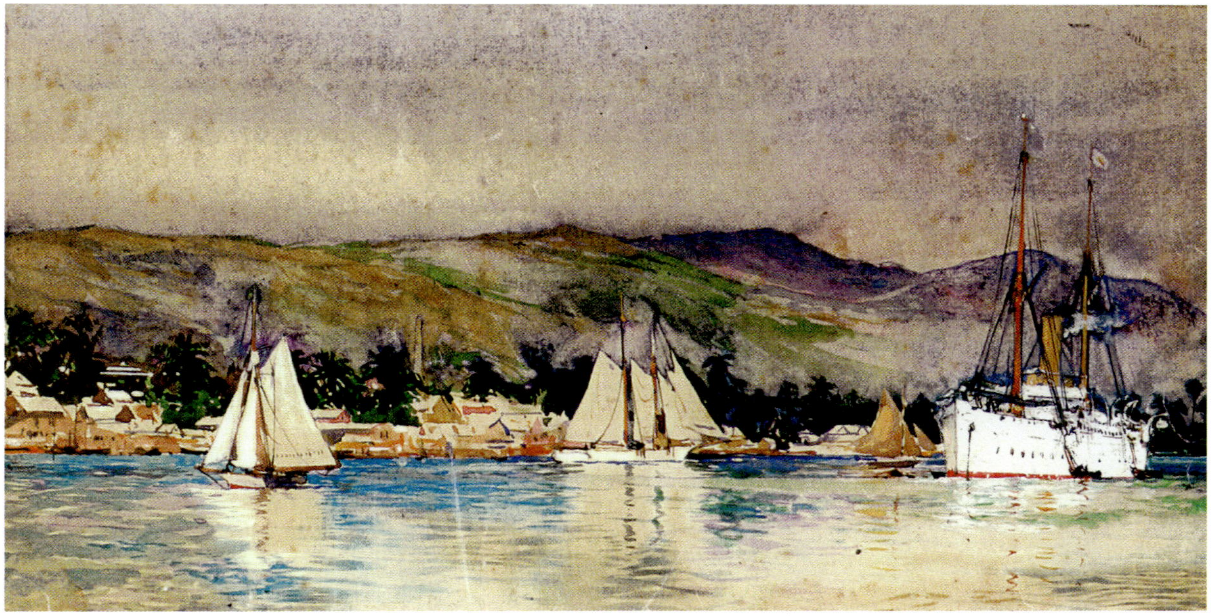

*Steam Yacht* Erin *Lying Off Jamaica*
*Charles Dixon, Watercolour, Signed*
J Morton Lee Fine Watercolours

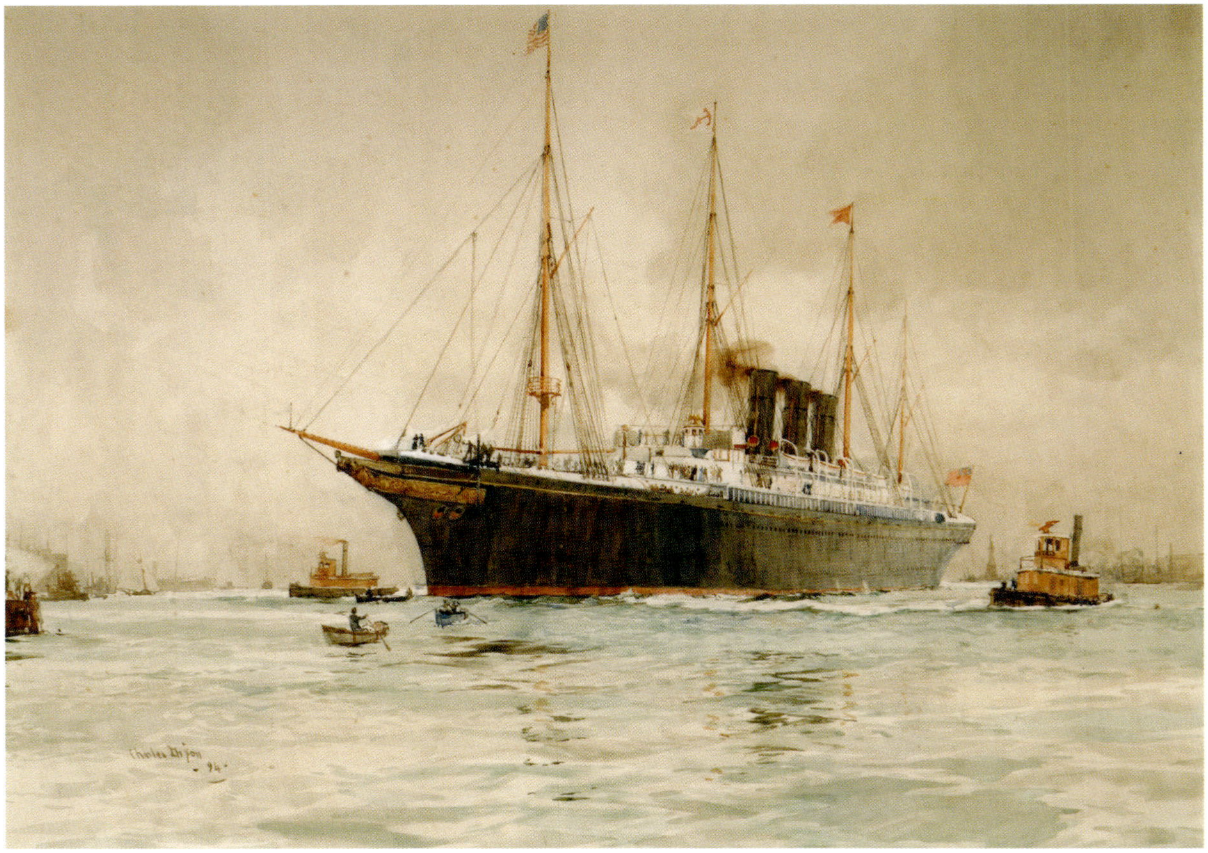

The City of Rome *Outbound from New York*
*Charles Dixon, Watercolour, Signed*
Private Collection

In 1899 the Spanish-American War had just ended and New York was celebrating the American victory with characteristic enthusiasm. During mid August that year Lipton arrived in New York Harbour with *Shamrock* – his first yacht to challenge for the Cup and Dixon was on board in readiness to paint 'on the spot' scenes of the America's Cup races due to commence in October. Moreover the timing of the visit was fortuitous for, in addition to enabling him to picture watercolours of the forthcoming action, it also allowed him the opportunity to record a major episode in America's maritime history when he painted 'New York Gives a Hero's Welcome to Admiral George Dewey, NY Harbour, Sept 29th 1899'. At this time Lipton and Dixon were aboard *Erin* in New York when Admiral Dewey of the US Navy arrived in honour and glory aboard his flagship, *Olympia*, after destroying a number of enemy vessels in Manila. The huge procession of yachts and steam vessels which had turned out to welcome Dewey was led on the port column by *Erin* and it was from this vantage point that Dixon would have painted his superb recording of the event. The scene so vividly portrayed by Dixon was probably the most colourful and exciting since John Paul Jones battled with the British off Flamborough Head in 1779 and is generally regarded as one of the finest examples of draughtsmanship, colour and movement that he ever painted. It was exhibited at the Royal Institute of Painters in Watercolours in 1900 (price £80) and in 1976 was reproduced as a limited edition colour print of 850 copies to mark 200 years of American history.

The years leading up to the First World War saw Charles Dixon's reputation as a marine painter of the utmost skill become firmly established, enhanced not only by a steady stream of entries at the Royal Academy, Royal Institute of Painters in Watercolours and his exhibitions at the Walker's Gallery, Bond Street in 1911, 1912 and 1913, but also the invitation he received from Sir Isadore Spielman, the English organiser of the great 1908 Franco-British exhibition held at the White City, London, to exhibit in the art section a large painting of Tower Bridge, a true symbol of Britain's pre-war power and strength. The exhibition was the biggest ever held in Britain and celebrated the *L'Entente Cordiale* which had been signed by the United Kingdom and France in 1904. As Dixon's popularity grew, so did the number of commissions received from many in the yachting and naval fraternities. Yet it was members of the Royal Family, with their love of sailing and service connections with the navy, who were to provide Dixon with the most prestigious of his commission work. King George V, in 1931, asked Dixon to produce for him a Christmas card of Cowes Week, and, in the same year Queen Mary purchased one of his exhibits at the RI. However, in 1929, Dixon received what was probably his most extraordinary and unusual commission, when a request arrived from St James' Palace for a miniature painting that could be hung in a doll's house being prepared as a gift for Queen Mary. It seems that this was intended to result in 'the most complete reproduction in miniature that has ever been achieved and would include every department of an English Country home of the present day, such as the King and Queen might live in'. One such department was the King's Library, which would contain a portfolio of drawings 'as representative of the best art of the period as is possible'. The portfolios were to be 2½ x 1¼ inches, and it was proposed that the drawing, either in pencil, pen and ink, or watercolour, be no more than 1½ x 1 inch. In his response, it seems that Dixon submitted not one but two watercolours, one of a sailing ship and the other of a steamer with barges, no doubt a Thames scene. Both these miniatures must have presented Dixon with something of a challenge, for he was at his most comfortable when working on a much larger scale but, given the formidable reputation of Queen Mary, he probably had no option but to comply! The miniature paintings now form part of the Royal Collection Trust, which includes nine other examples of Dixon's work and which are dispersed between Windsor Castle, Sandringham, the Royal Yacht *Britannia* and the Palace of Holyrood House. In 1934 Dixon was engaged on a Christmas card for the Prince of Wales – the drawing was unfinished.

# CHAPTER THREE
# A Highway of Nations

*'… In the part called The Pool vessels moored stem and stern and in the very strength of the tide formed a solid mass like an island covered with a forest of giant trees'* – **Joseph Conrad**

The nineteenth century was a boom period in the shipping industry and one that witnessed the transition from sail to steam propulsion, saw steel replacing timber in construction and the abandonment of traditional methods of ship building, so that by the end of the turn of the century and the beginning of the Great War, the Golden Age of Sail had almost come to an end. Thus, graceful looking sailing vessels with billowing canvas, which had once made their way silently and majestically from the heart of London to the Thames mouth and the sea, had been replaced by a very different scenario and one characterised by a frenetic mêlée of hooting steamers and tugs with high smoking funnels jostling each other for space in the congested waters. It was a time when traffic along the Thames, or as sailors called it – the London river – was probably more varied and colourful than of any other period, when out of the swirling mass of the heavily-polluted water around The Pool (the waterway extending from London Bridge through Tower Bridge), great hulks in black ochre and rust loomed above the multitude of smaller craft clustered along the Thames in profuse variety. Here were the steam coasters (the dirty British coaster with salt-caked stacks and cargoes of cheap tin trays so beloved by Masefield), three- and four-masted sailing ships loaded with wood or wool, red-sailed sprit-sail barges, the lorries of the river, carrying cheap bulk cargoes from the East Coast ports to London, and taking goods from foreign ships to towns along the estuary and above all, the most familiar sight along the Thames, sailing barges or 'stackies' which plied the river, supplying London with hay from Essex and Kent to fuel the Capital's horse-drawn transport.

*The Pool*
*Charles Dixon, Watercolour, 11½x32", Signed*
HAYNES FINE ART

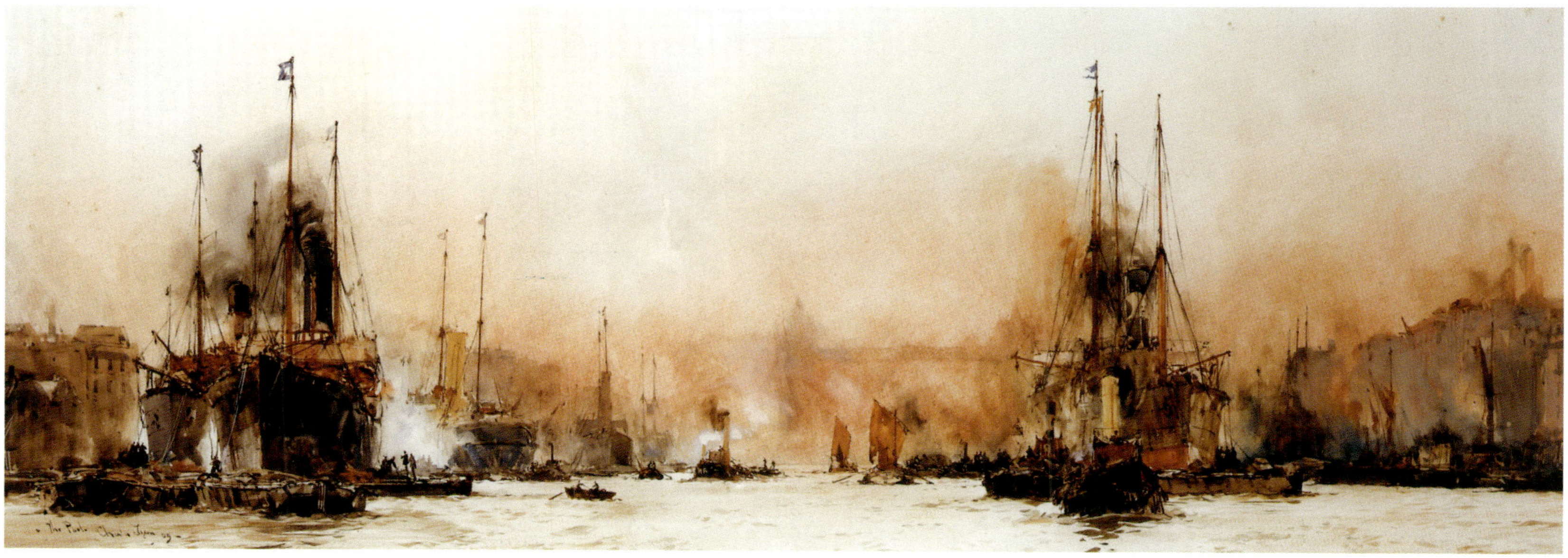

The whole scene is graphically described by W L Wyllie whose romantic metaphor 'A Highway of Nations' perfectly captures the significance of the Thames at the time as a major artery of commerce, with countless vessels and their cargoes arriving from all over the world. The true giants of the tidal Thames in those days were the passenger and cargo liners sailing to and from other ports in Europe, South Africa, South America, the Far East, Australia and the Antipodes. Even more numerous, if not so large, were the busy vessels which ran coastwise around the British Isles and the North Sea bringing coal, meat, steel, timber and a variety of consumer goods to London for distribution to other British markets. Wyllie had a phenomenal knowledge of the various aspects of the commercial life of the lower Thames, what took place on the river and its banks, as well as a deep understanding of the history which lay beyond the seamed and grubby face it offered the world, an ancient history dating back to the time of the Romans. Observing The Pool, the once busiest and most congested shipping terminal for the London merchants, where for centuries foreign shipping unloaded their cargoes and paid important dues to the Custom House, Wyllie, from the deck of his Thames barge *Ladybird*, wrote 'nothing surpasses in its way: men working like ants all over the ships and wharfs, the noise, the crush of shipping, the smoke and steam, the dumb barges drifting with tide and a man in white flannels rowing the lightest kind of outrigger. A Spanish steamer is unloading crates of oranges with an endless stream of porters walking up the sloping prow leaning forward to bring the weight of their heavy load more directly over their hips. Further down, the "fish carriers" are clustered thick around the pontoons and dolphins of Billingsgate. They have very high prows and are low in the water, rusty and scarred from grinding alongside boats on the Dogger Bank while picking up their catch for express delivery. Their funnels are white with salt spray off the stormy North Sea. When you meet a fish carrier on the river it's as well to keep clear of her because she is always in a hurry, storming out with the fast melting ice in her holds and storming out to get fresh herrings to the market and out onto Londoners' breakfast tables. Lying outside these unkempt busybodies, but in just as much hurry to unload their very special freights are unusual boats from Holland. They are unusual because unlike their black, smelly, rusty neighbours, their wooden hulls sparkle with gay colours and are brightly varnished. They are unusual too, for what they are unloading are live eels, fatter and more succulent than the English ones, especially good in eel pies. The fish have been sailed alive across the North Sea in unusual tanks built into the boats, which allow a constant flow of seawater over them. However, once the Dutchmen enter the estuary they have to anchor in Holy Haven and wait for a tug to fetch them because the water above that point, which has to continue to flow through, is so polluted it would kill their cargo'.

This crammed and relatively intimate world of London's port became a source of fascination to many late Victorian marine painters, for an artist would have been very feeble indeed not to have responded to the panorama so vividly described by Wyllie. Charles Dixon was one who did, returning time and time again, from his teenage years until he died, to paint with such passionate affection and understanding scenes of the tidal Thames from the panoply of shipping congregated in the upper Pool to Gravesend, generally regarded as the best of his watercolours and ones that linger in the memory. These are invariably inscribed with titles such as 'Below Tower Bridge', 'Greenwich Reach', 'Off Tilbury' and 'Blackwall Reach' and provide somewhat repetitive yet compelling images of the river as the Victorian era reached its zenith and London became the mercantile hub of Empire, with raw materials pouring in from every corner of the globe and manufactured goods filling the holds of every outbound ship. Furthermore London was the main terminal for the innumerable passenger lines which served every continent save North America. This was a time when its great commercial dockyards, which locations in London, particularly the Palace of Westminster and St Paul's, but in contrast to Marshall, he painted in a much tighter fashion, resulting in the meticulously fine and detailed watercolours which have now become much sought after. He exhibited from 1890, including the Royal Academy and RI and his work is represented in the British Museum.

Primarily a landscape and architectural painter, but one who also painted many views of the London river, the work of the amateur artist, the Rev Sir H J Medlycott (1841-1920) is less well known, but very competent. His exhibition venues included the RA and Society of British Artists. Another specialist

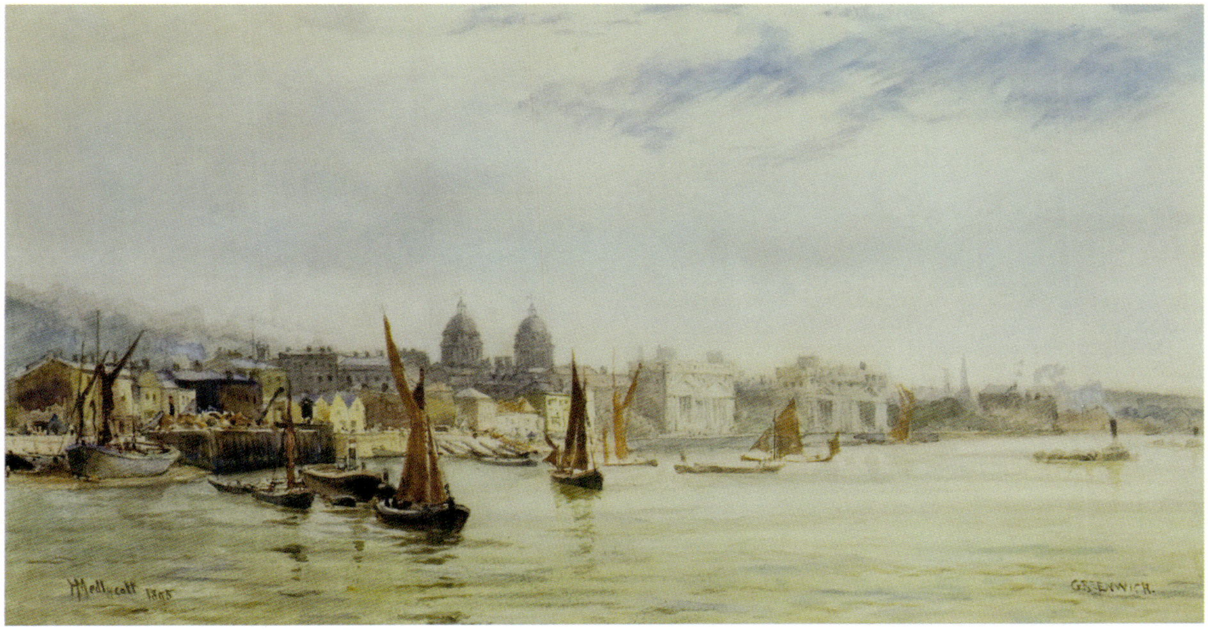

*Greenwich*
*H.J. Medlycott, Watercolour, 8¾x15",*
*Signed, inscribed and dated 1895*
PRIVATE COLLECTION

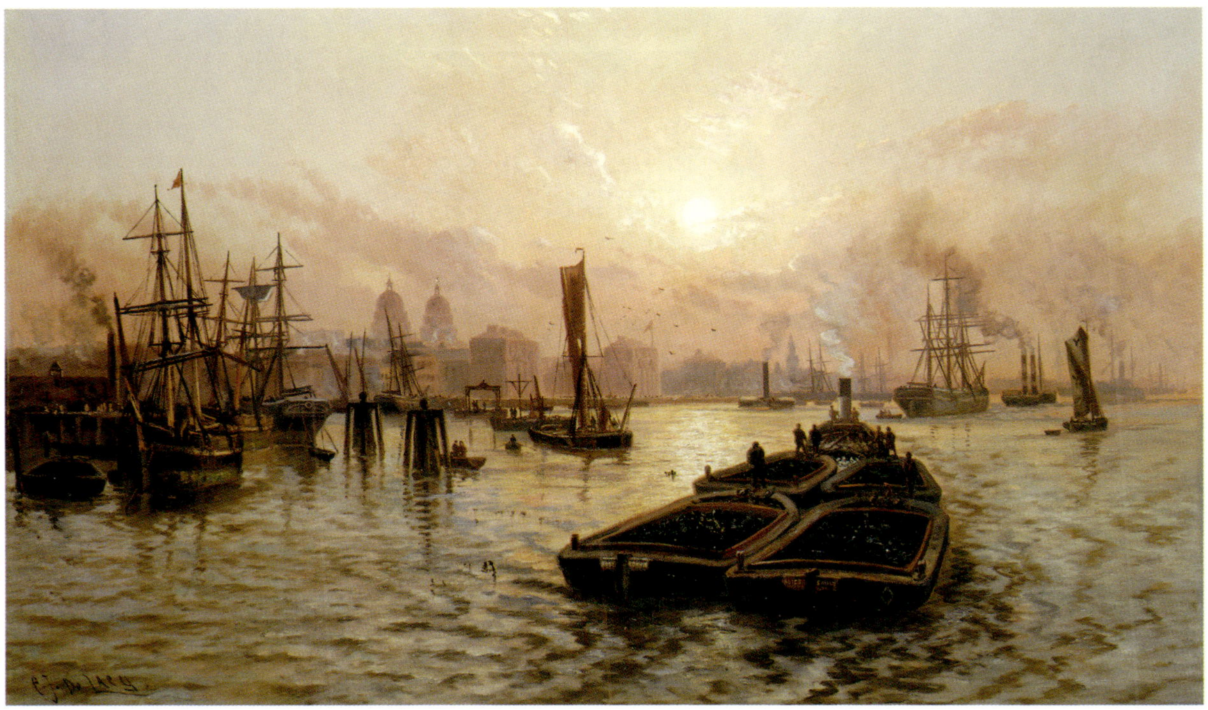

*Coal Barges on the Thames near Greenwich*
*Charles John de Lacy, Oil on Canvas, Signed*
N.R. OMELL GALLERY

marine painter, who concentrated on depicting scenes of the myriad of vessels working along the river in the last quarter of the nineteenth and first quarter of the twentieth centuries, is Charles John de Lacy (1856-1929). Born in Sunderland, he trained in London and, like Dixon and Wyllie, he worked as an illustrator for *The Graphic* and also *The Illustrated London News* which, from 1895, employed him as press artist and special correspondent. A great number of his pictures concern The Pool and the area around Limehouse and Greenwich Reach, his Thames scenes coming to the notice of the Port of London Authority who engaged him as their official artist. De Lacy was highly proficient in oil and watercolour and capable of working both on a large and very small scale, for he also painted shipping postcards for, among others, the White Star Line. Apart from the Royal Academy, de Lacy also exhibited in the provinces and the Royal Society of British Artists, and is credited with providing the illustrations for *A Book about Ships*, published in 1914 and *Our Wonderful Navy* in 1919.

In contrast to the other painters mentioned in this chapter, someone who opted for a rather different approach to his Thames and Medway subjects was Charles William Wyllie, RBA, ROI (1859-1923). The younger brother of William Lionel Wyllie, he too was an immensely gifted artist whose oil paintings enabled him to compete on equal terms with W L, but for him it was often the river folk themselves who supplied the main focus of his work, with the river merely the setting for a human rather than a nautical commentary. Like Dixon, growing up in London gave him an intimate knowledge of the river and, at the age of 13, he had his first painting, entitled 'The Evening Hour', shown at the Royal Academy; a remarkable achievement that even the precocious Dixon had been unable to emulate. In the footsteps of his brother, Charles attended Heatherley's Art School in London and his art bears some resemblance, producing work which was in every sense as painterly although in a freer style with usually a warmer sense of colour. Like Dixon, Charles also worked as an illustrator, mainly for *The Graphic*, but also *The Illustrated London News*, and during the First World War he served as a naval camouflage expert with the Royal Naval Volunteer Reserve. Between 1872 and 1904, he exhibited 47 works at the Royal Academy, of which a number reflect his long-standing association with the river. Although first and foremost a painter in oils, he also exhibited at the New Watercolour Society.

*Narrow Boats at a Lock*
*Charles W. Wyllie, Oil on Canvas, 36x28½", Signed and dated 1888*
ROYAL EXCHANGE ART GALLERY

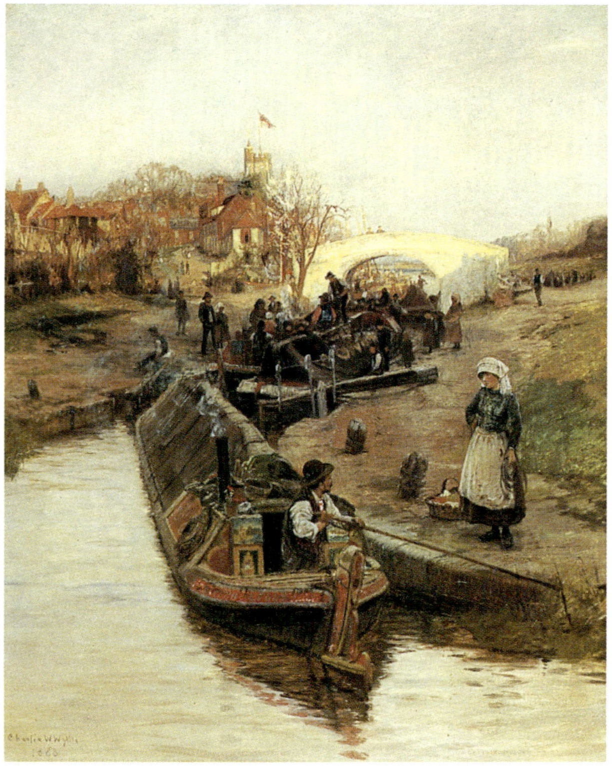

Generally acknowledged as one of Britain's outstanding marine artists of the twentieth century, references to the work of Norman Wilkinson (1878-1971) permeate each chapter of this book for his paintings encapsulate all the major genres of marine art. But for many admirers, it is the contribution he made in recording the war at sea during both the Great War and the Second World War that will remain the most memorable, and this is dealt with in more detail in the following chapter. He is included here, however, because during his long life he painted many fine oils of the London river in his painterly style and with an accomplished handling of colour. In his oil on canvas 'The Tower of London' Wilkinson shows the London river full of commercial activity, from tall-funnelled merchant ships to tugs and a splendid 1930s motor cruiser. All are overshadowed by the Tower with the sun shining through the clouds, for the cloud-scapes in Wilkinson's paintings are always vivid expressions of his art.

Born in Australia, Arthur James Weatherall Burgess, RI, ROI (1879-1957) was a marine artist of considerable talent who painted many scenes of the London river. Burgess studied art in Australia and later at St Ives, Cornwall. He exhibited at the Royal Academy from 1904 and at the Royal Institution of Oil Painters, the Royal Institute of

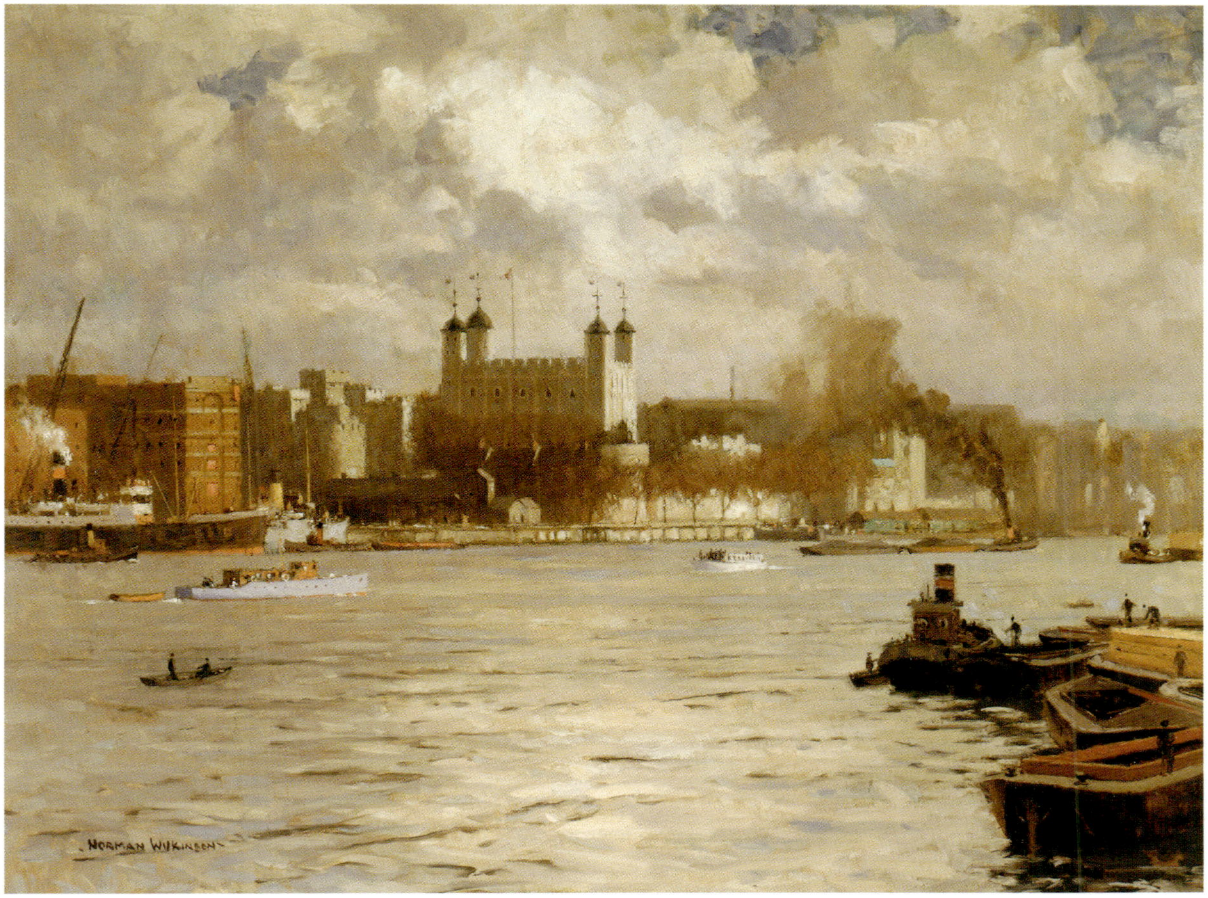


*The Tower of London*
*Norman Wilkinson, Oil on Canvas, Signed*
Royal Exchange Art Gallery

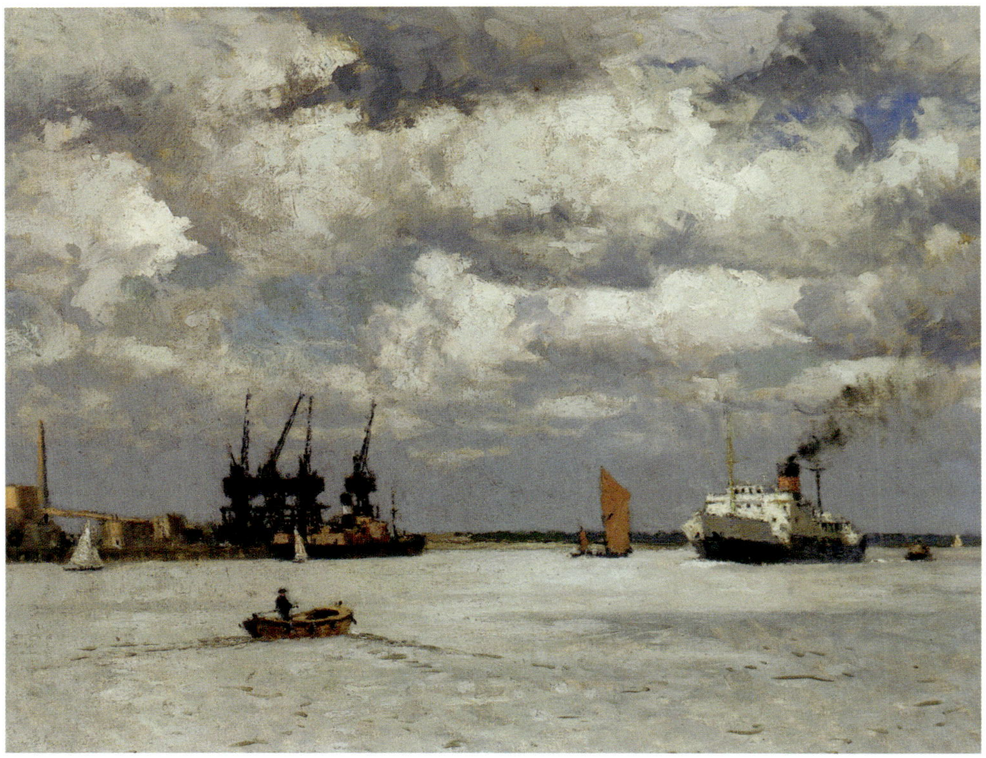

*The Lower River Below Gravesend*
*Norman Wilkinson, Oil on Canvas, 18x24",*
*Exhibited Fine Art Society 1959*
Royal Exchange Art Gallery

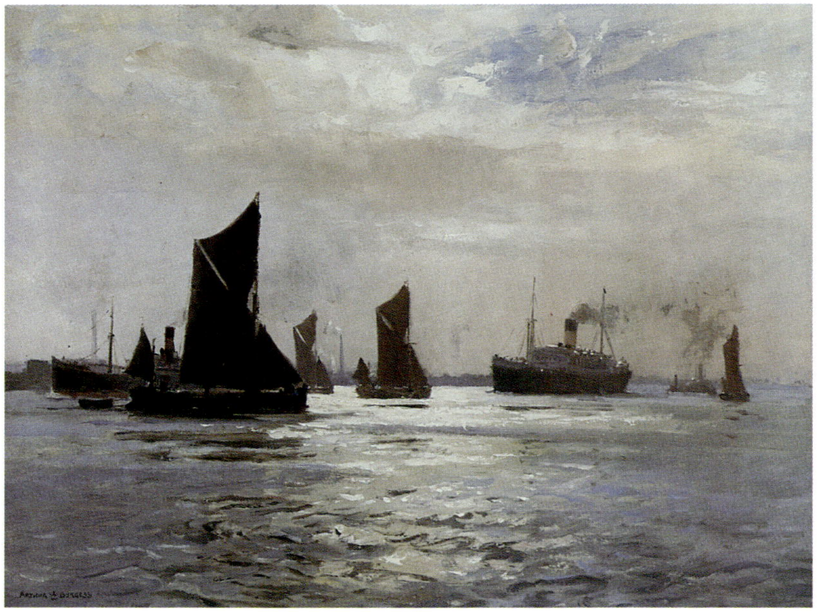

Painters in Watercolours and at the Paris Salon. Like many of his contemporaries, he combined easel painting with commercial art and worked as an illustrator for *The Graphic*, *The Illustrated London News* and *The Sphere*. A versatile artist, Burgess painted every conceivable type of maritime subject and his lifelong devotion to marine painting was instrumental in him becoming a founder member of the Society of Marine Artists and later a vice-president. In his oil 'On a Flowing Tide', Burgess shows sprit-sail barges under sail approaching a liner. These large trading vessels, sailed by 'a man and a boy', plied their trade on the Thames, the Medway and the South East coast of England, and in 1900 their numbers totalled close on 2,000.

*On a Flowing Tide*
*Arthur J. Burgess, Oil on Canvas, 18x24", Signed*
ROYAL EXCHANGE ART GALLERY

During the past twenty years, the work of Frederick William (Frank) Scarbrough (1863-1945) has become increasingly popular; a fact reflected in the prices now being achieved for his Thames scenes. Born in Boothby, Lincolnshire, he was the youngest son of a farmer. Details of his life are somewhat obscure, but it seems he spent some time in London recording, in his instantly recognisable style, scenes of shipping in The Pool. These usually show vessels in the river 'bow on' often in pairs, and although there seems to be a predictable sameness about them, they succeed in conveying an accurate snapshot of London's docks during its commercial heyday. Apart from his watercolour views of the Thames, Scarbrough also painted coastal harbour and estuary scenes from Scotland to Whitby Bay and East Anglia, and many of his north-eastern coastal subjects, which represent some of his best work, convey a loose, brooding impressionist freedom, contrasting sharply with his more typical views of The Pool. He died in his native county at Grantham at the age of 82.

Whilst the art of Dixon, W L Wyllie and Norman Wilkinson will always guarantee their place in the premier division of British marine painting, there were many other players whose names are linked with the London river, but whose work is generally less well known, such as Henry Branston Freer

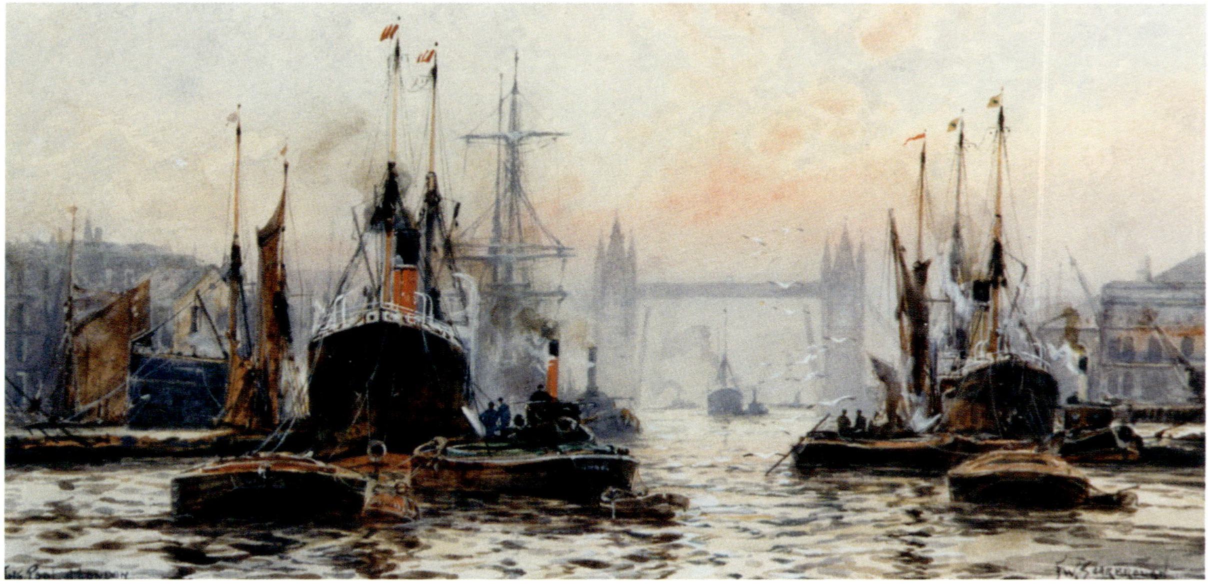

*Tower Bridge*
*Frank Scarbrough, Watercolour, 7½x15",*
*Signed and inscribed*
JOHN MORTON LEE FINE WATERCOLOURS

(1876-1947). For anyone considering the work of this very talented watercolour painter, it will be immediately apparent that the artist was influenced by W L Wyllie, with whom he came into contact whilst living in Rochester. Indeed, mention is made of this association in the biography of Wyllie *We Were One* written by Wyllie's wife. Apparently, Wyllie was painting four large canvases to raise funds for a new drill hall in Rochester and 'was assisted in this mammoth undertaking by H B Freer, a favourite pupil'. Noted for his Thames estuary scenes, his works are typical of the many Edwardian colourists who could give a sense of unsentimental occasion in depicting the ponderous workhorses of the river with their solemn, dark sails against the leaden Thames estuary sky. The Thames sailing barge was tailor made for the river. It was said they could sit wherever a duck could swim, as they were flat bottomed with no keel. 'Lee Boards', which hung like hinged fins from either side of the hull, prevented them from drifting in the wind and they were an integral part of the river traffic of the day. In this typical scene of barges on the Thames estuary, Freer's work is characterised by delicate and firm handling of the sea and sky and his favourite dusky red is prominent in the sails. Apart from Rochester, Freer also lived at Gravesend and between 1906 and 1915, he exhibited five pictures at the Royal Academy, including 'The River Medway'. He also produced artwork for shipping companies, notably the Aberdeen Line, his ship portraits appearing on a number of their postcards.

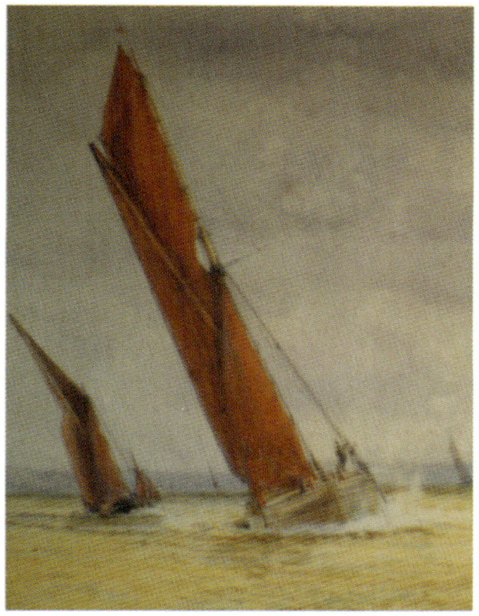

*Sea Reach (detail)*
*Henry Branston Freer, Watercolour, Signed*
PRIVATE COLLECTION

Although a prolific and accomplished marine artist, until recently little biographical information had been unearthed regarding William Minshall Birchall (1884-1941), another noted painter of the London river and whose work can sometimes show an affinity to that of Dixon, although it is more strongly reminiscent of W L Wyllie. It seems that Birchall, who was born of British parents in Iowa, USA, immigrated to London as a young man, eventually settling in Hastings where he lived and worked for most of his life. Certainly, he shared Dixon's love of all things maritime; his compositions showing lively watercolours of warships, liners and tea clippers. He seems to have employed the same effortless skill in producing many atmospheric scenes of the London river showing the usual panoply of sailing barques, steam ships and sprit-sail barges going about their daily business and often inscribed with titles such as 'The Gateway to London: Tower Bridge' and 'Old Father Thames'. Like Dixon, Birchall also worked as an illustrator but opted for a wide variety of nautical publications such as the magazine of the Navy League rather than the more high profile weekly illustrated newspapers of the day. Birchall's talent also caught the eye of the shipping lines for whom he painted postcards of their ships and these included the Orient, Cunard and Hamburg-Amerika Companies. It appears that throughout his relatively short life, he did not exhibit widely or indeed move in the same established artistic circles favoured by some of his contemporaries, but he painted during a period in the 1920s which brought to fruition a flourishing stable of marine artists whose work has become increasingly appreciated. Examples of his art are to be found in the National Maritime Museum, Greenwich, who hold five of his watercolours, and also the Peabody Museum of Salem in the USA. He sometimes used the pseudonym Frank Clifford, especially when signing work painted between 1916 and 1921.

A less familiar name, but whose watercolours of coastal scenes and views of shipping in the Thames estuary before the First World War bear some resemblance to those of Birchall, is William Stephen Tomkin (1861-1940). Tomkin was a sound draughtsman who exhibited at the RA in 1909. Like Dixon, his paintings seem to have found favour with Sir Thomas Lipton, but he never really exploited his work commercially, rather he worked as an illustrator, in 1889 joining the artists' department of Waterlow & Sons for whom he worked for over 40 years, producing many excellent brightly coloured designs for books and posters.

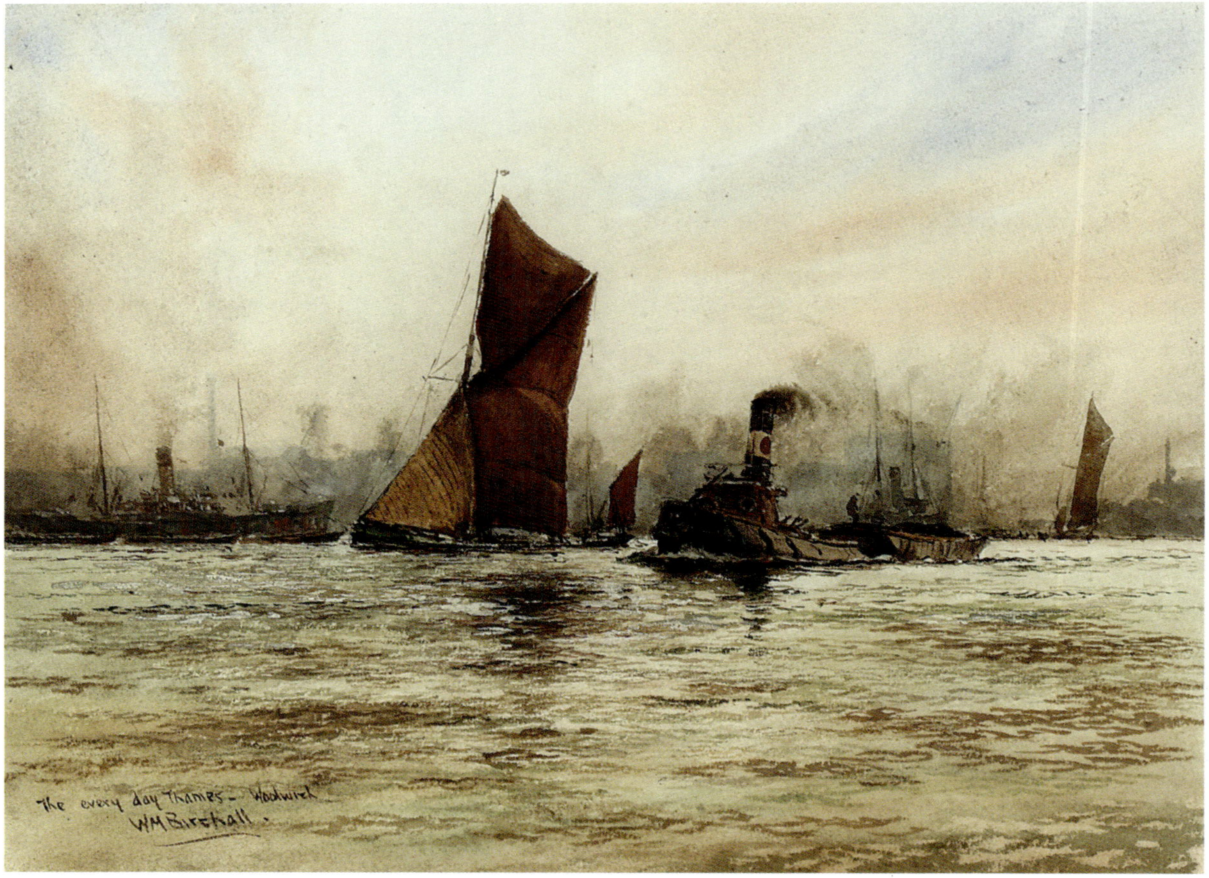


*The Everyday Thames, Woolwich*
*William M. Birchall, Watercolour, 10½x14⅝",*
*Signed and inscribed*
CHRISTIE'S IMAGES LTD

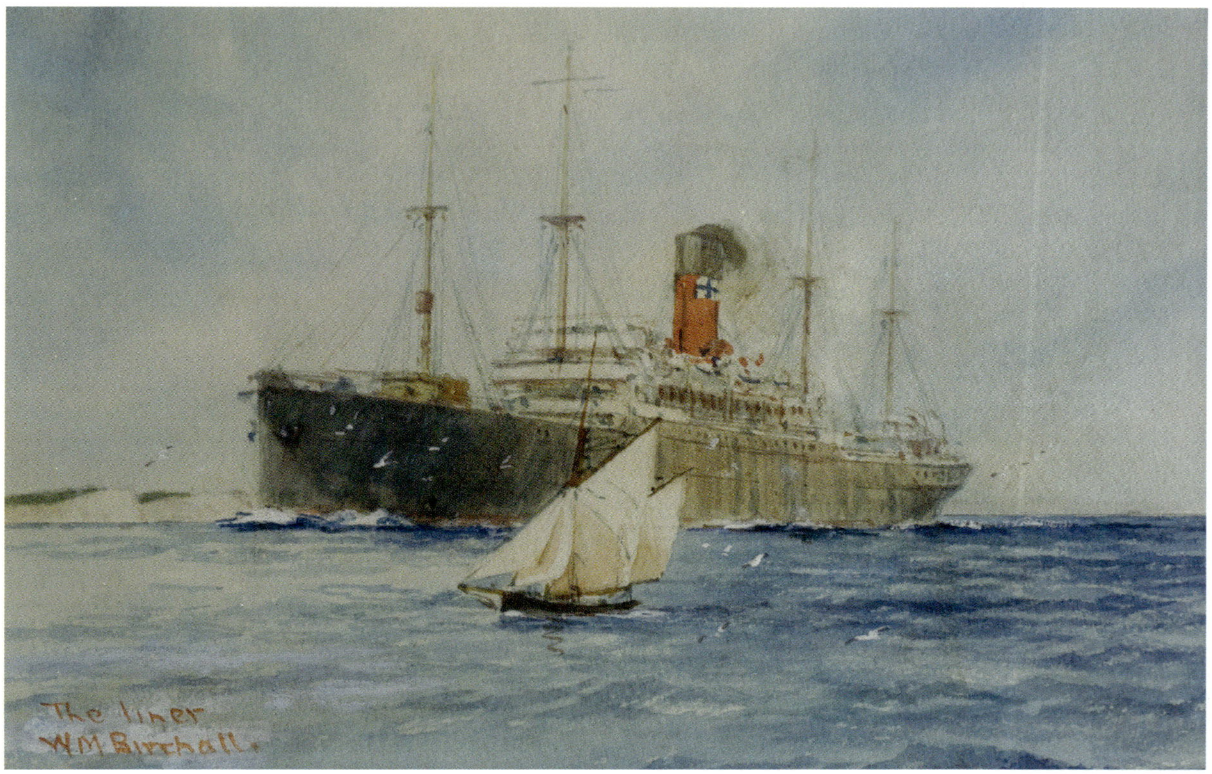


*The Liner*
*William M. Birchall, Watercolour, 5x7",*
*Signed and inscribed*
PRIVATE COLLECTION

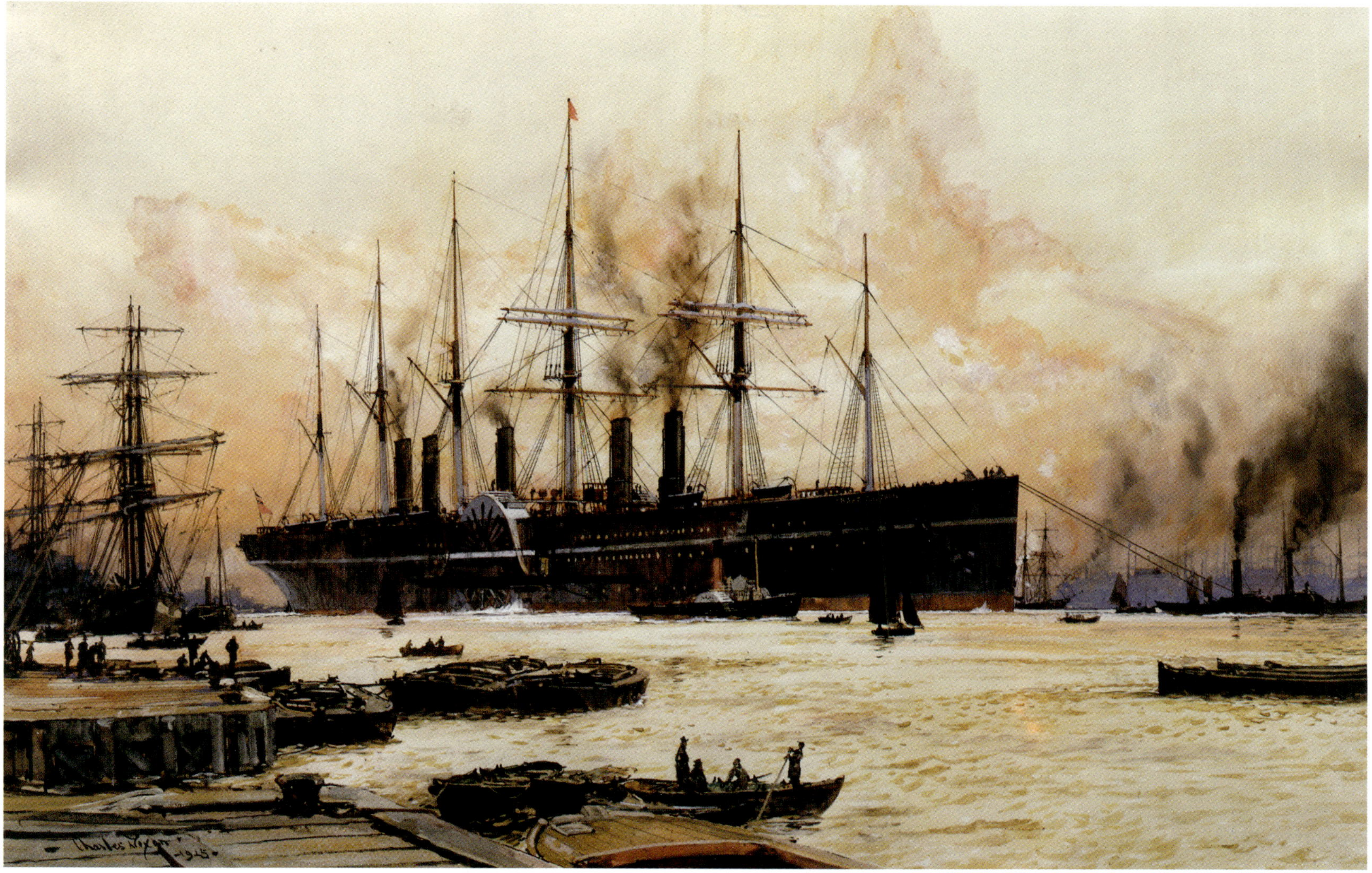

*The* Great Eastern
*Charles Dixon, Watercolour, Signed*
N.R. Omell Gallery

During its long history, the dockyards along the London river such as Deptford and Blackwall have given birth to many famous vessels but none more so than the mighty and controversial *Great Eastern*, which was launched at Millwall in 1858. In this fine rendering of the ship leaving Liverpool, Dixon has succeeded in depicting her monstrous bulk of 18,914 tons, dwarfing all around her as she is towed out into the Mersey. Although begun in 1853, the *Great Eastern* was not completed for another six years. She was five times larger than any vessel then afloat and Dixon's watercolour pays tribute to her indomitable designer and builder Isambard Kingdom Brunel. The success of Charles Dixon's scenes of the London river were largely due to the skill with which he applied the sombre colours of his palette to highlight its grimy industrial atmosphere; yet in his watercolour of 'H.M. Hospital Ship *Maine*' at anchor, he has ensured that the white hull and funnel of the ship dominate the composition, emitting a luminous contrast to the barges and other craft surrounding her.

Although it will be Dixon's paintings of the tidal river for which he will be best remembered, it seems that there were occasions, perhaps for some relief, when he returned to the upper reaches of the great waterway, which from around the 1880s became the playground of the well-to-do. This was a time when

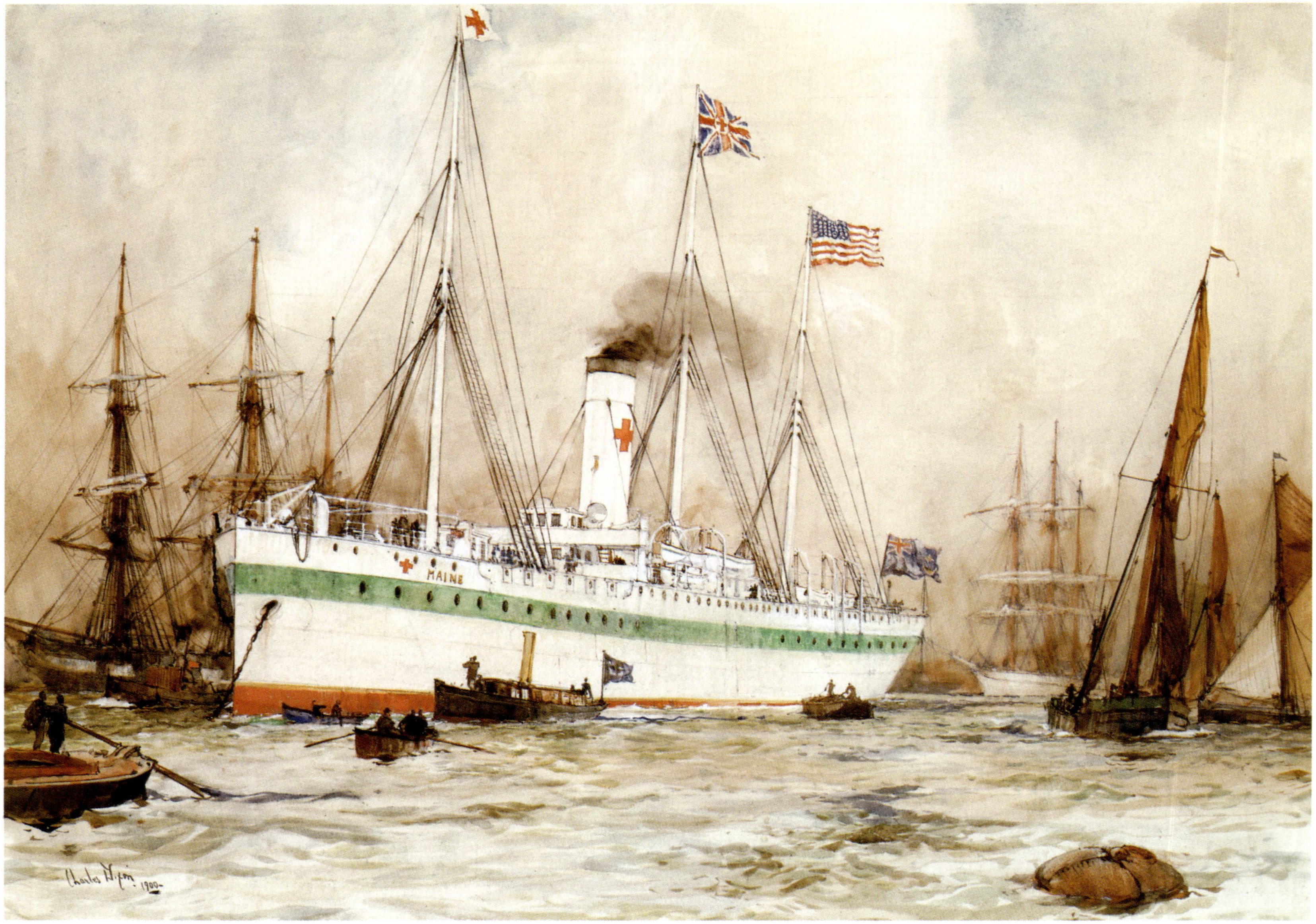

*HM Hospital Ship* Maine
*Charles Dixon, Watercolour, Signed*
PRIVATE COLLECTION

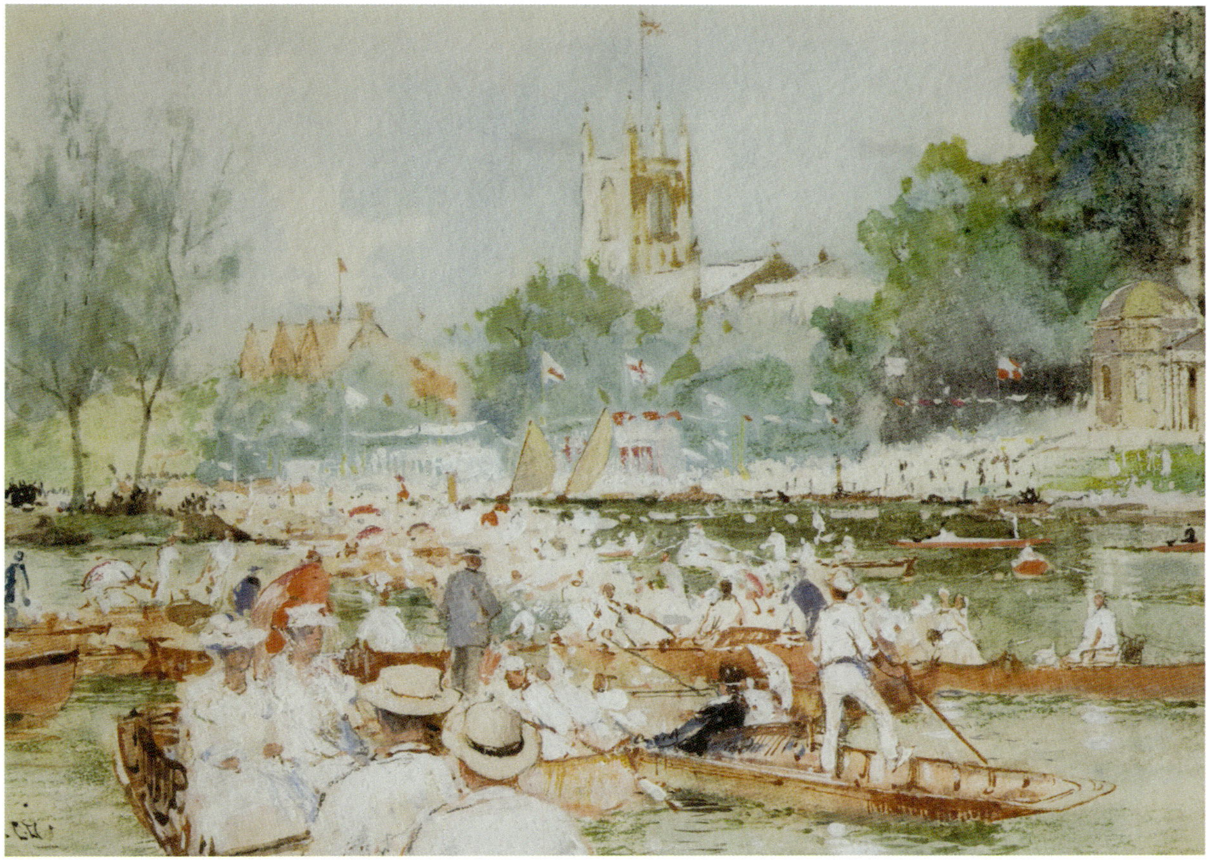

*The Sunbury Regatta*
*Charles Dixon, Watercolour,*
*Signed with initials, 4½x6¼″*
Private Collection

the sport of rowing and the age of regattas took over the river, a world away from the sweat and spice downstream. In a delightful little watercolour Dixon has succeeded in creating an image of summertime indolence in Edwardian England, in which he depicts 'The Sunbury Regatta'. The picture shows punts drifting lazily along the river with their catch of elegant parasoled ladies. Although not a cargo of the kind usually associated with Dixon's rendering of river traffic, it communicates all that special atmosphere and gentle warmth that river boating has come to symbolise.

Given Charles Dixon's prolific output in which his Thames scenes were predominant, it is no surprise that a number of these should have found their way into the collections of those city institutions so closely connected with the river. These include the Corporation of Trinity House, the Honourable Company of Master Mariners (a livery company of the City of London formed to promote the interests of the maritime profession, particularly the Merchant Navy) and also the Port of London Authority. The PLA holds several examples of Dixon's work, but it is 'Peace Pageant in the Pool of London, 4 August 1919', which is the most outstanding. In a huge oil on canvas (38″ x 86″), Dixon shows the Royal barge with King George V and the Royal Family aboard, heading the procession from the Custom House, whilst close by is the Admiralty barge with a gilded and winged sea horse forming the prow. The painting was exhibited at the Royal Academy in 1920.

At the end of Charles Dixon's life, the towering masts of the remaining sailing fleets on the world's oceans could still be seen on the London river, together with all forms of merchant steamships. There

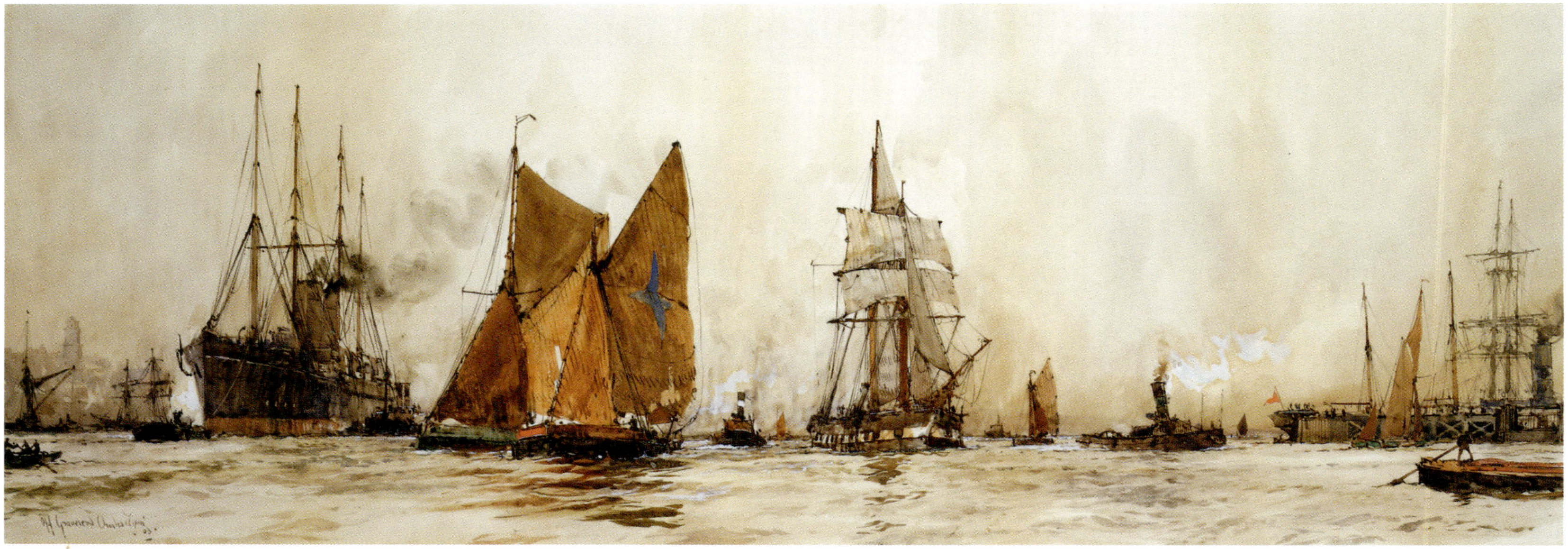

*Gravesend*
*Charles Dixon, Watercolour, Signed*
Private Collection

was constant noise, with people yelling, blasts from ships' horns and water boiling from the turmoil of thrashing screws, all of which added to the cacophony. However, should Charles Dixon and his contemporaries return to the London river today, they would, of course find the same classic landmarks such as the twin peaks of Greenwich Hospital, Tower Bridge or the single dome of St Paul's, but no longer the crowded wharves, the eternal din, the dusky sun or, as one art critic wrote, 'the vast clouds of smoke rolling skywards like the incense of some awful sacrifice', all of which serve to remind us how quiet the river is now compared with the scenes painted by Dixon a century ago.

Today, the tidal Thames is just another British river, admittedly less polluted now than in the last two centuries, yet sadly in every other aspect, it has fallen from its former greatness and lost its place in the national consciousness, and waterborne traffic is less than at any time in the last fifteen hundred years. Therefore, a debt is owed to Dixon, and his contemporaries for capturing these scenes of the tidal Thames so that those who see their pictures can delight in their realism and appreciate their documentary value, affirmation of the hours spent on the quayside at London docks.

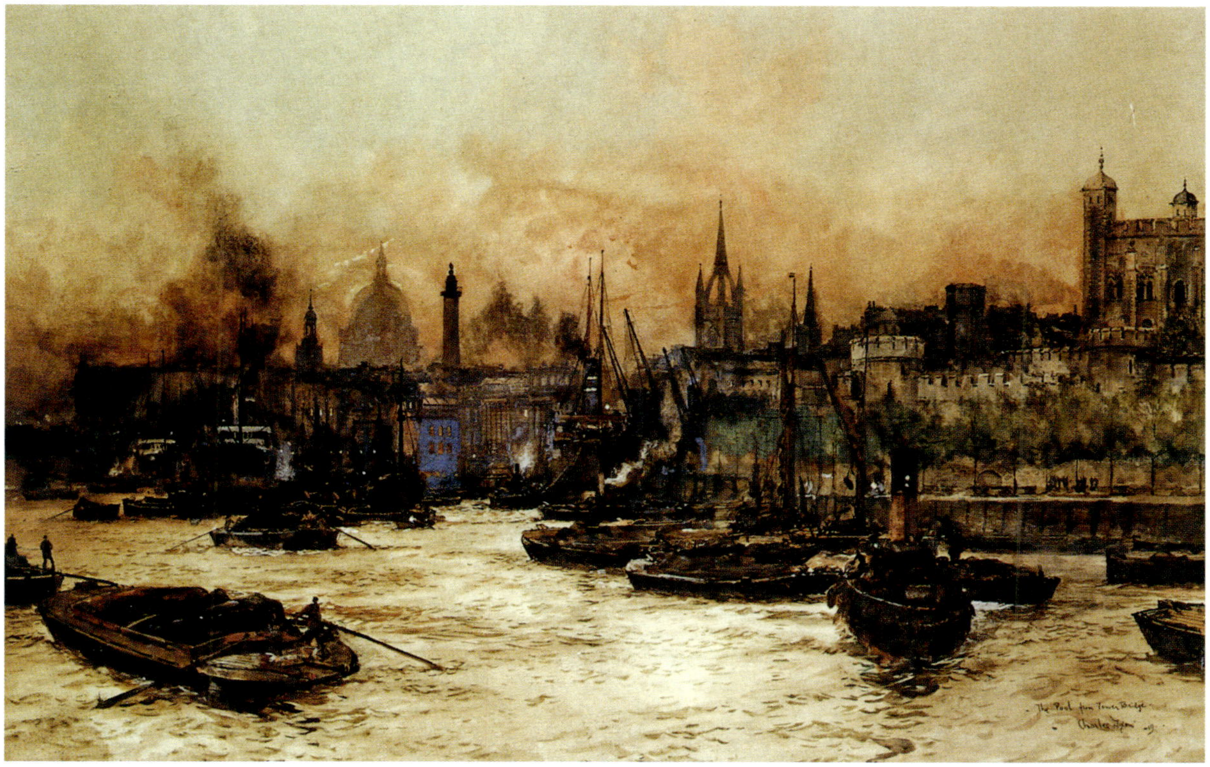

*The Pool from Tower Bridge*
*Charles Dixon, Watercolour with Bodycolour, 19¼x30¼", Signed, inscribed with title and dated '19*
SOTHEBY'S

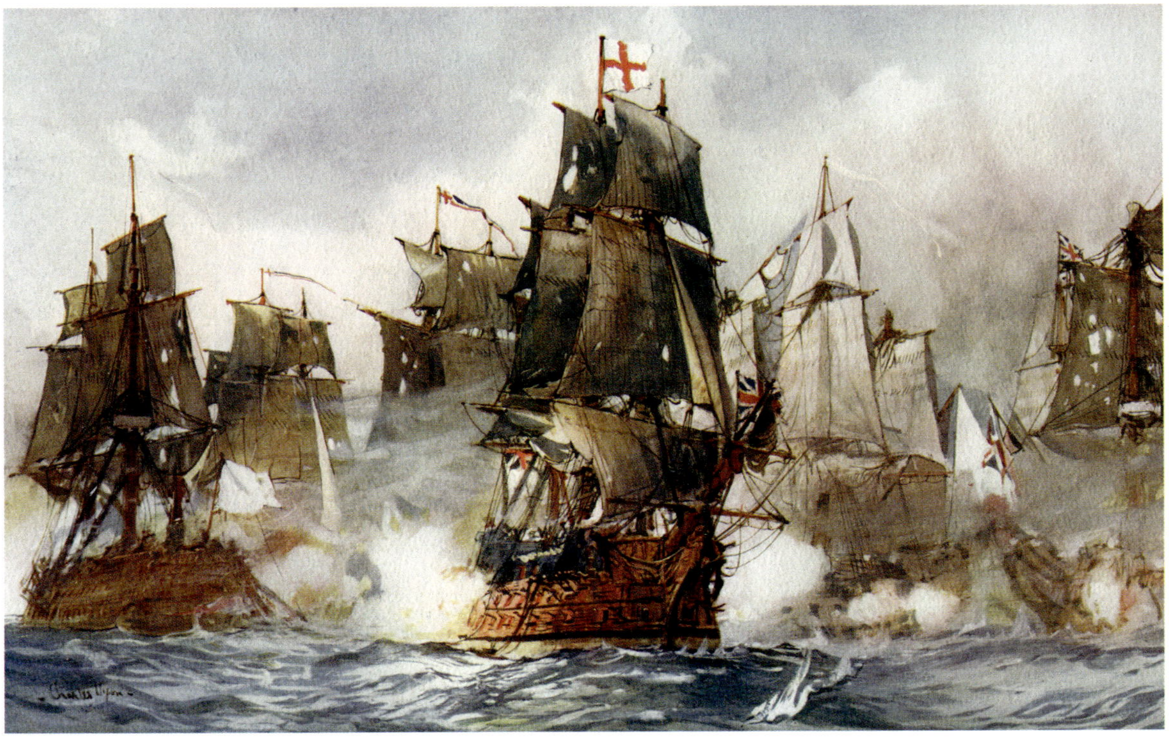

*Rodney's* Formidable *breaking the line, 1782.* Formidable *battleship, 1934 tons, launched Chatham*
*Charles Dixon, Illustration for* Britannia's Bulwarks

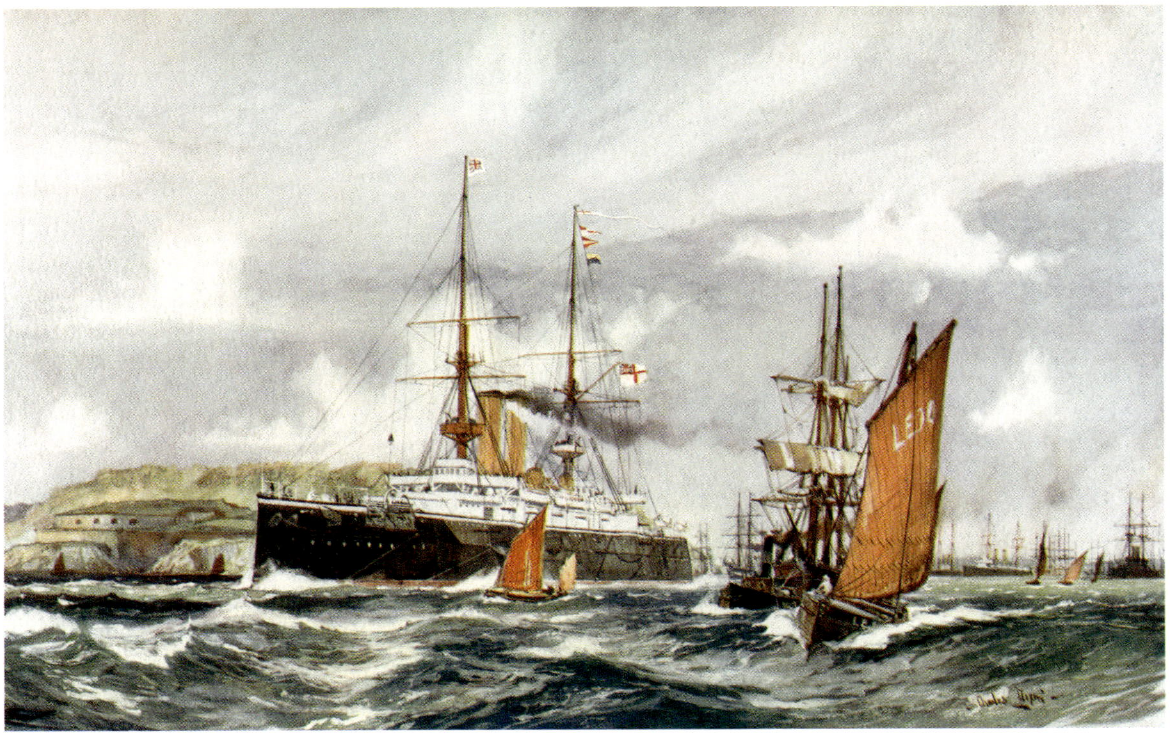

*HMS* Formidable *in Plymouth Sound.* Formidable *battleship, 15,000 tons, launched 17 November 1898, Portsmouth*
*Charles Dixon, Illustration for* Britannia's Bulwarks

# CHAPTER FOUR
# *Britannia's Bulwarks*

*'Wherever there is space to float a ship, we are sure to find you English in the way'* - **Napoleon**

Although Charles Dixon's reputation as a marine artist was built largely on his paintings of the tidal Thames and yachting, it is also the Royal Navy that has featured in much of his output, for he held a lifelong admiration for its achievements and traditions and believed unequivocally in the imperial power of Britain, in the Empire and the 'Senior Service'. This unswerving dedication, which has manifested itself in some of his most memorable paintings, notably those contained in the National Maritime Museum, Greenwich, may be divided into three areas, historical reconstructions of significant events involving the navy from Elizabethan times to the Napoleonic era, the Great Fleet reviews preceding the First World War, and potent scenes of the fury of battle at Jutland and its aftermath.

The present Royal Navy credits its foundation to the Saxon King Alfred the Great (849–c. 899) in response to the threat of Viking invasion, and the long list of illustrious episodes in its evolution from then up until the middle ages, and through to Nelson's victory at Trafalgar, had always been a source of great fascination for Dixon. His deep and knowledgeable interest in Britain's naval history became consolidated in a book with the splendidly patriotic title *Britannia's Bulwarks*, published in 1901. For this, Dixon was commissioned to paint all forty-eight colour plates which were based on the idea of linking 'the famous ships of glorious memory alongside their counterparts of the modern navy', thereby representing the navy, past and contemporary. Thus, 'Rodney's *Formidable* Breaking the Line', 1782, is juxtaposed with HMS *Formidable* in Plymouth Sound, circa 1900.

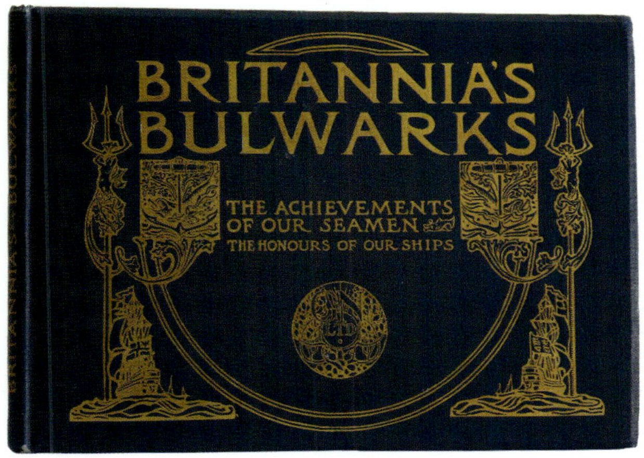


*The front cover of* Britannia's Bulwarks

In its introduction the book is described as 'a revelation of unsuspected possibilities for that eminent marine painter, Mr Charles Dixon, RI, who has prepared an admirably successful and beautiful series of watercolour pictures, which are produced with a fidelity of effect that would have been unattainable even a short time ago'. The compliment paid to Dixon is fully merited, for not only does it acknowledge his skill as a commemorative artist, but also as a ship portrait painter, each plate brilliantly encapsulating the colour, drama and character of the age, an interpretation of events seen uniquely through his imagination and executed with his bold, artistic flair. The book has now become a prized collector's item, but sadly often denuded of some of the colour plates which have been removed by dealers for selling individually or as sets. The illustrations are a vivid and nostalgic record of Empire and the Victorian Navy as epitomised in 'the veterans of the old trooping service'. The early Victorian period saw a considerable increase in Britain's colonial responsibilities and, especially after the rather haphazard experiences of the Crimean War and the Indian Mutiny, it was decided to build a group of specially designed steamships which could provide a regular service of troop transportation, primarily to India. The five ships, which were soon to become familiar to generations of British soldiers, were built in 1866 and were named *Crocodile, Euphrates, Juma, Malabar and Serapis*. Although built in different yards, each

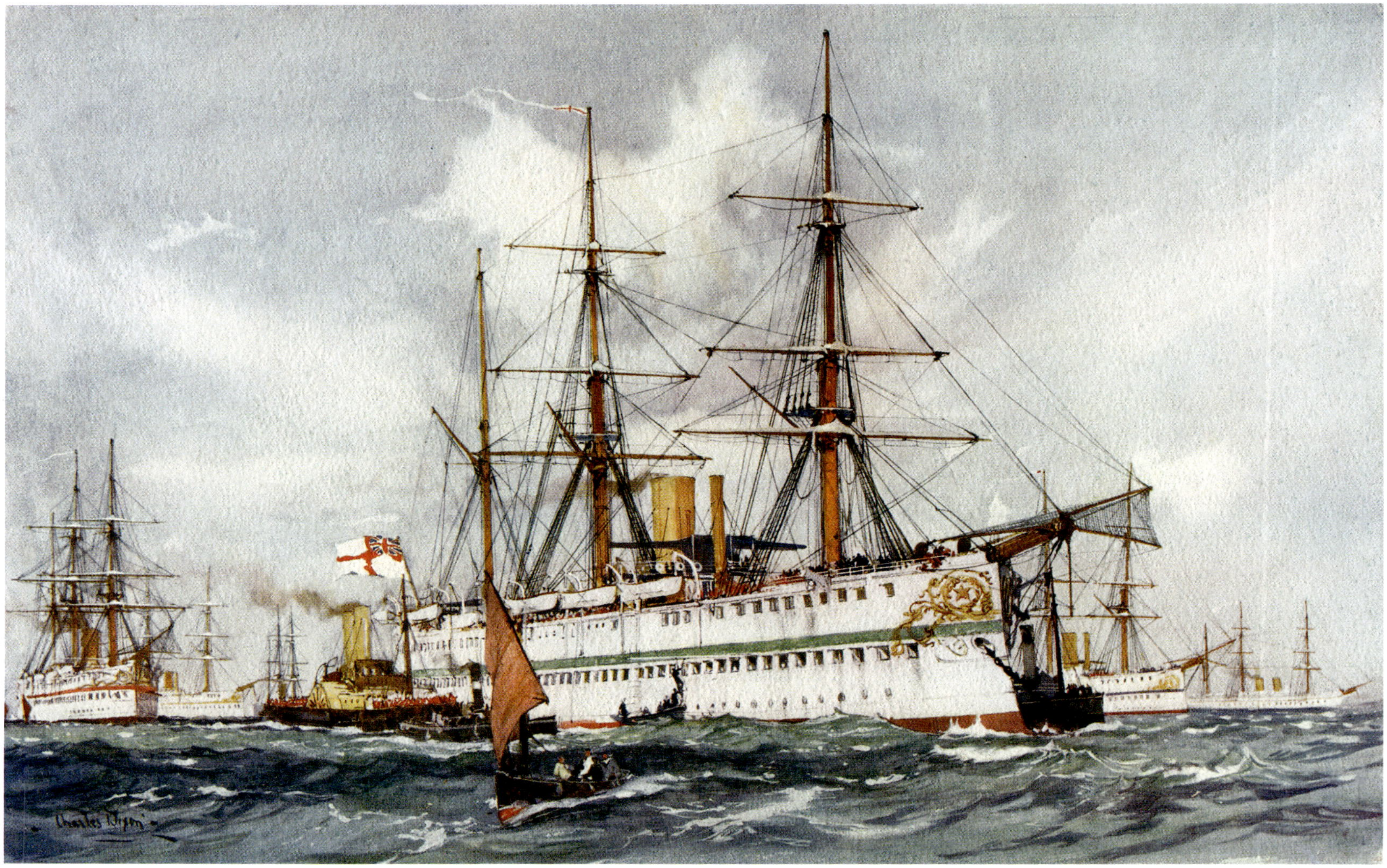


*The Veterans of the Old Trooping Service.* Serapis, *4173 tons*
*Charles Dixon, Illustration for* Britannia's Bulwarks

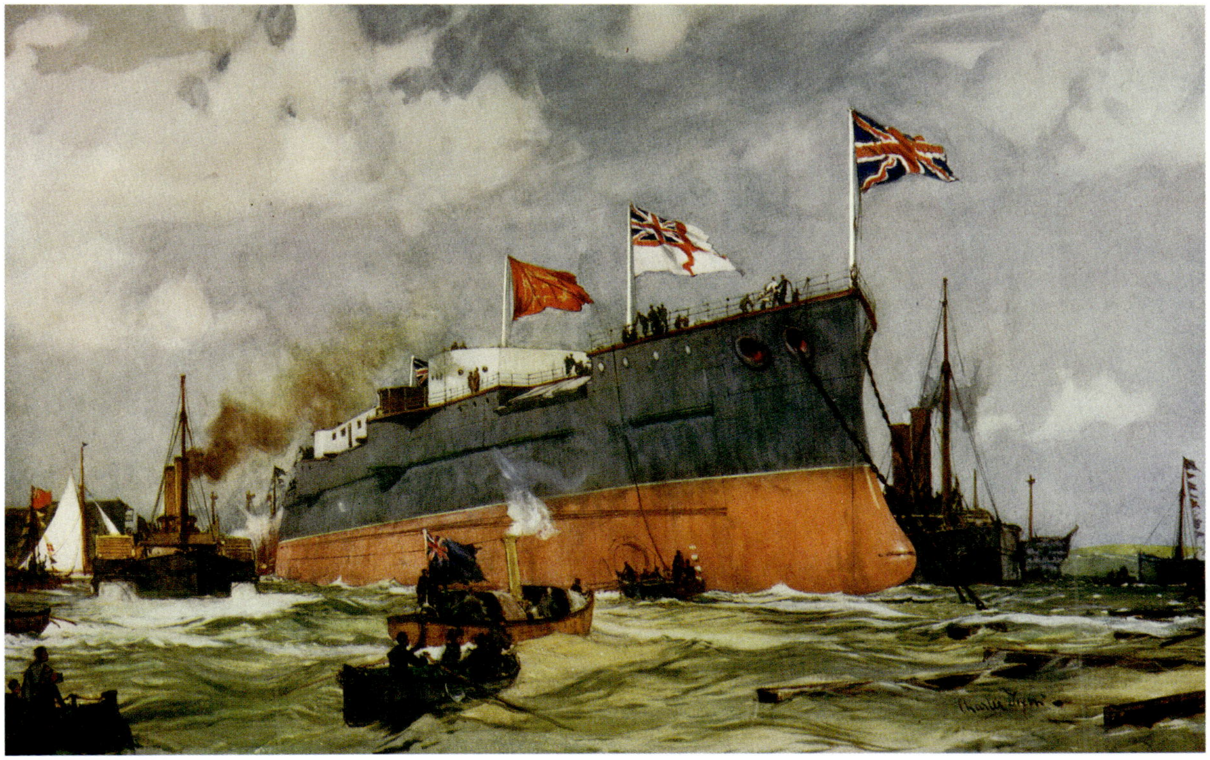

*The Launch of the* London *at Portsmouth 1899.* London *battleship, 1500 tons*
*Charles Dixon, Illustration for* Britannia's Bulwarks

was of the same design, dimensions and tonnage, and could accommodate a full battalion of infantry with its married families, numbering about 1,200 persons in all. Since their construction was paid for by the Indian government, the white-painted ships had the Star of India emblazoned upon their bows; in fact, they were all identical except for the coloured stripe painted along each hull which, in the case of *Serapis*, was green. Before the Suez Canal was opened, *Serapis* ran a Portsmouth to Alexandria service, but eventually, after years of continuous trooping, she was withdrawn in 1894 and broken up shortly afterwards.

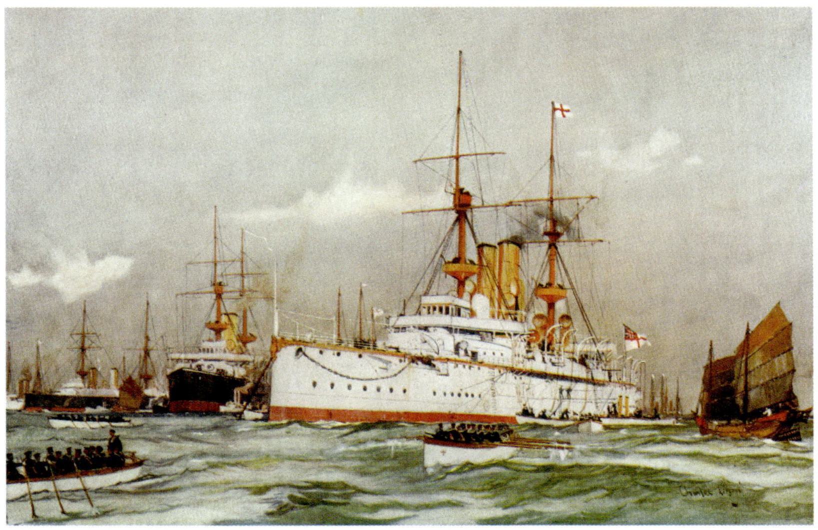

Centurion. *Sir Edward Seymour's flagship in the Far East, 1900.* Centurion *battleship, 10,500 tons, launched Portsmouth 1892*
*Charles Dixon, Illustration for* Britannia's Bulwarks

The launching of a capital ship has always been a cause for celebration throughout the long history of the Royal Navy, not least when iron replaced wood in the second half of the nineteenth century. Here in another splendid illustration taken from *Britannia's Bulwarks*, Dixon portrays the new vessel HMS *London* immediately after the launching ceremony; riding high in the water and dressed with the traditional ensigns of monarchy, the hull will soon be under tow to the fitting out basin.

During the high tide of British Imperialism, the Edwardian Navy had come to be regarded as the finest yacht club in the world, its flag-waving cruises to foreign ports occasionally interrupted by the need to send a gunboat to quell some misguided insurgent. For fifty years after the Crimean War 'send a gunboat' became an everyday phrase in British diplomacy and these small ships provided an important policing role. Traders, missionaries, consuls and governors

*The* Speedy *leaving Portsmouth.*
Speedy, *gunboat, launched Chiswick May 1893, 810 tons.*
*Charles Dixon, Illustration for* Britannia's Bulwarks

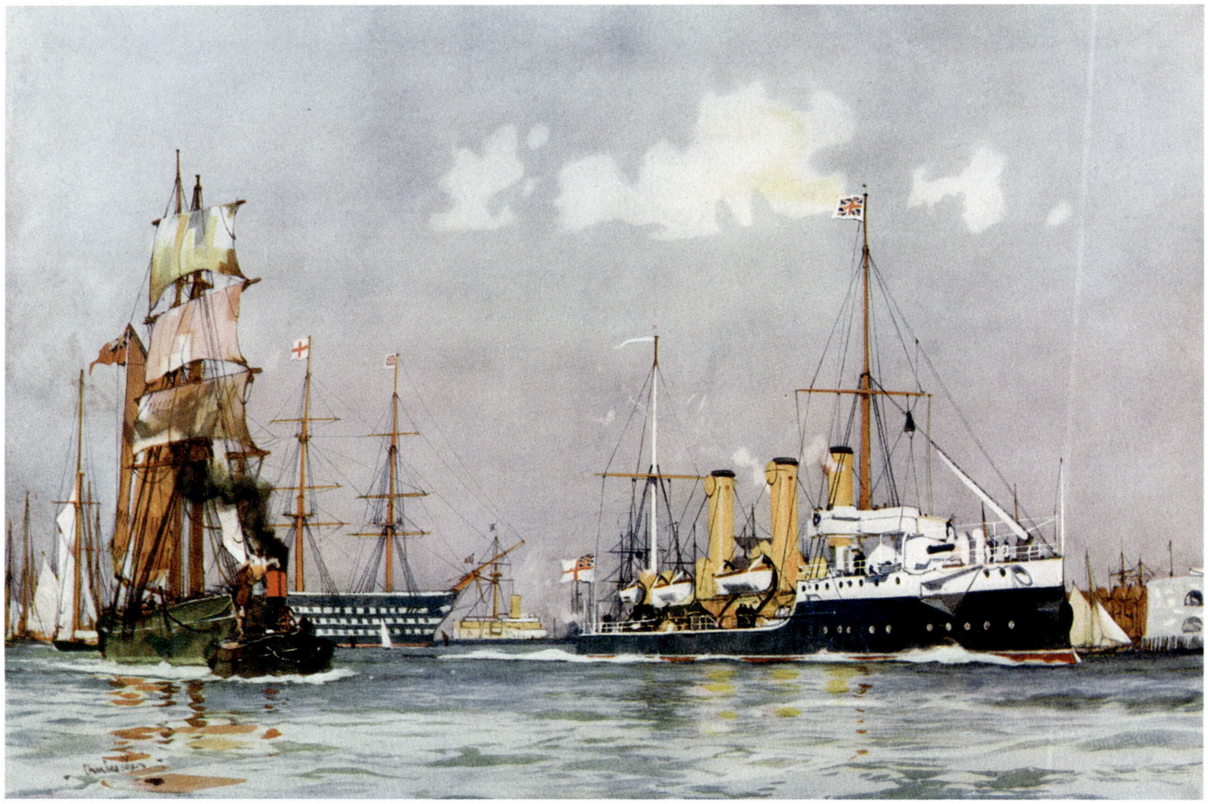

would send out cries for help all over the world from New Zealand to Brazil, Jamaica to Siam. Dr Livingstone on the Zambezi and British prisoners in Sierra Leone and Formosa were all helped or released without a shot fired, the mere appearance of the White Ensign sufficient to dispose of the trouble. From the end of the Victorian era until the beginning of the First World War, this situation remained largely unchanged. This power was witnessed not only in the navy flexing its muscles across the globe, but also at the magnificent spectacles of the great fleet reviews held between 1897 and 1915. These reviews were seen as an opportunity to demonstrate the importance of the nation's sea power and underscore the significance and responsibility of Empire. Fleet reviews had been held at Spithead intermittently since 1773 and recorded by artists of the calibre of John Cleveley (?-1790), Dominic Serres (1747-1786) and Francis Holman (1722-1793), but the event planned for the high summer of 1887, to mark the Golden Jubilee of Queen Victoria's accession, was intended to outshine all those which had gone before. In all, 135 vessels of all kinds were assembled, including 26 ironclads. On 23 July, 20,200 officers and men manned yards or lined decks to salute their Queen Empress as she progressed through the fleet in the Royal Yacht *Victoria & Albert*. It seems Her Majesty was clearly delighted with the day and afterwards declared herself as much touched by the loyalty of her sailors as she was impressed by the might of her navy, whose status and the pride it engendered reached its apotheosis. The seven miles of ships assembled at Spithead symbolised in a single place the integrity of Imperial power. By the end of the century 'all the nice girls loved a sailor' and every middle class child had a sailor suit for Sunday best. By that time too 52 per cent of all shipping around the world was owned by Britain, the second largest owner being the United States with 8 per cent. Ordinary folk might not have been unduly bothered by Empire, but they cared very much indeed about their fishing and merchant fleets and especially about the Royal Navy, which protected both. The Golden

Jubilee Review of 1887 was deemed such a success that ten years later an even larger and more spectacular event was planned. It was thus, on the afternoon of 26 June 1897, 165 British warships lay imposingly at anchor at Spithead. Strung out in five arrow-straight columns, each five miles in length, they included twenty one battleships, forty-two cruisers of various classes, thirty destroyers, twenty torpedo boats, along with various miscellaneous craft. Furthermore vessels representing 12 foreign powers were also present. The gathering was the most formidable ever assembled at a single anchorage and it exemplified the Royal Navy at the zenith of its power; the inclusion of so many battleships seen as confirmation of Britain's naval supremacy. Indeed, to the tens of thousands of exhilarated spectators who lined the shore, it was all the more impressive for the fact that it represented only half of the navy's strength, since not one ship had been recalled from the many foreign stations, where some 165 vessels were guarding British interests.

The occasion for this magnificent naval display was the Diamond Jubilee of Queen Victoria, whose reign had surpassed that of any other English Sovereign and during which period the British Empire had expanded until it encompassed eleven million square miles – one quarter of the globe. At this time Britain possessed the world's largest and most powerful navy, whose authority had not been challenged since Trafalgar, nearly a century earlier. Furthermore, since Nelson's victory in 1805 until the first sea action off Heligoland in 1914, the Royal Navy fleet had maintained the 'Pax Britannica' over the oceans of the world. This policy, to guarantee freedom of the sea for all, had not only brought with it a vast colonial empire, but had extended British influence around the world. In order to maintain its supremacy, Government policy mandated that the Royal Navy be equal in size to the navies of any two world powers that might seek to challenge it. 'The Royal Navy was the true bond of the Empire', observed *The Times*. 'Without it the Empire would be merely a loose aggregate of states'. And so it was appropriate that on this final day of a week of national celebrations, which included a great Jubilee procession through the streets of London, the culminating ceremony should be a review of Her Majesty's fleet at Spithead. Here, in his iconic painting of the review 'In Honour of Our Queen', which he probably did from one of the numerous small vessels on the perimeter, Dixon shows HMS *Renown* leading the line of Majestic class battleships, one of the many lines of capital ships with their freshly painted raven hulls gleaming darkly against bright red waterlines (ships of the Royal Navy were not painted grey until 1903). On the right of the painting is the Russian cruiser *Rosslyn*, while the white hulled American cruiser *Brooklyn*, newly completed, can be seen to the right and rear of the Royal Yacht, a truly international event. At precisely 2 o'clock the Royal Yacht *Victoria & Albert* edged her gilded prow out from the shore to be saluted by the waiting ships. On the quarter deck was the Prince of Wales, who was representing the Queen, and behind the Royal Yacht came a flotilla of vessels carrying the many assorted dignitaries. As the procession passed up and down the awesome ranks of warships, the guns thundered and the bands played 'God Save the Queen!' Then, as the Royal Yacht steamed back to Portsmouth, the anchorage resounded with the 165 ships companies cheering in unison. The men were cheering not only the Queen and her son, the future monarch, they were cheering the Royal Navy itself. The Prince of Wales, the entire Royal Family, innumerable foreign royalty and, in fact, everyone present agreed that it had been a triumphant day and one which, in the years ahead, would be seen as the apogee of British Imperial power. Dixon's painting of the review, which he exhibited at the Royal Academy in 1898, is probably one of his best known; a vast panorama of colour and pageantry in which he conveys all the stateliness and excitement of an unparalleled display of the impressive might of Britain's Imperial Navy.

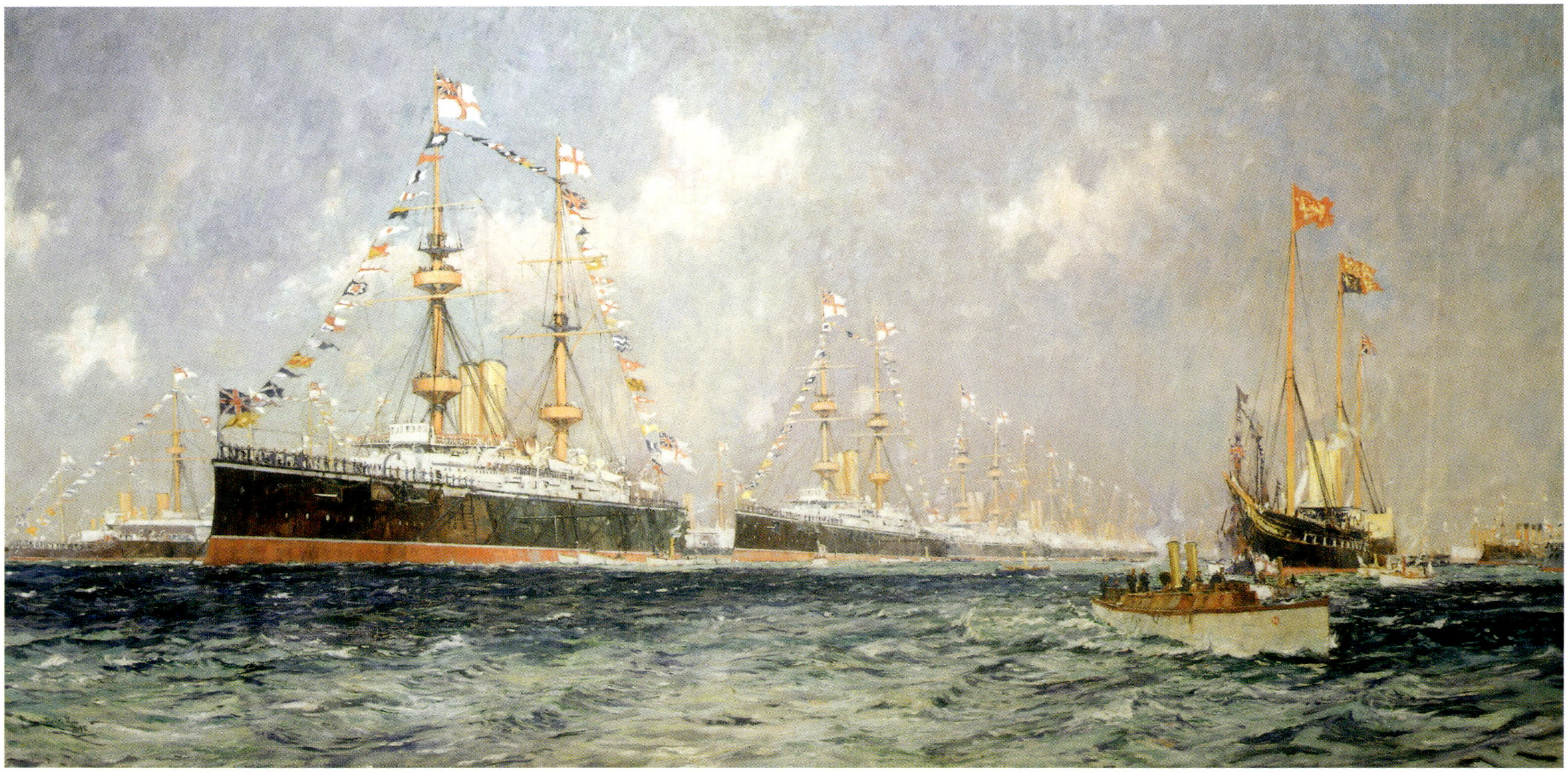

*'In Honour of Our Queen', Queen Victoria's Diamond Jubilee, 1897*
*Charles Dixon, Oil on Canvas, 37x73", Signed*
NATIONAL MARITIME MUSEUM

*The Royal Navy Ships present included the* Jupiter *and* Mars *which had been specially commissioned for this review. They were battleships of the newest type and the largest warships in the world.*

In 1901 Dixon returned to Portsmouth to record another important event in British history, although sadly one far removed from the joyous celebrations of the Diamond Jubilee four years earlier, for, on 22 January 1901, Queen Victoria's reign of sixty-four years ended with her death at her beloved Osborne House on the Isle of Wight. At sunset on 1 February 1901, escorted by eight destroyers, the Queen's body was carried ceremoniously to Portsmouth in the Royal Yacht *Alberta*, en route to London for her state funeral. The fleet, consisting of the channel and reserve squadrons, was moored in one line from Cowes to Spithead and, as *Alberta* entered Portsmouth harbour with the Royal Standard at half mast, the *Victory*, which had been the first ship of the Royal Navy on the accession of the young sovereign, saluted her passing. In his sombre rendering of the occasion, Dixon shows the *Alberta* passing the battleship, *Prince George*, at Spithead. As the tiny paddle vessel moved between the columns of the majestic ships at anchor, all with their crews mustered, and to the wail of boatswains' pipes, each warship fired a minute gun, for this was one of the country's last great displays of pomp and ceremony, the vivid sunset in Dixon's watercolour symbolising the end of the Victorian era.

During the period 1870 to 1910, royalty were more closely involved with the navy than at any time in its history, with three members of the Royal Family holding permanent commissions in the service.

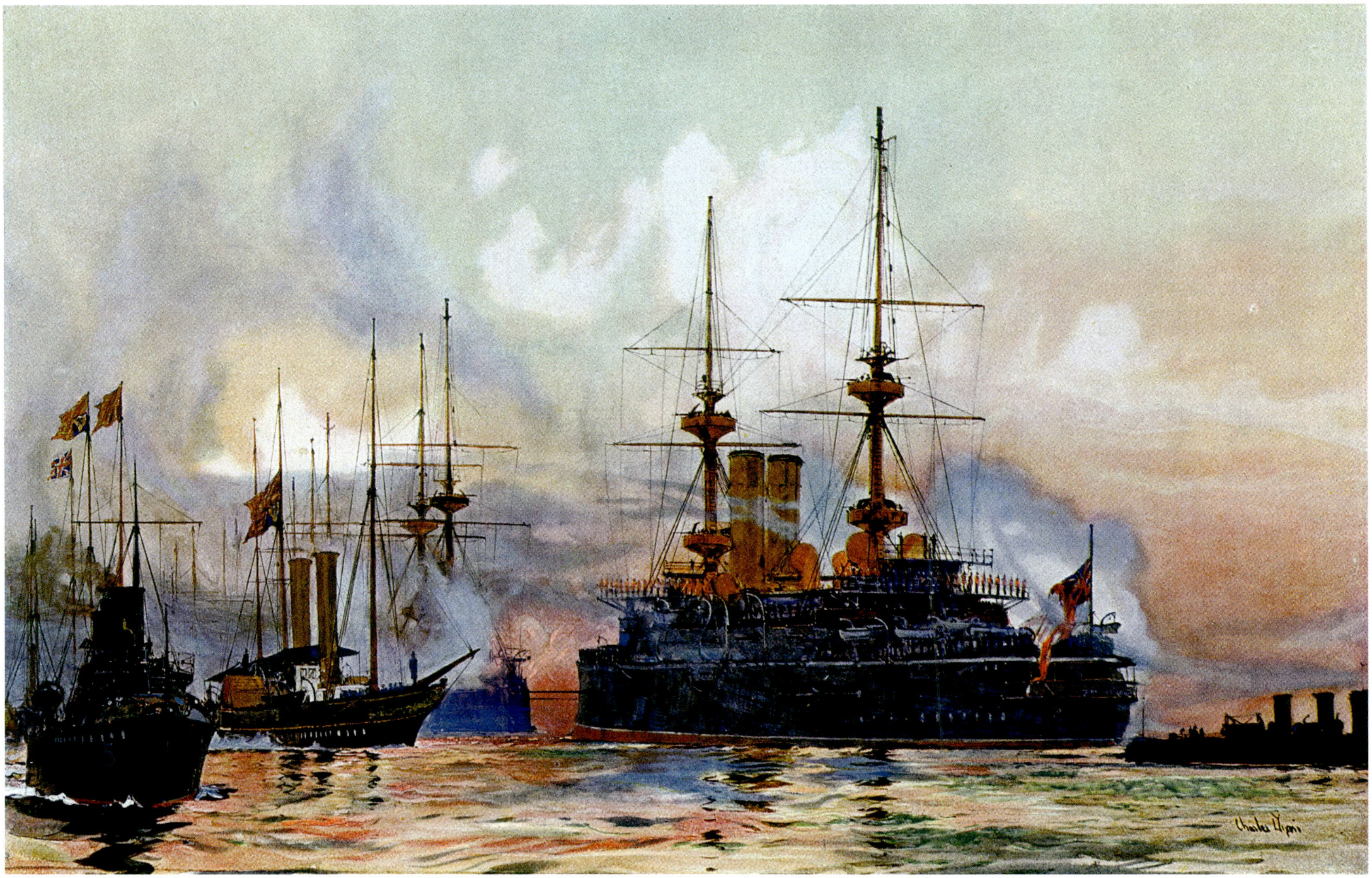

*The* Prince George *at Spithead: The Naval Requiem of Queen Victoria,* Prince George, *battleship, 14,900 tons, launched Portsmouth 1895. Charles Dixon, Illustration for* Britannia's Bulwarks

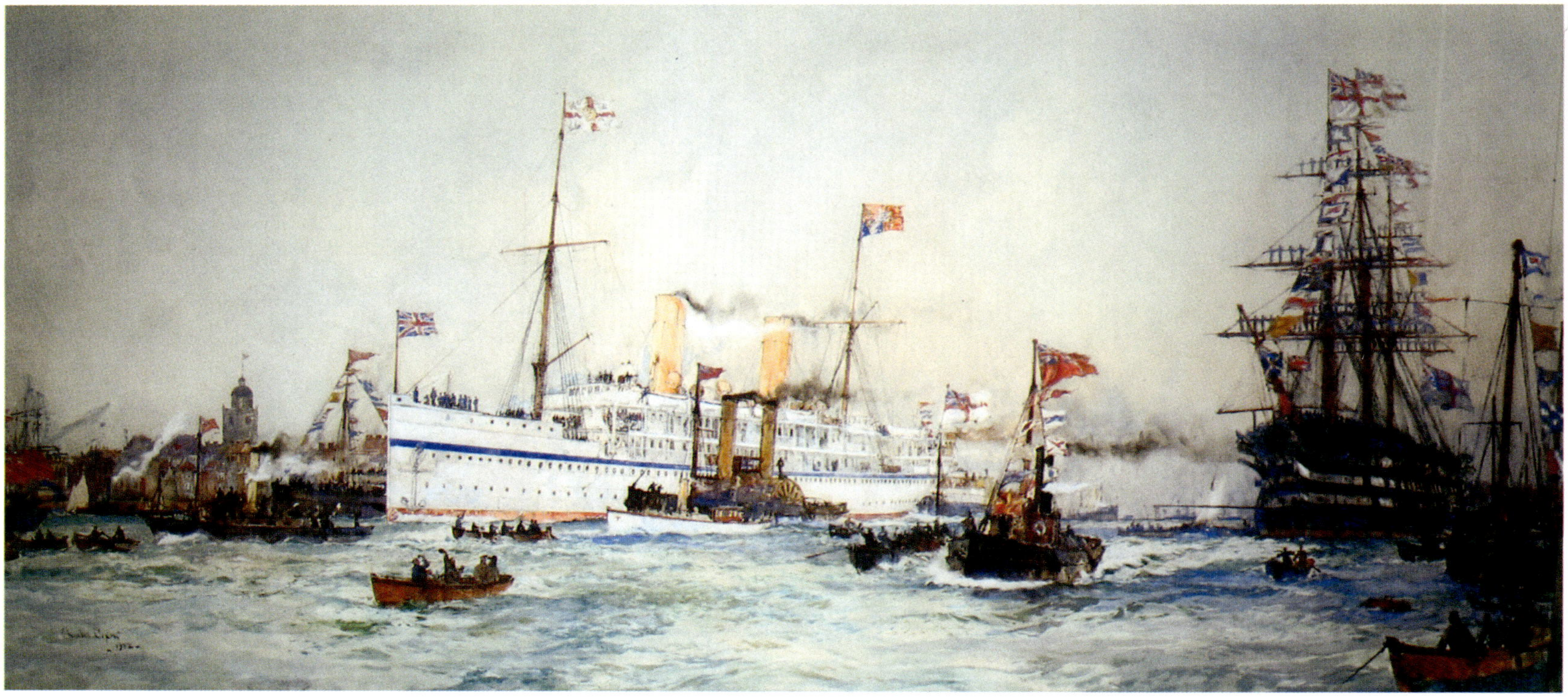

*HMS* Ophir *returning to Portsmouth*
*Charles Dixon,Watercolour and Gouache, 19x45", Signed and dated 1902*
BARON FINE ART

Furthermore, the great expansions of the Navy in the 1890s and again in the 1900s were given the seal of approval by the presence of royalty at important launchings; indeed, Edward VII, Queen Victoria's eldest son, who succeeded her, was particularly energetic and conducted the launch of HMS *Dreadnought* at Portsmouth in 1906. State visits were paid by royalty not only to major countries in the Empire such as India, Canada and Australia, but also to important strategic possessions, such as Gibraltar and Malta. In his splendid painting of HMS *Ophir* entering Portsmouth harbour on 1 November 1901, Dixon conveys a wonderful sense of occasion for the ship, formerly a liner of the Orient Line and chartered by the Admiralty for royal duties, was returning after her circumnavigation of the globe, with the Duke and Duchess of Cornwall and York (later King George and Queen Mary) on board. The royal couple had decided to accept an invitation to visit Australia to open the new Commonwealth Parliament as well as to express British thanks for the help given by the colonies during the South African war. Amidst great pomp and ceremony, she sailed from Portsmouth on 16 March. The voyage of 45,000 miles lasted over seven months and was the first overseas tour in the modern sense. As the Ophir sails into port, she is seen passing HMS *Victory* dressed overall with the yards manned, a testament to the feeling prevalent at that time, which was for Great Britain, the pinnacle of her great imperial days, Dixon at his lyrical best. The royal cruise of the *Ophir* was graphically recorded by a member of the crew, Petty Officer Harry Price, and a facsimile of his fascinating log was published in 1980.

Between 1870 and 1914 there were no less than 18 major royal fleet reviews, usually at Spithead, with just eight between 1815 and 1870. And apart from celebrating great national events such as a Jubilee or Coronation, as in 1887, 1897, 1902 and 1910, they were also held in honour of and to impress visiting Heads of State or to make some point of foreign policy, such as the celebrations of *L'Entente Cordiale*, which took place in Portsmouth in August 1905, to mark the centennial of the 100 years of peace between the French Republic and Great Britain, which followed the battle of Trafalgar. The occasion, which won for Edward VII the title of 'The Peacemaker', was unique in the history of the two nations. Since both parties were regarded as major maritime powers, the form of the exchange of missions which took place was mainly naval. Thus Royal Navy ships visited France and, on this side of the channel, there were reciprocal events; a major feature being the visit of the French fleet to Portsmouth. The scene depicted by Dixon shows the French C-in-C Admiral Crillard's flagship, the Massena, at the head of the fleet before taking up station at Spithead.

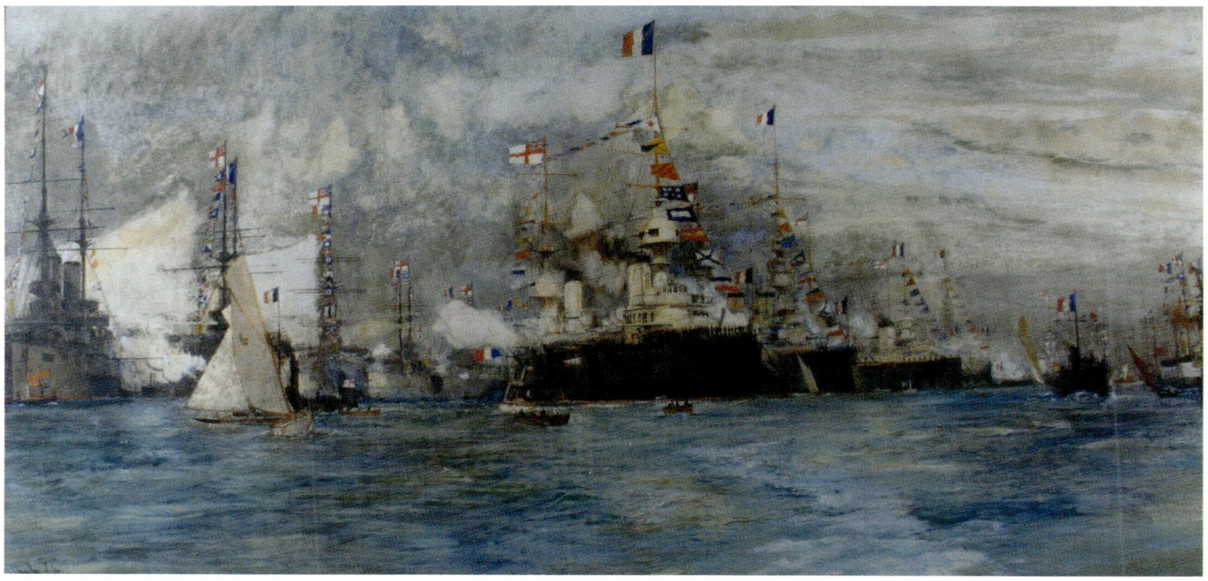

*'L'Entente Cordiale',*
*Review of the French Fleet, 1905*
*Charles Dixon, Watercolour, Signed*
PORTSMOUTH MUSEUM AND RECORDS SERVICE

When Edward, Prince of Wales, ascended the throne following Victoria's death, he was nearly sixty and had been 'a King in waiting'. However, his reign as King Edward VII lasted only until 1910, when he died aged 69. To celebrate the coronation of his successor, King George V, who had served in the Royal Navy for 15 years, another great naval review took place and once more Spithead provided the setting. 'Never before in the history of the world, has one been privileged to see such a powerful and numerous array of warships as the mighty armada of British and foreign vessels now gathered on the historic waters of Spithead in this year of our Lord, 1911, to celebrate the coronation of the British Sailor King, George V. It might be asked why Spithead is always selected for these great naval celebrations, and the answer is that there is no other waterway so conveniently situated and so famous as this particular place' – so said the official programme for the review. However, the 125 ships that packed the Solent for the review in 1911, which included 37 capital ships, were not the magnificent yet ageing vessels that Dixon painted in 1897 and later, such as the first class cruiser HMS *Ariadne* of 11,000 tons, seen leaving Portsmouth in 1902, but a new British fleet whose design had been based on the battleship HMS *Dreadnought*, launched in 1906. Her ten twelve-inch guns meant she could fight from beyond the range of any existing enemy and should she be unlucky enough to incur a direct hit, her eleven-inch armour plating (no other ship had more than seven inches) would protect her. Furthermore, radical steam turbine engines gave her twenty-one knots of speed, enough to outrun any warship afloat. Faster and more powerfully armed than any other ship in history, HMS *Dreadnought* represented such a quantum leap over her rivals in war at sea that she gave her name to a whole class of ship and soon the building race between Britain and Germany was on, as men-of-war slid down the ways in ever-increasing numbers. Portsmouth built a further 13 Dreadnoughts between 1907 and 1914 when, as the premier naval base in the world, it was the only dockyard capable of building an 18,000 ton naval ship, 500 feet long, and in secrecy. These big gun battleships were designed to guarantee continuing British supremacy at sea and were to the fore of another great display of British naval might at Spithead when, on 18 July 1914, King George V reviewed the fleet from his yacht, *Victoria & Albert II*, which included 24 Dreadnoughts, 35 pre-Dreadnoughts, 18 armoured cruisers, 31 light cruisers, 78 destroyers and hundreds of other vessels. One by one the squadrons sailed past to salute their monarch. But storm clouds were gathering on the horizon as Kaiser Wilhelm was building a mighty German fleet to rival the Royal Navy. On 4 August, Britain declared war on Germany and the holocaust of the first great world convulsion began.

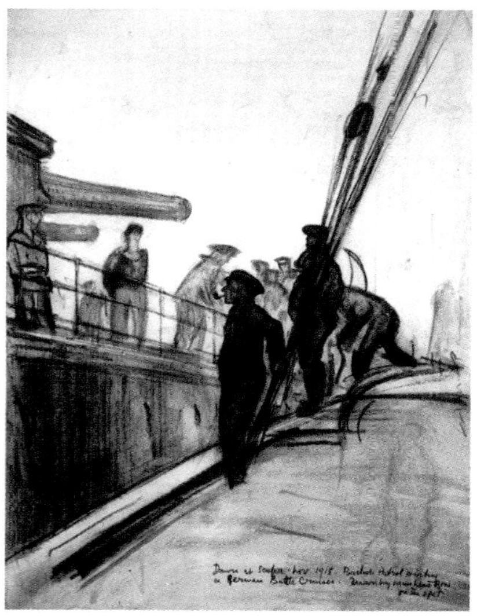

*Dawn at Scapa Flow*
*Muirhead Bone, Watercolour, 26¾x22¾"*
MINISTRY OF DEFENCE ART COLLECTION, LONDON
CROWN COPYRIGHT

As events taking place on the Western Front and at sea began to unfold, the immediacy of media reporting resulted in the first mass awareness of military and naval activity. The public were hungry for information about what was happening in their name and keen to obtain pictorial news of the action. Shortly after the war began, the Government set up a new department within the Foreign Office, known as the Department of Information, whose primary task was the production of publicity material which would deal with propaganda. However, it eventually became apparent that the format in which the information was being disseminated was not having the desired impact. As a consequence, it was decided that by employing a professional artist, capable of rendering the often complex emotional effects of the scenes he had been commissioned to draw, would be infinitely more effective. As a result, the first Official War Artist to be appointed was Muirhead Bone (1876-1953), a highly industrious and skilled painter and etcher. Like many of his artist contemporaries, Bone saw this as a unique opportunity to serve his country in the most effective way possible. There were also the benefits of temporary commissioned rank, which not only provided security clearance, but opportunities to travel. Muirhead Bone in March 1917 recording daily life at sea with the Grand Fleet.

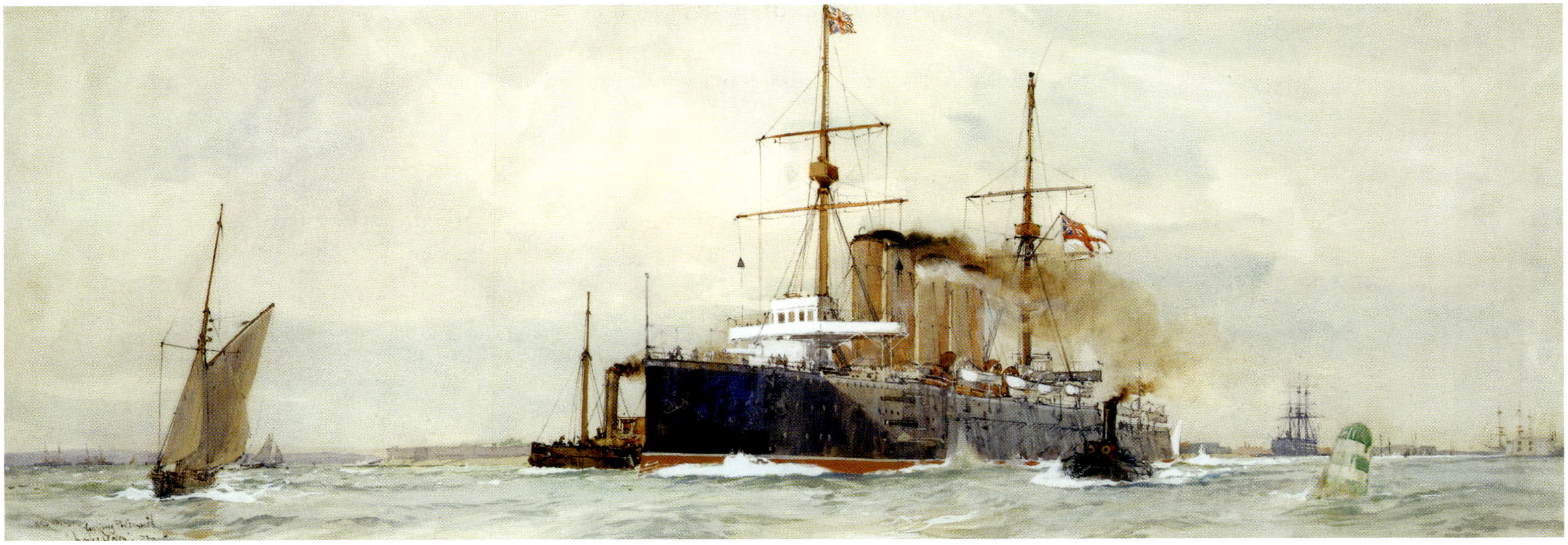

*HMS* Ariadne *leaving Portsmouth*
*Charles Dixon, Watercolour, 10½x30", Signed and dated '02*
PRIVATE COLLECTION

The artists employed to record events involving the Royal Navy and Royal Marines came under the auspices of the Admiralty and, in 1917, a special Admiralty Sub-Committee was convened to oversee their work; its overriding aim being to record 'every branch of the British Navy with regard to type of ships, bases and areas involved in naval operations'. One of the most distinguished of the artists to be appointed was Sir John Lavery, RA (1856-1941), better known for his portraits, figure subjects and landscapes, but who produced a large number of naval wartime paintings with his sensitive and impressionistic touch. The Imperial War Museum (IWM) has 61 oils by him, covering a broad range of military and naval subjects, predominantly those which feature the Royal Navy at sea but navy-related life ashore as well. Along with W L Wyllie and F W Wood he was present at the surrender of the German High Seas Fleet.

Also a Royal Academician and whose skill was put to good use as an official naval artist in the Great War is Philip Connard, RA (1875-1958). A painter in oil and watercolours his naval pictures include a variety of craft, but also figure studies, portraits and dramatic events. He was also a contributing artist in the Second World War. Eighty of his pictures are held in the IWM. The museum also contains examples of the work of Robert Henry Smith (active 1906–1920), who served initially as able seaman in the Great War and was subsequently commissioned Lieut. RNVR as Naval artist. He painted in oil and watercolours and was also an etcher and illustrator. Three large oils by him in the IWM show dramatic scenes of action at Jutland. Another artist who served as a naval officer during the Great War is Lt. Geoffrey S Allfree, RNVR (1889-1918), who was appointed an Official War Artist. A painter in oil and watercolours some 50 examples of his work are in the IWM, some of which are reminiscent of the work of Charles Pears. He was drowned on active service in 1918. It seems inevitable that the work of Charles Pears (1873-1958) should be strongly represented in the IWM, which contains over a hundred oils, watercolours and drawings by this prolific artist and whose service as an Official War Artist spanned both World Wars. The National Maritime Museum, Greenwich also holds examples of his work, mainly subjects of the Great War. Both the quality of art and the passion with which it was presented by these artists and their contemporaries were formidable. In 1918, the Ministry of Information was disbanded, but the concept of the War Artist was completely established.

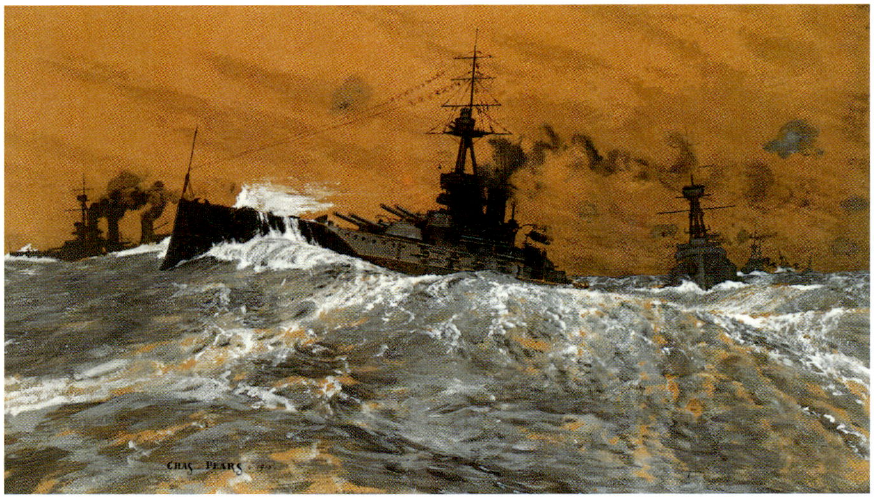

*Capital Ships in a Gale*
*Charles Pears, Oil on Paper, 13x22", Signed and dated 1915*
Royal Exchange Art Gallery

In 1939, the threat of war again turned into a reality; the question of art and its role in the future hostilities needing to be addressed. The outcome was the creation of the War Artists' Advisory Committee who, by appointing respected artists, would produce a pictorial record of the war. Lessons had been learned from the First World War and the importance of appointing artists at the earliest possibility had been clearly acknowledged. Amongst the plethora of war artists appointed were Stephen Bone (1904-1958), who served as a Hon. Lieut. RNVR, 1942-1945. The son of Muirhead Bone, he inherited his father's wide ability and his work is featured in the collection of The National Maritime Museum and the IWM. Other early appointments include Charles Cundall (1890-1971), Roland Vivian Pitchforth (1895-1982) and Richard Eurich (1903-1992), all of whom were given the honorary rank of Captain, Royal Marines. Eric Ravilious (1903-1942) was another of that select band of Hon. Captains, RM. Appointed in 1939, he gave the nation many superb watercolours of the navy at war, exemplified in 'Dangerous Work at Low Tide' which shows a team of Royal Marines considering tactics before making safe a magnetic mine; his emphatic light and shade vividly transmitting a remarkable sense of stillness in the face of danger. Not all war artists painted from first-hand experience, but Ravilious was one of those who wished to be in the thick of events. He was killed on active War Artists' service off Iceland, 1942. According to one source, in all some 30 artists were recording marine events and personnel in the 1914-18 war and about 40 more in the Second World War. Although the numbers are imprecise what they all achieved was the creation of lasting visual records of the endeavours of Britain's Royal and Merchant Navies during the dark days of both conflicts.

*Dangerous Work at Low Tide*
*Eric Ravilious, Watercolour, 28x37",*
MINISTRY OF DEFENCE ART COLLECTION, LONDON
CROWN COPYRIGHT

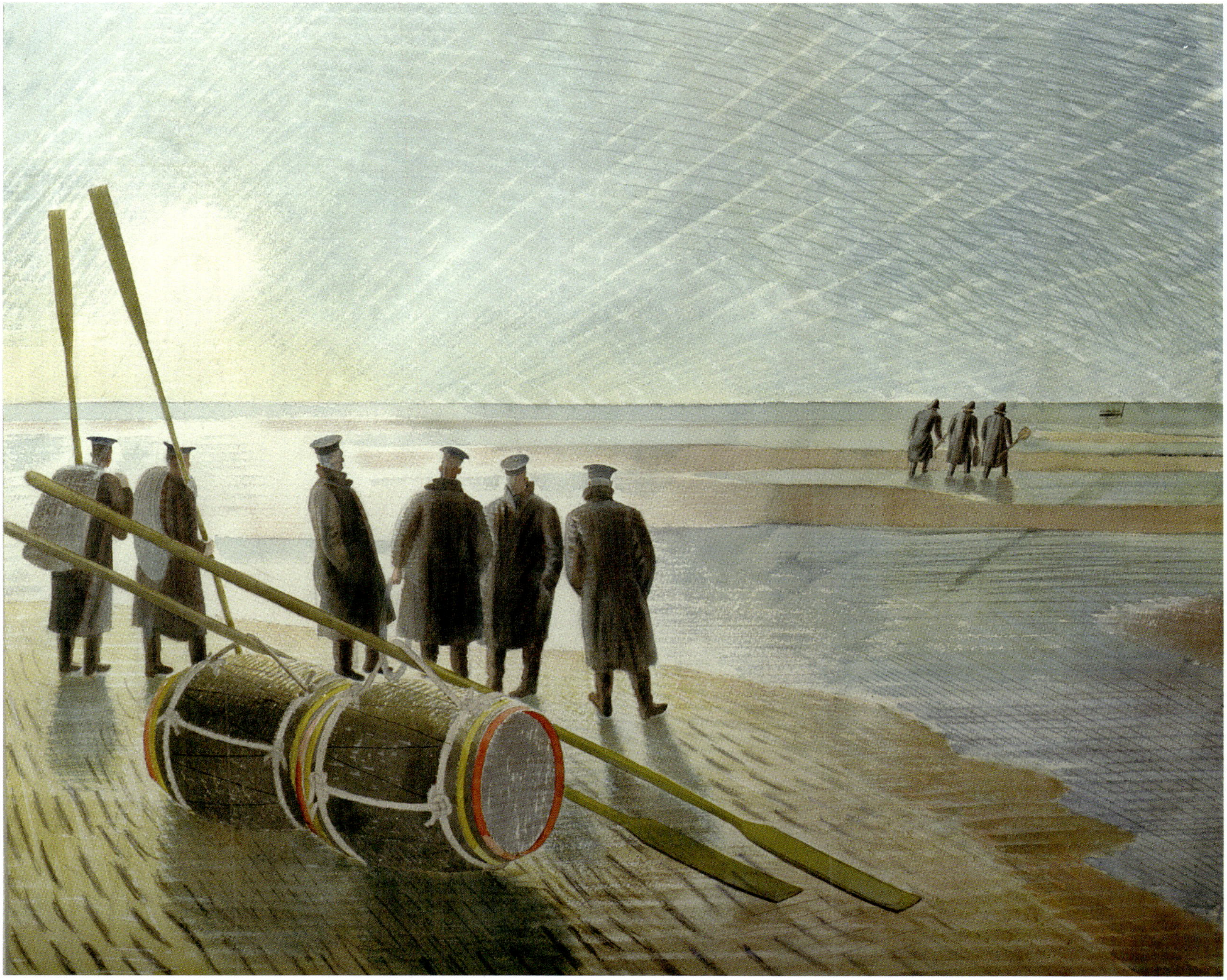

Although Charles Dixon, or for that matter W L Wyllie, did not serve as official War Artists, they nevertheless performed an important role by recording significant events of the war at sea through their illustrations for *The Illustrated London News*, *The Sphere* and *The Graphic*. These were often worked up from sketches made on the spot by naval personnel and by using their well-honed graphic skills and imaginative flair were able to produce accurate and realistic images of the action taking place (Wyllie in particular enjoying a good deal of latitude through his friends at the Admiralty). One subject of the war which epitomises these qualities in many of Dixon's paintings, is the Dardanelles Campaign and the landings at Gallipoli. During the First World War, Turkey had aligned herself to Germany and, as part of Britain's war strategy, it was intended to assemble a combined naval and military force to attack, invade and occupy the strategically important Gallipoli Peninsula. The landings at Gallipoli were intended to open up a second front in the Middle East and ultimately lead to the capture of Istanbul. This would secure safe passage for the vital trade with Russia. A multinational force gathered in Egypt; joining the ANZACs (Australian and New Zealand Army Corps) were the British 29th Division and 10th Division from Kitchener's army, the Royal Naval Division, Royal Marines, the French Oriental Expeditionary Corps and four Senegalese battalions. The time spent gathering this force meant any element of surprise was lost. The Turkish Infantry, supported by the German 5th Army, consisted of no less than 84,000 men. On the landing beaches the Allied Forces were hopelessly exposed to Turkish machine gun fire from the Fortress and, of the first 200 men to disembark, only twenty-one made it to the beach. Six Victoria Crosses would be awarded to sailors and infantry for the action at 'V' Beach, and a further six to soldiers of the Lancashires at 'W' Beach. Beach-heads were slowly established, but at great cost to both sides. Over the coming months, offensive and counter-offensive led to a stalemate. Conditions were appalling; a storm struck the Peninsula in late November which lasted for three days. The trenches were so waterlogged that soldiers drowned and unburied corpses were washed into the lines. A blizzard followed in early December, resulting in more deaths from exposure. The situation was untenable and a full withdrawal was completed by January 1916.

In his large and stunning watercolour 'Anzac', Dixon has recreated the action at V Beach, Cape Helles on 25 April 1915. The 4,000 tonne SS *River Clyde*, an old collier, is beached, having carried over 2,000 soldiers, mainly from the Royal Munster Fusiliers, 2nd Division and the Hampshire Regiment. The ominous Fort of Sedd el Bahr, meaning 'Key to the Sea' overlooks the scene. The painting was exhibited at the Royal Academy in 1916. In the same year, it was also shown at an exhibition of war paintings, held by the Fine Art Society, London, together with another Gallipoli painting by Dixon 'The Yeomanry at Gallipoli'. It would seem from the exhibition catalogue that both paintings received critical acclaim, but especially 'Anzac', described as 'a scene that Mr Dixon (aided by details given to him by many who took part in it) has depicted with a fidelity and vividness which those who have seen it consider to be more than remarkable'. The painting was reproduced by the Fine Art Society at a cost of one guinea. Perhaps the horror of the whole ill-fated campaign is best summed up by Dixon's poignant inscription on one of his three 1916 entries at the RI – 'V Beach – the most terrible of all the Landings'. 'The Sinking of L15' and a number of other Gallipoli subjects by Dixon are held by the IWM.

It was, however, the war at sea per se that became the main focus of Dixon's First World War output and it was not long after the commencement of hostilities that he painted an episode which occurred on 14 September 1914, when the armed merchant cruiser *Carmania*, a former Cunard liner taken over by the navy, fought a duel in the South Atlantic against the German armed merchant cruiser *Cap Trafalgar* which she sank. A similar event took place in 1916 with another thrilling encounter between a British armed

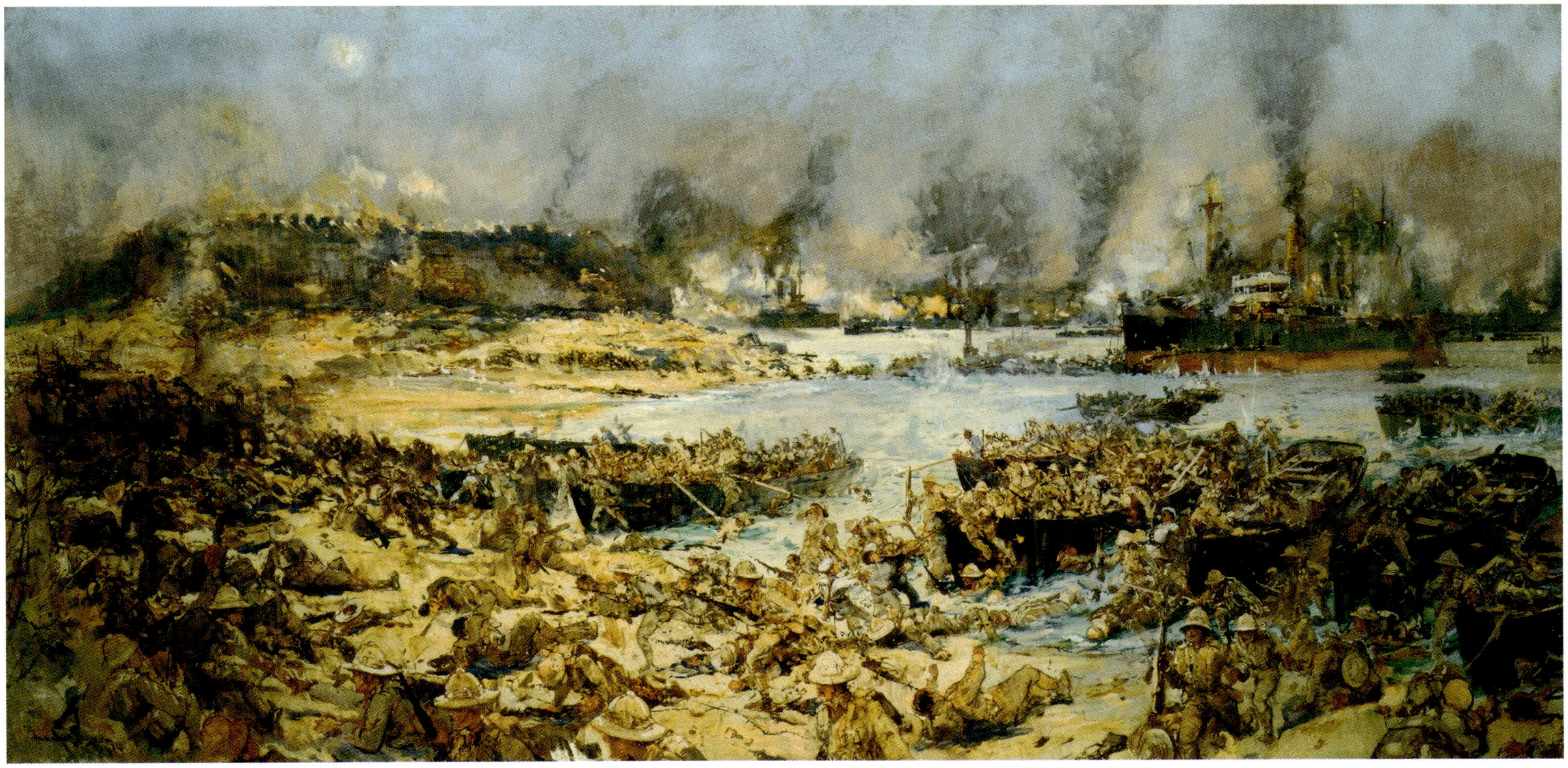

*Anzac*
*Charles Dixon, Watercolour and Gouache, 35½x71½", Signed and dated 1916*
SOTHEBY'S

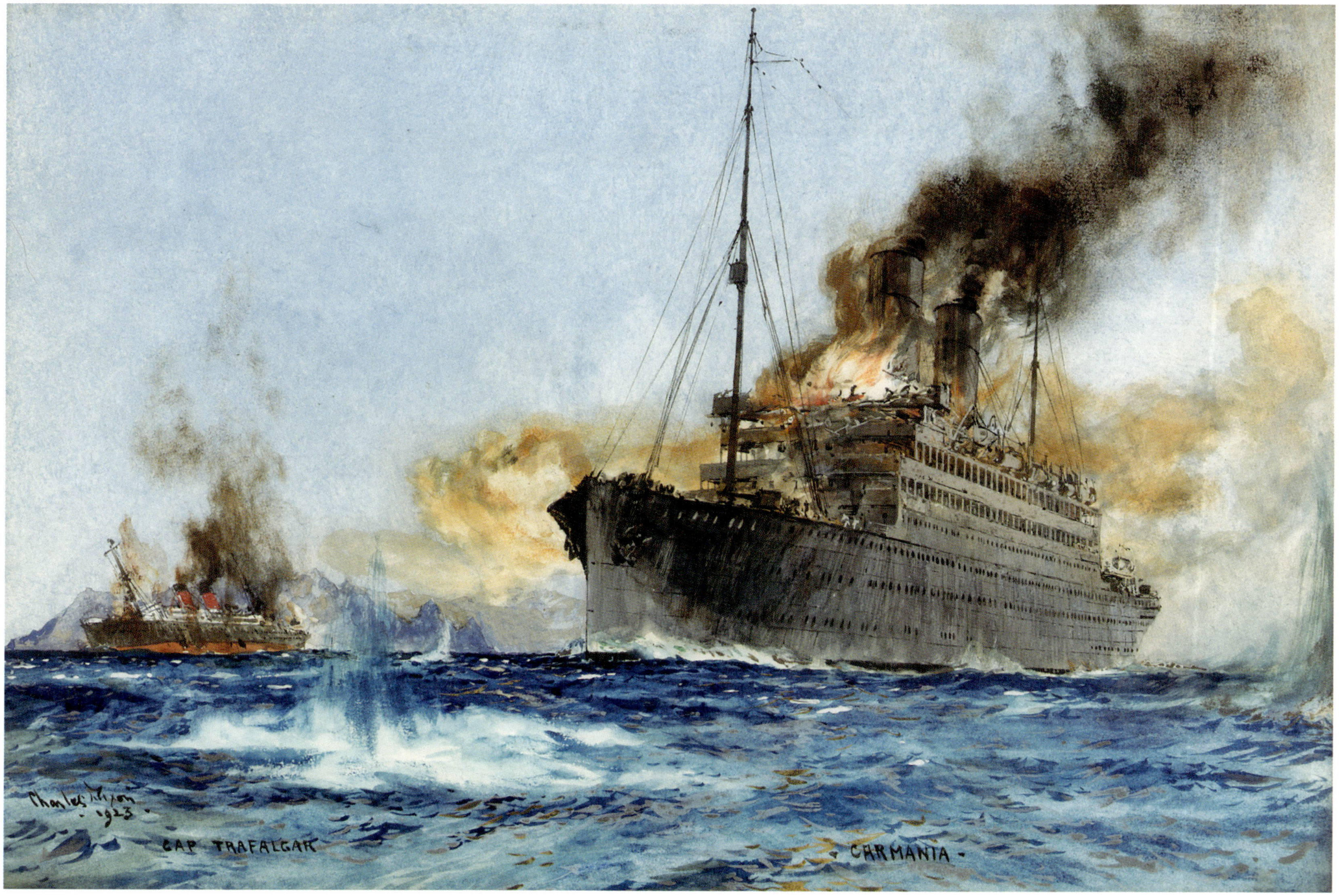


Carmania *Sinking* Cap Trafalgar *off Trinidad, 14 September 1914*
*Charles Dixon, Watercolour, Signed and dated 1923*
NATIONAL MARITIME MUSEUM, GREENWICH

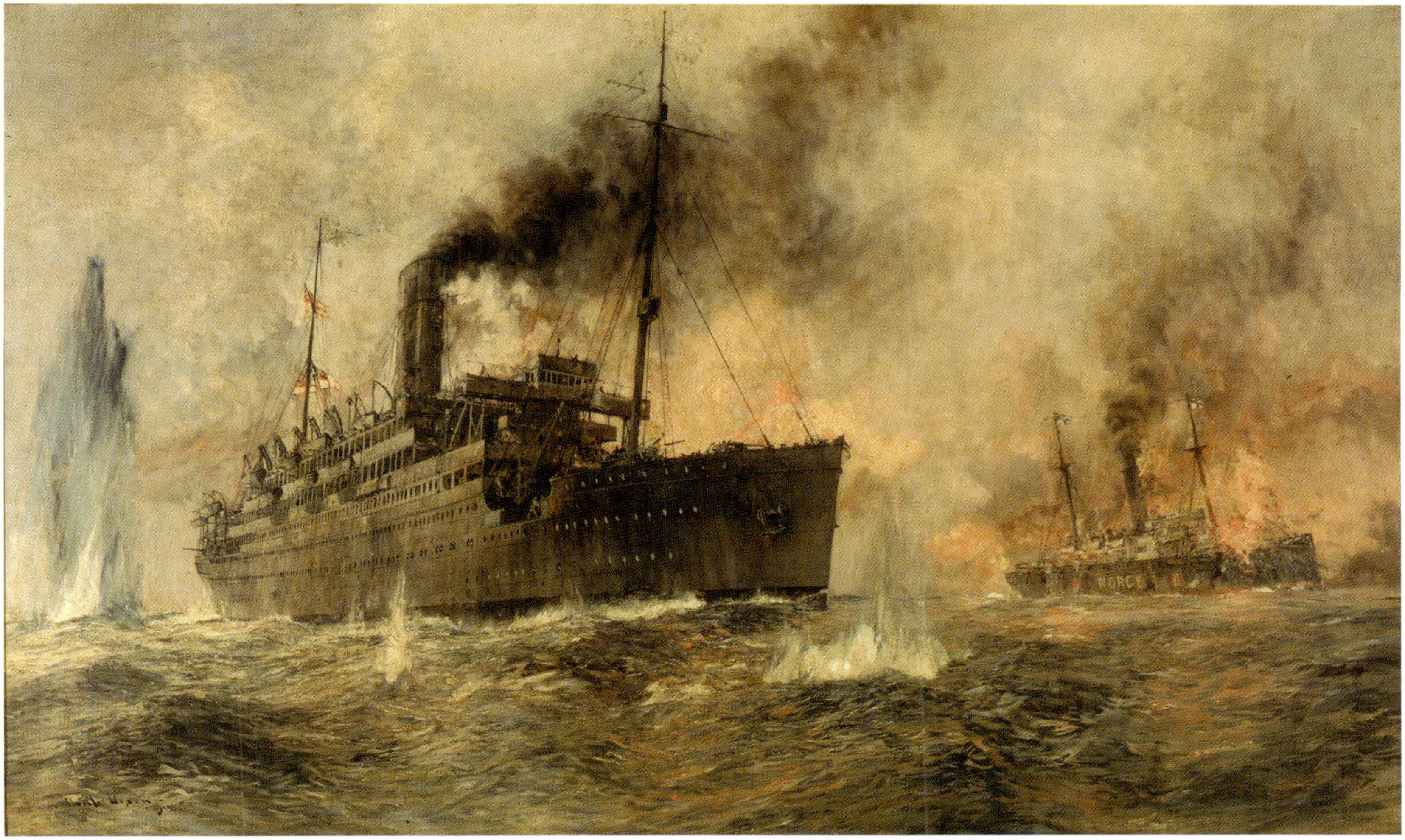

*The Fight Between the* Alcantara *and* Grief*, 1916*
*Charles Dixon, Oil on Canvas, Signed and dated 1923*

merchant cruiser, the *Alcantara*, an ex-Royal Mail Packet ship, and the German raider *Grief* in the North Sea on 29 February 1916. *Alcantara* was due to leave her patrol in the Skagerrak (which separates Danish Jutland from Norway) for Liverpool on 29 February, but was ordered to intercept a disguised Norwegian merchant ship. This was, in fact, *Grief*, a German raider. *Alcantara* spotted the raider at 08.45 and was about to send a boarding party when *Grief* opened fire, causing great damage to the British vessel. In the ensuing exchange, *Grief* was also hit and caught fire. As *Alcantara* listed to port, the order was given to abandon ship and she sank within two hours. *Grief* burned furiously and sank at 13.00. *Alcantara* lost 72 men and Grief 280. The oil painting, which depicts the action at the beginning of the encounter, was presented to the Merseyside Maritime Museum in 1963 by the Royal Mail Shipping Company. Apart from skirmishes such as this, it was the period between August 1914 and January 1915 that witnessed more full-scale encounters between British and German ships when the Royal Navy was engaged in the battles of Heligoland Bight, Coronel, the Falkland Islands and Dogger Bank which, Coronel apart, resulted in successful outcomes for the British Squadrons involved. They were however a prelude to the 'big one' – Jutland – the greatest naval engagement of the war, for this was the set piece when the battle fleets of Britain and Germany met for the first and last time; the eventual confrontation taking place between the British Grand Fleet and the German High Seas Fleet on 31 May 1916. Soon, within the confined area of the North Sea, no fewer than 148 British and 99 German ships of various kinds, funnels belching black smoke, engaged in the only full-scale surface battle of the war, in which the battle cruisers on each side were fiercely engaged, together with their supporting flotillas. When night fell, with the fleets no longer in immediate contact, the British felt confident of a successful engagement with the enemy ships the following morning, but in fact gave them the opportunity to escape and run for home.

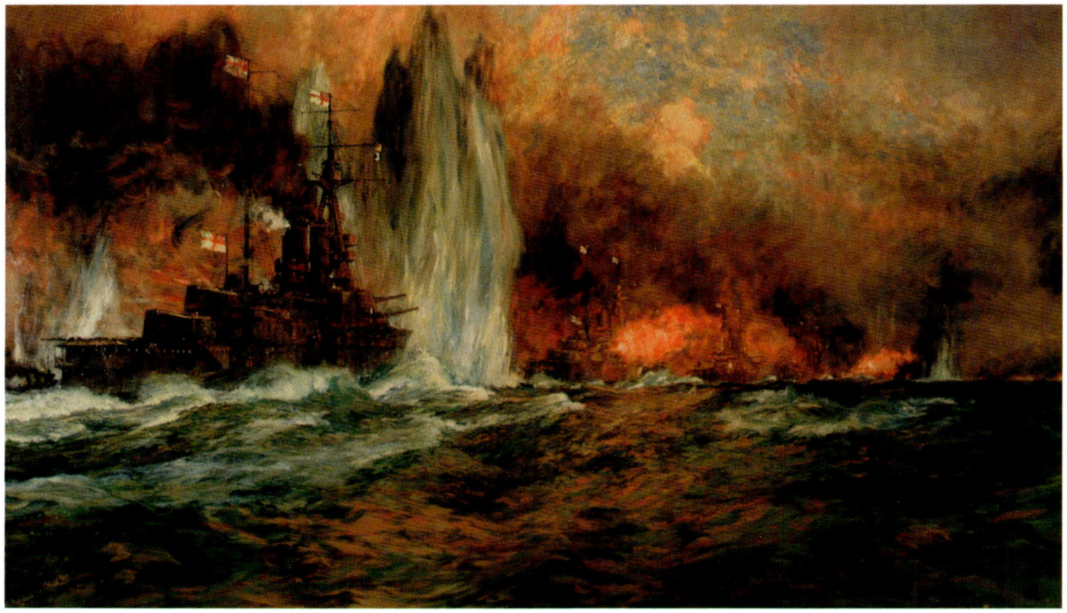

*The Battle of Jutland*
*Charles Dixon, Oil on Canvas, 41¼x70¾", Signed and dated 1916*
Blackburn Art Gallery

As regards the outcome of Jutland, certainly the German High Seas Fleet inflicted far more damage than it had received, having lost a battleship, a battle cruiser, four cruisers and five destroyers against the British loss of three battle cruisers, three cruisers and eight destroyers. Moreover the navy had lost 6,097 men to Germany's 2,545. The moral shock resulting from Jutland was considerable for the British public, shaken by the dreadful casualties on the Western Front and expecting another Trafalgar, who had to accept that her navy had come off worst. However, whilst statistically the Germans might have a case for declaring Jutland a victory, in reality the real honour went to the Royal Navy for, apart from several abortive sorties after Jutland, the remainder of the German fleet spent the rest of the war penned up in its port, never again to put to sea with the intention of engaging the Grand Fleet.

In 1918, the culmination of the war at sea between the British and German navies resulted in the main proportion of the German surface fleet steaming to Scapa Flow to surrender – eleven battleships, five battle cruisers, eight cruisers and fifty destroyers. The internment of the German High Seas Fleet took

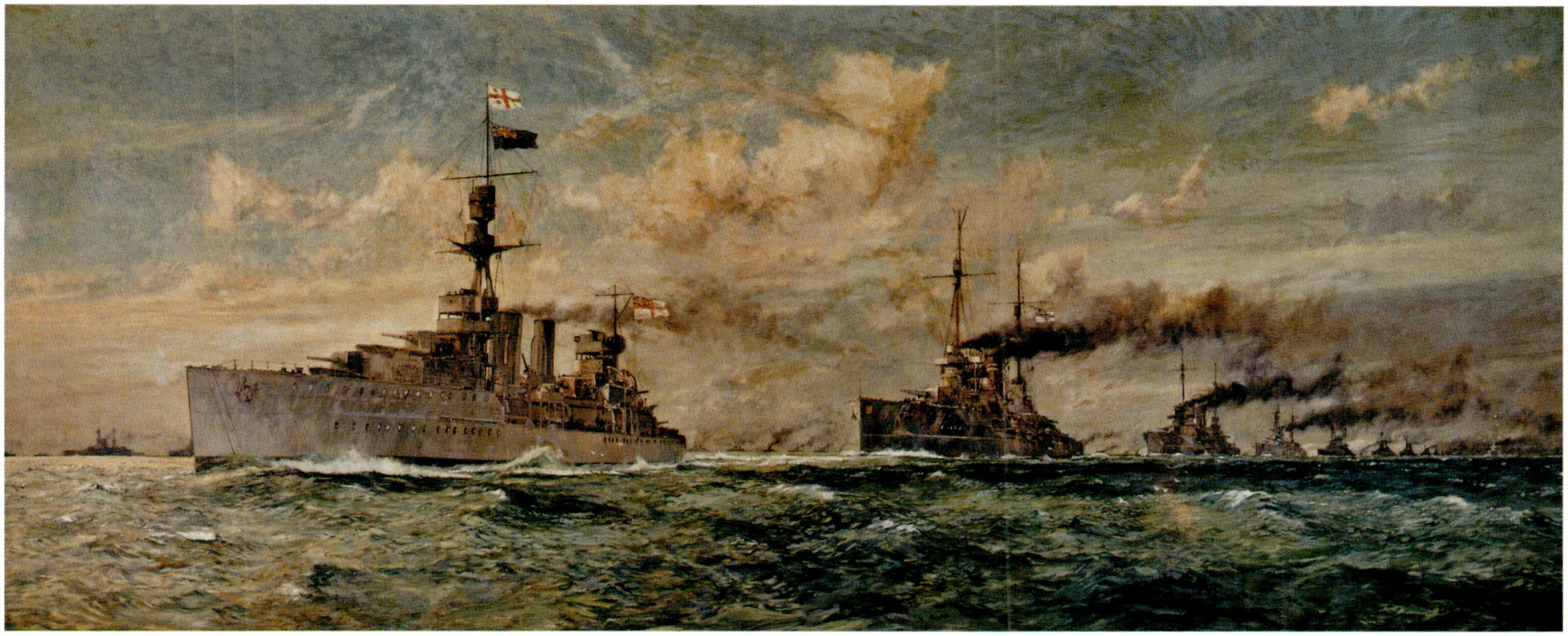

*HMS* Cardiff *Leading the Surrendered German High Seas Fleet*
*Charles Dixon, Oil on Canvas, Signed*
National Maritime Museum

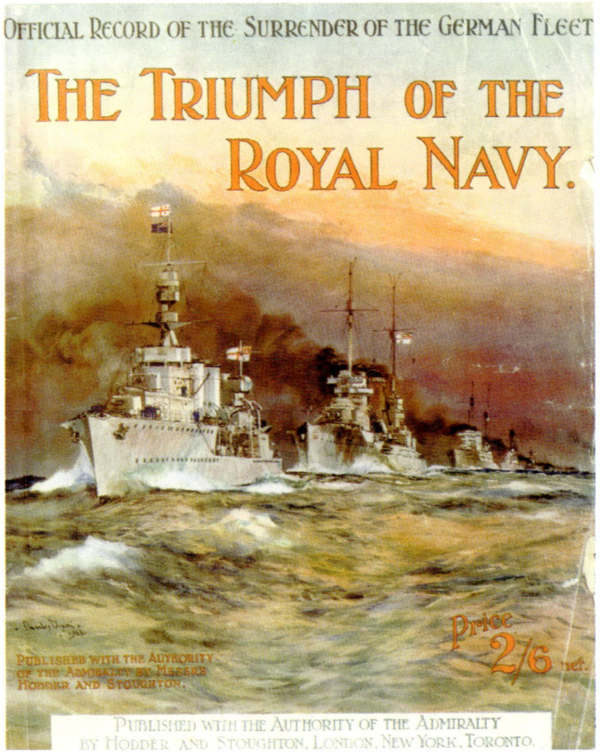


*The Triumph of the Royal Navy*
*Charles Dixon, Illustration for the*
The Illustrated London News and Sketch
*Signed and dated 1918*
PUBLISHED BY HODDER AND STOUGHTON

place on 21 November 1918 and a watercolour of the event featured on the cover of *The Illustrated London News and Sketch* with its bold jingoistic heading 'The Triumph of the Royal Navy', its journalistic sense of excitement and occasion so characteristic of Dixon's war paintings which were exactly in tune with the spirit prevailing in Britain at the time. This was an inglorious end for the proud German Navy and, when the ships were scuttled the following year by their crews, an Admiralty signal struck the right note when it stated 'the surrender of the German Fleet, accomplished without shock of battle, will remain for all time the example of the wonderful silence and sureness with which sea power attains its ends'. The cost, however, was enormous. In just over four years, the staggering total of 4,837 allied merchantmen had gone to the bottom. The tonnage represented was 11,135,000; of that amount by far the greater proportion had fallen to the submarine and the mine.

Although high tribute is due to the Royal Navy for its achievements between 1914 and 1918, when 41 officers and men were awarded the Victoria Cross, the way in which the mercantile marine continued to sail their ships during the long and painful phases of the war at sea, with none of the publicity which was given to the armed forces, was beyond praise. Throughout the war Dixon produced many illustrations for the news magazines of the day, which featured dramatic accounts of the vital role played by the Merchant Navy, these graphic drawings often appearing as the centrefold in order to convey all the drama of the subject. Between 1914 and 1918 Dixon continued to show work at the Royal Academy, the war giving rise to evocatively titled entries such as Dixon's 'The Wounded Warrior : Jutland 1916' when patriotic subjects became a desirable element in the Academy.

After the war and based on photographic evidence, sketches and accounts from those actively involved, Dixon produced a series of paintings, mainly watercolours, which are housed in the National Maritime Museum, Greenwich, and form the largest single collection of Dixon's First World War output. Known as 'The Bourne Collection', at one time these were owned by Mr Hollingsworth of Bourne and Hollingsworth, the one time Oxford Street, London store, and passed to Mr Stafford Bourne, his nephew, who bequeathed them to the museum in 1928. The subjects represented in the collection range from major dramatic events such as 'Windy Corner', Jutland, defence sinking between 6.07pm and 6.18pm 31st May 1916 to the raid on Zeebrugge '*Vindictive* alongside the Mole, Zeebrugge, April 23rd, 1918, 12.30am'. In this watercolour Dixon depicted one of the most daring naval actions of the whole war, when Admiral Sir Roger Keyes led a naval task force to the Belgian port of Zeebrugge with the intention of blockading the Bruges Canal and so reducing the flow of U-boats into the North Sea. His force included the cruiser, HMS *Vindictive*, two passenger ferries carrying additional marines, and three old warships which had previously been filled with concrete. At Zeebrugge, the marines first went ashore to take possession of the Mole and engage German defences. Then Keyes manoeuvred the three concrete-filled ships into the entrance to the Channel, placed them sideways on and then scuttled them. Whilst this was going on, a British submarine managed to edge its way under a viaduct connecting the Mole with the mainland and once the crew had abandoned the submarine, it was exploded and the viaduct destroyed. As soon as the marines were on board the *Vindictive*, they withdrew under the cover of a smoke screen. The deed ensured that the German troops defending the Mole could not be reinforced. In truth the raid had little effect on the movement of the U-boats in and out of Zeebrugge, but the epic

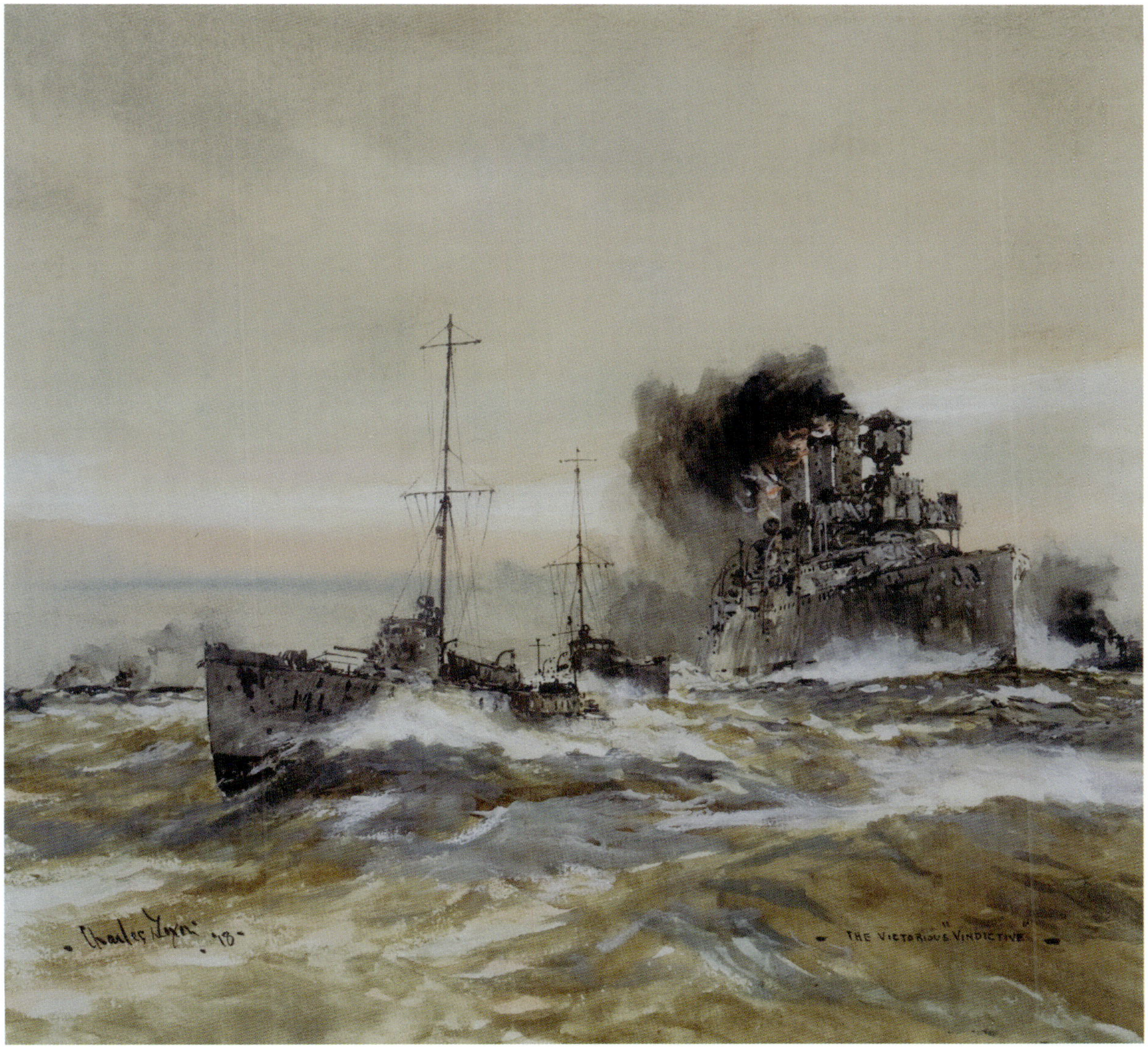


*The Victorious* Vindictive
*Charles Dixon, Watercolour, 9½x10½" Signed, inscribed and dated 19(18)*
PRIVATE COLLECTION

action, which had taken place on St George's Day, did much to boost the morale of the nation. Winston Churchill later referred to the raid as 'an episode unsurpassed in the history of the Royal Navy'. Furthermore, it was an event which won the Victoria Cross for eight of those brave men who took part.

Jutland apart, there was no major surface action at sea between 1914 and 1918; moreover the crisis of the sea war came in the increasing and sinister menace of the submarine, for the Germans had quickly discovered the skill of their U-boat commanders against men-of-war; merchantmen and liners were still easier victims and in defiance of the Hague Convention of 1907, which forbade the destruction of any ship without warning and first ensuring the safety of both passengers and crew, unrestricted submarine warfare by Germany continued unabated until 7 May 1915, when the U20 had sunk the liner, *Lusitania*, in the Irish Sea with the loss of 1,198 lives. This so outraged world opinion that the German High Command felt obliged to restrain their U-boat commanders, although this situation did not last through the war, with unrestricted attacks by Germany beginning once more in February 1917, depicted by Dixon in his drawing of 'The Sinking of the *Glenart Castle*', torpedoed in the Bristol Channel, within the 'free

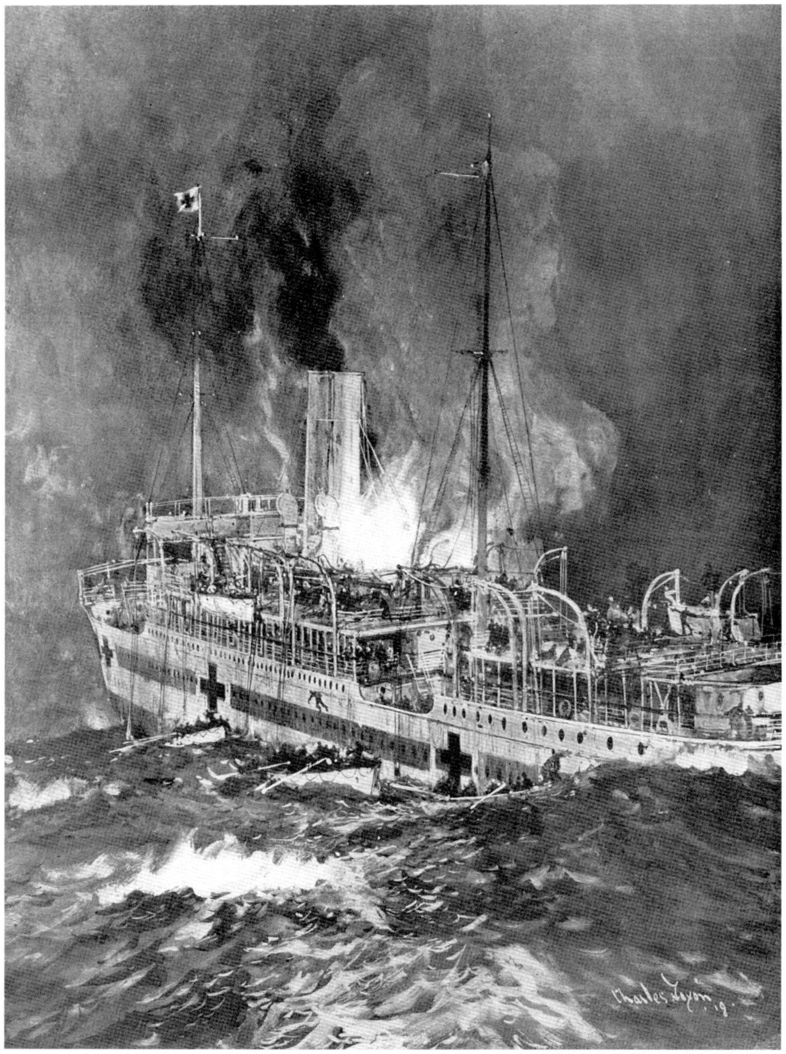


*The Sinking of the* Glenart Castle
*Charles Dixon, Illustration for* The Graphic, *9 March 1918*

Area' on 26 February 1918, which he did for *The Graphic*. The *Glenart Castle* was one of over 70 British vessels, mainly liners, which had been converted for a variety of uses as hospital ships, troopships and armed merchant cruisers, in fact all belligerents lost liners to Government duties at this time, and indeed since when Cunard's *Queen Elizabeth II* was requisitioned at the time of the Falklands campaign.

By the autumn of 1917 German U-boats had sunk, under appalling conditions of suffering, two and three quarter million tons of allied shipping and one measure designed by the Admiralty to counter this offensive, was the Q-ship, designed so that an innocent and helpless looking merchant vessel would give every appearance of being at the submarine's mercy and some of her crew would ostentatiously take to the boats – when the surfaced U-boat came close to the Q-ship, either to put a boarding party aboard or to sink her, secret guns would suddenly appear on the Q-ship's side and that would inevitably be the end of the U-boat. Unfortunately attempts to use disguised craft to attack U-boats enjoyed temporary but diminishing success for the Germans soon became more cautious and would torpedo anything suspicious without warning. Dixon's watercolour at Greenwich of the HM Topsail Schooner, *Prize*, sinking UB85 on 30th April 1918, is of particular interest since it resulted in Lt Sanders, RNR, receiving the Victoria Cross for his action.

Throughout the British Isles there are many landmarks and references which serve to remind us of the nation's maritime past, from the shipbuilding heritage of Belfast, Newcastle and the Clyde, the commercial ports of Cardiff, Bristol, Liverpool and Southampton, and the once thriving fishing industries of the North East and Cornwall. However, as far as the Royal Navy is concerned, one is immediately mindful of the great royal dockyards of Devonport, Chatham, and Portsmouth, for they are the potent symbols of Britain's naval heritage. Devonport, to the west of Plymouth, was established as a naval base in 1691 and the city is steeped in the history of some of Britain's greatest seafarers. Thus, Sir Francis Drake, the greatest of all Elizabethan seafarers, set sail from Plymouth in 1577 for his three year circumnavigation of the world. Sir Walter Raleigh also set sail from Plymouth to Carolina in 1584, as did the Pilgrim Fathers in 1620 and, at a later date, Captain James Cook. The first royal dockyard on the banks of the River Medway was founded at Chatham in 1570 by Elizabeth I and down the centuries the great names of maritime history, Drake, Hawkins and Nelson, sailed from here. Furthermore, it was the birthplace of many of the navy's famous ships, including Nelson's great flagship, HMS *Victory*, launched on 7 May 1765. However, for over 800 years it was Portsmouth which became the principal home of the Royal Navy, the dockyard being the largest industrial complex in the world for much of the long period of British supremacy at sea. In 1495 the world's first dry dock was built at Portsmouth and 1509 saw the first ship built there, the 600 ton *Peter Pomegranate*. It was also in 1509 that the ill-fated *Mary Rose* was commissioned in this historic place and where her remains can be seen today. The size and scale of its facilities dominated the naval scene for generations and its presence embodied security for the nation.

The activities in and around these dockyards and harbours provided an abundance of subject matter for the marine artist, but none more so than Portsmouth. In his book *Hampshire*, published in 1909, Telford Varley wrote "to describe Portsmouth adequately would be to write the history of the British Navy. In Portsmouth the navy confronts you at almost every turn – not merely in the harbour, the dockyard, the old *Victory*, the Garrison Church – but even on Southsea beach amongst the trippers, it is the navy first and the navy always, and this is as it should be. Portsmouth and the navy are rightly inseparable, even if not interchangeable terms. To understand and appreciate Portsmouth, it should be approached from the sea. As you round the point, the town, with its towers, spires and long sea walls, lies spread out before you. The waters are alive with craft, large and small, active, vicious looking tugs, little fussy launches and 'Pickford steamers', coasting ketches and brown-sailed smacks, and away beyond the spit forts on the right, some three- or four-masted dull grey ironclads, looming huge and sombre far out in the channel".

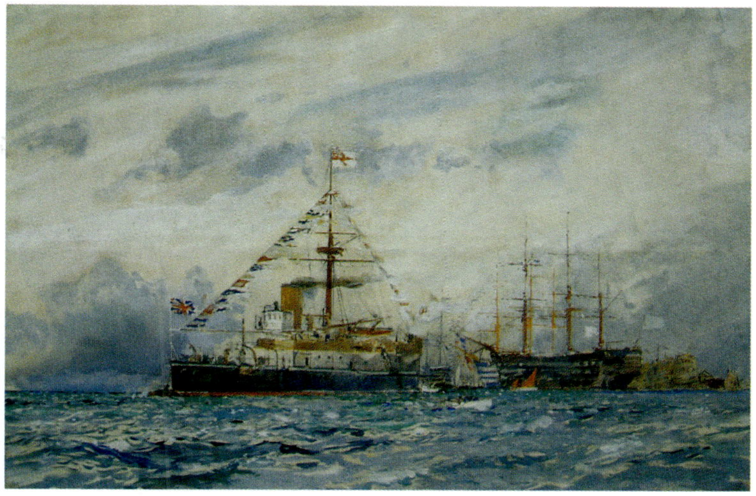

*HMS* Victory *and HMS* Hero *at Portsmouth*
*Charles Dixon, Watercolour, Signed Charles Dixon*
*HMS* Hero *was a turret ship built in 1885 in Chatham and after 1907 was used as a target ship, sunk as such in 1908.*
PRIVATE COLLECTION

*NB This watercolour provided the cover illustration for the exhibition of Dixon's work at the Hampton Hill in 1973.*

From this wonderfully evocative description of Portsmouth before the First World War, it is easy to understand its enormous appeal to artists such as Dixon, W L Wyllie, Frank Watson Wood and Alma Burlton Cull, all of whom not only used it as a vehicle for their work, but also chose to live in the vicinity. Indeed, Wyllie's house at the entrance to the harbour, enabled him to paint in surroundings that could not possibly have been richer in the history, lore and evolution of the Royal Navy. From 1906 until his death in 1931, with the sea a few feet from his studio, very few ships left the harbour

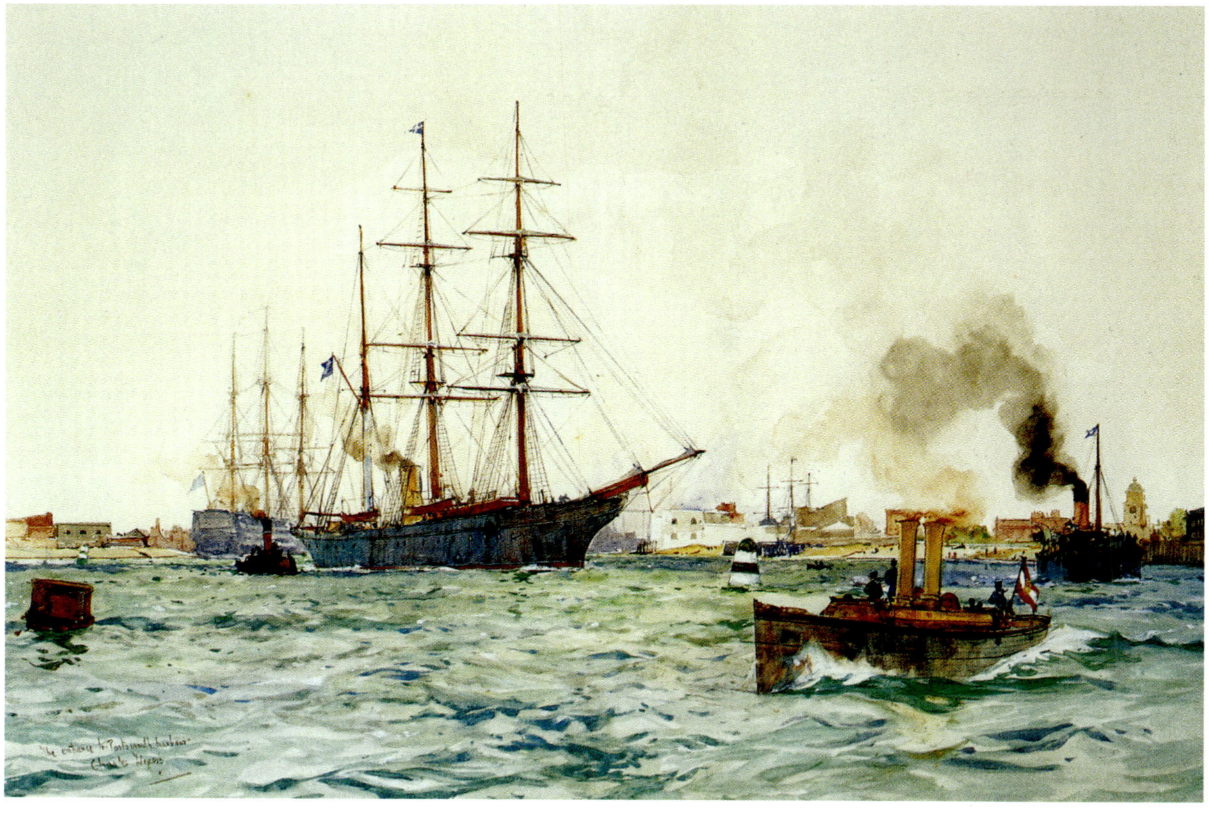

*The Entrance to Portsmouth Harbour.*
*The steam yacht* Valhalla *with HMS* Victory
*Charles Dixon, Watercolour,*
*Signed and inscribed with the title, 15x21¼"*
BARON FINE ART

without being seen by Wyllie or his eldest son, Harold (1880-1973), also a marine artist, who inherited his father's love of ships, albeit not so much in the contemporary scene as in the development of the sailing ship in naval history. He exhibited ten paintings at the Royal Academy, all of which were reconstructions of historical sea battles and reflect his father's deep interest in nautical history and HMS *Victory* in particular. W L Wyllie's obsessive desire to paint the sea and anything that floated on it, embraced every type and size of vessel of the Royal Navy, and the British fleet at the time of the First World War provided him with the material for not only some of his best watercolours, which he painted during the latter part of his life, but also for the illustrations he did for *Sea Fights of the Great War* and *More Sea Fights of the Great War*, which were published in 1919. On several occasions throughout the war Wyllie travelled with the Grand Fleet by special licence in order to make drawings such as those he sketched whilst aboard the battleship HMS *Revenge*, depicting the British and German fleets as they steamed up to their internment at Scapa Flow. Like Dixon, throughout his life he maintained a devout belief in the invincibility of the navy and Empire and it is undoubtedly a reflection of the esteem in which Wyllie was held by the Royal Navy that, after his funeral in Portsmouth Cathedral, his coffin was carried up Portsmouth Harbour by a naval cutter, lent by HMS *Nelson*, Flagship of the Atlantic fleet and rowed by sea scouts of the troop he had founded, to be buried in Portchester churchyard. On the way, as the cutter drew abreast of each battleship, a bugle call rang out, the ships' company saluted and the colours were lowered to half mast.

Born in Croydon, Alma Claude Burlton Cull (1880-1931) was another marine artist who moved to the Portsmouth area where he found the perfect conditions to paint many fine studies of important naval vessels of his day. Cull was the son of the artist, James Allanson Cull, and for a while lived at Harrow on the Hill, but little information exists about his life. His work is generally less well known than the paintings of Dixon and Wyllie, but as a portrayer of ships of the Royal Navy in the first quarter of the twentieth century, he was able to display a skill unsurpassed by either men, recording the massive armoured Dreadnoughts of the Grand Fleet with the grave panache echoed by Winston Churchill's description of British warships passing through the straits of Dover in July 1914. Observed with metaphors mixed to potent effect, Churchill described them as 'scores of gigantic castles of steel wending their way across the misty, shiny sea, like giants bowed in anxious thought'. Cull's studies of warships are meticulously accurate and beautifully drawn and he was able to achieve a marvellous sense of light in his subjects, whether they were big capital ships forging through long swells and throwing off clouds of spray or vessels lying serenely in a quiet anchorage. His style is similar to that of Wyllie and he excelled in creating delicate colour harmonies, while effortlessly conveying the power of the ships he sought to record. Cull's main exhibition period was between 1906 and 1927, during which he had pictures shown at the Royal Institute of Painters in Watercolours, The Walker Art Gallery, Liverpool and the Alpine Gallery in London. Surprisingly he exhibited only twice at the Royal Academy where in 1912, he showed the large oil 'Send out your big Warships to guard your big waters', which was painted for HRH the Prince of Wales and is now in the collection of the National Maritime Museum. Sadly, Cull died young, at the age of fifty, on 27 January 1931 at Lee on Solent, Hampshire. Unfortunately, many of his paintings which had been put into storage in nearby Portsmouth, were destroyed by enemy bombs on the city during the Second World War and are consequently rare, but three of his oils and seventy watercolours are preserved at Greenwich. Because his paintings appear so infrequently on the market, they have become much sought after by discerning collectors willing to pay quite high prices to secure an example by arguably the finest portrayer of ships of the Royal Navy of the period.

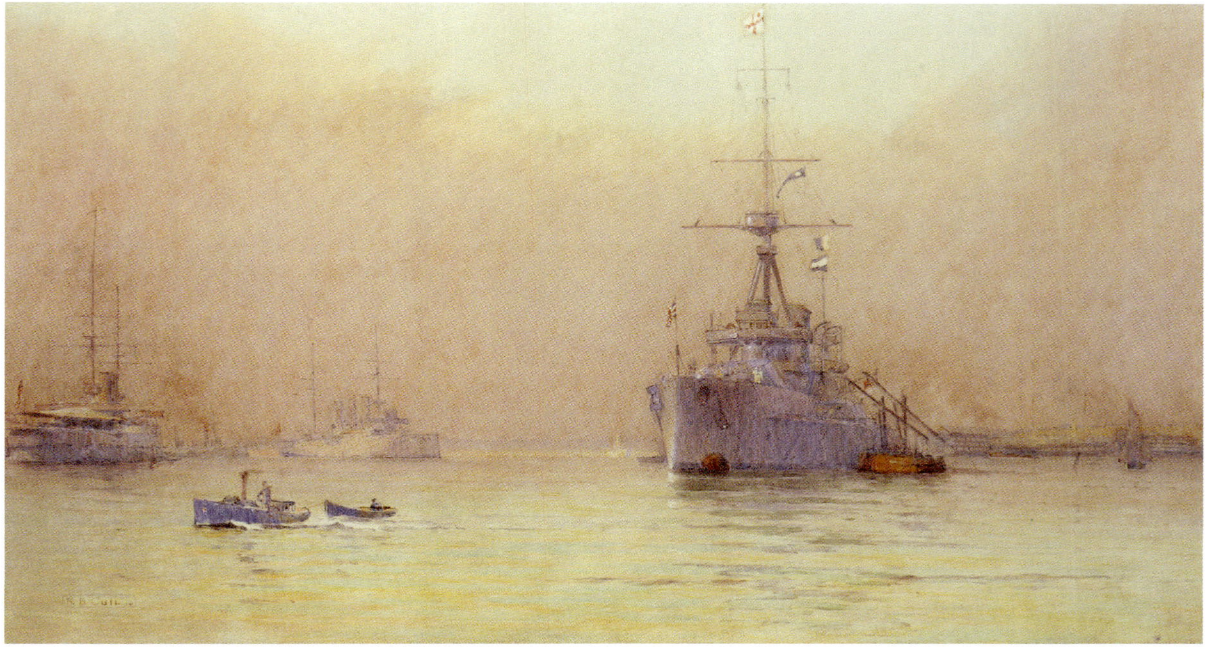

*A 1902 Battleship Refitting at Portsmouth*
*Alma B. Cull, Watercolour, Signed and Dated 1908*
N.R. Omell Gallery

A Scottish artist, who also painted portraits of Royal Navy ships around the period when Cull, Wyllie and Dixon were active in Portsmouth, is Frank Watson Wood (1862-1957). After studying at the Berwick on Tweed School of Art and the Academie Julian in Paris, he taught at the Newcastle School of Art, but left the North East in 1900 when he moved to Portsmouth. It was here that he concentrated on naval subjects, accepting many commissions from Naval Officers for portraits of their ships and of naval exercises, but also some of the great fleet reviews. By the end of the First World War, his career as a naval artist had become firmly established and in 1918 he was invited with W L Wyllie, Charles de Lacy and Sir John Lavery aboard the Grand Fleet flagship, HMS *Queen Elizabeth*, to cover the surrender of the German High Seas fleet and he later made a number of sketches of the German ships before the scuttling. After the war he often travelled abroad and in 1938 he accompanied King George VI and Queen Elizabeth on their Canadian tour as official artist. He painted some oils, but worked mostly in

*The Hamoaze, Plymouth*
*Frank Watson Wood, Watercolour, Signed*
Maritime Prints and Originals

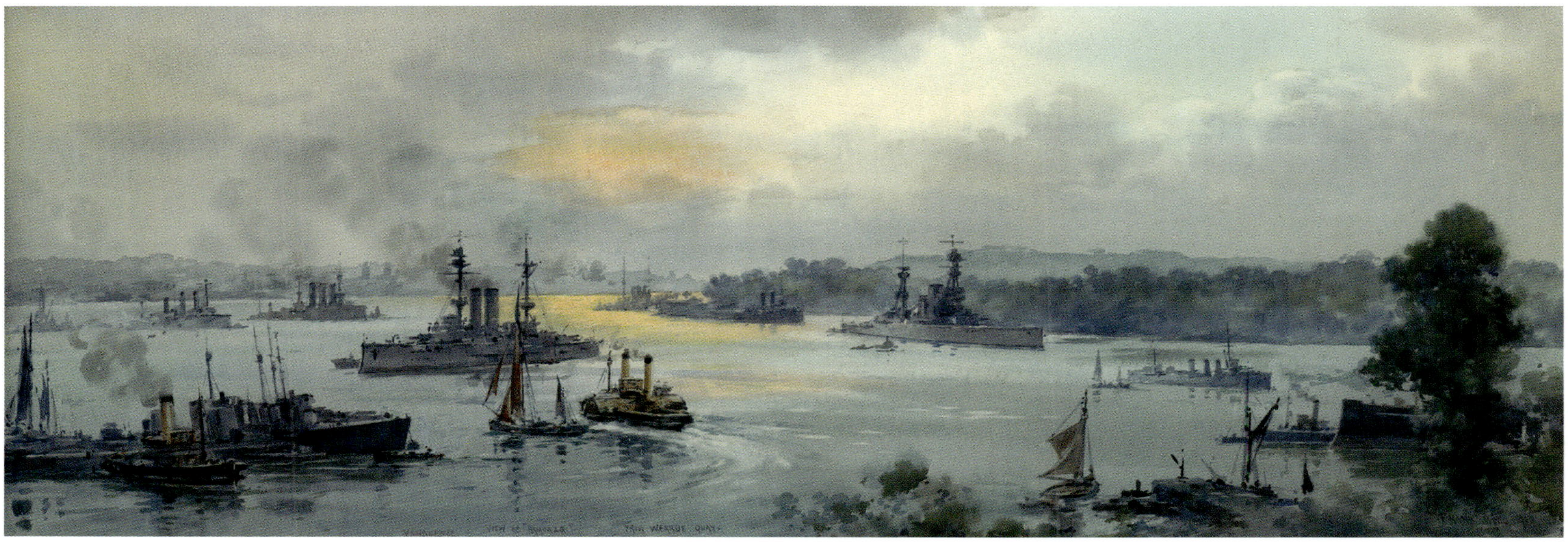

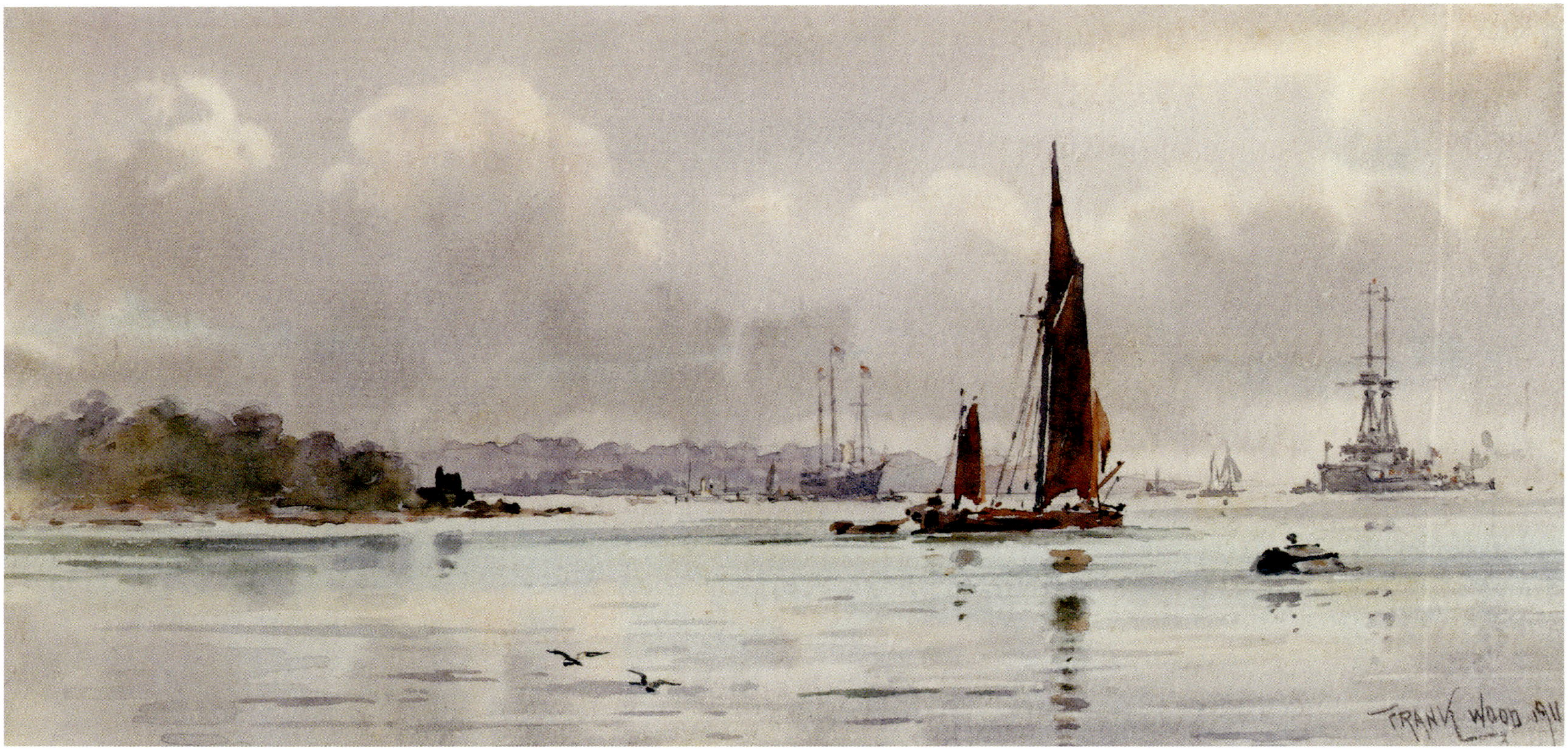


*The Royal Yacht* Victoria & Albert *off Cowes*
*Frank Watson Wood, Watercolour, Signed*
JOHN MORTON LEE FINE WATERCOLOURS

watercolours, often using an elongated format, similar to that employed by Dixon, usually showing some of the great battleships and cruisers in harbour, mainly Portsmouth, but also naval activity at Devonport, with big capital ships at anchor or entering or leaving Plymouth Sound. Although he painted similar subjects to Cull, he practised a much looser style and used higher colouring, often a somewhat obtrusive light blue predominating. His watercolours have a simplicity about them, not unlike those by Eduardo de Martino (1838-1912). Between 1890 and 1930, Wood painted yachting scenes at Cowes and on one occasion, Tsar Nicholas II of Russia bought work from him whilst visiting at the height of the season. He exhibited at the Glasgow Institution, the Royal Society of Artists and the Royal Academy and a number of his pictures are in the National Maritime Museum, Greenwich.

Although relatively unknown, another marine painter, much influenced by naval scenes at Portsmouth and also Chatham, was Irwin John Bevan (1852-1940). Unlike Dixon, Wyllie and Cull, he was not born into an artistic family, but came from a wealthy background with railway interests in South Wales. From an early age Bevan took a keen interest in nautical matters, becoming a member of the Royal Naval reserve and through his enthusiasm for sailing coupled with his hobby of painting came into contact with W L Wyllie when they both lived in the Medway area. It seems they became close friends, Bevan marrying Wyllie's sister-in-law. After Rochester, they lived for a time on the Norfolk Broads, and later settled in Bedford and it was here that Bevan developed his painting and illustrative work on a full time basis. At the outbreak of the First World War, he became an official war artist and later collaborated with Wyllie on the first of Wyllie's wartime publications *Sea Fights of the Great War*. Bevan also wrote and illustrated *Trafalgar,* which was published in 1908. Proficient in both watercolour and oils, watercolour seems to have been his preferred medium, often with a preponderance of soft blues – his pictures are usually signed 'I Bevan' in red and painted in an elongated format. During his long life, he produced a

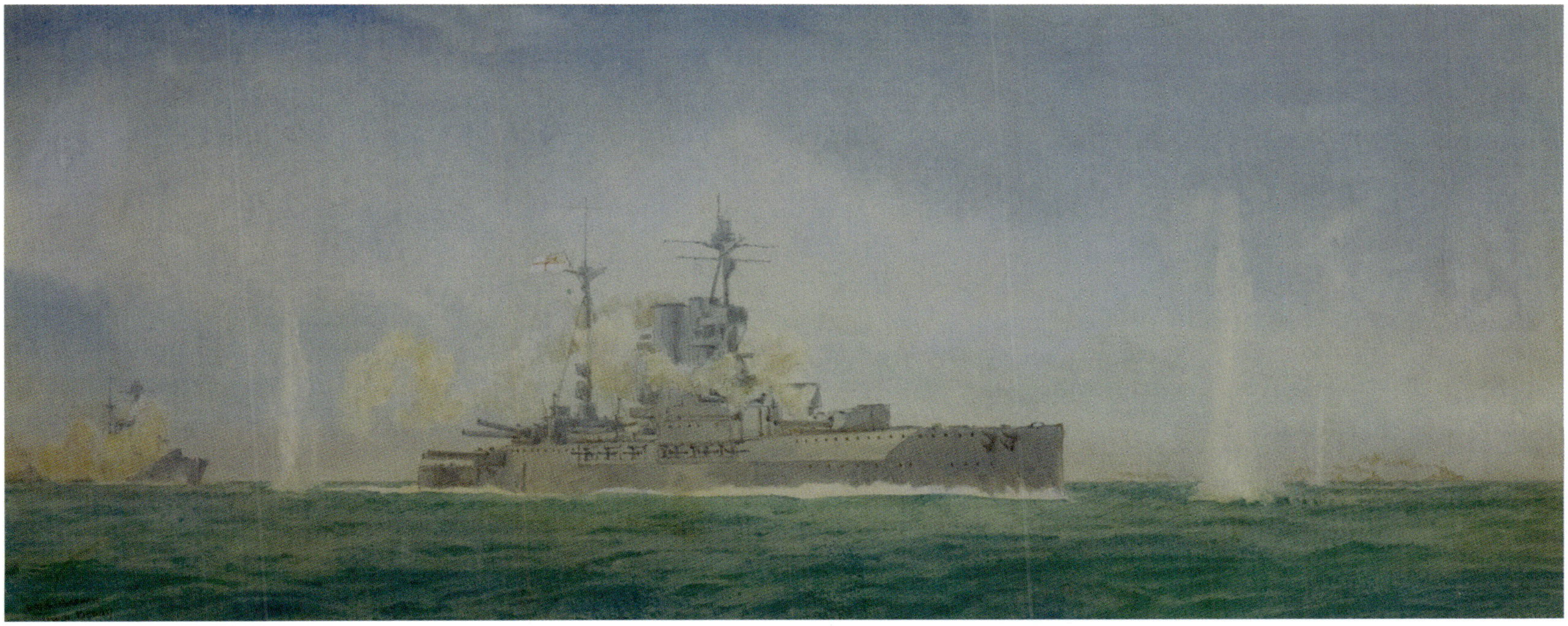

large number of paintings of contemporary and also historical naval subjects, which demonstrate his ability to skilfully depict nautical detail and historical fact, particularly the action between British and American naval vessels over the period 1740-1850 and these form part of the collection of his work in the Mariners' Museum, Newport News, Virginia, USA. His paintings are also represented in the American Naval Academy, the National Maritime Museum, Greenwich and the Guildhall Museum, Rochester, Kent. In 1908, 1909 and 1915, he had pictures shown at the Royal Academy.

*HMS* Barham *at the Battle of Jutland*
*Irwin John Bevan, Watercolour, 7¼x18½", Signed*
PRIVATE COLLECTION

A rather more familiar name and one of Britain's most gifted marine artists of the twentieth century, who painted many scenes depicting the Royal Navy during the First and Second World Wars, is Frank Henry

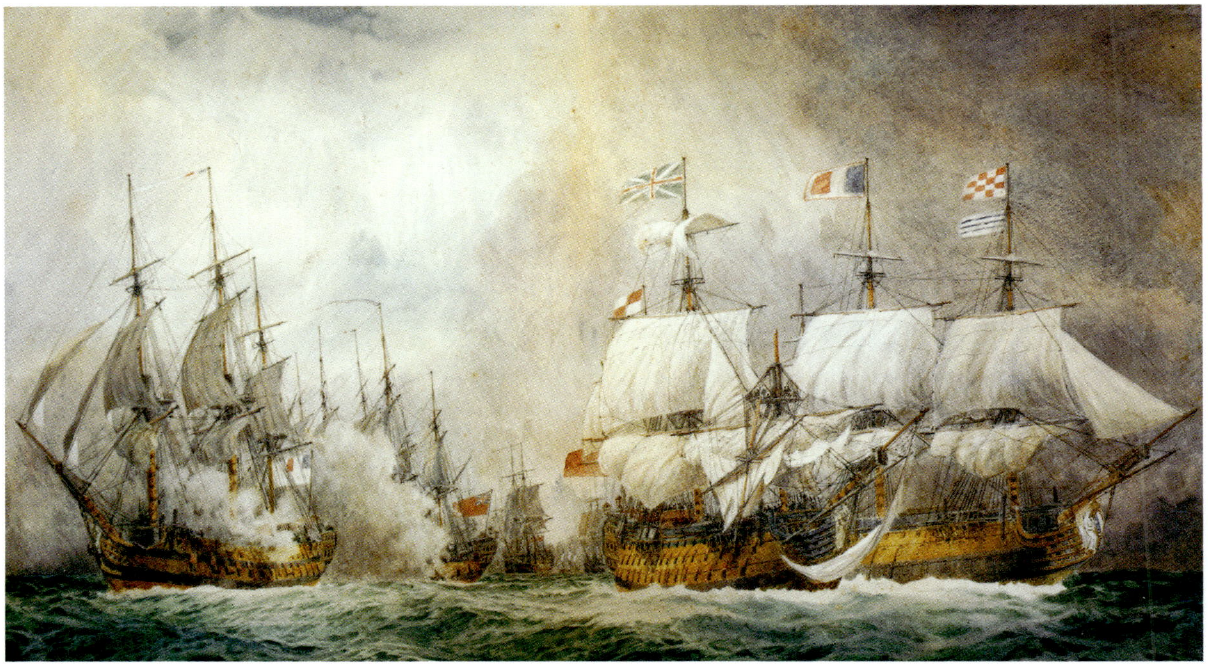

*The Glorious 1st of June*
*Irwin John Bevan, Watercolour, Signed*
PRIVATE COLLECTION

Mason, RI (1887-1965) - a Northcountry man born at Seaton Carew in County Durham. After an education at the training ship, HMS *Conway*, Mason pursued a career as a marine engineer in the shipbuilding industry working at Hartlepool. During the First World War, he served as a Lieutenant in the RNVR in the North Sea and was also stationed in Malta and Egypt. During the Second World War, he served in the Directorate of Camouflage, Naval Division and was appointed an official war artist, a task for which his early involvement in the navy made him particularly suitable and fifty-six of his pictures, many taken from his time in the Middle East, are now in the Imperial War Museum. For a time Mason studied at his local art school in Scarborough and it seems he had some involvement with the colony of artists along the coast at Staithes, where he was a regular visitor and painted studies of the local fishing fleet. Though executed with a free hand, his paintings were always factually accurate, his nautical background enabling him to produce vivid records of events very much from a naval man's point of view at a time when Britain's navy was expanding and her ports were bustling. Mason was one of the most prolific and versatile artists of his time, for he painted in oil, watercolour and was also an

*The Monitor vessels* Severn *and* Mersey *Engaging the German Battlecruiser* Konigsberg *on the Rufiji River, German East Africa*
*Frank H. Mason, Oil on Canvas, 15x21", Signed*
N.R. Omell Gallery

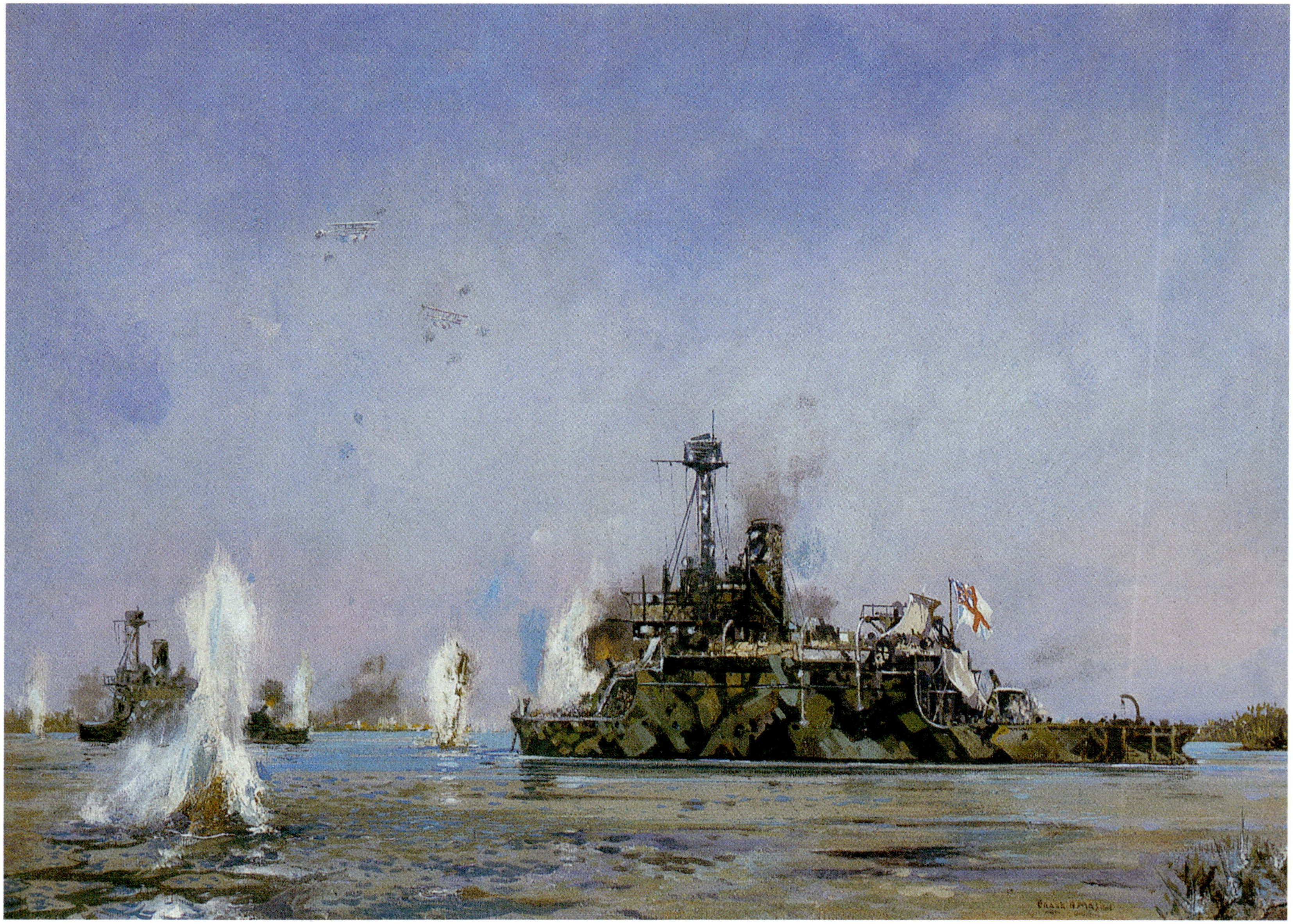

accomplished etcher. From time to time during his long life he embarked on a number of extensive sketching tours and Venice seems to have been a favourite place, his views around the lagoon displaying a strong impressionistic style. Mason's choice of subjects was wide and included merchant shipping, yachting and scenes of the Royal Navy at war. Like Dixon, he also had a penchant for historical naval subjects and it was the dash of romance which Mason added to his concern for authenticity which ensured the lasting popularity of his historical reconstructions of men-of-war, widely distributed as prints and cover pictures for books and magazines. His clarity of line and vision also meant that Mason was much in demand as a poster designer, at one time for Players 'Senior Service' cigarettes. According to the assessment by H Clifford Smith of the Victoria and Albert Museum, his stature as a painter just prior to the Great War, was 'a little above Dixon and a little below Norman Wilkinson'. He exhibited at the Royal Academy from 1900 and examples of his work may be found at Dundee Art Gallery, Gray Art Gallery, Liverpool and also the National Maritime Museum, Greenwich, where an exhibition of his work was held in 1973.

In many ways the career of Frank Mason resonates with that of Norman Wilkinson CBE, RI, ROI (1878-1971), often regarded as the doyen of British marine painters. As a boy, Wilkinson lived at Southsea, where the proximity of Portsmouth harbour and Spithead, alive with shipping, were ideal for a youth whose whole interest was ships and the sea. After training at the Portsmouth School of Art, he gained some nautical experience and made trips in colliers from Portsmouth along the North East coast, but it was a career as a painter and illustrator, rather than a seafarer, which beckoned and resulted in a move to London and eventual employment with *The Illustrated London News*, which he refers to in his autobiography, *A Brush with Life*. "My first drawing to appear in the ILN was one in 1898, the subject, picket boats, guarding the Royal Yacht at night in Portsmouth Harbour, Queen Victoria being on board, the excitement of buying a copy on the Friday to see if it had been accepted, can hardly be described". Certainly well before the First World War Wilkinson had made his mark as a fine painter of ships, and one of his pictures had gone down with the *Titanic* in 1912. During the war, Wilkinson obtained a commission as a Lieutenant in the Royal Navy Volunteer Reserve and, like Frank Mason, commanded a motor patrol boat. It was at this time that he put forward the idea of dazzle painting of ships as a means of confusing the aim of German gunners and torpedo men, and this concept was generally accepted by both the Naval and Merchant fleets. This resulted in many thousands of British and Allied ships owing their safety to this artwork which was entirely the outcome of Wilkinson's original thinking, no doubt enhanced by his knowledge of seamanship in the RNVR. Like Dixon, W L Wyllie, A Briscoe and Charles Pears, Wilkinson was a keen yachtsman and after the war he became honorary marine painter to the Royal Yacht Squadron. In 1944 at the age of 66 and a veteran of the Great War he was not an official war artist in World War II, but remained active and was present at the Normandy invasion, sketching from the destroyer, HMS *Jarvis*. It was from these sketches, which were executed with a sure hand and fine realism, that he produced some of his 'war at sea' series, a set of 53 mostly oil paintings of naval incidents of the war, the fruit of some two and a half years work. These were exhibited at the National Gallery and presented to the nation by the artist. They are now housed in the National Maritime Museum in

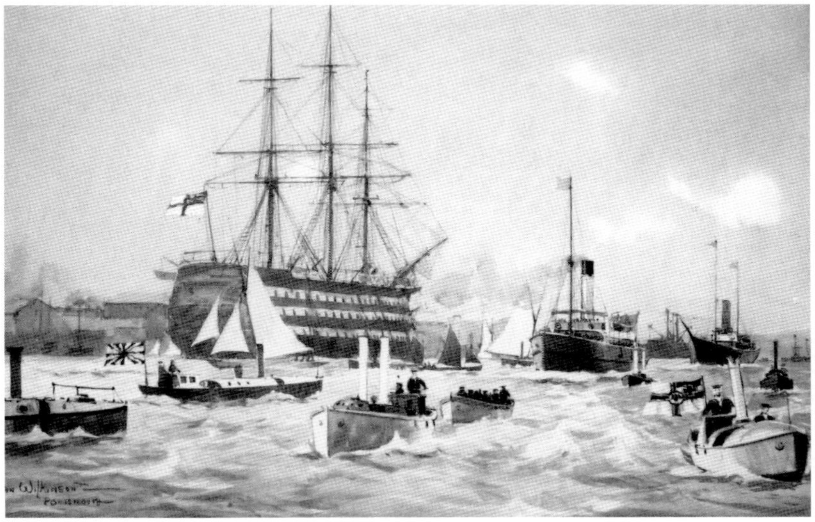

*A Busy Portsmouth Harbour c.1902*
*Norman Wilkinson,*
*Monochrome Watercolour, Signed*
Private Collection

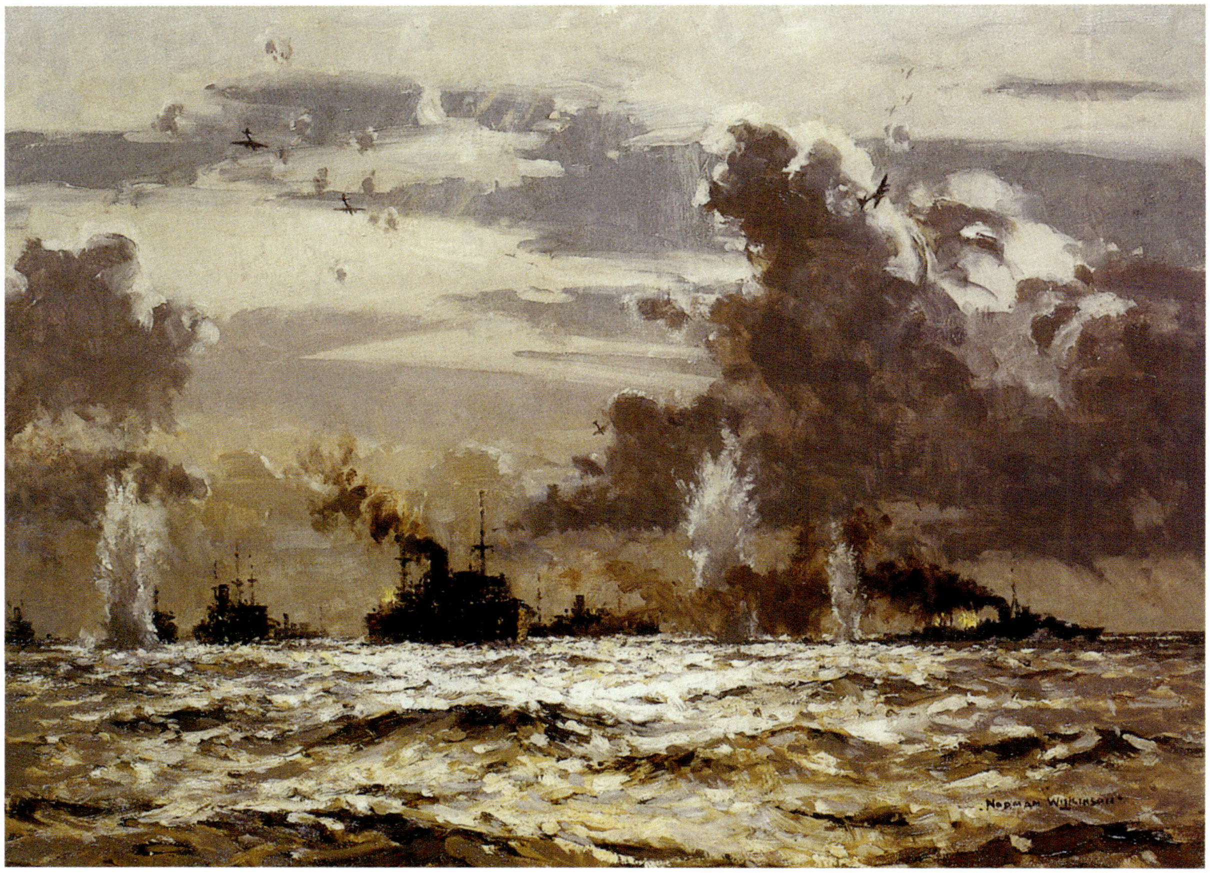

*A Convoy of Merchant Ships Escorted by Royal Navy Destroyers and Frigates Under Aerial Attack*
*Norman Wilkinson, Oil on Canvas, 26x36", Signed*
*Exhibited Royal Academy 1941*
*No 305 entitled 'Convoy'*
Royal Excahnge Art Gallery

Greenwich, but examples of Wilkinson's war pictures may also be found in the Imperial War Museum. Wilkinson was highly skilled as an oil and watercolour artist and produced a number of dry point etchings, but for many he will be best remembered for his advertising work as a poster designer, which was commissioned by the many shipping and railway companies and with whom he achieved a considerable measure of success. He exhibited at virtually all the major art institutions in Britain, including the Royal Academy where, in 1941, he exhibited one of his many World War II subjects, 'Convoy'.

A Surgeon Lt in the Royal Navy in WWI, Oscar Parkes (1885-1958) eventually became known as a highly respected naval historian, specialising in the technical design and development of the battleship. His excessive knowledge extended to other classes of warships which were in commission during his life, especially between the two wars. Principally a painter in watercolours, marine painting appears to have become an adjunct to his interests and he became a skilful practitioner in the rendering of naval ship portraits. Seven of his paintings are in the Imperial War Museum, including two oils, one depicting the Hospital Ship *Karapora* and also the Royal Hospital Ship *Somali*. Little is known about the life of Charles Eddowes Turner (1883-1965), other than he was an illustrator of the same generation as Charles Dixon and who also worked for *The Illustrated London News* and *The Sphere*. In the Second World War, he painted naval actions for these magazines, which were usually reproduced as double page spreads. During the Second World War his position as Captain in the Fleet Air Arm offered a unique opportunity for him to record his first hand experiences in the war. His

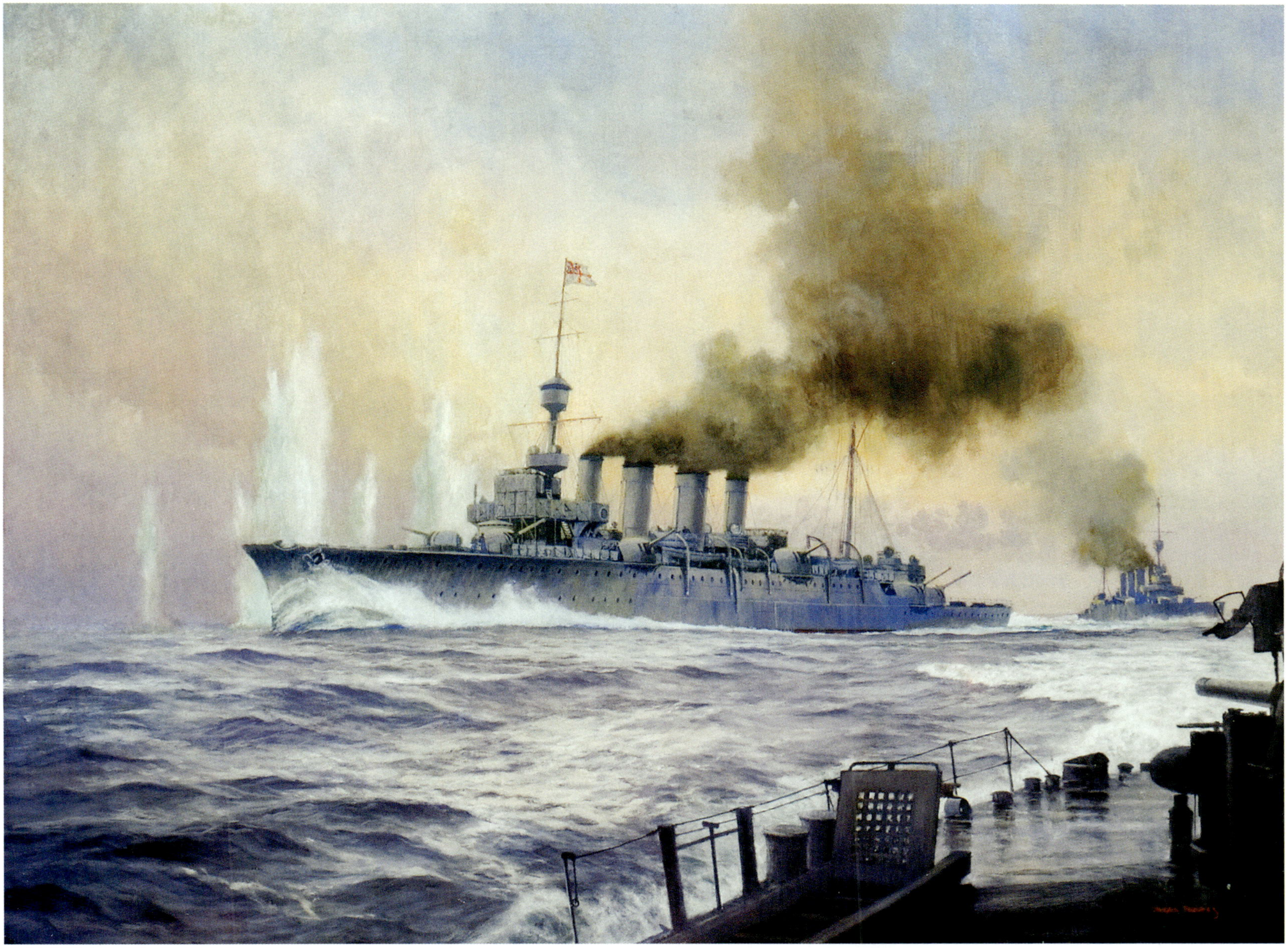

paintings in oils and watercolour demonstrate his skill in creating fresh and realistic compositions not only in his naval subjects, but in other facets of his work as an illustrator of shipping posters and postcards. The National Maritime Museum has eight examples of his work, including 'Sinking of the *Bismarck*, 27 May 1941' and he is also represented at the IWM. Turner had a great capacity of painting dramatic naval actions, the details of which are usually well observed. An artist who painted naval subjects in oil and watercolour, the work of George Cochrane Kerr (Fl 1873-1907) is somewhat reminiscent of W L Wyllie, with whom he may have come into contact when he moved from London to Rochester, for Wyllie lived on the Medway from 1886 until 1906. Between 1878 and 1897, Kerr exhibited thirteen marine and coastal views at the Royal Academy, including 'Greyhounds of the British Navy' and 'A Modern Convoy in Time of War'. He also exhibited at the new Watercolour Society and examples of his work are to be found at the NMM.

*HMS* Southampton,
*Battle of Jutland 31 May 1916*
*Oscar Parkes, Oil on Canvas, 30x40", Signed*
Royal Excahnge Art Gallery

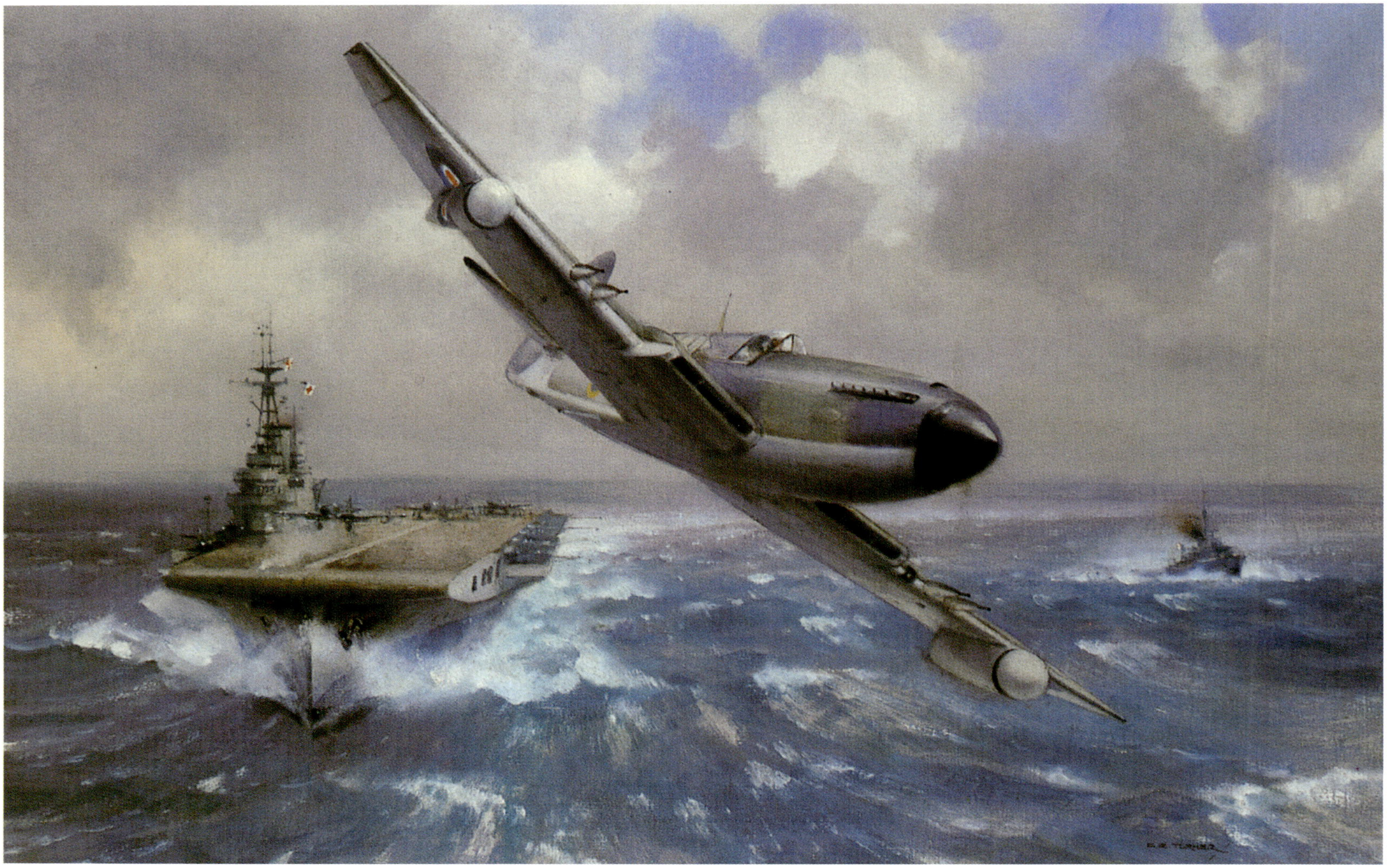

*À Fairey Firefly MK IV Naval Reconnaissance Fighter taking off from the Aircraft Carrier* Indefatigable *in the Pacific*
*Charles E. Turner, Oil on Canvas, 20x30", Signed*
N.R. Omell Gallery

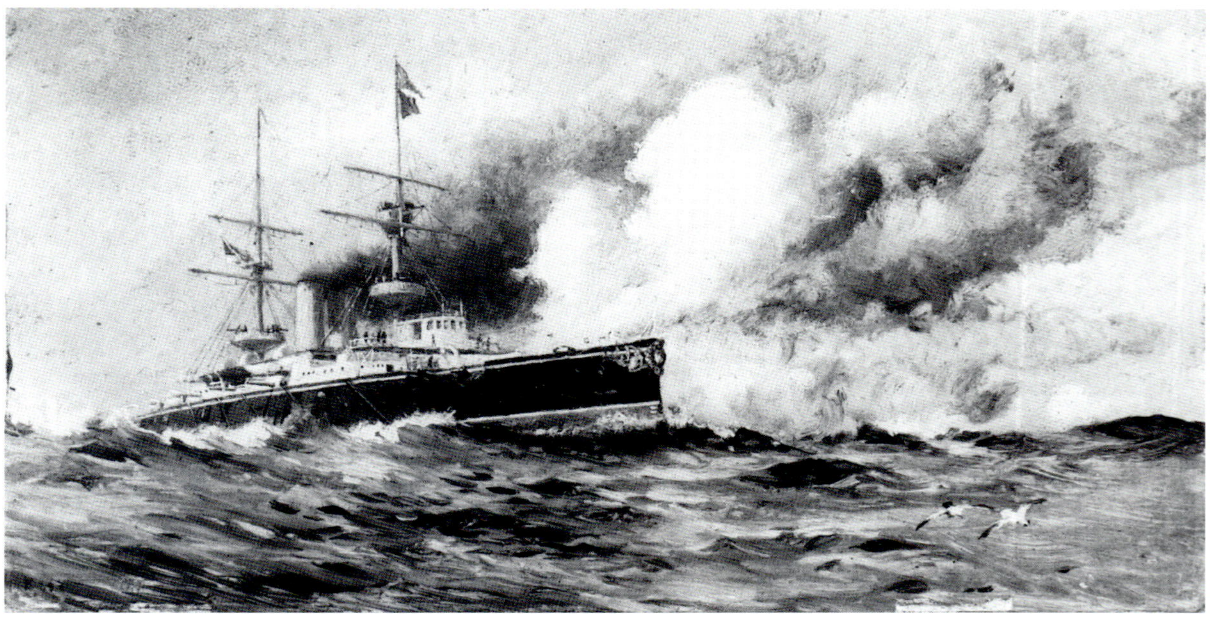

*A Dreadnought Under Full Steam*
*George Cochrane Kerr,*
*Oil on Panel, 7¾x14¾", Signed*
N.R. Omell Gallery

Born on Vancouver Island, Canada, the son of a Royal Navy engineer officer, the work of Lt Commander Rowland Langmaid (1897-1956) is closely associated with Portsmouth. Apparently, during his posting there in the 1920s whilst serving with the navy, he became acquainted with W L Wyllie, who gave him some lessons in the technique of etching. This seems to have had a deep influence on Langmaid's subsequent work which, although extremely competent, never achieved the same level of technical control so evident in Wyllie's plates. He appears to have fallen victim to 'Geddes Axe' in the early 20s when the personnel of the Royal Navy was greatly reduced. In the Second World War Langmaid rejoined and served for the most part in the shore base HMS *Nile* in Egypt. It was here that he was appointed a 'local' war artist to the Mediterranean fleet by the C-in-C Admiral Sir Andrew Cunningham and this resulted in a book about its operations call 'The Med', which he wrote and illustrated and which was published in 1948. He also wrote and illustrated *The Kings' Ships through the Ages*, which was published in 1937. Although Langmaid is best known as an etcher, many of which were done during his time at Portsmouth, he also produced some very skilful examples of naval ships in watercolour and occasionally oils. The National Maritime Museum has a collection of seventeen of his wartime paintings during his spell in the Mediterranean eg. 'Convoy from Crete' 1941 and his work is also held at the IWM and the MoD art collection. He exhibited three paintings at the Walker Art Gallery, Liverpool and one at the Royal Academy, 'HMS *Repulse* Wearing the Standard of HRH The Prince of Wales entering Portsmouth Harbour', and was a member of the Royal Society of Marine Artists. Because of the seemingly boundless opportunities available to serving officers such as Langmaid to paint ships and events featuring the Royal Navy in peace time and War, it is hardly surprising that there were a number of other twentieth century naval officer painters who produced excellent studies of their ships, notably Commander Eric Tufnell, RN (1888-1978) whose watercolours have always attracted a strong following with those having served with the Royal Navy and RNVR. Tufnell served in both wars in a number of branches and his work shows great attention to detail, as does that of Captain Thomas H. Hand, RN (born 1870), who lived in Southsea and between 1909 and 1921 painted ships of the Royal Navy and other marine subjects in watercolour.

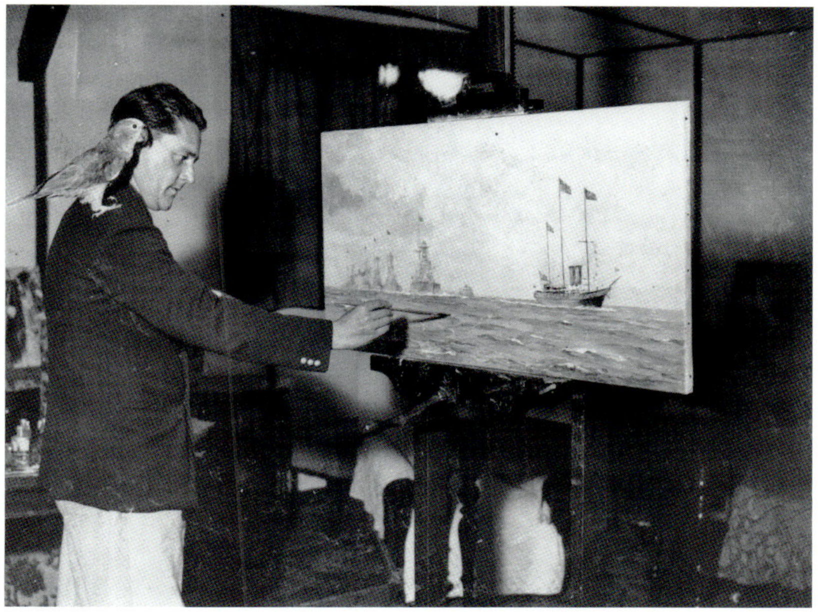

*Rowland Langmaid*
RICHARD MARTIN GALLERY

The achievements of Dixon, Wyllie, Wood, Cull, Wilkinson and others in recording important events in the history of the Royal Navy from the late nineteenth century up until the Second World War has consolidated their place in the upper echelons of British marine painting, but it must be remembered that there were also a number of other marine artists, less exalted, but who painted in the Portsmouth area around the same period. These artists were capable of producing well observed and atmospheric scenes of the lively activity in and around the harbour, but their paintings are familiar usually only to those with a more local knowledge. Some were amateurs, such as William Charles Cluett (1868-1958); born in Portsea, he worked in the dockyard and painted many small, finely detailed studies of naval vessels, which are usually titled and dated on the reverse and for which he had a good market in the area, and may account for the reason

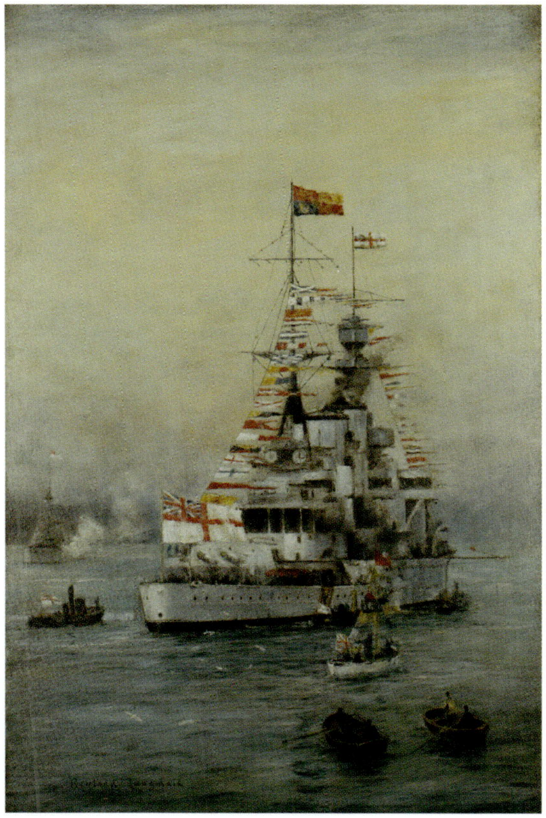

*HMS* Renown *Wearing the Standard of HRH The Prince of Wales*
*Rowland Langmaid, Oil on Canvas, 30x40"*
MARITIME PRINTS AND ORIGINALS

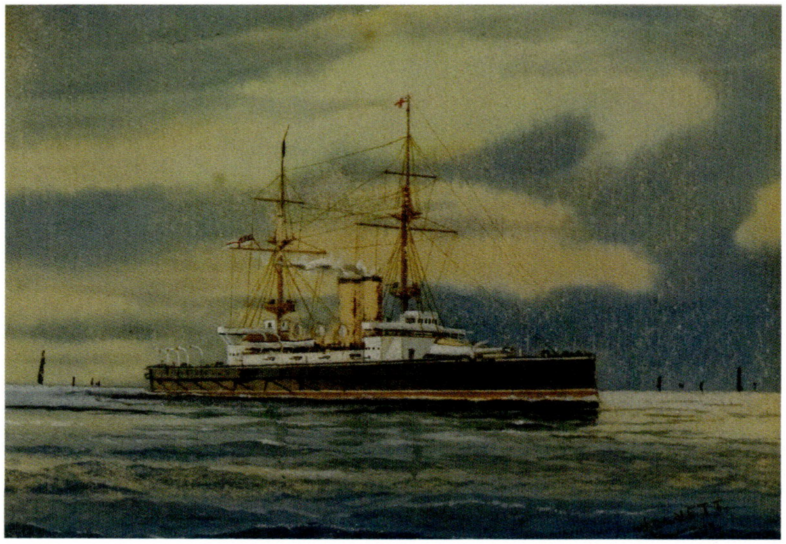

*HMS Majestic*
*W. Cluett, Watercolour, 4¾x6½″, Signed*
Private Collection

that he did not exhibit. Another minor, yet equally proficient Portsmouth watercolour artist, who produced charming miniature ship portraits showing Royal Navy vessels of the Victorian navy, often as a set, was W Sutton (c. 1900), who was active around the turn of the century and whose work bears a close similarity with that of Cluett, possibly they were one and the same.

Although relatively unknown outside his home town of Gosport, Martin Snape (1852-1930) was primarily a marine artist who painted scenes of Portsmouth Harbour and the waterfront at Gosport on the opposite side, but his work also includes natural history subjects. However, he is best known for his vivid portrayal of the ever-changing scene in and around Portsmouth, often characterised by his studies of hulks against a background of yachts and the might of the navy. He exhibited seventeen pictures at the Royal Academy between 1874 and 1901. In this rather loose and impressionist watercolour of HMS *St Vincent* in Portsmouth harbour, the pale winter sun is reflected on the icy pools of water on the Gosport mudflats, and were often a feature of his harbour scenes.

As the nineteenth century wore on, there remained a constant demand for what became the mass produced ship portrait which proliferated in response to Britain's growing prosperity and naval supremacy and came to be regarded as an important element in marine painting. The majority of ship portraitists were extremely knowledgeable about the technical detail of the vessels they depicted, indeed

*HMS* St Vincent *in the Frozen Harbour*
*Martin Snape, Watercolour,*
*Signed and dated February '04*
Richard Martin Gallery

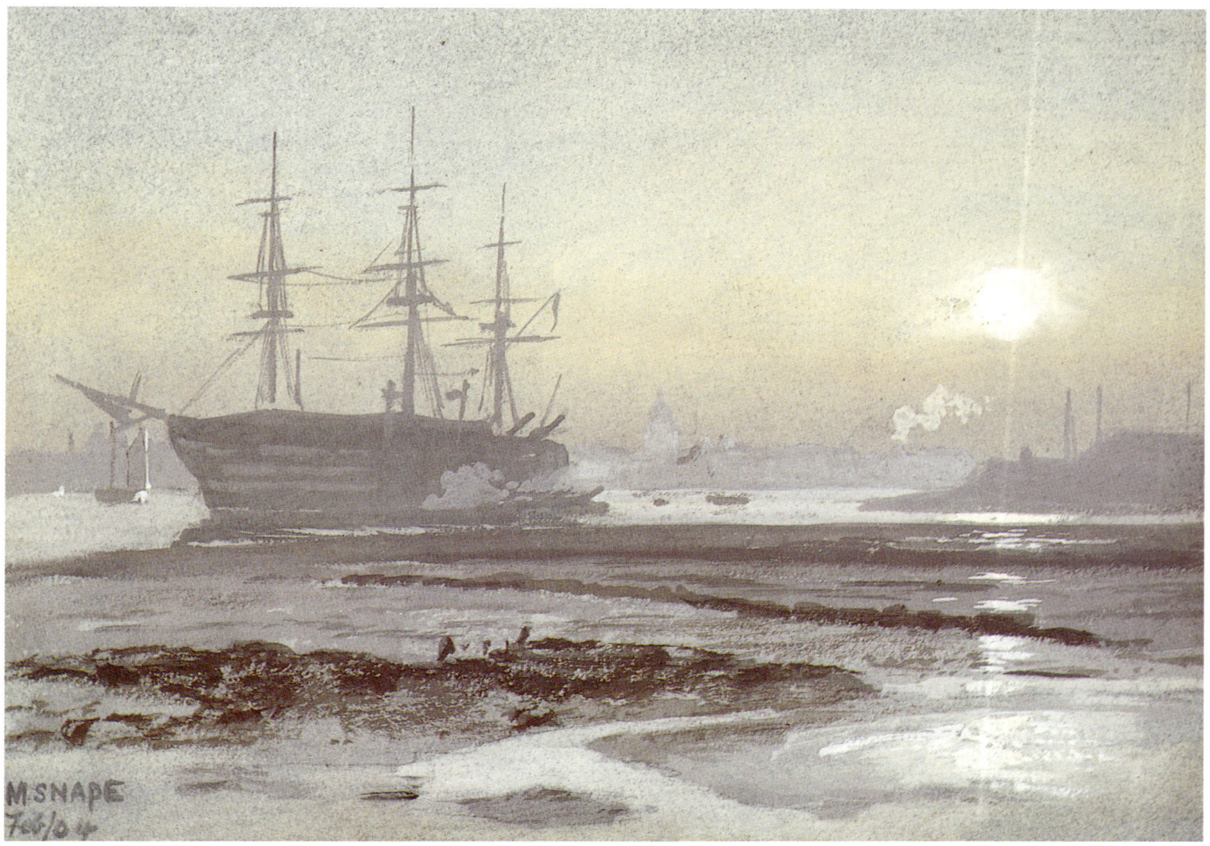

a number of them probably had dockyard or sea-going experience. The level of detail includes everything about the vessel from such things as the shape of the hull, the figurehead, position of deck houses, her armament, to the intricacies of the rigging being accurately portrayed. They were, however, usually done to a formula – a standard port or starboard profile either at sea or against a background; sometimes a generalised coastline, but more often a specific location. During the heyday of sail and steam, the demand for portraits of naval ships was met in no small measure by two specialist marine painters, William E Atkins (1842/3-1910) and William Frederick Mitchell (1854-1914), both of whom were able to include Queen Victoria among their patrons and who worked in Portsmouth where their paintings found favour with ship's officers keen to acquire pictures of their vessels. William Edward Atkins was born in Portsea, the son of George Henry Atkins, also a local marine artist, from whom it seems William learned to paint, specialising in watercolours of ships, usually on a large scale. During the 1870s he was appointed as the Portsmouth correspondent and marine artist of *The Graphic* and held this appointment for about ten years when, due to ill health, he was succeeded by W L Wyllie. Atkins'

*Portsmouth Harbour and Dockyard c.1875*
*William Edward Atkins, Watercolour, Signed*
PORTSMOUTH MUSEUM AND RECORDS SERVICE

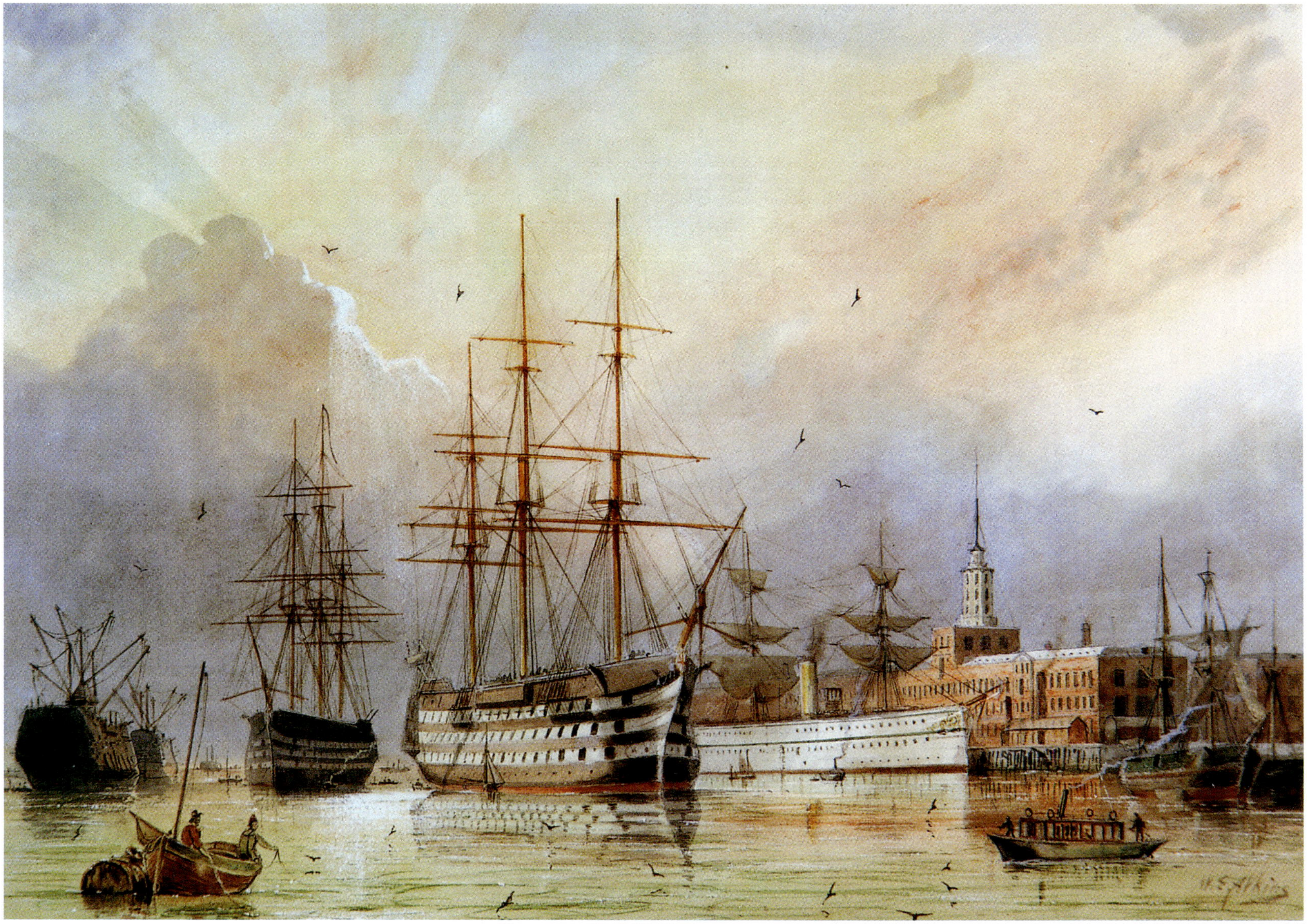

output was prodigious and he continued to work, albeit at a slower pace, up until the turn of the century. The National Maritime Museum has a large watercolour by him, 'Spithead Review 1878' (21" x 46"), and examples of his work may also be found in the Portsmouth City Museum.

Even more prolific than Atkins, William Frederick (Fred) Mitchell (1854-1914) also lived for most of his life in close proximity to the Royal Navy's principal base at Portsmouth, for it was here at Griffins, a bookshop strategically positioned on the hard near the main entrance to the dockyard, that he too received commissions for his work from naval officers. Mitchell was profoundly deaf and it is reported that the shop acted as an intermediary. Mainly a water colourist, he numbered all his ship portraits up to a staggering figure in excess of three thousand five hundred. Mitchell was a faultless draughtsman and his work is characterised by a meticulous attention to detail for his patrons demanded from him absolute accuracy of rigging and superstructure and appreciated these qualities far more than aesthetic ones. The correct setting of particular sails and the degree of tension which controlled them was of greater interest to a naval patron than a beautiful sunset. His watercolours are usually on a small scale, sometimes of a postcard size (he painted cards for P&O and White Star lines) for this was more practical to hang in a somewhat cramped ship's cabin. The convention was to show the vessel from the side, in profile and beam view, but Mitchell often depicted vessels 'portbow'. As well as contemporary ships, Mitchell also painted some of the old time vessels, such as the *Royal George* and the *Great Harry*. Coloured lithographs of these paintings were produced about 1870 and have become quite rare and desirable. A number of his watercolours are preserved in the National Maritime Museum, Greenwich, and his subjects typically range from wooden three-decked vessels to the 'new' gun terraced armoured steamships which succeeded them thirty years later. Examples of his watercolours are beautifully

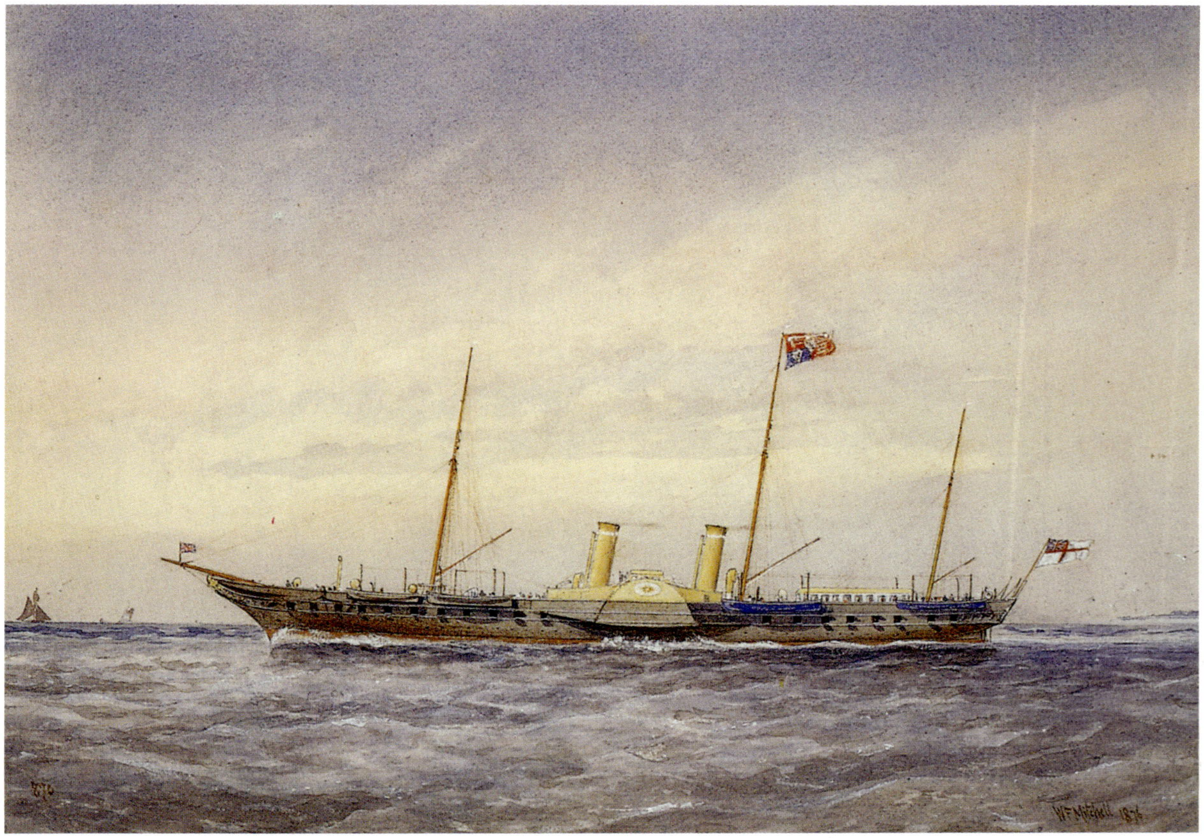

*The Royal Yacht* Osborne
*Frederick W Mitchell, Watercolour, 9¾x13¾", Signed and dated 1976*
Royal Exchange Art Gellery

illustrated in the six volumes of *Her Majesty's Navy*, published in 1892. Mitchell also drew for Brasseys, *The Naval Annual* and in 1905 with W C Symons published *The British Navy Past and Present*. An example of his work may also be found in the Mariners' Museum, Newport News, Virginia, USA. Fred Mitchell died in Ryde, Isle of Wight in 1914 and with his parting left a legacy of great importance to all those interested in the history of the Victorian navy; many of the ships he painted having no surviving visual record. Although his work as a ship portraitist is less well known than Atkins and Mitchell, the finely painted watercolours and excellent draughtsmanship of Charles William Fothergill, who was active during the latter part of the nineteenth century, have much to commend them. Fothergill's speciality was depicting men o'war in either Devonport or Portsmouth. He also worked along the River Dart and produced watercolours of some of the old 'Wooden Walls' moored in the river, including HMS *Britannia*, a training ship which preceded the R.N.C., Dartmouth. He exhibited at the Suffolk Street Galleries in London, where one of his exhibits was titled 'At the Mouth of the Dart' 1880, and in 1900 he exhibited at the Royal Academy. The ship portrait, usually of pre-dreadnought Royal Navy vessels in Portsmouth harbour, was also the forté of Mackenzie Thomson, a marine artist in watercolour, who was active around the same time as Fothergill. He, too, was a meticulous draughtsman, but his output nowhere near matched that of Mitchell or Atkins. Another marine artist who worked around Portsmouth, although at a later period than Atkins, Thomson, Mitchell and Snape, was Kenneth Yockney (1881-1965), who after the 1939-45 war produced charming watercolours of Portsmouth harbour. Yockney studied at the Slade School in London and was a good draughtsman, clearly evident in some of his neatly drawn pencil sketches of early twentieth century warships. He lived at Ryde, Isle of Wight from where he worked well into the twentieth century. He did not exhibit his pictures at the major exhibitions, preferring instead to sell them locally through Percy Beer, an art dealer in Portsmouth. It seems he

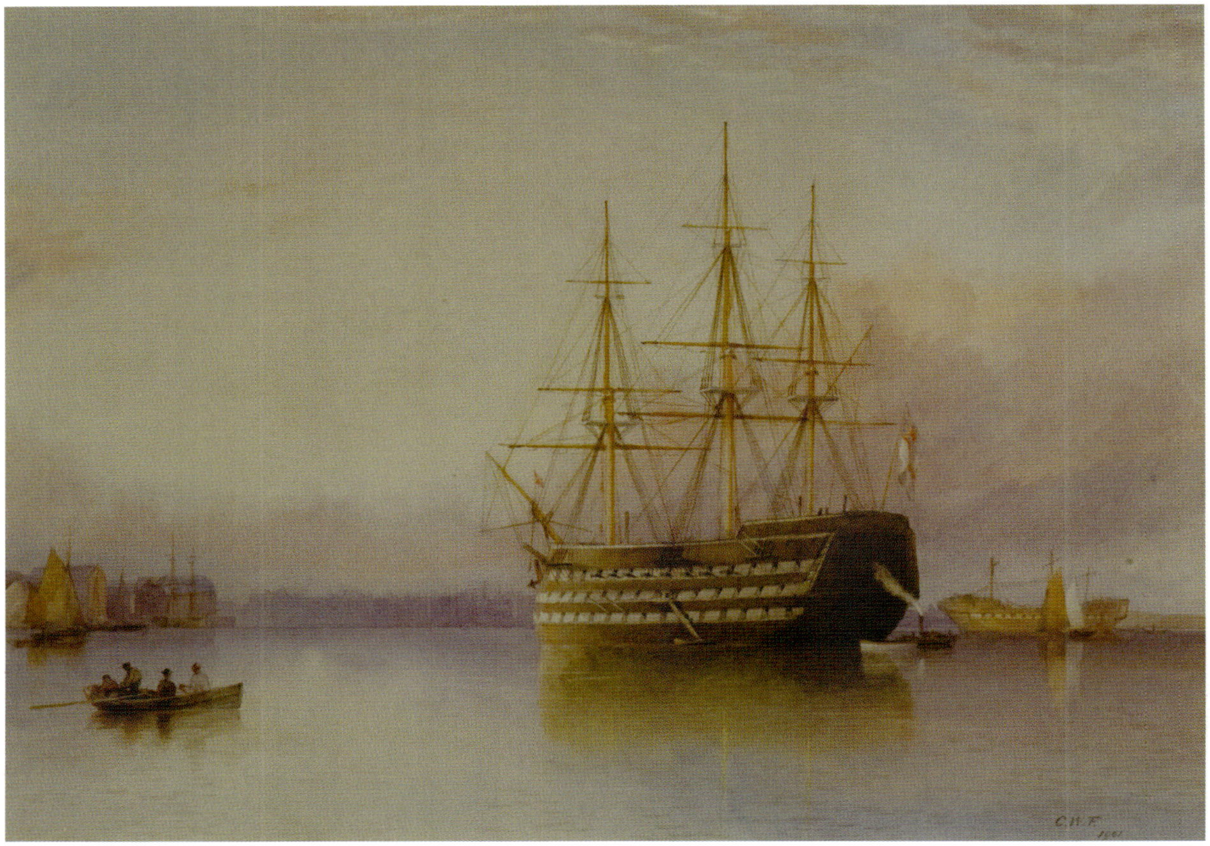

*Man O' War, Plymouth*
*C W Fothergill, Watercolour, 9¾x13¾",*
*Signed and dated 1901*
PRIVATE COLLECTION

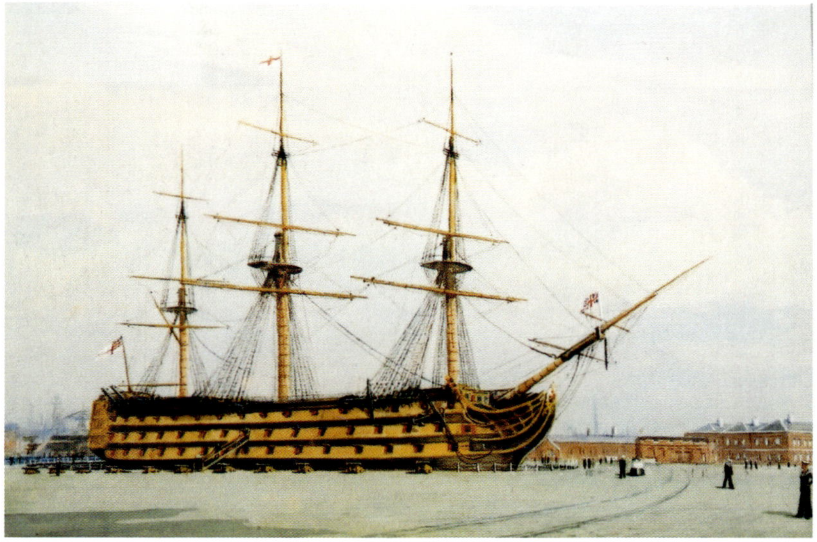

*HMS* Victory *c.1960*
*Kenneth Yocksey, Watercolour,*
John Morton Lee Fine Watercolours

scorned wealth and had no real ambition to promote his work, which as far as is known he never signed. A prolific artist who painted coastal and harbour subjects, many including Portsmouth, was Sydney Goodwin (1867-1944). Goodwin, who lived at Southampton for some years, was the nephew of Albert Goodwin, also a watercolourist. In 1917 he moved from the south coast to Dublin, where he continued to paint his atmospheric watercolours, some of which were exhibited at the Royal Hibernian Academy. However, Portsmouth continued to be a favourite subject, and one which he went on to paint well into the 1930s.

In 1938 Portsmouth was the venue for what has become known as 'The Big Marine Show', when many prominent marine artists, such as Charles Pears, Roland Langmaid and Cecil King (1881-1942), exhibited pictures set in Portsmouth. King was an official naval artist in 1918 and later became active in organising marine exhibitions between 1935 and 1938. Born in Portsmouth, Preston Cribb (1876-1927) illustrated ships of the Royal Navy there before and after the Great War. His later career was spent in Birmingham, where he also practiced as an etcher and illustrator. Like King, he too exhibited at the Royal Academy and ROI.

For over 400 years the Royal Navy has permeated every level of British society, stretching back through the mists of time from Nelson, Hawkins, Drake and Raleigh to Alfred the Great. Although in the twenty-first century we now find a very different navy to that recorded by Charles Dixon, its reputation continues to gather respect and admiration not only in Britain, but throughout much of the world, epitomised by the Falklands campaign when never before in its history has the navy been so immediately ready to answer the nation's call and seldom has it met its task with such fortitude. As the premier base of the Royal Navy, it seems appropriate that much of this chapter has centred on Portsmouth and those artists who painted scenes of the harbour in peace and in war during the end of the nineteenth century and the first quarter of the twentieth century. It was undoubtedly a period when Portsmouth had been the focus of a mighty naval power, a centre for warship design, construction and repair as well as providing the huge logistical support necessary for what has been, at various times, a Royal Navy capable of global deployment. However it is now known for another role, as a maritime heritage centre of world importance and although visitors will find far fewer warships compared to the massive ironclads and dreadnoughts witnessed by Dixon, Wyllie and Cull, they will see the *Mary Rose*, HMS *Victory* and HMS *Warrior*, ships which have become the surviving embodiment of the long and distinguished history of the Royal Navy, spanning the era of wood, iron, sail and steam.

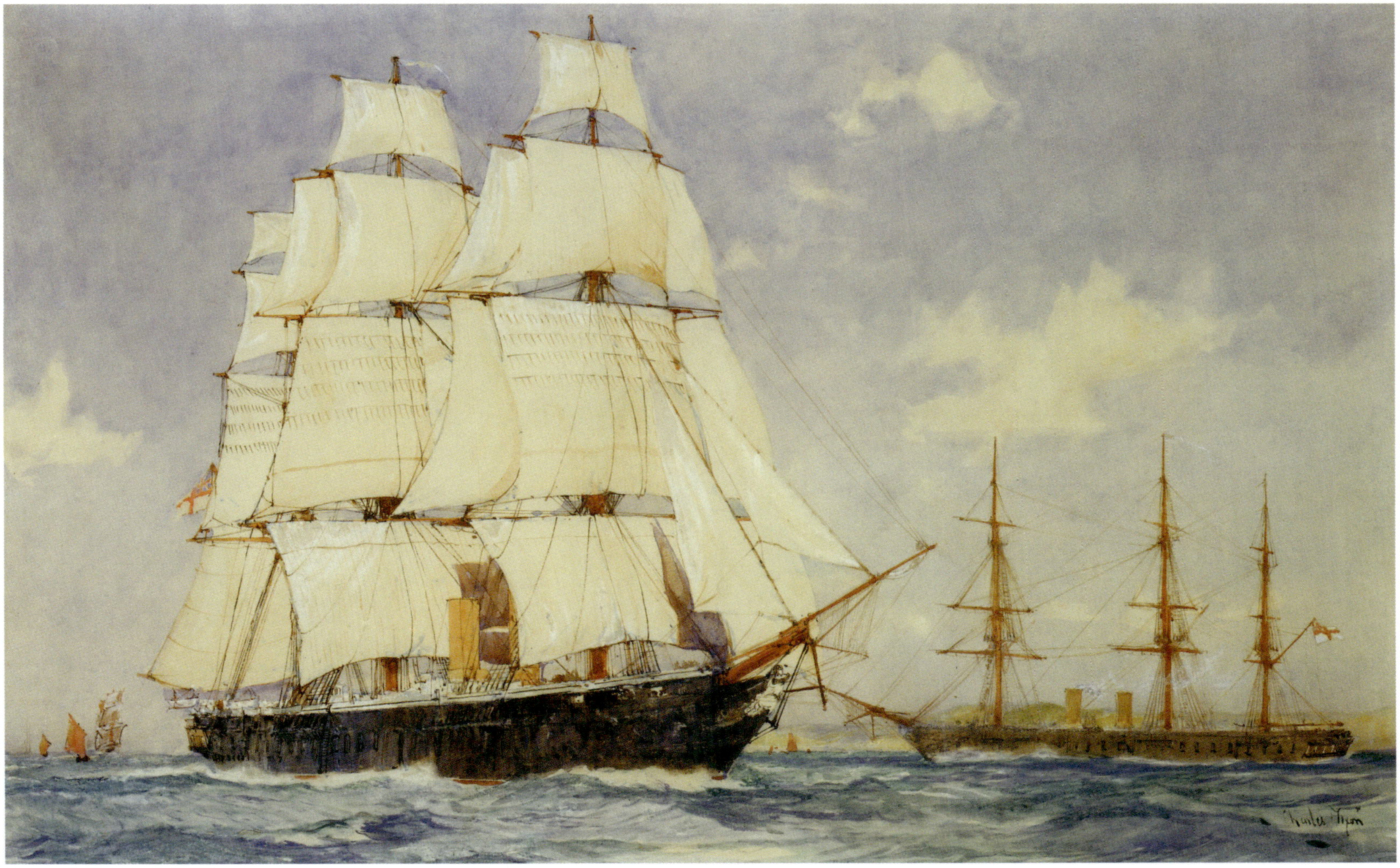

*Britain's First Two Ironclads. HMS* Warrior *and HMS* Blackprince
*Charles Dixon, Watercolour, 14½x23", Signed*
*Illustration for* Britannia's Bulwarks

HMS *Warrior* and HMS *Blackprince* were the worlds first ocean-going iron armoured ships and for many years were the pride of the Channel fleet. At the time of their completion in 1860 and 1861 they were the most powerful warships afloat, having an impregnable battery and a faster speed than their immediate rival, the French frigate *Gloire*.

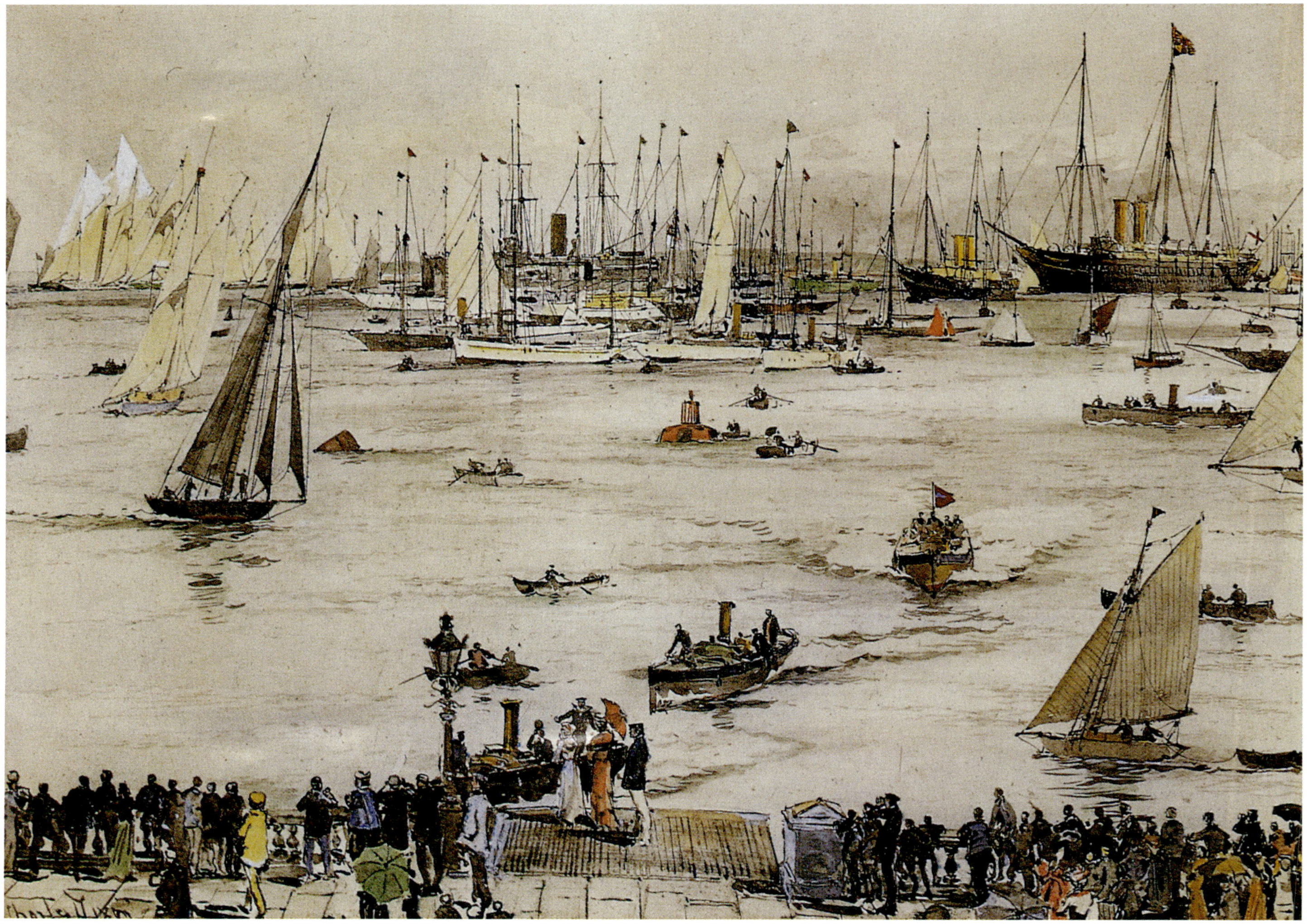

*Beginning of Cowes Week. August 1904*
*Charles Dixon, Watercolour and Ink, 12½x17½", Signed and inscribed on reverse*
ROYAL EXCHANGE ART GALLERY

# CHAPTER FIVE
# The Art of Yachting

*'After Goodwood – Cowes. And so the London Season ends at the sea. One of Society's charming paradoxes'*
The Graphic, *3 August, 1912.*

For almost four hundred years yachting, or boating for pleasure rather than trade, has attracted the interest of marine artists whose paintings have ensured that yachting art has become firmly established as a sub-genre of marine painting. However, in charting the development of yachting art in Britain, or indeed marine art in general, it is important to acknowledge that it was the Dutch artists, Willem Van de Velde, the elder (1611-1693) and his son, Willem (1633-1707), whose drawings provide some of the earliest images of the sport, one which has fascinated artists to the present day.

Much has been written about the history of yachting and it is beyond the scope of this book to replicate that in any detail, suffice to say that the origins of organised yacht racing started off the Dutch coast in the early 1600s, when King Charles was said to have developed a taste for it while in exile in the Netherlands, and it is he who is credited with introducing the yacht to Britain after the Restoration in 1661. The first recorded race was held on the Thames that year between the King and his brother. These early yachts were mainly used to transport the King and his courtiers, but they also took part in the occasional race – a tradition that was maintained by the Hanoverian monarchs and those that followed. Furthermore, royal interest in yachting and yacht racing encouraged the aristocracy to follow suit and its popularity as a sport increased throughout the course of the eighteenth century. Following her accession in 1837, the young Queen Victoria bought Osborne House on the Isle of Wight. Situated on a hill overlooking the East Bank of the Medina river, it was from here that the Sovereign's interest in yachting and her love for Cowes, home of the nearby Royal Yacht Squadron, ensured that the Solent, the narrow strip of water between the island and the south coast, would remain the major focus of British sailing. It also provided the setting for the most important yacht race in the history of the sport, for the Royal Yacht Squadron, founded in 1815, and the New York Yacht Club, formed in 1844, had been in contact discussing the possibility of an American yacht crossing the Atlantic to take on the pride of British yachting. In response, the Schooner *America* was built and sailed to Cowes, arriving off the Isle of Wight on 1 August 1851. This was the year of the Great Exhibition, the Royal Navy ruled the waves, the Empire girdled the globe and British yachtsmen were confident of their superiority, yet it was the Schooner *America* that immediately defeated the British cutter *Lavernock*. After this display, the other British yachtsmen were slow to offer a challenge, with the Americans adamant that they would only race for a wager in order to recoup some of their costs. Eventually, on 22 August, the Americans agreed to take part in a race around the Isle of Wight against the British yachts for a 100 guinea cup. The story of that race is legend, and the outcome only too well known, as the *America*, which was the clear winner, became the most famous yacht in history. Such an ignominious defeat awoke the British from their complacency, for everyone in England thought it was important to avenge the American victory and regain the trophy, which became known as the America's Cup. The preoccupation was to dominate British yachting throughout the Edwardian era and beyond, and eventually led to Sir Thomas Lipton, a name inextricably linked with the history of the Cup, to mount the first of his five challenges to restore British pride, an endeavour in which Charles Dixon too was to play his part.

Thomas Lipton was the second son of an impoverished Irish family who had immigrated to Scotland. At the age of 10 he left school to help his family and at the age of 15 went to find work in the United States. During this time he managed to save enough money to return to Glasgow, where he opened his first grocery shop and success soon followed success, for a succession of entrepreneurial business ventures, not least his tea plantations in Ceylon made him a multi-millionaire by the time he was in his mid-40s.

Lipton was a generous man who, as a result of one particular philanthropic gesture, came to the notice of the Prince of Wales and the two became good friends. As a companion to the Prince, who was an ardent sportsman and an enthusiastic member of Europe's aristocratic yachting community, Lipton soon became swept up in the excitement of sail and it was undoubtedly Edward who suggested Lipton should challenge for the America's Cup. Lipton, who had not shown any interest in yachting before 1888, realised that trying to win the trophy would reward him on two fronts. Despite his recent elevation to the Peerage, his fortune and a Prince's friendship, the majority of the aristocracy refused to acknowledge him. Fitting out a large yacht and taking it to the United States ought to open some hitherto closed doors for her owner. The other was a commercial advantage. A challenge would provide Lipton and his products with some profitable publicity in the American market and victory for the son of an Irish immigrant would do much to restore British prestige. On 6 August 1898, Lipton issued his challenge to the New York Yacht Club to race for the Cup. This was in the name of the Royal Ulster Yacht Club, as the Royal Yacht Squadron had not deigned to admit him as a member. A year later his green-hulled *Shamrock* was towed across the Atlantic by Lipton's luxury steam yacht, *Erin*, and on board was Charles Dixon, who Lipton had commissioned to paint on the spot scenes of the races. *Shamrock*'s arrival in New York Harbour must have been an exciting event for the 26-year-old Dixon, who would have been thrilled to accompany Lipton on his pursuit of yachting glory. However, this was not to be for the American defender succeeded in defeating Shamrock in three straight races.

Far from deterred, Lipton vowed to mount another challenge and in 1901 he returned with *Shamrock II* and, once again, he looked to Charles Dixon to capture the thrill of the action with *Shamrock* versus the same *Columbia* that had defeated her predecessor. Although Dixon had been commissioned by Lipton to paint scenes of the racing, he was also using the opportunity to send images back to London for the popular illustrated weekly magazines and newspapers, such as the pen and ink drawing he did, conveying his admiration and enthusiasm for the new yacht, with the inscription 'Hooray to *Shamrock* – she's a fine boat, the best ever built – CD, New York, Sept 30th'. The drawing was sent to *The Sphere* and no doubt was meant to generate a sense of optimism in British followers, but unfortunately this was to be short lived, for although all three races were close run, it was the American yacht that won on each occasion. Although the disappointment of a second defeat would have been too much to bear for most, not so the indefatigable 'Jolly Tea Merchant', who declared 'I will return' and in 1903 he sailed back across the Atlantic in *Shamrock III*, again accompanied by Dixon, eager to record a successful challenge for his patron, although this was to be denied, for *Shamrock* was beaten in three successive races, a humiliating defeat by the defender *Reliance.*

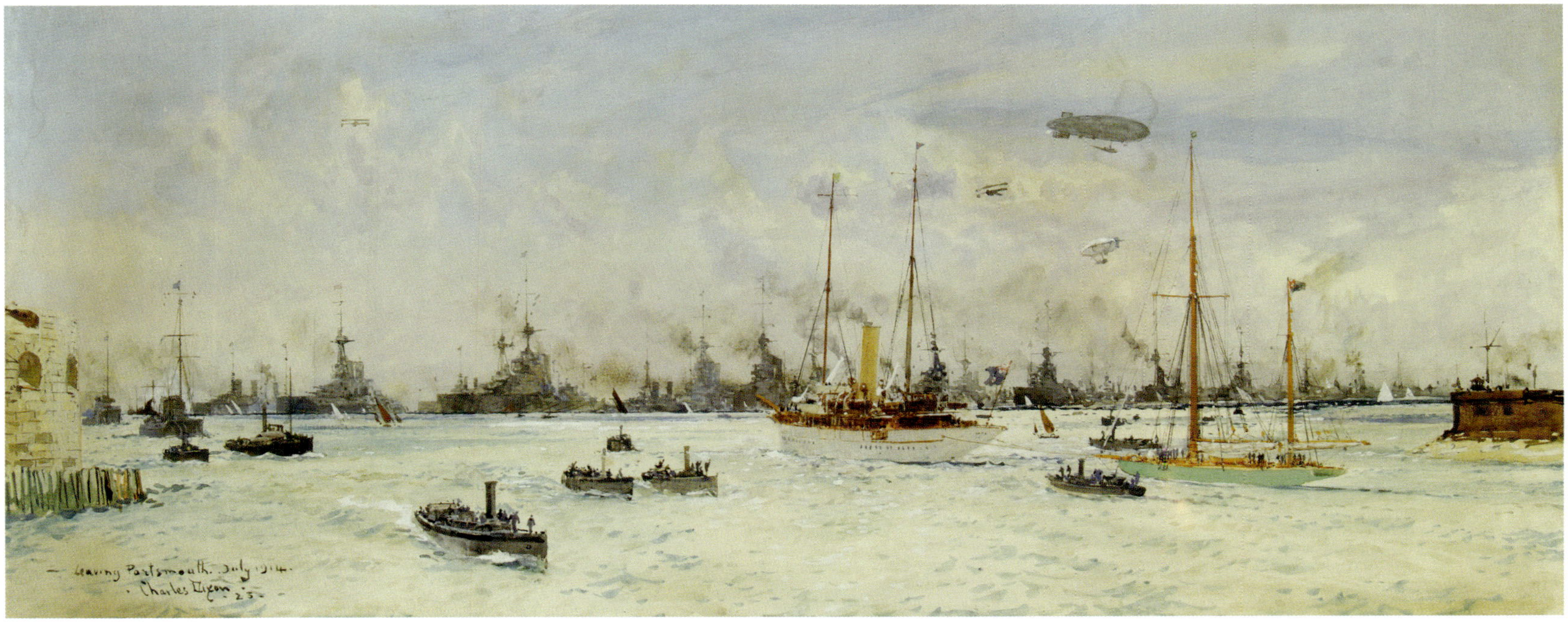

Shamrock *leaving Portsmouth for New York being towed by S.Y.* Erin *and Passing the Fleet Review 1914*
*Charles Dixon, Watercolour, Signed*
CULTURE AND SPORT GLASGOW (MUSEUMS)

After a gap of some eleven years, Lipton had regained his enthusiasm and decided to try again, but the late summer of 1914 saw the outbreak of World War One and it was at this time that Dixon was en route to New York with *Erin* and *Shamrock IV* to prepare for Lipton's fourth attempt. It seems that whilst on passage, *Erin*'s radio intercepted a message from one German cruiser to another, which stated that war had been declared between Britain and Germany. *Erin*'s master then contacted a British cruiser in the vicinity and, to escape possible attack by German submarines, towed *Shamrock* to Bermuda and then on to Brooklyn Navy Yard, New York, where she waited out the conflict. The intervention of the war meant that Lipton had to bide his time until 1920 for *Shamrock IV* to have her chance against the American defender *Resolute* and it seemed that on this occasion Lipton's hope of winning the big trophy would be fulfilled when, for the first time in the history of the Cup, a five series race had reached the fifth race. For Lipton, his ambition of victory came tantalisingly close, only for *Shamrock* to lose the final race with *Resolute* the clear winner. The defeat was a huge setback for Lipton, but tenacious to the end, he was determined to achieve that elusive victory and in the summer of 1930 arrived in Newport, Rhode Island with *Shamrock V*, again accompanied by Dixon. The 1930s series was to be determined by four wins out of seven races, but once more the outcome was all too familiar, for the American defender *Enterprise* won a clean sweep of four races, leaving *Shamrock* a badly beaten boat.

Later Vanderbilt, the skipper of the winning yacht, wrote 'our hour of triumph, our hour of victory is all but at hand, but it is so tempered with sadness that it is almost hollow. Uppermost in our minds is a feeling of sympathy for that grand old sportsman'. Lipton's defeat seemed a melancholy and anticlimactic finish to a great era in yachting and one in which his contribution had been immense. Although he proclaimed that he would try again, he never did. He was corresponding with the New York Yacht Club about the possibility when, on 2 October 1931, at the age of 81, he died – only a few

Shamrock *Passing Through Traffic on Arrival at America*
*Charles Dixon, Watercolour, 9⅞x20", Signed and dated 1899*
CULTURE AND SPORT GLASGOW (MUSEUMS)

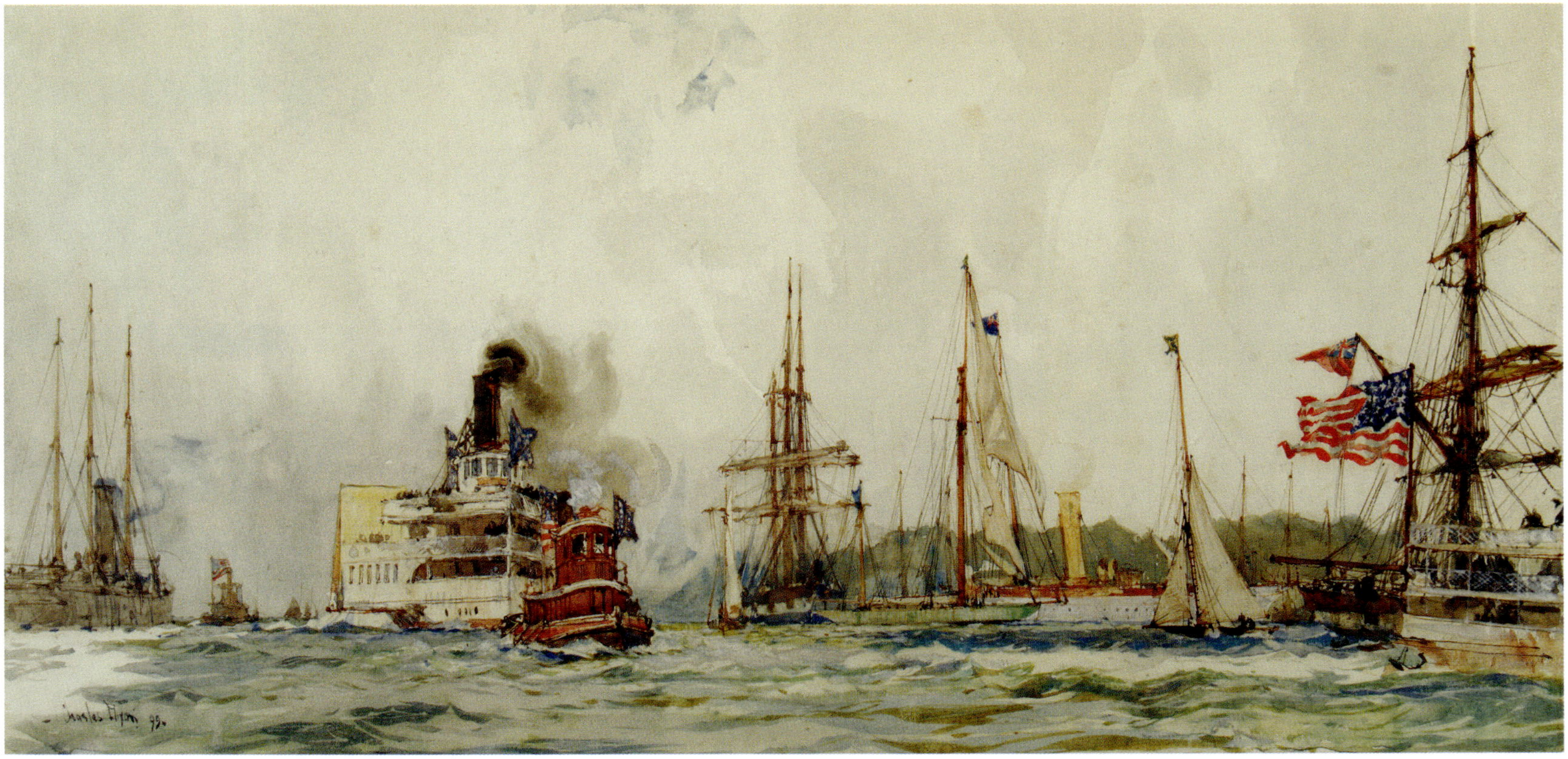

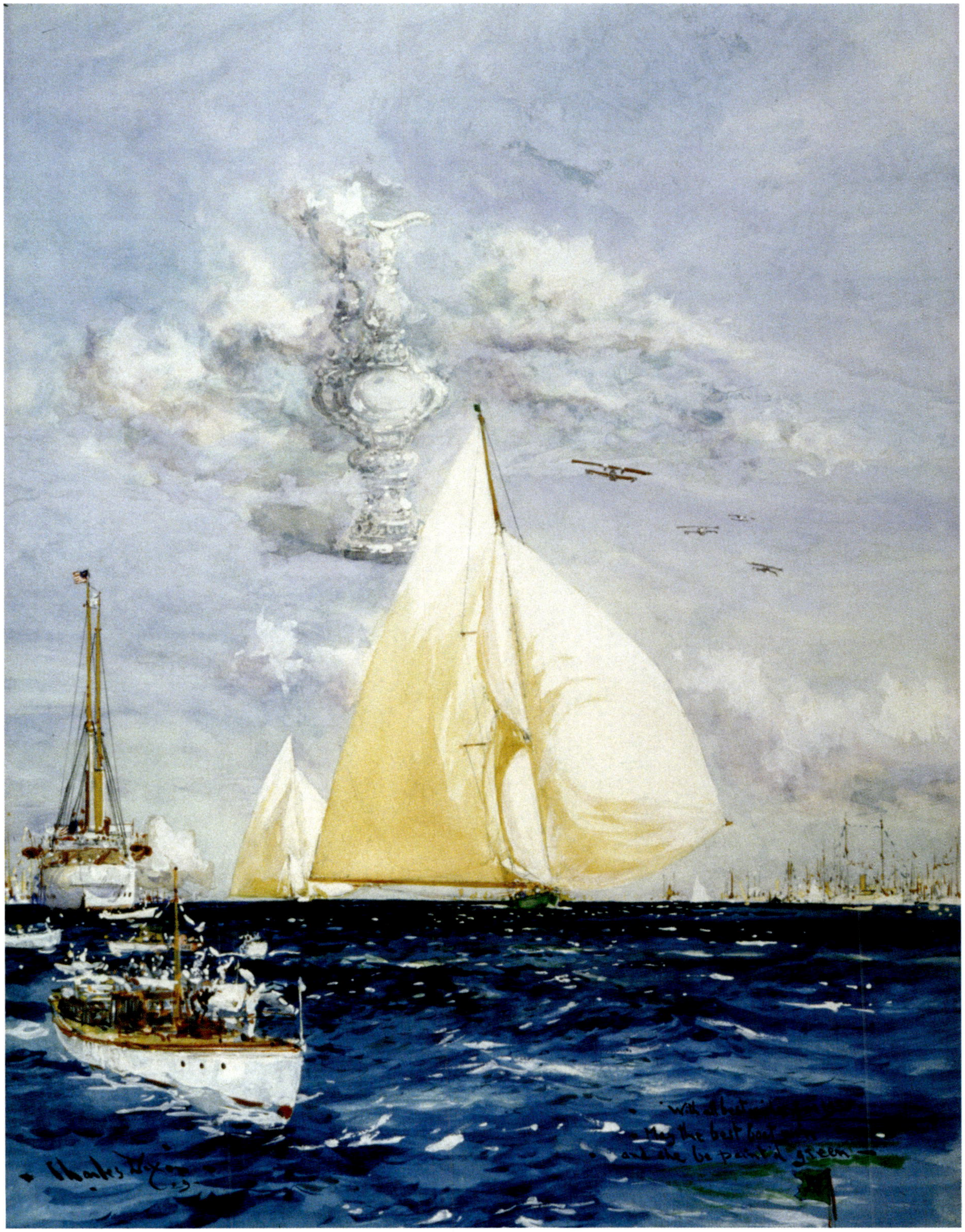


Shamrock V *Running Before the Wind, Aircraft Following with Vision of America Cup in Clouds off Cowes*
*Charles Dixon, Watercolour, Signed*
CULTURE AND SPORT GLASGOW (MUSEUMS)

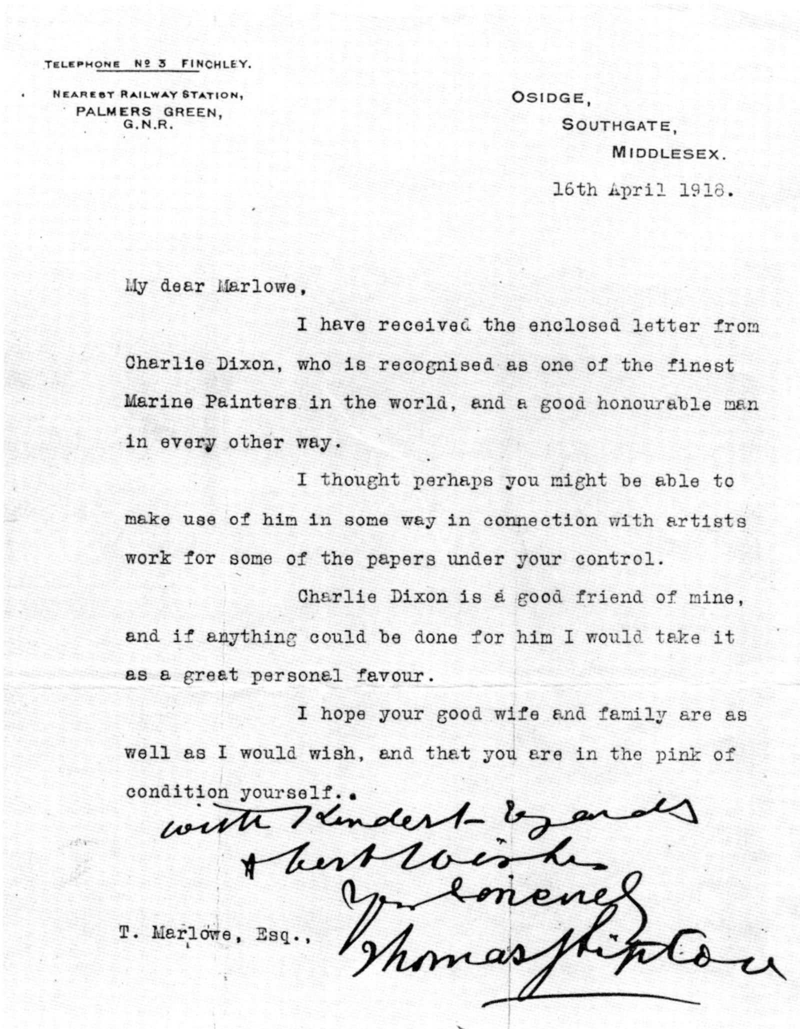

TELEPHONE No 3 FINCHLEY.

NEAREST RAILWAY STATION,
PALMERS GREEN,
G.N.R.

OSIDGE,
SOUTHGATE,
MIDDLESEX.

16th April 1918.

My dear Marlowe,

I have received the enclosed letter from Charlie Dixon, who is recognised as one of the finest Marine Painters in the world, and a good honourable man in every other way.

I thought perhaps you might be able to make use of him in some way in connection with artists work for some of the papers under your control.

Charlie Dixon is a good friend of mine, and if anything could be done for him I would take it as a great personal favour.

I hope your good wife and family are as well as I would wish, and that you are in the pink of condition yourself..

with kindest regards
& best wishes
Yours sincerely
Thomas J Lipton

T. Marlowe, Esq.,

*Copy of a reference for Charles Dixon from Sir Thomas Lipton*

months after he had been honoured by being elected at last to the Royal Yacht Squadron. Upon his death, Lipton left a large collection of yachting memorabilia including trophies, photographs and paintings to Glasgow Museums and a part of this bequest includes 17 works, mainly watercolours which Dixon painted for Lipton during a friendship that lasted for over thirty years. The circumstances which led to the beginning of their long relationship are not known, but what is clear is that, throughout, Lipton had a high regard for the artist as reflected in the warm sentiments expressed in a reference for employment which he did for Dixon in 1918. It is easy to see how Dixon's bold, vibrant and colourful paintings would have appealed to Lipton for they were, in a sense, a reflection of his own persona, yet despite the part that Dixon played in Lipton's yachting endeavours, strangely no reference is made of this in either his autobiography or in any of the many biographies written about his fascinating life.

Like many of his marine artist contemporaries, not only was Charles Dixon a fine painter, but also an accomplished yachtsman, indeed it has been suggested that perhaps the most virile form of marine painting often lies in the work of artists who are themselves sailors, communicating experiences in seamanship and deriving their inspiration from 'the lonely sea and the sky'. It is no coincidence therefore that so many great English marine artists were professional seamen or shipwrights before turning to painting. Thomas Luny and C Stanfield were in the Royal Navy, W J Huggins served in the East India Company and N Pocock and D Serres were Masters of trading vessels; George Chambers Snr spending seven years at sea. Throughout his life, Dixon's love of painting and all things maritime was matched only by his passion for sailing and it was his knowledge of the sea that often provided the unique driving spirit within his most successful yachting subjects, for his lightness of touch combined with the joyous colouring which is always a characteristic of his work, perfectly captures the levity of the Edwardian summer.

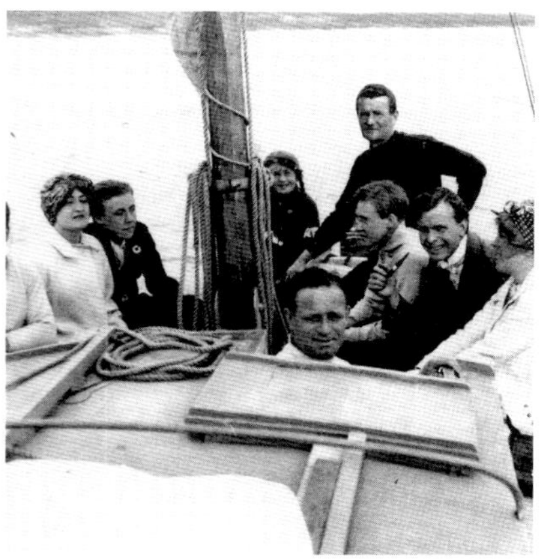

*Photograph of Charles Dixon sailing with family and friends. (Ada is seated on the left of the photo).*

Whilst it is not known where Dixon began to develop his interest in sailing, his long association with Itchenor meant that he relished any opportunity to travel down from London to the pretty Sussex village where pleasure sailing activities are reported to date back to the seventeenth century, when King Charles II kept his boat *Fubs* there. Apart from farming, shipbuilding has always played a prominent role in the history of Itchenor. Although the majority of men-of-war to sail from Sussex were built at Shoreham, the boatyards of Itchenor were responsible for some notable craft, most significantly HMS *Chichester* (902 tons) in 1785. It was from Itchenor where Dixon could truly indulge his love of the sport, either cruising around the south coast with family and friends or racing *Phaedora* his green-hulled Itchenor 16 foot class boat with the sailing club. Although not a founder, Dixon appears to have been a stalwart member and actively involved in its formation in 1927. The history of the club contains several references to his association, such as 'the occasion he raced another member to East Head (the entrance to Chichester

Harbour) for a bottle of Guinness' and also 'the special gift of a very charming painting that Dixon presented to the club' at the opening of the clubhouse in 1932. The watercolour, depicting a race and inscribed "Who's going to win the Cup this Year?" still hangs in the club bar. Somewhat surprisingly this seems to be the only tangible record of a membership which must rank as one of the club's most distinguished.

Given its many attractions for the marine artist and yachtsman, it is hardly surprising that many of Dixon's watercolours and sketches were done at Itchenor where he loved to paint and often accepted commissions from friends and members of the sailing community to produce pictures of their boats at club regattas or lying serenely at their moorings. With their eye for detail, his patrons always demanded complete accuracy in the way he depicted their yachts in action, but knew that in Dixon they could be confident that his sailor's instinct and local knowledge would bring freshness to his work and that their paintings would always be full of well observed movement, such as in 'Two Minutes to Go', showing preparations for the start of a race at Itchenor Sailing Club. It was however wealthy owners keen to immortalise their large and

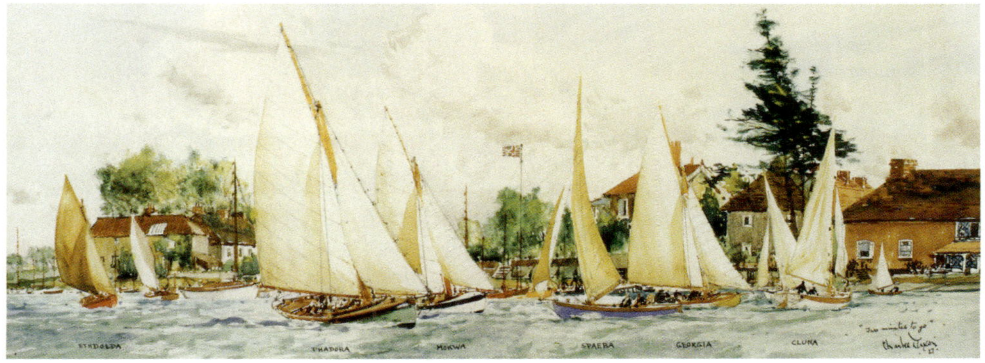


*Two Minutes to Go*
*Charles Dixon, Watercolour, Signed and inscribed*
PRIVATE COLLECTION

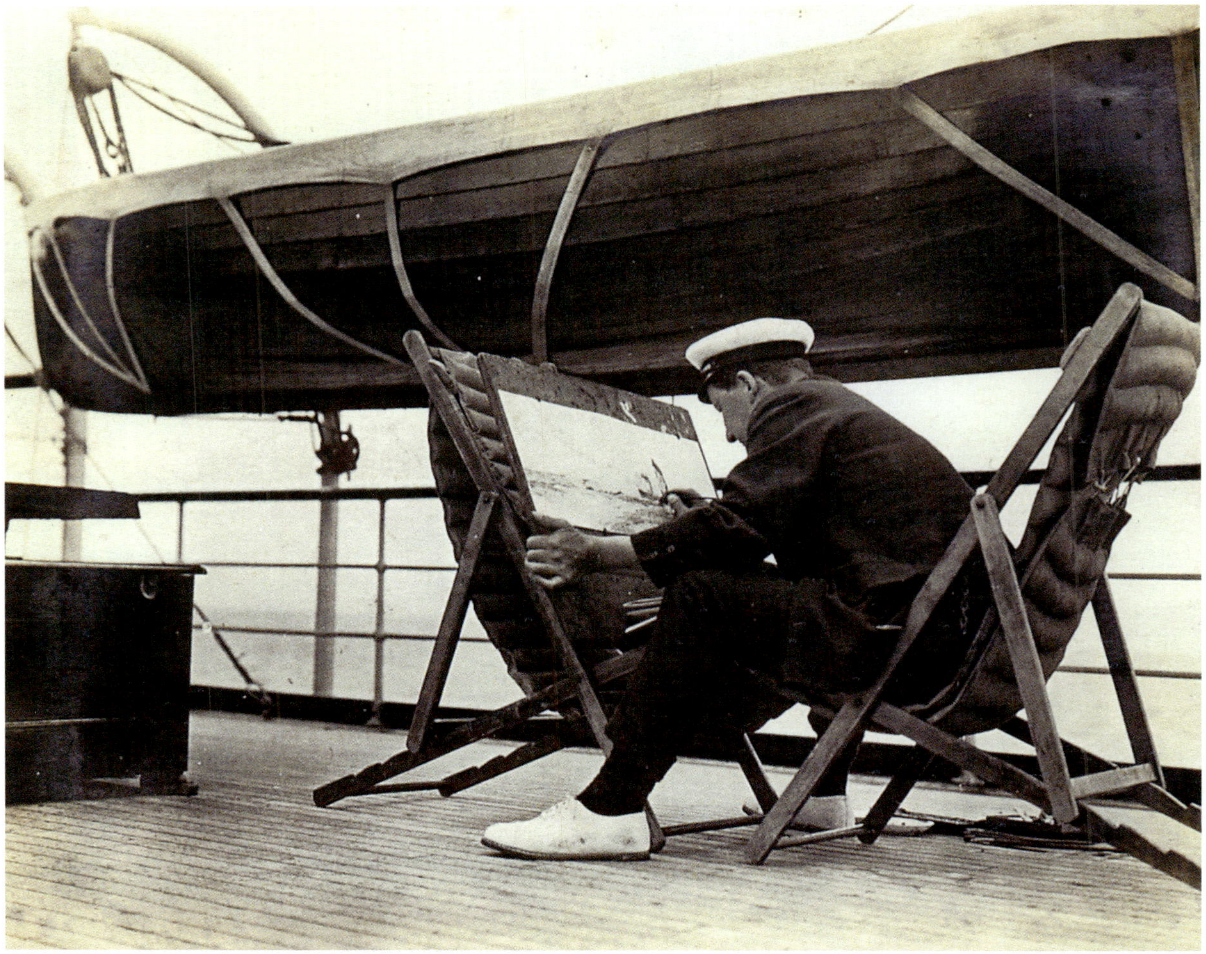

*Photograph of Charles Dixon painting on board steam yacht* St Serf*, 1916.*

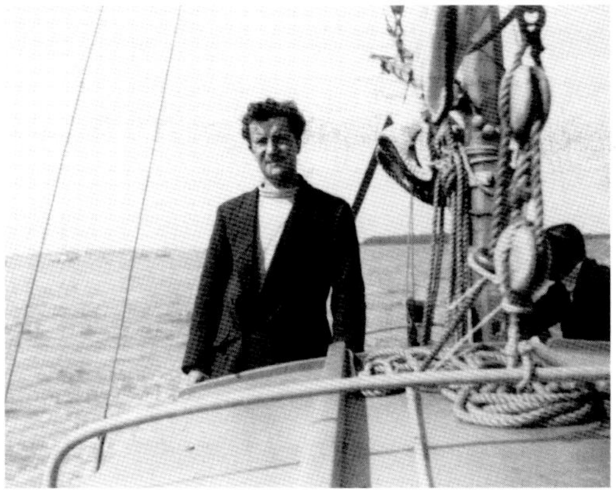

*Dixon on his yacht*

opulent yachts such as the steam yacht *St Serf* that provided Dixon with his more lucrative commissions, often with the prospect of a leisurely cruise and, during the summer of 1916, Dixon is seen at work on board *St Serf*, as a guest of Mr T Mordey, JP, a wealthy South Wales dry dock owner. In the photograph Dixon is putting the final touches to a painting of the yacht lying off Ben Nevis in Fort William, which he subsequently presented to Mr Mordey's father on the occasion of his 71st birthday. In 1922 Dixon sent his patron a Christmas card in the form of a watercolour sketch of *St Serf* with the charming inscription 'To Mr and Mrs Mordey from Charles Dixon 1922 and wishing you sunny skies, fair wind and tide and freights for Xmas and 1923' adding 'and smooth sea for Mrs Mordey'. Perhaps not surprisingly, Dixon spent some time around the Scottish coast, for apart from the Solent it was here that his more famous patron, Sir Thomas Lipton, watched his various *Shamrocks* during their trial races prior to setting off across the Atlantic to compete once again for the America's Cup. Time spent in Scottish waters also meant that Lipton and Dixon were able to take in other racing events taking place around the coast and, of course, enjoy the hospitality of clubs, such as the Royal Clyde Yacht Club, which was established in 1856 and hosted the most prestigious regatta of the season, which Dixon has depicted in 'The First Race of The Royal Clyde Yacht Club's Regatta, off Hunter's Quay, 1905'. Naturally, Lipton wanted Dixon to ensure maximum coverage of his yachts preparing for another challenge. His drawings were illustrated in the weekly magazines who needed illustrators who could make sense of the details of the race and then convey them to the public, thereby adding to the growing sense of expectation of readers that perhaps this would be the year when the Cup would come home.

*The America's Cup Challenger on her trials: The* Shamrock *off Cowes*
*Charles Dixon, Illustration for the* Graphis*, 22 July 1899*

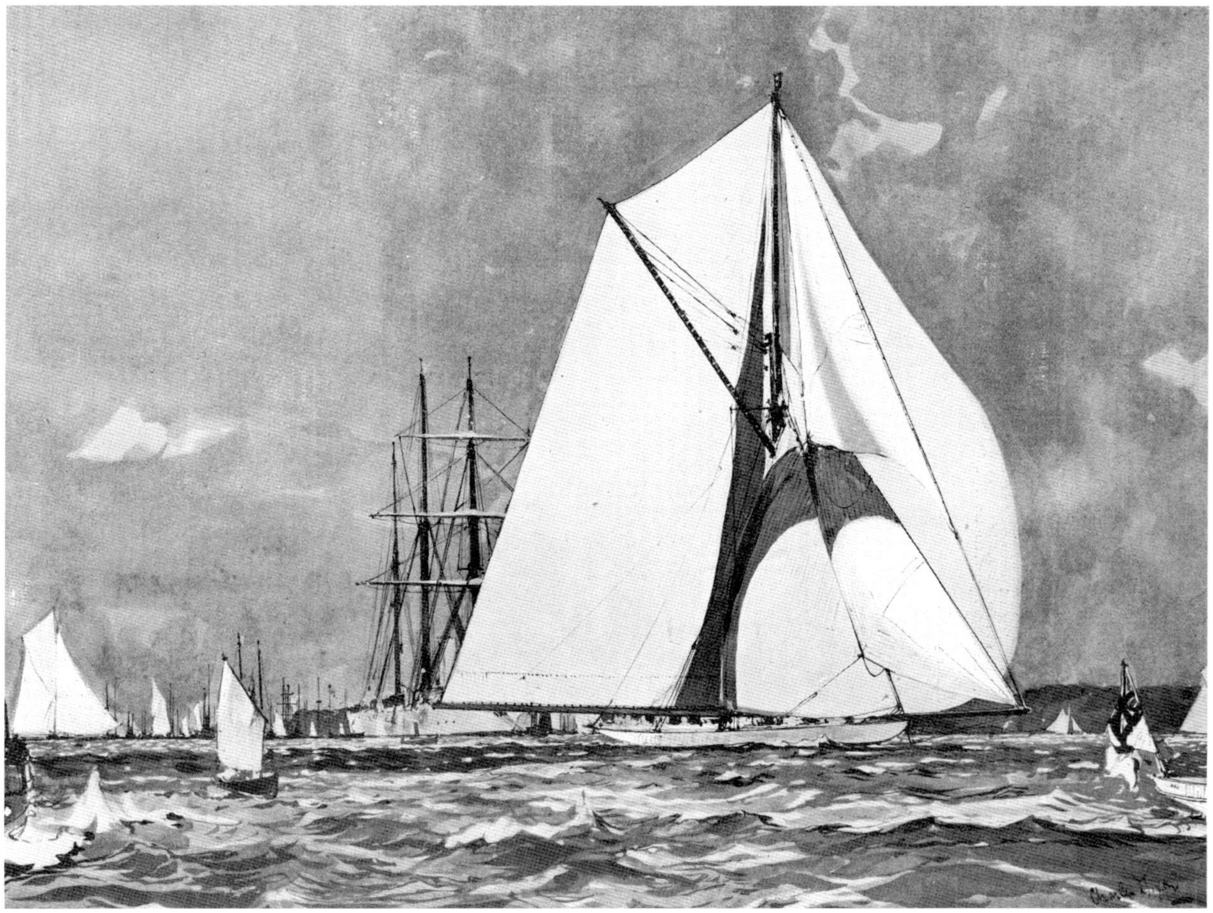

Arguably Britain's greatest ambassador of twentieth century marine painting, the popularity of the work of Montague Dawson (1845-1973) continues unabated. Noted for his large oils of clipper ships ploughing through blue seas under full canvas, this speciality subject has attracted admirers and collectors around the world, especially the United States. To some critics however his work became facile and repetitive, yet early in his career he produced a number of fine yachting subjects such as this superb watercolour of a gaff-rigged cutter running before a fresh breeze, her rigging and sails rendered with the usual meticulous attention to detail expected from someone with his experience as a yachtsman and Lt, RNVR in the first war.

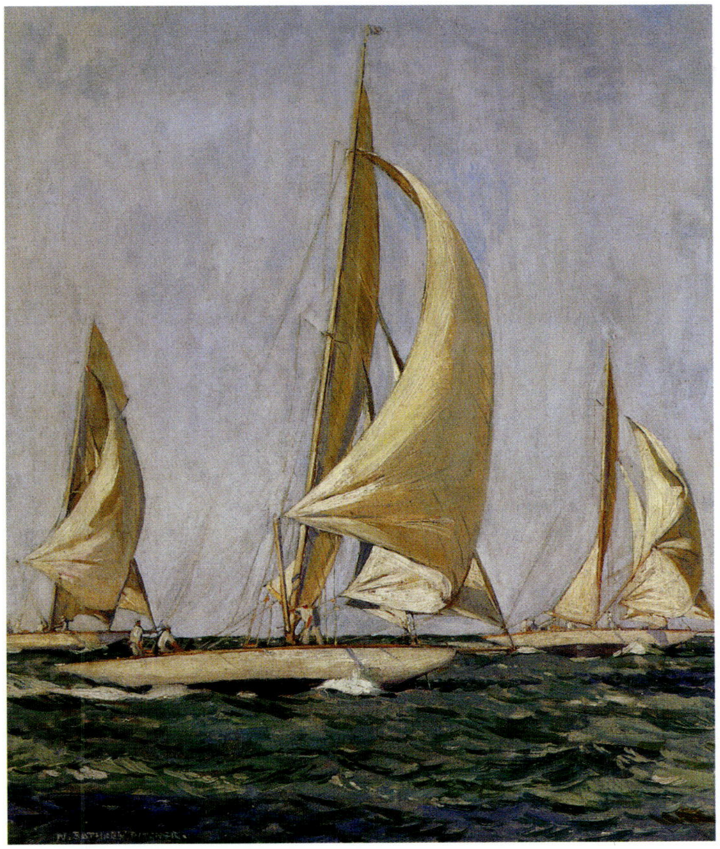

*A Yacht Race*
*Neville Sotheby Pitcher,*
*Oil on Canvas, 20½x16", Signed*
ROYAL EXCHANGE ART GALLERY

A painter of landscapes and genre scenes as well as a seascaper, Neville Sotheby Pitcher (flourished 1907-1959) lived in London during the first quarter of the 20th Century before moving to the small and more tranquil coastal town of Rye in East Sussex in 1925. He was a founder member of the Royal Society of Marine Artists and apart from exhibiting with their society, he had thirteen paintings hung in the Royal Academy between 1912 and 1942. A versatile artist, Pitcher painted in oils and watercolours and exhibited with both the Royal Institute of Painters in Watercolours and the Royal Institute of Oil Painters. During the Second World War he served with the Royal Naval Reserve and after the war he returned to live in Rye, where he died in 1959.

The careers of Sotheby Pitcher and another marine painter of the same period, Claude Muncaster (1903-1974) show similarities since both were members of the Royal Society of Marine Artists and also served with the Royal Navy; Muncaster, like a number of marine artist contemporaries, specialising as a camouflage adviser during the Second World War. Born in Sussex, he was the son of the painter Oliver Hall and changed his name to Muncaster in 1923 to avoid confusion with his father. In the 1920s Claude Muncaster spent time at sea, which included sailing on the four-masted barque *Olivebank*, on which he rounded Cape Horn. His first-hand knowledge of life aboard a windjammer resulted in some of his best paintings in oil and watercolour, but particularly those which show deck scenes similar to those rendered by Arthur Briscoe. He exhibited at the Royal Academy and his work may be found in the Tate Gallery and many other public collections. To write a chapter on yachting without reference to Norman Wilkinson would be remiss in the extreme for not only was he too a keen and experienced yachtsman, but in 1919 he became Honorary Marine Painter to the Royal Yacht Squadron. Like Dixon, he was in New York to cover Sir Thomas Lipton's second attempt to bring back the America's Cup and his sketches were sent back for inclusion in *The Illustrated London News*, for whom he

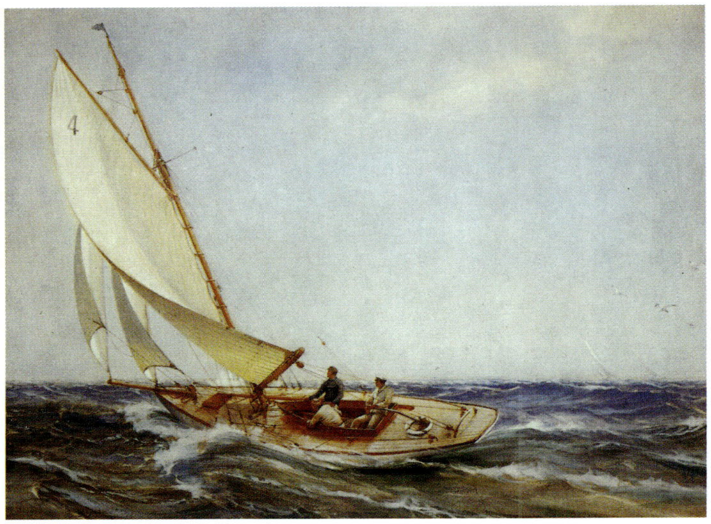

*A Gaff Rigged Day Boat*
*Running Before the Wind*
*Montague Dawson,*
*Watercolour, Signed*
ROYAL EXCHANGE ART GALLERY

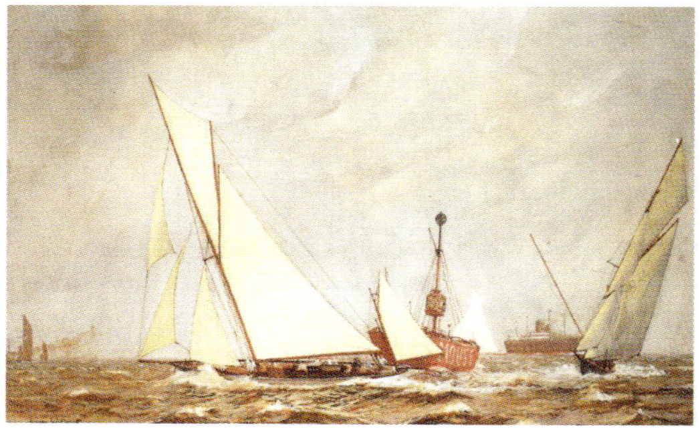

*Yachts rounding the 'Mouse' Lightship*
*Norman Wilkinson, Watercolour, 13½x21¼", Signed*
Royal Exchange Art Gallery

worked until 1915. Examples of his yachting pictures, particularly those which featured King George V's *Britannia*, are included in the British Royal Collection and the National Maritime Museum.

For anyone admiring the paintings of David Cobb (born 1921), it would be hard to discern any influence by Charles Dixon in his style, yet it is Dixon who has been acknowledged as having played a catalytic role in Cobb's artistic development, for it was his early encouragement and inspiration which ultimately led to the young David Cobb embarking on what has been a long and distinguished career as a painter. Like Dixon, Cobb was largely self-taught and throughout his life he became a dedicated marine artist whose work, mainly in oils, has encompassed a wide repertoire of marine subjects. In keeping with many of his fellow marine artists, Cobb has been a keen yachtsman and there are parallels between his life and, for instance, that of Arthur Briscoe, for both owned and lived on their own boats and had also seen active service in the Royal Navy, albeit in different ways. Throughout his career, Cobb has fulfilled a number of important roles; at one time becoming president of the Royal Society of Marine Artists and he was also appointed Marine Painter to the Royal Yacht Squadron. David Cobb is now retired, that is if a painter ever retires, but latterly he has made an important and telling pictorial record of the aftermath of the Falklands conflict when, following the

*The* Dorade *Sets a Cracking Pace*
*David Cobb, Oil, 20x24", Signed*
Royal Exchange Art Gallery

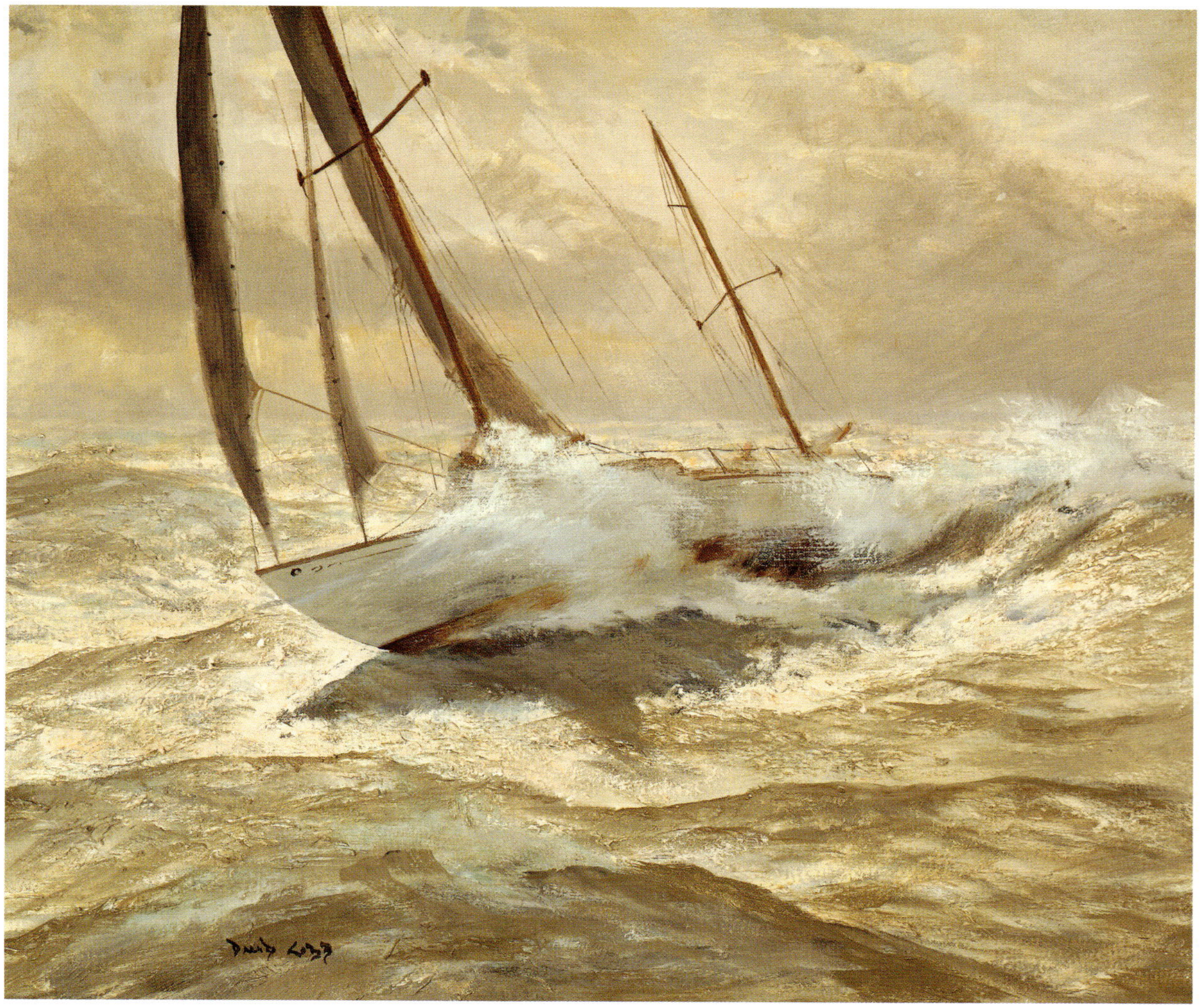

Argentinian surrender in 1982, he was engaged as an Official War Artist. Examples of his work are in the National Maritime Museum and also the Royal Navy Museum at Portsmouth, for whom he painted a large collection of the naval side of the two world wars. Cobb's late contemporaries, Leslie Wilcox (1904-1982) and John Chancellor (1925-1984), both excelled at painting historic yachts, including yachts of the 16th and 17th Centuries and another talented English yachting artist, Deryck Foster (born 1924) painted historic yachting scenes in which the influence of Montague Dawson is particularly discernable. If 'King of the Clipper Ships' is the sobriquet often used to describe Dawson, then 'Painter of the America's Cup' would be an entirely fitting mantle for Dixon, for this was an event which played such a major part in his artistic life. Never exactly a poor man's sport, it is now more than ever the preserve of the super rich wishing to challenge for the most prestigious of yachting trophies, currently held by Switzerland, a fact that would no doubt bemuse Dixon but also cause some dismay at Britain's continued lack of success or indeed participation. However, his disappointment would surely be offset by the magnificent achievements of Britain's sailors during the Olympic Games of 2008. Furthermore, he would have little difficulty in connecting with the many British yachting artists who took on the baton, coming to prominence in the second half of the twentieth century and who have sought their inspiration in the

Endeavour II *v* Ranger
*Martyn Mackrill, Oil on Canvas, Signed*
Royal Exchange Gallery

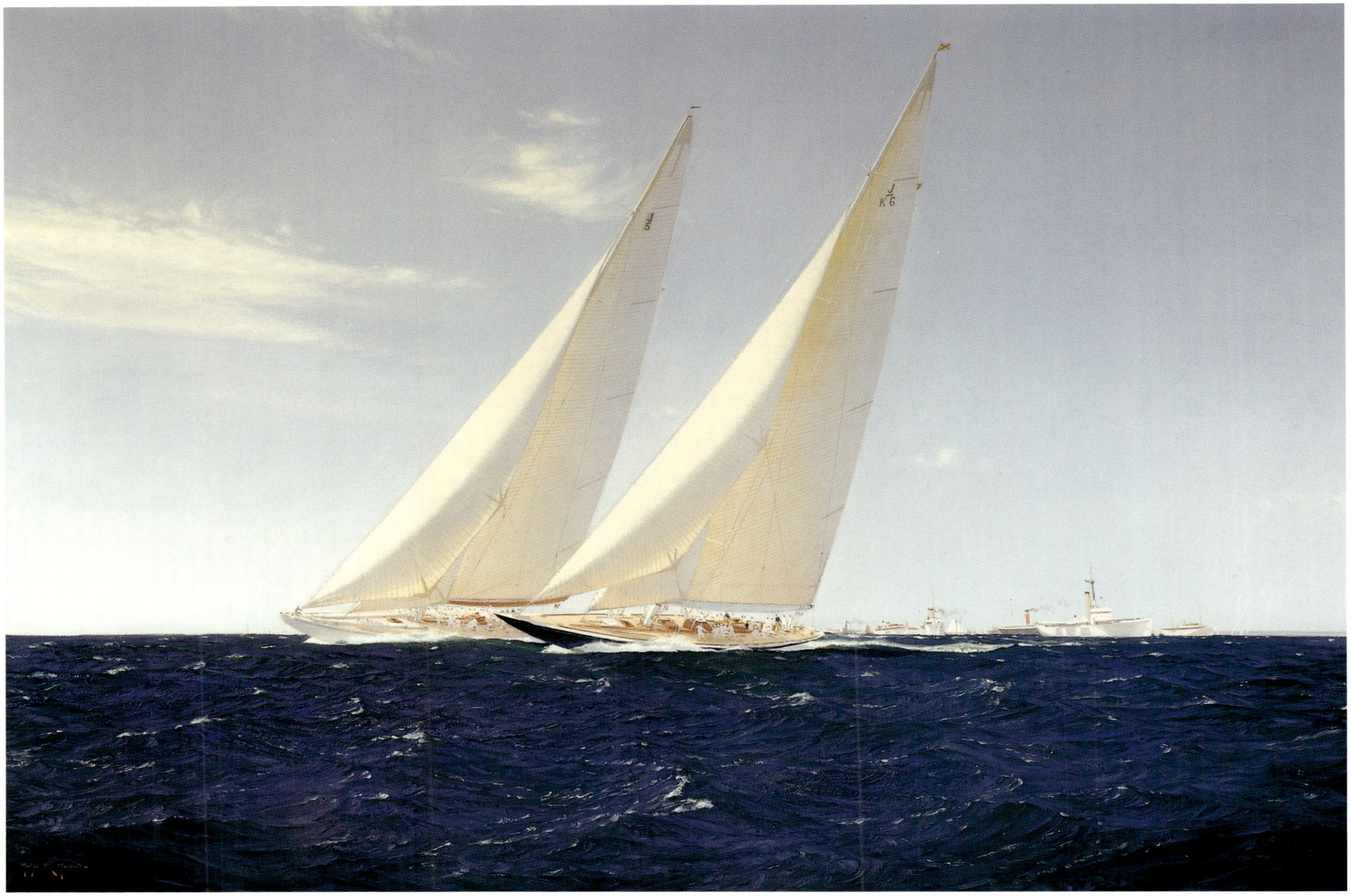

past, the glory of the big class yachts continuing to remain a subject for the nostalgic paintings of seasoned painters such as Michael Vaughan (b 1940), J Steven Dews (b 1949), Tim Thompson (b 1951), and Martyn Mackrill (b 1962) who, as a self confessed traditionalist, openly acknowledges the influence of Dixon and others of that Golden Era. Like Dews, Mackrill's depiction of the great classic yachts of the Edwardian period show a remarkable attention to detail, the images appearing more like photographs than paint of canvas. In his superb oil of the 1937 America's Cup race, Mackrill shows *Endeavour II* and *Ranger* both heading for the line about 30 seconds before the starting gun is fired. This was to be the last America's Cup match off Newport, Rhode Island using the J class yachts, but once more resulting in defeat for the British challenger, for *Endeavour II* was up against *Ranger*, the greatest J class ever built and whose superior design proved decisive.

Given Charles Dixon's great love of sailing and his close association with all of Sir Thomas Lipton's challenges for the America's Cup, it seems a poignant coincidence that he was buried on the same day in 1934 when, following the defeat of *Shamrock V* and the death of Sir Thomas Lipton, a new challenger came to the fore – Sir Thomas Sopwith with his *Endeavour*, which was making her mark to bring the trophy back to England and which came closest of any British challenge to winning the elusive trophy; beaten in the series of seven races by the American defender, *Rainbow*.

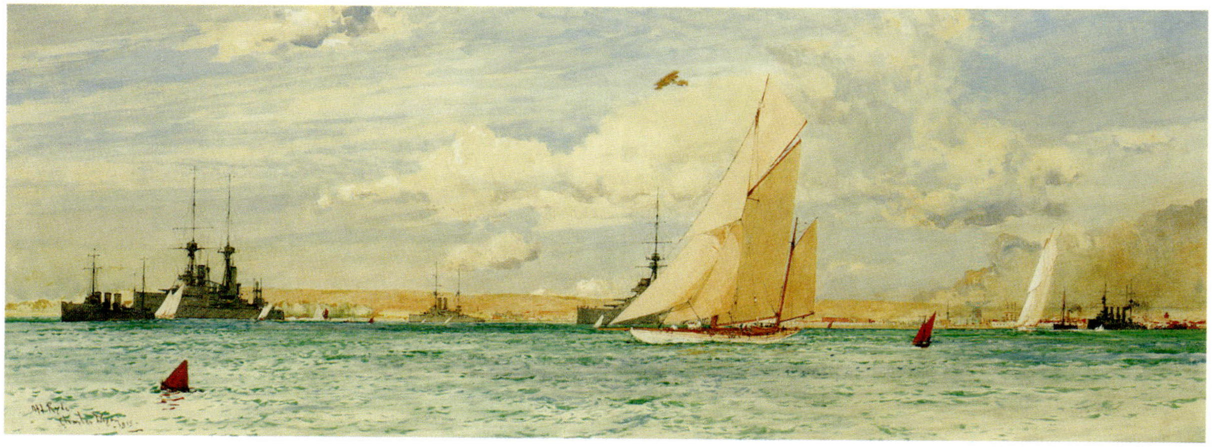

*Yacht Racing Off Ryde*
*Charles Dixon, Watercolour,*
*10½x29½", Signed and dated 1913*
SOTHEBYS

# Farewell

Of the three principal themes found in Charles Dixon's considerable output, the navy, yachting and the tidal Thames, it was undoubtedly the London river which formed the bedrock of his art, his views of the river traffic from the Tower to Blackwall, chronicled with such faithful integrity during a working life spanning 46 years. Since he painted his first exhibits for the Royal Academy, two centuries have passed during which Britain has witnessed the demise of her domination as a world naval and trading power. However, rather than lament its passing, a debt of gratitude is owed to Dixon and others for leaving such accurate and nostalgic pictorial records, which so vividly evoke a lost world in Britain's maritime history.

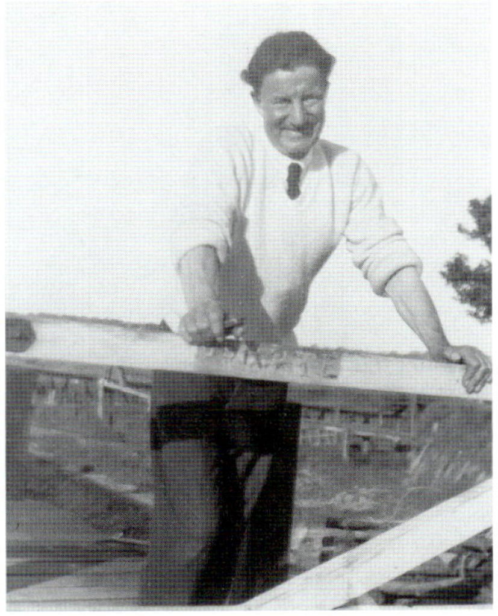

*Charles Dixon at Pierpoint 1934*

The artistic legacy left by Dixon's enduring devotion to marine painting has undoubtedly secured his place among the finest marine painters of the 20th Century, yet, despite the recognition afforded him during his life as a gifted professional artist, he was a modest and somewhat reticent man, who seems to have preferred to shun the limelight enjoyed by some of his contemporaries. Thus, not for him an honorary service commission as war artist or appointment as marine painter to one of the more prestigious yacht clubs, he seems to have been happy to the end, applying himself to his art with customary vigour. Indeed it is perhaps inevitable that the reputation of a thriving artist should derive from the work produced during the latter part of his life. In 1934, the year of his death, Dixon exhibited five pictures at the Royal Academy, after which the art critic of the *Daily Telegraph* wrote, "his best work showed no falling off in power of expression" and who considered the best of the five works sent in that year to be 'the Starting Gun 1675', depicting the start of a yacht race at the time of Charles II.

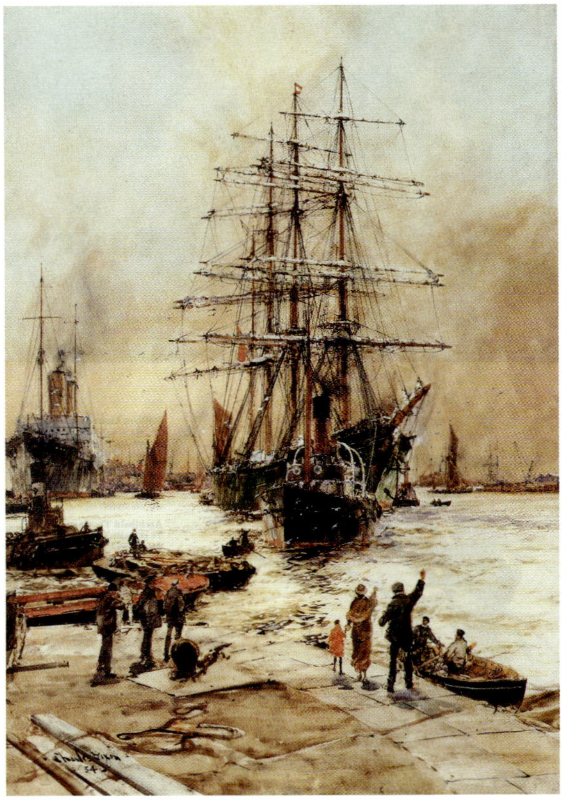

*Farewell*
*Charles Dixon, Watercolour, 30x21",*
*Signed and dated 1934*
BOURNE GALLERY

At the age of 61, Charles Dixon died at his home in Itchenor on 12th September 1934. His death was reported in national and local newspapers throughout the British Isles and had not gone unnoticed much further afield, including the Colonies, with obituaries appearing in the *Victoria Times* and the *Montreal Daily Star*, with its heading 'noted old country marine artist dies'. He was interned in the churchyard of the beautiful Little Parish Church of St Nicholas, Itchenor and, according to the report of the service in the *Hampshire Daily Telegraph*, Portsmouth, 'he was buried with an informality and quietness which would have exactly suited his temperament, amid surroundings which he loved'.

# Appendix I

**Public and Other Collections holding Works by Charles Dixon**

**United Kingdom**
Aberdeen Maritime Museum
Birkenhead: Williamson Art Gallery and Museum
Blackburn Museum and Art Gallery
Blackpool: Grundy Art Gallery
Bournemouth: Russell Coates Art Gallery and Museum
Bury: Bury Art Gallery
Cardiff: National Museum of Wales
Glasgow: Kelvingrove Art Gallery and Museum
Liverpool: The Walker Art Gallery
Liverpool: The Merseyside Maritime Museum
London: National Maritime Museum, Greenwich
London: Imperial War Museum
London: Victoria and Albert Museum
London: Docklands Museum
Newport City Art Gallery and Museum
Portsmouth: Royal Naval Museum
Portsmouth City Art Gallery and Museum
Sheffield: Graves Art Gallery
Sunderland Museum and Art Gallery
Swansea: Glyn Vivian Art Gallery
Ulster: Folk and Transport Museum

**Other Collections**
Royal Collection Trust – Buckingham Palace
Corporation of Trinity House – London
Honourable Company of Master Mariners - London
Port of London Authority
P&O Heritage Collection – London
Royal National Lifeboat Institute
Royal Northern & Clyde Yacht Club
Royal Yacht Squadron, Cowes, I.O.W.
The Royal Yacht *Britannia*, Leith, Edinburgh

**Overseas**
Australia: The Mitchell Library, Sydney, New South Wales
New Zealand: Government War Art Collection
Canada: The Marine Museum, Toronto
USA: Mystic Seaport Museum, Connecticut
USA: Mariners Museum, Newport News, Virginia

Fossilien eines bestimmten Zeitalters, wie etwa die Überreste von Dinosauriern aus dem Mesozoikum, findet man nur in Gestein, das in dieser Zeit entstanden ist. Das schränkt die Auswahl der Fundorte schon beträchtlich ein. Geologen erstellen bei der Suche nach Mineralen und anderen Bodenschätzen wie Kohle, Öl und Erzen geologische Karten. Dieses Material ist für Paläontologen, die oftmals Seite an Seite mit den Geologen in Vermessungstrupps arbeiten, von unschätzbarem Wert. Aus den Karten ist der Typ und das ungefähre Alter der obersten Gesteinsschichten zu ersehen. Ein großer Teil der Festlandoberfläche unserer Erdkugel ist bisher allerdings noch nicht kartiert. Ebenfalls eine große Hilfe für die heutigen Fossilienjäger sind Luftvermessungen und verschiedene Arten von Aufnahmen aus Flugzeugen und Satelliten, darunter normale, bei sichtbarem Licht aufgenommene Fotos und Bilder von infraroter, ultravioletter und anderer Strahlung. Mit Hilfe dieser Fotografien lassen sich potenzielle Fossilienstätten in sehr abgelegenen, noch nicht untersuchten Gebieten ermitteln.

Viele der Gebiete, in denen die berühmtesten Fossilienfundstätten der Welt liegen – die Wüste Gobi oder Teile des mittleren Westens der USA –, sind so genannte „Badlands". Das sind raue Landschaften, in denen das Gestein frei an der Oberfläche liegt und durch die Extreme der Elemente unablässig erodiert. Der heißen Sonnenstrahlung bei Tage folgt eine kalte oder frostige Nacht, gelegentliche Überschwemmungen oder Sandstürme sprengen und zerfressen das Gestein, so dass immer neue Schichten freigelegt werden. Der Boden wird entweder vom Wind davongetragen oder vom Regen weggespült, deshalb wachsen hier nur wenige Pflanzen und der Fels bleibt nackt. Andere ausgezeichnete Fundstätten sind felsige Küsten, See- oder Flussufer, wo Wellen, Wind und Regen an den Klippen oder dem zutage liegenden Gestein nagen und Steinfälle immer wieder neue Gesteinsformationen bloßlegen. In Bergwerken, Steinbrüchen, bei Abtragungsarbeiten für den Straßen- und Eisenbahnbau und bei Großbauten wie etwa Dämmen verursachen Maschinen die Erosion. Solche Orte werden regelmäßig von Fossilienjägern aufgesucht, die auf der Suche nach frisch zutage geförderten und interessant aussehenden Überresten sind.

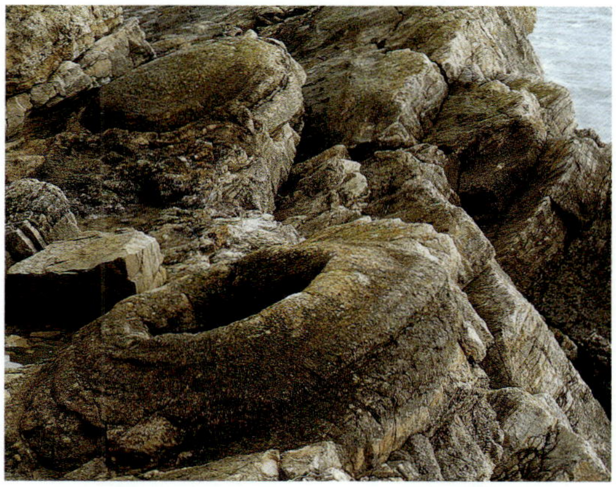

**OBEN** Manche Felsen wie diese versteinerten Bäume bei Lulworth an der Südostküste Englands sind größtenteils konservierte organische Überreste.

**UNTEN** An der Dinosaur Cove in der Nähe von Melbourne (Australien) wurde das Känguru auf dem Schild durch einen Dinosaurier ersetzt. Auf diesem Gelände wurden viele sensationelle Fossilfunde gemacht, doch Zugang und Arbeitsbedingungen sind dort nicht einfach.

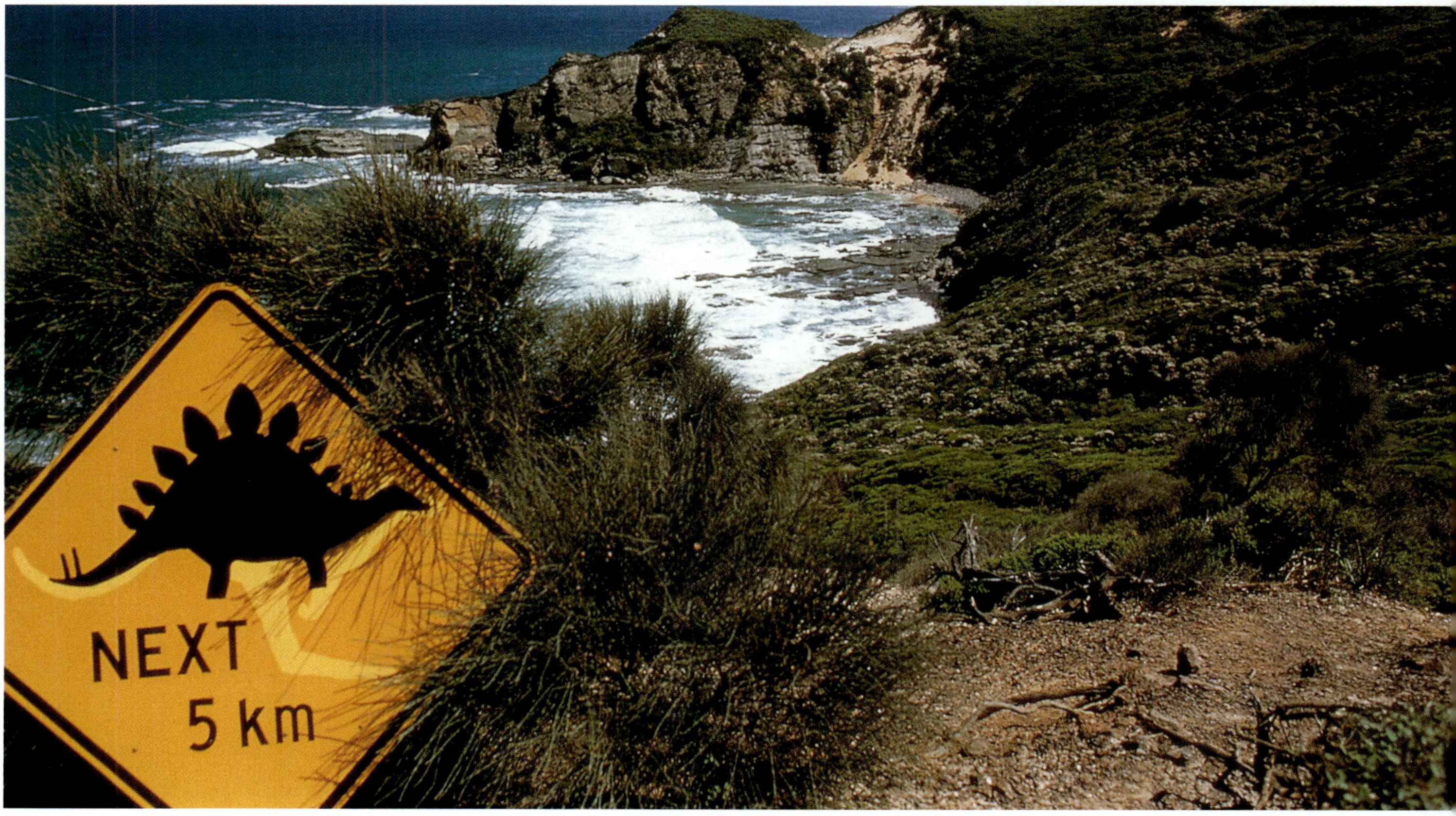

# DIE DATIERUNG VON FOSSILIEN

***Wie alt ist ein Fossil? Zum Feststellen des Alters eines Fossilfundes gibt es verschiedene Methoden. Diese werden in zwei große Gruppen eingeteilt – in die relative oder vergleichende und in die absolute Altersbestimmung. Bei der relativen Datierung vergleicht man Fossilien und die Gesteine, in welche die Funde eingebettet sind, miteinander um festzustellen, welche jünger oder älter sind. Die Schichten von Sedimentgesteinen beispielsweise sind so aufgebaut, dass die jüngsten in der Regel näher an der Oberfläche und die älteren tiefer liegen. Natürlich gibt es auch Ausnahmen. Mitunter können Gesteinsschichten durch Erdbewegungen so stark geneigt werden, dass sie regelrecht umkippen, ältere Gesteine und Fossilien also näher an die Oberfläche gelangen.***

In vielen Regionen haben sich Sedimentgesteine in einer typischen Abfolge von Arten und Schichtstärken abgelagert, die genau erforscht ist. Passt man Steine und Fossilien aus einer kleinen Probe oder einem Kernstück dieser Struktur, vielleicht nur zwei oder drei Schichten, in diese bekannte Gesamtabfolge ein, kann man sie genau datieren. Überreste von Lebewesen, die zahlreich und weit verbreitet waren, sich von der Natur gut konservieren ließen und so über lange Zeiträume erhalten blieben, nennt man „Leitfossilien". Beispiele dafür sind beschalte oder gepanzerte Meerestiere wie die Trilobiten aus dem Kambrium oder die Ammoniten und Belemniten aus dem Jura (siehe Seiten 42, 45 und 49). An Veränderungen der Schalen- oder Panzerformen und Muster lässt sich ihre Zugehörigkeit zu einem bestimmten Zeitraum ablesen. Dieses Wissen liefert uns Anhaltspunkte für die Datierung anderer, weniger bekannter Fossilien, die zusammen mit ihnen gefunden wurden. Auch winzige Relikte jener Foraminiferen (Kammerlinge) genannten Wasserlebewesen oder der widerstandsfähigen Pollenkörner der Pflanzen werden zur Altersbestimmung herangezogen.

**UNTEN** Diese Querschnittansicht von einem Sandsteinfelsen, der einst der sandige Grund eines Flachmeeres war, lässt eine deutliche Schichtung erkennen. Die Bänder treten dank der verschiedenen Farbtöne eisenhaltiger Minerale hier besonders deutlich und reizvoll hervor.

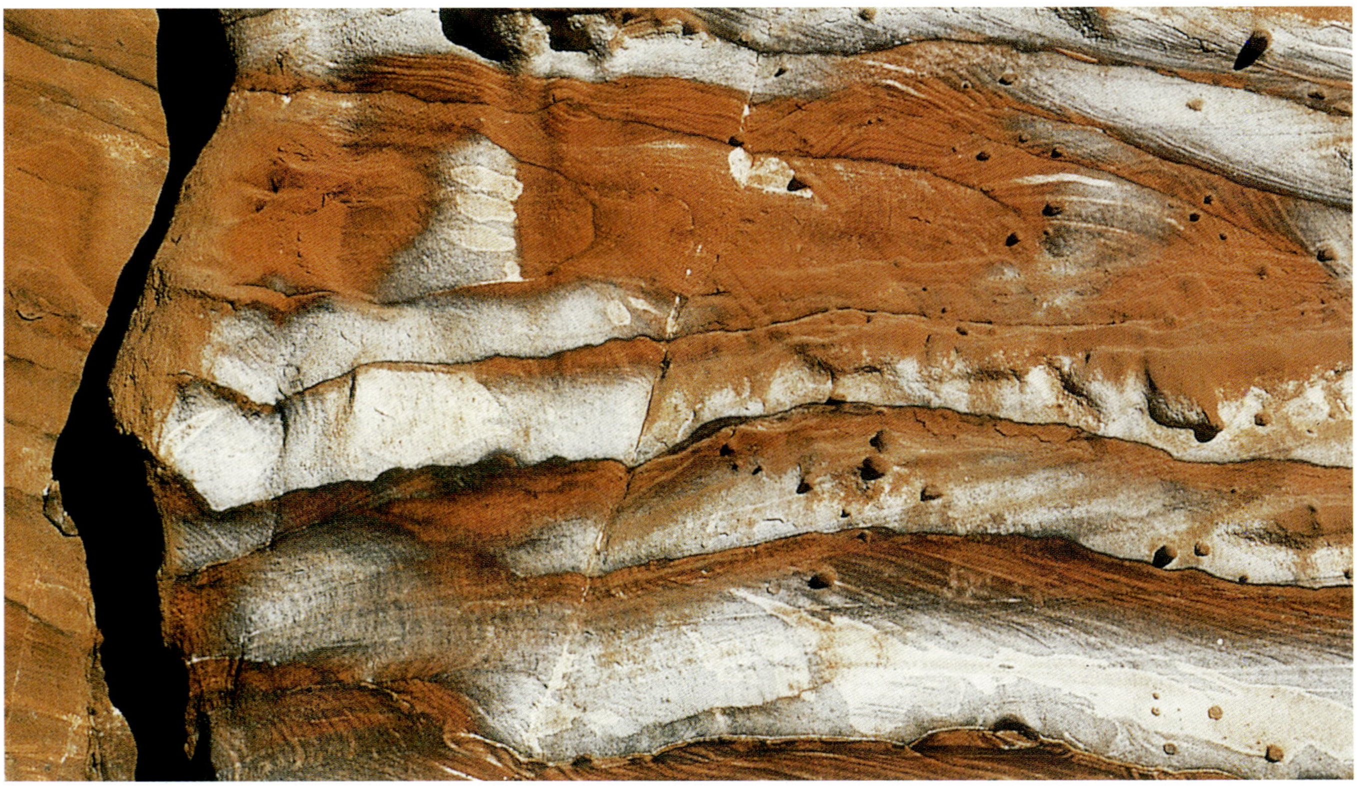

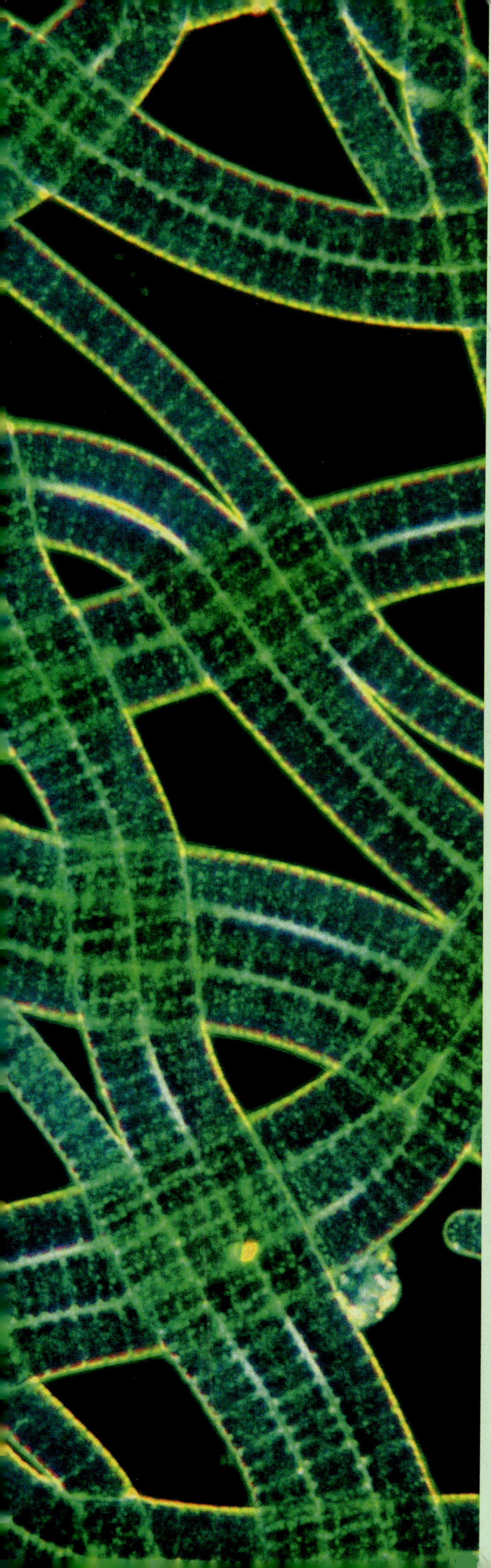

# Kapitel Eins

# Frühes Leben

*Die Erde war während des Paläozoikums von frühen Tierarten bevölkert, deren Vielfalt von meeresbewohnenden Würmern und Quallen bis zu den ersten Geschöpfen reichte, die sich auf dem Land bewegten.*

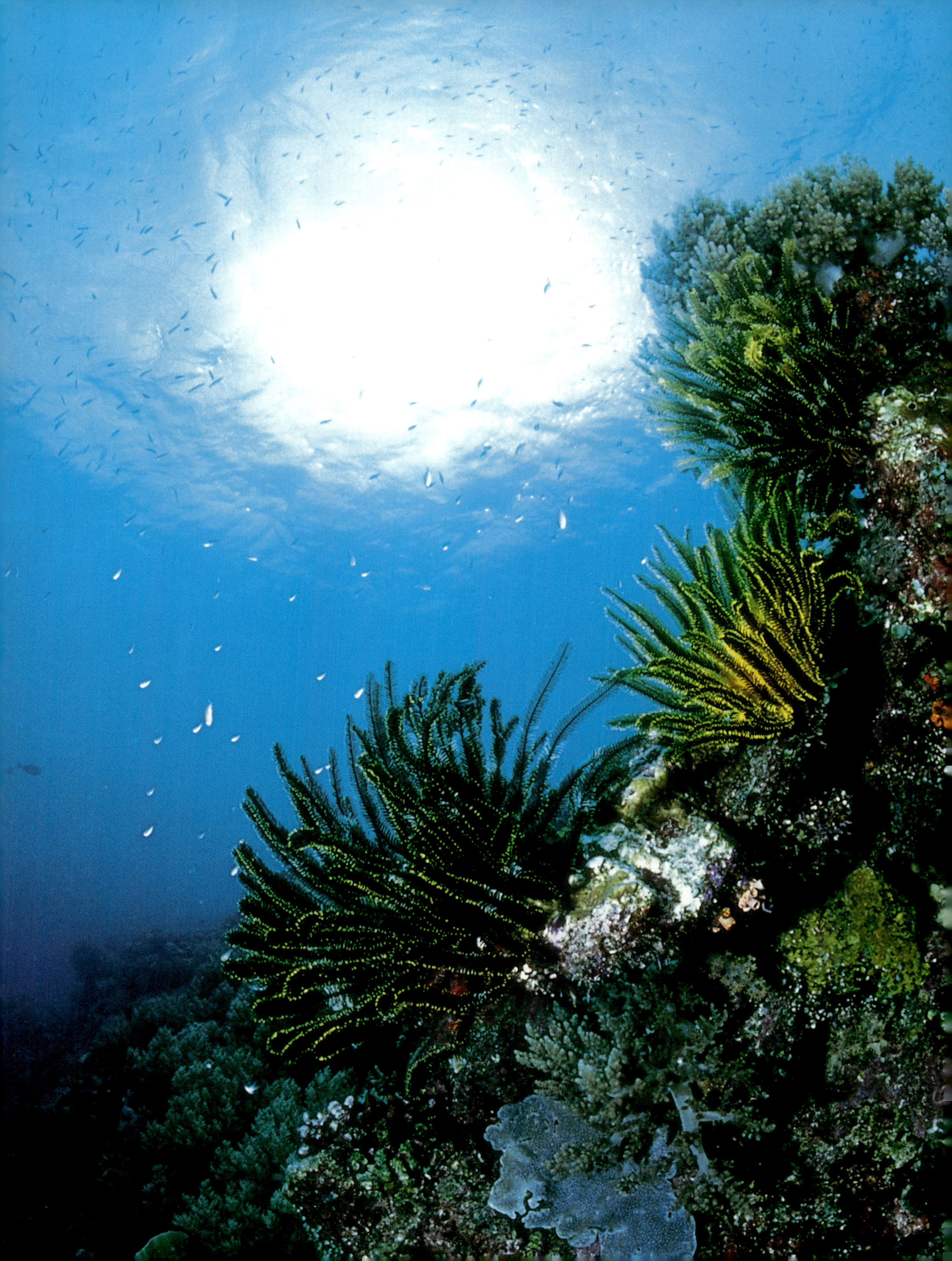

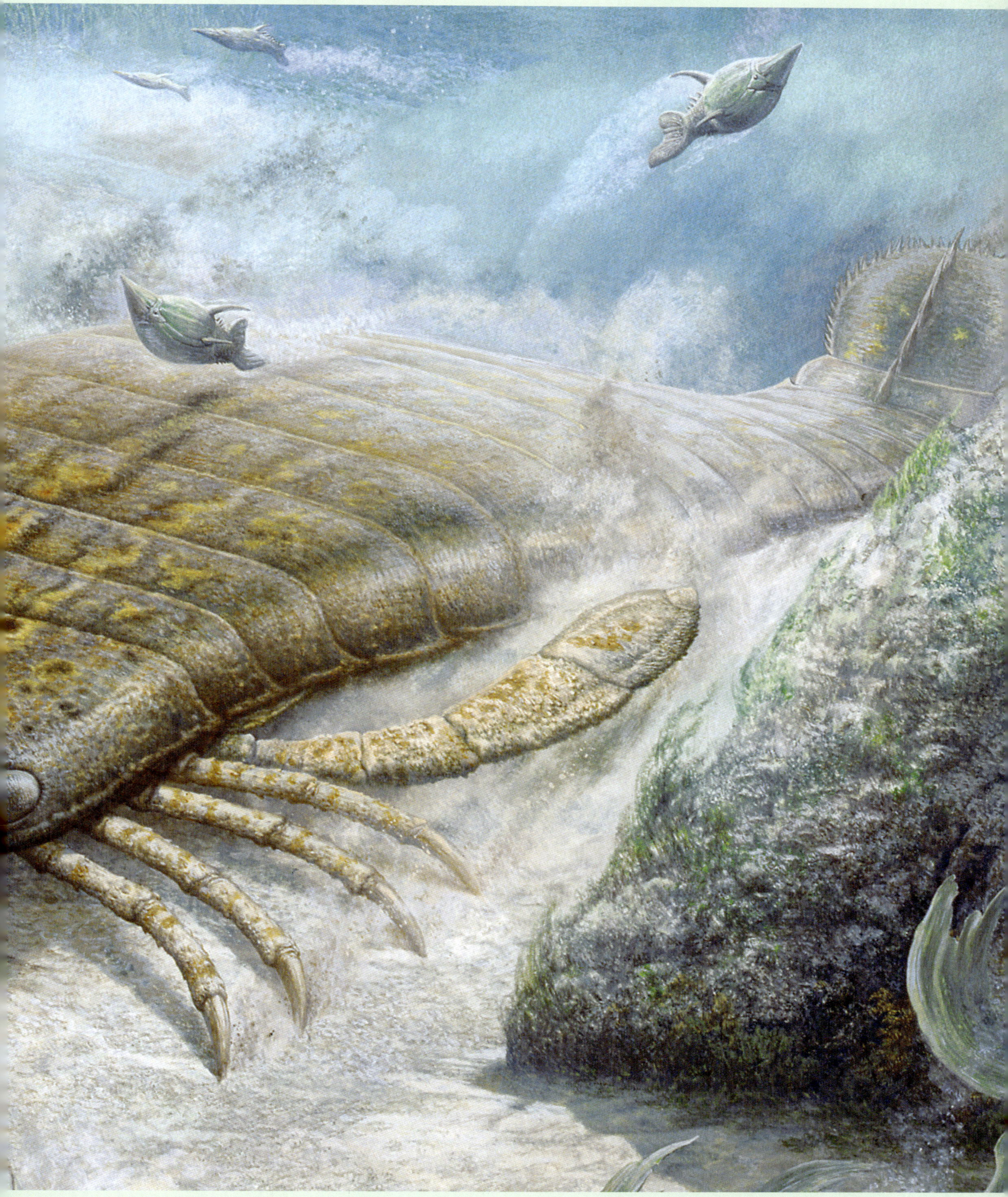

# Ampyx und Pliomera

Zu den bekanntesten prähistorischen Tieren zählen die Trilobiten. Ihr Name bedeutet „dreilappig" und weist auf die äußere Erscheinung der Lebewesen hin. Ihr Körper bestand aus drei Teilen oder Lappen, die durch zwei lange, vom Kopf- bis zum Schwanzschild reichende Furchen voneinander getrennt waren. Äußerlich ähnelten die Trilobiten den rezenten Kellerasseln, die bevorzugt unter feuchter Rinde leben. Kellerasseln sind Krustentiere, Verwandte der Krebse und Garnelen (siehe Seite 50); Trilobiten zählen nicht zu den Krustentieren, obgleich sie einen großen Teil der Arthropoden ausmachen, zu denen die Krustentiere und die Spinnen, die Insekten und die Skorpione gehören. Sie liefen oder schwammen mit Gliederfüßen (siehe Seite 46) und sie besaßen als Erste Augen angemessener Größe, die ihre Umgebung vermutlich deutlich abbilden konnten.

*Ampyx* gehörte zu den kleineren und früheren Trilobitenformen. Die Tiere hatten ungefähr die Größe eines menschlichen Daumens und waren leicht gebaut. Ihr dünner Körperpanzer war vorn zu einem langen Sporn und an den Vorderseiten zu zwei nach hinten weisenden dornartigen Fortsätzen ausgezogen. Vermutlich durchsiebten die Tiere den auf dem Meeresboden abgelagerten Schlamm und Sand nach genießbaren Nahrungspartikeln und gruben sich zum Schutz tiefer in den Grund ein. *Pliomera* war ebenfalls klein und lebte auch im Ordovizium, vor rund 450 Millionen Jahren. Dieses Tier besaß keine Panzerfortsätze, dafür saßen an seinem Kopf eingekerbte Kämme; rollte das Tier sich zusammen, umschlossen sie das hintere Körperende, so dass die verwundbare Bauchseite in dem gekrümmten Körperpanzer geschützt lag (siehe unten).

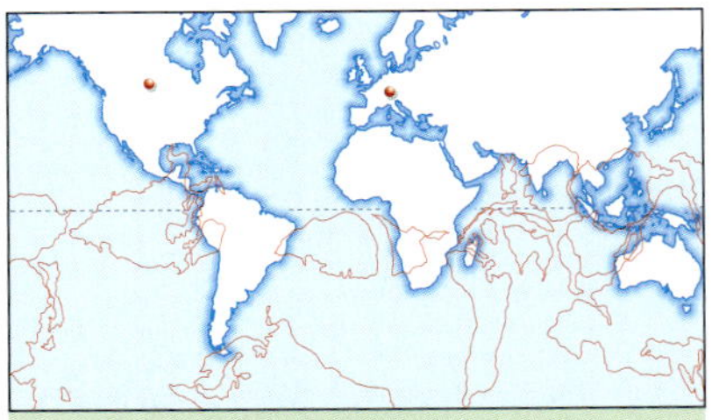

**ÜBERSICHT (TIERE)**

***Ampyx***

**Bedeutung des Namens:** Ungefähr zwei

**Periode:** Ordovizium

**Hauptgruppe:** Arthropoda (Trilobita)

**Länge:** 4 Zentimeter

**Nahrung:** Kleine genießbare Partikel

**Fossilfundstätten:** In Europa und Nordamerika

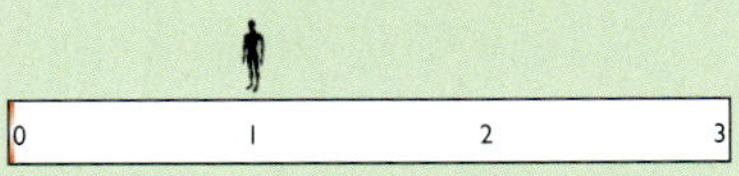


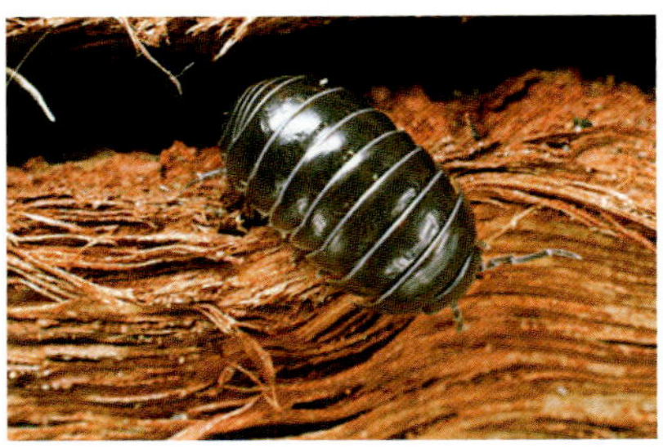

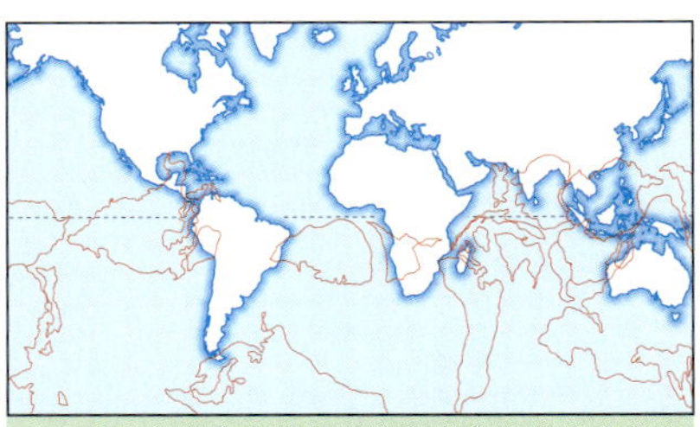

**ÜBERSICHT (TIERE)**

***Pliomera***

**Bedeutung des Namens:** Monströs(eres Wesen)

**Periode:** Ordovizium

**Hauptgruppe:** Arthropoda (Trilobita)

**Größe:** Bis 5 Zentimeter

**Nahrung:** Partikel auf dem Meeresboden

**Fossilfundstätten:** Hauptsächlich in der westlichen Hemisphäre

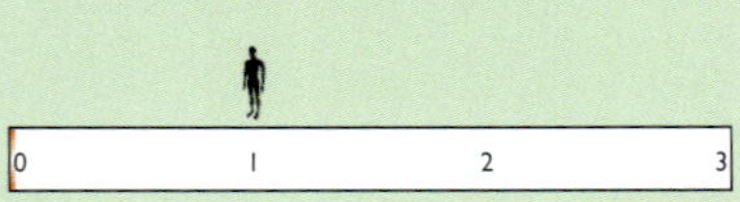


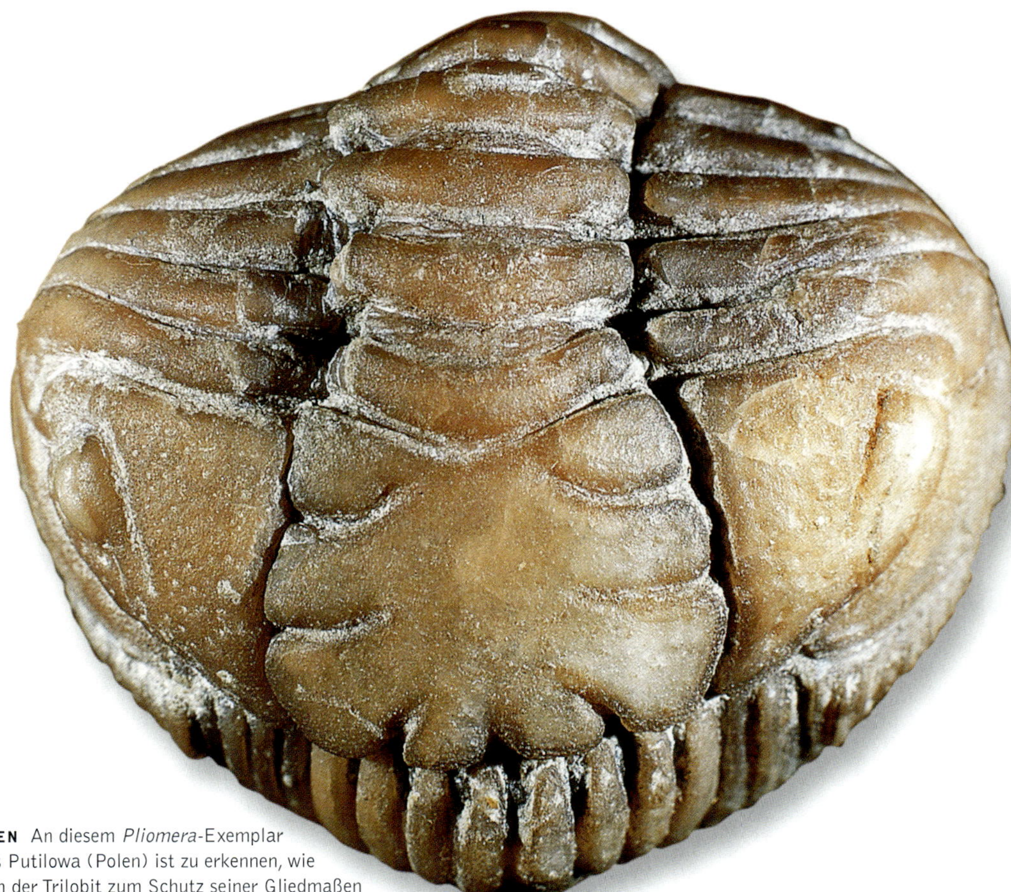

**OBEN** An diesem *Pliomera*-Exemplar aus Putilowa (Polen) ist zu erkennen, wie sich der Trilobit zum Schutz seiner Gliedmaßen und der gesamten Bauchseite zusammenrollte.

**LINKS** Die rezenten Kellerasseln sind – wie einst auch die Trilobiten – Arthropoden. Auch wenn keine enge Verwandtschaft mit den Trilobiten besteht, können sie sich bei Gefahr ebenfalls zu einer Kugel zusammenzurollen.

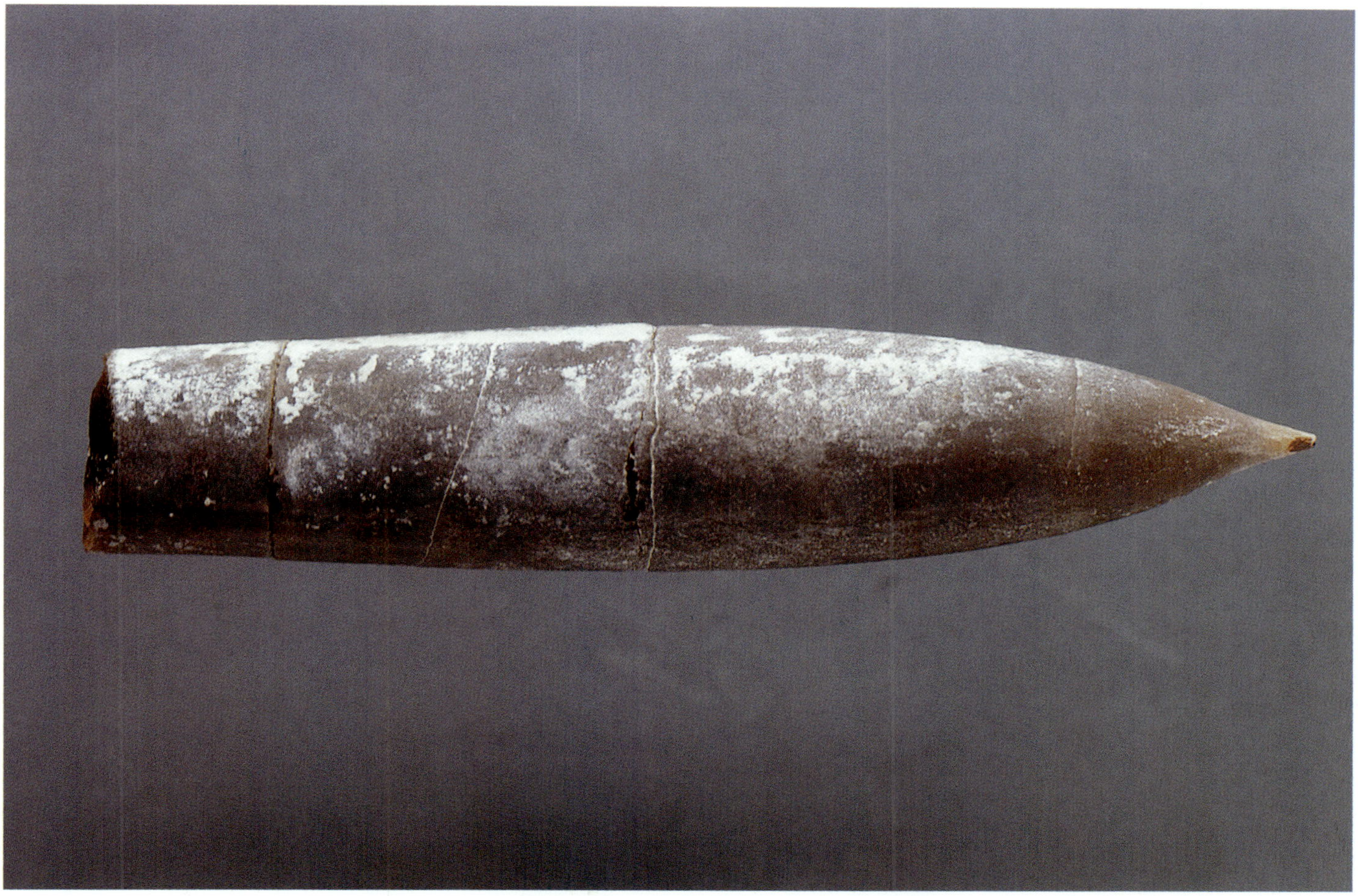

# Gonioteuthis

Wie die großäugigen schnellen Jäger auf den vorhergehenden Seiten war auch *Goniotheutis* eine Form der Mollusken, die wir Cephalopoden (Kopffüßer) nennen. Das Tier gehörte zur Untergruppe der Belemniten, die die ordovizischen Meere binnen kurzem mit Hunderten verschiedener Arten bevölkerten. Wie die Ammoniten (siehe Seite 42) erlosch diese Ordnung der Kopffüßer in der Kreidezeit allmählich und war am Ende dieser Periode schließlich verschwunden. In dieser Zeit, in der Oberkreide, lebte *Gonioteuthis*. Er war verhältnismäßig klein, sein Körper wurde nur 15–20 Zentimeter (ohne Tentakeln) lang.

Die Belemniten ähnelten zu Lebzeiten wahrscheinlich einer rezenten Kopffüßergruppe, den Kalmaren. An beiden Seiten ihres lang gestreckten, stromlinienförmigen Körpers befand sich ein flügel- oder flossenartiger Auswuchs. Am Kopf saßen seitlich zwei große Augen und in der Mitte ein horniger Schnabel, den zehn lange Tentakeln umgaben; die Tentakeln waren bei manchen Belemnitenformen auf der gesamten Länge mit Haken oder Saugorganen besetzt. Erhalten geblieben sind nur die Gehäuse, die die Tiere nicht umhüllten, sondern in deren Körper steckten. Diese Innenskelette hatten ein kegelförmiges Gehäuse (Phragmokon) in der Körpermitte und einen langen, schlanken Fortsatz (Rostrum), der in das spitz zulaufende Körperende auslief. An manchen Fundorten liegen Tausende dieser fossilierten Rostren. Neben längeren, schlankeren, dolchähnlichen Rostren findet man auch kürzere, breitere, die der Volksmund „Donnerkeile“ nennt. Die Bezeichnung „Belemniten“ wurde nach der Gehäuseform von dem griechischen Wort *bélemnos* abgeleitet, was „Blitz“ oder „Geschoss“ bedeutet.

**OBEN** Auf der Isle of Wight vor der Südküste Englands und auch an anderen Orten findet man „Donnerkeile“ zu Hunderten. Es handelt sich dabei um den fossilierten hinteren Teil des Innenskeletts eines Belemniten. Ein modernes Äquivalent dazu ist der Schulp der Tintenschnecken.

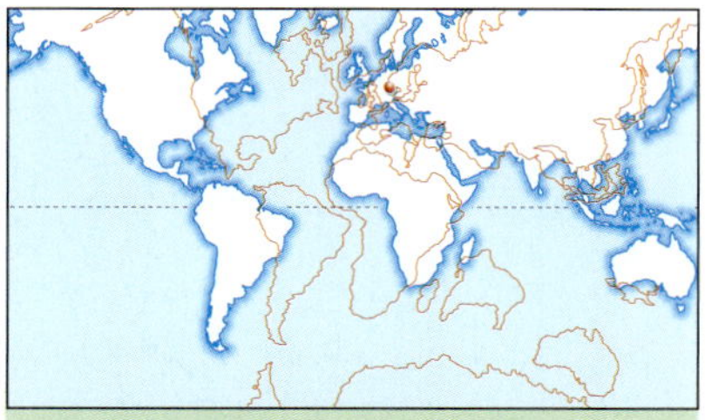

**ÜBERSICHT (TIERE)**
***Gonioteuthis***

**Bedeutung des Namens:** Schmalkalmar, Schlankkalmar
**Periode:** Kreide
**Hauptgruppe:** Mollusca
**Größe:** Körperlänge (ohne Tentakeln) bis 20 Zentimeter
**Nahrung:** Kleine Tiere
**Fossilfundstätten:** U. a. in Europa

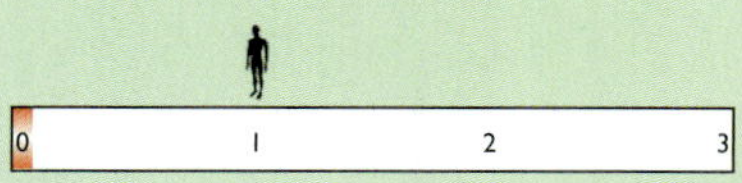

# Aeger und Eryon

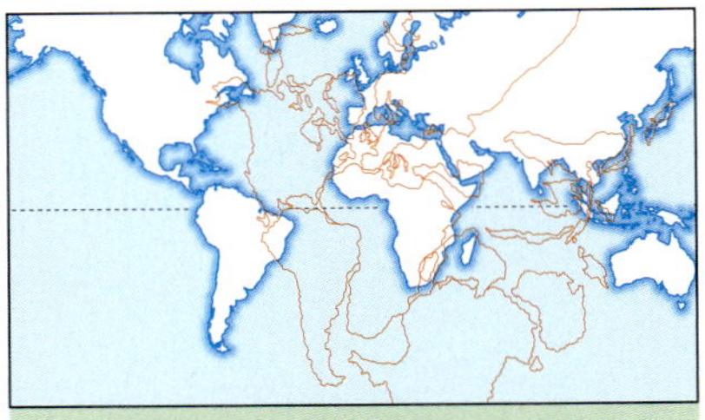

**ÜBERSICHT (TIERE)**

***Aeger***

**Bedeutung des Namens:** Garnele

**Periode:** Trias bis Jura

**Hauptgruppe:** Arthropoda (Crustacea)

**Größe:** 12 Zentimeter

**Nahrung:** Kleine genießbare Bissen

**Fossilfundstätten:** Weltweit

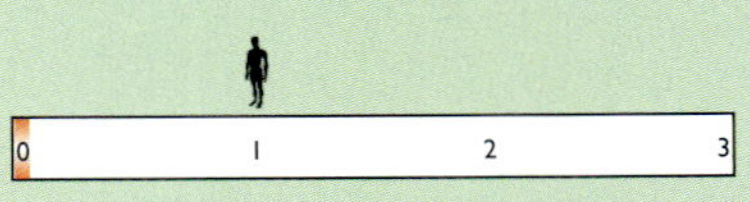


Innerhalb der Arthropoden (siehe Seite 46) gibt es die große Gruppe der Crustacea (Krusten- oder Krebstiere). Von ihr existieren heute mehr als 40 000 Spezies, die einen Großteil des Lebens in den Meeren beherrschen. Ihre Fossilgeschichte reicht mehr als 550 Millionen Jahre, bis ins Präkambrium, zurück. Eine der größten Untergruppen der Krustentiere bilden die Decapoden (Zehnfußkrebse). Zu ihnen gehören die kleinen und großen Garnelen, die Hummer, Krabben und Flusskrebse.

*Aeger* war eine prähistorische Garnele aus der Periode des Jura, in der die Land bewohnenden Dinosaurier ihre Blütezeit erlebten. Überreste der Tiere hat man in vielen Gegenden gefunden; sie belegen, dass sich ihre Merkmale von denen der rezenten Garnelen im Großen und Ganzen nur wenig unterscheiden. Die heutigen Garnelen haben auf der Stirn noch immer den langen, spitz zulaufenden Fortsatz (Rostrum), sehr lange Fühler (Antennen), einen Kopf und Thorax umschließenden Panzer und scherenartig endende Gliedmaßen, mit denen sie kleine Nahrungspartikel und Aasstücke vom Meeresboden aufsammeln.

*Eryon* war eine Art Stachelhummer, der vor rund 150–100 Millionen Jahren, in der Zeit des Jura und der Unterkreide, lebte. Er war etwas kleiner als eine Menschenhand und besaß einen breiten, abgeflachten Kopfschild (Cephalothorax), an den sich ein gegliederter, biegsamer schwanzartiger Hinterleib anschloss. Seine vier Beinpaare endeten in Scheren, deren vorderste die größten waren, und die Schwanzspitze hatte die Form eines Fächers. Wenn *Eryon* seinen Schwanz mit einer kurzen, schnellen Bewegung unter den Körper bog, wurde das Tier mit einem Ruck zurückgestoßen, was ihm bei Gefahr eine rasche Flucht ermöglichte. *Eryon* war möglicherweise der Vorfahr einer der letzten großen Gruppen von Krustentieren, sie sich entwickelten und die erstmals im Jura auftauchten – der Urahn der Krabben.

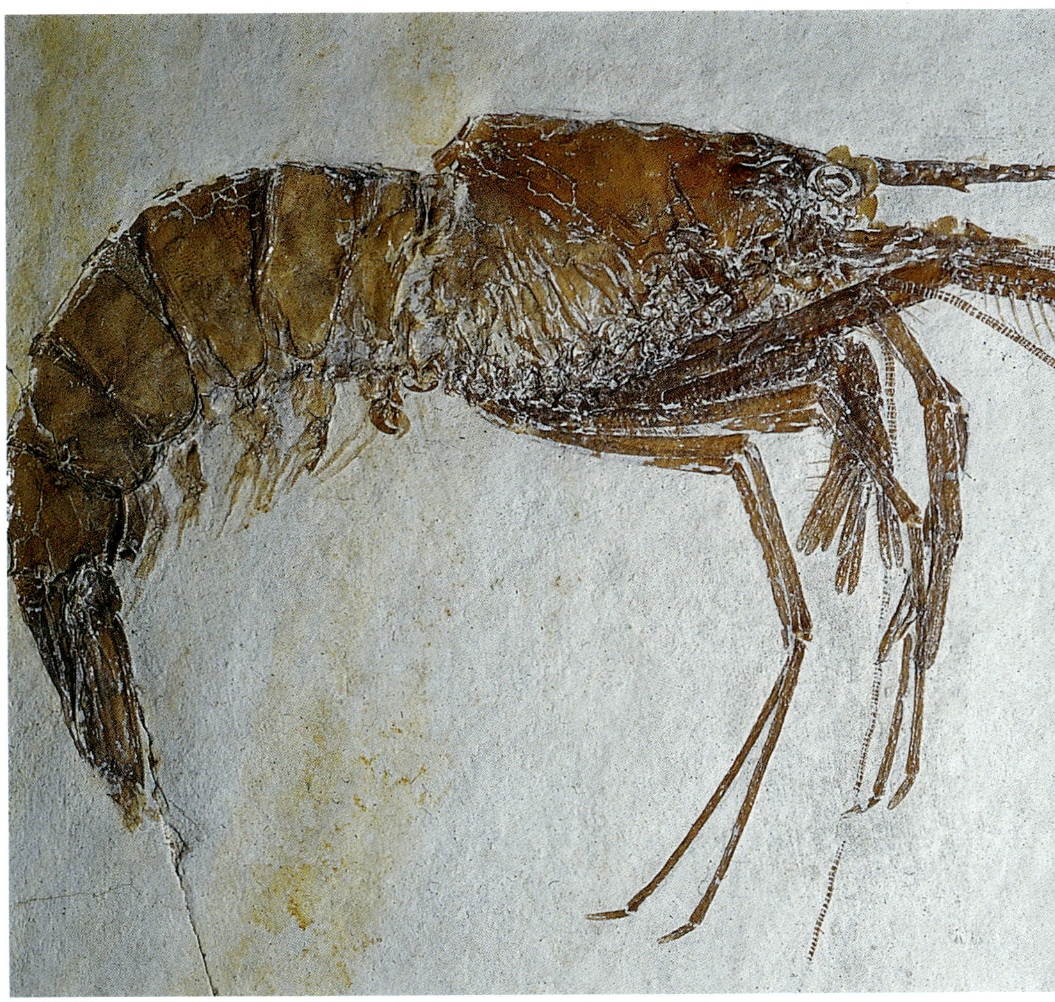

**RECHTS** Dieses schöne Exemplar der fossilen Garnelenart *Aeger tipularius* ordnet man dem Mittleren Jura zu, sein Alter wird auf 170 Millionen Jahre geschätzt. Es wurde in Süddeutschland gefunden. Sein Körperbau ähnelt dem seiner heute lebenden Verwandten stark.

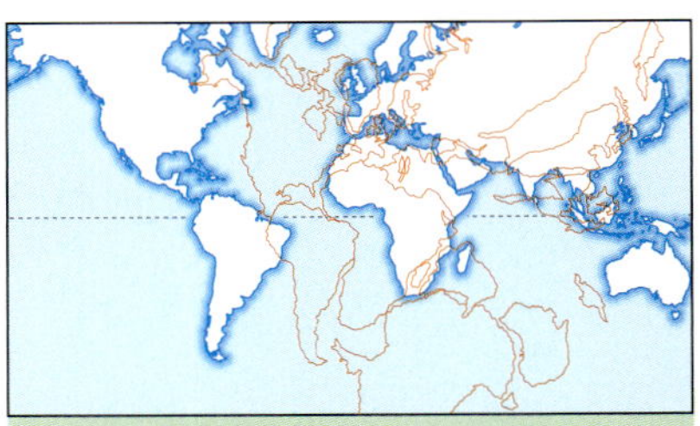

**ÜBERSICHT (TIERE)**

***Eryon***

**Bedeutung des Namens:** Rotes (Tier)

**Periode:** Jura bis Kreide

**Hauptgruppe:** Arthropoda (Crustacea)

**Größe:** 10 Zentimeter

**Nahrung:** Materiepartikel vom Meeresboden, Aas

**Fossilfundstätten:** Vor allem auf der Nordhalbkugel

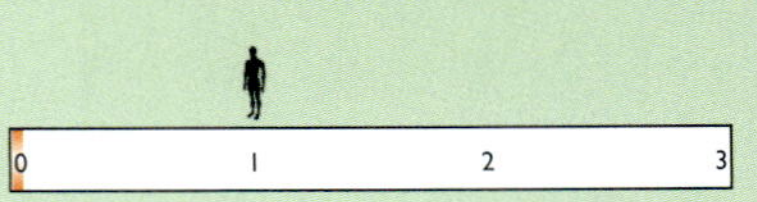

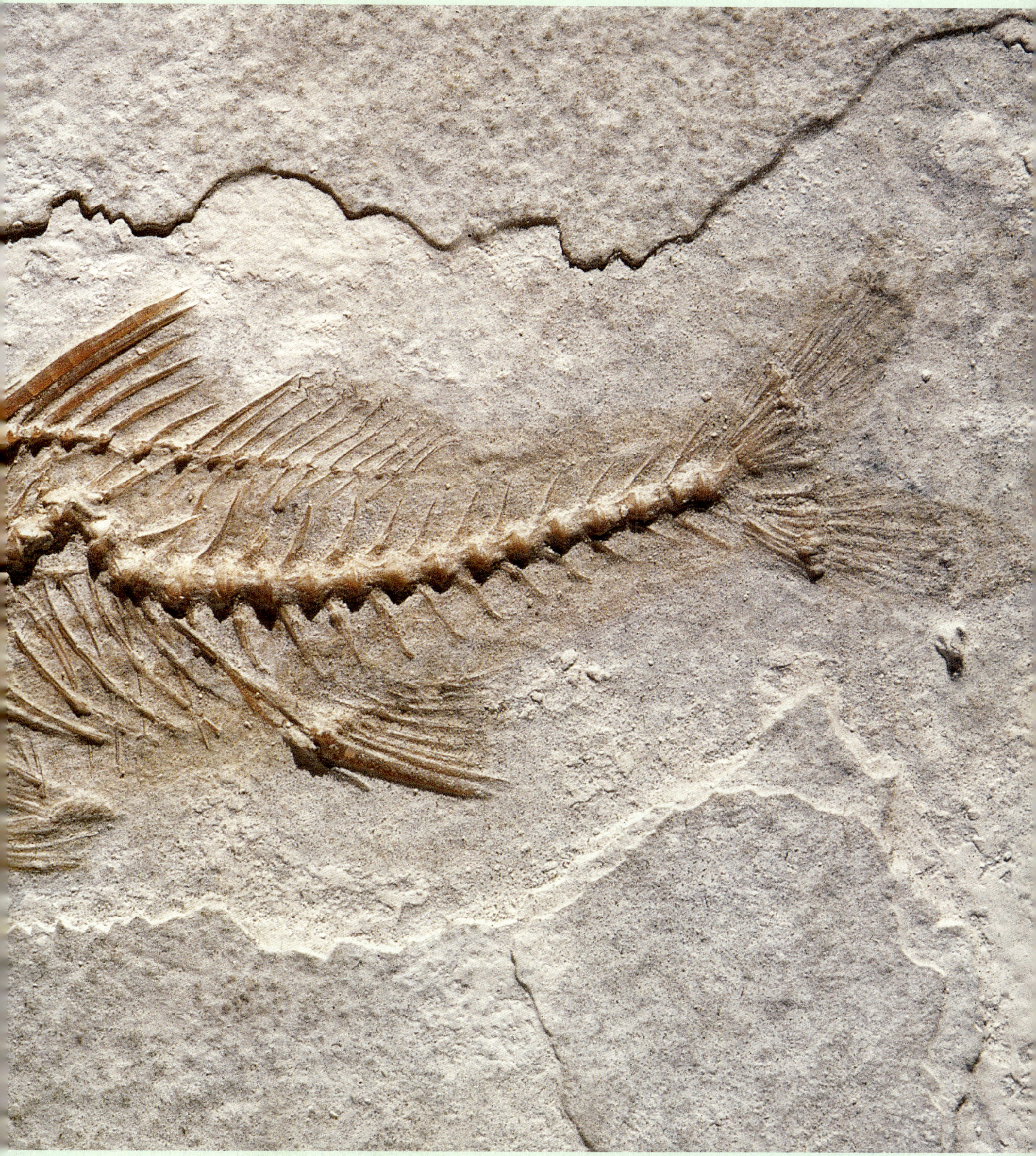

# Hemicyclaspis

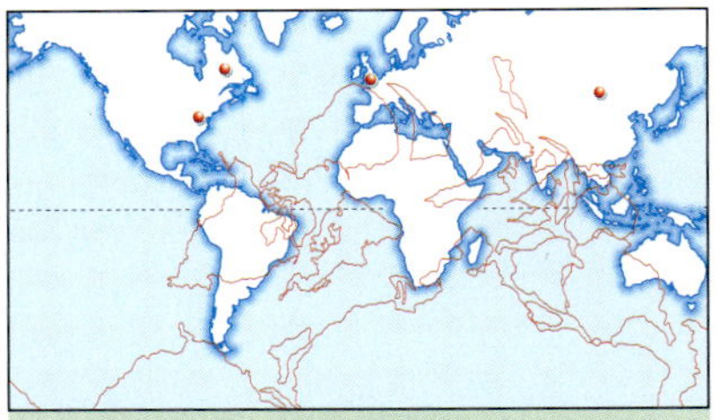

**ÜBERSICHT (TIERE)**

***Hemicyclaspis***

**Bedeutung des Namens:** Halbrunder Schild, halbrunde Platte

**Periode:** Obersilur, Unterdevon

**Hauptgruppe:** Osteostraci (Cephalaspida)

**Länge:** 13 Zentimeter

**Nahrung:** Partikel aus dem Schlamm des Meeresbodens

**Fossilfundstätten:** In Europa (England), Asien, im Osten Kanadas und der USA

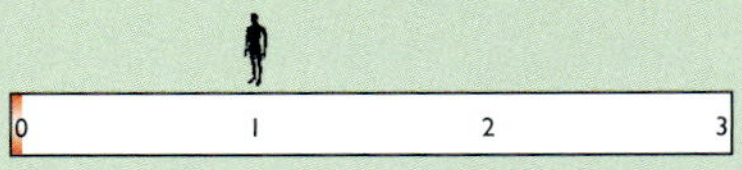


Die ältesten Fische aus dem Oberordovizium ähnelten in ihrer Körperform im Großen und Ganzen ihren heutigen Pendants. Sie besaßen allerdings keine echten paarigen Brust- und Bauchflossen, die den rezenten Fischen zur Stabilisierung und Steuerung dienen, und ihnen fehlten auch echte Kiefer. Diese ersten Fische werden Agnathen (Kieferlose) genannt. Sie hatten einen Saug- oder Raspelmund, der entweder rund oder schlitzförmig war. Es gab mehrere Hauptgruppen sowie vielgestaltige Spezies. Die meisten waren kleiner als eine Menschenhand. Zum Schutz vor Seeskorpionen und anderen starken Jägern trugen viele Arten in die Haut engebettete Knochenplatten. Dieses Merkmal hat diesen Lebewesen zu der Bezeichnung Ostracodermen (Schalenhäuter) verholfen.

*Hemicyclaspis* war nur 12–13 Zentimeter groß. Sein flacher, abgeplatteter Körper weist darauf hin, dass er zu den bodenlebenden Meerestieren gehörte. *Hemicyclaspis* existierte vom Obersilur an – bereits vor 420 Millionen Jahren –, sein Lebensraum war wahrscheinlich das Süßwasser. Er trug einen halbkreisförmigen knöchernen Kopfschild. Mit seinem Saugmund vorn an der Unterseite sammelte er aus dem Schlamm und Sand des Meeresbodens genießbare Partikel auf. Am oberen Teil des Kopfes befanden sich zwei dicht stehende Augen, weiter unten am Kopfschild saß links und rechts je ein flossenartiges Gebilde. Den Körper umschlossen Segmente aus schmalen, gewölbten Knochenplatten, die sich leicht gegeneinander neigen ließen. Der Körper verjüngte sich hinten zu einer Spitze, an deren Unterseite sich ein Lappen spannte, der wie ein Schwanz funktionierte. Ein steifer flossenartiger Auswuchs auf dem Rücken sorgte für Stabilität, wenn *Hemicyclaspis* – wie die rezenten Fische – seinen Körper in einer Kombination aus Schlängel- und Schwimmbewegungen von einer Seite zur anderen bog, um am See- oder Flussgrund entlangzupflügen oder sich dicht über dem Untergrund zu bewegen.

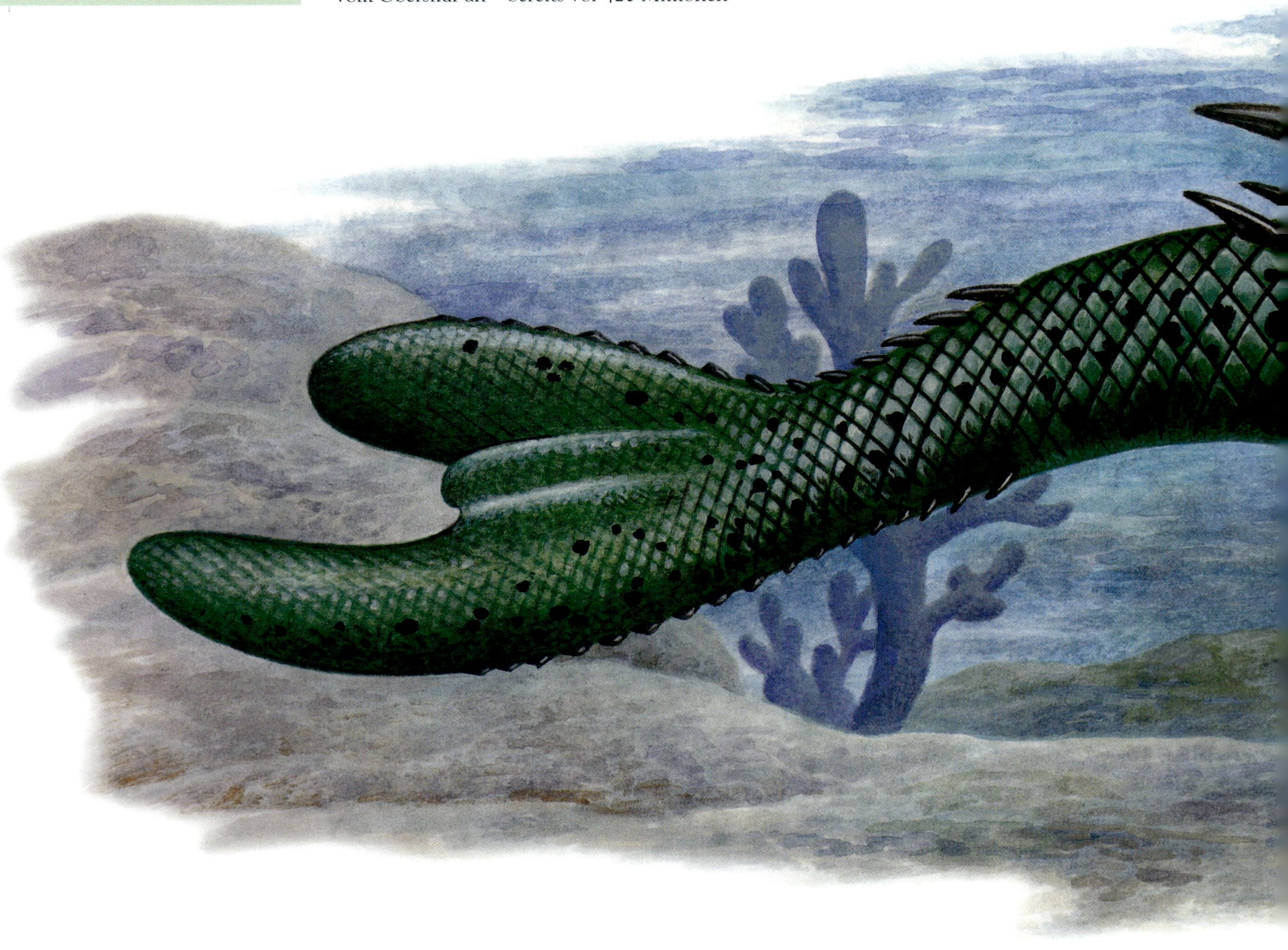

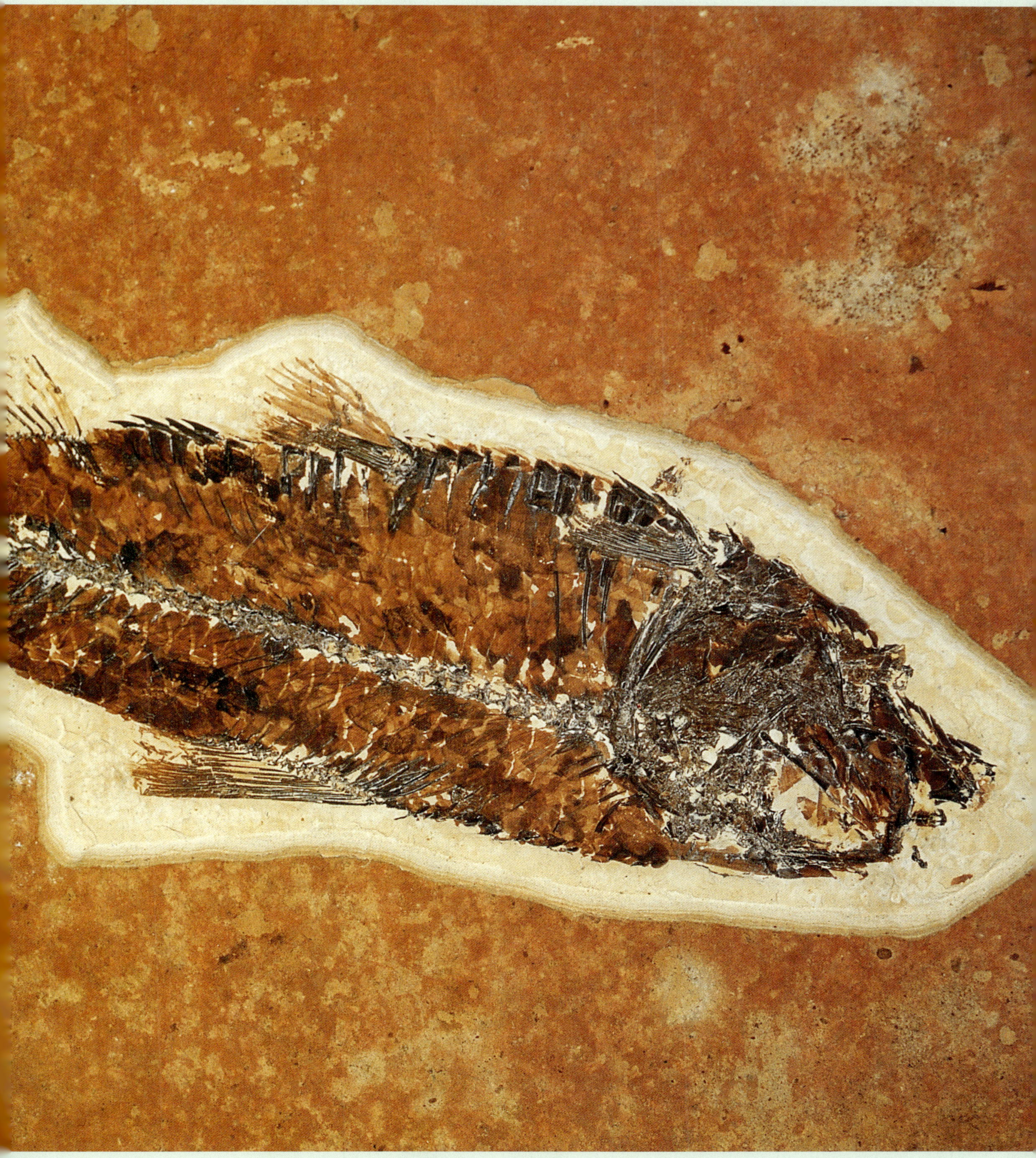

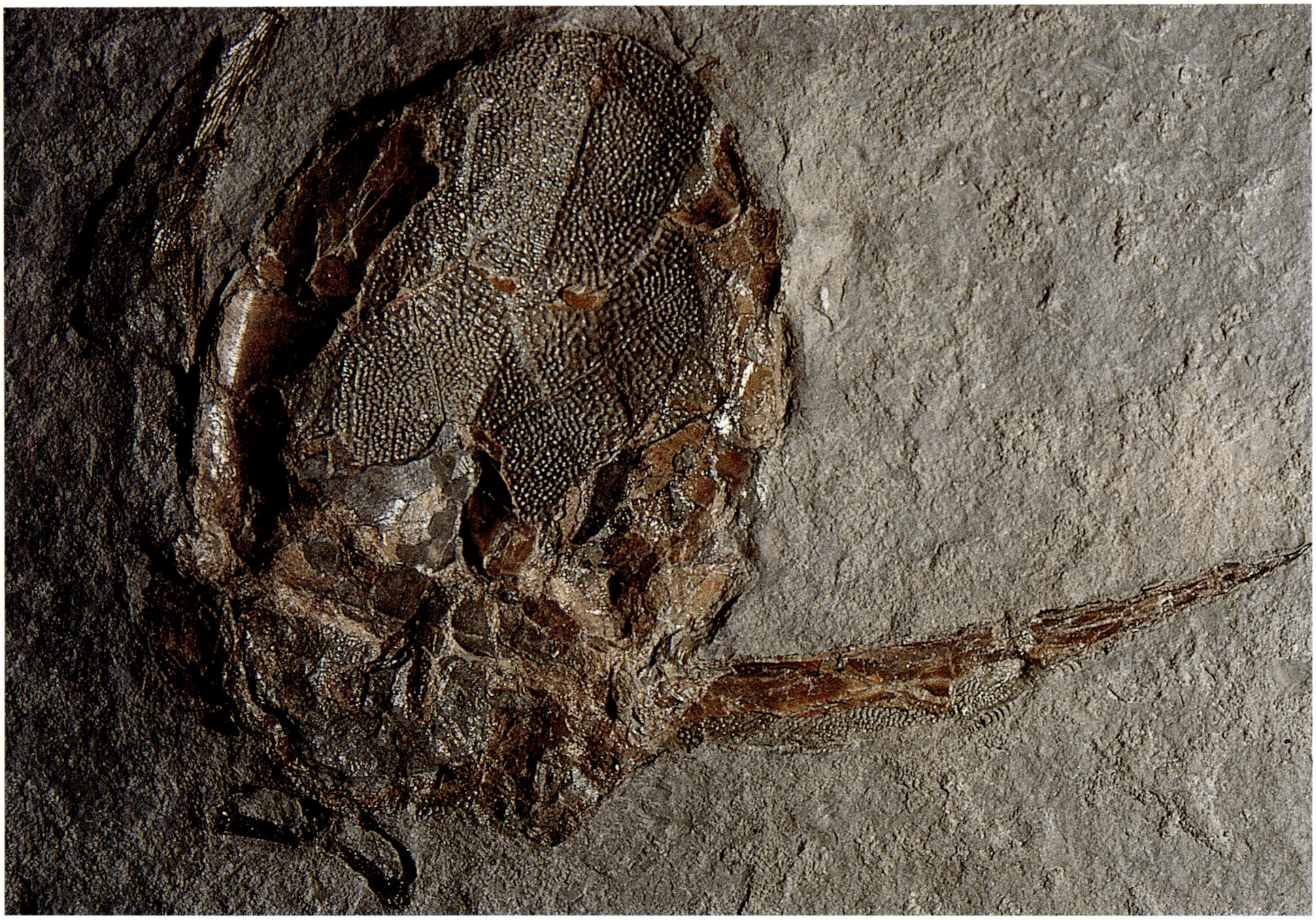

# BOTHRIOLEPIS

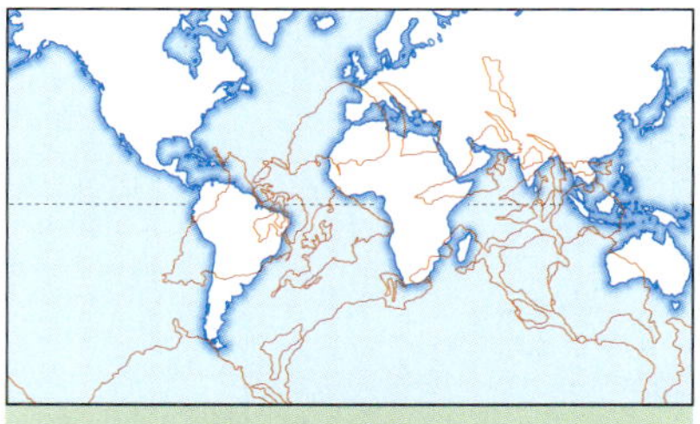

**ÜBERSICHT (TIERE)**
***Bothriolepis***
**Bedeutung des Namens:** Furchenschuppe
**Periode:** Oberdevon
**Hauptgruppe:** Placodermi (Antiarchi)
**Länge:** Bis zu 1 Meter
**Nahrung:** Kleine Nahrungsbrocken, Aas
**Fossilfundstätten:** Weltweit

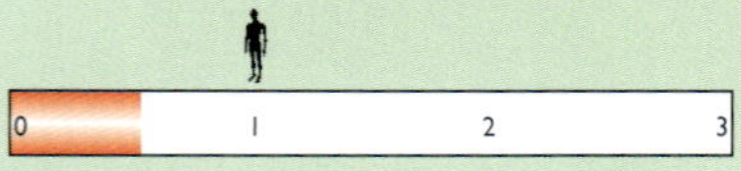


Dieser Fisch gehörte wie der massige *Dunkleosteus* zur Gruppe der Placodermen. Die Placodermen erschienen im Obersilur, sie zählten zu den ersten Fischen mit echten Kiefern und symmetrisch paarigen Seitenflossen. *Bothriolepis* lebte wie die meisten Panzerfische im Devon, der dem Obersilur folgenden Periode – vor über 350 Millionen Jahren. Kopf und Rumpf des Tieres waren durch gewölbte Knochenplatten geschützt. Von seinem riesigen Verwandten *Dunkleosteus* unterschied er sich allerdings deutlich, denn er war kleiner, nur etwa einen Meter lang, hatte einen flachen, unten abgeplatteten Körper und seine Augen saßen fast an der höchsten Stelle des Kopfes. Diese Gestalt ist charakteristisch für bodenlebende Fische. *Bothriolepis* bewegte sich wahrscheinlich nur langsam voran und siebte und sortierte dabei mit seinem Maul, das nur schwach entwickelte Kiefer hatte, kleine Tiere und andere genießbare Materie aus dem Sand und Schlamm heraus.

Das Seltsamste an *Bothriolepis* waren seine zwei „Arme". Es handelte sich dabei um Brustflossen, die wie bei den meisten Fischen beiderseits des Rumpfes, unten hinter dem Kopf, saßen. Diese Flossen waren lang und schlank und wurden von gegliederten Panzern aus miteinander verbundenen Knochenröhren gebildet. Sie wurden vielleicht zum Kriechen im Wasser benutzt, doch die Winkel der „Arm"glieder und deren Beweglichkeitsgrad erscheinen ungeeignet dafür. Vielleicht stocherte und grub der Fisch mit den „Armen" im Gewässergrund, um versteckte Nahrungsteilchen aufzuspüren und zu lockern. Einer anderen These zufolge benutzte *Bothriolepis* diese Körperteile um an Land von einem Gewässer zum anderen zu kriechen. In Gesteinen aus Süßwasser- und Meereshabitaten wurden nämlich Überreste dieser Fische gefunden, und Fossilvergleiche lassen darauf schließen, dass *Bothriolepis* möglicherweise einfache Lungen besaß, mit denen er Sauerstoff aus der Luft aufnahm (siehe Seite 68, *Dipterus*).

**OBEN** Die eigenartigen Brustflossen des *Bothriolepis* waren zu gegliederten Röhren umgebildet – zu welchem Zweck ist unklar.

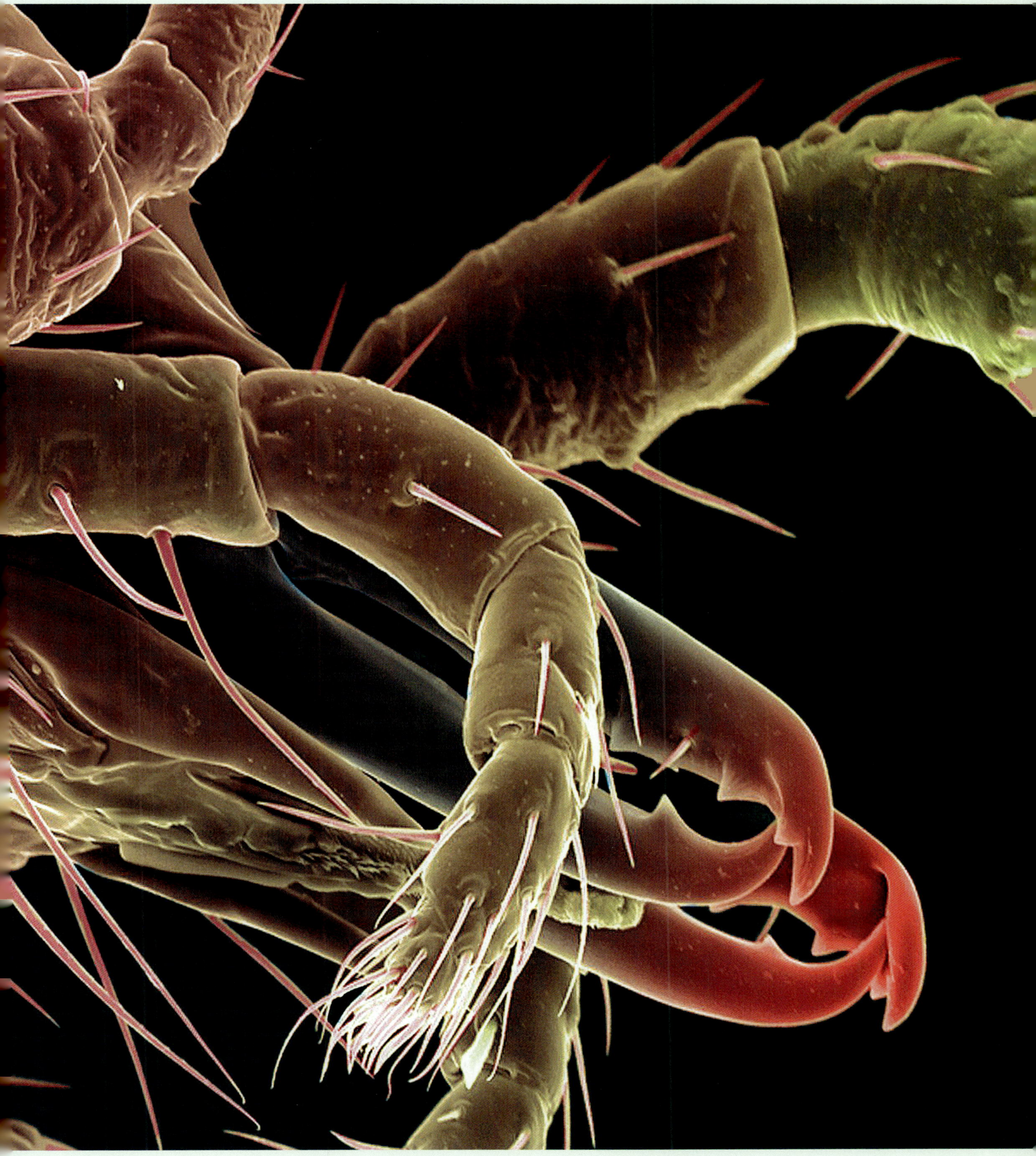

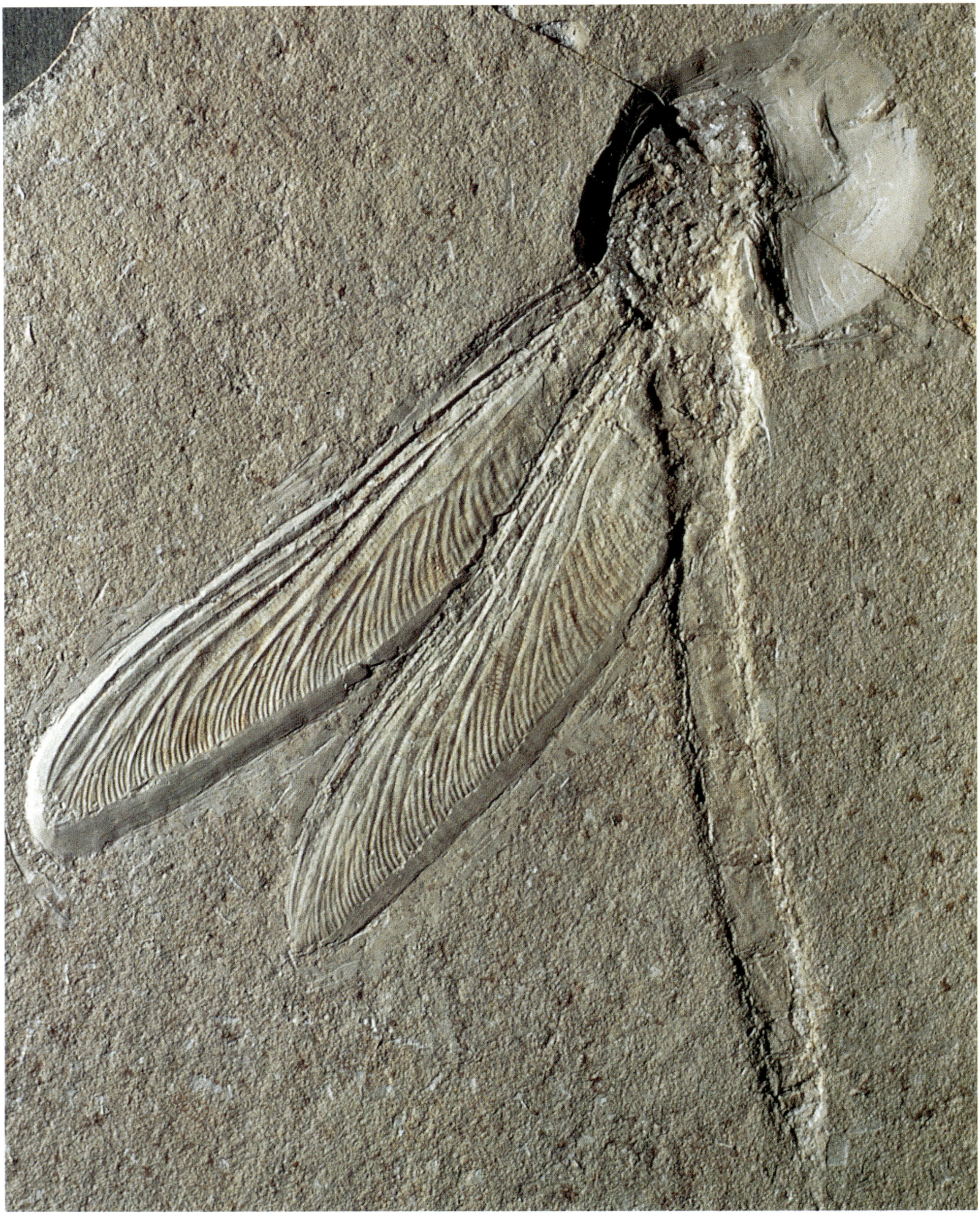

# Meganeura

In der Zeit des Oberkarbon herrschte auf dem größten Teil der Landmassen unserer Erde reichlich Feuchtigkeit und Wärme vor. Dieses Klima förderte das rasche Wachstum ausgedehnter Wälder aus riesigen Farnen und anderen Pflanzen. Auch die Tiere dieser Zeit, beispielsweise *Arthropleura* (siehe unten), erreichten eine enorme Größe. Zwischen den großen Pflanzen flog auch *Meganeura*, das größte Insekt aller Zeiten, umher. Es handelte sich um eine Art Libelle aus der Gruppe der Odonata oder Wasserjungfern. Libellen gehören zu den ältesten Fluginsekten; sie erschienen vor rund 320 Millionen Jahren und weisen einen bis heute größtenteils unveränderten Flügelbau auf. Da sie im Unterschied zu den meisten anderen geflügelten Insekten ihre Flügel nicht im rechten Winkel bewegen und längs über dem Rücken zusammenlegen können, müssen sie sie seitwärts nach außen halten.

*Meganeura* erreichte eine Länge von 35 Zentimetern, die Flügel maßen von einer Spitze zur anderen 70 Zentimeter. Die Lebensweise des Tieres unterschied sich höchstwahrscheinlich nicht von der rezenter Libellen. Das Insekt war ein schneller Räuber, der sich blitzschnell und akrobatisch drehen und wenden, mit seinen riesigen Augen Beute aufspüren und das Opfer mit seinen Beinen wie mit einem Korb einfangen konnte. Die Beute wurde später, wenn *Meganeura* sich auf irgendeinem Sitzplatz ausruhte, zu den kräftigen Beißwerkzeugen geführt, zerrissen und aufgefressen. Die Beine der Urlibelle waren, verglichen mit denen der heutigen Libellen, länger und kräftiger und hatten fast die Größe einer Menschenhand. Vielleicht machte *Meganeura* auch im Sturzflug Jagd auf Kakerlaken und andere am Boden lebende Insekten.

Die Insekten traten vor über 400 Millionen Jahren auf und zählten vermutlich zu den ersten Gruppen kleiner Tiere, die das Land besiedelten. Unter den frühen Formen der Landlebewesen befanden sich prähistorische Versionen der Silberfische, der Borstenschwänze sowie der flugunfähigen Kakerlaken und Ohrwürmer. Die Fähigkeit des Fliegens kam möglicherweise vor rund 350 Millionen Jahren, zu Beginn des Karbon, auf. Einige der bekanntesten rezenten Insekten erschienen verhältnismäßig spät. Das trifft beispielsweise auf die Bienen und die Wespen zu, die sich erst mit der Kreidezeit entfalteten; ihre rapide Entwicklung in dieser Periode hing wahrscheinlich mit dem Erscheinen der Blütenpflanzen zusammen.

**LINKS** Diese fossilierte Libelle aus einer mit *Meganeura* verwandten Gattung wurde im feinkörnigen Solnhofener Plattenkalk gefunden. Das Tier lebte im Jura.

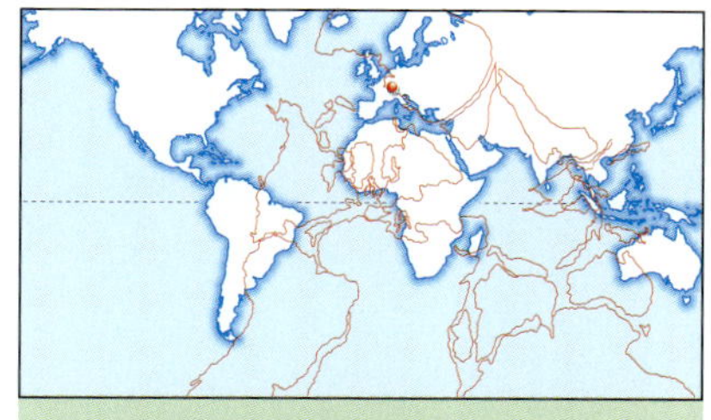

**ÜBERSICHT (TIERE)**
***Meganeura***
**Bedeutung des Namens:** Großes Fadenwerk (auf die Flügel bezogen)
**Periode:** Oberkarbon
**Hauptgruppe:** Arthropoda (Insecta)
**Länge:** Körper einschließlich Kopf 35 Zentimeter
**Nahrung:** Fluginsekten
**Fossilfundstätten:** In Europa

# Arthropleura

Zu den ersten Landbewohnern gehörten auch die Myriopoden aus der großen Gruppe der Arthropoden oder Gliederfüßer (siehe Seite 46). Deren heutige Vertreter sind beispielsweise die Diplopoden (Doppelfüßer) und die Chilopoden (Hundertfüßer). Als eine Urform der Doppelfüßer kann man *Arthropleura* betrachten. *Arthropleura* lebte lange nachdem die ersten Lebewesen ihrer Art an Land erschienen waren. Das Tier erreichte eine außergewöhnliche Körpergröße. Die heute existierenden riesigen Doppelfüßer in den Tropen werden nur selten größer als 25 Zentimeter. *Arthropleura* dagegen war bis zu zwei Meter lang, dabei aber recht breit und nicht sehr hoch, so dass das Tier einem „laufenden Tisch" glich. Es lebte im Karbon, vor mehr als 300 Millionen Jahren, und war – auch wenn es nicht den Seeskorpionen (siehe Seite 52), den riesigen Wasser bewohnenden Arthropoden, gleich kam – der größte landlebende Gliederfüßer, den die Wissenschaft aus dieser Zeit kennt.

*Arthropleura* besaß einen breiten Körperpanzer aus gelenkig verbundenen schmalen Segmenten, der an den Seiten von breiten Dornen gesäumt war. Oberflächlich ähnelte das Tier der Kellerassel von heute oder vielleicht einem Trilobiten, doch diese waren Vertreter anderer Arthropodengruppen. Unter dem Panzer befanden sich die Mundwerkzeuge, die sich zum Sortieren und Zerkauen weicher Nahrung, vielleicht pflanzlicher Materie, eigneten. Das Karbon war eine Zeit der warmen Sümpfe und der „Kohlewälder". Riesige Farngewächse und andere üppige Vegetation bedeckten das Land wie ein Teppich und lieferten Pflanzenfressern aller Art unermessliche Mengen an Nahrung. *Arthropleura* besaß rund sechzig gegliederte Laufbeinpaare – zwei Paar an jedem Körpersegment –, die das schwere Tier trugen. Doppelfüßer sind nicht mit den Hundertfüßern zu verwechseln, die nicht zwei, sondern nur ein Beinpaar je Segment haben und ausgesprochen räuberisch leben.

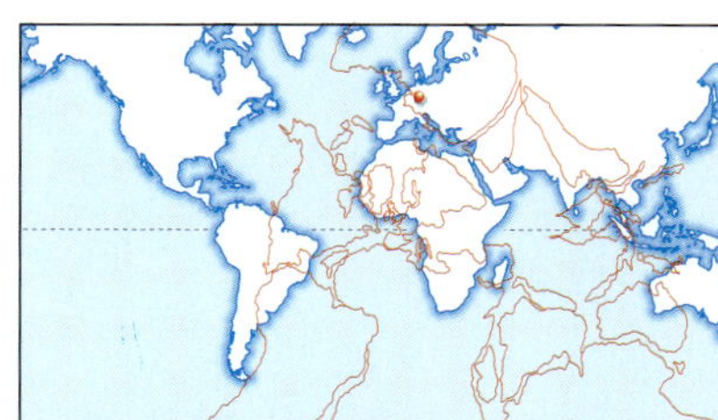

**ÜBERSICHT (TIERE)**
***Arthropleura***
**Bedeutung des Namens:** Gliederseiten
**Periode:** Karbon
**Hauptgruppe:** Arthropoda (Diplopoda)
**Länge:** Bis 2 Meter
**Nahrung:** Pflanzliche Materie
**Fossilfundstätten:** In Deutschland

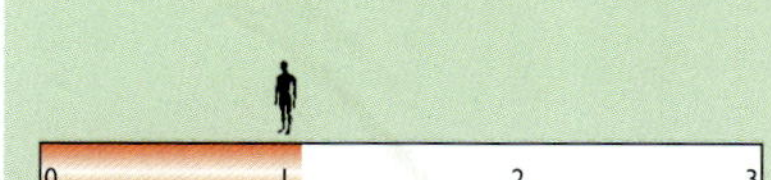

# Aysheaia und Rhyniella

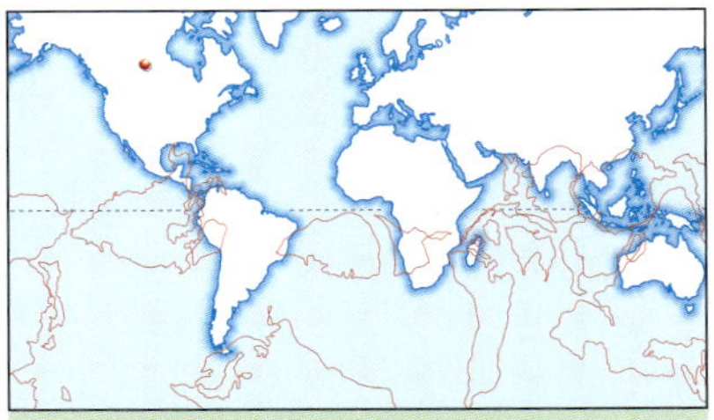

**ÜBERSICHT (TIERE)**

***Aysheaia***

**Bedeutung des Namens:** Nach dem Berg Ayshea benannt

**Periode:** Kambrium

**Hauptgruppe:** Onychophora

**Länge:** Wenige Zentimeter

**Nahrung:** Vermutlich Schwämme und verrottende Materie

**Fossilfundstätten:** In Kanada

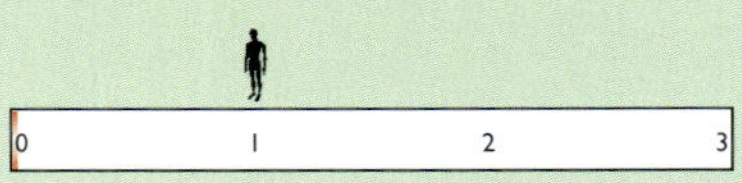


Die größte Tiergruppe der heutigen Zeit ist die der Insekten; ihr Artenreichtum übersteigt bei weitem die Gesamtzahl der Spezies aller anderen Lebewesen. Ihr Ursprung liegt allerdings im Dunkeln. Die Insekten gehören wie Krebstiere, Spinnen, Skorpione, Doppelfüßer und Hundertfüßer, wie die ausgestorbenen Trilobiten und alle anderen Lebewesen mit gegliederten Extremitäten zu den Arthropoden (siehe Seite 46), und die Gliederfüßer gehen möglicherweise auf einen gemeinsamen Vorfahren zurück, der im Kambrium, vor mehr als 500 Millionen Jahren, existierte und vermutlich ein inzwischen ausgestorbener Wurm war. Eine Vorstellung davon, wie ein „Wurmgliederfüßer", eine Zwischenform von Wurm und Arthropod, vielleicht ausgesehen haben mag, vermittelt uns *Aysheaia* aus dem fossilienreichen Burgess-Schiefer in Kanada, der aus dem mittleren Kambrium stammt (siehe Seite 38). *Aysheaia* besaß den segmentierten Körper eines Wurms, doch auch zwanzig zweireihig angeordnete Stummelfüßchen. Das Tier ähnelte den rezenten Onyphoren (Stummelfüßer), die im Unterschied zum Meeresbewohner *Aysheaia* an Land lebten. Deren Beine bewegen sich hydraulisch, durch den Druck körpereigener Flüssigkeit, wie der Körper eines Wurms, und obwohl sie keine Gelenke besitzen, funktionieren sie doch als Laufbeine.

*Rhyniella* hatte Ähnlichkeit mit den Springschwänzen, heute lebenden insektenartigen Lebewesen, die wie *Rhyniella* ungeflügelt sind. Manche Klassifikationen stellen die Springschwänze zu den Insekten, andere lassen sie als eigenständige, eng mit den Insekten verwandte Gruppe der Collembolen (Springschwänze) erscheinen. Springschwänze sind – von uns größtenteils unbemerkt – in großer Zahl in vielen Lebensräumen, vor allem im Boden und in Laubstreu zu Hause. Sie ernähren sich von pflanzlichem oder tierischem Abfall. Die meisten sind kleiner als dieses „o". *Rhyniella* war größer, etwa einen Zentimeter lang, und lebte wahrscheinlich ebenfalls von Pflanzenresten.

**RECHTS** Die heutigen Collembolen (Springschwänze) haben sich gegenüber ihren Pendants aus dem Devon, die Wegbereiter für das Leben an Land waren, kaum verändert.

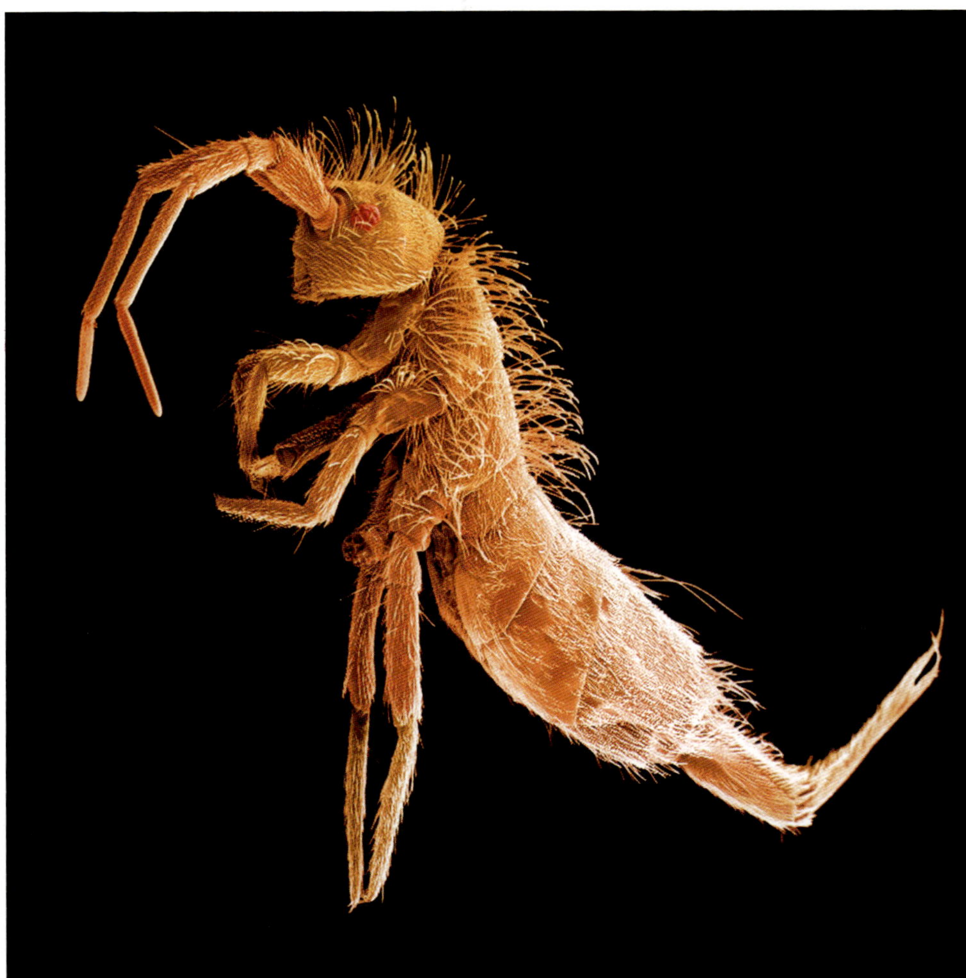

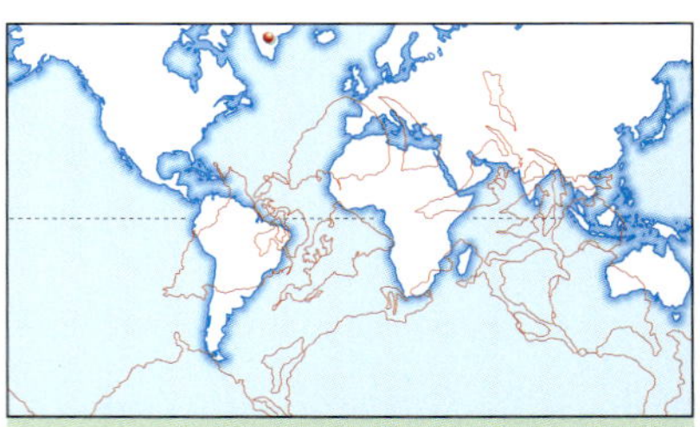

**ÜBERSICHT (TIERE)**

***Rhyniella***

**Bedeutung des Namens:** Kleinschnabel

**Periode:** Devon

**Hauptgruppe:** Arthropoda (Insecta)

**Größe:** 1 Zentimeter

**Nahrung:** Pflanzliche und tierische Reste

**Fossilfundstätten:** In Grönland

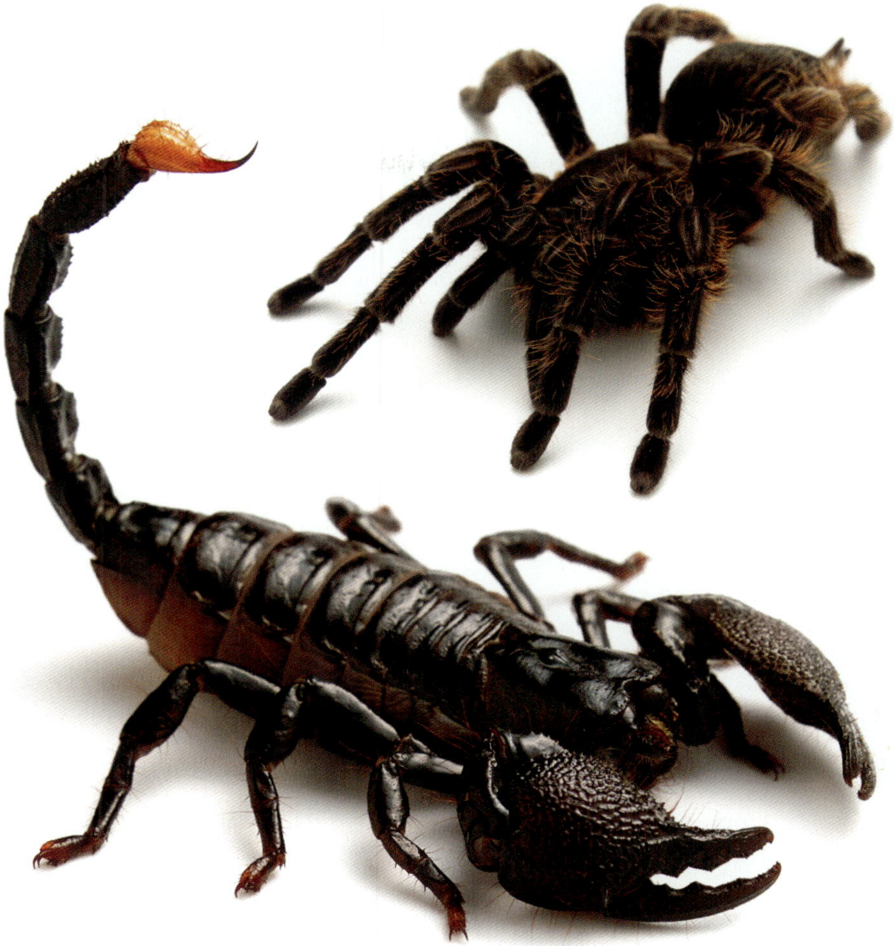

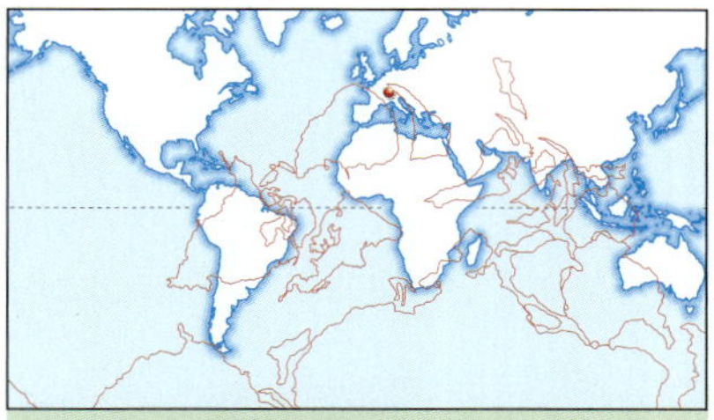

**ÜBERSICHT (TIERE)**
***Arthrolycosa***
**Bedeutung des Namens:** Wolf(sspinne) mit Gelenken
**Periode:** Karbon
**Hauptgruppe:** Arthropoda (Arachnida)
**Größe:** Körper einschließlich Kopf 5 Zentimeter
**Nahrung:** Kleinere Tiere
**Fossilfundstätten:** In Europa

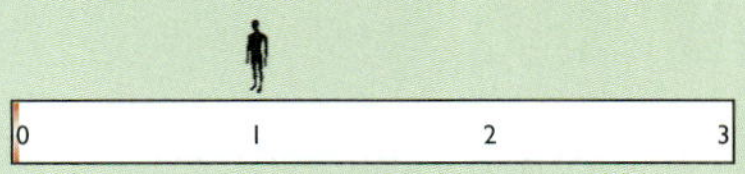


**LINKS OBEN** Die rezenten Taranteln gehören zur Gruppe der Mygalomorphen. Sie gelten als „wenig entwickelt", weil sie noch viele Merkmale ihrer prähistorischen Verwandten, darunter auch *Arthrolycosa*, besitzen.

**LINKS UNTEN** *Palaeophonus* hätte den heutigen Skorpionen in den meisten charakteristischen Merkmalen geähnelt, denn er besitzt große Greifscheren, vier Beinpaare und einen gebogenen Schwanz mit spitzem Giftstachel am Ende.

# Palaeophonus und Arthrolycosa

In diesem Buch war bereits an verschiedenen Stellen die Rede von den Cheliceraten aus der Gruppe der Arthropoden. Es ging dabei unter anderem auch um die Furcht erregenden Eurypteriden oder Seeskorpione (siehe Seite 51). Bei diesen Tieren handelte es sich nicht um echte Skorpione, die in der Dunkelheit umherstreifen und ihren Giftstachel emporrecken – wenngleich auch die echten Skorpione eine sehr lange Stammesgeschichte haben. Einer ihrer frühen Vertreter war *Palaeophonus*. Er war etwa so lang wie ein menschlicher Finger, besaß große Greifarme und starke Kieferklauen, mit denen er seine Beute zerteilte. Sein schmaler, schwanzartiger Hinterkörper endete in einer Spitze, mit der er vermutlich sein Gift in Beutetiere oder Feinde injizierte. Früher hielt man *Palaeophonus* für ein Landlebewesen, doch ihm fehlten die Luftöffnungen zum Atmen, wie sie bei Land bewohnenden Typen vorhanden sind, und lebte deshalb wahrscheinlich im Wasser.

Die Skorpione gehören zu einer Untergruppe der Scherenfüßer, zu den Arachniden, die über vier Laufbeinpaare verfügen. Im Karbon erschienen noch mehr Arachniden an Land – die Spinnen.

Ein typisches Beispiel aus dem Karbon war die nahezu handgroße *Arthrolycosa*. Dieses frühe Lebewesen ähnelte von Anfang an stark den heutigen Spinnen, insbesondere den Wolfsspinnen. Die frühesten Spinnen machten auf ihren acht Beinen Jagd auf Beute; erst spätere Vertreter fingen ihre Nahrung mit Netzen. Die beiden kürzeren Gliedmaßen zu beiden Seiten des Kopfes waren Kiefertaster, mit denen *Arthrolycosa* ihren Weg suchte.

*Arthrolycosa* besaß acht über die Vorderseite des Kopfes verteilte Augen. Darunter in der Mitte saßen zwei hauerartige Kieferklauen, an denen die Beutetiere aufgespießt wurden.

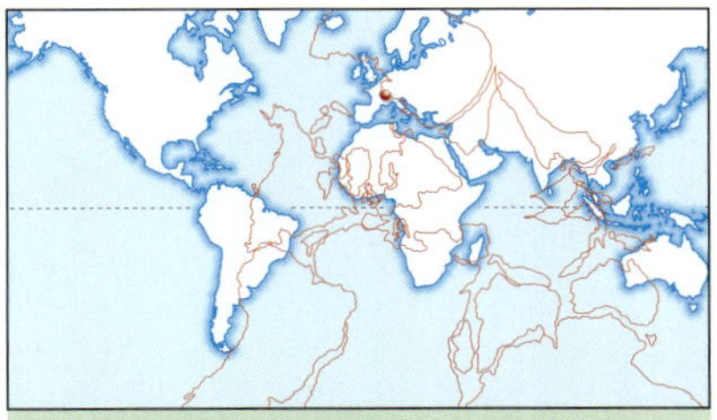

**ÜBERSICHT (TIERE)**
***Palaeophonus***
**Bedeutung des Namens:** Mörder aus dem Altertum
**Periode:** Obersilur
**Hauptgruppe:** Arthropoda (Arachnida)
**Länge:** 7–8 Zentimeter (mit Schwanz, ohne Greifscheren)
**Nahrung:** Kleine Beutetiere
**Fossilfundstätten:** In Europa

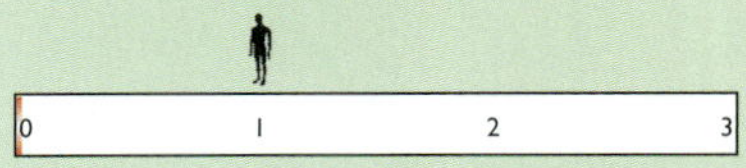

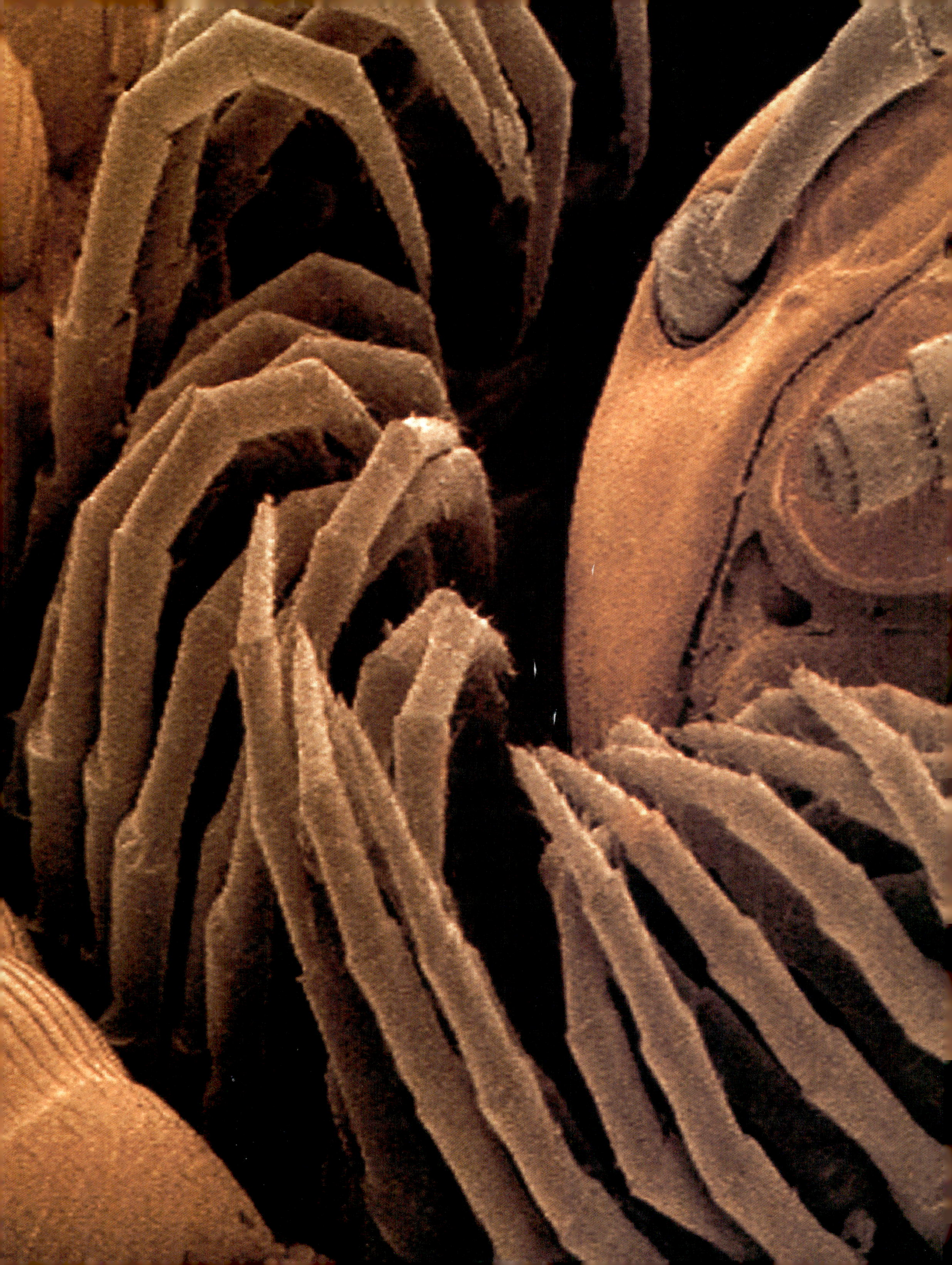

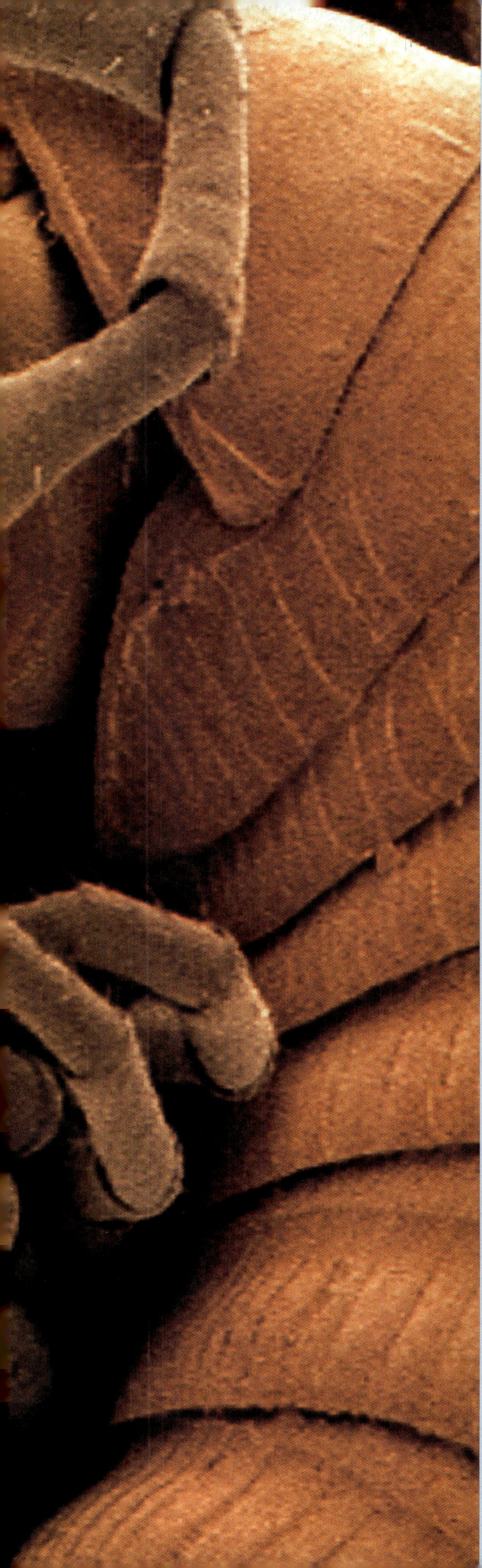

KAPITEL ZWEI

# DIE EROBERER DES FESTLANDS

*Vor rund 400 Millionen Jahren, im Devon, setzte die Wanderung wasserlebender Geschöpfe auf das Land ein. Die Tiere wanden und schlängelten sich aus dem nassen Element heraus, schoben sich durch die Sümpfe und bewegten sich dann auf trockenes Land. Vor 230 Millionen Jahre, am Ende des Perm, war schließlich der Weg für die Entwicklung der Dinosaurier geebnet.*

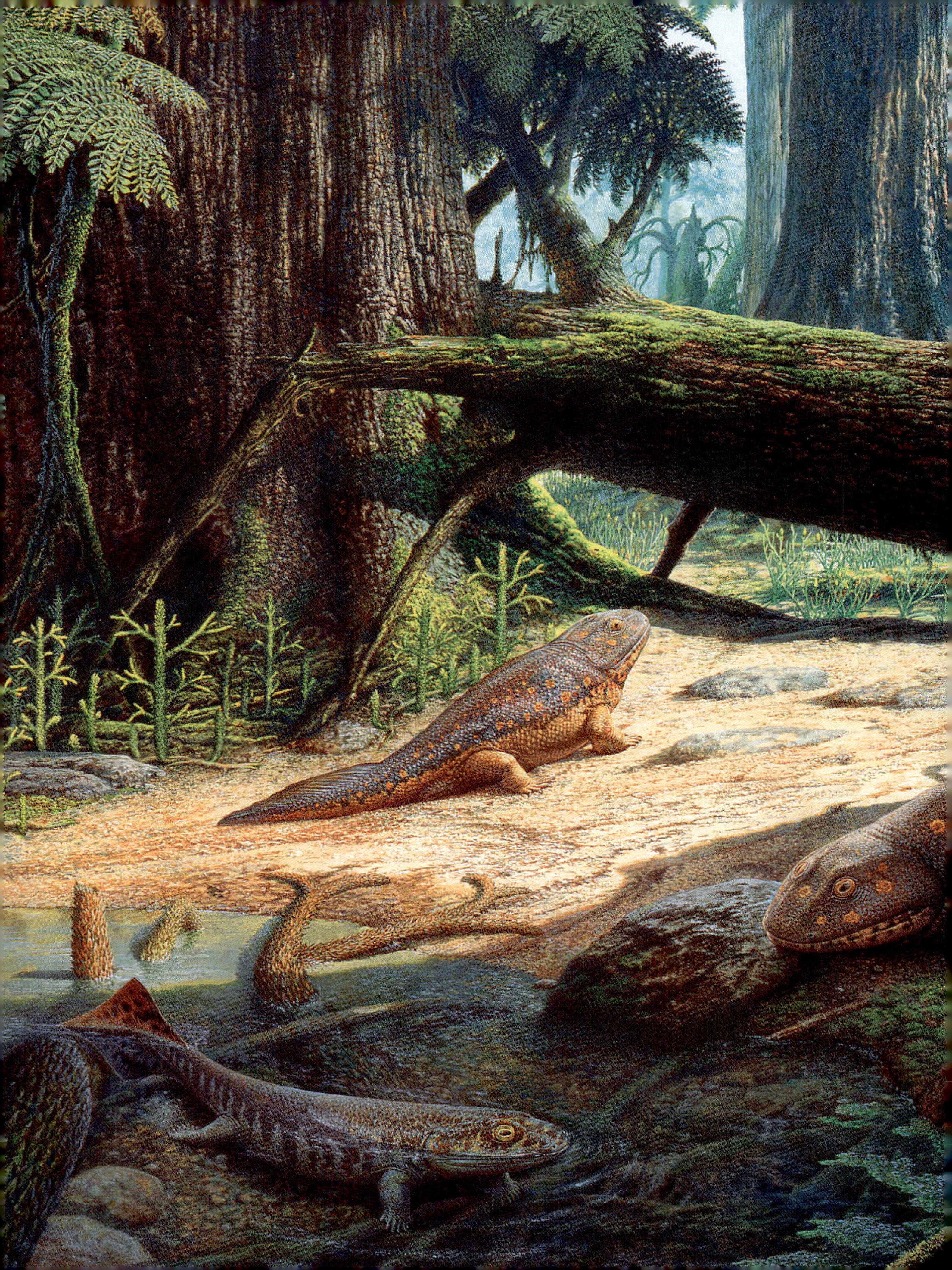

# AUS DEM WASSER HERAUS

***Viele populärwissenschaftliche Veröffentlichungen zur Vorgeschichte beginnen mit den Dinosauriern, was vielleicht den Eindruck erweckt, diese Tiere seien die ersten Landlebewesen oder gar die frühesten Kreaturen überhaupt gewesen. Die Wirbeltiere gewöhnten sich aber weit über 100 Millionen Jahre vor dem Erscheinen der ersten Dinosaurier an das Leben auf dem Land. Und schon lange vor dieser Zeit krochen Milben, Doppelfüßer, Skorpione, Insekten und andere Wirbellose auf dem Trockenen umher oder kletterten auf die prähistorischen Pflanzen. Die Wanderung von Wirbeltieren aus dem Wasser auf das Land war – im buchstäblichen Sinn wie auch für die Evolution – ein großer Schritt. Dieser Schritt erschloss den Tieren gänzlich neue Lebensräume, wo sich größere landlebende Wesen bei kaum vorhandener Konkurrenz den neuen Nahrungsquellen und Umweltbedingungen anpassen konnten.***

## VON DER FLOSSE ZUM BEIN

Ein Schlüsselereignis in der Evolution war die Entwicklung der Fischflossen zu Gliedmaßen, die sich zum Laufen eigneten. Diese Veränderung nahm ihren Anfang bei bestimmten Sarcopterygiern oder Fleischflossern, einer Gruppe, die noch heute in den Quastenflossern und Lungenfischen fortlebt (siehe Kapitel Eins). Die Flossen dieser Tiere besaßen eine Basis aus Knochen und Muskeln, die Form und Bewegung der Flossenfläche steuerten. Bei einigen Fleischflossern vergrößerte sich die Basis allmählich, während der Flossenteil schrumpfte, da die Fische das Anhängsel benutzten um sich von Flächen abzustoßen, die härter waren und einen größeren Widerstand boten als Wasser. Die Knochen wurden länger und die Muskulatur kräftiger, bis die Flosse schließlich verschwunden war und der Fleischlappen zu einem Bein wurde.

## TETRAPODEN

Die Anzahl der Gliedmaßen bei den ersten Landwirbeltieren geht auf die bei Fischen üblichen zwei Flossenpaare, die Brust- und die Bauchflossen, zurück. Das Ergebnis der oben beschriebenen Veränderung waren also Tiere mit vier Beinen, die Tetrapoden (Vierfüßer). Einige ihrer frühesten Exemplare, die im Oberdevon, vor mehr als 360 Millionen Jahren, lebten, werden auf den folgenden Seiten vorgestellt. Früher nahm man an, die Vierfüßer seien ausgesprochene „Landläufer" gewesen, da die treibende Kraft hinter der Entwicklung von Flossen zu Gliedmaßen die Notwendigkeit war, beim Austrocknen eines Tümpels zum nächsten zu kriechen. Neuere Untersuchungen lassen jedoch den Schluss zu, dass sich die Vierfüßer durchaus im Wasser entwickelt haben können. Ihre Gliedmaßen waren anfangs keine Laufbeine, sondern Paddel zum Schwimmen oder zum Beiseiteschieben von Wasserpflanzen. Erst später wagten sich die Tetrapoden wirklich aus ihrem Wassermilieu hinaus aufs Trockene, als aus den Paddeln Beine wurden.

## DAS LEBEN AUF TROCKENEM LAND

Die Laufgliedmaßen waren nur eines von vielen Merkmalen, die die Vierfüßer zur Eroberung des trockenen Landes brauchten. Weitere Besonderheiten waren Lungen, die im Unterschied zu den Kiemen den Sauerstoff nicht aus dem Wasser filterten, sondern durch Einatmen von Luft gewannen. Lungen waren nichts gänzlich Neues – verschiedene Gruppen von Fischen hatten diese Organe bereits entwickelt, vielleicht um in warmen, unbewegten Tümpeln mit sauerstoffarmem Wasser durch das zusätzliche Luftholen ihren Sauerstoffbedarf zu decken. (Verschiedene Arten Luft schluckender Fische, beispielsweise der weltweit größte Süßwasserfisch Arapaima aus der Gruppe der Knochenzüngler, tun das noch heute.) Ein weiteres Erfordernis für das Leben an Land war eine Haut, die verhinderte, dass Feuchtigkeit und Körperflüssigkeit an der Luft zu schnell verloren gingen, was im Wasser kein Problem gewesen war. Die meisten frühen Tetrapoden waren Lebewesen, die man vielleicht als „Amphibien" bezeichnen könnte, obgleich „Amphib" in neueren Klassifikationen ein ungenauer, beschreibender Begriff für verschiedene Tiergruppen ist. Eine Veränderung, die diese „Amphibien" wahrscheinlich nicht meisterten, war die Fortpflanzung außerhalb des Wassers. Sie lebten in ihrem Jugendstadium, als Larven, noch immer im Wasser. Die völlige Unabhängigkeit von diesem Lebensraum kam erst später, als die Reptilien auftraten, die beschalte Eier legten (siehe Seite 88).

**VORHERGEHENDE SEITE** Farbige REM-Aufnahme eines zusammengeringelten *Brachydesmus superus* in 15-facher Vergrößerung. Die Arthropoden, zu denen die Doppelfüßer zählen, waren die ersten Landlebewesen.

**LINKS** Tetrapoden (vierbeinige Wirbeltiere) der Gattung *Ichthyostega* an einem Tümpel zwischen Riesenfarnen und ähnlichen Urzeitpflanzen der feuchtwarmen devonischen Wälder, die es einst auf dem Gebiet des heutigen kalten Grönland gab.

# Ichthyostega und Acanthostega

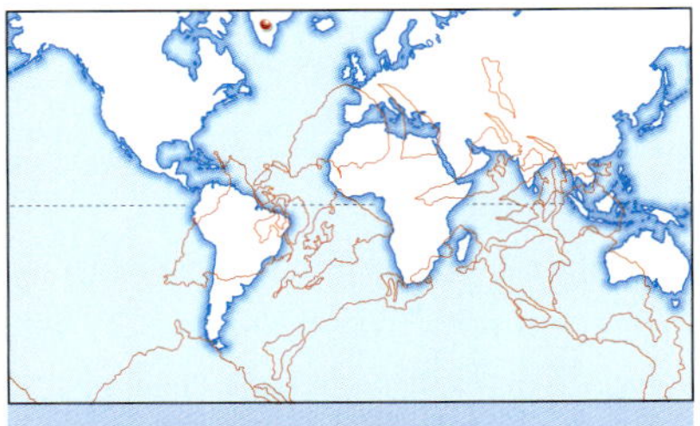

**ÜBERSICHT (TIERE)**

***Ichthyostega***

**Bedeutung des Namens:** Fischplatte

**Periode:** Oberdevon

**Hauptgruppe:** Tetrapoda

**Länge:** 1 Meter

**Nahrung:** Tiere

**Fossilfundstätten:** In Grönland

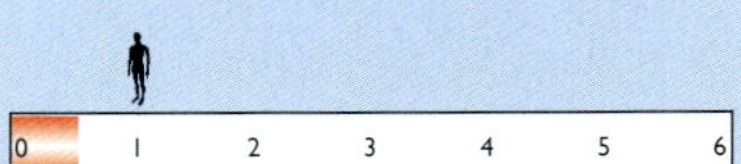


*Acanthostega* und *Ichthyostega* zählen zu den ersten vierbeinigen Wirbeltieren. In früheren Klassifikationen stellte man beide zur Gruppe der Labyrinthodonten, den ersten Formen der Amphibien (siehe Seite 78). Labyrinthodont bedeutet „Labyrinthzähne" und weist auf die Faltenstruktur des sehr harten Zahnschmelzes dieser Tiere hin. Die Zähne von *Acanthostega* und *Ichthyostega* sind eines der Merkmale, die beide mit den Fischen verbinden, die wahrscheinlich ihre Vorfahren waren – Osteolepiformen wie *Eusthenopteron* und *Panderichthys* aus der Gruppe der Fleischflosser.

*Acanthostega* erreichte eine Körperlänge von fast einem Meter und ähnelte äußerlich einem großen breitmäuligen Wassermolch oder Salamander. Seine Gliedmaßen waren für eine bequeme Fortbewegung an Land vermutlich nicht stark genug, sondern dienten als Schwimmpaddel oder halfen dem Tier, sich durch die Sümpfe zu schieben. Das breite Maul hatte mit kleinen scharfen Zähnen bestückte Kiefer, und der Schwanz trug an Ober- und Unterseite flache, lange Flossen. Das Tier besaß Kiemen, konnte aber bestimmt auch atmen.

*Ichthyostega* war etwas länger und massiger als *Acanthostega* und lebte auch im Süßwasser. Beide existierten etwa in der gleichen Zeit – im Oberdevon, vor rund 360 Millionen Jahren, und im selben Gebiet, dem heutigen Grönland. *Ichthyostega* war stärker gebaut und besaß vor allem vorn kräftigere Gliedmaßen. Er galt viele Jahre lang als wichtigster Vorfahr der heutigen Tetrapoden, doch stellt man ihn aufgrund der Einzelheiten seines Skelettaufbaus heute allgemein auf einen Seitenzweig des Stammbaums der Vierfüßer. Seine Hinterbeine endeten in sieben Zehen; *Acanthostega* hatte an den Vorderbeinen acht Zehen. Noch älter als diese beiden war der Vierfüßer *Elginerpeton*, dessen fast 370 Millionen Jahre alten Überreste in Schottland gefunden wurden.

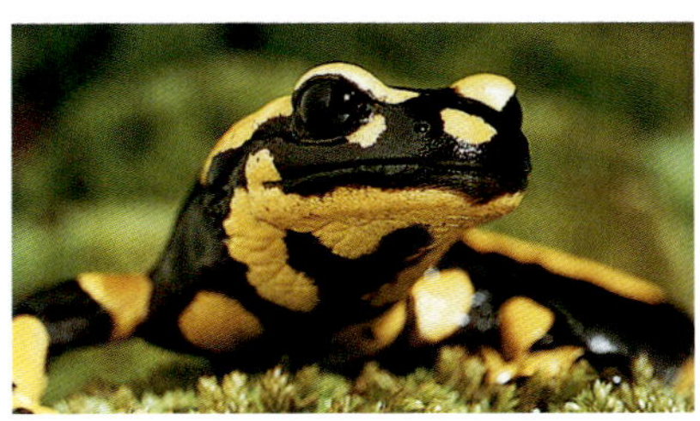

**OBEN** Vertreter der rezenten geschwänzten vierbeinigen Amphibien sind Molche und Salamander wie dieser Feuersalamander.

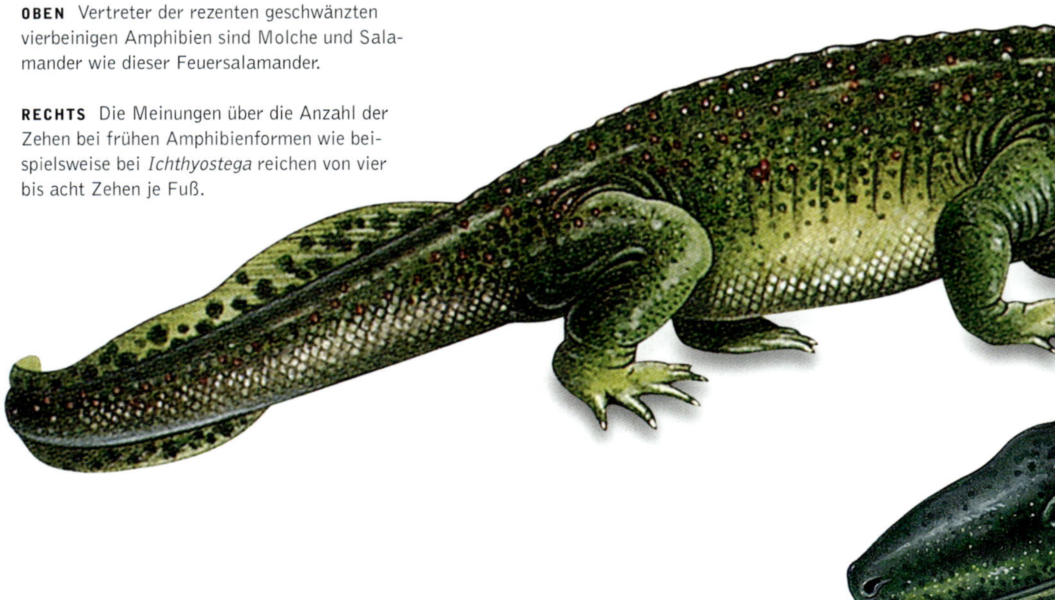

**RECHTS** Die Meinungen über die Anzahl der Zehen bei frühen Amphibienformen wie beispielsweise bei *Ichthyostega* reichen von vier bis acht Zehen je Fuß.

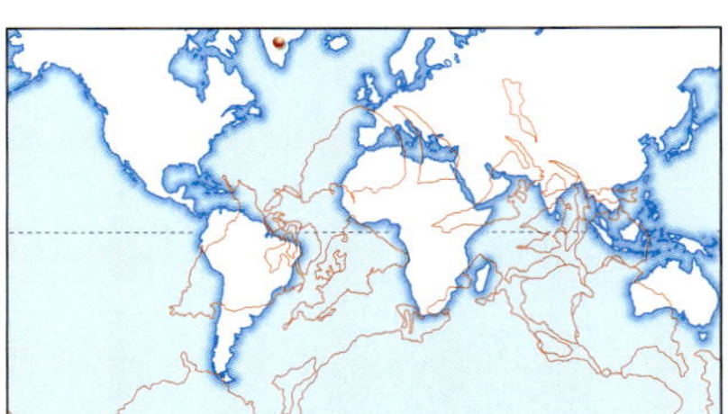

**ÜBERSICHT (TIERE)**

***Acanthostega***

**Bedeutung des Namens:** Stachel- oder Dornenplatte

**Periode:** Oberdevon

**Hauptgruppe:** Tetrapoda

**Länge:** 1 Meter

**Nahrung:** Tiere

**Fossilfundstätten:** In Grönland

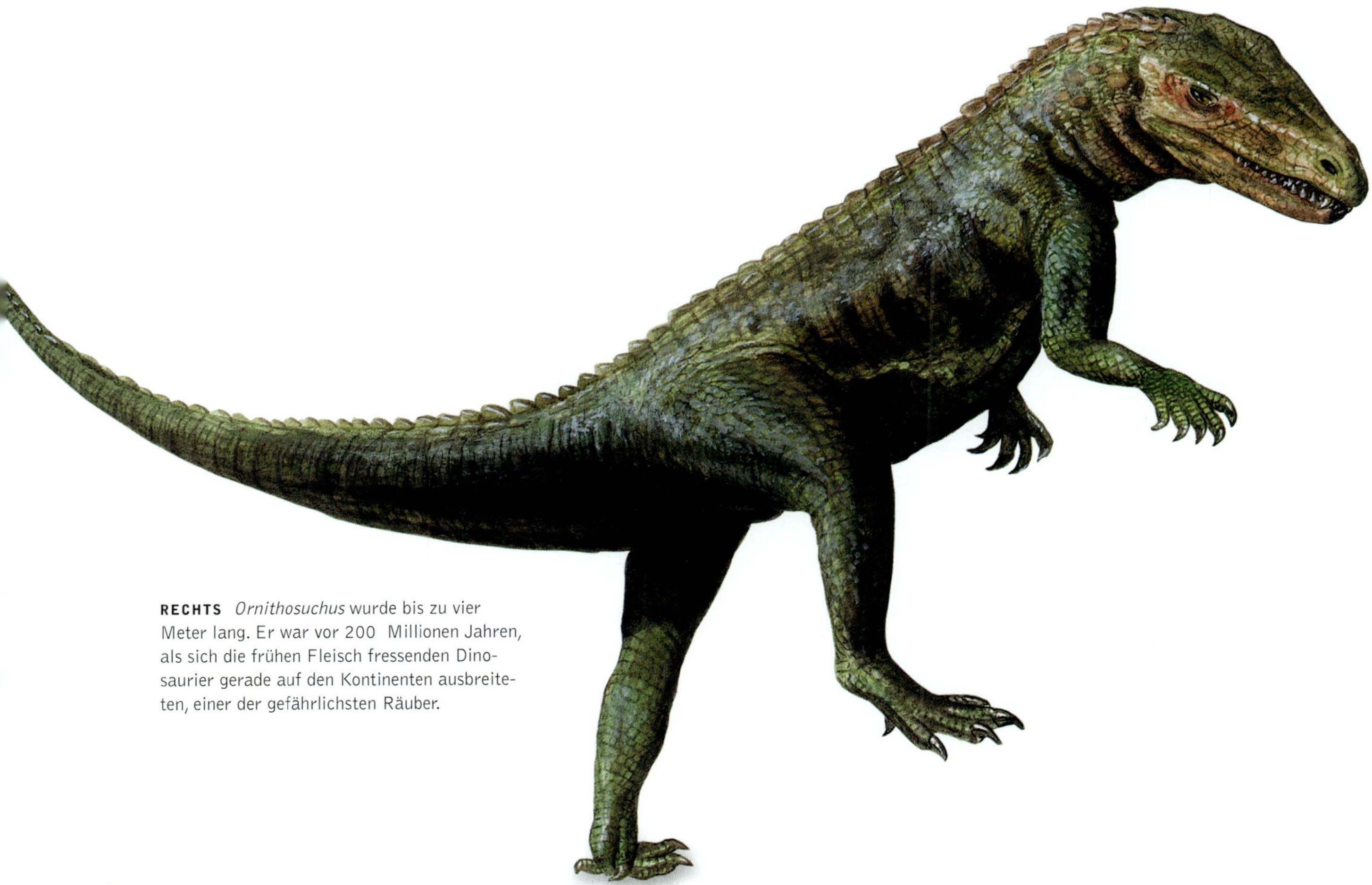

**RECHTS** *Ornithosuchus* wurde bis zu vier Meter lang. Er war vor 200 Millionen Jahren, als sich die frühen Fleisch fressenden Dinosaurier gerade auf den Kontinenten ausbreiteten, einer der gefährlichsten Räuber.

# ORNITHOSUCHUS

*Ornithosuchus*, das „Vogelkrokodil", war weder ein Vogel noch ein Krokodil. Er gilt heute als Archosauromorph (wie gegenüber erklärt) oder nach älteren Klassifikationen als thecodontes Reptil. Unabhängig davon, welche Zuordnung die richtige ist, war *Ornithosuchus* eng verwandt mit der Gruppe der Archosaurier, zu der die Dinosaurier und die Krokodile zählen. Früher betrachtete man ihn sogar als Dinosaurier, und zwar als einen ihrer ältesten Vertreter. Er besaß jedoch verschiedene Merkmale, die für Dinosaurier untypisch waren, darunter die Anordnung der Schädelfenster, der Bau der unteren Wirbelsäule und die Art der Verbindungen zu den Beckenknochen; die fünf Zehen an den Füßen und insbesondere die Details seines Sprunggelenks: dem Sprungbein (Astragulus) fehlten die nach oben gerichteten Vorsprünge und Verlängerungen, die charakteristisch für die meisten Dinosaurier waren.

Seinen Namen erhielt *Ornithosuchus* 1877 von dem britischen Paläontologen Thomas Henry Huxley. Huxley ist noch heute als Anhänger Charles Darwins und der von Darwin und anderen Wissenschaftlern aufgestellten Theorie über die Evolution durch natürliche Auslese berühmt. Er entdeckte damals an fossilen Resten des *Ornithosuchus* Merkmale, die ihn an Eigenarten bei Krokodilen und Vögeln erinnerten.

Einen nachgebildeten *Ornithosuchus* könnte man auf den ersten Blick fälschlicherweise für einen frühen Theropoden oder Fleisch fressenden Dinosaurier halten. Er konnte sich auf allen vieren bewegen, aber auch aufgerichtet auf seinen Hinterbeinen laufen, die größer und kräftiger als die Vorderbeine waren. Die Hinterbeine standen senkrecht unter dem Körper, wie es charakteristisch für die Dinosaurier war. Die lange Schnauze des *Ornithosuchus* barg kräftige Kiefer mit spitzen Zähnen zum Zerbeißen und Zerreißen der Beute.

In Europa, hier vor allem in Schottland, sowie in Südamerika wurden Fossilien mehrerer ähnlicher Reptilien entdeckt. Ihre Körperlänge reicht von lediglich einem halben Meter bis über drei Meter, und die meisten der Funde weisen ähnliche Körperproportionen auf wie *Ornithosuchus*.

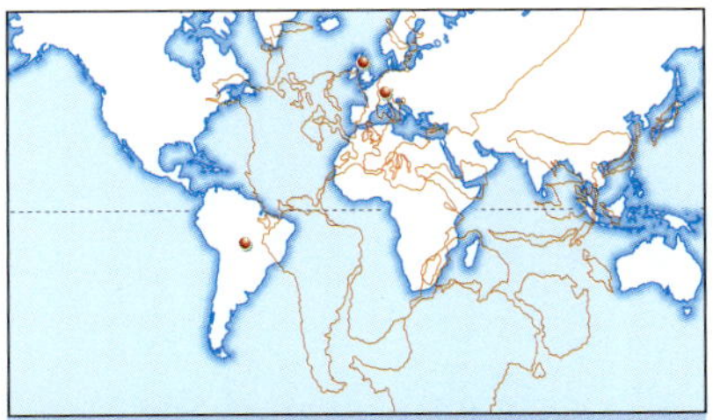

**ÜBERSICHT (TIERE)**
***Ornithosuchus***
**Bedeutung des Namens:** Vogelkrokodil
**Periode:** Mittlere bis Obere Trias
**Hauptgruppe:** Reptilia
**Länge:** Kopf–Schwanz 2 Meter
**Nahrung:** Beute mittlerer Größe
**Fossilfundstätten:** In Großbritannien, in anderen Teilen Europas und in Südamerika

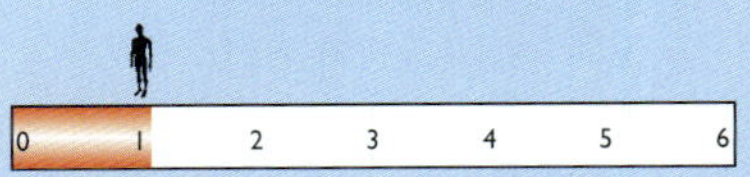

# VOR DEN DINOSAURIERN

*Vor dem Zeitalter der Dinosaurier und bis in die Anfänge dieser Zeit hineinreichend existierten die Synapsiden, die wir mitunter auch säugetierähnliche Reptilien nennen. Frühe Formen der Synapsiden wie beispielsweise die Pelycosaurier waren noch reptilähnliche Geschöpfe – wechselwarme Tiere mit schuppiger Haut und seitlich am Körper sitzenden Gliedmaßen –, von denen manche hohe Hautsegel auf dem Rücken trugen. Spätere Typen wie die Cynodonten ähnelten den Säugetieren schon viel mehr, sie besaßen eine behaarte Haut und waren Warmblüter.*

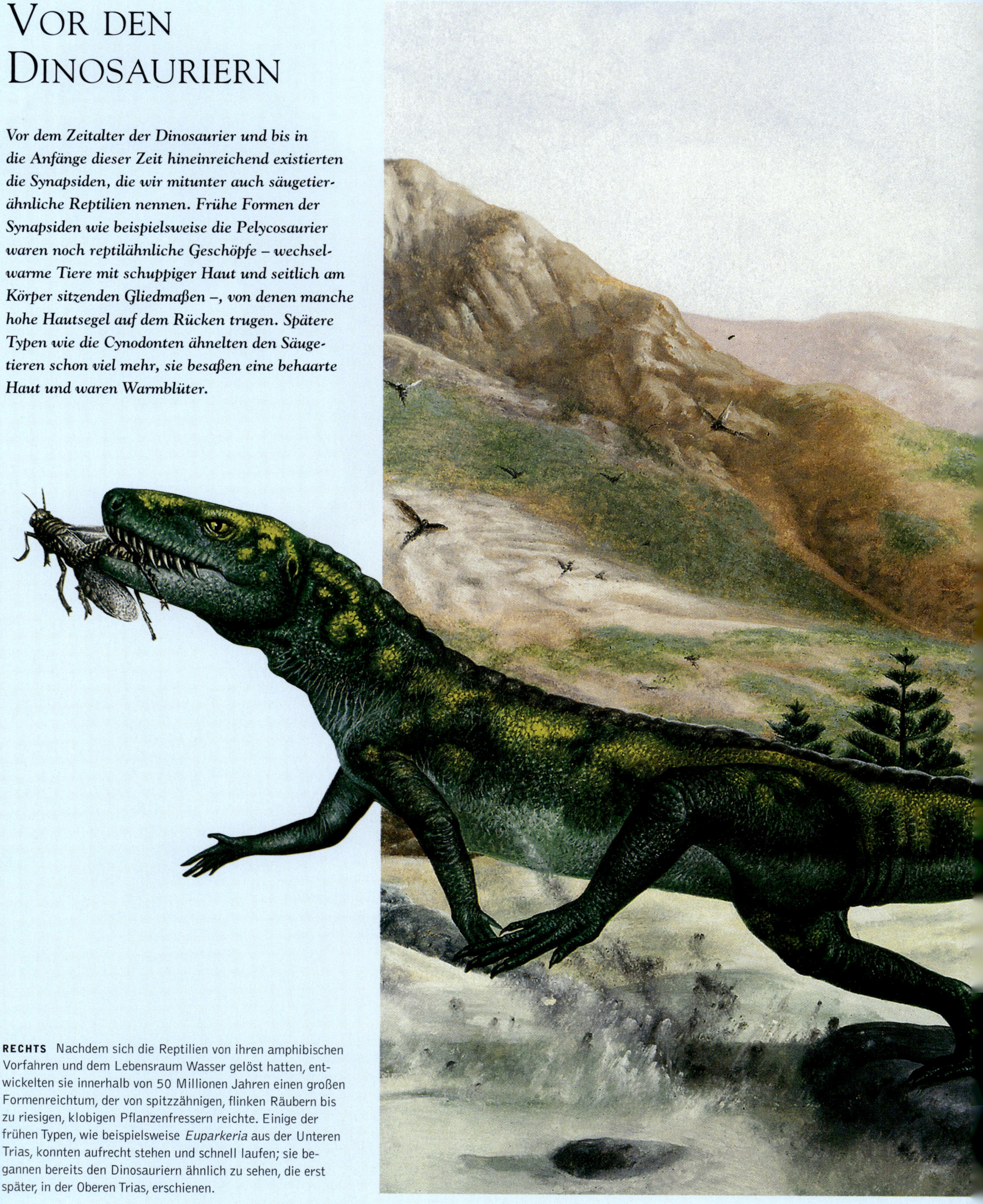

**RECHTS** Nachdem sich die Reptilien von ihren amphibischen Vorfahren und dem Lebensraum Wasser gelöst hatten, entwickelten sie innerhalb von 50 Millionen Jahren einen großen Formenreichtum, der von spitzzähnigen, flinken Räubern bis zu riesigen, klobigen Pflanzenfressern reichte. Einige der frühen Typen, wie beispielsweise *Euparkeria* aus der Unteren Trias, konnten aufrecht stehen und schnell laufen; sie begannen bereits den Dinosauriern ähnlich zu sehen, die erst später, in der Oberen Trias, erschienen.

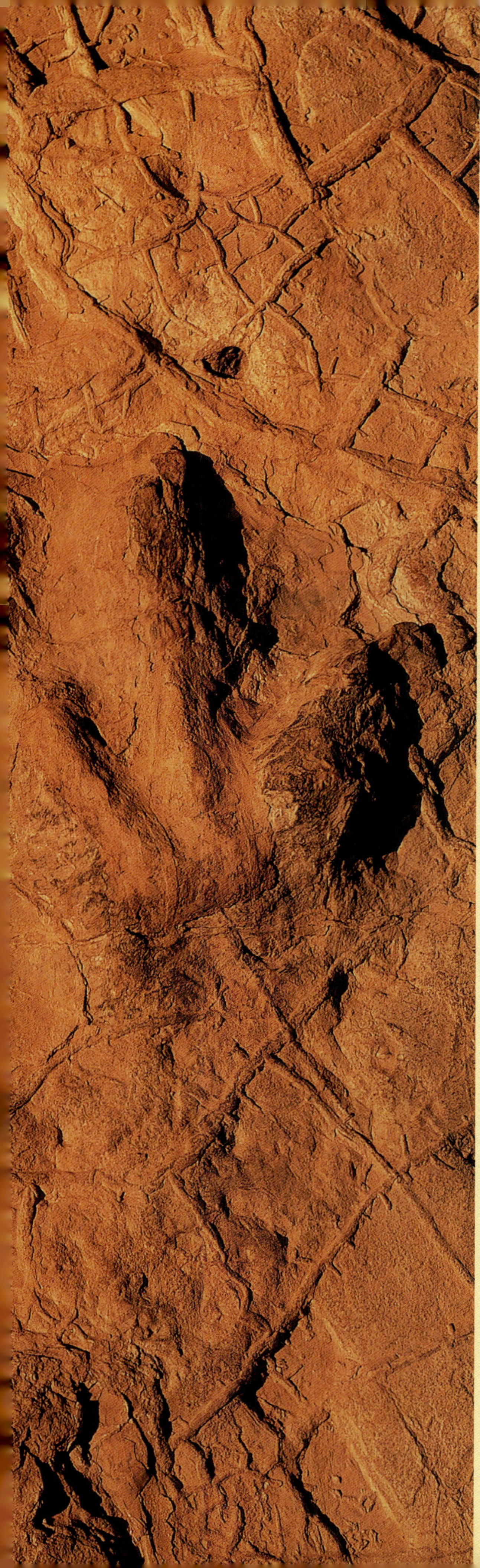

KAPITEL DREI

# DIE ERSTEN DINOSAURIER

*In der Oberen Trias entwickelten sich Reptilien, die das Leben auf dem Festland mehr als 160 Millionen Jahre lang – länger als irgendeine andere Tiergruppe – beherrschten.*

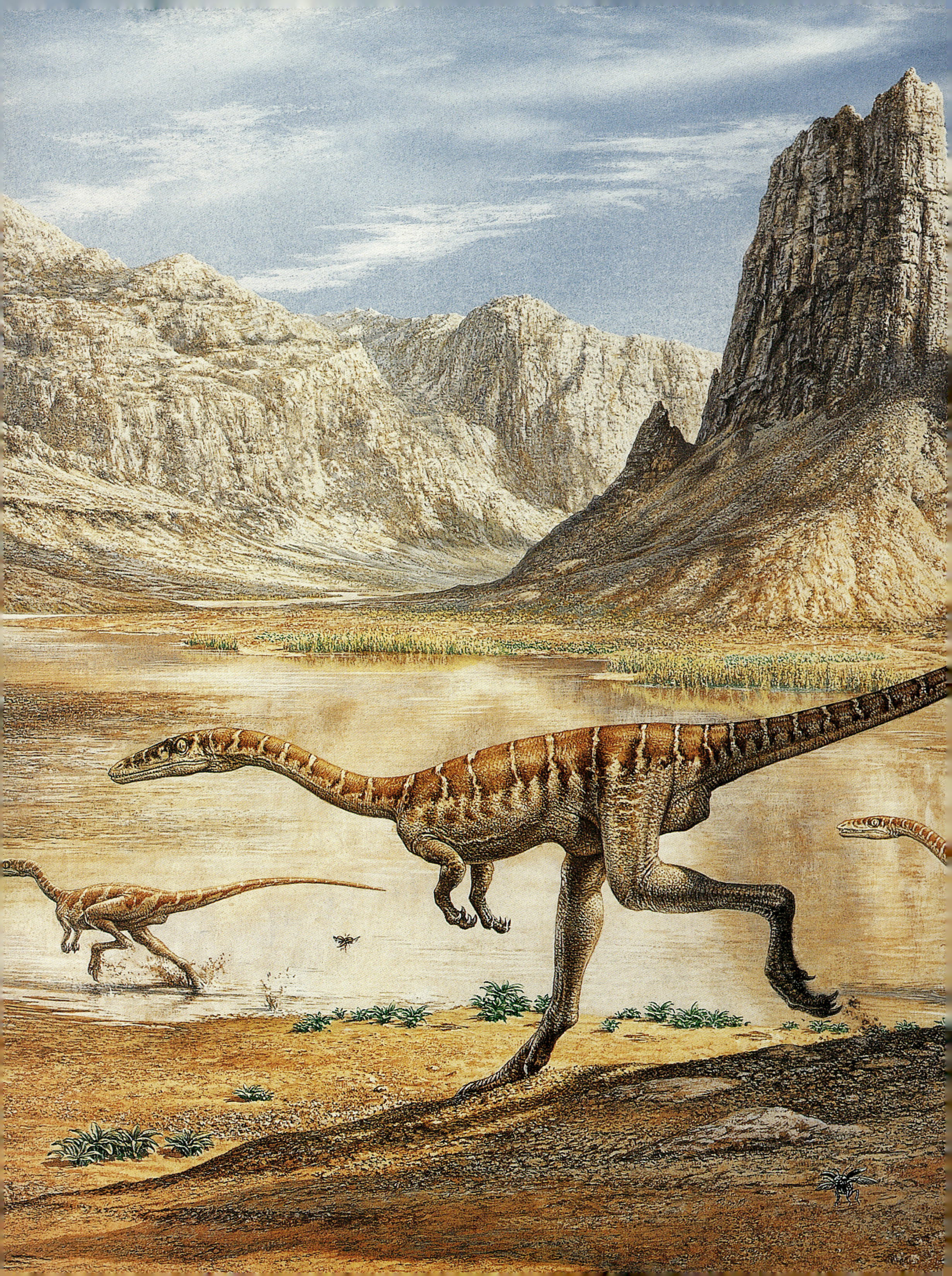

# Was sind Dinosaurier?

***Was war eigentlich ein Dinosaurier? War das ein wildes, schrecklich brüllendes Tier mit grüner Haut und bluttriefendem Maul? Vielleicht war es so, doch unter den Fossilien hat man bislang keinen Hinweis entdeckt, der diese Vorstellung begründen würde. Dinosaurier definiert man aufgrund bestimmter Merkmale ihrer Überreste, was in der Hauptsache Knochen, Zähne, Krallen und Hörner sind. Wichtig hierbei sind Schädel- und Skelettknochen – der obere Teil des Schädels, der obere Knochen der Gliedmaßen (Humerus), die vorderen Zehen („Finger"), das Becken (Pelvis), das Schienbein (Tibia) und die Fußwurzelknochen (Tarsalia).***

## Merkmale der Dinosaurier

Es gibt einige Fossilmerkmale, die dem Laien klein und unbedeutend scheinen mögen. Das ist beispielsweise beim Becken (Pelvis) der Fall. Am Hüftbein befindet sich eine schüsselförmige Hüftgelenkpfanne (Acetabulum), in die der kugelige Kopf (oder das obere Ende) des Oberschenkelbeins (Femur) passt. Diesen allgemeinen Aufbau des Hüftgelenks finden wir bei allen Wirbeltieren. Die Hüftgelenke bei Dinosauriern unterscheiden sich jedoch von denen anderer Reptilien in dreierlei Hinsicht. Erstens wies die Pfanne einen Rand auf, der am oberen Teil stärker als am unteren war. Dieser Hüftpfannenrand ruhte auf dem kugelförmigen Oberschenkelkopf. Zweitens war der Oberschenkelkopf rechtwinklig vom Femurschaft abgesetzt. Drittens war die Hüftgelenkpfanne keine geschlossene, vollständig vom Knochen umgebene Vertiefung, sondern war „offen", denn an der tiefsten Stelle befand sich ein Loch oder Fenster. Zu den für Dinosaurier typischen Merkmalen gehören zwar noch rund zehn weitere Details, die dem flüchtigen Beobachter gar nicht auffallen, doch die Bedeutung eines Beckenknochens bei einem Fossilienfund kann man gar nicht hoch genug bewerten.

## Aufrechtes Stehen

Die oben genannten Skelettmerkmale ergeben ein Hüftgelenk, das in der Reptilgruppe nur bei den Dinosauriern vorkommt. Äußerlich zeigt es sich an der Stellung des Beines zum Rumpf. Dinosaurier hatten eine „aufrechte Haltung" – im Stand befand sich das Bein mit durchgedrücktem, geradem Kniegelenk direkt unter dem Rumpf. So wurde die Körpermasse effektiv und auf natürlich ausgewogene Weise getragen. Im Gegensatz dazu zeigten die meisten anderen Reptilien einen „gespreizten Stand", wie es bei den heutigen Echsen zu beobachten ist – das Bein sitzt schräg am Körper, sein oberer Teil ist seitwärts, der untere Teil nach unten gerichtet. Dieser Aufbau erfordert mehr Muskelkraft, denn er verhindert, dass das Tier bei der Fortbewegung seine Energie rationell nutzt. So mag denn die aufrechte Haltung einer der Gründe für den entwicklungsgeschichtlichen Erfolg der Dinosaurier gewesen sein.

## Der Ursprung der Dinosaurier

Die in Südamerika und insbesondere in Argentinien gefundenen fast 230 Millionen Jahre alten Überreste gehören zu den ältesten Dinosaurierfossilien, die der Wissenschaft bekannt sind. Wie auf den nächsten Seiten zu erfahren ist, gehörten die meisten dieser Dinosaurier zu den Theropoden, räuberisch lebenden Tieren, die sich ständig auf ihren zwei großen hinteren Gliedmaßen fortbewegten, kleinere Vorderextremitäten („Arme") und lange, spitze Zähne besaßen, mit denen sie ihre Beute zerlegten. Um mögliche Vorfahren dieser Dinosauriertypen ging es bereits im vorhergehenden Kapitel. In jüngster Zeit wurden auf Madagaskar Fossilien anderer früher Sauriertypen, der Prosauropoden, entdeckt, wodurch das Bild nun komplizierter geworden ist. Die Funde könnten die Ursprünge der Dinosaurier weiter in die Vergangenheit, in die Mittlere Trias, rücken. Fast unmittelbar nach ihrem Erscheinen begannen die Dinosaurier sich auszubreiten und sich in vielerlei Formen und Größen zu entwickeln, was verheerende Auswirkungen auf die Tierwelt ihrer Zeit hatte.

**VORHERGEHENDE SEITE** Die Abdrücke eines dreizehigen Saurierfußes, von denen jeder größer als ein Essteller war, wurden im US-Bundesstaat Utah in einem rund 150 Millionen Jahre alten Gesteinsblock mit seltsam geometrischen Austrocknungsrissen entdeckt. Sie stammen von einem großen Theropoden. Zu den Theropoden gehörte auch der gewaltige, Furcht erregende *Allosaurus*.

**LINKS** Wachsam und flink wie Vögel jagt eine kleine Gruppe schlanker, zierlicher *Coelophysis*-Dinosaurier über ein trockenes Hochland, das heute zum Territorium von New Mexico gehört. *Coelophysis* ist einer der bekanntesten frühen Dinosaurier aus der Zeit vor 225 Millionen Jahren.

# Eoraptor

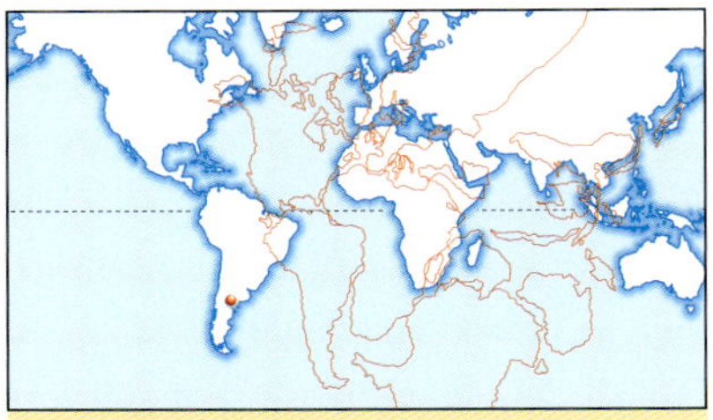

**ÜBERSICHT (DINOSAURIER)**
***Eoraptor***
**Bedeutung des Namens:**
Dieb in der Dämmerung, Dämmerungsjäger
**Periode:** Mittlere bis Obere Trias
**Hauptgruppe:** Theropoda
**Länge:** 1 Meter
**Gewicht:** 3–15 Kilogramm
**Nahrung:** Kleine Tiere
**Fossilfundstätten:** In Argentinien

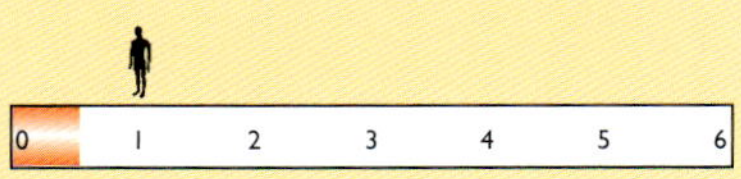


Zu den ältesten Dinosaurierfossilien, die man bisher entdeckt hat, gehören die Überreste des *Eoraptor*. Sie wurden auf rund 228 Millionen Jahre datiert. Die Fossilien waren 1991 in Argentinien, in den Anden vorgelagerten Bergzügen, von Grabungstrupps aus der Umgebung und von der University of Chicago freigelegt und zwei Jahre später von Paul Sereno und dessen Mitarbeitern von der Universität benannt worden. Die Schichten aus Vulkanasche, auf die man im Zusammenhang mit der Entdeckung gestoßen war, ermöglichten schließlich auch eine verhältnismäßig genaue Schätzung des Fossilalters.

*Eoraptor* war ein kleiner Theropode, ein Vertreter der Fleisch fressenden Dinosaurier. Mit seinen Körperproportionen – langer, schlanker Kopf und Hals, langer, sich verjüngender Schwanz, kurze Vordergliedmaßen und lange, kräftige Hinterextremitäten zum Laufen und Rennen auf zwei Beinen – ähnelte er vielen der späteren räuberisch lebenden Typen. Die Zähne an der Vorderfront des Kiefers waren ungewöhnlich blattförmig und nicht die spitzen, messerscharfen Dolche oder speerartigen Zacken, wie sie für Fleisch fressende Dinosaurier typisch sind.

Man kann *Eoraptor* als kleinen frühen, primitiven Theropoden sehen, der genau dem entsprach, was man als einen der ersten „Zweige" des Fleischfresser-Astes am Evolutionsbaum der Dinosaurier erwarten könnte. Er besaß leichte Röhrenknochen, die jenen des etwas späteren und viel bekannteren *Coelophysis* ähnelten. *Eoraptor*, ein schlanker, schneller, behender Räuber, machte vermutlich Jagd auf kleine Beutetiere wie beispielsweise Echsen und andere kleinere Reptilien und vielleicht auch auf große Insekten und Würmer. An seinen Vordergliedmaßen trug er je fünf Zehen; dieses Merkmal weist *Eoraptor* als frühen Theropoden aus, denn die Anzahl der Zehen verringerte sich bei späteren Theropoden auf drei oder gar zwei. An den Zehen saßen scharfe Krallen, mit denen *Eoraptor* wohl im Boden wühlte oder seine Beute packte. Weniger wahrscheinlich ist, dass er Aasfresser war und sich an den Kadavern verendeter oder sterbender größerer Reptilien gütlich tat, denn für diese zähe Nahrung waren seine Zähne nicht geschaffen. Sie waren vielmehr klein, spitz und nach hinten gebogen und damit besser zum Greifen und Zerteilen kleiner Beutetiere geeignet.

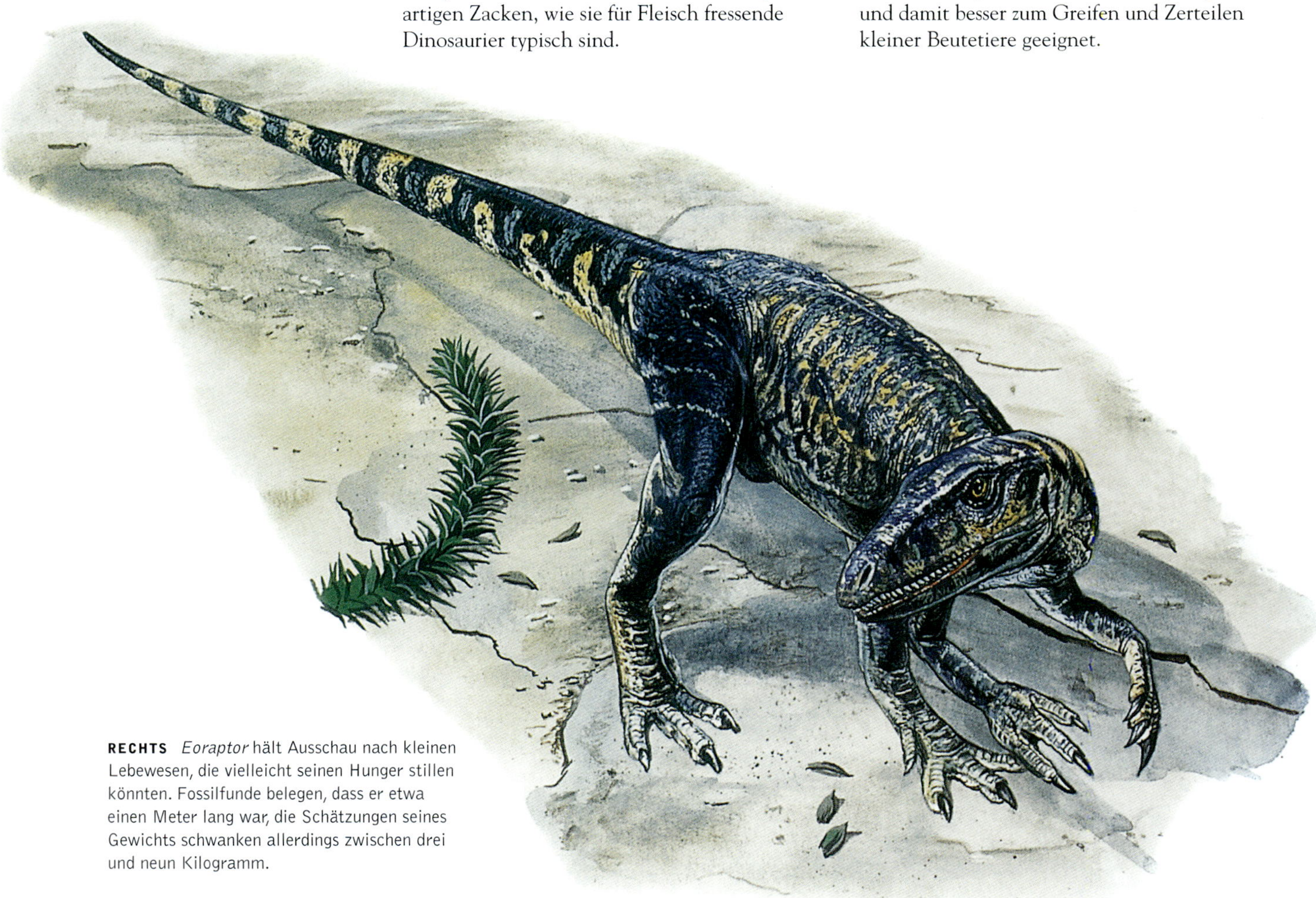

**RECHTS** *Eoraptor* hält Ausschau nach kleinen Lebewesen, die vielleicht seinen Hunger stillen könnten. Fossilfunde belegen, dass er etwa einen Meter lang war, die Schätzungen seines Gewichts schwanken allerdings zwischen drei und neun Kilogramm.

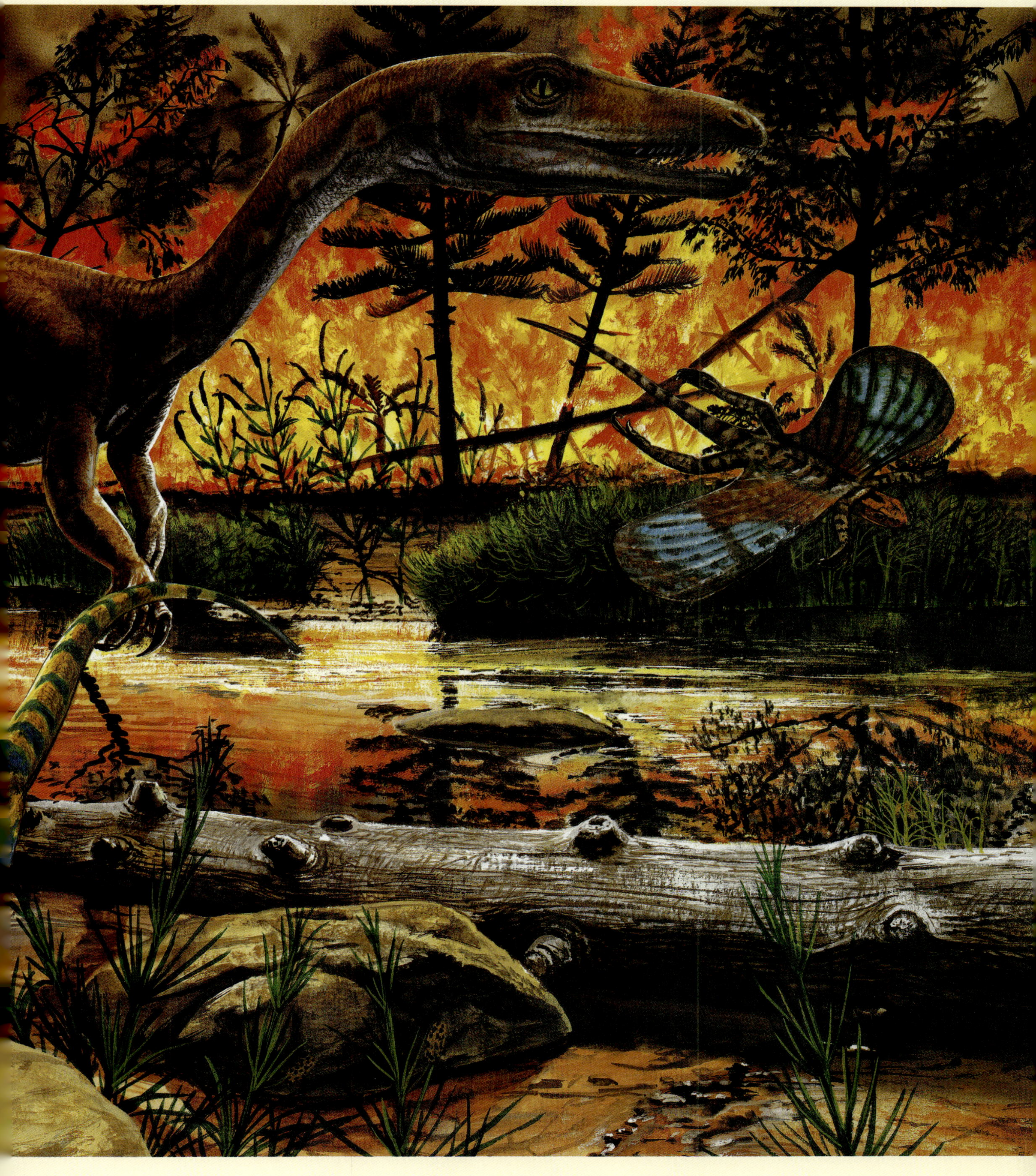

# SEGISAURUS

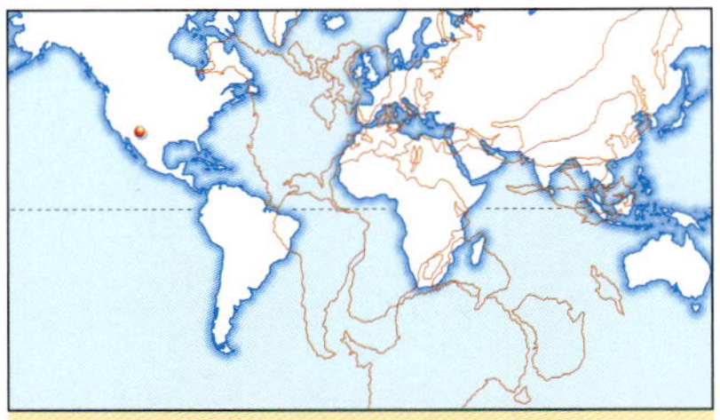

**ÜBERSICHT (DINOSAURIER)**

***Segisaurus***

**Bedeutung des Namens:** Segi-Reptil (nach dem Fundort benannt)

**Periode:** Unterer Jura

**Hauptgruppe:** Theropoda

**Länge:** 1 Meter

**Gewicht:** 5 Kilogramm

**Nahrung:** Kleine Tiere

**Fossilfundstätten:** In den USA (Arizona)

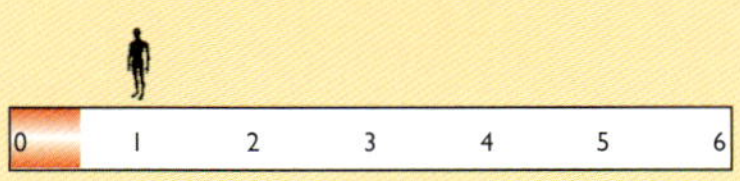


*Segisaurus* ist weniger bekannt als *Coelophysis* (siehe Seite 121), da Fossilien von ihm nicht in der Fülle wie bei *Coelophysis* erhalten geblieben sind. Das erste Exemplar des Tieres, das wir heute *Segisaurus* nennen, wurde 1933 in der Nähe des Segi Canyon in Arizona, in einem Navajo Sandstone genannten Gebiet ausgegraben und 1936 beschrieben und benannt. Das Skelett war allerdings nicht vollständig, denn es fehlte beispielsweise der Kopf mit den so aussagekräftigen Zähnen. Die lückenhaften Überreste bestanden aus Teilen der vorderen und hinteren Gliedmaßen, Bruchstücken des Beckens sowie einigen Rippen und Rückenwirbeln. Aus diesen Teilen wurde *Segisaurus* als Theropode (Fleischfresser) nachgebildet, der *Coelophysis* ähnelte, jedoch kleiner als dieser war und wahrscheinlich zu den Ceratosauriern, einer Untergruppe der Theropoden, gehörte.

*Segisaurus* konnte mit seinen langen Hinterbeinen und dreizehigen Füßen vermutlich sehr schnell laufen und hielt dabei die kürzeren, scharfkralligen Finger wohl dicht vor der Brust. Die schlanken Proportionen der fossilen Knochen belegen, dass dieser Dinosaurier leicht gebaut und in der Lage war, sich bei dem Verfolgen eines Beutetiers plötzlich umzudrehen, wobei er seinen Schwanz – Gegengewicht und Ruder zugleich – zur Seite schnellen ließ und auf diese Weise dem Körper ruckartig eine neue Bewegungsrichtung gab. Vielleicht fing er Libellen, Grillen und andere große Insekten oder kleine Wirbeltiere wie Frösche und Echsen. Da von *Segisaurus* aber bisher keine Zähne und Kieferknochen gefunden worden sind, kann man nur anhand von Vergleichen mit anderen, besser bekannten Verwandten, insbesondere mit *Coelophysis*, auf die Ernährungsgewohnheiten des Tieres schließen.

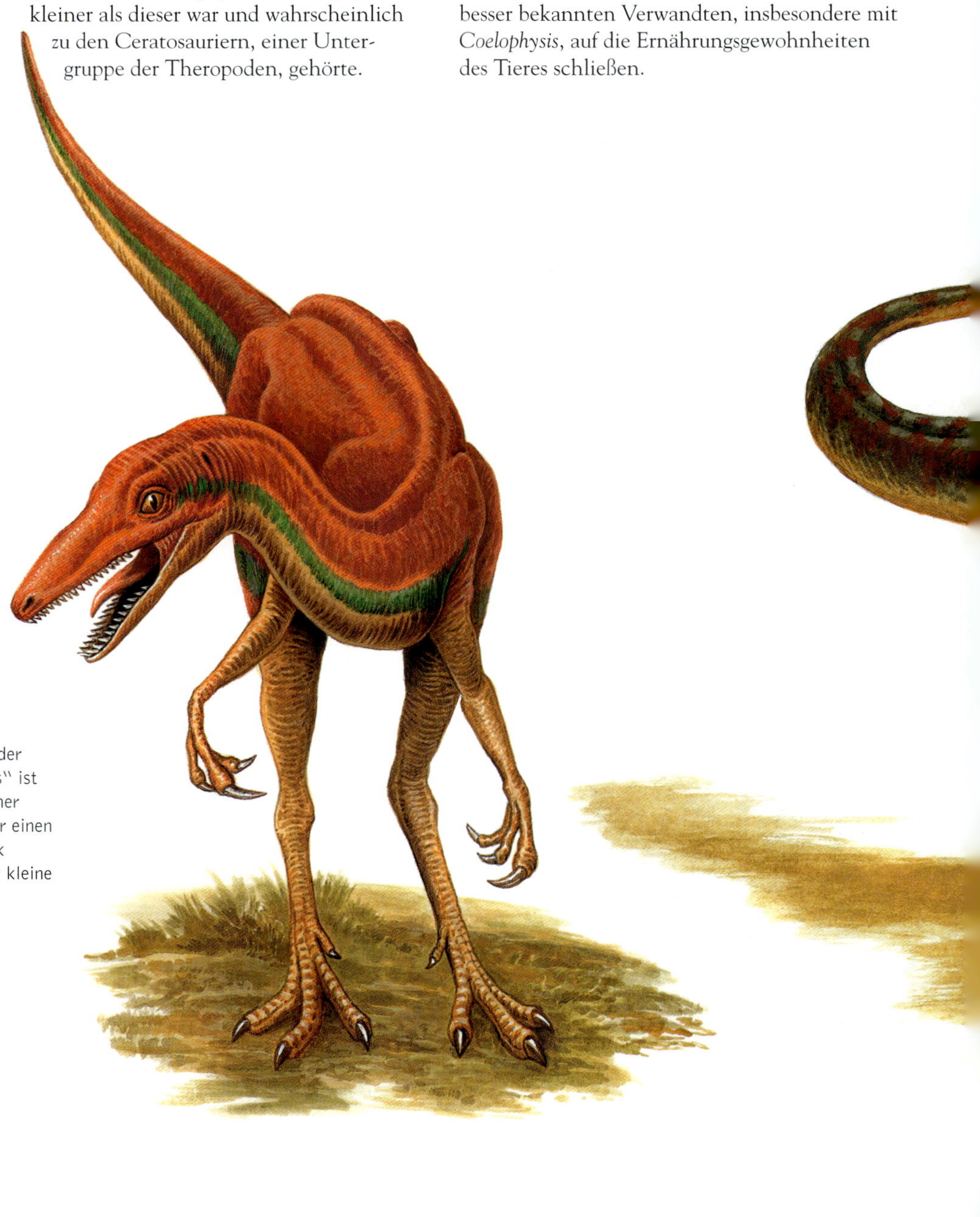

**RECHTS** Die Nachbildung des Kopfes, der Kiefer und der Zähne des „Segi-Reptils" ist größtenteils hypothetisch. Ziemlich sicher ist jedoch, dass dieser frühe Dinosaurier einen sehr leichten Körperbau hatte und dank wacher Sinne und schneller Reaktionen kleine Beutetiere fangen konnte.

# MELANOROSAURUS

*Melanorosaurus*, der 1924 offiziell nach seinem Fundort benannt wurde, war – zusammen mit *Plateosaurus* – viele Jahre lang einer der wenigen Pflanzen fressenden Dinosaurier aus dem Zeitraum von Oberer Trias bis zum Unteren Jura, die die Wissenschaft kannte. Jüngere Entdeckungen, insbesondere in Südamerika, wo beispielsweise *Riojasaurus* ausgegraben wurde, haben unser Wissen über die Entwicklung und Verbreitung dieser bedeutenden frühen Gruppe großer Dinosaurier, der Prosauropoden, mittlerweile jedoch erweitert. Das betrifft insbesondere die Ähnlichkeiten zwischen den südafrikanischen Prosauropoden wie *Melanorosaurus* und den Fossilfunden in Südamerika, die daher rühren können, dass die beiden Kontinente in der Trias unmittelbar aneinandergrenzten.

*Melanorosaurus* war ein recht typischer Vertreter der Prosauropoden, auch wenn seine Größe die der meisten anderen Prosauropoden übertroffen haben mag. Er hatte einen kleinen Kopf, Hals und Schwanz waren lang, der Körper wuchtig, und mit seinen vier sehr stämmigen Gliedmaßen trottete er wohl mehr durch seine Welt als das er ging. Die Stärke seiner Beinknochen lässt auf Anpassungen – vier breite fünfzehige Füße – an ein Körpergewicht von mindestens einer Tonne schließen. Da die hinteren Gliedmaßen länger waren, verlief die Rückenlinie vom Becken zur Schulter geneigt. Die Gesamtlänge des Dinosauriers wird auf sieben bis zwölf Meter geschätzt. Vermutlich weidete *Melanorosaurus* baumhohe Pflanzen ab, indem er wie andere Prosauropoden seinen langen Hals nach Farnwedeln, jungen Koniferennadeln, Knospen, Trieben und sonstigen weicheren Pflanzenteilen reckte. Verglichen mit *Plateosaurus* war er aber wahrscheinlich kaum in der Lage seine Vorderbeine vom Boden zu heben und sich, gestützt auf seinen Schwanz, auf die Hinterbeine zu stellen, um höher wachsende Nahrungsquellen zu erreichen.

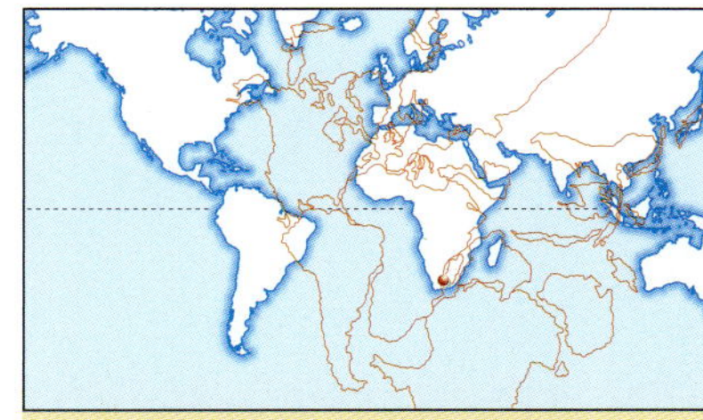

**ÜBERSICHT (DINOSAURIER)**

***Melanorosaurus***

**Bedeutung des Namens:** Black-Mountain-Reptil

**Periode:** Obere Trias, Unterer Jura

**Hauptgruppe:** Prosauropoda

**Länge:** 10 Meter

**Gewicht:** 1 Tonne

**Nahrung:** Pflanzen, besonders hochwachsende

**Fossilfundstätten:** Südafrika

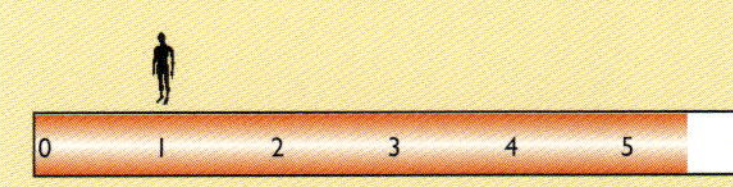


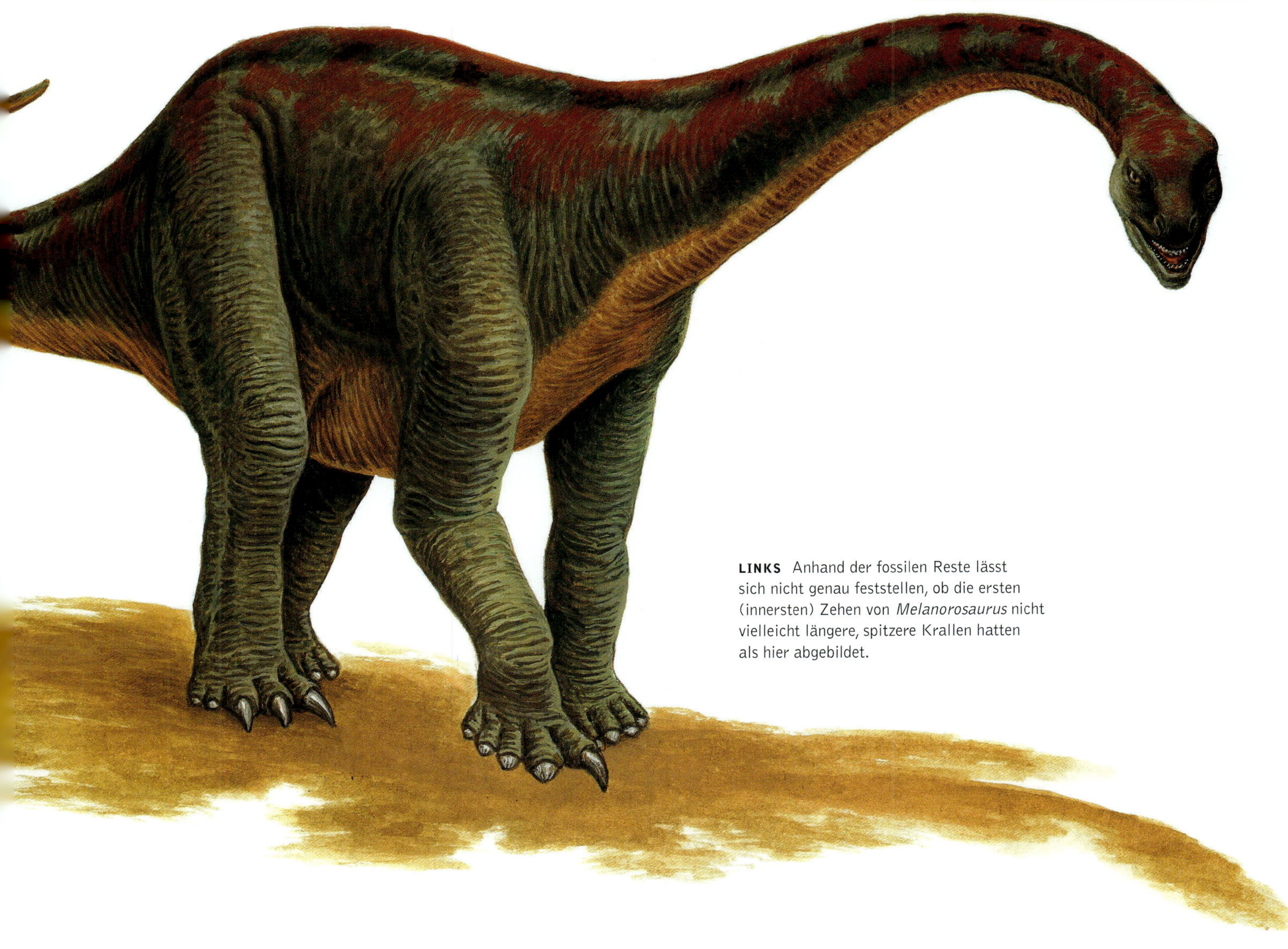

**LINKS** Anhand der fossilen Reste lässt sich nicht genau feststellen, ob die ersten (innersten) Zehen von *Melanorosaurus* nicht vielleicht längere, spitzere Krallen hatten als hier abgebildet.

# THECODONTOSAURUS

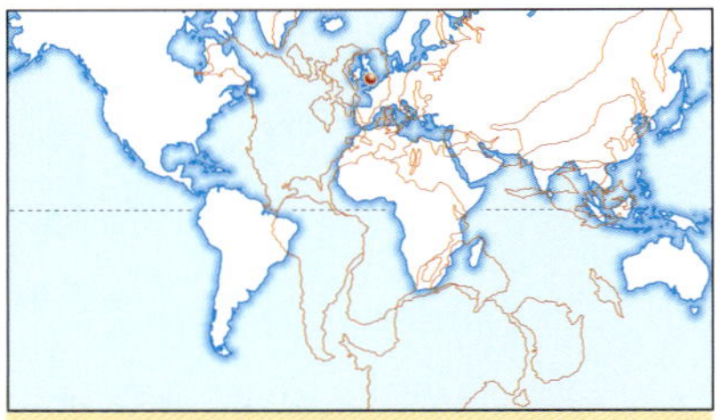

**ÜBERSICHT (DINOSAURIER)**
***Thecodontosaurus***
**Bedeutung des Namens:** Grubenzähniges Reptil
**Periode:** Unterer Jura
**Hauptgruppe:** Möglicherweise Prosauropoda (diese Zuordnung wird von manchen Fachleuten nicht anerkannt)
**Länge:** 2,2 Meter
**Gewicht:** 10 Kilogramm
**Nahrung:** Pflanzen
**Fossilfundstätten:** In England und Wales

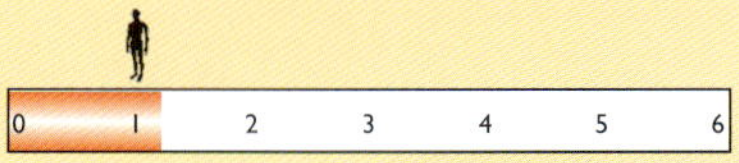


Der Name dieses Dinosauriers weist auf Zähne hin, die in Zahngruben im Kieferknochen sitzen; er sollte nicht mit der großen Reptiliengruppe der Thecodontier verwechselt werden, die man jetzt Archosauromorphe (siehe Seite 102) nennt. Eine solche Ähnlichkeit der Namen mag heute zwar ärgerlich erscheinen, doch *Thecodontosaurus* erhielt seinen offiziellen Namen schon vor langer Zeit, nachdem man bei Bristol im Südwesten Englands in Gesteinsspalten zerbrochene fossilierte Überreste von ihm entdeckt hatte. Das war im Jahr 1843, kurz nachdem für die gesamte Tiergruppe die Bezeichnung Dinosaurier geprägt worden war. In jenen Tagen waren die wissenschaftlichen Ansichten über prähistorische Tiere und deren Klassifizierung noch weit von den heutigen Systemen entfernt.

*Thecodontosaurus* war ein ziemlich kleiner, Pflanzen fressender Dinosaurier, der meistens auf seinen Hinterbeinen stand und ging. Die kürzeren, schwächeren Vorderbeine könnte er in der Luft gehalten und nur dann zur Fortbewegung benutzt haben, wenn er auf allen vieren umhersprang oder sich nach unten beugte um niedrig wachsende Pflanzen abzuweiden. In dieser Hinsicht ähnelte *Thecodontosaurus* einem viel besser bekannten und weiter verbreiteten verwandten Prosauropoden, dem *Anchisaurus*. An den Füßen hatte er jeweils vier Zehen und an jeder „Hand" fünf Finger, wobei der Daumen eine besonders lange Kralle trug. Er besaß einen langen Schwanz, Hals und Kopf waren verhältnismäßig klein, die an den Schneiden sägeartigen Zähne blattförmig. *Thecodontosaurus* gilt wie *Anchisaurus* bei manchen Fachleuten als kleiner, früher Typ eines Prosauropoden. Entwicklungsgeschichtlich stellt er eine Sackgasse dar, denn seine Gruppe starb schon nach kurzer Zeit aus.

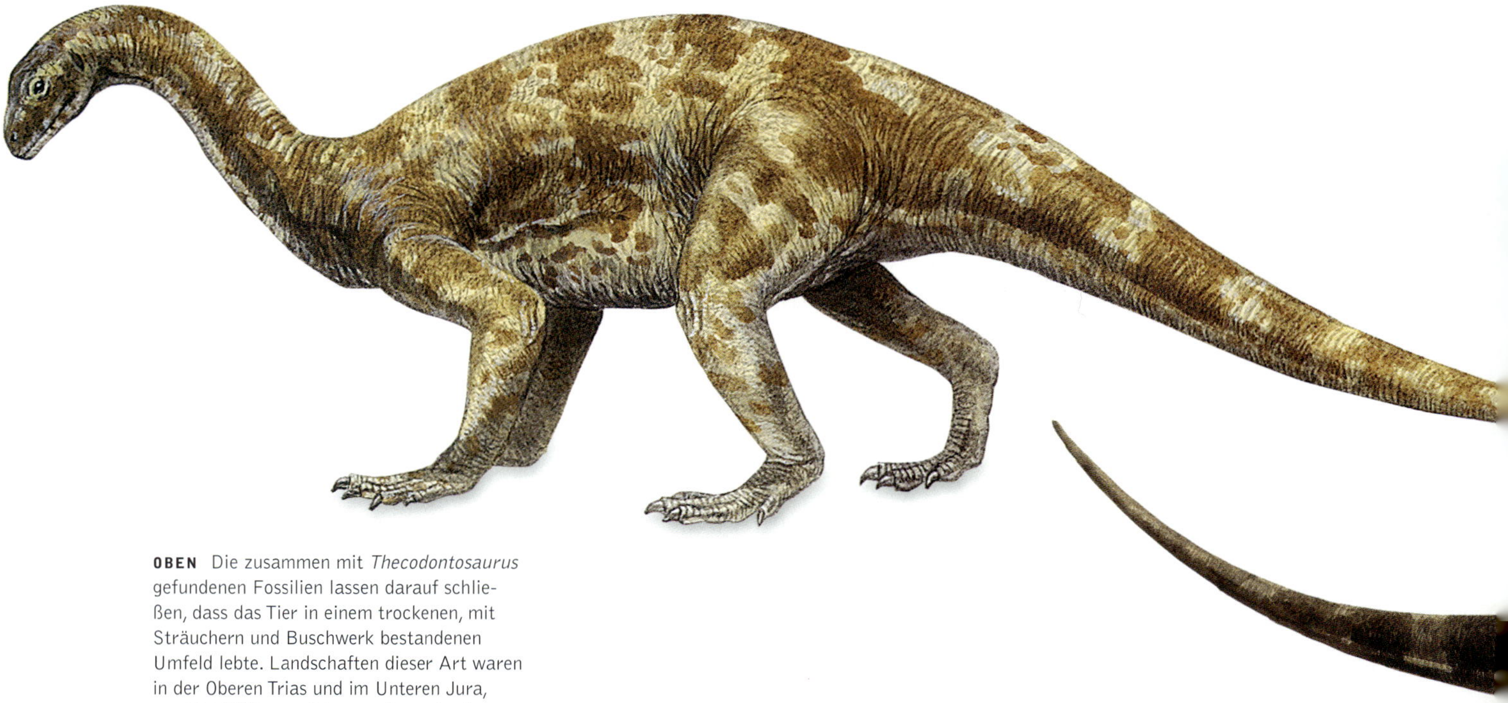

**OBEN** Die zusammen mit *Thecodontosaurus* gefundenen Fossilien lassen darauf schließen, dass das Tier in einem trockenen, mit Sträuchern und Buschwerk bestandenen Umfeld lebte. Landschaften dieser Art waren in der Oberen Trias und im Unteren Jura, vor 200 Millionen Jahren, sehr verbreitet.

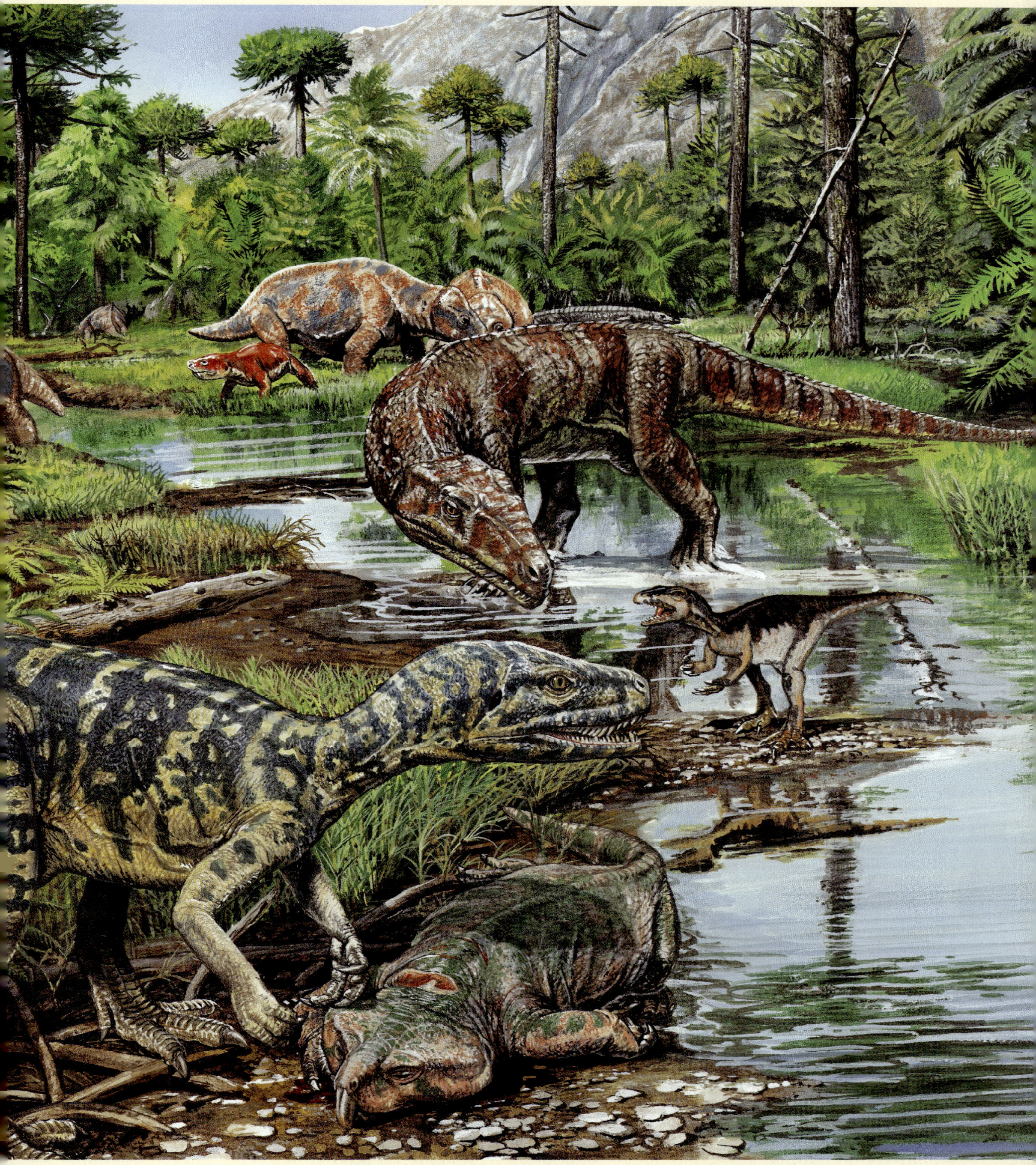

# MUSSAURUS

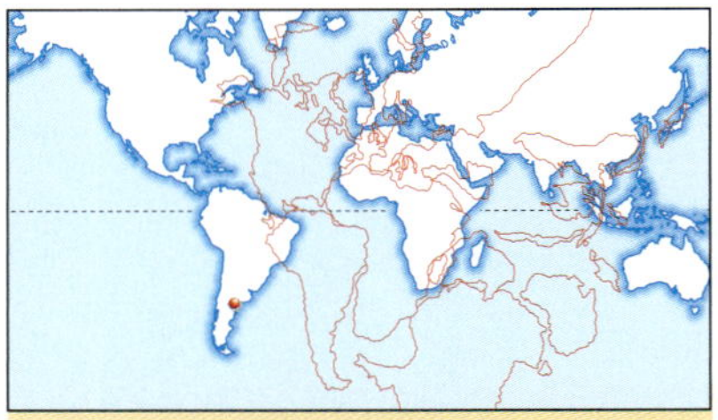

**ÜBERSICHT (DINOSAURIER)**
***Mussaurus***
**Bedeutung des Namens:** Mausreptil
**Periode:** Obere Trias
**Hauptgruppe:** Prosauropoda
**Länge:** 3 Meter
**Gewicht:** 150 Kilogramm
**Nahrung:** Pflanzen
**Fossilfundstätten:** In Argentinien

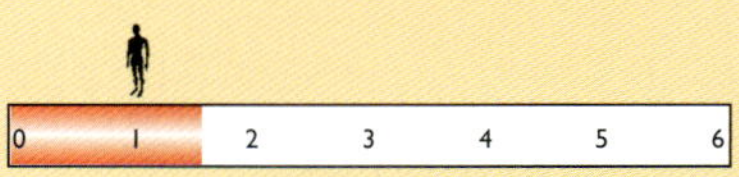


*Mussaurus* war ein Dinosaurier aus der Gruppe der Prosauropoden – ein massiger, vierbeiniger Pflanzenfresser mit kleinem Kopf, langem Hals und langem Schwanz, der äußerlich anderen Prosauropoden ähnelte. Weshalb gaben die argentinischen Paläontologen José Bonaparte und Martin Vince 1979 diesem drei Meter langen und 150 Kilogramm schweren Urtier dann einen Namen, der „Mausreptil" bedeutet? *Mussaurus* war nur von den fossilierten Überresten kleiner Jungtiere bekannt, die bei weitem nicht vollständig sind. Eine aus den Bruchstücken zusammengesetzte Nachbildung zeigt, dass *Mussaurus*, wenn auch nicht so klein wie eine echte Maus, so doch zumindest rattengroß war – jedes Jungtier hatte einschließlich des langen Schwanzes und des etwa daumengroßen Schädels eine Länge von rund 20 Zentimetern. Einige waren zum Zeitpunkt ihres Todes gerade erst geschlüpft; andere lagen als Embryos noch in ihrer schützenden Eihülle, als die Fossilierung einsetzte.

Erstaunlich an den *Mussaurus*-Fossilien, die in den 1970er Jahren in der argentinischen Provinz Santa Cruz entdeckt wurden, ist die Kleinheit der erhalten gebliebenen Details. Die Kiefer enthalten Reihen von Zähnen, die kaum größer als Stecknadelköpfe sind, die Knöchel und Fußknochen haben nur Reiskorngröße. Das sind unter allen Dinosaurierarten die kleinsten relativ vollständigen Exemplare, auf die man bislang gestoßen ist.

Etwas später hat man Fossilien ausgewachsener Tiere eindeutig identifiziert, auch wenn es sich dabei nur um unvollständige Überreste handelte. Auf diesen Relikten und den aus Fossilbelegen bekannten Größenbereichen anderer Dinosaurier sowie aus den Wachstumsraten rezenter Reptilien basieren die gegenwärtigen Schätzungen der oben angegebenen Größe eines adulten *Mussaurus*. In derselben Provinz und in denselben Gesteinsschichten wie *Mussaurus* hat man auch *Coloradisaurus*, einen anderen Dinosaurier, ausgegraben, dessen Alter auf rund 215 Millionen Jahre geschätzt wird. Es ist nicht auszuschließen, dass es sich dabei um die ausgewachsene Spielart eines *Mussaurus* handelt. Allerdings ist über *Coloradisaurus* noch wenig bekannt, da man bisher nur den Schädel und die Kiefer gefunden hat.

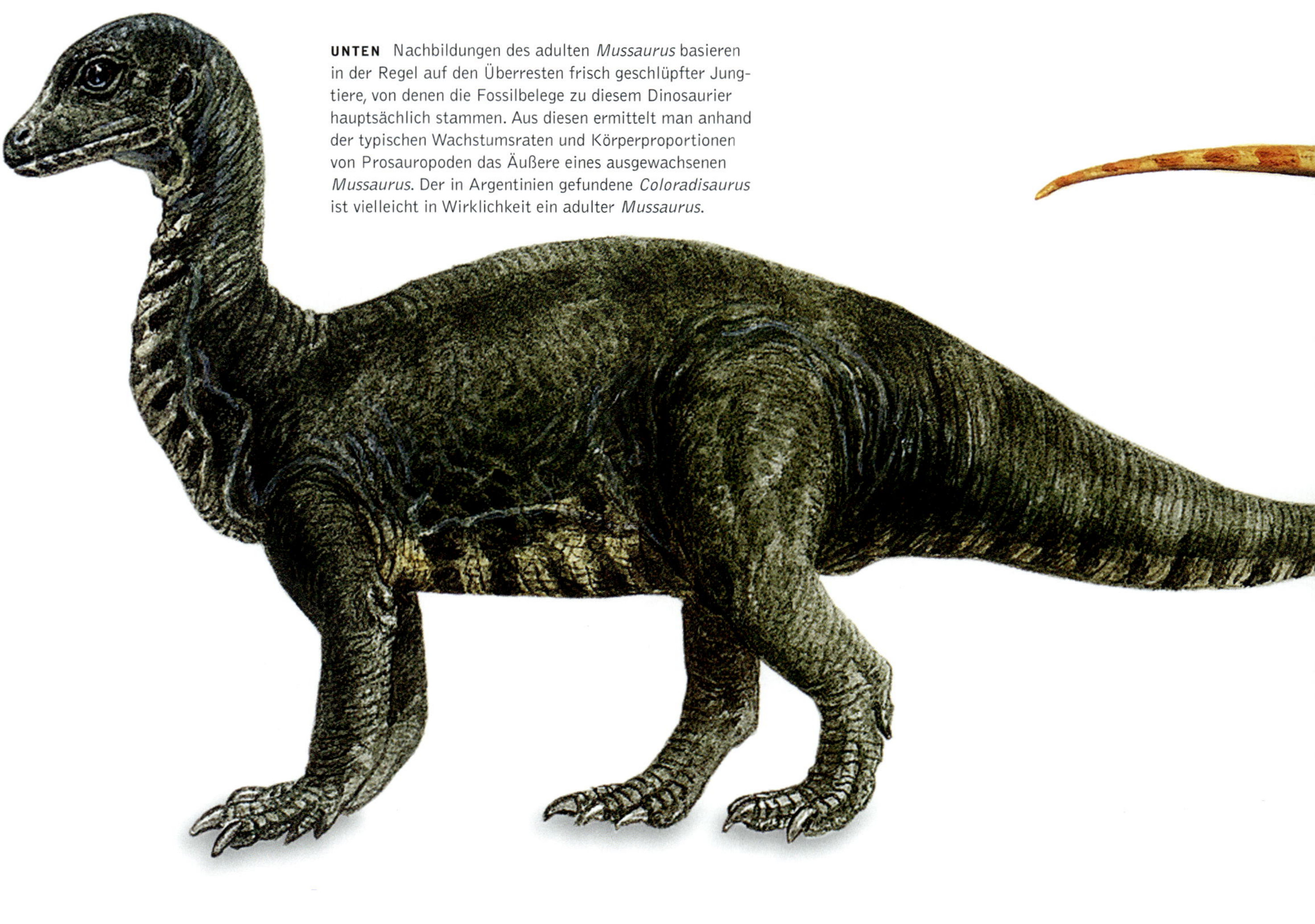

**UNTEN** Nachbildungen des adulten *Mussaurus* basieren in der Regel auf den Überresten frisch geschlüpfter Jungtiere, von denen die Fossilbelege zu diesem Dinosaurier hauptsächlich stammen. Aus diesen ermittelt man anhand der typischen Wachstumsraten und Körperproportionen von Prosauropoden das Äußere eines ausgewachsenen *Mussaurus*. Der in Argentinien gefundene *Coloradisaurus* ist vielleicht in Wirklichkeit ein adulter *Mussaurus*.

# Anchisaurus

*Anchisaurus*, der etwa die Größe eines großen Hundes hatte, gebührt die Ehre der erste Dinosaurier zu sein, der in Nordamerika, genauer im Connecticut Valley, entdeckt und in der wissenschaftlichen Literatur auf der Grundlage seiner fossilen Reste offiziell beschrieben wurde. Das war bereits 1818, und die Geschichte hat seitdem verschiedene Wendungen genommen. Eine Zeit lang galten die Skelettteile als Relikte eines uralten menschlichen Wesens. In den 1850er Jahren erkannte man in ihnen die Überreste eines Reptils, allerdings nicht unbedingt die eines Dinosauriers – die Gruppe der Dinosaurier war erst wenige Jahre zuvor, 1841, offiziell benannt und anerkannt worden. 1885 gab Othniel Charles Marsh einem anderen Satz von Fossilien, die diesmal aus Massachusetts stammten, den Namen *Anchisaurus*. 1912, fast ein Jahrhundert nachdem die oben erwähnten Reste erstmals beschrieben worden waren, identifizierte man sie schließlich als die eines *Anchisaurus*.

*Anchisaurus* lebte vor etwa 195 Millionen Jahren. Er hatte den typischen Körperbau eines Prosauropoden, sein Kopf war klein, Hals und Schwanz waren lang. Der Rumpf und die Gliedmaßen waren allerdings schlanker als bei größeren Prosauropoden wie beispielsweise *Plateosaurus* oder *Massospondylus*. Der *Anchisaurus* bewegte sich vermutlich langsam hüpfend wie ein Känguru auf allen vieren fort und suchte dabei am Boden nach Pflanzen. Trotzdem konnte sich *Anchisaurus* vielleicht auf seinen Hinterbeinen aufrichten, wenn er sehr schnell laufen wollte. An den vorderen Gliedmaßen saßen jeweils fünf Finger, deren erster – vielleicht zur Verteidigung – eine große gebogene Kralle trug. Die Hinterfüße waren mit vier Zehen ausgestattet, die alle eine große, nagelartige Kralle trugen. Wie viele Prosauropoden besaß auch *Anchisaurus* kleine, blattförmige Zähne mit sägeartig gezackten Schneiden, die sich gut zum Abstreifen von Blättern und Farnwedeln eigneten. Sein Lebensraum war ein tiefes Tal mit vielen pflanzenumsäumten Seen.

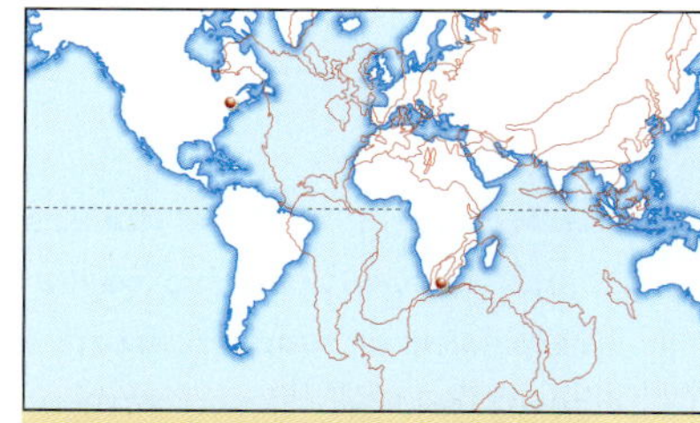

**ÜBERSICHT (DINOSAURIER)**
***Anchisaurus***
**Bedeutung des Namens:** Nahe bei einem Reptil
**Periode:** Unterer Jura
**Hauptgruppe:** Prosauropoda
**Länge:** 2,5 Meter
**Gewicht:** 35 Kilogramm
**Nahrung:** Pflanzen
**Fossilfundstätten:** In den USA (Connecticut Valley in Massachusetts), möglicherweise in Südafrika

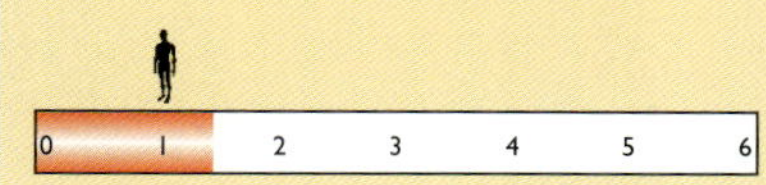


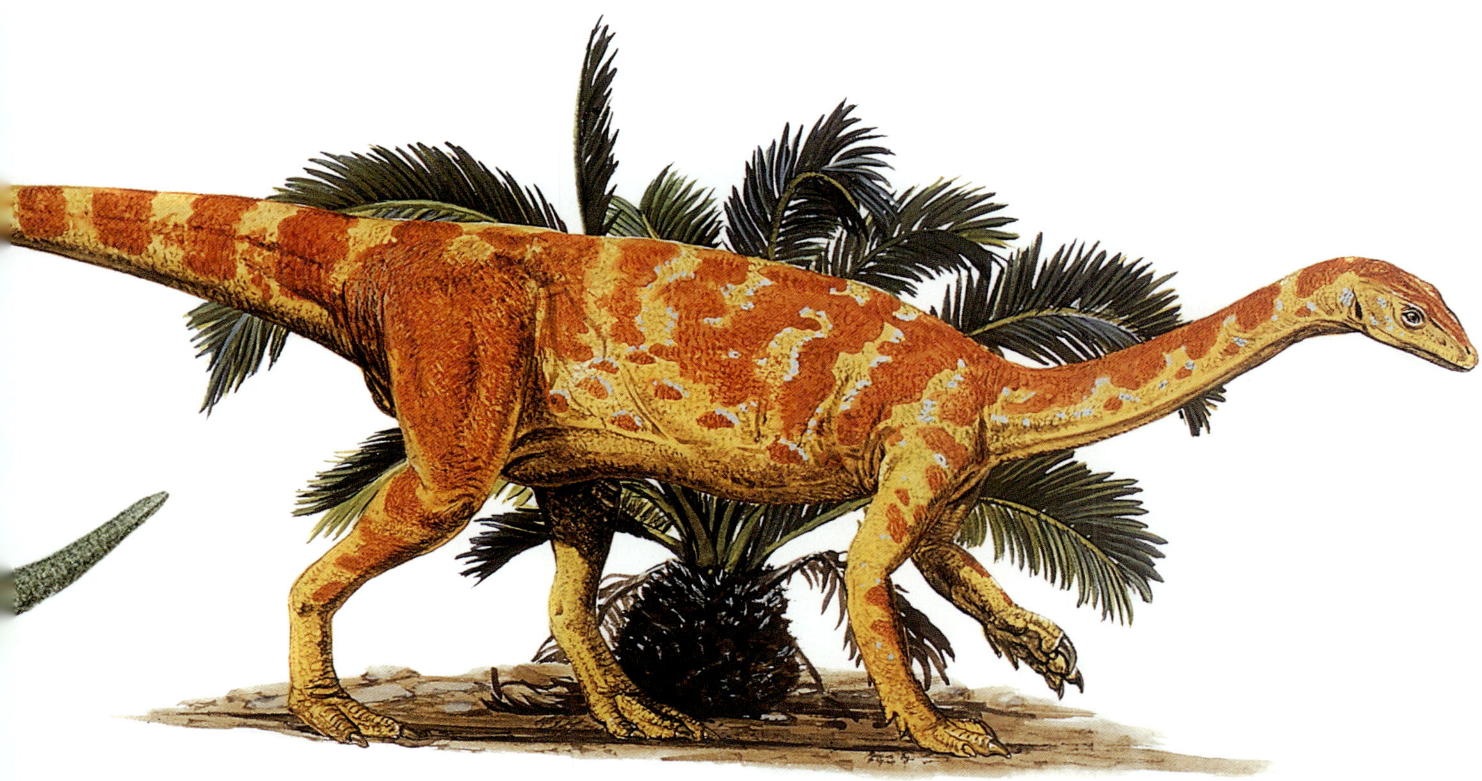

**OBEN** *Anchisaurus* war einer der kleineren Prosauropoden und unter diesen auch eines der Tiere mit dem leichtesten Körperbau. Auf der Suche nach neuen Nahrungsquellen konnte er vermutlich über große Entfernungen traben oder hüpfen.

# DIE LANDSCHAFT IN DER TRIAS

*Die Trias vor 250 – 203 Millionen Jahren war überall auf der Erde eine Zeit der Wärme. Die Kontinente bildeten eine riesige Landmasse, die wir heute die Pangäa nennen. An ihren Küstenstreifen wuchsen Farne, Palmfarne und Koniferen, von feuchten Winden umweht, doch im Innern des Doppel-Superkontinents gab es riesige Gebiete, die lediglich mit Buschwerk und Gesträuch bestanden oder einfach nur Wüste waren. In diese Welt kamen die ersten Dinosaurier.*

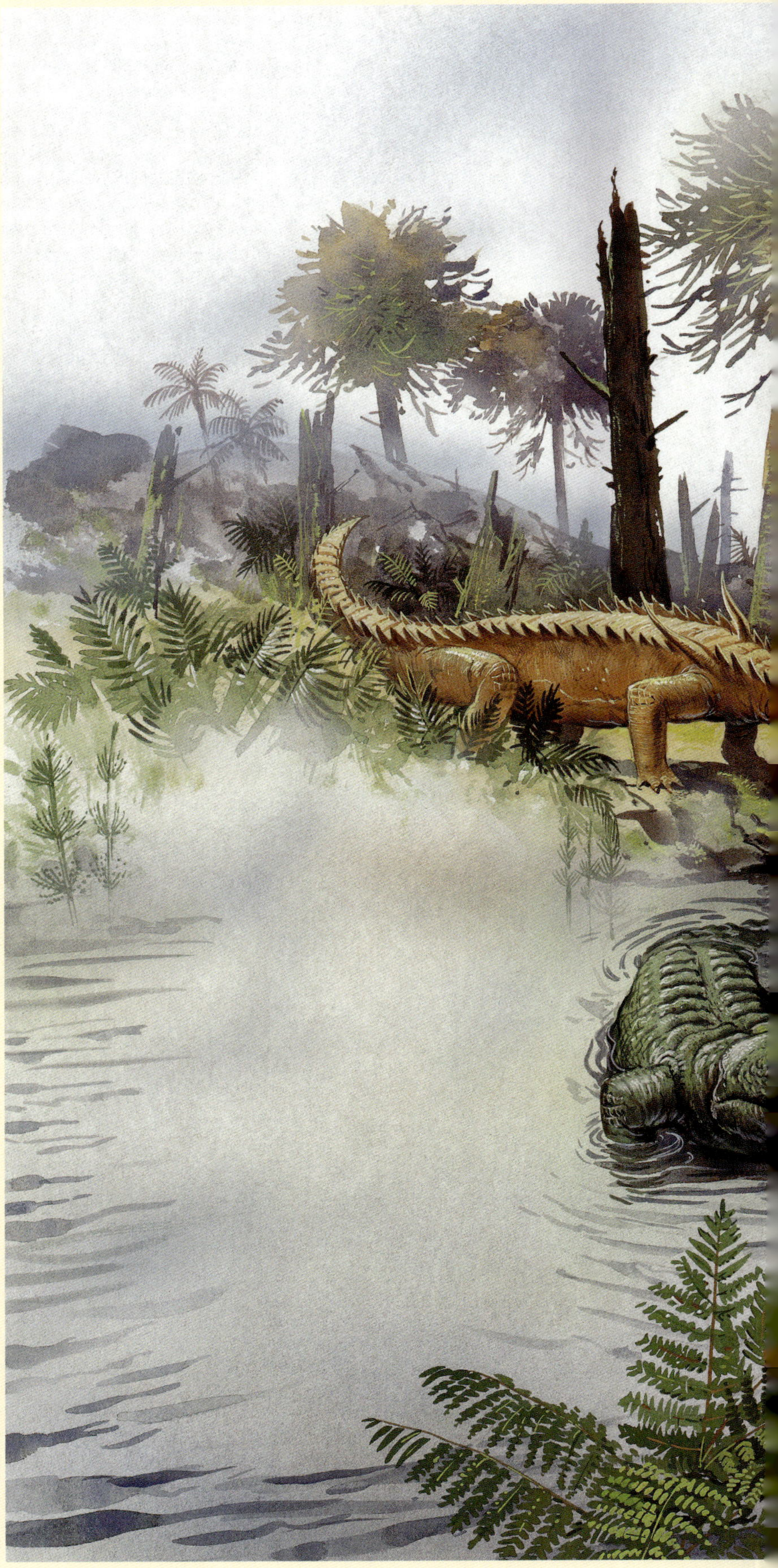

**RECHTS** In der Oberen Trias zogen die in den trockenen Landschaften verstreuten Tümpel und Wasserlöcher genau wie heute viele Tiere an. In der Szene, die hier nachgestellt wurde, erhebt sich ein krokodilartiger Phytosaurier aus dem Wasser, was eine kleine Gruppe *Coelophysis*-artiger Theropoden (rechts im Vordergrund) einzuschüchtern scheint. Links im Hintergrund steht am Tümpelrand ein Pflanzen fressender Aetosaurier, dessen Rücken mit zwei Dornenreihen bewehrt ist; rechts verlässt ein großer Pareiasaurier das Wasser, um dann zwischen den Bäumen zu verschwinden.

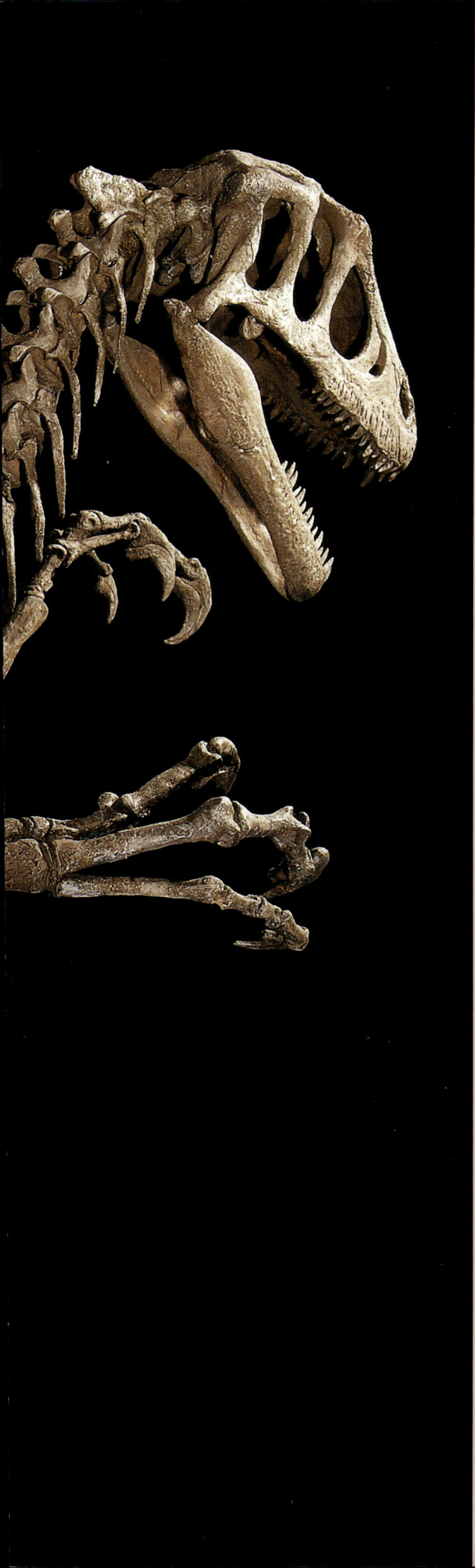

# Kapitel Vier

# Die kleinen Fleischfresser

*In unserer Zeit gibt es die Wildkatze, das Hermelin, den Fuchs, den Indischen Mungo und ähnliche Säuger als räuberisch lebende Tiere. Die Rolle kleinerer, aber dennoch tödlicher Räuber spielten im Mesozoikum verschiedene Dinosaurier. Da die Tiere damals größer waren, übertrafen manche dieser kleineren Fleischfresser selbst die heutigen Tiger und Bären!*

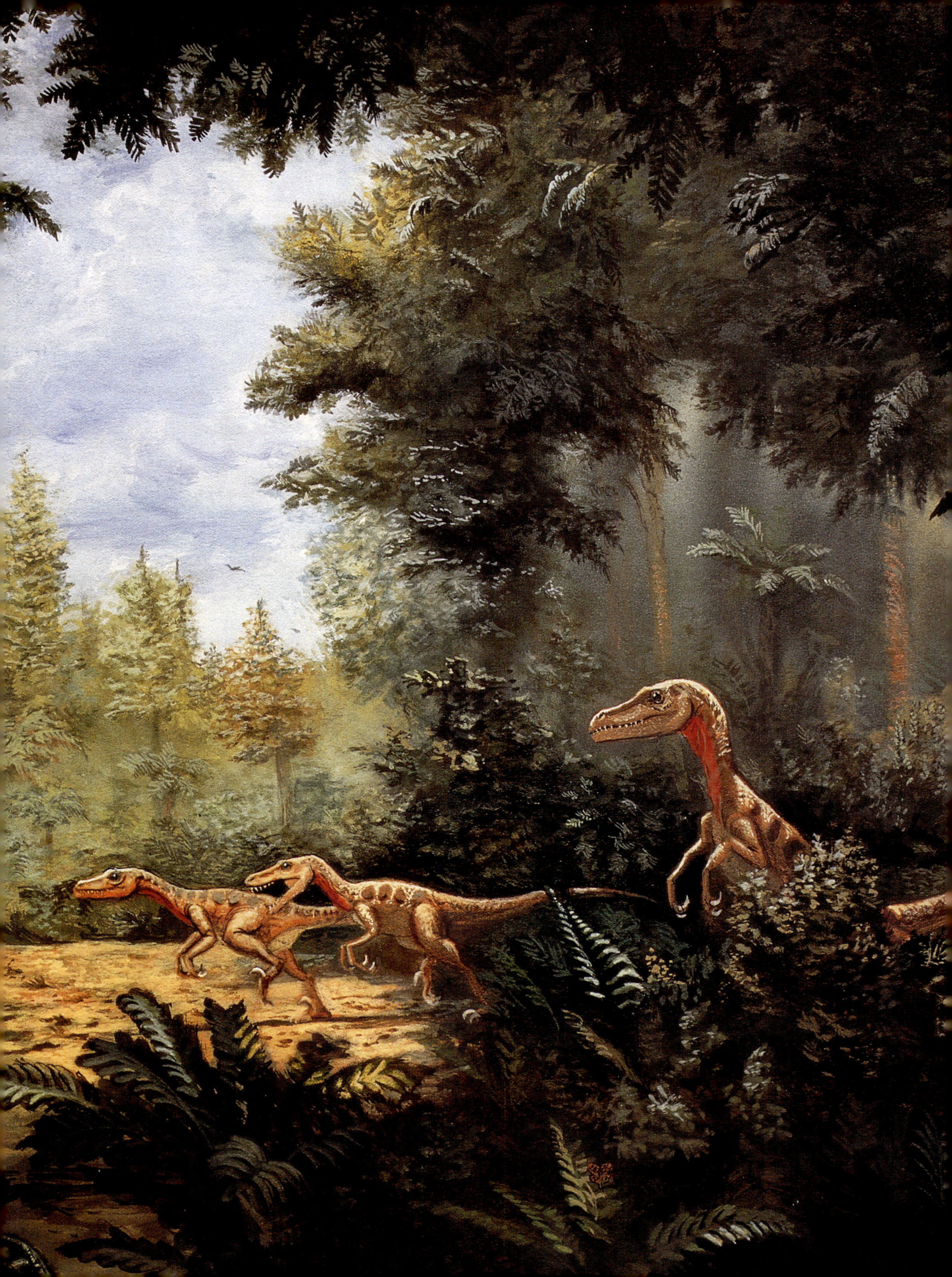

# INGENIA

Dieser Dinosaurier wird für gewöhnlich als Oviraptoride bezeichnet, d.h. er weist viele Ähnlichkeiten mit *Oviraptor* (siehe gegenüber) auf und ist möglicherweise ein naher Verwandter von diesem. *Ingenia* war vielleicht etwas kleiner, die Körperlänge lag wohl näher bei 1,5 als bei 2 Metern. Die meisten bekannten Körpermerkmale ähneln denen von *Oviraptor*, und *Ingenia* lebte auch etwa zur gleichen Zeit, vor rund 80 Millionen Jahren, in der gleichen Gegend, auf dem Gebiet der heutigen Mongolei. Seinen offiziellen Namen erhielt das Tier 1981. Wovon es sich ernährte, ist wie bei *Oviraptor* unklar. *Ingenia* mag vielleicht ein Allesfresser gewesen sein, der nach jeder Art Nahrung pickte und alles Fressbare aufhackte – Käfer, Eier, hartschalige Tiere wie Muscheln oder Schnecken, andere kleine Tiere und sogar Wurzeln und Samen. Vielleicht handelte es sich auch um einen Aasfresser, der sich an Fleisch und Knochen von Kadavern gütlich tat, wie es heute Geier und Kondor tun, oder um einen Pflanzenfresser. Der schnabelartige Kiefer war vermutlich wie bei den rezenten Vögeln von einer Hornscheide umgeben, die das hakenförmige Fresswerkzeug an den Kanten noch schärfer machte.

Besser als *Ingenia* ist der Theropode *Oviraptor* bekannt. Bestimmte fossilierte Schädel mit tiefen, zahnlosen, wie Papageienschnäbel geformten Kiefern, die denen des *Oviraptor* ähneln, aber nur einen sehr kleinen oder überhaupt keinen Schnauzenkamm tragen, wurden früher als Überreste von *Oviraptor*-Jungtieren identifiziert. Begründet wurde die Zuordnung damit, dass Kämme, Hörner und ähnliche Körpermerkmale bei Jungtieren sehr klein gewesen sein müssen und erst mit dem Heranwachsen eines Individuums schneller an Größe zunahmen, so wie es auch in der heutigen Tierwelt zu beobachten ist. Andere Details veranlassten die Fachleute jedoch dazu, einige Schädel der neueren Gattung *Ingenia* zuzuordnen. Die Untersuchungen von *Ingenia*-Fossilien wurden in den letzten Jahren fortgesetzt. Die Ergebnisse, gepaart mit neuen Erkenntnissen über die Konstruktion und die Aufgaben des Schnabels bei rezenten Vögeln, favorisieren die Variante, dass *Ingenia* ein Pflanzenfresser war.

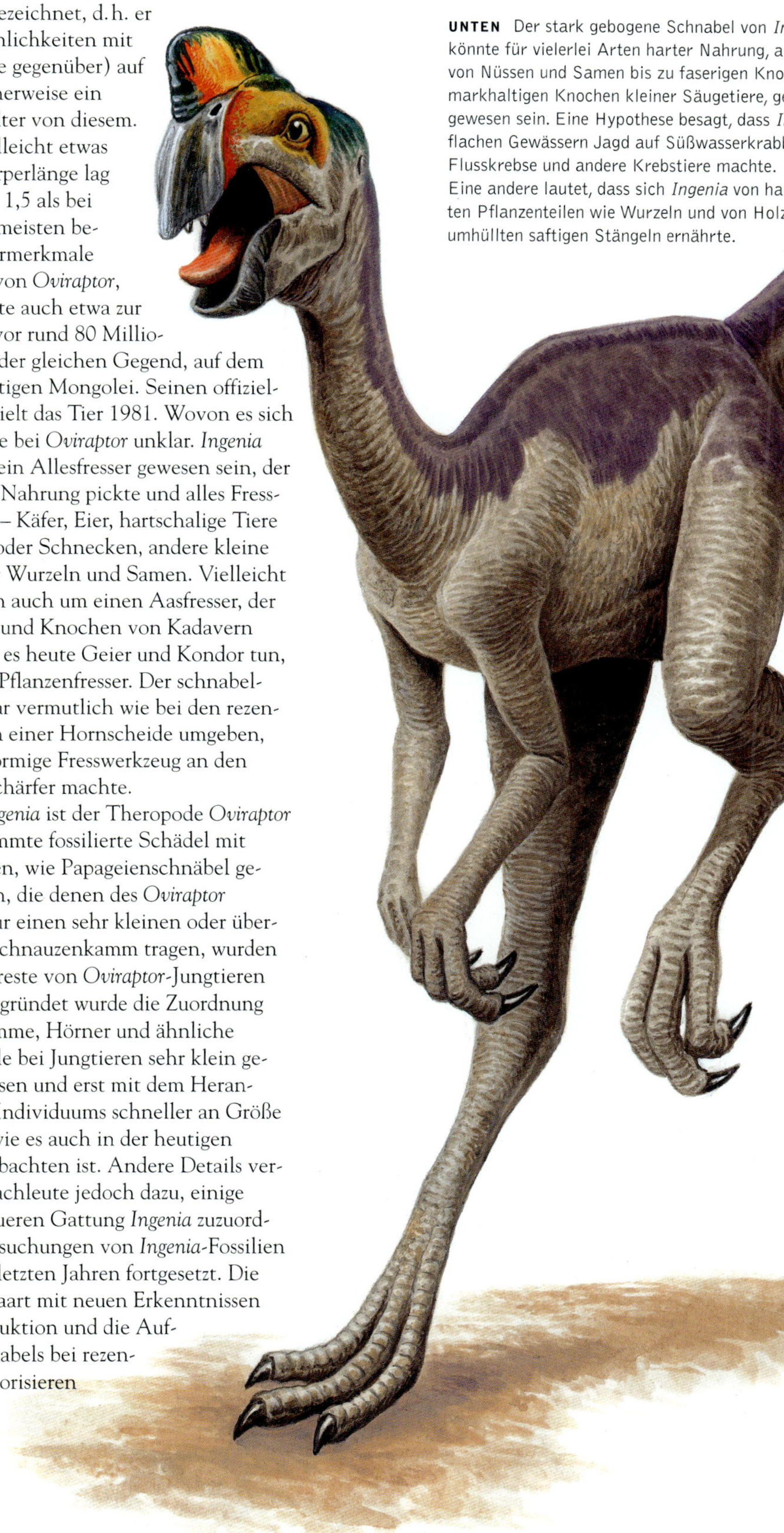

**UNTEN** Der stark gebogene Schnabel von *Ingenia* könnte für vielerlei Arten harter Nahrung, angefangen von Nüssen und Samen bis zu faserigen Knorpeln und markhaltigen Knochen kleiner Säugetiere, geeignet gewesen sein. Eine Hypothese besagt, dass *Ingenia* in flachen Gewässern Jagd auf Süßwasserkrabben, Flusskrebse und andere Krebstiere machte. Eine andere lautet, dass sich *Ingenia* von harten Pflanzenteilen wie Wurzeln und von Holz umhüllten saftigen Stängeln ernährte.

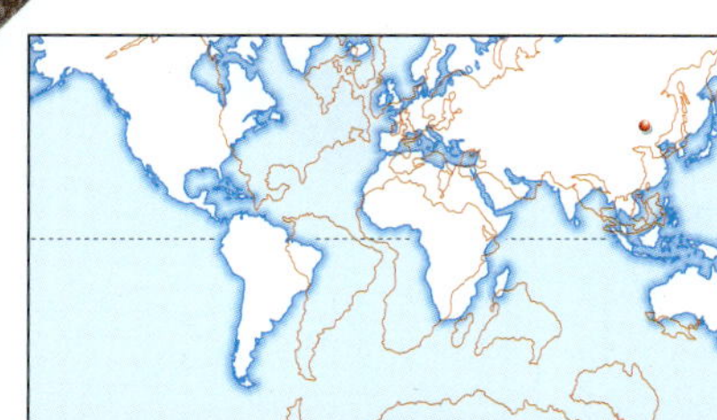

**ÜBERSICHT (DINOSAURIER)**
***Ingenia***
**Bedeutung des Namens:** Nach dem Fundort, der mongolischen Ingeni-Khobur-Senke, benannt
**Periode:** Oberkreide
**Hauptgruppe:** Theropoda
**Länge:** 1,5 – 2 Meter
**Gewicht:** 25 Kilogramm
**Nahrung:** Unklar
**Fossilfundstätten:** In der Mongolei

# Saurornitholestes

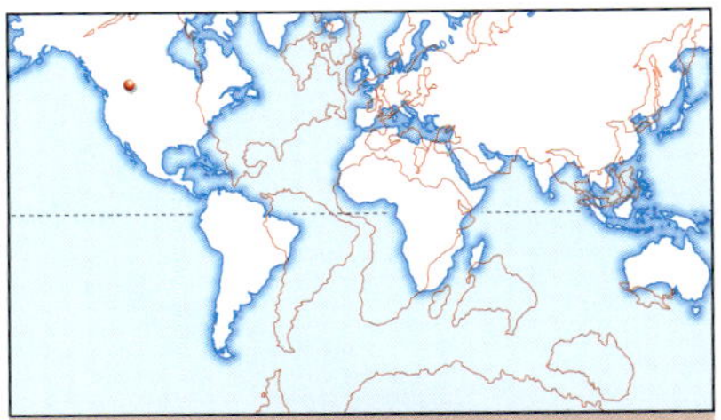

**ÜBERSICHT (DINOSAURIER)**
***Saurornitholestes***
**Bedeutung des Namens:** Vogelräuber-Reptil, vogelartiges Räuberreptil
**Periode:** Oberkreide
**Hauptgruppe:** Theropoda
**Länge:** 1,8 – 2 Meter
**Gewicht:** 5 – 20 Kilogramm
**Nahrung:** Kleine Tiere
**Fossilfundstätten:** In Kanada (Alberta)

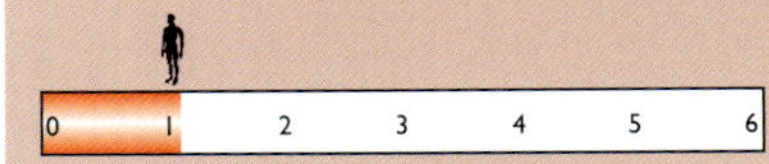


Der schnelle, Fleisch fressende *Saurornitholestes* war ein Vertreter der Dromaeosaurier oder Raptoren, der in der letzten Phase der Kreidezeit in Nordamerika existierte; seine Fossilien sind 75 – 73 Millionen Jahre alt. Zu dieser Zeit durchstreiften die großen Raubdinosaurier wie beispielsweise der Furcht erregende *Albertosaurus* und der noch mächtigere *Tyrannosaurus* das Gebiet des heutigen Nordamerika. *Saurornitholestes* war hundertmal kleiner als diese Giganten und hätte stehend einem erwachsenen Menschen nur bis zur Hüfte gereicht. Dennoch war er für seine Beute – wahrscheinlich kleine Wirbeltiere wie Echsen, Schlangen und Frösche und vielleicht Vögel sowie etwa rattengroße Säugetiere, von denen wir wissen, dass sie zu der Zeit in dem Gebiet existierten – genauso tödlich wie seine riesigen Zeitgenossen.

*Saurornitholestes* wies einige Ähnlichkeiten mit *Velociraptor* (siehe Seite 154) auf und gilt als dessen nordamerikanisches Pendant. Er wurde 1978, über fünfzig Jahre später als *Velociraptor* von Hans-Dieter Sues benannt. Zu den wichtigsten Fossilien, die man von *Saurornitholestes* entdeckte, gehörten Teile des Schädels, einige Zähne und Teile von Knochen der vorderen Gliedmaßen. Man nimmt wohl nicht zu Unrecht an, dass das Tier ein Zweifüßer war und sich ausschließlich auf seinen langen, kräftigen, aber schlanken Hinterbeinen fortbewegte. *Saurornitholestes* war vom Kopf bis zur Schwanzspitze zwei Meter lang. Da von ihm kein vollständiges Skelett vorliegt, schwanken die Schätzungen zu Körperbau und Gewicht zwischen fünf Kilogramm und dem Vierfachen davon. Einer anderen, früheren These zufolge ähnelte *Saurornitholestes* eher einem *Troodon* (siehe Seite 154), hatte mächtige Greifhände und vielleicht ein großes Hirn, das ihn zum Lernen und zu verhältnismäßig intelligentem Verhalten befähigte. Weitere Untersuchungen zeigten dann größere Ähnlichkeiten mit *Velociraptor* als mit *Troodon*.

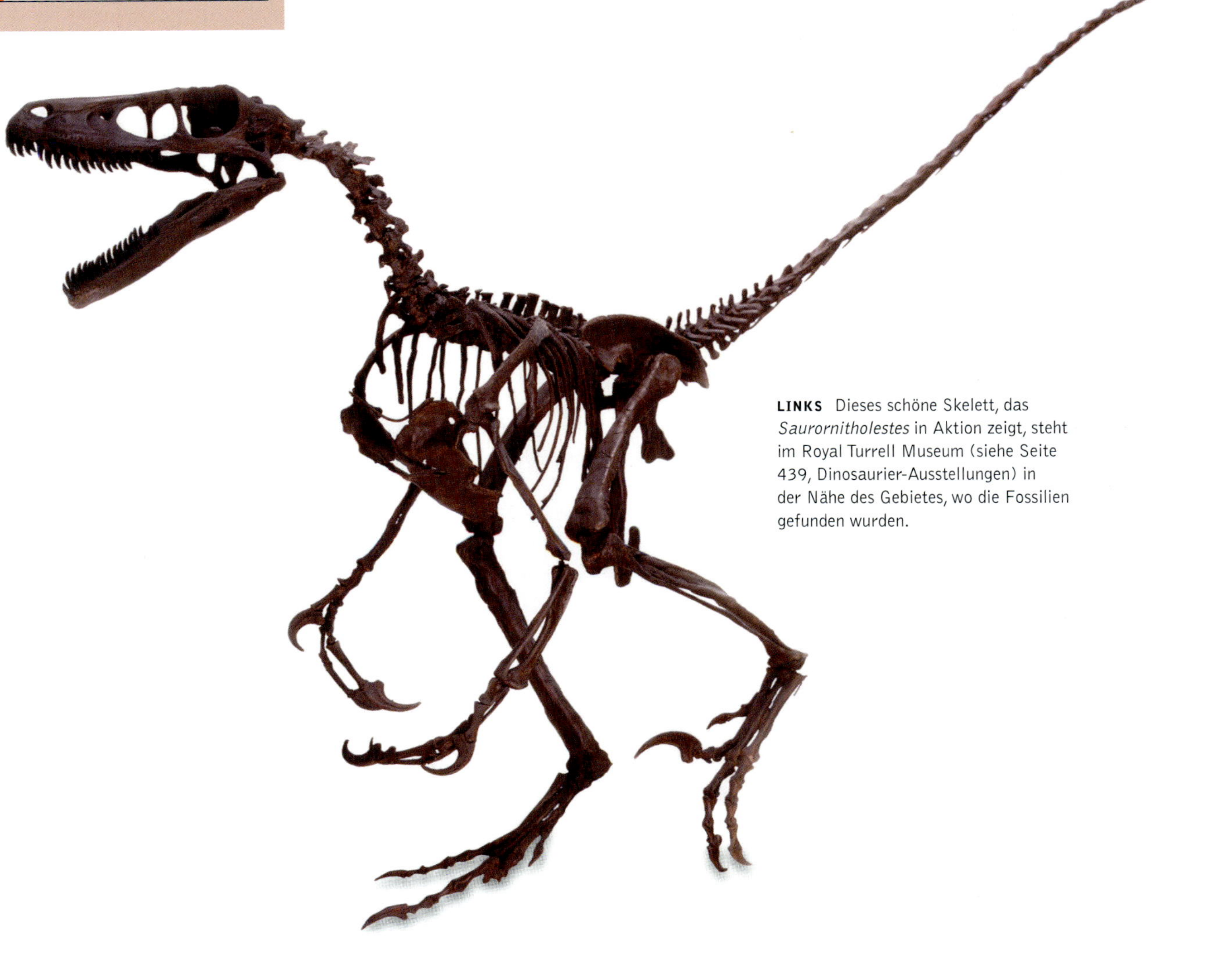

**LINKS** Dieses schöne Skelett, das *Saurornitholestes* in Aktion zeigt, steht im Royal Turrell Museum (siehe Seite 439, Dinosaurier-Ausstellungen) in der Nähe des Gebietes, wo die Fossilien gefunden wurden.

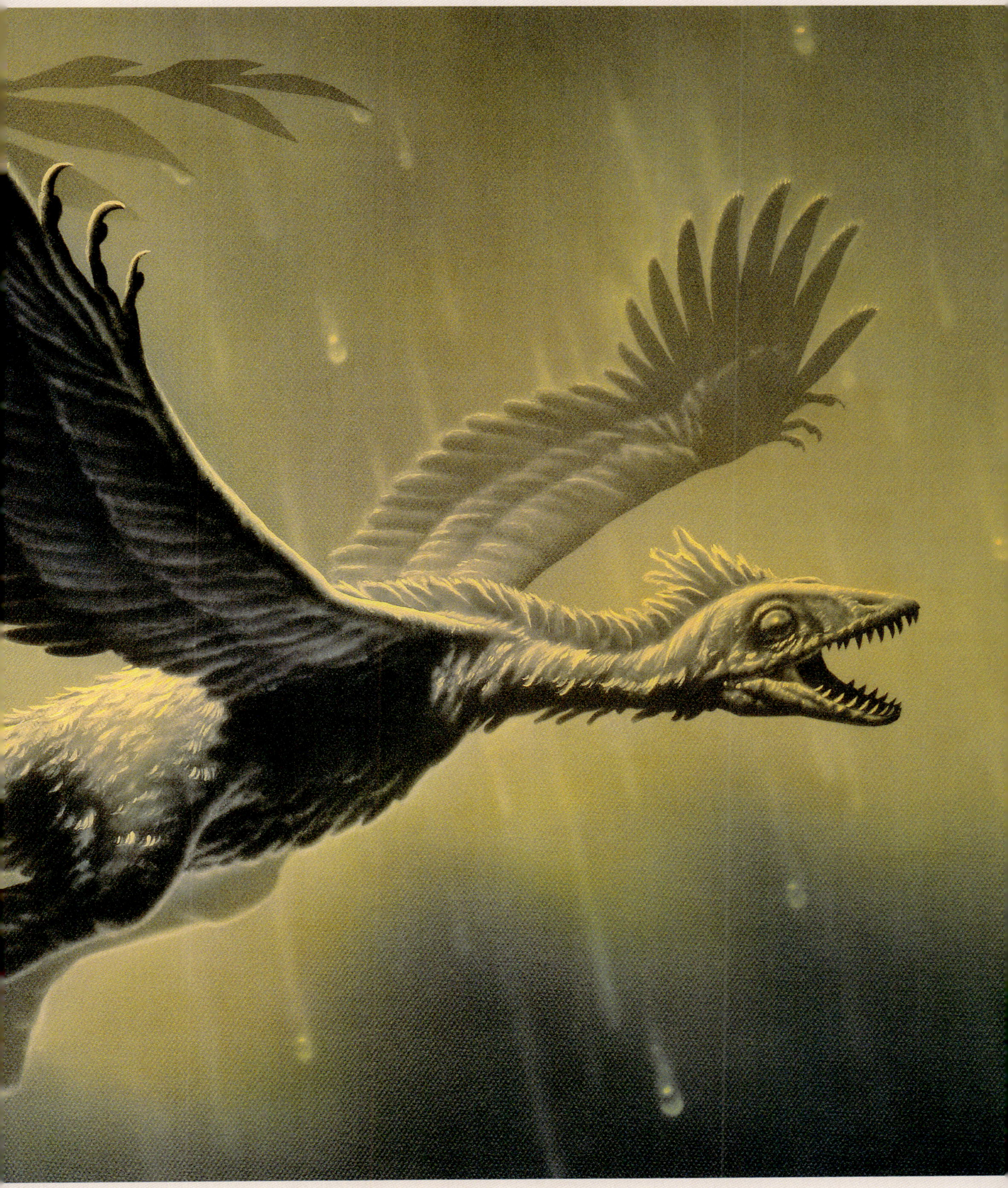

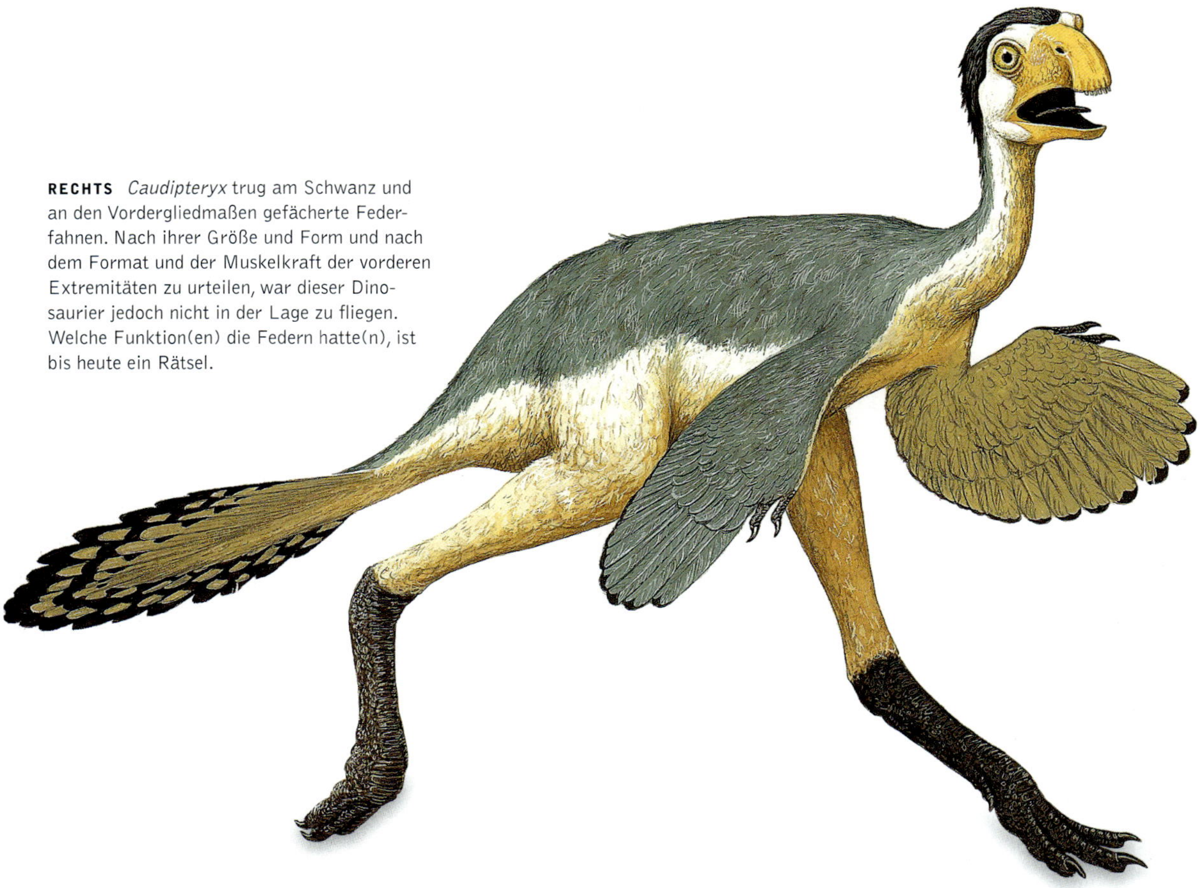

**RECHTS** *Caudipteryx* trug am Schwanz und an den Vordergliedmaßen gefächerte Federfahnen. Nach ihrer Größe und Form und nach dem Format und der Muskelkraft der vorderen Extremitäten zu urteilen, war dieser Dinosaurier jedoch nicht in der Lage zu fliegen. Welche Funktion(en) die Federn hatte(n), ist bis heute ein Rätsel.

# CAUDIPTERYX

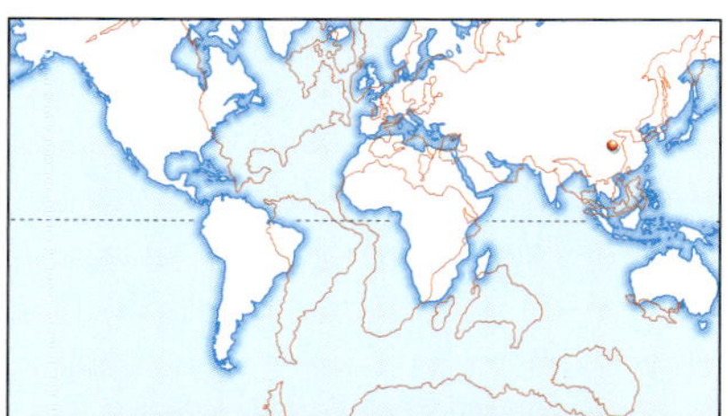

**ÜBERSICHT (DINOSAURIER)**
***Caudipteryx***
**Bedeutung des Namens:** Schwanzflügel, Schwanzfeder
**Periode:** Unterkreide
**Hauptgruppe:** Theropoda
**Länge:** 80 Zentimeter
**Gewicht:** 5 Kilogramm
**Nahrung:** Abwechslungsreich, vielleicht Tiere und Pflanzen
**Fossilfundstätten:** In China

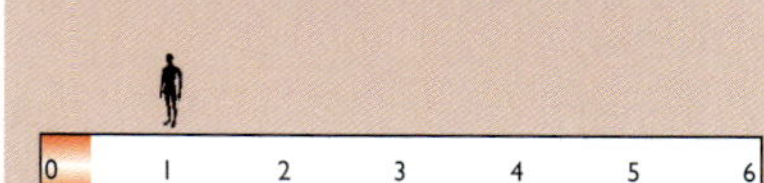


Dieses Tier ist seit der Beschreibung seiner aus der Provinz Liaoning stammenden Fossilien im Jahr 1998 Gegenstand wissenschaftlicher Diskussionen. Bei der Bestimmung der Fossilien kam man zu unterschiedlichen Ergebnissen und identifizierte diese als Überreste eines sehr ungewöhnlichen Sprosses der Gruppe kleiner Theropoden, als flugunfähigen Nachkommen bisher unbekannter Dinosaurier und sogar als Nachfahren von Vögeln, die sich von flugfähigen zu flugunfähigen Tieren entwickelt hatten. *Caudipteryx* lebte etwas später als *Archaeopteryx*, der älteste flugfähige Vogel, konnte also kein Vorfahre jener Gruppe sein. Wahrscheinlich gehörte er zu einer Gruppe von Dinosauriern, die keine Nachfahren – ganz gleich ob bei Reptilien oder Vögeln – hinterlassen haben.

Die verschiedenartigen Merkmale dieses Tieres sind sicherlich verwirrend. Ein Teil des Skeletts ähnelt in Aufbau und Proportionen einem generalisierten kleinen räuberischen Dinosaurier. Der Schwanz und auch die Vorderextremitäten sind jedoch extrem kurz, obgleich *Caudipteryx* genau wie viele andere Dinosaurier an jeder „Hand" drei lange bekrallte Finger hatte. Der Kopf ist lang und das Maul wie bei *Oviraptor* (siehe Seite 160) mit einem gebogenen Schnabel versehen. Am Oberkiefer vorn sitzen spitze Zähne, die nur wenig herausstehen und fast wie eine Fransenkante aussehen. Die langen, schlanken Beine eignen sich zur schnellen Fortbewegung; einige ihrer Knochen und Gelenke ähneln denen von *Oviraptor*, während andere Teile angeblich mehr den Beinen eines typischen Vogels der Jetztzeit ähneln.

Das vielleicht bizarrste Merkmal sind die Federn. Die an den Vordergliedmaßen und am Schwanz sitzenden Federn weisen Fahne und Kiel auf, wie es allgemein bei den Flugfedern eines Vogels der Fall ist. Die am Schwanzende sind bis zu zwanzig Zentimeter lang und fächerförmig ausgebreitet. Dennoch waren die Federn nicht im Detail wie echte Flugfedern ausgebildet, und aus der Größe und Stärke der vorderen Gliedmaßen ist zu schließen, dass *Caudipteryx* flugunfähig war. Der Großteil des Körpers scheint wie bei *Sinosauropteryx* (siehe Seite 165) mit Flaum oder faserigen Daunenfedern bedeckt gewesen zu sein.

# Therizinosaurus

In den späten 1940er Jahren fand eine sowjetisch-mongolische Forschungsexpedition, die in der Wüste Gobi nach Fossilien suchte, einige seltsame Knochenkrallen von riesiger Größe. Man glaubte, diese Krallen stammten von einem Dinosaurier oder einem ähnlich großen Tier, und so erhielt das ansonsten unbekannte Wesen 1954 den Namen *Therizinosaurus* – „Sensenreptil". In den 1950er und 1960er Jahren tauchten in Zentralasien weitere Krallen sowie Teile einer Vorderextremität und Bruchstücke einer hinteren Gliedmaße auf. Aus späteren Funden in China zogen Fachleute den Schluss, dass die Knochen zu einer Gruppe ähnlicher Dinosaurier gehörten, die unter der Sammelbezeichnung Therizinosaurier bekannt wurden. Zu den Therizinosauriern gehören auch der 1993 entdeckte *Alaxasaurus* sowie *Beipiaosaurus*, auf den man 1996 stieß. Diese jüngeren Funde lieferten weitere Einzelheiten zu dem Gesamtbild – die Ergebnisse sind wirklich erstaunlich.

*Therizinosaurus* war ein riesiger Theropode, d.h. er passt in die Gruppe der Fleischfresser, obwohl er vielleicht eher wie eine Giraffe oder ein Gorilla nur von Pflanzen gelebt hat.

*Therizinosaurus* existierte vor 75 – 70 Millionen Jahren und war einer der jüngeren Vertreter seiner Gruppe. Die drei Finger an den Vordergliedmaßen waren mit je einer gewaltigen, leicht gebogenen, abgeflachten Kralle versehen, die sich zu einer scharfen Spitze verjüngte. Die Kralle am ersten Finger war mit über sechzig Zentimetern Länge die größte; die gesamte Vordergliedmaße war 2,5 Meter lang. Der Hals war riesig, der Kopf klein und mit einem Schnabelmund versehen, der Körper tonnenförmig, das Becken breit, die hinteren Gliedmaßen waren stämmig und hatten breite, kurze Füße, die in vier Zehen endeten. *Therizinosaurus* kann riesengroß, über zehn Meter lang oder hoch und mit Flaumfedern bedeckt gewesen sein.

Es ist denkbar, dass die Therizinosaurier als Gruppe Verwandte von *Oviraptor* (siehe Seite 160) waren. Über ihre Lebensweise streiten sich die Fachleute. Vielleicht reckten sie ihre langen Hälse um in den Bäumen nach Früchten und anderen Pflanzenteilen zu picken und zu schnappen. Ihre Krallen mögen als eine Art Rechen zum Heranholen von Nahrung oder zur Verteidigung gedient haben oder waren ein Zeichen des Ranges innerhalb einer Gruppe sowie der Geschlechtsreife (wie die stark verlängerten Eckzähne eines Walrosses); vielleicht rissen sie damit Termitenbauten und Ameisenhügel auf, wie es heute der Große Ameisenbär mit seinen starken Klauen tut. Ebenfalls „Sensenreptilien" waren *Segnosaurus*, *Nanshiungosaurus*, *Erlikosaurus* und *Enigmosaurus*. Die Hinweise auf eine Körperdecke aus Federn stammen hauptsächlich von den Fossilien des *Beipiaosaurus*.

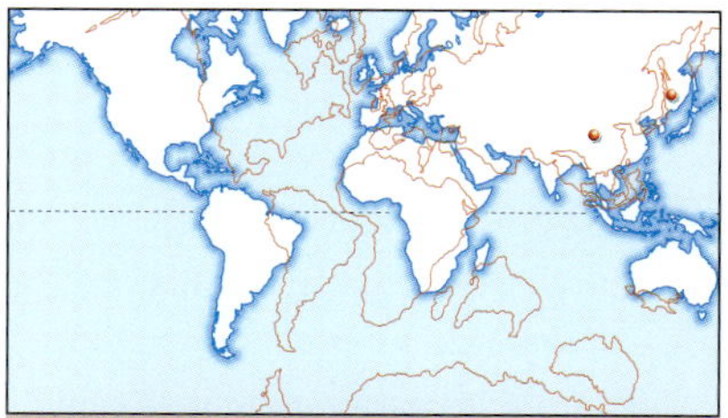

**ÜBERSICHT (DINOSAURIER)**

***Therizinosaurus***

**Bedeutung des Namens:** Sensenreptil

**Periode:** Oberkreide

**Hauptgruppe:** Theropoda

**Länge:** 10 Meter und mehr

**Gewicht:** Rund 1 Tonne

**Nahrung:** Vielleicht Pflanzen

**Fossilfundstätten:** In Zentral- und Ostasien

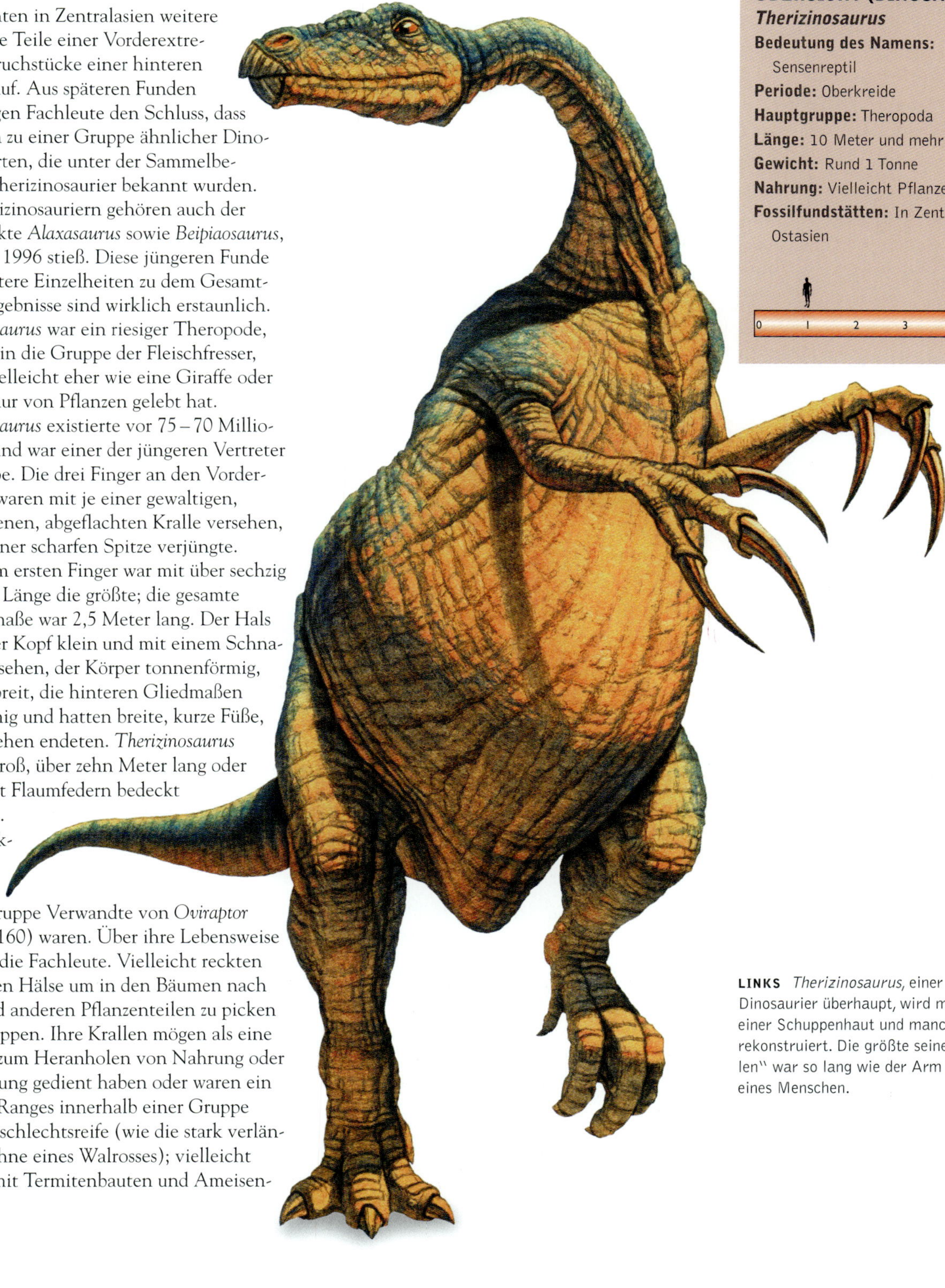

**LINKS** *Therizinosaurus,* einer der seltsamsten Dinosaurier überhaupt, wird mitunter mit einer Schuppenhaut und manchmal mit Federn rekonstruiert. Die größte seiner „Sensenkrallen" war so lang wie der Arm und die Hand eines Menschen.

# VÖGEL ALS DINOSAURIER

*Es gab eine Zeit, da wir jedes Lebewesen, das Federn besaß, als Vogel betrachteten. In jüngerer Zeit entdeckte Relikte von gefiederten Dinosauriern haben uns allerdings zum Umdenken veranlasst. Vielleicht bildeten sich die Federn ursprünglich als Wärmeisolation, als „Netz" zum Einfangen kleiner Beutetiere oder zur Tarnung heraus. Die Flugfähigkeit entwickelte sich erst später, als die Baumkletterer ihre Sturzflüge zu steuern lernten oder schnelle Läufer mit ihren Vordergliedmaßen schlugen, um bei der Verfolgung einer Beute oder auf der Flucht vor Räubern in die Höhe zu springen. Verwirrend mag sein, dass Vögel nach der modernen Klassifizierung nicht als größere, den Reptilien oder Säugetieren gleichwertige Gruppe, sondern als Untergruppe der Dinosauria gelten. Daher sind Vögel in Wirklichkeit lebende warmblütige, gefiederte Dinosaurier.*

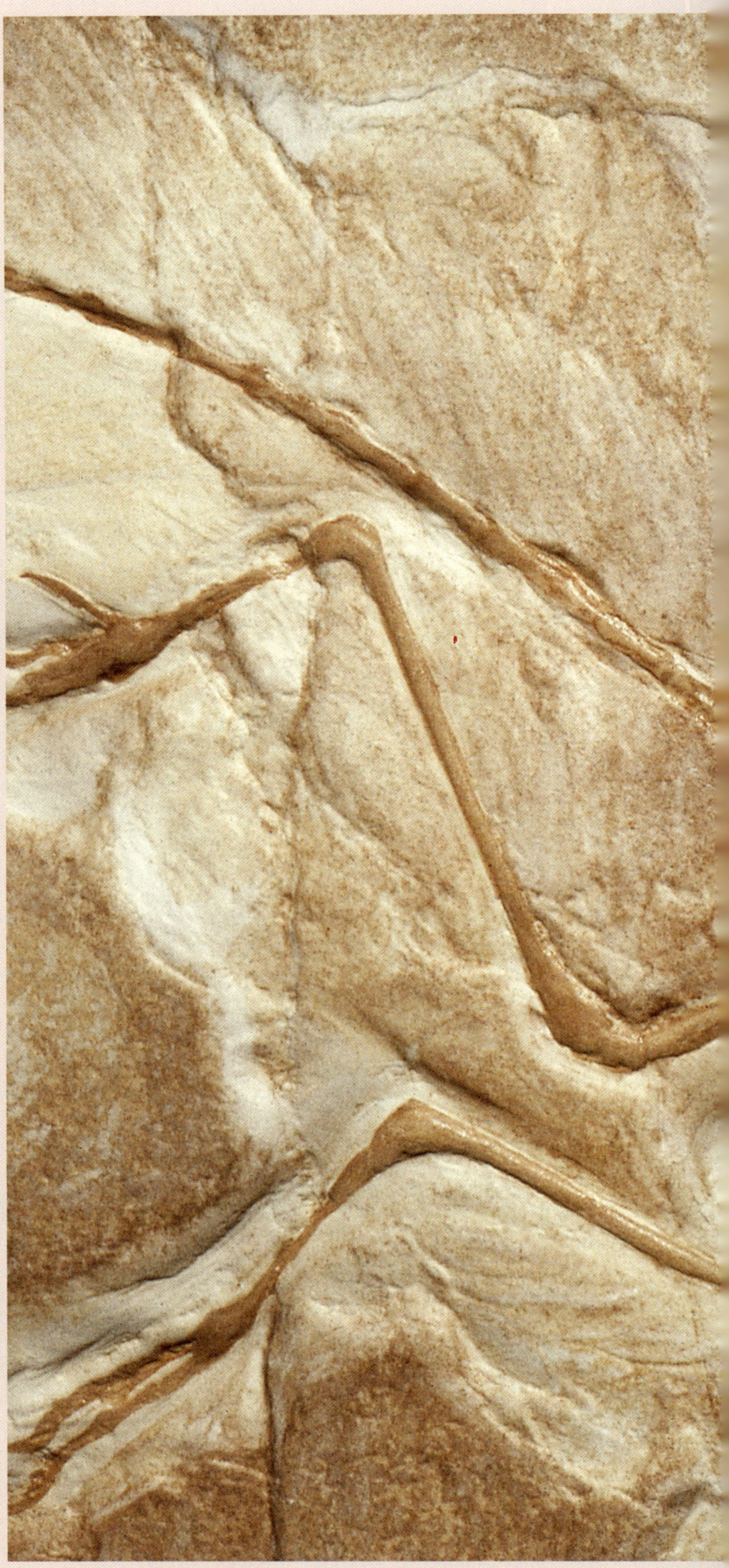

**RECHTS** Eines der weltweit berühmtesten und wertvollsten Fossilien zeigt Archaeopteryx sehr gut erhalten in der typischen Todeshaltung, die entsteht, wenn sich die Halssehnen nach dem Verenden des Tieres verkürzen und den Kopf nach oben und über den Rücken ziehen. Der lange, knöcherne Schwanz ragt nach links oben. Rechts oben und in der Mitte unten sieht man die fächerförmigen Abdrücke der Flügelfedern.

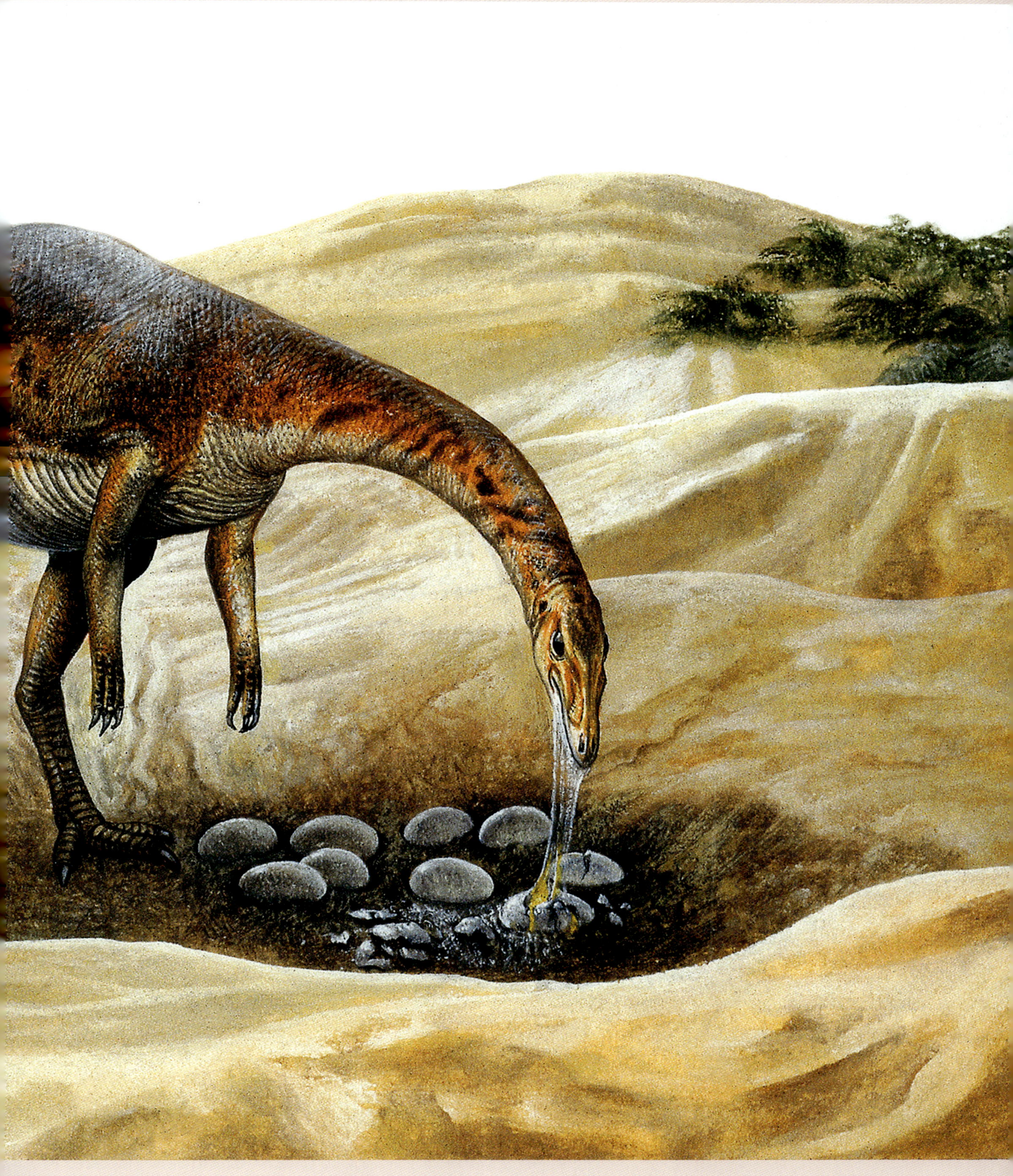

# Liaoningornis und Protarchaeopteryx

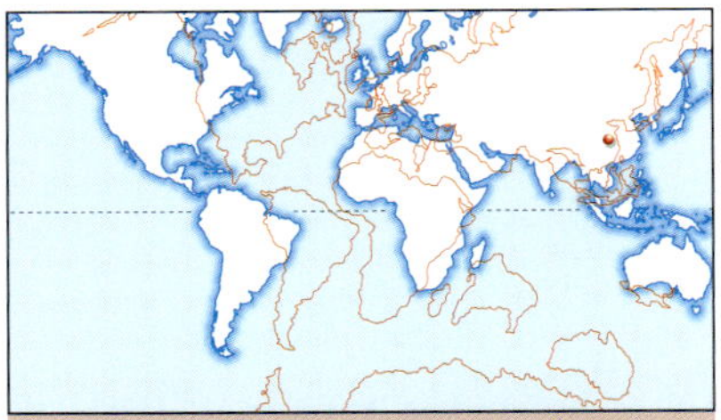

**ÜBERSICHT (VÖGEL)**
***Liaoningornis***
**Bedeutung des Namens:** Liaoning-Vogel
**Periode:** Unterkreide
**Hauptgruppe:** Aves (Vögel)
**Länge:** Schnabel–Schwanz 15 bis 18 Zentimeter
**Nahrung:** Wahrscheinlich Allesfresser
**Fossilfundstätten:** In China

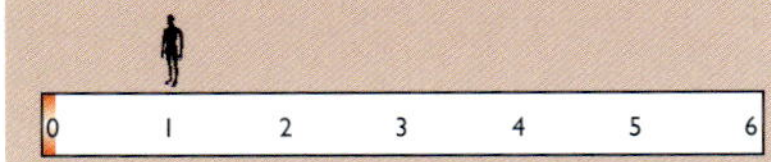


Seit den 1990er Jahren ist die nordostchinesische Provinz Liaoning eine der ergiebigsten Gegenden für die Entdeckung von Fossilien aus dem Zeitalter der Dinosaurier. Zu den Funden, die dort gemacht wurden, gehören *Confuciusornis* (siehe vorhergehende Seite), *Liaoningornis* und *Protarchaeopteryx*. An einer Fundstätte scheint einst eine Katastrophe, vermutlich ein Vulkanausbruch, fast alles Leben in der Umgebung ausgelöscht zu haben; sie hat uns eine Art „Momentaufnahme" von der damaligen Situation geliefert. Einige Fachleute hielten die Fossilien zunächst für die Reste von Lebewesen aus dem Oberen Jura und schätzten sie auf vielleicht 150 Millionen Jahre. Andere hingegen vertraten die Ansicht, die Relikte stammten aus der Unterkreide und seien 130–120 Millionen Jahre alt. Jedenfalls haben die Entdeckungen eine intensive Diskussion ausgelöst. Vor allem die Fossilien von *Liaoningornis* und *Protarchaeopteryx* lassen sich schwer interpretieren und stellen viele bestehende Vorstellungen über Reptilien und Vögel in Frage (siehe Seite 170).

*Liaoningornis* war ein früher, etwa sperlingsgroßer Vogel. Er besaß einen sehr hohen Brustkamm, einen Auswuchs auf dem Brustbein, an dem die für den Schwingenflug wichtigen großen Brustmuskeln verankert waren. Dieses Merkmal und andere Einzelheiten lassen darauf schließen, dass *Liaoningornis* mehr den rezenten Vögeln ähnelte und nicht zu den älteren Gruppen gehörte, zu denen *Archaeopteryx* und *Confuciusornis* zählten. Wenn es sich so verhielt, kann *Liaoningornis* der älteste wirklich „moderne" Vogel sein. Auch *Protarchaeopteryx* hielt man anfangs für einen Vogel; wie sein Name schon sagt, schienen bestimmte Merkmale darauf hinzuweisen, dass er eine Art Vorfahr von *Archaeopteryx* (siehe Seite 172) war. Er lebte allerdings viel später als *Archaeopteryx* und ist wahrscheinlich kein Vogel, sondern ein Dinosaurier. Der Fleischfresser oder Theropode konnte nicht fliegen, trug aber an den Armen, fast am gesamten Rumpf und an seinem kurzen Schwanz – hier fächerartig angeordnete – Federn. Vielleicht dienten sie der Wärmeisolation seines warmblütigen Körpers und/oder hatten lediglich eine optische Funktion während der Paarungszeit (siehe Seite 168).

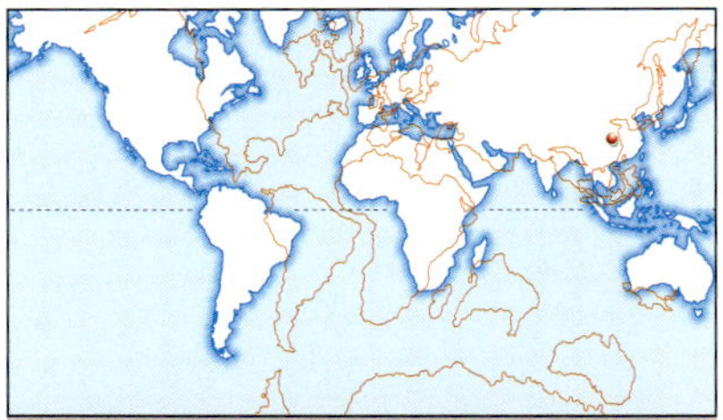

**ÜBERSICHT (VÖGEL)**
***Protarchaeopteryx***
**Bedeutung des Namens:** Vor Archaeopteryx
**Periode:** Unterkreide
**Hauptgruppe:** Theropoda
**Länge:** 70 Zentimeter
**Nahrung:** Wahrscheinlich kleine Beutetiere oder Nahrung eines Allesfressers
**Fossilfundstätten:** In China

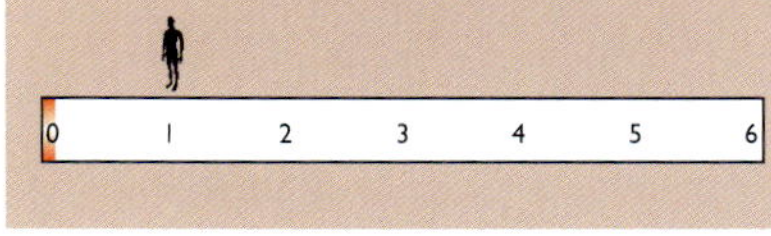


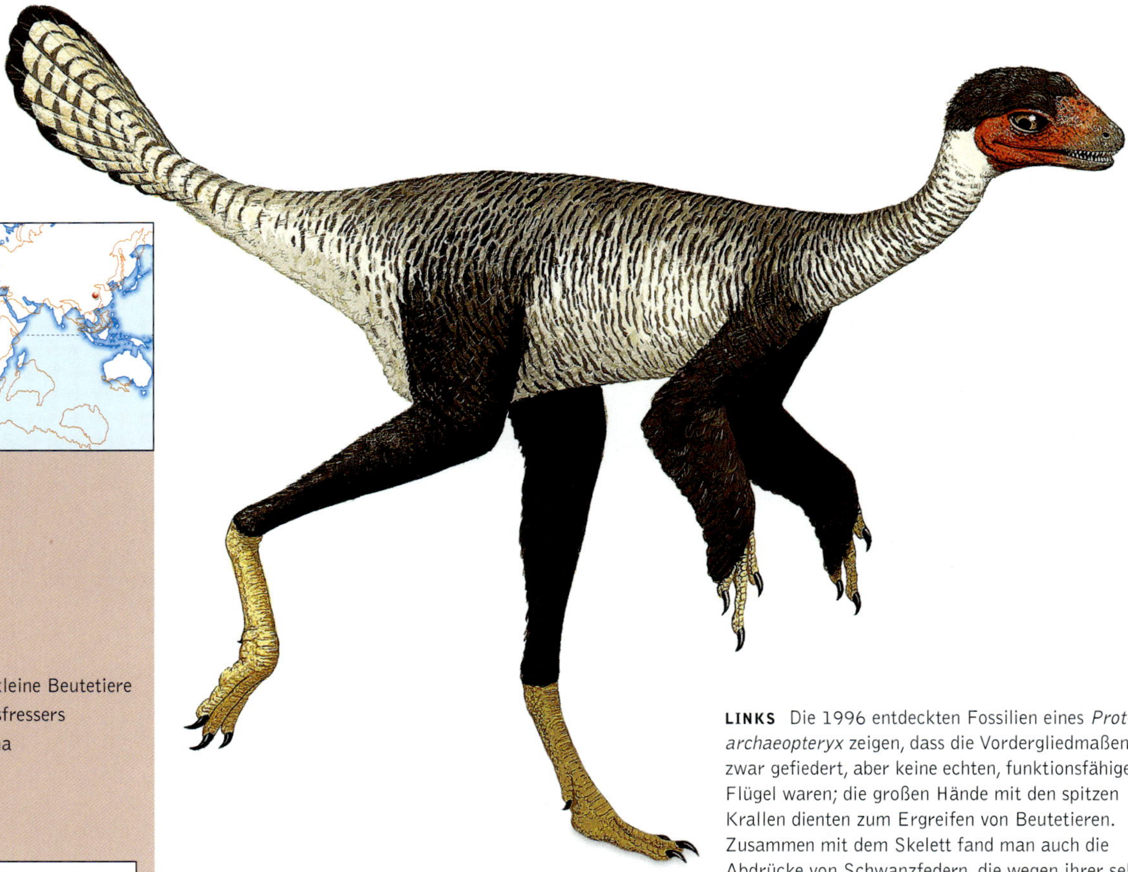

**LINKS** Die 1996 entdeckten Fossilien eines *Protarchaeopteryx* zeigen, dass die Vordergliedmaßen zwar gefiedert, aber keine echten, funktionsfähigen Flügel waren; die großen Hände mit den spitzen Krallen dienten zum Ergreifen von Beutetieren. Zusammen mit dem Skelett fand man auch die Abdrücke von Schwanzfedern, die wegen ihrer seltsamen Lage von einigen Experten aber für die Federn eines anderen Tieres gehalten werden.

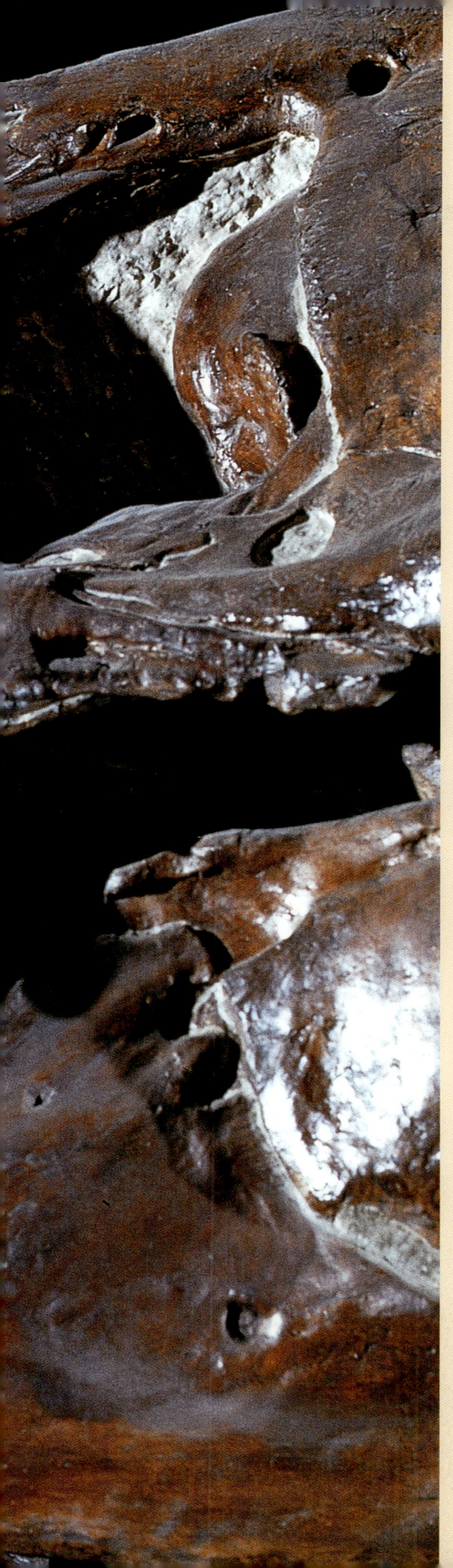

KAPITEL FÜNF

# GROSSE RAUB-DINOSAURIER

*Die größten Fleischfresser, die je auf der Erde gelebt haben und hier auf Pirsch gingen – Allosaurus, Tyrannosaurus und Gigantosaurus – wirken noch heute, mehr als 65 Millionen Jahre nach ihrem Aussterben, Furcht erregend.*

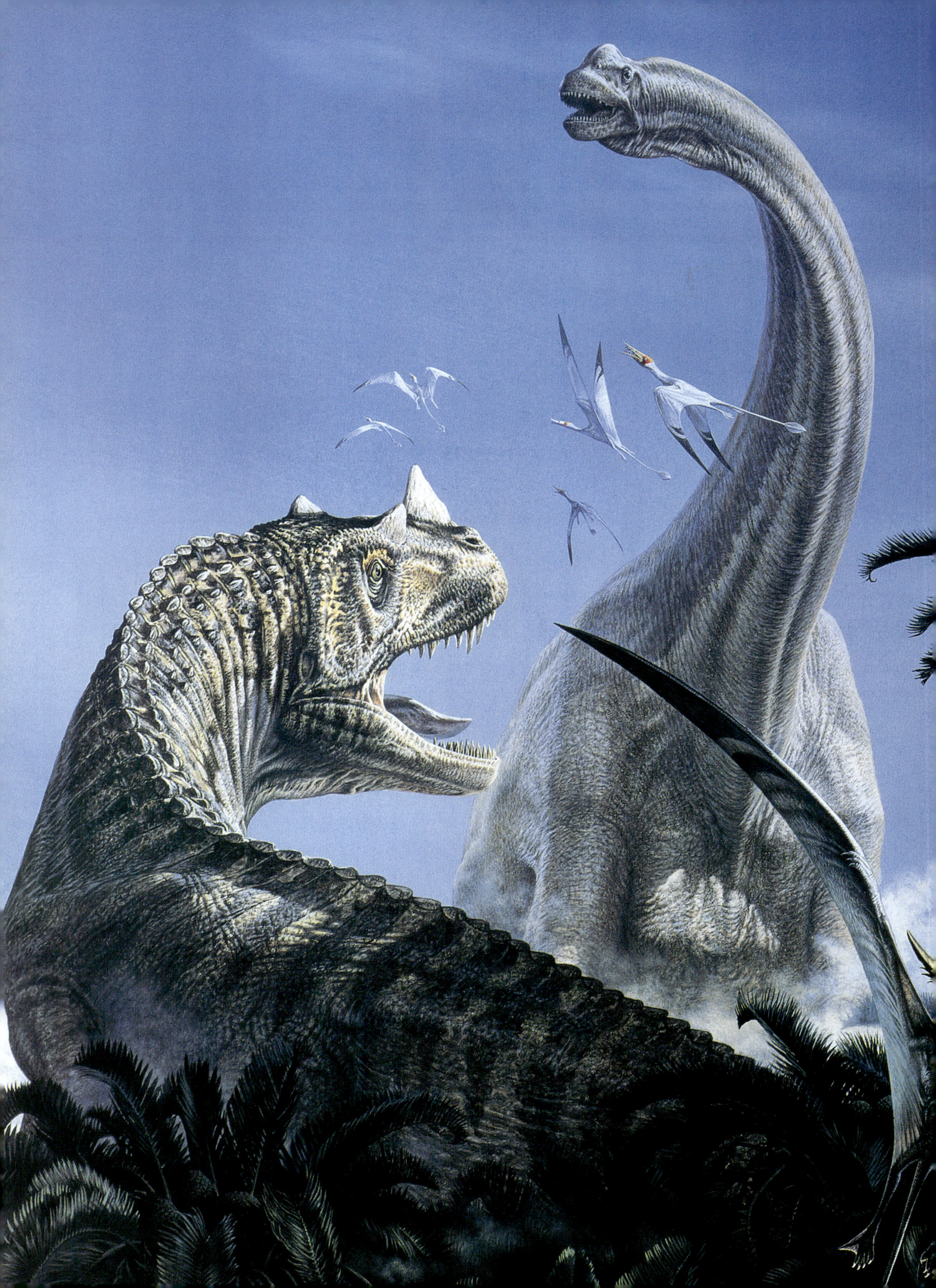

# DIE GRÖSSTEN FLEISCHFRESSER

***Zu den Theropoden gehören alle räuberisch lebenden Dinosaurier – große wie kleine. Bei den Theropoden gab es mehrere Untergruppen, deren Vertreter die größten Land bewohnenden Jäger waren, die die Welt je gesehen hat. Bemerkenswert ist jedoch, dass in den prähistorischen Meeren noch gigantischere Räuber wie etwa der Pliosaurier Liopleurodon existierten und dass ähnliche Riesen – die Pottwale, die mit ihrer Körpermasse die größten Raubdinosaurier um ein Mehrfaches übertreffen – auch die heutigen Ozeane durchstreifen.***

## WIE GROSS WAREN DIE GROSSEN?

Die großen Theropoden waren um ein Mehrfaches größer als die heutigen Rekordhalter unter den landlebenden Jägern wie etwa der Grizzlybär oder der Sibirische Tiger, die beide weniger als eine Tonne wiegen. Der bekannte *Tyrannosaurus* Nordamerikas wog mehr als fünf Tonnen, und *Giganotosaurus*, dessen Fossilien erst viel später in Südamerika entdeckt worden sind, war noch eine oder zwei Tonnen schwerer. Jüngste Fossilfunde, die ebenfalls aus Südamerika stammen, deuten darauf hin, dass es Tiere von noch gewaltigerer Größe gab.

## GRUPPEN GROSSER JÄGER

Die großen Fleischfresser stammten aus verschiedenen Untergruppen der Dinosaurier. Eine dieser Untergruppen waren die Ceratosaurier mit Vertretern wie *Dilophosaurus*, *Carnotaurus* und *Ceratosaurus* selbst. Der Name Ceratosaurier bedeutet „gehörntes Reptil", doch nicht alle Ceratosaurier trugen Hörner, wohingegen viele Nicht-Ceratosaurier Hörner besaßen. Die Raubdinosaurier konnten sich vor allem im Jura durchsetzen, verschwanden danach aber auf den nördlichen Kontinenten allmählich. Ihren Platz nahmen die Tetanurer oder „Starrschwänze" wie *Eustreptospondylus*, *Megalosaurus*, *Spinosaurus* und *Allosaurus* ein. Später im Zeitalter der Dinosaurier erschienen noch größere Tenaturen wie *Giganotosaurus* und ganz am Schluss *Tyrannosaurus* (siehe Seiten 187 und 202).

## JÄGER ODER AASFRESSER?

Heute wird viel über die Frage debattiert, ob die Riesen in erster Linie Jäger oder Aasfresser waren. Falls Letzteres zutrifft, könnten diese Tiere den großen Herden riesiger Pflanzen fressender Dinosaurier gefolgt sein und sich an jedem leichten Opfer, tot oder verendend, alt oder jung, krank oder verletzt, gütlich getan haben. Wenn sie aber Jäger waren, jagten sie dann aus dem Hinterhalt oder verfolgten sie ihre Beute? Pirschten sie sich an eine potenzielle Beute heran, lauerten ihr auf und überfielen dann das überraschte Tier, oder verfolgten sie das Opfer beharrlich, bis es ermüdete und langsamer wurde? Fossilierte Fußspuren zeigen uns, dass Dinosaurier wie *Tyrannosaurus* sowohl rennen als auch gehen konnten. Unklar ist jedoch, ob sie langsam und bedächtig umherstampften oder sich schneller fortbewegten. Die Schätzungen zu ihrer Höchstgeschwindigkeit reichen von weniger als zwanzig bis mehr als fünfzig Kilometer pro Stunde. Die Zähne und Schädel vieler großer Fleischfresser erscheinen sehr kräftig gebaut; so konnten sie der Beanspruchung durch kämpfende und sich wehrende Beutetiere standhalten. Auch die Hälse waren stark gebaut, damit die Tiere ihre Köpfe ruckartig bewegen und drehen konnten, wenn sie beispielsweise große Fleischstücke aus ihrer Beute herausrissen.

## ANGEPASSTER APPETIT

Vielleicht mussten sich die großen Raubdinosaurier zu ihren Lebzeiten gar nicht zwischen Auflauern, Verfolgung oder Aasfressen entscheiden. Denkbar ist, dass sie wie die heutigen Hyänen, Schakale und Wölfe einfach jede günstige Gelegenheit nutzten, die ihnen über den Weg lief. Neuere Entdeckungen von *Tyrannosaurus*-Fossilien lassen darauf schließen, dass die Tiere in Familien oder größeren Gruppen lebten. Die Vorstellung von einem ausgehungerten Rudel dieser Fleischfresser, von denen einige auf der Lauer liegen, einige ein Beutetier verfolgen und andere, vielleicht die Jungtiere, Aas fressen, ist wirklich überwältigend.

**VORHERGEHENDE SEITE** Die Zähne des *Tyrannosaurus* waren fünfzehn Zentimeter lang, nach hinten gekrümmt und sägeblattartig. Ihre unterschiedliche Größe rührte vom Rhythmus der Erneuerung her; war ein Zahn abgebrochen oder ausgefallen, wuchs an seiner Stelle ein neuer nach, so dass die Kiefer stets mit einem Durcheinander von Zähnen in unterschiedlichen Wachstumsphasen bestückt waren. Diese Art des Zahnwechsels ist auch bei rezenten Reptilien, z. B. bei Krokodilen, zu beobachten. Die Erneuerung fand nicht wie etwa beim Menschen im Ganzen statt.

**LINKS** Ein hungriger *Ceratosaurus* nähert sich einem hoch aufragenden *Brachiosaurus*. Das Zusammentreffen in dieser Szene aus dem Oberen Jura (vor etwa 150 Millionen Jahren) hat einen Schwarm Pterosaurier der Gattung *Rhamphorhynchus* aufgeschreckt.

# DASPLETOSAURUS

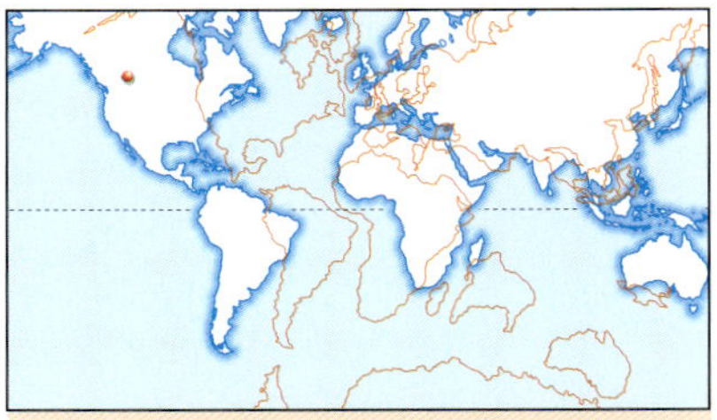

**ÜBERSICHT (DINOSAURIER)**
***Daspletosaurus***
**Bedeutung des Namens:** Schreckliches Reptil, schreckliches Fleisch fressendes Reptil
**Periode:** Oberkreide
**Hauptgruppe:** Theropoda
**Länge:** 9–10 Meter
**Gewicht:** 3 Tonnen
**Nahrung:** Große Beutetiere, Kadaver
**Fossilfundstätten:** In Kanada (Alberta)

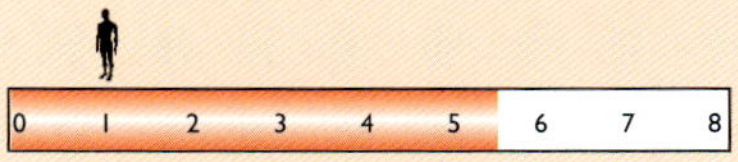


Die ersten Fossilien dieses großen, starken, kräftig gebauten Raubdinosauriers fand 1921 Charles M. Sternberg in der Gegend von Steveville am Red Deer River in der kanadischen Provinz Alberta. Sie galten zunächst als Überreste eines *Gorgosaurus*, eines dem *Tyrannosaurus* ähnelnden Dinosauriers, der bereits 1914 entdeckt und benannt worden war. 1970 berichtete der amerikanische Paläontologe und Dinosaurier-Experte Dale Russell über eine umfassende Untersuchung dieser Dinosauriertypen in Westkanada, in deren Folge die leichter gebauten Exemplare von *Gorgosaurus* neu als *Albertosaurus* klassifiziert wurden. Andere Exemplare mit kräftigerem oder robusterem Körperbau benannte man in *Daspletosaurus* um. Seitdem hat es mehrmals Vorschläge gegeben, *Daspletosaurus* als schwerere maskuline Form einer der *Albertosaurus*-Arten oder aber als einen kleineren Vorfahren des etwas jüngeren und größeren *Tyrannosaurus* einzuordnen. Für eine Klärung der Frage bedarf es wohl weiterer Fossilbelege.

Der Furcht erregende *Daspletosaurus* lebte vor etwa 75–72 Millionen Jahren. Fossilien anderer Tiere sowie Pflanzenreste, die zusammen mit den Relikten dieses Dinosauriers gefunden wurden, lassen darauf schließen, dass *Daspletosaurus* in einem marschigen oder sumpfigen Lebensraum existierte. Das Tier besaß mehrere bemerkenswerte Charakteristika. Seine Zähne gehören zu den längsten Dinosaurierzähnen überhaupt; ihre Kronen (der das Zahnfleisch überragende Zahnteil) maßen zwanzig Zentimeter oder mehr. Sie saßen wie zwei Reihen großer, nach hinten gekrümmter Dolche in den starken Kiefern des massigen Kopfes; das deutet darauf hin, dass *Daspletosaurus* ein sehr kräftiger Jäger war, der selbst die härtesten Brocken wie etwa Hadrosaurier und vielleicht *Triceratops* angreifen konnte. Seine Vordergliedmaßen waren klein, doch im Verhältnis gesehen größer als bei fast allen anderen Tyrannosauriern. *Daspletosaurus* trug wie mehrere andere große Theropoden auch kleine „Hörner“, von denen je eines knapp über und genau vor den Augen saß.

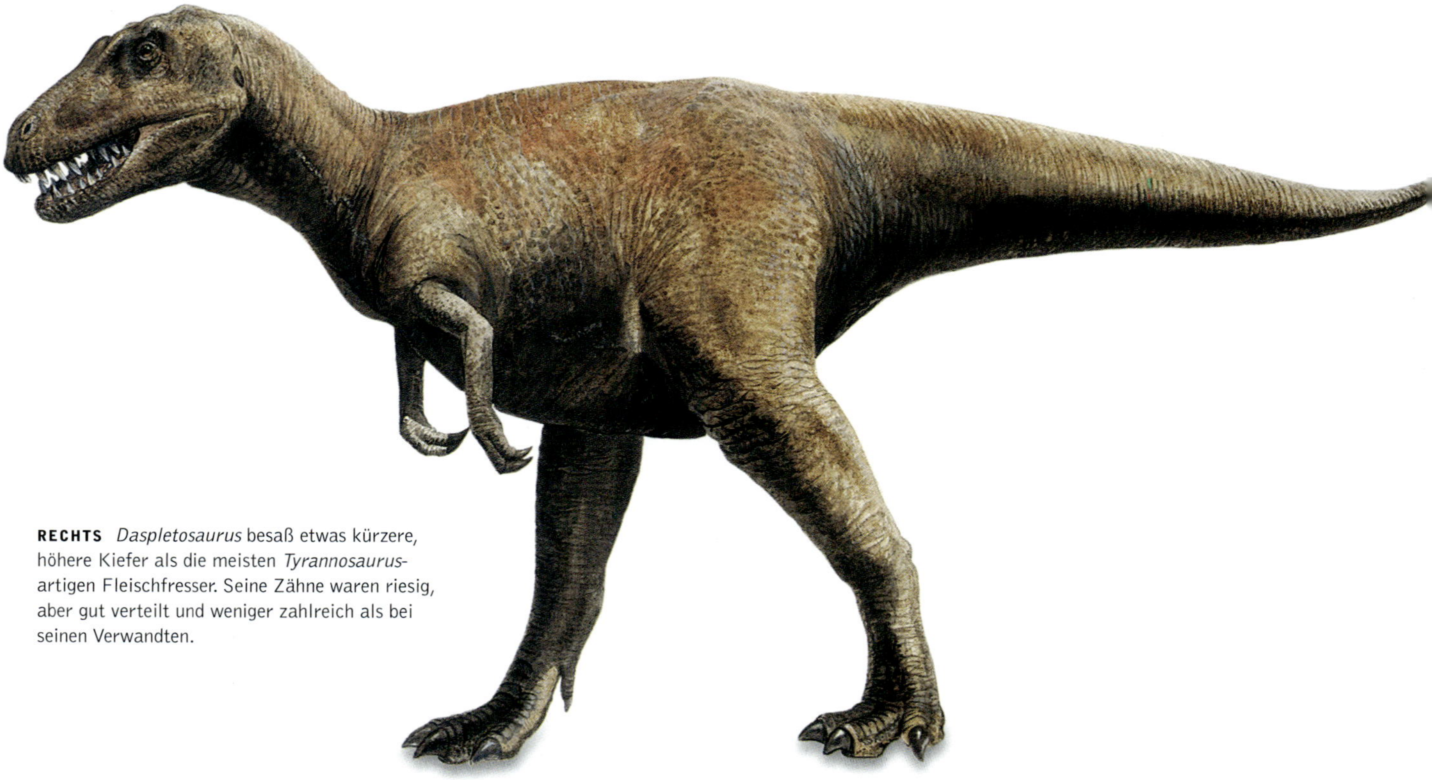

**RECHTS** *Daspletosaurus* besaß etwas kürzere, höhere Kiefer als die meisten *Tyrannosaurus*-artigen Fleischfresser. Seine Zähne waren riesig, aber gut verteilt und weniger zahlreich als bei seinen Verwandten.

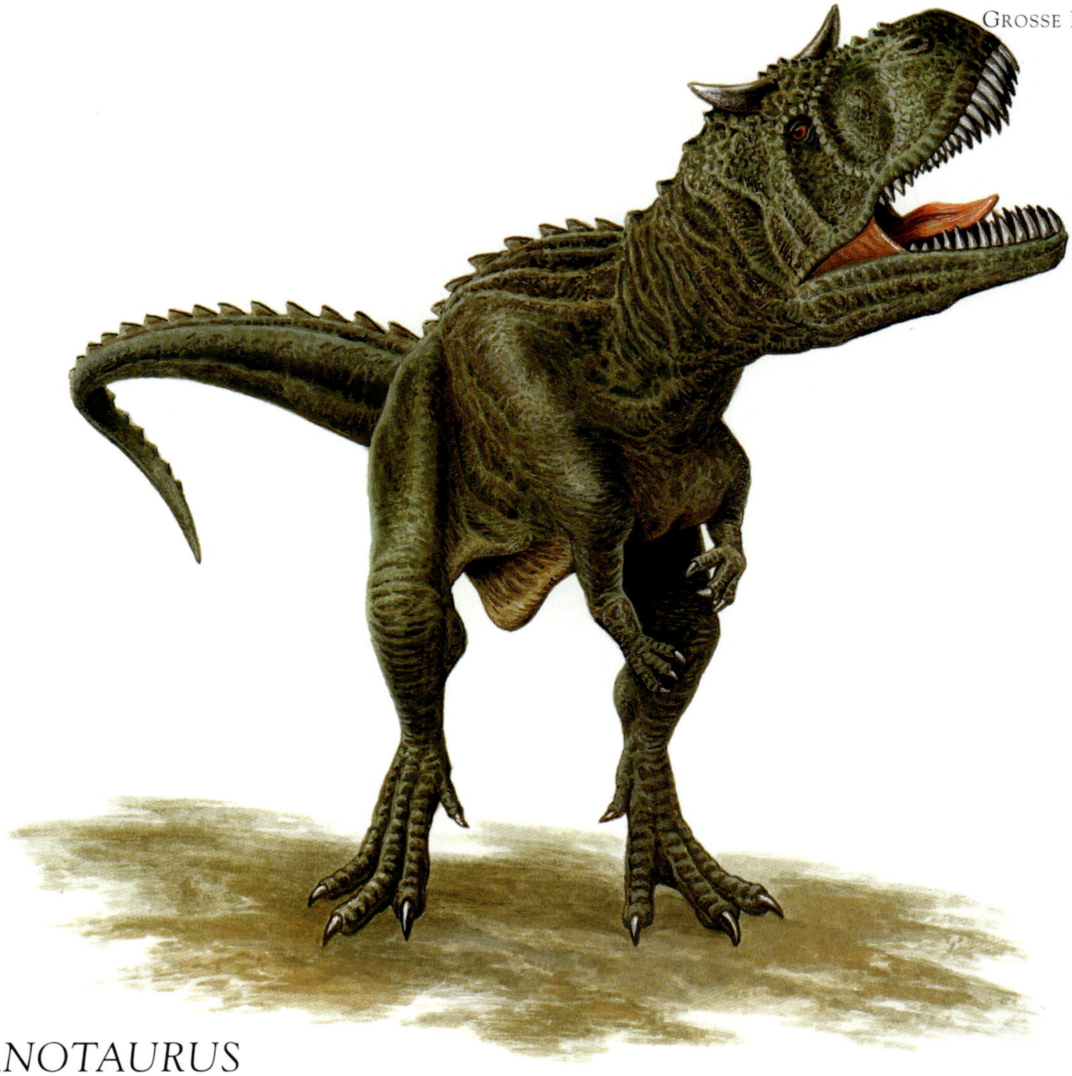

# CARNOTAURUS

*Carnotaurus* war ein großer Theropode der Kreidezeit. José Bonaparte benannte ihn 1985 auf der Grundlage fast vollständiger Skelettüberreste, die man in der fossilienreichen argentinischen Provinz Chubut ausgegraben hatte. Die Untersuchungen zeigten, dass *Carnotaurus* ein Verwandter von *Abelisaurus* war, den Bonaparte und seine Mitarbeiter bereits 1985 wissenschaftlich benannt hatten. Die Abelisauriden stellten eine Theropodengruppe dar, deren Vertreter zwar als primitiv einzustufen sind, die aber dennoch eine lange, durch die Kreidezeit sich hinziehende Geschichte hatten. Die Beute des *Carnotaurus* bestand möglicherweise aus jungen, alten oder kranken Pflanzenfressern wie dem Sauropoden *Chubutisaurus*, der von Fossilien aus etwa der gleichen Zeit und Region bekannt ist. Über die Nahrung des *Carnotaurus* gibt es aufgrund der eigenartigen Kieferproportionen des Tieres allerdings ganz verschiedene Ansichten.

Bei *Carnotaurus* saß über beiden Augen ein kleiner kegelförmiger Vorsprung, der wie ein Kuhhorn aussah. Die Augen selbst waren verhältnismäßig klein, doch sie blickten – was bei Dinosauriern ungewöhnlich war – nicht ausschließlich zur Seite, sondern teilweise auch nach vorn, was dem Tier das räumliche Sehen zur genauen Einschätzung von Entfernungen ermöglichte. Die kurze, hohe Schnauze verlieh dem Gesicht eine abgerundete Form, die Kiefermuskeln waren stark. Der Unterkiefer wirkte dagegen seltsam mickrig und nicht sehr kräftig, die Zähne waren kleiner und schwächer als man bei einem so großen Kopf erwartet hätte. Die fast lächerlich kleinen Vordergliedmaßen übertrafen sogar die des *Tyrannosaurus* (siehe Seite 202) mit ihrer Winzigkeit. Der Schwanz war überlang und verjüngte sich ganz allmählich zum Ende hin. Bei den auf 100–95 Millionen Jahre geschätzten Überresten des *Carnotaurus* hatte man Abdrücke gefunden, die eine unebene Haut mit Reihen flacher, klumpiger Schuppen an den Seiten und auf dem Rücken sowie runde, scheibenartige Schuppen zeigen.

**OBEN** Die seltsamen flügelartigen Brauenhörner sowie der im Verhältnis zu dem hohen oberen Schädelteil schmale, mickrige Unterkiefer kennzeichnen *Carnotaurus* als einen ungewöhnlichen großen Theropoden aus der Gruppe der Abelisauriden.

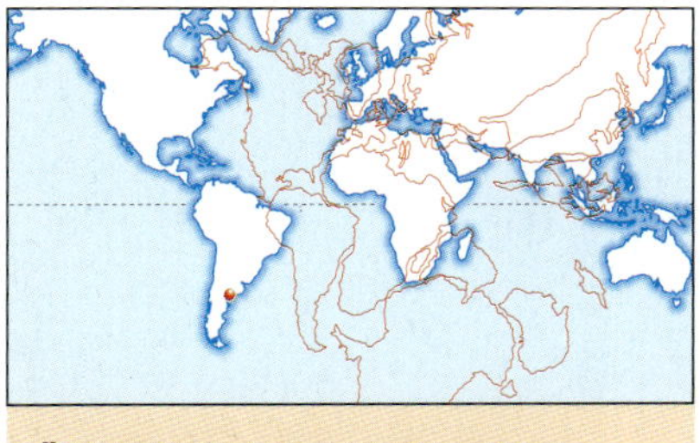

**ÜBERSICHT (DINOSAURIER)**

***Carnotaurus***

**Bedeutung des Namens:** Fleisch fressender Bulle

**Periode:** Mittlere Kreidezeit

**Hauptgruppe:** Theropoda

**Länge:** 7,5 Meter

**Gewicht:** 1 Tonne

**Nahrung:** Tiere

**Fossilfundstätten:** In Argentinien

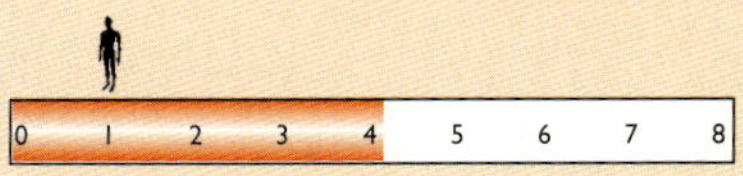

# SCHNELLE LÄUFER

*Anhaltspunkte für die Geschwindigkeit, mit der sich die verschiedenen Dinosaurier fortbewegen konnten, erhält die Wissenschaft aus vielerlei Quellen. Aufschlussreich sind vor allem die Größe und die Proportionen der Extremitätenknochen, die unebenen Stellen am Skelett, die uns zeigen, wo einst die Muskeln ansetzten sowie fossilierte Bewegungsspuren, an denen wir die Schrittlänge zwischen den einzelnen Fußabdrücken erkennen. Aus Hinweisen dieser Art schließt man heute, dass einige Straußdinosaurier damals durchaus schneller gewesen sein können als die heutigen Strauße und Laufgeschwindigkeiten von über achtzig Kilometern pro Stunde erreichten.*

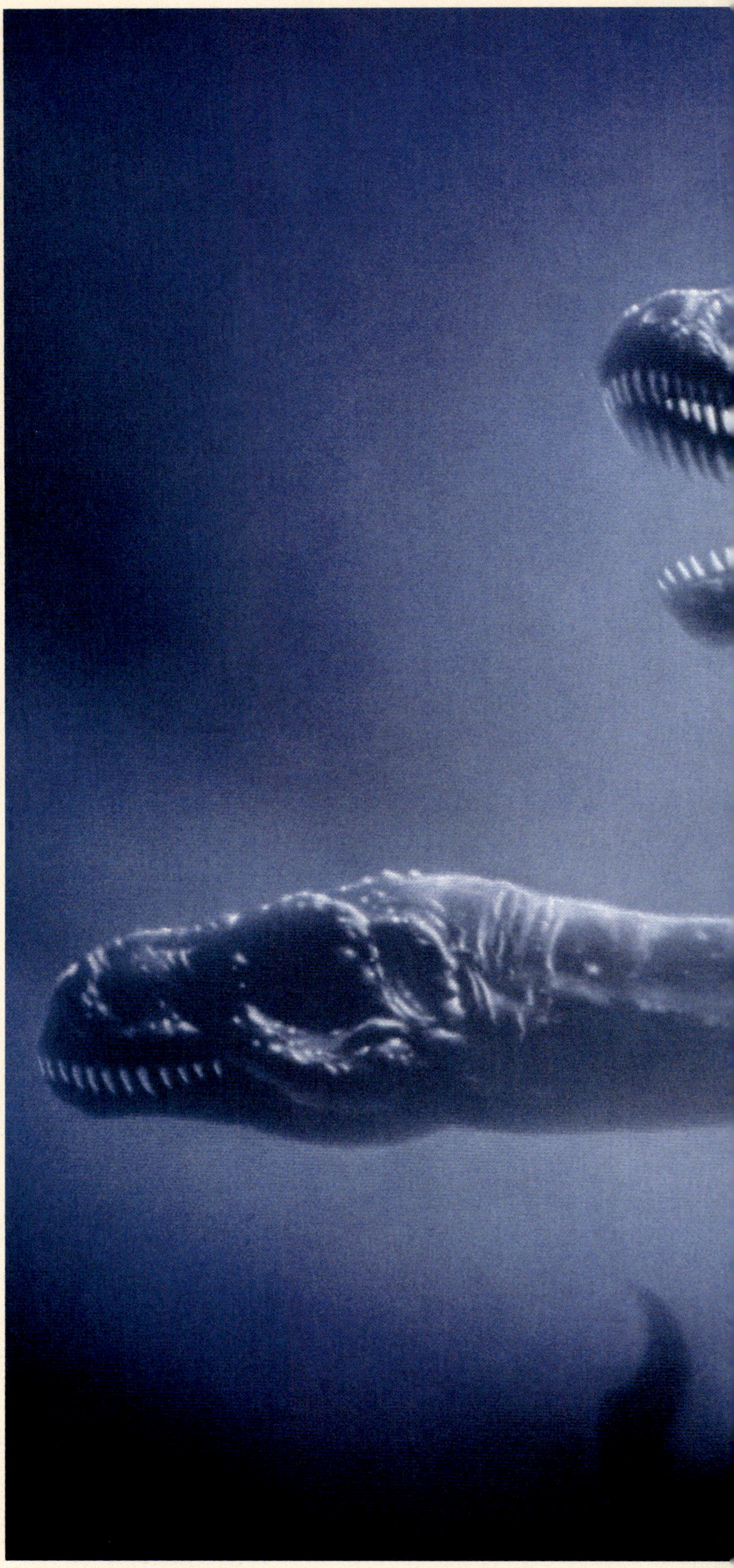

**RECHTS** Megaraptoren bei der Verfolgung einer Beute. Der bisher größte Fund eines „raptorartigen Dinosauriers" wurde in Patagonien, dem südlichsten Teil Südamerikas, gemacht. Die 33 Zentimeter lange Zehenkralle des Tieres ist hier deutlich zu sehen.

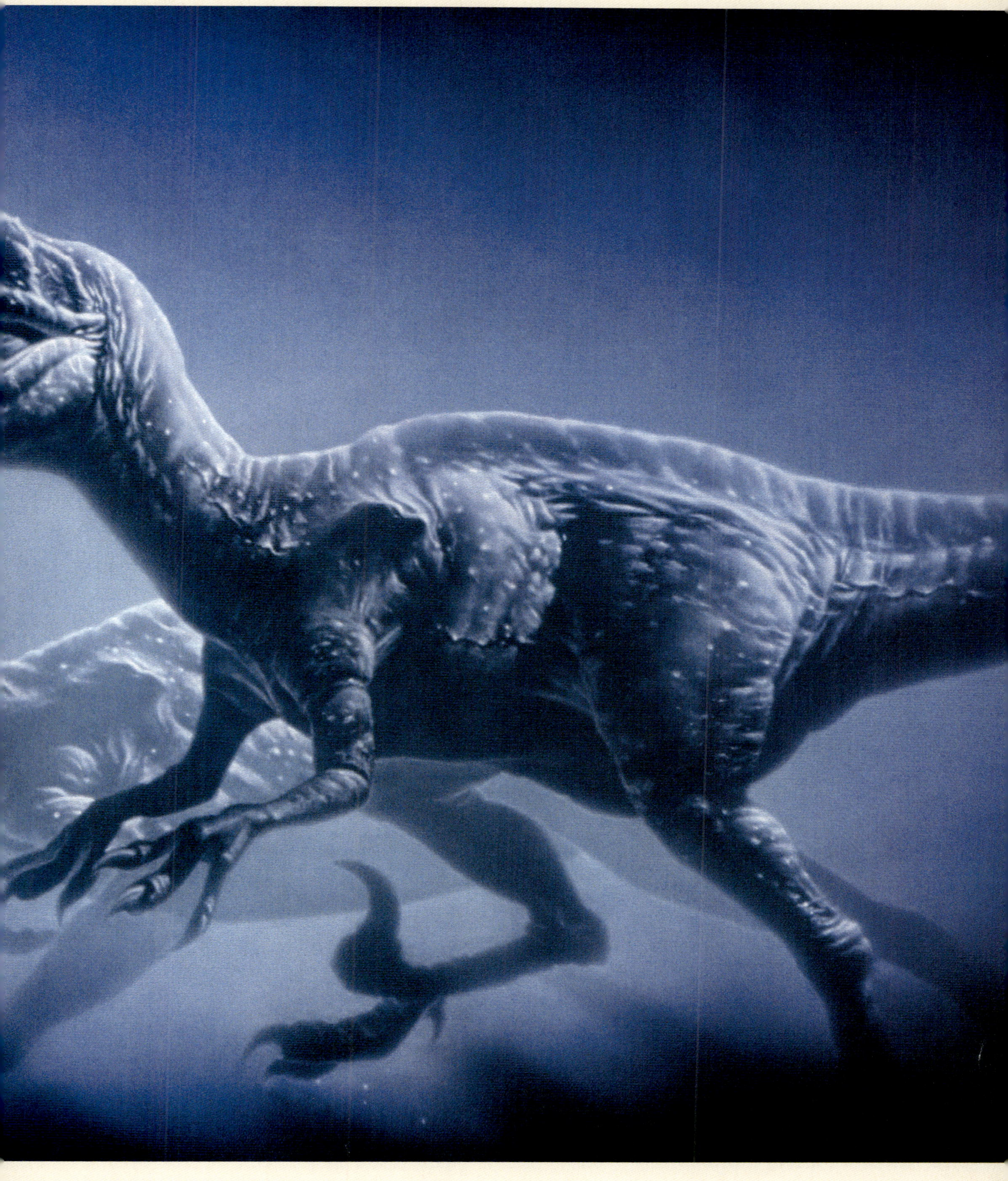

# DILOPHOSAURUS

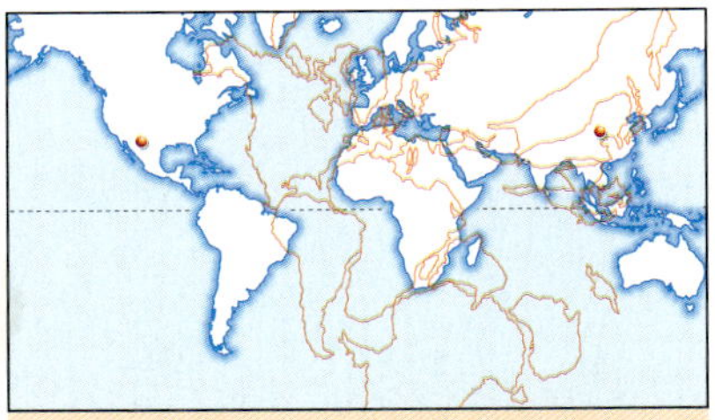

**ÜBERSICHT (DINOSAURIER)**
***Dilophosaurus***
**Bedeutung des Namens:** Zweikamm-Reptil, Doppelkamm-Reptil
**Periode:** Unterer Jura
**Hauptgruppe:** Theropoda
**Länge:** 6 Meter
**Gewicht:** 400 Kilogramm
**Nahrung:** Tiere
**Fossilfundstätten:** In den USA (Arizona), möglicherweise in China

0 1 2 3 4 5 6 7 8

Dieser mittelgroße bis große Fleischfresser gehört zu den wenigen seines Typs, die der Wissenschaft durch reichlich vorhandene Überreste gut bekannt sind. Die Fossilien sind fast 200 Millionen Jahre alt, stammen also aus der Zeit des Unteren Jura, und weisen *Dilophosaurus* als einen der ältesten großen Raubdinosaurier aus. *Dilophosaurus* gehört zur Gruppe der Ceratosaurier (siehe gegenüber). Überreste dieses Tieres wurden im US-Bundesstaat Arizona und möglicherweise auch in der chinesischen Provinz Yunnan gefunden. Unter den amerikanischen Exemplaren befinden sich drei Individuen, die zusammen fossiliert wurden; denkbar ist, dass sie einst als Rudel auf Jagd waren. Die Benennung des *Dilophosaurus* durch den amerikanischen Paläontologen Sam Welles bedurfte zweier Versuche. Die drei Exemplare aus Arizona waren 1942 ausgegraben worden, nachdem Jesse Williams, ein Angehöriger der Navajo, Fachleute zu dem Fundort geführt hatte. Welles untersuchte die Fossilien und beschrieb sie 1954 als eine neue Spezies der Gattung *Megalosaurus*. 1964 sah er sich durch weitere Entdeckungen von Fossilien dieser Kamm tragenden Dinosauriertypen – auf einige war Welles selbst gestoßen – veranlasst, die Tiere von *Megalosaurus* zu unterscheiden. 1970 gab er ihnen dann den neuen Namen *Dilophosaurus*.

*Dilophosaurus* war etwa sechs Meter lang, verhältnismäßig schlank und wog vermutlich weniger als eine halbe Tonne. Sein Name bezieht sich auf die beiden Kämme, die seinen Kopf zierten. Bei diesen schräg über den Augen aufragenden Gebilden handelte es sich um bogenförmige Knochenwülste, die so groß wie ein Drittel eines Esstellers, dabei aber kaum so stark wie ein Teller waren. Die Kämme erwiesen sich als derart dünn und zerbrechlich, dass sie zu Lebzeiten des Tieres vermutlich nur eine optische oder symbolische Wirkung hatten und vielleicht ein Geschlechtsmerkmal und/oder ein Zeichen der Geschlechtsreife waren. Dem *Dilophosaurus* zugeordnete Bewegungsspuren zeigen nur die Abdrücke von den Krallen und eine Schrittlänge von etwa zwei Metern. Eine Variante des *Dilophosaurus* ist in dem Film *Jurassic Park* zu sehen; im Unterschied zu dem Filmmonster spuckte das echte Tier vermutlich kein Gift und besaß auch keinen Nackenschild.

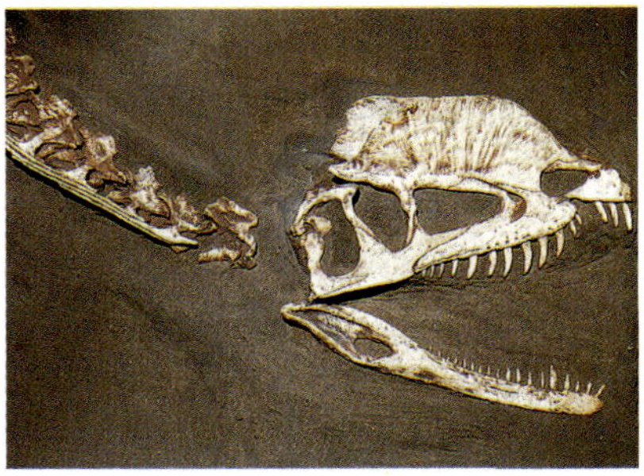

**OBEN** Der fossilierte Schädel eines *Dilophosaurus* mit der Seitenansicht eines Kopfkammes, die die Höhe dieses Körperteils verdeutlicht.

**RECHTS** Bei diesen Dinosauriern der Gattung *Dilophosaurus* handelt es sich vielleicht um zwei Männchen, die während der Paarungszeit um Weibchen kämpfen.

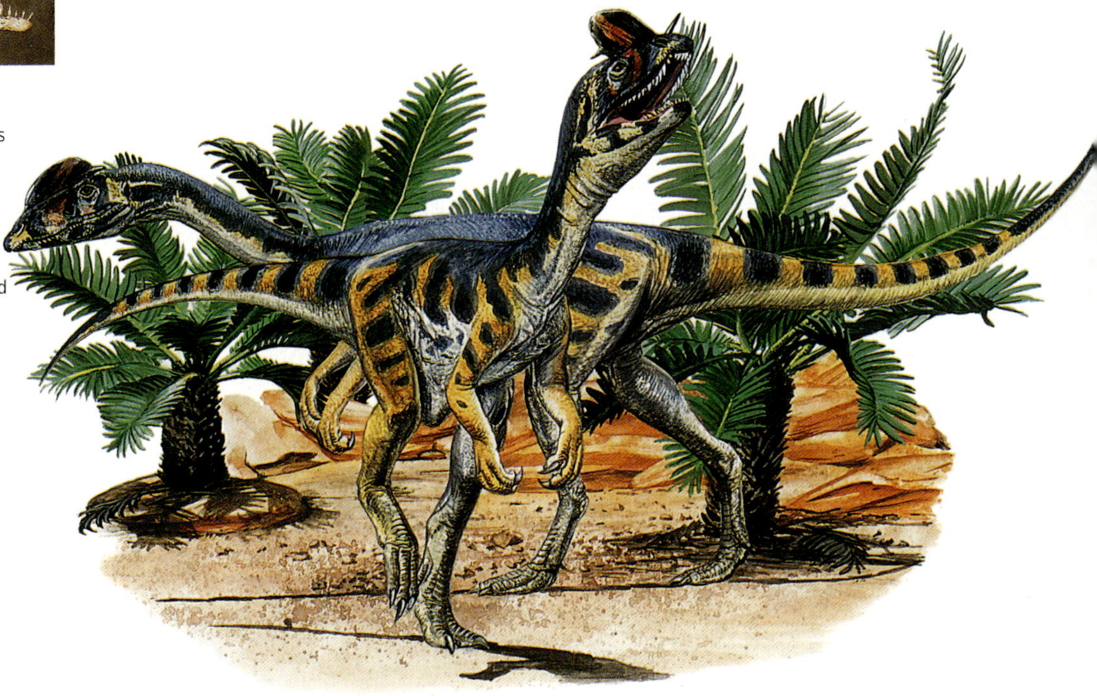

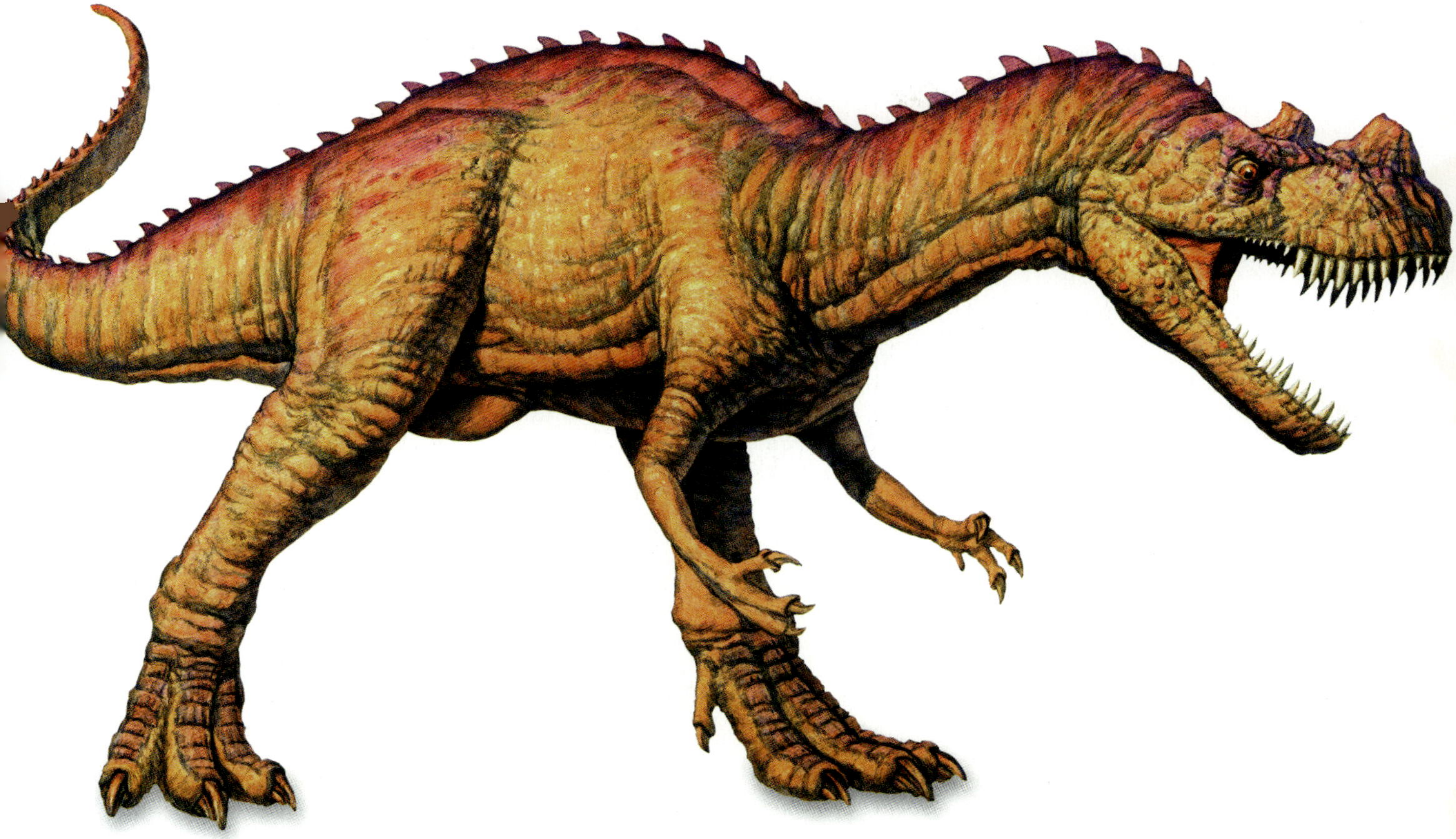

# CERATOSAURUS

*Ceratosaurus* war der um einen oder zwei Meter kleinere Rivale des *Allosaurus*, des größten Raubdinosauriers Nordamerikas im Oberen Jura. Seinen Namen verdankt er dem kurzen vorspringenden Horn auf der Nase. Außer diesem Horn trug *Ceratosaurus* über beiden Augen einen wulstartigen Kamm. Der Theropode war ein gefährlicher Jäger, er wog fast eine Tonne und war damit schwerer als jeder Bär, jede Großkatze oder jeder andere landlebende Fleischfresser der Jetztzeit.

*Ceratosaurus* wurde 1884 von dem amerikanischen Fossiliensucher Othniel Charles Marsh benannt. Marsh waren besonders die großen stachelartigen Fortsätze ober- und unterseits der Schwanzwirbel aufgefallen. Aus einem Vergleich dieser Schwanzform mit der eines Krokodils schloss er, dass der 150 Millionen Jahre alte *Ceratosaurus* möglicherweise ein guter Schwimmer gewesen war und in Sümpfen gelebt hatte.

Der so früh in der wissenschaftlichen Geschichte der Dinosaurier eingeführte Name des *Ceratosaurus* wurde dann einer der großen Untergruppen der Theropoden (Raubtierfuß-Dinosaurier) gegeben. Den Ceratosauria sind über zwanzig Species zugeordnet. Die Ceratosaurier, zu denen *Coelophysis* und *Dilophosaurus* (siehe gegenüber) gehören, sind die älteren Pendants einer weiteren großen Theropodengruppe, der Tetanurae. Trotz einiger primitiver Merkmale des Beckens und anderer Körperteile, beispielsweise der vier – statt drei und bei jüngeren Theropoden nur noch zwei – Zehen an den Vordergliedmaßen muss *Ceratosaurus* ein aktiver Räuber gewesen sein. Auffallend waren seine riesigen fangartigen Zähne und die kräftigen hinteren Laufbeine. Fossilfunde, bei denen Überreste einzelner Vertreter der Gattung *Ceratosaurus* neben den Knochen mehrerer Tiere der Gattung *Allosaurus* lagen, deuten darauf hin, dass *Ceratosaurus* allein auf Jagd ging und *Allosaurus* im Rudel umherstreifte. *Ceratosaurus*-Fossilien sind inzwischen auch in Portugal und möglicherweise in Ostafrika identifiziert worden.

**OBEN** Über die Funktion des eigenartigen Nasenhorns des *Ceratosaurus* konnte sich die Fachwelt bisher noch nicht einigen. Da das Horn als Waffe vermutlich zu klein und zu schwach war, diente es möglicherweise als Zeichen der Geschlechtsreife und der Fortpflanzungsbereitschaft oder war ein geschlechtsspezifisches Merkmal.

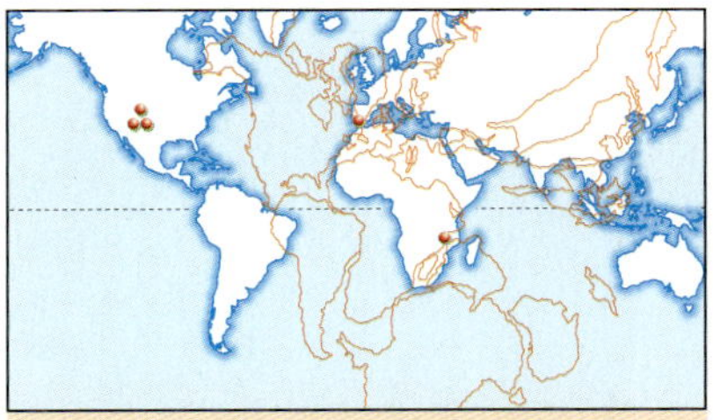

**ÜBERSICHT (DINOSAURIER)**
***Ceratosaurus***
**Bedeutung des Namens:** Gehörntes Reptil
**Periode:** Oberer Jura
**Hauptgruppe:** Theropoda
**Länge:** 6 Meter
**Gewicht:** 700–850 Kilogramm
**Nahrung:** Tiere
**Fossilfundstätten:** In den USA (Colorado, Utah, Wyoming), in Portugal, möglicherweise in Afrika

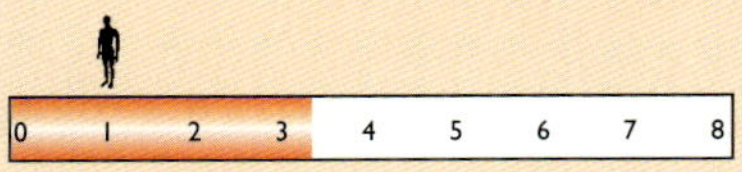

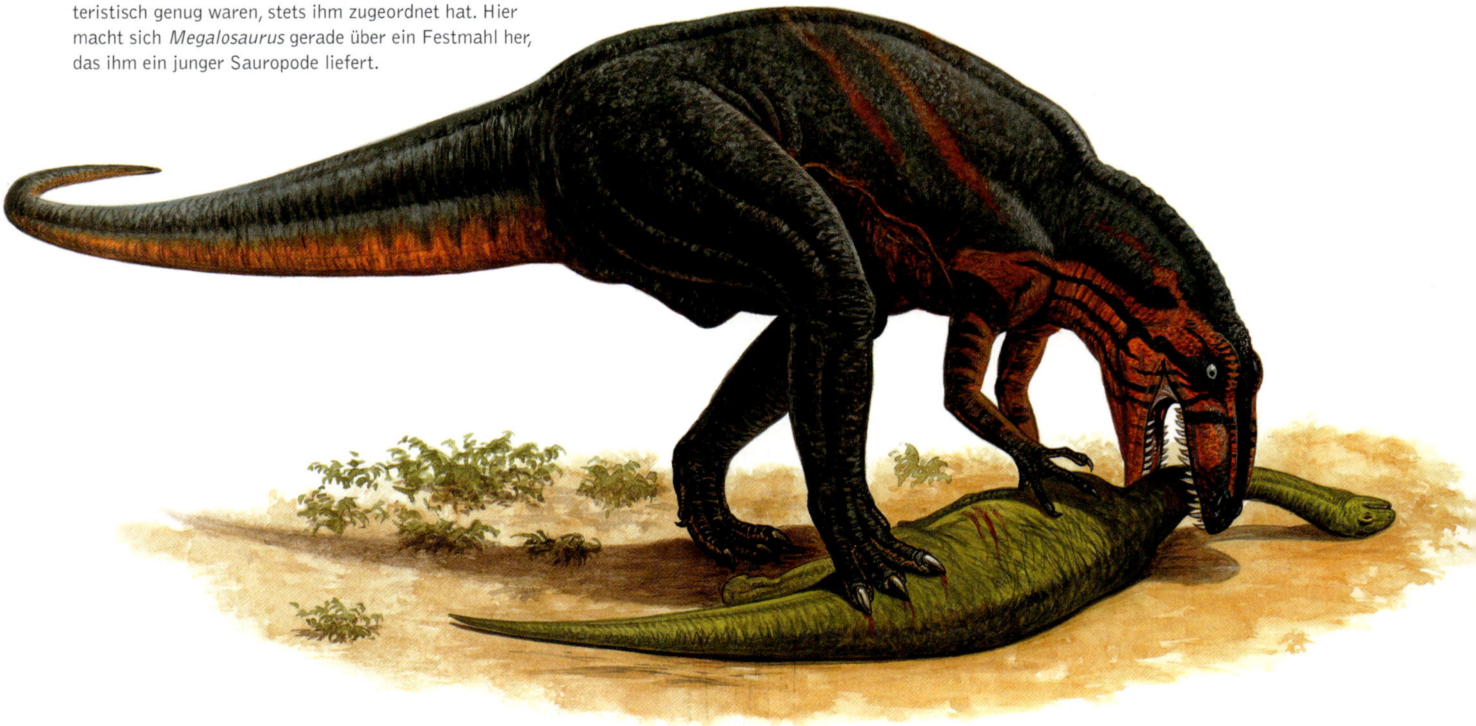

**RECHTS** *Megalosaurus* wird etwas drastisch auch der „Abfalltonnen-Dinosaurier" genannt, weil man über fünfzig Jahre lang die Fossilien aller großen Fleischfressertypen, die für einen eigenen Namen nicht charakteristisch genug waren, stets ihm zugeordnet hat. Hier macht sich *Megalosaurus* gerade über ein Festmahl her, das ihm ein junger Sauropode liefert.

# MEGALOSAURUS

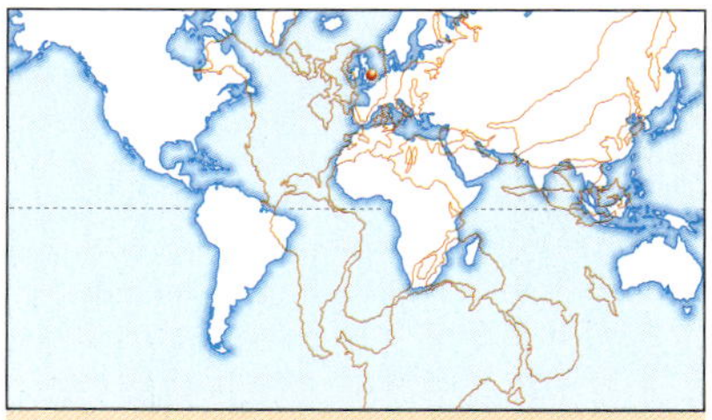

**ÜBERSICHT (DINOSAURIER)**

***Megalosaurus***

**Bedeutung des Namens:** Großreptil

**Periode:** Mittlerer Jura

**Hauptgruppe:** Theropoda

**Länge:** 9 Meter

**Gewicht:** 1 Tonne

**Nahrung:** Größere Tiere

**Fossilfundstätten:** In England

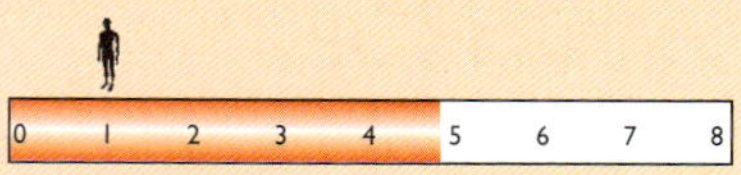


*Megalosaurus*, das „Großreptil", nimmt unter all den Lebewesen, die wir inzwischen unter der Bezeichnung Dinosaurier kennen, eine geachtete, aber verwirrende Position ein. Er war der erste, der einen offiziellen, wissenschaftlichen Namen erhielt; den Namen gab ihm 1824 William Buckland. Und als man 1841 die Dinosauria als eigenständige Reptiliengruppe anerkannte, war *Megalosaurus* gewissermaßen ein Gründungsmitglied. Dann wurde mehr als ein halbes Jahrhundert lang nahezu jedes große Reptil seines Typs, das wie ein Räuber mit Fangzähnen aussah und nicht charakteristisch genug erschien um anders genannt zu werden, zu einem *Megalosaurus* gemacht. Detaillierte Untersuchungen und Vergleiche beendeten die Verwirrung um dieses Tier jedoch nach und nach. Verschiedene Exemplare, die einst als *Megalosaurus* galten, darunter auch mehrere hier erwähnte Tiere, wurden als andere Theropoden klassifiziert und umbenannt.

Heute wird *Megalosaurus* als großer Raubdinosaurier aus dem Mittleren Jura, als früher Tetanure oder „Starrschwanz" aus der Gruppe der Theropoden (siehe Seite 183) klassifiziert. Wegen seines Platzes in der Geschichte der Paläontologie und in der Gruppe der Dinosaurier ist er weithin bekannt, doch andererseits wissen wir nur wenig über ihn, da die Fossilien, die ihm nach Jahrzehnten der Diskussion nun noch zugeordnet werden, nur bruchstückhaft und nicht sehr zahlreich sind. Die von Buckland untersuchten originalen Kieferteile zeigen lange ältere Zähne, daneben neue, gerade aus dem Knochen hervorbrechende Ersatzzähne sowie interdentale Platten, die die Zähne voneinander trennen. Die frühen Funde enthielten auch Abschnitte der Wirbelsäule, Teile des Beckens sowie Knochen der hinteren Gliedmaßen. Sie wurden in den Steinbrüchen bei Stonesfield in der Grafschaft Oxfordshire entdeckt. Andere Fossilien des *Megalosaurus* waren bereits seit den 1670er Jahren bekannt. Der wichtigste damalige Fossilfund war das runde oder knöchelförmige untere Ende des Oberschenkelbeins, das vermutlich von *Megalosaurus* stammte. Über das Relikt wurde 1673 von Robert Plot berichtet; Plot fertigte davon 1676 auch eine Zeichnung an. Die Zeichnung existiert noch, doch das originale Fossil ist nicht mehr auffindbar.

# SPINOSAURUS

*Spinosaurus*, einer der ungewöhnlichsten großen Raubdinosaurier, zeichnete sich durch ein riesiges segelartiges Gebilde auf dem Rücken aus. Dieses Gebilde war vermutlich ein großer Hautlappen, der von langen, aus der Wirbelsäule emporragenden Fortsätzen, den Wirbelfortsätzen, gehalten wurde. *Spinosaurus* gehörte außerdem zu den größten Raubdinosauriern, da er es hinsichtlich seiner Länge selbst mit *Tyrannosaurus* aufnehmen konnte, allerdings einen leichteren Körperbau als dieser aufwies. Fossilien dieses Tieres wurden erstmals 1912 in Ägypten, in der Nähe einer Oase, gefunden und drei Jahre später von dem deutschen Paläontologen Ernst Stromer von Reichenbach beschrieben und benannt. Die wenigen Überreste wurden zur sicheren Aufbewahrung nach München gebracht, während eines Bombenangriffes im Zweiten Weltkrieg jedoch zerstört. Seither bauen alle Spekulationen über Größe, Körperbau und Lebensweise von *Spinosaurus* auf den Dokumenten zu diesen ersten Fossilexemplaren und auf neueren Funden aus Marokko auf.

Das ungewöhnliche „Segel", das an seinem höchsten Punkt fast zwei Meter über der Wirbelsäule stand, diente vielleicht der Regelung der Körpertemperatur und/oder als eine Art Blickfang für Artgenossen des anderen Geschlechts (siehe Seite 107). In der mittleren bis späten Kreidezeit, vor 100–90 Millionen Jahren, scheint es im Gebiet des heutigen Nordafrika einen entwicklungsgeschichtlichen Trend zu solchen Segeln gegeben zu haben. Der Pflanzen fressende *Iguanodon*-artige *Ouranosaurus* (siehe Seite 266) und vielleicht auch der Sauropode *Rebbachisaurus* besaßen nämlich ebenfalls ein Rückensegel. Gestützt auf die wenigen Hinweise von *Spinosaurus*-Fossilien vermutet man, dass das Tier eine lange, flache Schnauze hatte, die der von *Baryonyx* und *Suchomimus* ähnelte und vielleicht ebenfalls zum Fangen von Fischen geeignet war. Die Zähne sind schmal, spitz und wenig gezackt, aber nicht so zahlreich wie bei *Baryonyx*. Daraus schließt man, dass der kräftige *Spinosaurus* mit seinen schlanken und weniger muskulösen Körperproportionen sich vom weichen Fleisch verwesender Kadaver ernährte.

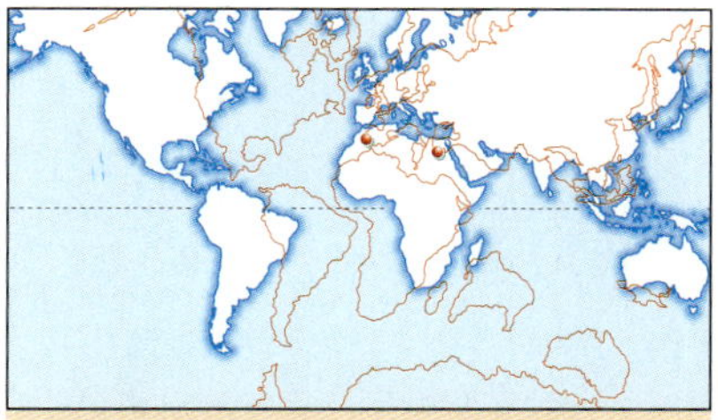

**ÜBERSICHT (DINOSAURIER)**
***Spinosaurus***
**Bedeutung des Namens:** Stachelreptil, Dornreptil
**Periode:** Mittlere und obere Kreide
**Hauptgruppe:** Theropoda
**Länge:** 12–14 Meter
**Gewicht:** 3 Tonnen
**Nahrung:** Tiere
**Fossilfundstätten:** In Ägypten und Marokko

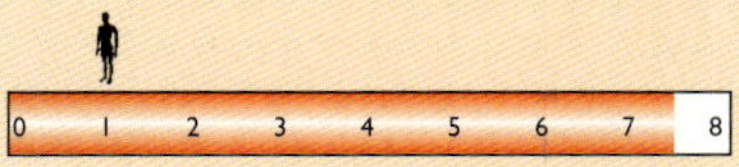


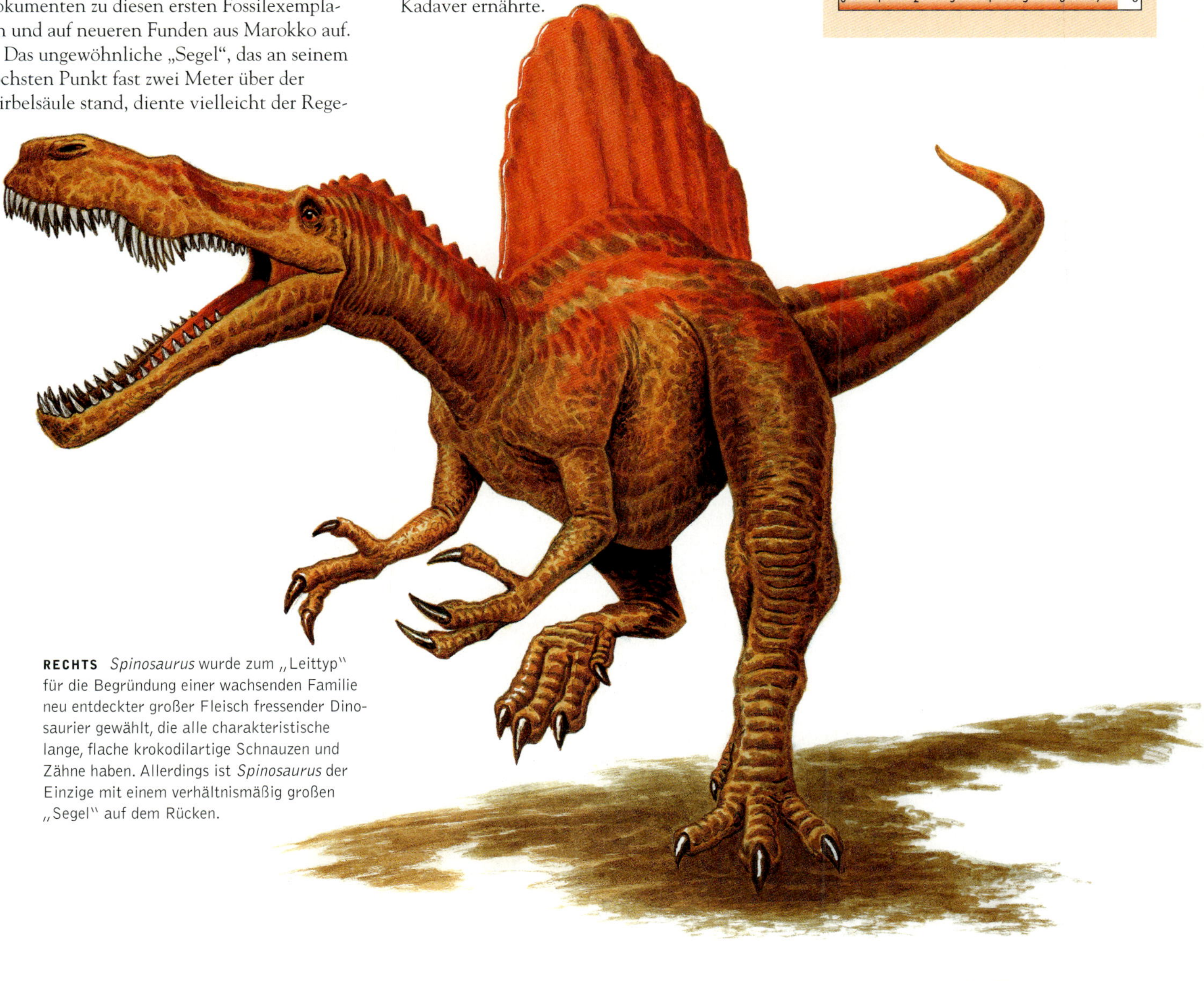

**RECHTS** *Spinosaurus* wurde zum „Leittyp" für die Begründung einer wachsenden Familie neu entdeckter großer Fleisch fressender Dinosaurier gewählt, die alle charakteristische lange, flache krokodilartige Schnauzen und Zähne haben. Allerdings ist *Spinosaurus* der Einzige mit einem verhältnismäßig großen „Segel" auf dem Rücken.

# Die Segelrücken

*Große Gebilde auf dem Rücken, die wie Segel, Lappen oder Flossen geformt waren, hat es bei den Dinosauriern und auch bei anderen Gruppen von Landwirbeltieren, beispielsweise bei Pelycosauriern wie Dimetrodon, in mehreren, voneinander unabhängigen Fällen gegeben. Es scheint, dass das „Segel" zur Vergrößerung der Körperoberfläche diente und dabei nur ein Minimum an Fleisch und anderem Körpergewebe enthielt. Als Funktion dieser Gebilde wird heute bevorzugt die Temperaturregelung angenommen. Demnach wirkte das „Segel" wie ein umkehrbarer Wärmetauscher. Es nahm Wärme aus der Umwelt auf, wenn der Körper des Tieres kälter als seine Umgebung war und strahlte überschüssige Wärme ab, um bei hohen Temperaturen die Überhitzung des Körpers zu verhindern.*

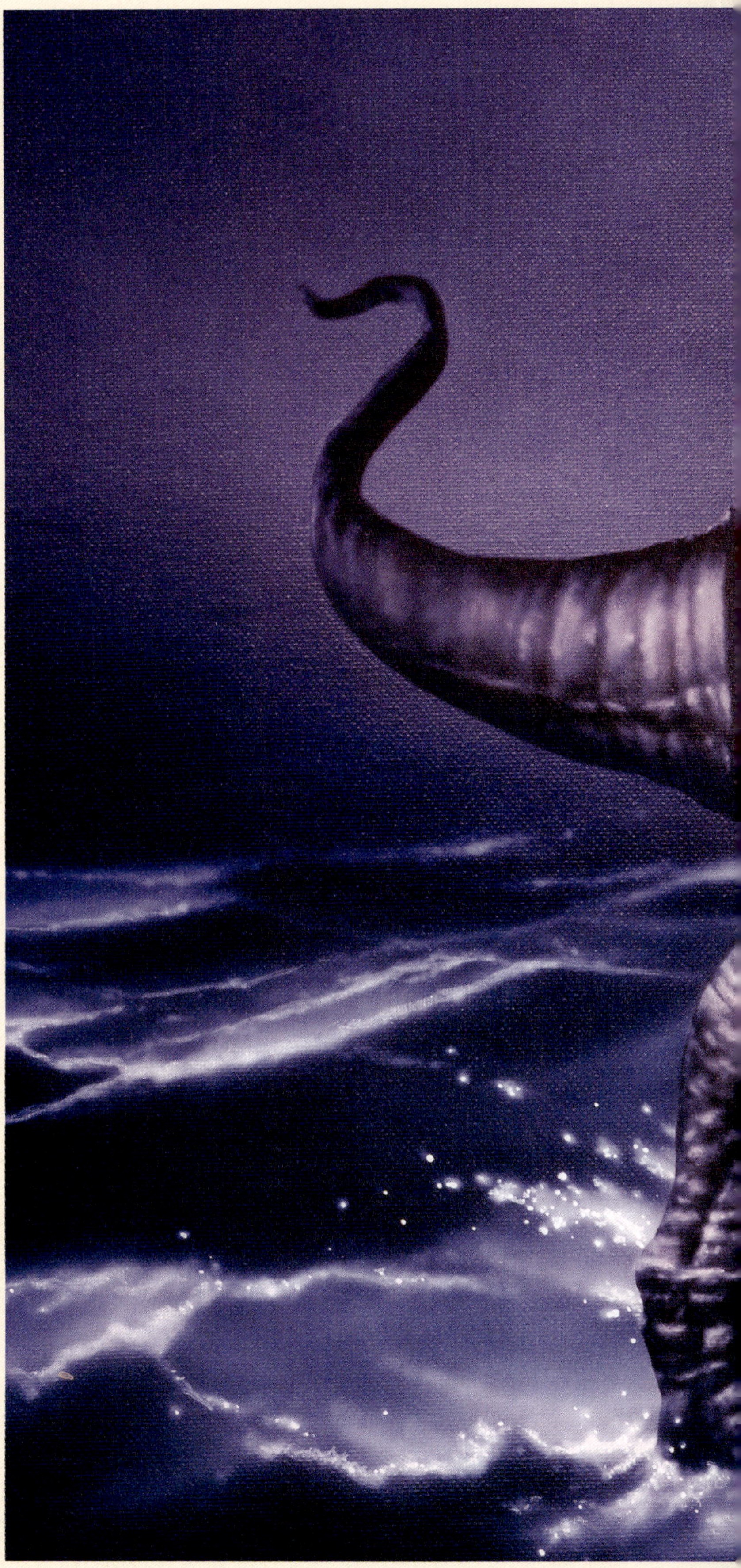

**RECHTS** Hier rennt ein *Spinosaurus* wohl bei der Verfolgung eines Beutetiers platschend durch flaches Wasser. *Spinosaurus* zählt nicht allein wegen seiner gewaltigen Größe, der ungewöhnlichen Kieferform und natürlich wegen seines flossenartigen Rückensegels zu den faszinierendsten Dinosauriern, sondern auch aufgrund der Tatsache, dass der größte Teil seiner Fossilien für die Wissenschaft verloren gegangen ist (siehe vorhergehende Seite).

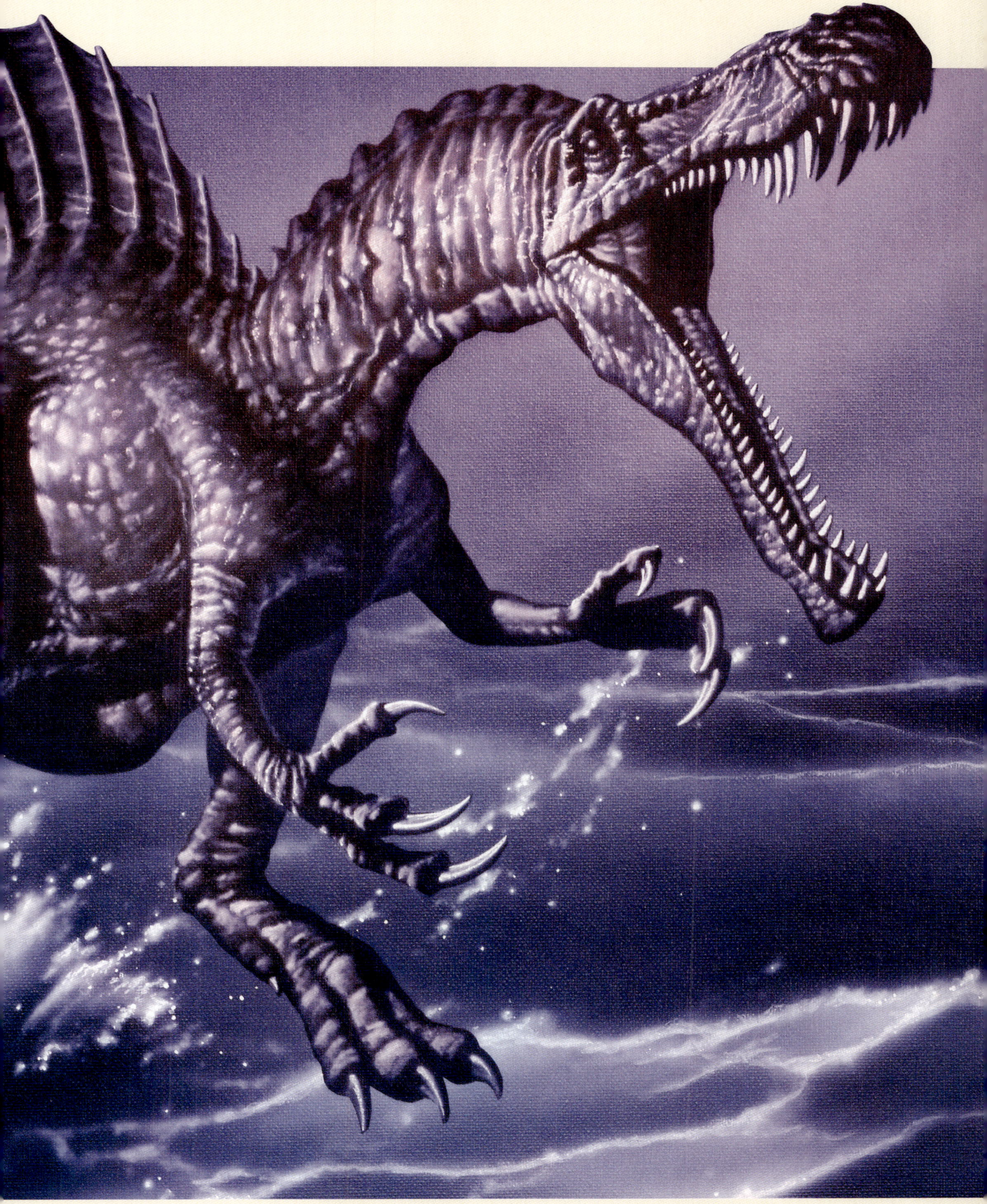

# TYRANNOSAURUS

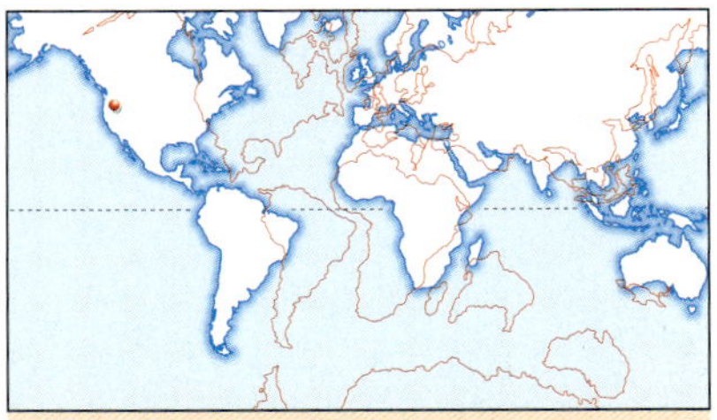

**ÜBERSICHT (DINOSAURIER)**
***Tyrannosaurus***
**Bedeutung des Namens:** Tyrannenreptil
**Periode:** Oberkreide
**Hauptgruppe:** Theropoda
**Länge:** 12 Meter
**Gewicht:** 6 Tonnen
**Nahrung:** Große Tiere
**Fossilfundstätten:** Im westlichen Nordamerika

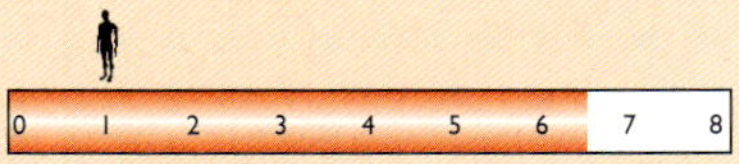


Über das „Tyrannenreptil", eines der berühmtesten nichtmenschlichen Lebewesen unseres Planeten, sind ganze Bücher, viel größer als dieses hier, geschrieben worden. *Tyrannosaurus* gilt zwar nicht mehr als der größte landlebende Räuber überhaupt, ist dank seiner zahlreichen, ausgiebig untersuchten Fossilien aber trotzdem berühmt. Er gehörte zu den letzten Dinosauriern, die von der Erde verschwanden. 1990 wurde in South Dakota ein fast komplettes und teilweise mumifiziertes Exemplar gefunden, bei dem es sich um riesiges Weibchen handelte, das dann nach seiner Entdeckerin Susan Hendrickson den Spitznamen „Sue" erhielt. „Sue" und weitere *Tyrannosaurus*-Individuen von anderen, nahe gelegenen Fundorten haben viele wertvolle neue Hinweise über den gewaltigen Fleischfresser geliefert; „Sue" ist jetzt im Field Museum in Chicago ausgestellt. In diesem Kapitel werden verschiedene Aspekte der Sinneswahrnehmung, der Lebensweise, der Jagdmethoden, der Ernährung und der Verhaltensmuster des *Tyrannosaurus*, hierbei auch die Vorstellung, dass diese Dinosaurier im Rudel jagten, erörtert.

*Tyrannosaurus* hatte einen gewaltigen Kopf, sein Schädel war 1,4 Meter lang, doch die Schädelfenster in den Knochen verringerten das Gewicht des Kopfes. Er besaß mehr als fünfzig riesige, spitze Zähne mit gezackten Schneiden, von denen einige über zwanzig Zentimeter lang waren und eine breite Basis hatten, was darauf schließen lässt, dass diese Zähne einer starken Beanspruchung gewachsen waren. Das riesige Maul ließ sich so weit öffnen, dass es einen erwachsenen Menschen von heute hätte verschlingen können. Auch der dicke, kräftige Hals legt den Schluss nahe, dass gewaltige Kräfte am Werk waren, wenn *Tyrannosaurus* von seiner Beute Fleischstücke abbiss und abriss. Die vorderen Gliedmaßen, häufig als winzig und nutzlos abgetan, waren dennoch sehr muskulös, und die beiden Finger am Ende trugen spitze, scharfe Krallen. Das Elefantengewicht des *Tyrannosaurus* ruhte auf den drei Zehen der vogelartigen Füße, die den Boden nur mit ihren starkkralligen Spitzen berührten.

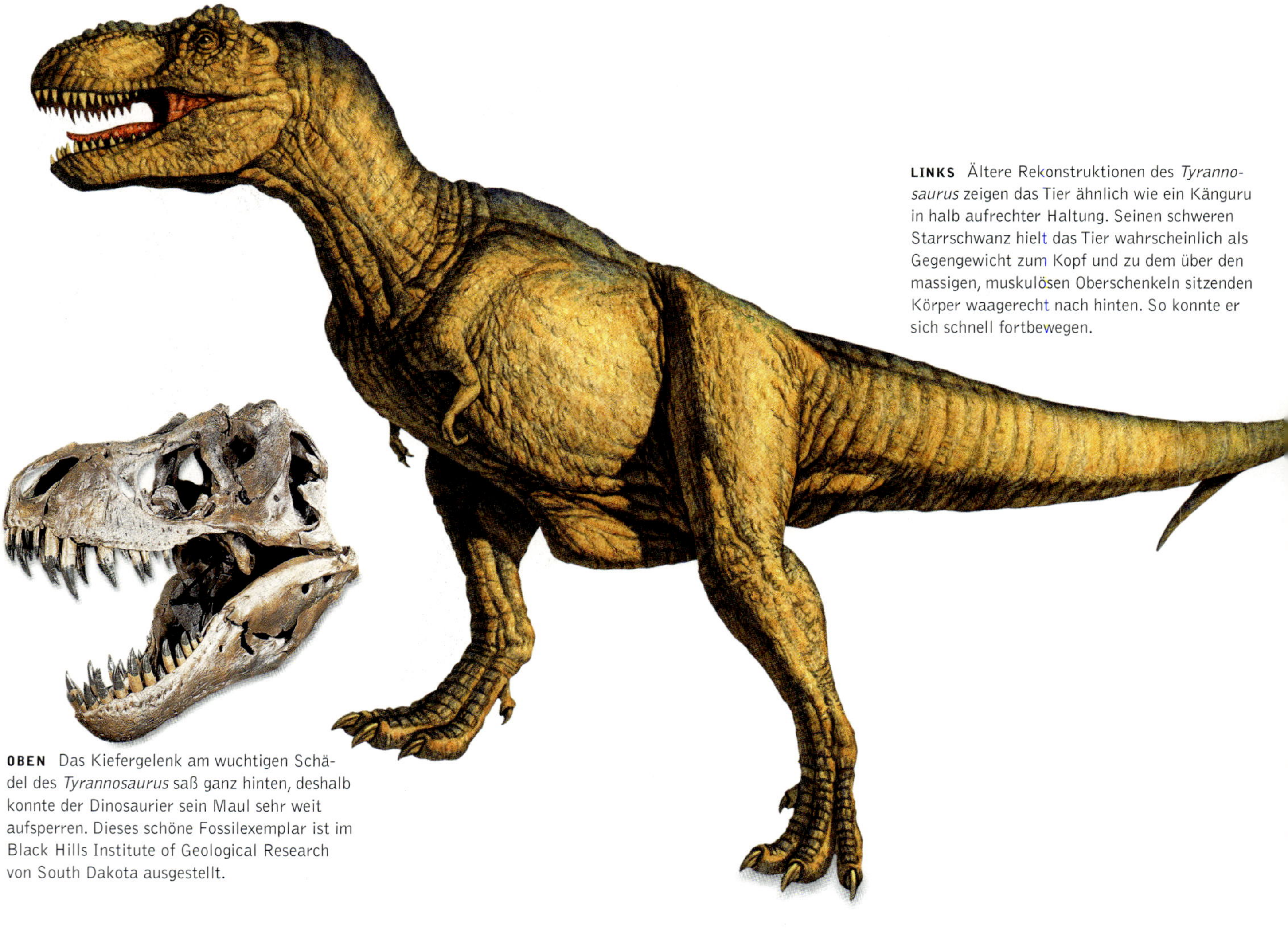

**LINKS** Ältere Rekonstruktionen des *Tyrannosaurus* zeigen das Tier ähnlich wie ein Känguru in halb aufrechter Haltung. Seinen schweren Starrschwanz hielt das Tier wahrscheinlich als Gegengewicht zum Kopf und zu dem über den massigen, muskulösen Oberschenkeln sitzenden Körper waagerecht nach hinten. So konnte er sich schnell fortbewegen.

**OBEN** Das Kiefergelenk am wuchtigen Schädel des *Tyrannosaurus* saß ganz hinten, deshalb konnte der Dinosaurier sein Maul sehr weit aufsperren. Dieses schöne Fossilexemplar ist im Black Hills Institute of Geological Research von South Dakota ausgestellt.

**UNTEN** *Tarbosaurus*, der hier Jagd auf einen jungen Ornithopoden macht, findet man in vielen neuen Klassifikationen als eine Spezies der Gattung *Tyrannosaurus*. Eine andere sehr ähnliche asiatische Gattung ist *Alectrosaurus*.

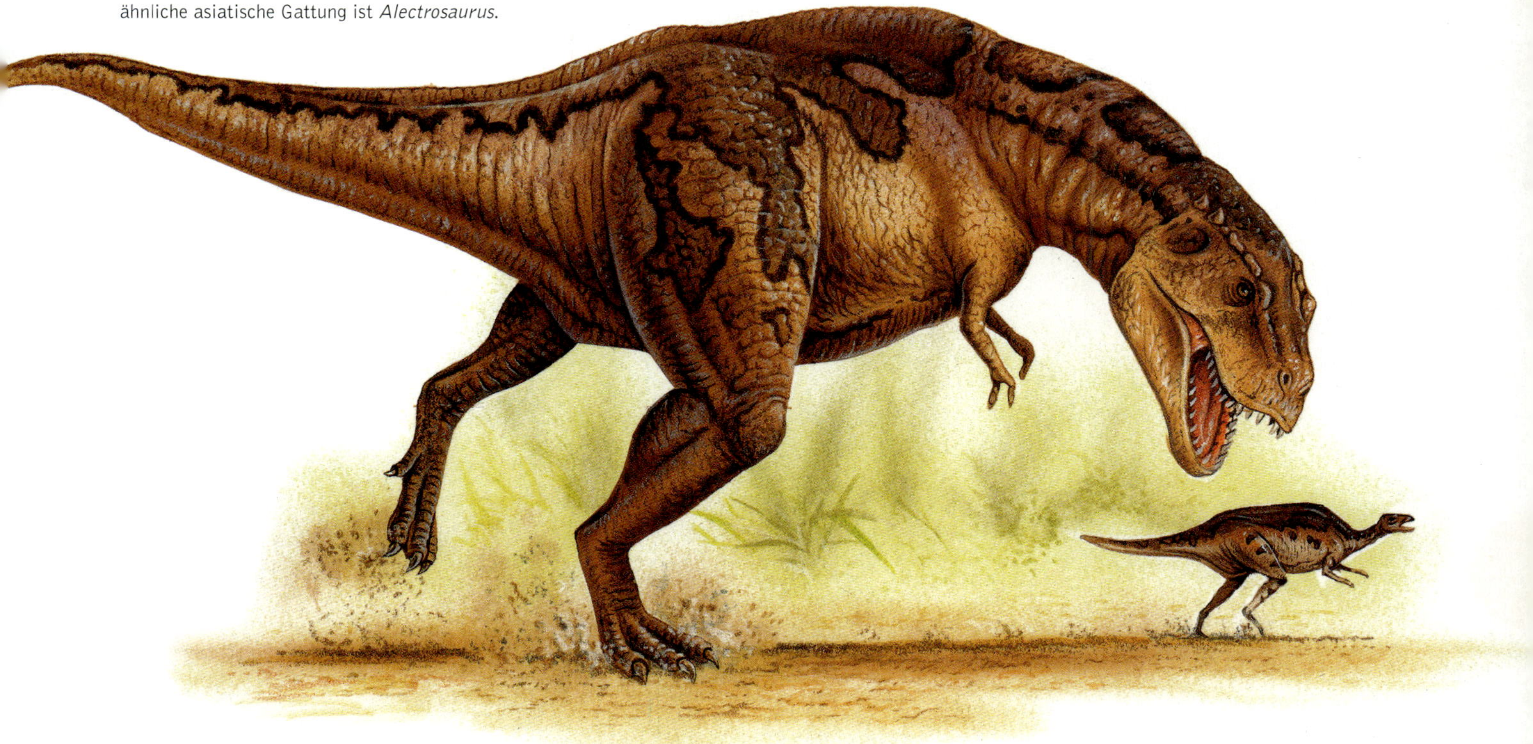

# TARBOSAURUS (TYRANNOSAURUS BATAAR)

Viele Jahre lang galt *Tarbosaurus* als das etwas kleinere ostasiatische Pendant und als Zeitgenosse des *Tyrannosaurus* (siehe gegenüber). Seine Existenz wurde durch Fossilien aus dem Nemegt-Becken im mongolischen Teil der Wüste Gobi nachgewiesen; an der Fundstätte wurden bei einer sowjetischen Expedition Überreste von vermutlich sieben Individuen ausgegraben. 1955 wurden die Fossilien von Evgenij Aleksandrovič Maleev als Spezies einer neuen Gattung – *Tarbosaurus* – beschrieben und *Tarbosaurus bataar* benannt.

Allerdings gab es schon zu Beginn auch die Meinung, dass dieser Dinosaurier dem *Tyrannosaurus* so stark ähnelt, dass man ihn auch so nennen müsste. Wären die Fossilien des *Tarbosaurus* in Nordamerika und nicht in Asien ausgegraben worden, so hieß es, hätte man sie der Gattung *Tyrannosaurus* – allerdings nicht der bekanntesten Art *Tyrannosaurus rex* – zugeordnet. Heute betrachten viele Fachleute den Namen *Tarbosaurus* als ungültig. Das Tier, für das sie sprechen, wurde neu als Vertreter der Gattung *Tyrannosaurus* und als eines von zwei verschiedenen Arten, *Tyrannosaurus bataar* und *Tyrannosaurus efremovi*, klassifiziert.

*Tarbosaurus/Tyrannosaurus* besaß die Kraft und alle Waffen eines großen Theropoden – ein riesiges Maul, lange, spitze Zähne, starke Kiefer, große Augen und eine große Nase zum Wittern von Beutetieren, winzige Vordergliedmaßen, massive Hinterbeine und einen langen, dicken Schwanz als Gegengewicht. Er unterscheidet sich von *Tyrannosaurus* durch seine Größe und einige Details an den Schädelknochen. Ein neuer Fund in Thailand deutet darauf hin, dass die Tyrannosaurier schon lange vor ihrem Erscheinen in Nordamerika in Asien existierten. Der neue Tyrannosauriertyp wird nach dem früheren Landesnamen Siam *Siamotyrannus* genannt. Seine Fossilien stammen aus der Unterkreide und sind rund 120 Millionen Jahre alt. Vielleicht hat die Ausbreitung in dieser Gruppe nicht, wie von einigen Fachleuten bisher angenommen, von Nordamerika nach Asien, sondern umgekehrt stattgefunden.

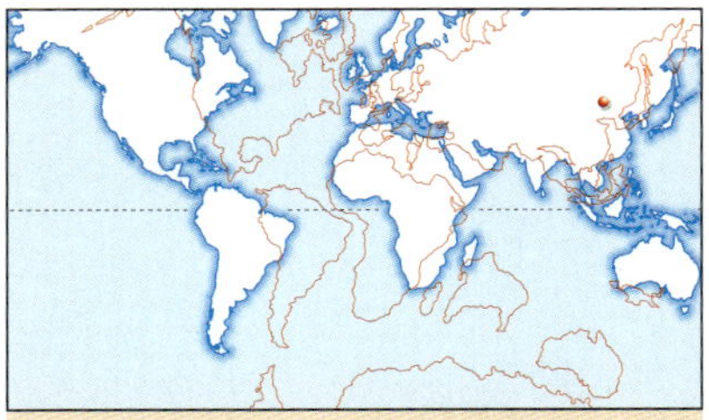

**ÜBERSICHT (DINOSAURIER)**
***Tarbosaurus (Tyrannosaurus bataar)***
**Bedeutung des Namens:**
Alarmierendes Reptil
**Periode:** Oberkreide
**Hauptgruppe:** Theropoda
**Länge:** 10 Meter
**Gewicht:** 4 Tonnen
**Nahrung:** Große Tiere
**Fossilfundstätten:** In der Mongolei

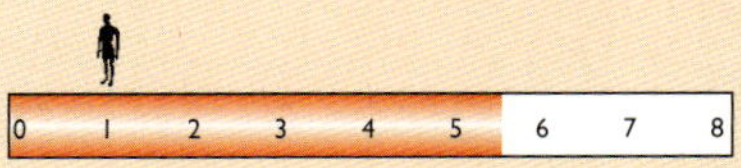

# ALIORAMUS

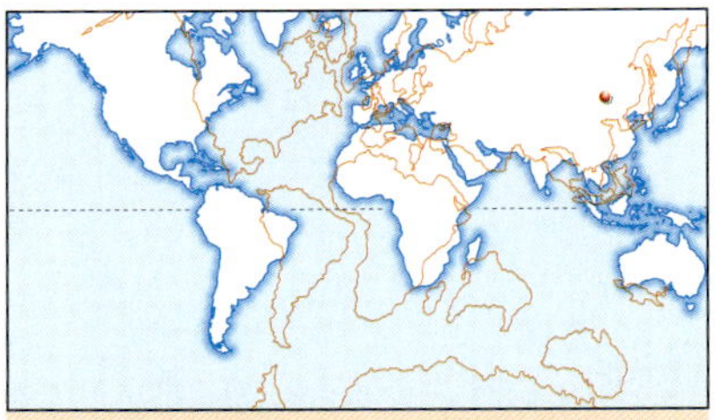

**ÜBERSICHT (DINOSAURIER)**

***Alioramus***

**Bedeutung des Namens:** Anderer Zweig

**Periode:** Oberkreide

**Hauptgruppe:** Theropoda

**Länge:** 6 Meter

**Gewicht:** 1 Tonne

**Nahrung:** Tiere

**Fossilfundstätten:** In der Mongolei

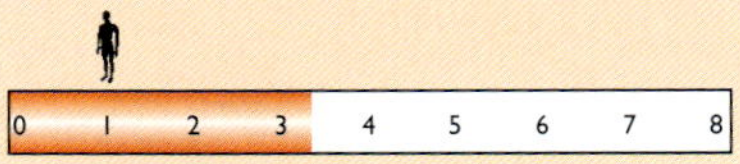


Dieser mittelgroße Raubdinosaurier ist hauptsächlich durch einen unvollständigen Schädel und Teile von Fußknochen bekannt. Er gilt als ein ungewöhnlicher Verwandter der letzten großen Gruppe Fleisch fressender Dinosaurier, der Tyrannosaurier. Er lebte gegen Ende des Zeitalters der Dinosaurier, vor 70–65 Millionen Jahren. Benannt wurde er 1976 nach Fossilfunden in der Mongolei von dem sowjetischen Fossilienexperten Sergej Michajlovič Kurzanov, der später auch mit seinen Untersuchungen und Bewertungen des viel kleineren und möglicherweise gefiederten Theropoden *Avimimus* (siehe Seite 164) Aufmerksamkeit erregte.

Die wirkliche Körpergröße von *Alioramus* ist zwar schwer zu bestimmen, da es bislang keine Überreste von Bein- oder Rumpfknochen gibt, doch man geht davon aus, dass das Tier viel kleiner als seine großen Tyrannosaurier-Verwandten, trotzdem aber ein großer und kräftiger Jäger und viel größer als die meisten landlebenden Fleischfresser der Jetztzeit war. Einige Fachleute mutmaßen, dass *Alioramus* sechs Meter Länge erreichte und etwa eine Tonne wog. Seine fossilierten Fußknochen belegen, dass er leichter und wahrscheinlich schneller als die größeren Theropoden war. Seine Laufgeschwindigkeit überstieg nach Expertenschätzungen vierzig Stundenkilometer. Der Körperbau und die Proportionen – winzige Arme, lange, starke Hinterbeine und ein langer, starrer Schwanz – waren typisch für die Tyrannosaurier.

Ungewöhnlich war der Kopf. Seine Form ist von einem unvollständigen Schädel bekannt, der lang und flach war und eine verlängerte Schnauze hatte; die meisten Tyrannosaurier hingegen besaßen einen hohen Schädel mit kürzerer Schnauze. Weitere Besonderheiten waren die knöchernen Vorsprünge – vier kleine höckerartige „Hörner", die in einer Reihe auf dem Nasenrücken standen, sowie weiter oben je einen Höcker über beiden Augen. *Alioramus* war vielleicht nicht der beherrschende Raubdinosaurier seiner Umgebung. Vermutlich teilte er Lebensraum und Zeit, das Ostasien der späten Kreidezeit, mit der viel größeren Tyrannosaurierart, die man früher als *Tarbosaurus* kannte.

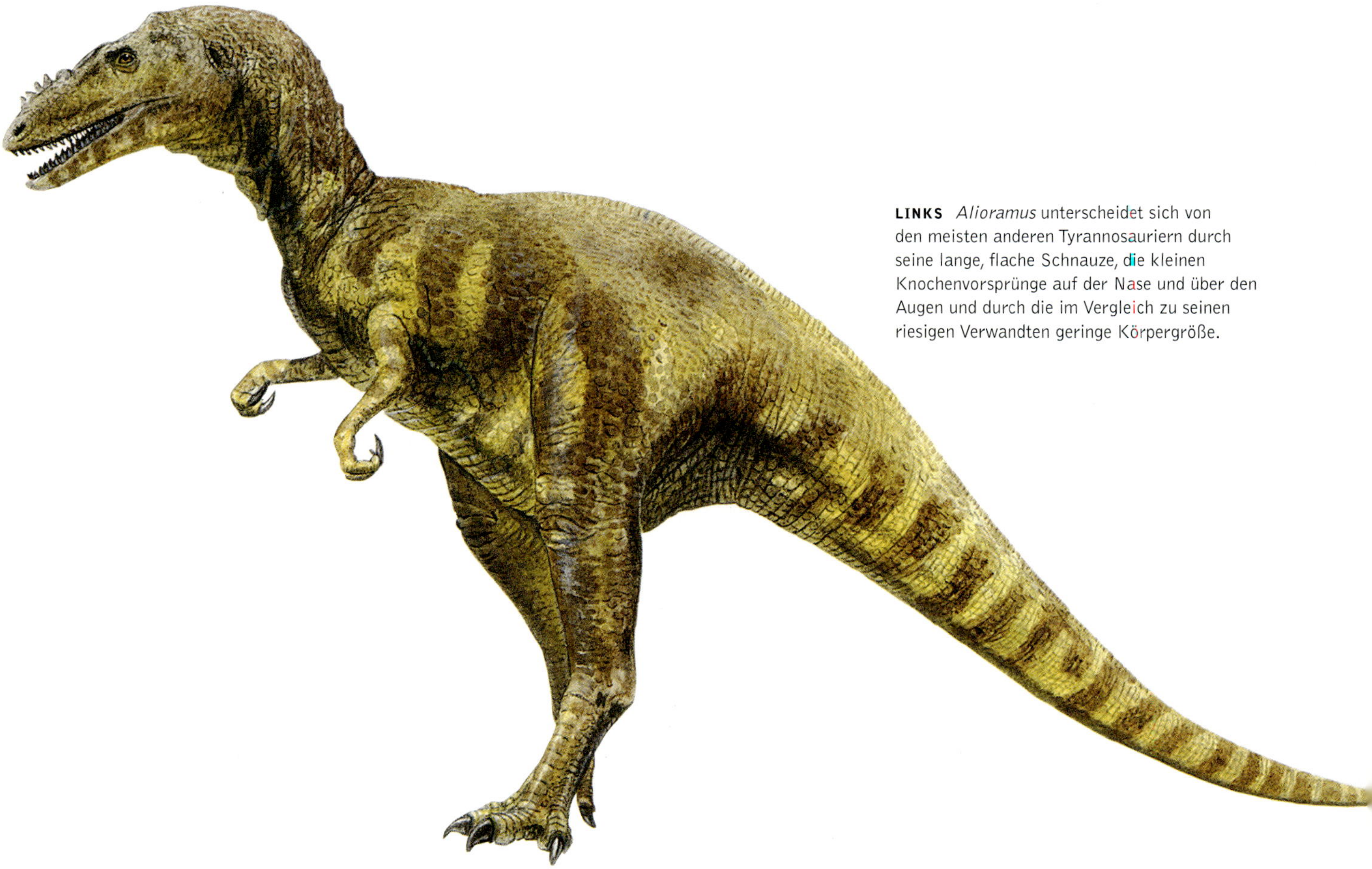

**LINKS** *Alioramus* unterscheidet sich von den meisten anderen Tyrannosauriern durch seine lange, flache Schnauze, die kleinen Knochenvorsprünge auf der Nase und über den Augen und durch die im Vergleich zu seinen riesigen Verwandten geringe Körpergröße.

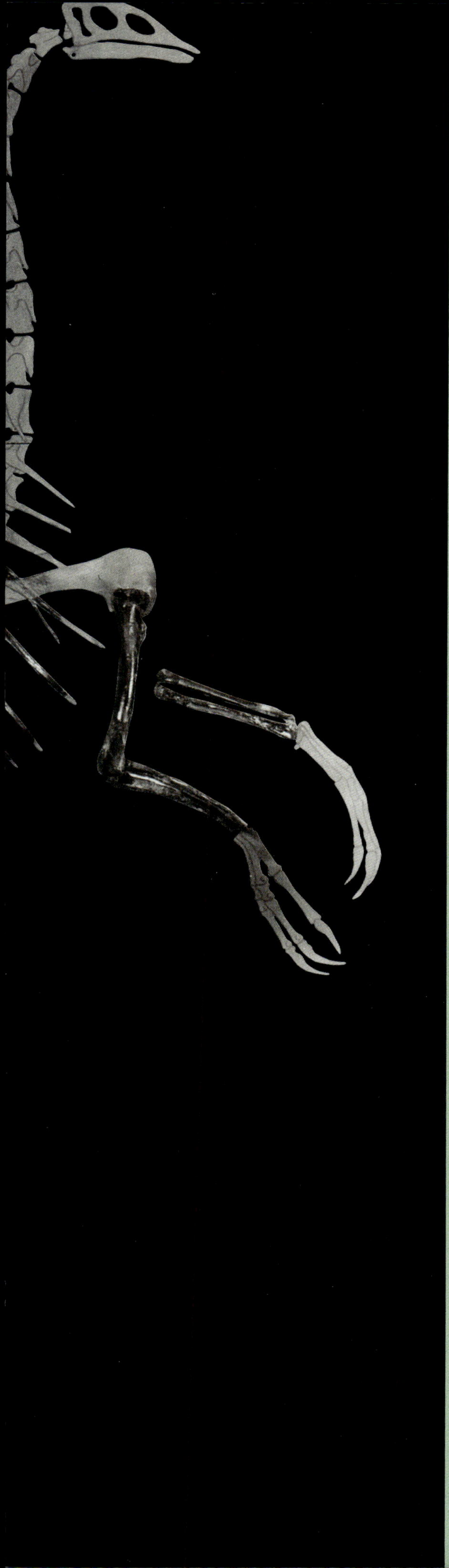

# Kapitel Sechs

# Strauss-dinosaurier

*Zu den seltsamsten Dinosauriergruppen gehörten die Ornithomimosaurier, die Vogelnachahmer unter den Dinosauriern. Die meisten besaßen keinerlei Zähne und pickten ihre Nahrung mit dem Schnabel auf.*

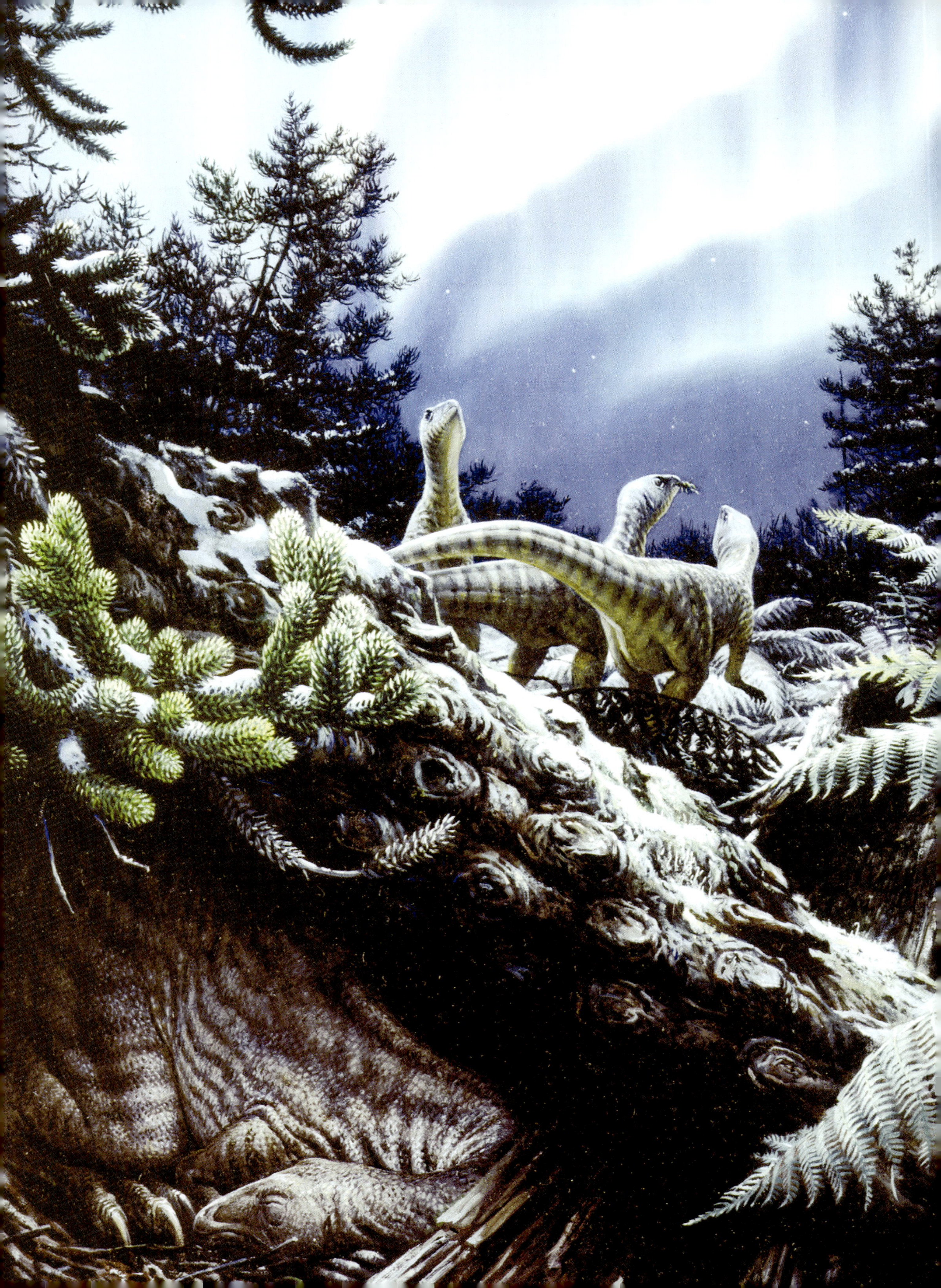

# WIE EIN VOGELSCHNABEL

***Bei verschiedenen Dinosaurierarten endete der Mund in einer schnabelartigen Vorderfront, wie es bei den großen Pflanzenfressern Triceratops und Stegosaurus der Fall war. Bei den Fleischfressern hingegen entwickelten nur die Ornithomimosaurier ein solches Merkmal. Ihr Name, der „Vogelnachahmer-Reptil“ bedeutet, weist u. a. auf das Vorhandensein eines Schnabels hin. Die fossilierten Reste solcher Schnäbel bestehen aus Knochen, die den Ober- und den Unterkiefer bilden und lang und flach wie eine Nadelzange sind. Die meisten Typen besaßen keinerlei Zähne (siehe auch unten). Die Kieferknochen müssen wie bei den heutigen Vögeln von Hornscheiden umgeben gewesen sein. Das Horn wuchs ständig nach, wodurch die abgenutzten Stellen ersetzt wurden und der innen liegende Knochen geschützt lag. Das Hornmaterial könnte auch scharfe Kanten oder Wülste entlang der Kiefer gebildet haben, so dass der Schnabelbesitzer seine Nahrung nicht einfach nur zerquetschte, sondern auch zerschneiden konnte.***

## WIE EIN STRAUSS

Vogelschnäbel weichen in ihrer Größe und Form stark voneinander ab. Verglichen mit den Vögeln der Jetztzeit wiesen die Schnäbel der Ornithomimosaurier die größte Ähnlichkeit mit denen der rezenten Strauße auf. Tatsächlich erinnern nicht nur der Schnabel, sondern auch Kopf, Hals und Hintergliedmaßen der Ornithomimosaurier an die Strauße von heute. Einer der bekanntesten Ornithomimosaurier trägt den Namen *Struthiomimus*, der „Straußnachahmer“ bedeutet, und die gesamte Gruppe der Ornithomimodinosaurier wird häufig als Straußdinosaurier bezeichnet. Davon sollte man sich allerdings nicht irreführen lassen. Die Ähnlichkeiten zwischen Straußdinosauriern und den Straußen sind entwicklungsgeschichtliche Zufälle und keine Anzeichen naher Verwandtschaft. Zwischen den Dinosauriern und den namengebenden Vögeln gibt es bedeutende Unterschiede; schließlich handelt es sich bei den Straußdinosauriern um prähistorische Reptilien und nicht um rezente Vögel. Die Vordergliedmaßen eines Straußes sind flügelartig, während Straußdinosaurier ziemlich lange Arme hatten, die unter dem Körper baumelten und in spitzkralligen Fingern endeten, die scharren, graben und greifen konnten. Der Körper eines Straußes ist mit Federn bedeckt, wohingegen es bisher keinen brauchbaren Fossilbeleg irgendeiner Art gibt, aus dem ersichtlich ist, ob die Straußdinosaurier wie die meisten Reptilien Schuppen oder wie einige Dinosaurier und alle Vögel Federn besaßen.

## VERHALTENSMUSTER

Trotz der Unterschiede deuten die Ähnlichkeiten doch darauf hin, dass die Straußdinosaurier einst ähnlich wie die heutigen Strauße lebten. Sie bewegten sich wahrscheinlich mit gemessenen Schritten durch die Landschaft, dabei suchten ihre Augen, die dank der langen Beine und des langen Halses von einer hohen Warte ausschauen konnten, die Umgebung nach Nahrung und Feinden ab. Nahte Gefahr, nahm ein Straußdinosaurier Zuflucht zu seiner wichtigsten Überlebensmethode – er rannte davon. Die Knochen der Gliedmaßen und die Rekonstruktion der Muskulatur deuten darauf hin, dass Ornithomimosaurier wahrscheinlich die schnellfüßigsten Dinosaurier überhaupt waren. In dieser Hinsicht konnten manche mit dem heutigen Strauß mithalten oder die achtzig Stundenkilometer, die bei dem Vogel schon gemessen wurden, sogar noch übertreffen. Entdeckte ein Ornithomimosaurier etwas Fressbares, beugte er wahrscheinlich Hals und Kopf nieder und pickte die Nahrung auf. Andernfalls konnte er mit seinen Vordergliedmaßen kleine Beutetiere wie Echsen und winzige Dinosaurierjunge ergreifen. Die Strauße von heute sind meisterhafte Allesfresser. Als Nahrung dient ihnen so gut wie alles – die Blätter, Stängel, Triebe und Knospen der Pflanzen sowie Eier, Insekten, Larven und andere kleine Tiere. Dass sich Straußdinosaurier auf die gleiche Weise ernährten, ist durchaus denkbar.

## EVOLUTION

Die Straußdinosaurier erschienen auf der Erde als eine der letzten Dinosauriergruppen. Die meisten lebten gegen Ende der Kreidezeit, der größte Teil ihrer Fossilien wurde auf den nördlichen Landmassen – in Nordamerika, Europa und Ostasien – gefunden. Sie hatten noch Zähne, von denen sechzig an der Vorderseite des Oberkiefers und einhundertvierzig Stück vorn im Unterkiefer saßen, die allesamt jedoch nur winzig klein waren. Das zeigt, wie bei den Straußdinosauriern allmählich die normalen Dinosaurierzähne verloren gingen, während die Schnäbel sich immer stärker herausbildeten. Die Gruppe scheint noch in der Entwicklung und Ausbreitung begriffen gewesen zu sein, als das große Massenaussterben einsetzte und ihr ein jähes Ende bereitete (siehe Seiten 407–409).

**VORHERGEHENDE SEITE** An dieser Skelettnachbildung sind die typischen Merkmale der Ornithomimosaurier – ein unpassend wirkender Kopf, schlaksige Vordergliedmaßen, lange, kräftige Hinterbeine und ein überlanger Schwanz – deutlich zu erkennen.

**LINKS** Hier hat sich ein australischer Straußdinosaurier *Timimus* zum Überwintern unter einen Baumstamm gelegt. In der Nähe ziehen kleine Ornithopoden, darunter *Leaellynasaura*, durch den farnbestandenen Wald, wie er typisch für die mittlere Kreidezeit war. Die ganze Szene wird von Südlichtern *(Aurora australis)*, gewaltigen Leuchterscheinungen aus der hohen Atmosphäre, erhellt.

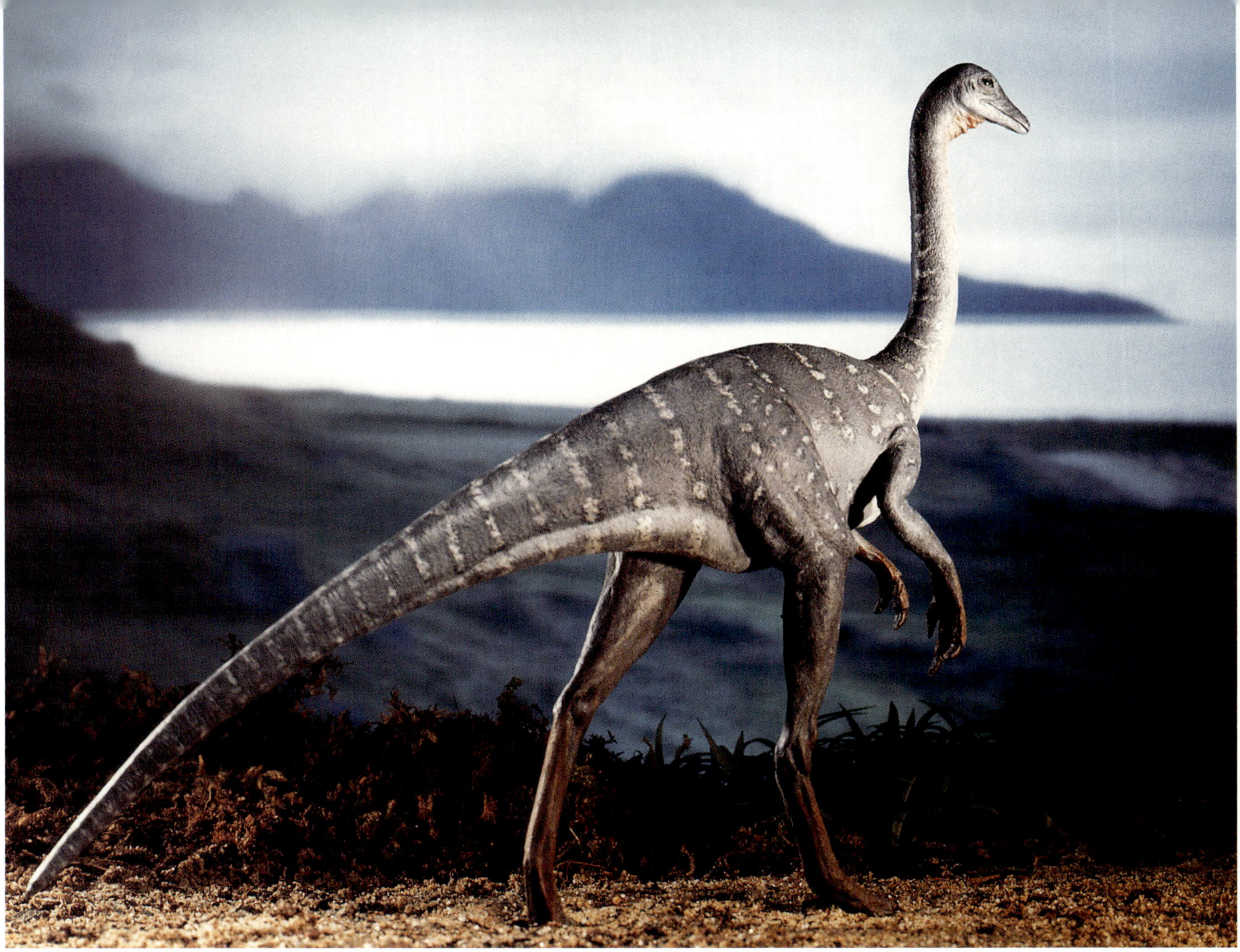

# ORNITHOMIMUS

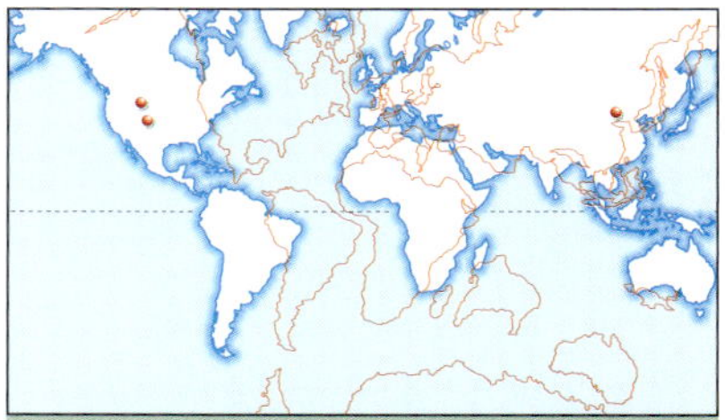

**ÜBERSICHT (DINOSAURIER)**

***Ornithomimus***

**Bedeutung des Namens:** Vogelnachahmer, Vogelvortäuscher

**Periode:** Oberkreide

**Hauptgruppe:** Theropoda

**Länge:** 4–6 Meter

**Gewicht:** 130–160 Kilogramm

**Nahrung:** Wahrscheinlich Allesfresser

**Fossilfundstätten:** Im Westen der USA, möglicherweise in der Mongolei

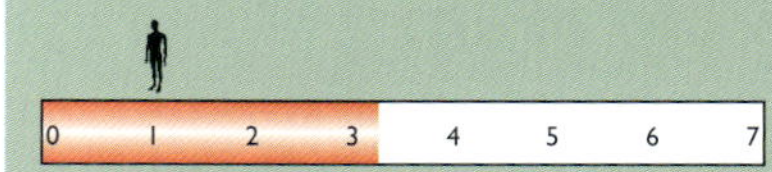


Die wissenschaftliche Geschichte der Straußdinosaurier begann 1890 mit einer Art Urknall. Damals benannte der bedeutende Paläontologe Othniel Charles Marsh auf der Grundlage von Fossilien, die ein oder zwei Jahre zuvor von George Cannon in Denver (US-Bundesstaat Colorado) und von John Bell Hatcher im Bundesstaat Montana ausgegraben worden waren, drei Spezies der Gattung *Ornithomimus*. Marsh vermutete damals, dass es sich bei den Fossilien um Überreste vogelartiger Reptilien und wahrscheinlich um Ornithopoden aus derselben großen Dinosauriergruppe handelte, zu der auch der viel größere *Iguanodon* gehört. 1892 folgten Funde von zwei weiteren Arten, doch zu dieser Zeit hatte Marsh bereits erkannt, dass diese Dinosaurier wahrscheinlich Theropoden, d.h. Raubtierfuß-Dinosaurier, waren. Nach weiteren Fossilfunden und einigen Verwechslungen mit *Struthiomimus* übernahm *Ornithomimus* seinen Platz als Gründungsmitglied einer neu klassifizierten Gruppe, der Ornithomimosaurier („Vogelnachahmer-Reptilien") oder Straußdinosaurier.

*Ornithomimus* besaß alle für die Straußdinosaurier typischen Merkmale: einen schlanken Körperbau; Röhrenknochen; einen langen, flachen Schädel; einen zahnlosen Schnabel; große Augen und ein großes Hirn; starke Vordergliedmaßen mit drei bekrallten Greiffingern; extrem lange, schlanke Hinterbeine, die von einer kräftigen Beckenmuskulatur bewegt wurden; sehr lange Mittelfußknochen; an jedem Fuß drei große, den Boden berührende Zehen; einen langen, dünnen Schwanz mit bis zu vierzig Schwanzwirbeln. Er zählte zu den größeren Vertretern seiner Gruppe und war mit rund fünf Metern etwas länger als *Struthiomimus*. Die Schätzungen seiner Körperlänge schwanken allerdings zwischen weniger als vier bis mehr als sechs Meter. Weitere Fossilfunde von ihm sind in der Mongolei sowie in Nordamerika vorläufig identifiziert worden. *Ornithomimus* war wie die meisten Straußdinosaurier wahrscheinlich ein Allesfresser.

**OBEN** In dieser aufrechten Haltung war *Ornithomimus* gut über zwei Meter hoch, größer als ein erwachsener Mensch. Wenn er schnell lief, hielt er Kopf und Hals wahrscheinlich tiefer und den Schwanz höher, so dass sie mit dem Rumpf in einer waagerechten Flucht lagen und eine lange, pfeilartige Silhouette ergaben.

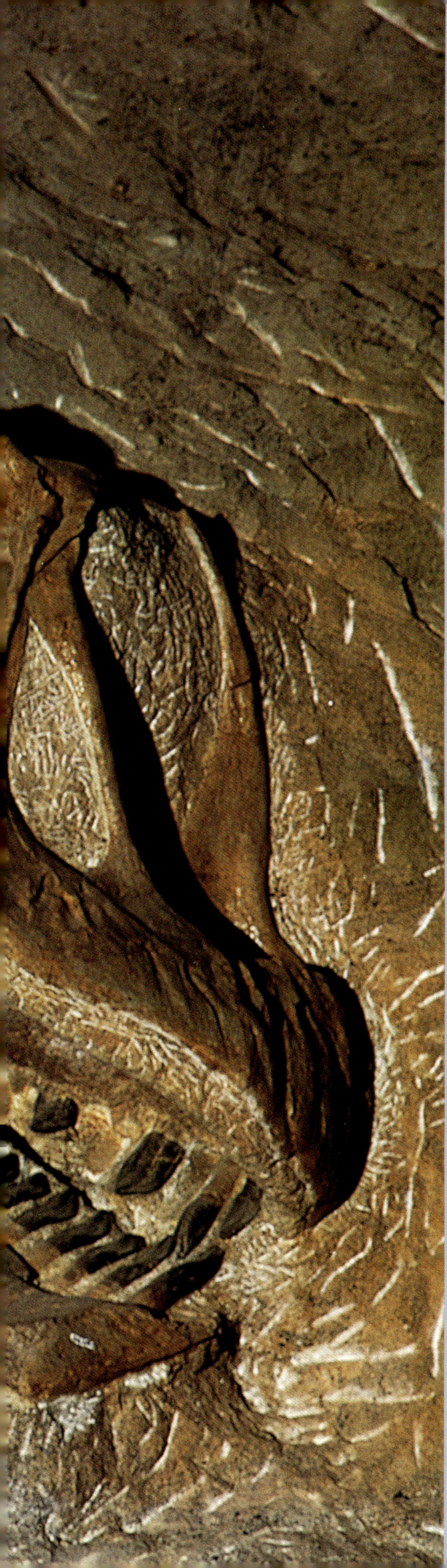

## Kapitel Sieben

# Die Riesen

*Groß, größer, am größten – wie es scheint, wird in gewissen Abständen unter den gewaltigsten Tieren, die je die Erde mit ihren Schritten erschüttert haben, immer wieder ein neuer Rekordhalter entdeckt.*

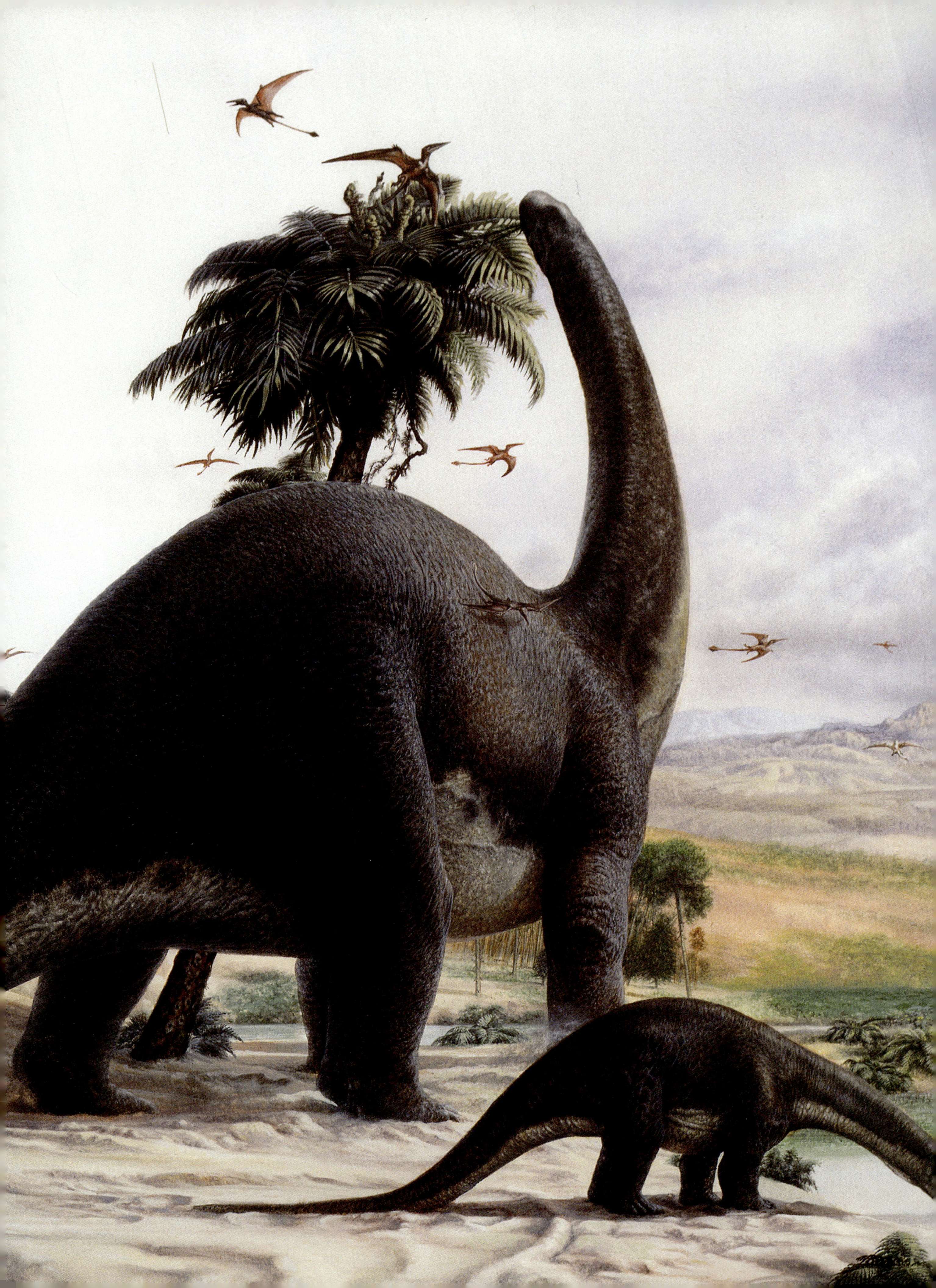

# REKORDBRECHER

*Die Konkurrenz zwischen Säugetieren und Dinosauriern um den Titel des größten Tieres, das je existiert hat, ist viel stärker, als es noch vor einigen Jahren schien. Neue Fossilfunde von Riesendinosauriern aus der Gruppe der Sauropoden, beispielsweise des Argentinosaurus, besagen, dass diese Reptilien den großen Walen der Jetztzeit wie etwa dem Blauwal im Wettbewerb um den obersten Rang nicht nachstehen. Im Verlauf des Zeitalters der Dinosaurier gab es mehrere große Sauropodengruppen, und jede dieser Gruppen hatte ihre Riesen. Die Diplodociden waren außergewöhnlich lang, sie erlebten ihre Blütezeit im Oberen Jura und hauptsächlich in Nordamerika. Ebenfalls in dieser Zeit existierten in Nordamerika sowie in Europa und Asien Camarasaurus und dessen Verwandte, die sich – von großen bis zu riesigen Geschöpfen – stark voneinander unterschieden. Die Brachiosauriden besaßen besonders lange Vorderbeine, auch sie konnten sich in der Zeit des Oberen Jura in Nordamerika, Europa und Afrika durchsetzen. In der folgenden erdgeschichtlichen Periode, der Kreide, erschienen auf fast allen Kontinenten die Titanosauriden, die sich dann vor allem in Südamerika ausbreiteten.*

## VORTEILE DER GRÖSSE

Weshalb eigentlich wurden die Sauropoden so riesig und erreichten eine mehr als zehnmal so große Körpermasse wie die Elefanten, die größten Landlebewesen der Jetztzeit? Einen größeren Körper zu haben, bringt mehrere Vorteile mit sich. Einer davon ist die verbesserte Fähigkeit zur Selbstverteidigung. Größere Dinosaurier besaßen mehr Masse und Kraft, die sie in die Lage versetzten Räuber abzuwehren. Sie konnten ihre langen Schwänze wie große Peitschen oder ihre langen Hälse wie riesige Totschläger schwingen oder sich mit ihrem massigen Körper gegen einen Feind lehnen und ihn dadurch zu Tode quetschen. Immerhin brachten es die meisten Räuber, selbst die größten Fleisch fressenden Dinosaurier, nicht einmal auf ein Fünftel des Gewichts der größten Sauropoden.

## WÄRMESPEICHERUNG

Ein weiterer Vorteil könnte in der Regelung der Körpertemperatur gelegen haben. Einer der Hauptfaktoren, der die Energieabgabe eines warmen Gegenstandes an seine kühlere Umgebung beeinflusst, ist das Verhältnis zwischen Oberfläche und Volumen dieses Gegenstandes. Je größer die Oberfläche im Vergleich zum Volumen ist, desto schneller wird Wärmeenergie abgeführt. Da größere Objekte eine bezüglich ihres Volumens viel kleinere Oberfläche besitzen als kleinere Gegenstände, verringert sich der Wärmeverlust bei zunehmender Körpergröße. Das könnte für die Sauropoden wichtig gewesen sein, wenn sie „wechselwarm" oder genauer gesagt ektotherm waren, d. h. wenn sie ihre Körpertemperatur durch Wärme aus der Umgebung erhöhten. Hatte ein riesiger Dinosaurier tagsüber Sonnenwärme aufgenommen, speicherte er in seinem Körperinneren einen großen Teil davon für die kalte Nacht. Ein Dinosaurier mit höherer Körpertemperatur blieb beweglich und wachsam, wenn er Nahrung suchte oder mit Feinden aneinander geriet.

## NACHTEILE DER GRÖSSE

Ein sehr großer Körper hat natürlich auch Nachteile. Beispielsweise erhöht sich die Menge der Knochen, die gebraucht wird um den Körper zu stützen, überproportional zum Gewicht. Zum Fortbewegen der massigen Gestalt ist eine kräftigere Muskulatur nötig – auch hier ist wieder ein außerordentlicher Zuwachs erforderlich. Die lebensnotwendigen Nahrungsmengen steigen ins Gigantische, und es wird schwierig mit einem verhältnismäßig kleinen Kopf ausreichend pflanzliche Materie aufzunehmen, um dem gewaltigen Verdauungsapparat Nachschub zu liefern. Auch die Natur könnte damals belastet worden sein, da bestimmte Pflanzen in solch großen Mengen verbraucht wurden, dass sie schließlich verschwanden, insbesondere dann, wenn die riesigen Sauropoden in Herden lebten – und vieles an den Fossilbelegen deutet darauf hin, dass dies der Fall war. Die Sauropoden erlebten ihre Blütezeit im Oberen Jura, dessen feuchtwarmes Klima ein rasches Pflanzenwachstum begünstigte. Dennoch müssen damals ganze Gebiete kahl gefressen und von aller verwertbaren Vegetation entblößt gewesen sein, was bedeutete, dass die Herde weiterziehen musste.

**VORHERGEHENDE SEITE** Dieser Schädel eines *Camarasaurus* ist am Dinosaur National Monument in Utah zu sehen. Der Sauropode besaß einen hohen Schädel mit drei großen Öffnungen an beiden Seiten – vorn die riesigen Nasenlöcher, dann die Augenhöhlen und etwas weiter hinten die schräg unter den Augenhöhlen gelegene Schädelfenster, in denen sich die Kiefermuskulatur wölbte.

**LINKS** Umherziehende Sauropoden, die die Gegend nach neuen Weidemöglichkeiten absuchten, müssen ein Furcht erregender Anblick gewesen sein. Zahlreiche Beispiele von fossilierten Fußabdrücken zeigen, dass diese gewaltigen Dinosaurier in losen Gruppen unterwegs waren.

# Barosaurus

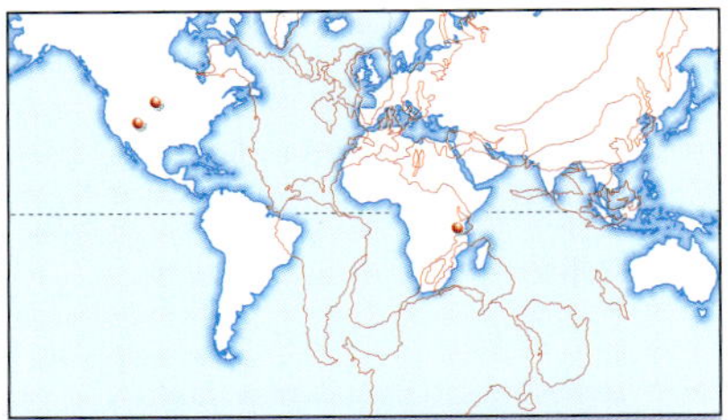

**ÜBERSICHT (DINOSAURIER)**
***Barosaurus***
**Bedeutung des Namens:** Schweres Reptil
**Periode:** Oberer Jura
**Hauptgruppe:** Sauropoda
**Länge:** 27 Meter
**Gewicht:** 30 Tonnen
**Nahrung:** Pflanzen
**Fossilfundstätten:** Im Westen der USA, in Tansania

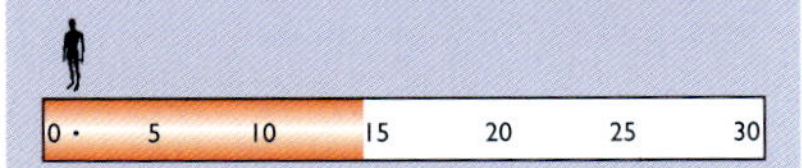


*Barosaurus* ist einer der zahlreichen Sauropoden, die während der „Wildwestjagden auf Dinosaurier" im späten 19. Jahrhundert in Nordamerika entdeckt wurden. Seinen Namen erhielt er 1890 von Othniel Charles Marsh. Der Name *Barosaurus* wird auch für Exemplare mit der früheren Bezeichnung *Tornieria* verwendet. 1922 begann ein Trupp unter Leitung von Earl Douglas vom Carnegie Museum mit Ausgrabungsarbeiten im Carnegie Quarry (US-Bundesstaat Utah), in deren Verlauf die Fossiliensucher drei nahezu vollständige *Barosaurus*-Skelette zutage förderten. Earl Douglas hatte bereits früher auf demselben Gelände Reste eines *Apatosaurus* ausgegraben und war auch 1915 an der Einrichtung des dortigen Dinosaur National Monument beteiligt gewesen. Weitere *Barosaurus*-Fossilien wurden in South Dakota gefunden, später kamen aus dem ostafrikanischen Tansania Teile eines Schädels und der Vordergliedmaßen sowie andere Bruchstücke eines Exemplars hinzu, die man ebenfalls der Gattung *Barosaurus* zuordnete.

*Barosaurus* war ein großer, jedoch ziemlich unverkennbarer Sauropode vom Typ des *Diplodocus*. Er lebte im Oberen Jura, vor rund 150 Millionen Jahren. Genau gesagt, ähnelte *Barosaurus* in vielerlei Hinsicht stark dem *Diplodocus* selbst (siehe gegenüber), wies aber trotzdem kleine Unterschiede zu diesem auf – viel längere Rückenwirbel, einen kürzeren Schwanz und einen deutlich längeren Hals. Wie *Diplodocus* besaß auch er insgesamt fünfzehn Halswirbel, doch bei ihm waren einige mehr als einen Meter lang. Wegen der Mulden und Höhlungen in den Knochen muss der Hals insgesamt verhältnismäßig leicht gewesen sein. Von den vermutlich 27 Metern Gesamtlänge des Pflanzenfressers nahmen Hals und Schwanz wohl mehr als vier Fünftel ein. Man geht davon aus, dass *Barosaurus* einen kleinen Kopf hatte, auch wenn bisher kein Schädel von ihm entdeckt worden ist. Im New Yorker American Museum of Natural History kann man ein „Mutterskelett" von *Barosaurus* besichtigen, das sich auf seinen Hinterbeinen zu enormer Höhe aufgerichtet hat, um ein Jungtier vor einem kleinen Allosaurus zu schützen. Der Kopf des Skeletts würde bei dieser Körperhaltung bis ins fünfte Stockwerk eines Hauses reichen.

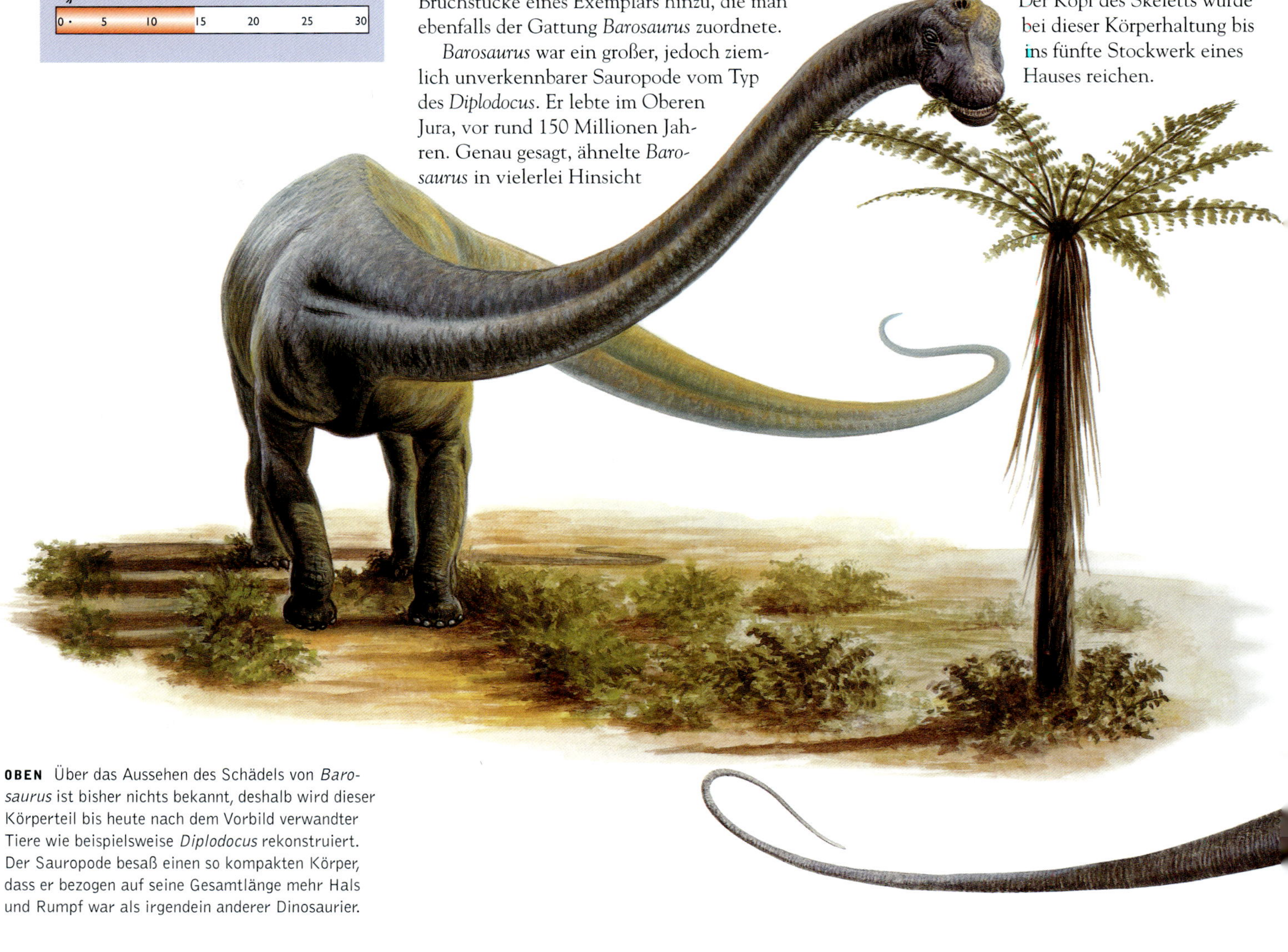

**OBEN** Über das Aussehen des Schädels von *Barosaurus* ist bisher nichts bekannt, deshalb wird dieser Körperteil bis heute nach dem Vorbild verwandter Tiere wie beispielsweise *Diplodocus* rekonstruiert. Der Sauropode besaß einen so kompakten Körper, dass er bezogen auf seine Gesamtlänge mehr Hals und Rumpf war als irgendein anderer Dinosaurier.

# DIPLODOCUS

Manche Dinosaurier, die uns von neueren Entdeckungen fragmentarischer Überreste bekannt sind, waren womöglich länger als *Diplodocus* (siehe Seiten 222 und 224), doch dieser oberjurassische Riese ist noch immer so ziemlich der längste Dinosaurier, den wir von fast vollständigen Fossilexemplaren kennen, und besitzt auch noch immer den mit dreizehn Metern längsten bekannten Schwanz. 1877 fand Sam Williston in der Nähe von Canyon City die unvollständigen Überreste eines Urtieres, die im Jahr darauf von Othniel Charles Marsh den Namen *Diplodocus* erhielten. Zweiundzwanzig Jahre später wurde im Albany County des US-Bundesstaates Wyoming ein weniger fragmentarisches Exemplar gefunden. Der Name *Diplodocus* bedeutet „Doppelbalken" und bezieht sich angeblich auf die Schwanzwirbel, von denen es mehr als siebzig gab. Die Wirbel im Mittelabschnitt des Schwanzes hatten an der Unterseite je einen Fortsatz, der vorn und hinten einen längs liegenden Sporn oder Balken trug und wie ein umgekehrtes T mit sehr kurzem Hauptstrich aussah. Zum Schwanzende hin wurde die Form der Wirbel einfacher, an der peitschenartigen Schwanzspitze waren die Wirbel nur noch einfache Stäbe.

Nach *Diplodocus* wurde eine ganze Gruppe von Sauropoden mit ähnlicher Schädelform benannt. Die Stirn eines solchen Schädels war flach und fiel zu einer etwas stumpfen Schnauze ab; die Stiftzähne standen an der Vorderseite des Ober- und des Unterkiefers und funktionierten beim Abstreifen des Laubes wie ein Kamm oder Rechen. Neuere Untersuchungsergebnisse lassen allerdings vermuten, dass Dinosaurier dieses Typs ihren Kopf nicht sehr hoch heben konnten. Die Nasenlöcher saßen hoch oben an der Stirn, fast zwischen den Augen. An jedem der vier Füße saßen wie bei den meisten Sauropoden fünf Zehen, wobei nur die erste Zehe eine richtige Kralle trug. Die Schlankheit der Beine und des Rumpfes deutet darauf hin, dass *Diplodocus* trotz seiner enormen Länge verhältnismäßig leicht war und wohl nur etwa zehn bis fünfzehn Tonnen wog. Neuere Funde von Hautabdrücken, die wahrscheinlich von *Diplodocus* stammen, zeigen eine Stachelreihe entlang des Rückens.

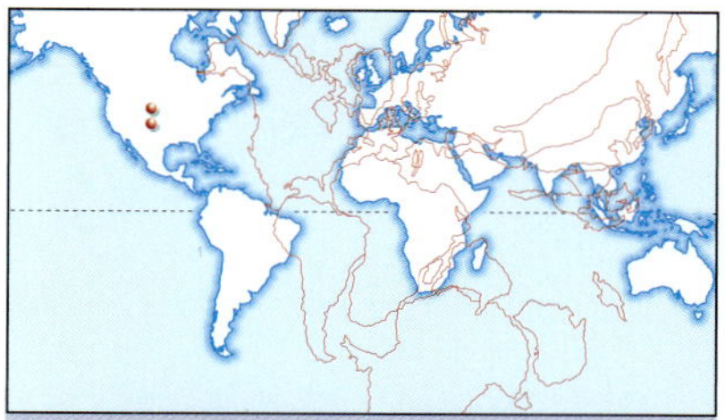

**ÜBERSICHT (DINOSAURIER)**
***Diplodocus***
**Bedeutung des Namens:**
Mit Doppelbalken
**Periode:** Oberer Jura
**Hauptgruppe:** Sauropoda
**Länge:** 27 Meter
**Gewicht:** 10–15 Tonnen
**Nahrung:** Pflanzen
**Fossilfundstätten:**
In den USA (Colorado, Wyoming)

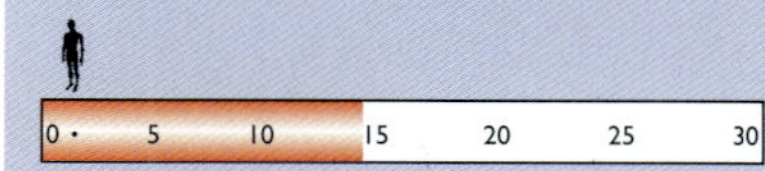


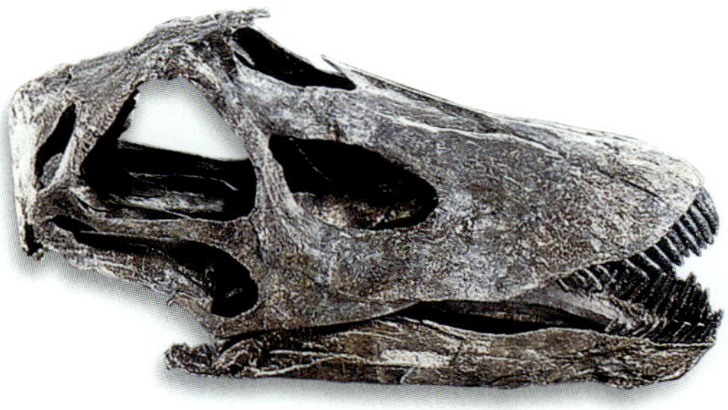

**RECHTS** Der flache, langschnäuzige Schädel des *Diplodocus*. Die Vorderfront des Mundes ist von Stiftzähnen gesäumt.

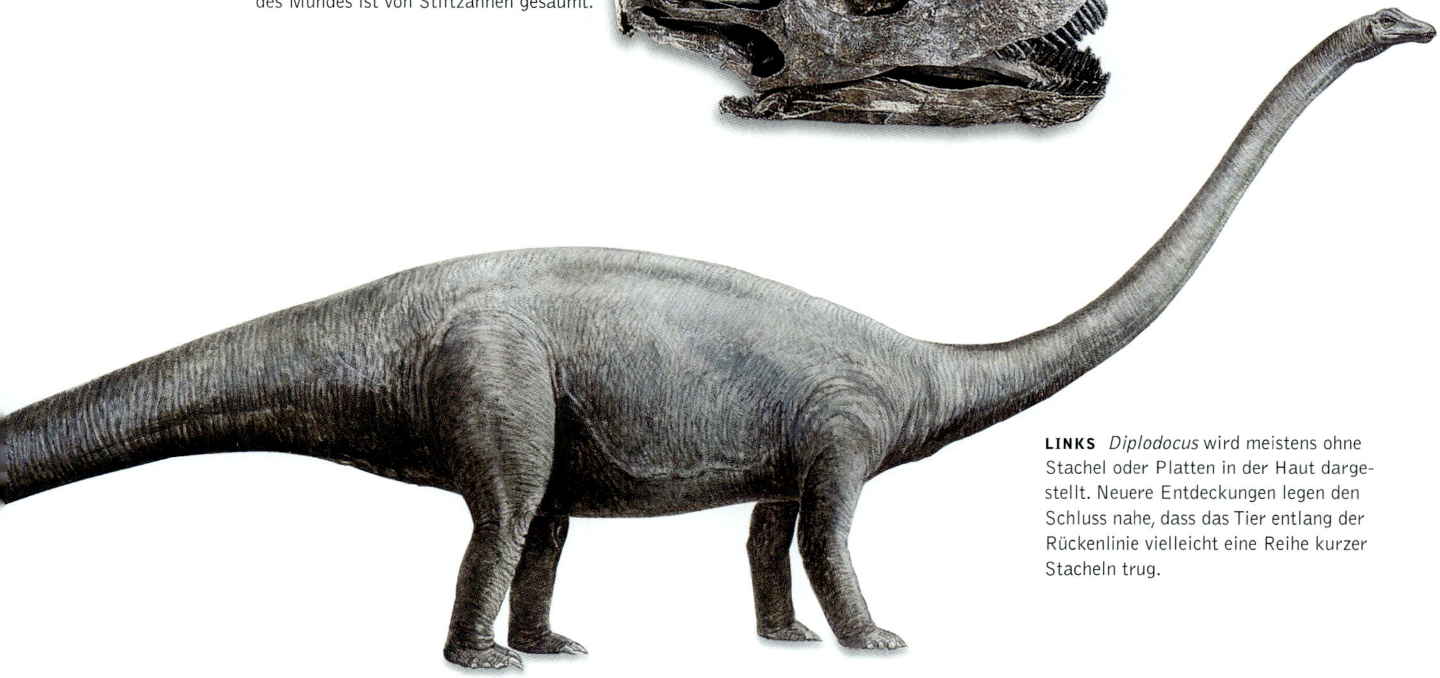

**LINKS** *Diplodocus* wird meistens ohne Stachel oder Platten in der Haut dargestellt. Neuere Entdeckungen legen den Schluss nahe, dass das Tier entlang der Rückenlinie vielleicht eine Reihe kurzer Stacheln trug.

# Supersaurus

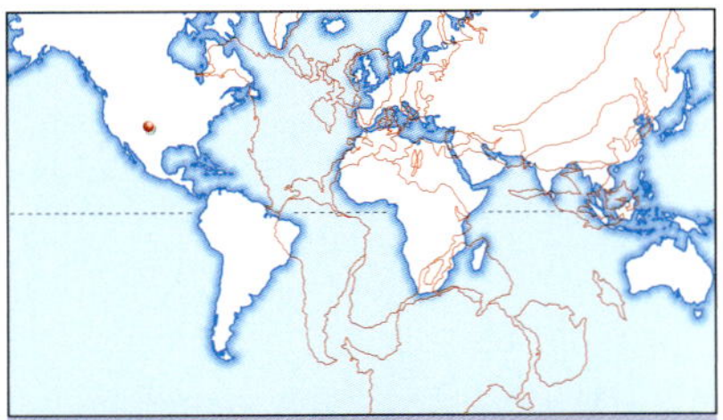

**ÜBERSICHT (DINOSAURIER)**
***Supersaurus***
**Bedeutung des Namens:** Superreptil
**Periode:** Oberer Jura
**Hauptgruppe:** Sauropoda
**Länge:** Schätzungsweise 30 – 40 Meter
**Gewicht:** Schätzungsweise 30 – 50 Tonnen
**Nahrung:** Pflanzen
**Fossilfundstätten:** In den USA (Colorado)

0 5 10 15 20 25 30

*Supersaurus* war ein Sauropode vom Typ des *Diplodocus*, er lebte in der Zeit des Oberen Jura in Nordamerika. Fossilien dieses Tieres wurden erstmals 1972 von James Jensen ausgegraben, aber erst 1985 benannt. Das geborgene Skelettmaterial reicht aus um zu belegen, dass es sich um die Reste eines wirklich riesigen Urtieres handeln muss, das wahrscheinlich über dreißig, möglicherweise aber fast vierzig Meter lang war und fünfzig Tonnen wog. Allein die Schulterblätter sind mit 2,4 Metern Länge viel größer als ein erwachsener Mensch. Die Rippen messen drei Meter und einzelne Halswirbel sind 1,4 Meter lang. Leider sind die Überreste verstreut und bei weitem nicht so vollständig wie etwa bei *Brachiosaurus* oder anderen Riesen, und deshalb kann über die wirklichen Abmessungen vorläufig nur spekuliert werden.

*Supersaurus* lebte wahrscheinlich wie andere Sauropoden, schwang stundenlang seinen langen Hals, um seinen massigen Körper „aufzutanken" und zu diesem Zweck riesige Mengen pflanzlicher Nahrung zu sammeln, die er unzerkaut verschluckte. Falls er in der Lage war, seinen Kopf nach oben zu strecken, könnte er sogar Blätter in fünfzehn Meter Höhe gefressen haben. Dieser Dinosaurier wird in die Familie der Diplodociden gestellt, die sich durch einen langen, peitschenartigen Schwanz und stiftförmige Zähne auszeichnen. Zu seinen Verwandten gehören *Amargasaurus*, *Apatosaurus*, *Barosaurus* und der ähnlich riesige *Seismosaurus*. Von James Jensen wurde auch *Ultrasauros*, ein weiterer Riese, als *Supersaurus*-Verwandter vorgeschlagen, doch dessen Name gilt heute bei vielen Dinosaurierexperten als unzutreffende Bezeichnung für einen Zufallsfund, der im US-Bundesstaat Colorado gemacht wurde und in Wirklichkeit aus einem Fossilienmix von *Supersaurus* und *Brachiosaurus* (siehe Seite 232) bestand.

**UNTEN** *Supersaurus* gehört zu den zahlreichen Sauropodenriesen, die wir von verhältnismäßig wenigen überdimensionalen Fossilien kennen. Er war vermutlich ein Vertreter der Familie der Diplodociden und ist einer der Anwärter auf den Titel „Längster Dinosaurier".

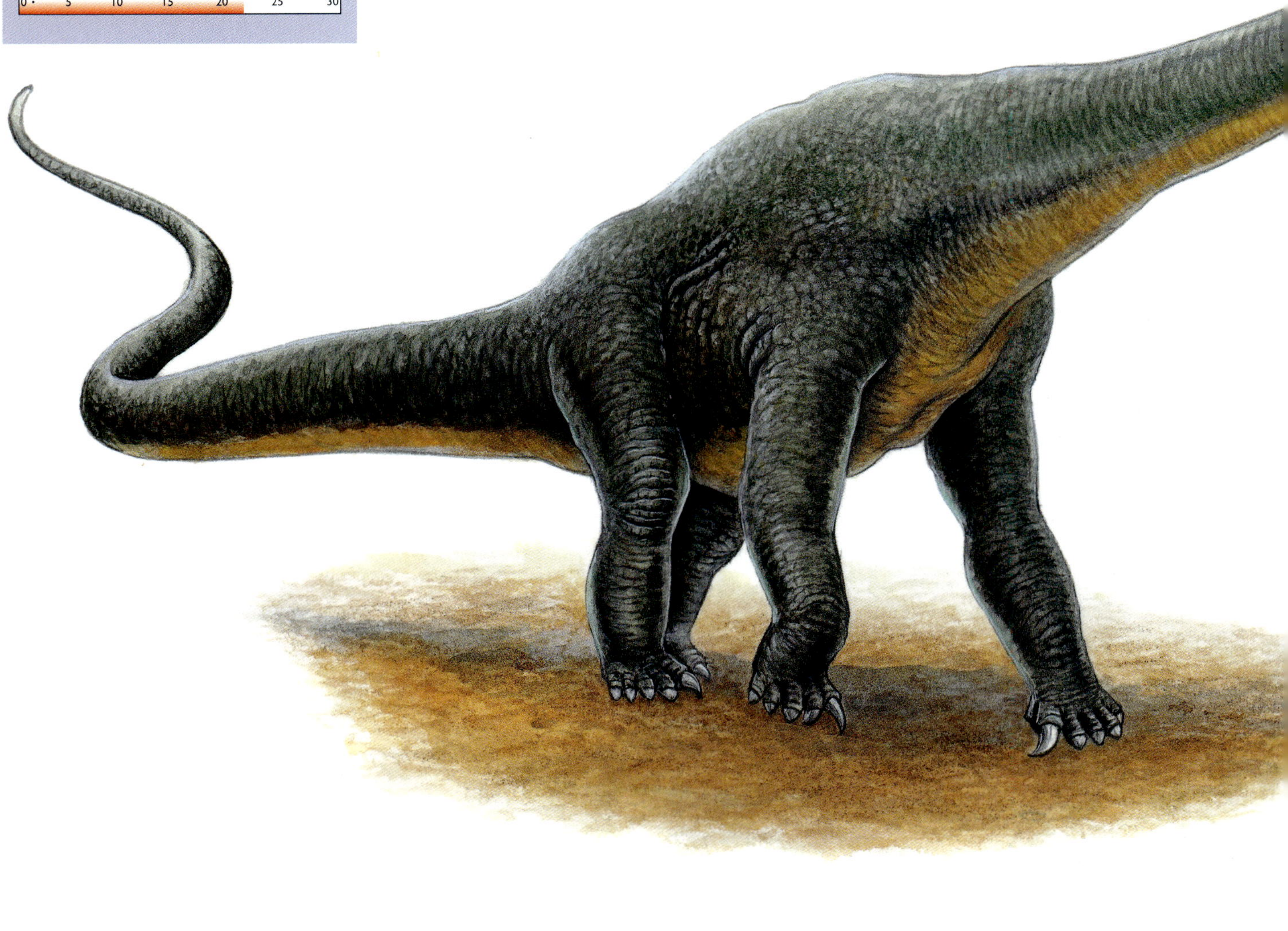

**UNTEN** Die sehr spärlich vorhandenen Fossilien des *Dicraeosaurus* zeigen eine seltsame Mischung von Merkmalen verschiedener Sauropodengruppen, darunter der Diplodociden und der Cetiosauriden. Besonders auffallend ist, dass das Tier anders als die meisten Sauropoden nur wenige Hals- und Schwanzwirbel besaß – am Hals vielleicht nur zwölf –, wodurch der Rumpf verhältnismäßig lang wirkte.

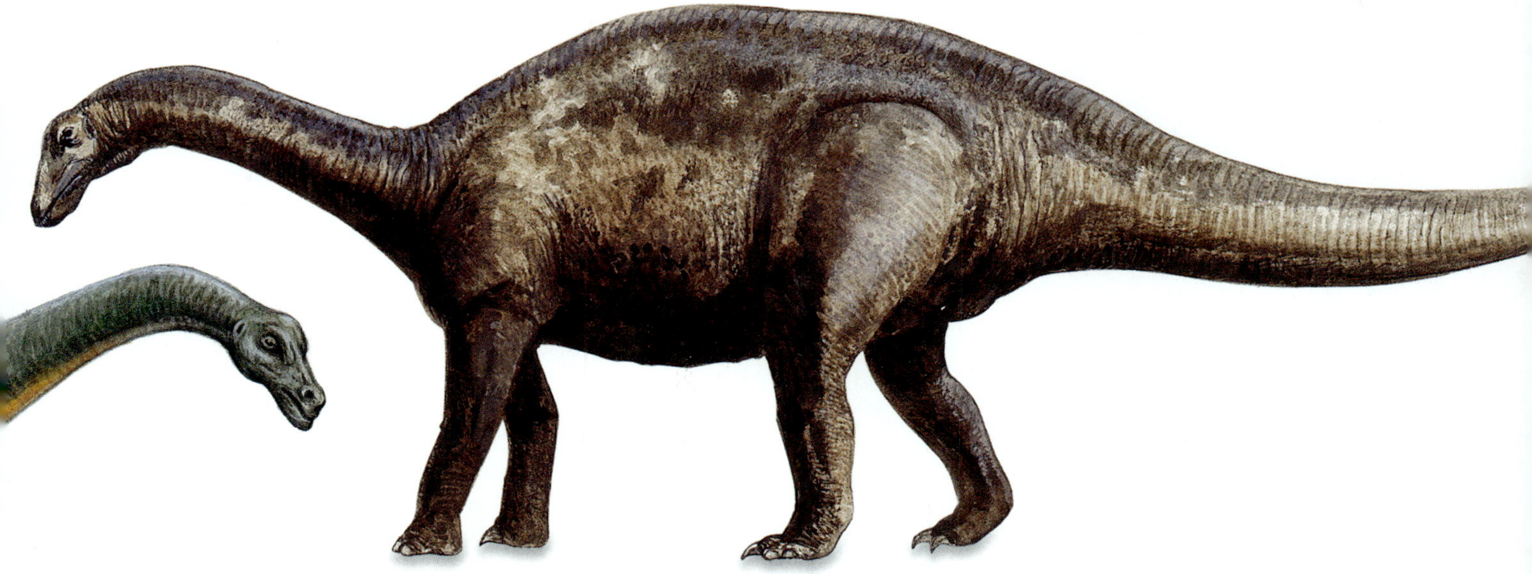

# Dicraeosaurus

Diesen Sauropoden aus dem Oberen Jura könnte man als für seine Gruppe mittelgroßes Tier einstufen, obgleich er viel länger als irgendein Landlebewesen der Jetztzeit war. Überreste des *Dicraeosaurus* wurden während der deutschen Tendaguru-Expeditionen ausgegraben, bei denen man in den Jahren 1908 bis 1912 im damaligen Deutsch-Ostafrika (später Tanganjika, heute ein Teil Tansanias) nach Fossilien suchte. Der Fund bestand aus vielen Skeletteilen, unter denen sich auch ein gut erhaltener Schädel befand.

Im Tendaguru-Bergland entdeckte man viele weitere Fossilien, die heute sehr bekannt sind, darunter Reste eines *Brachiosaurus* und eines *Kentrosaurus* (des „Stachelreptils"), eines afrikanischen Verwandten des *Stegosaurus*. Die Fossilien wurden 1914 von Werner Janensch, dem damaligen Direktor des Museums für Naturkunde in Berlin, untersucht und benannt (siehe auch Seite 245).

*Dicraeosaurus* ist abwechselnd der Familie der Diplodociden und seiner eigenen Gruppe, den Dicraeosauriden, zugeordnet worden. Er zeigt auch Ähnlichkeiten mit dem südamerikanischen Sauropoden *Amargasaurus* (siehe Seite 230). Die „zwei Gabeln" im Namen von *Dicraeosaurus* beziehen sich auf die Y-förmigen Dornfortsätze der Rückenwirbel. Diese Fortsätze trugen wahrscheinlich einen Kamm aus dicker Haut oder ein dünneres, flaches segelartiges Gebilde, das verschiedene Aufgaben gehabt haben könnte, also etwa der Temperaturregelung und/oder als optisches Signal diente. (Mögliche Funktionen dieser Segel werden auf Seite 107 erörtert.)

Der Schädel zeigt die typischen Merkmale eines Diplodociden: die Augen sitzen weit oben, ebenso die fast zwischen den Augen liegenden Nasenlöcher; die Schnauze ist lang, flach und wie ein Pferdemaul geformt; die Zähne sind dünn, fast stiftartig, und sitzen in zwei bogenförmigen Gruppen rund um die Vorderfront der Kiefer.

Der Schwanz mit den gegabelten Fortsätzen unterhalb einiger Wirbel war nicht so lang und peitschenartig wie der Schwanz des mit *Dicraeosaurus* verwandten Sauropoden *Diplodocus*.

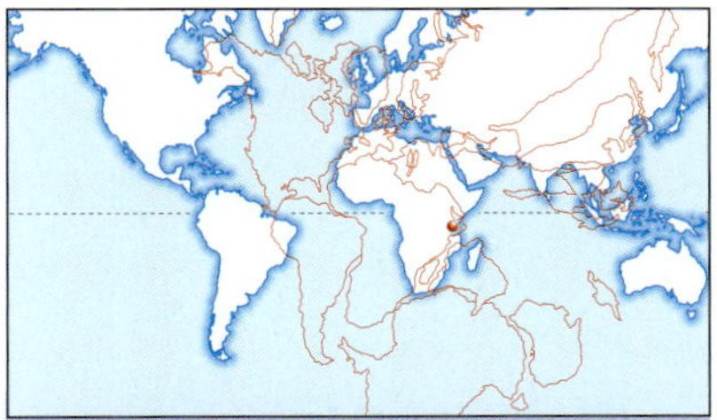

**ÜBERSICHT (DINOSAURIER)**
***Dicraeosaurus***
**Bedeutung des Namens:** Gegabeltes Reptil
**Periode:** Oberer Jura
**Hauptgruppe:** Sauropoda
**Länge:** 13 – 20 Meter
**Gewicht:** 10 Tonnen
**Nahrung:** Pflanzen
**Fossilfundstätten:** Tansania

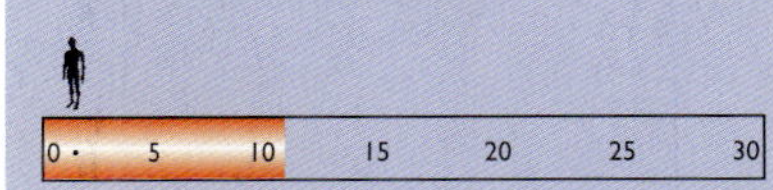

# Seismosaurus

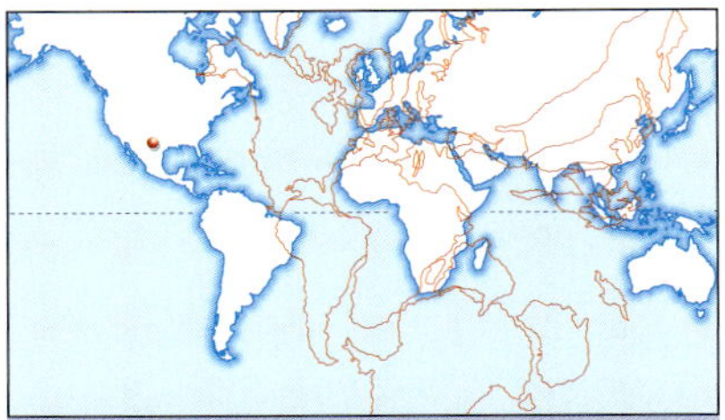

**ÜBERSICHT (DINOSAURIER)**
***Seismosaurus***
**Bedeutung des Namens:**
Erdbebenreptil
**Periode:** Oberer Jura
**Hauptgruppe:** Sauropoda
**Länge:** Schätzungsweise 35 – 52 Meter
**Gewicht:**
Schätzungsweise 30 – 50 Tonnen
**Nahrung:** Pflanzen
**Fossilfundstätten:**
In den USA (New Mexico)

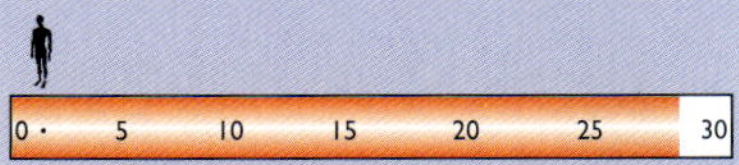


In den 1990er Jahren konnte die Wissenschaft über viele neu entdeckte Riesendinosaurier berichten. Eine der Entdeckungen war *Seismosaurus*, der diesen Namen erhielt, weil er mit jedem Schritt, sei es beim Dahintraben oder gar im Galopp, den Boden vermutlich wie ein Erdbeben erschütterte. Die Überreste aus dem Oberen Jura wurden 1991 von David Gillette in New Mexico entdeckt. Sie bestanden aus Teilen der Rückenwirbel, einigen Rippen, aus Fragmenten des Beckens und anderen Stücken. Die Rückenwirbel gehören mit je 1,8 Meter zu den längsten, die man je gefunden hat. Bei den Fossilien lagen auch zahlreiche glatt geschliffene runde Gastrolithe, so genannte Magensteine. Die Dinosaurier schluckten Steine, die das Zerkleinern der unzerkauten Nahrung in ihrem Muskelmagen unterstützten.

Aufgrund gewisser Ähnlichkeiten vermutete man, *Seismosaurus* vertrete keine eigene Gattung, sondern sei eigentlich eine überdimensionale Form oder Spezies der Gattung *Diplodocus* (siehe Seite 223). Merkmale der Rückenwirbel, darunter die spornartigen Fortsätze unterhalb der Wirbel, und andere fossilierte Knochen identifizieren *Seismosaurus* als Sauropoden vom Typ des *Diplodocus*, der wie dieser vor rund 155 – 144 Millionen Jahren lebte. *Seismosaurus* und andere Funde aus den 1990er Jahren haben freilich dazu beigetragen, *Diplodocus* von seiner Position als längster Dinosaurier und Landbewohner, den es je gab, zu verdrängen. Schätzungen auf der Grundlage der wenigen Überreste besagen, dass *Seismosaurus* bis zu zweiundfünfzig Meter lang war, was fast das Doppelte der Gesamtlänge von *Diplodocus* – siebenundzwanzig Meter – ist; nach anderen Berechnungen erreichte er vierzig oder vielleicht nur fünfunddreißig Meter. Die Schätzungen seines Gewichts variieren ähnlich – von dreißig bis zu achtzig Tonnen –, obgleich *Seismosaurus* als schlanker, leichter Diplodocid vermutlich nicht die riesengroße Körpermasse der Sauropoden vom Typ des *Brachiosaurus* besaß.

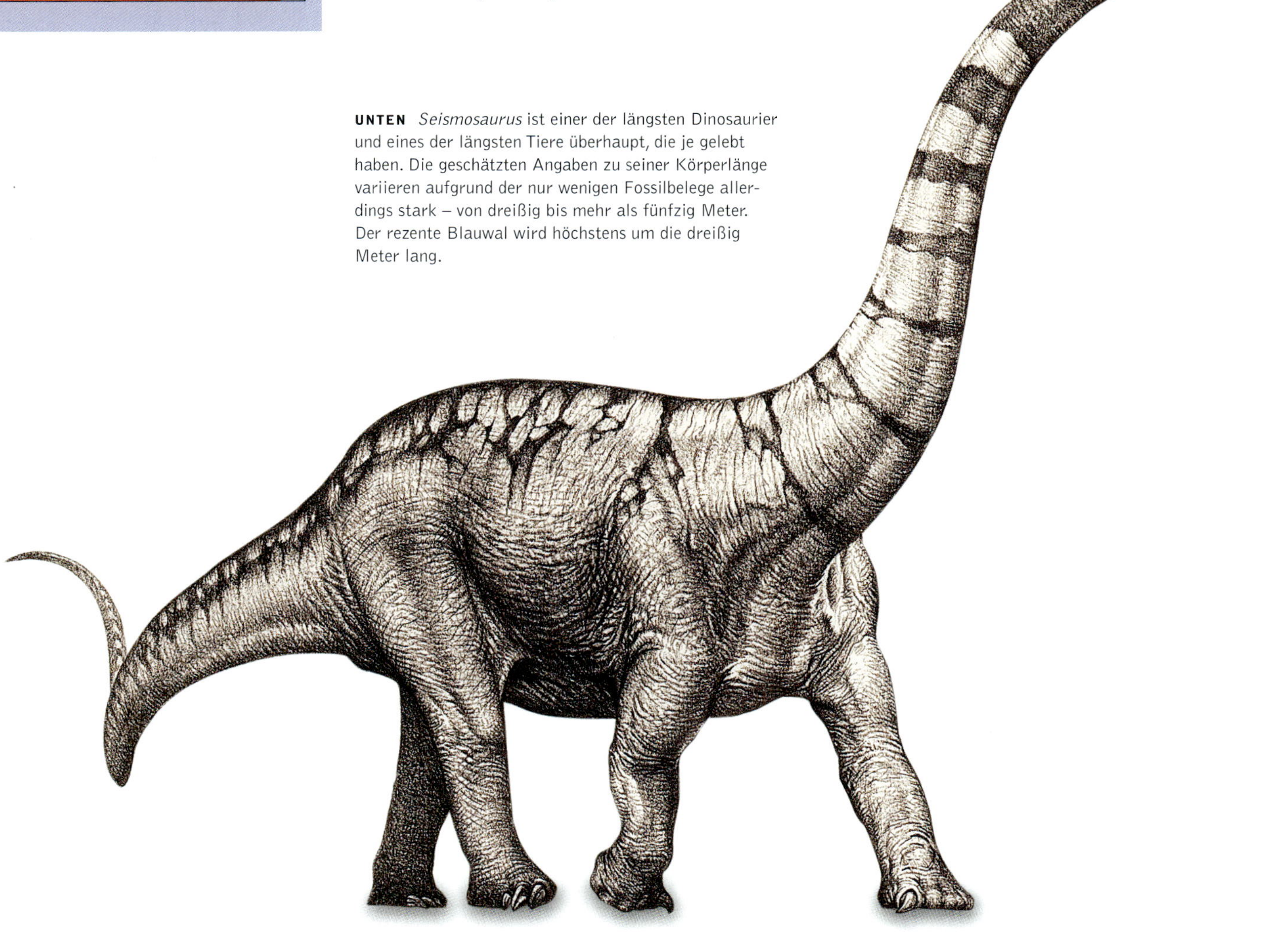

**UNTEN** *Seismosaurus* ist einer der längsten Dinosaurier und eines der längsten Tiere überhaupt, die je gelebt haben. Die geschätzten Angaben zu seiner Körperlänge variieren aufgrund der nur wenigen Fossilbelege allerdings stark – von dreißig bis mehr als fünfzig Meter. Der rezente Blauwal wird höchstens um die dreißig Meter lang.

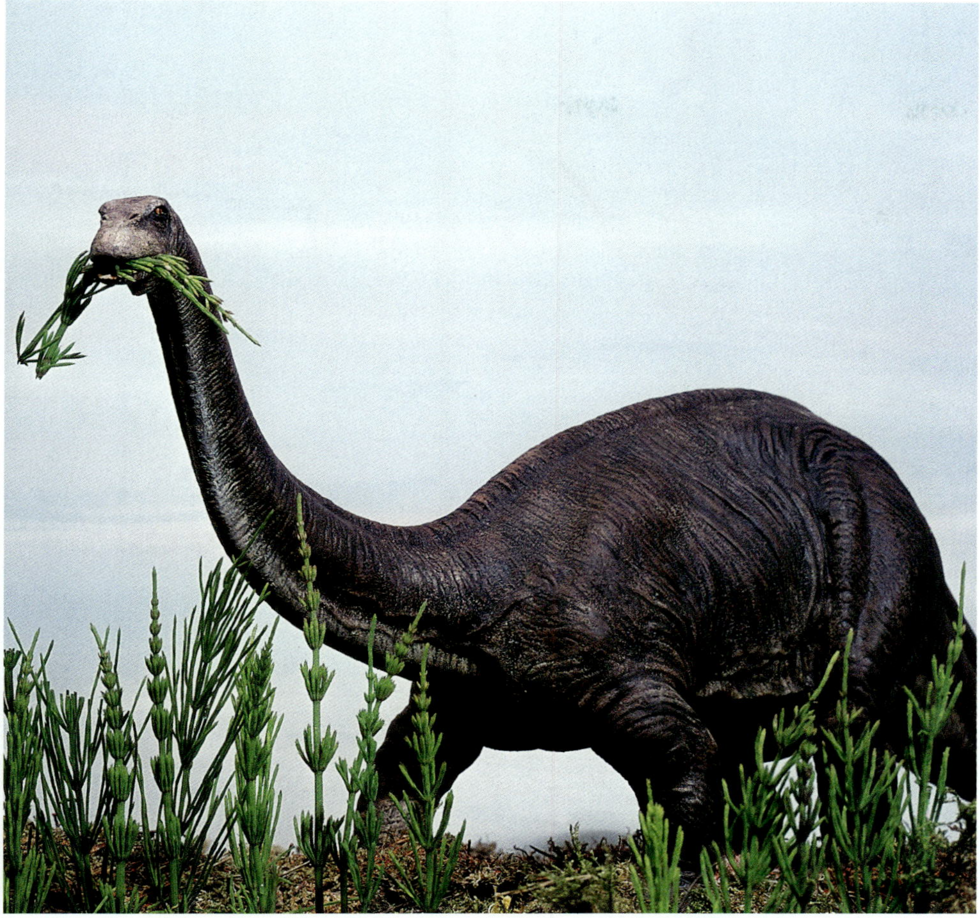

**LINKS** Der Pflanzenfresser *Apatosaurus* muss genau wie die meisten Riesensauropoden den größten Teil seiner Zeit mit der Nahrungsaufnahme zugebracht haben. Mit seinen stiftartigen Zähnen zog und harkte er unablässig pflanzliche Materie in sein Maul, die er unzerkaut in seinen riesigen Magen schluckte.

# APATOSAURUS (BRONTOSAURUS)

*Brontosaurus* gehört zu den bekanntesten Dinosauriern überhaupt, dennoch existiert sein Name wissenschaftlich betrachtet gar nicht. Das Tier, zumindest seinen Namen, gab es aber früher, als Othniel Charles Marsh 1879 zwei große Sauropodenskelette aus Como Bluff im US-Bundesstaat Wyoming beschrieb und den berühmten Namen mit der Bedeutung „Donnerechse" prägte. Zwei Jahre zuvor hatte Marsh schon einen anderen riesigen Sauropoden nach Überresten, die von Arthur Lakes in Gesteinen bei Morrison im US-Bundesstaat Colorado entdeckt worden waren, beschrieben und *Apatosaurus* genannt. Zu diesem Schwung früher Sauropodenfunde gehörte auch *Atlantosaurus*, ein weiterer Name, den Marsh prägte – für Fossilien, die er bereits als *Titanosaurus* beschrieben hatte. Nachdem er festgestellt hatte, dass der Name *Atlantosaurus* bereits in Gebrauch war, musste er eiligst eine Änderung vornehmen. In die allgemeine Verwechslung war auch *Camarasaurus*, ein weiterer Sauropode, verwickelt. Nach und nach wurde klar, dass *Apatosaurus*, *Brontosaurus* und *Atlantosaurus* Vertreter ein und derselben Gattung waren, und so erhielt der erste Name, der auch als erster in die wissenschaftliche Literatur eingegangen war, den Vorrang. Die Bezeichnung *Brontosaurus* wurde aus den offiziellen Listen gültiger Dinosauriernamen gestrichen, lebt in den Vorstellungen der Öffentlichkeit seither aber trotzdem weiter.

*Apatosaurus* war ein naher Verwandter des *Diplodocus*, er lebte in der gleichen Zeit, dem Oberen Jura, und in der gleichen Gegend des nordamerikanischen Westens. Er war jedoch kürzer und kräftiger und wahrscheinlich mehr als doppelt so schwer als *Diplodocus*. Über viele Jahre hinweg wurde rund ein Dutzend fossilierter Skelette ausgegraben und untersucht, doch über die Form des Schädels erlangte man erst 1975 Aufschluss, als Jack MacIntosh und David Berman etwas mehr Klarheit in die Verwirrung brachten. Ein neuer Schädelfund zeigte, dass *Apatosaurus* nicht den langen, gerundeten Schädel des *Camarasaurus* besaß, wie bis dahin angenommen. Sein Kopf war vielmehr flach und kurzschnäuzig, die Nasenlöcher saßen weit oben, fast zwischen den Augen, und seine Zähne waren schwach und stiftförmig. Mit diesen Merkmalen ähnelte er *Diplodocus*.

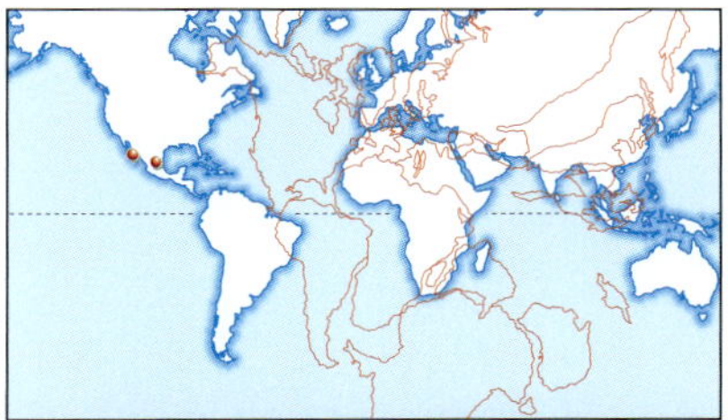

**ÜBERSICHT (DINOSAURIER)**
***Apatosaurus***
**Bedeutung des Namens:** Trügerisches Reptil
**Periode:** Oberer Jura
**Hauptgruppe:** Sauropoda
**Länge:** 21–23 Meter
**Gewicht:** 25–35 Tonnen
**Nahrung:** Pflanzen
**Fossilfundstätten:** Im Südwesten der USA, in Mexiko (Niederkalifornien)

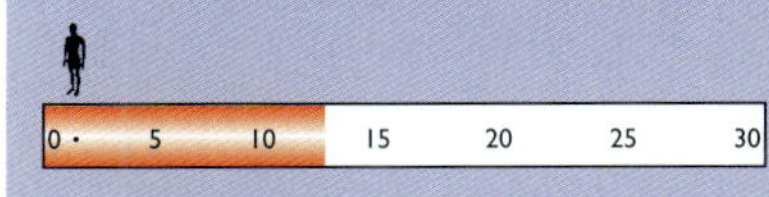

# Wie eine Herde Elefanten, nur grösser

*Es gibt viele Belege dafür, dass verschiedene Sauropoden in Gruppen oder Herden zusammenlebten. An vielen Fundstätten liegen auf kleiner Fläche die Überreste mehrerer Exemplare unterschiedlichen Alters – von Jungtieren bis zu ausgewachsenen Sauropoden – beisammen. Auch fossilierte Fußspuren weisen darauf hin, dass einst ganze Gruppen von Tieren unterwegs waren. Bei den Spuren fällt auf, dass in der Mitte kleine und an der Seite größere Abdrücke liegen. Nahmen die ausgewachsenen Tiere damals ihre Jungen zum Schutz in die Mitte?*

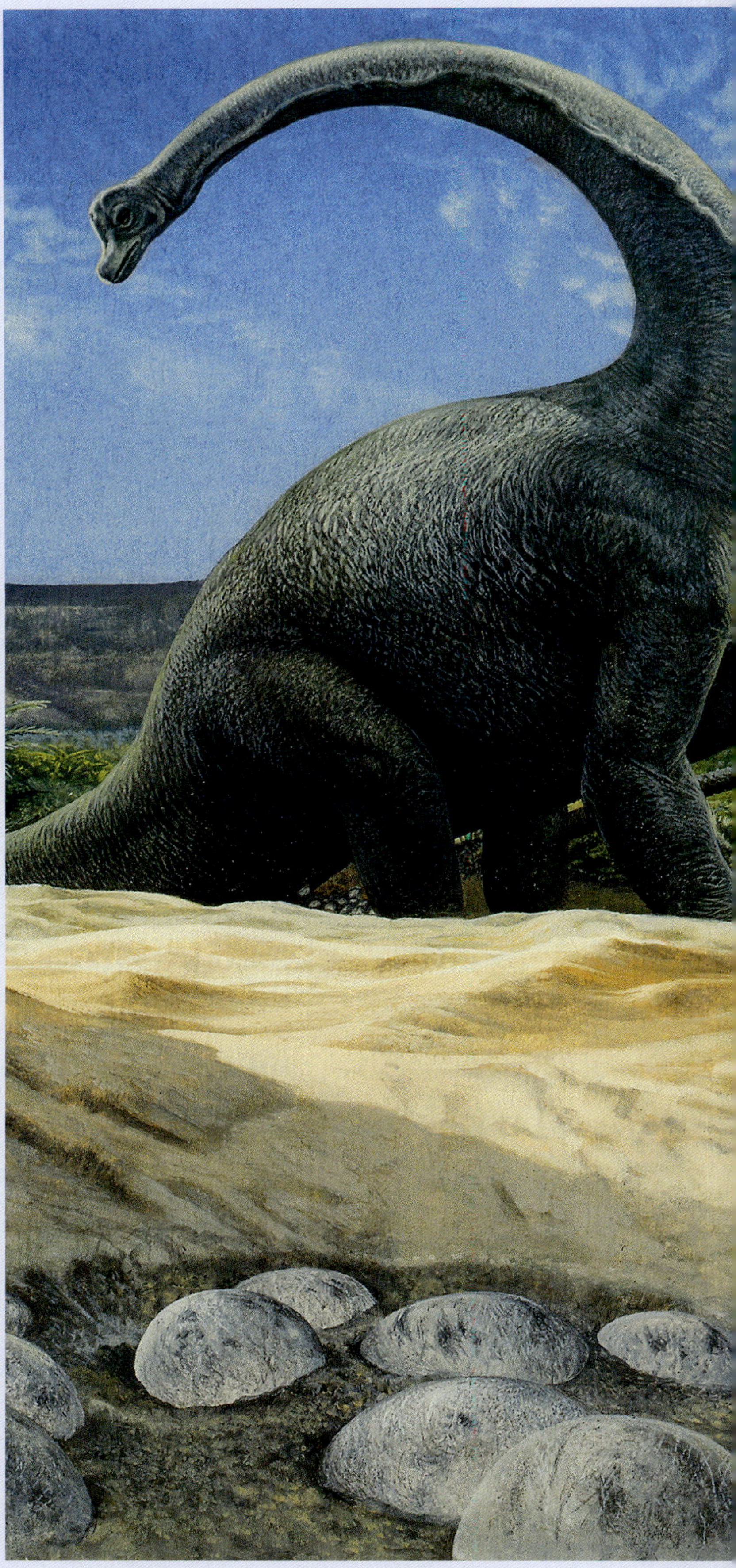

**RECHTS** In diesem hypothetischen Szenario aus dem Oberen Jura versammeln sich Sauropoden vom Typ des *Brachiosaurus* an ihrer althergebrachten Brutstätte. Im Hintergrund wiegen und umschlingen ein Weibchen und ein Männchen ihre Hälse beim Paarungsritual. Das Weibchen auf der linken Seite legt seine Eier in eine Vertiefung, die es zuvor in den Boden gescharrt hat. Das Gelege im Vordergrund wird schon bald von dem riesigen Fuß eines anderen Weibchens mit Sand zugeschüttet sein und dann von der trockenen Wärme ausgebrütet werden.

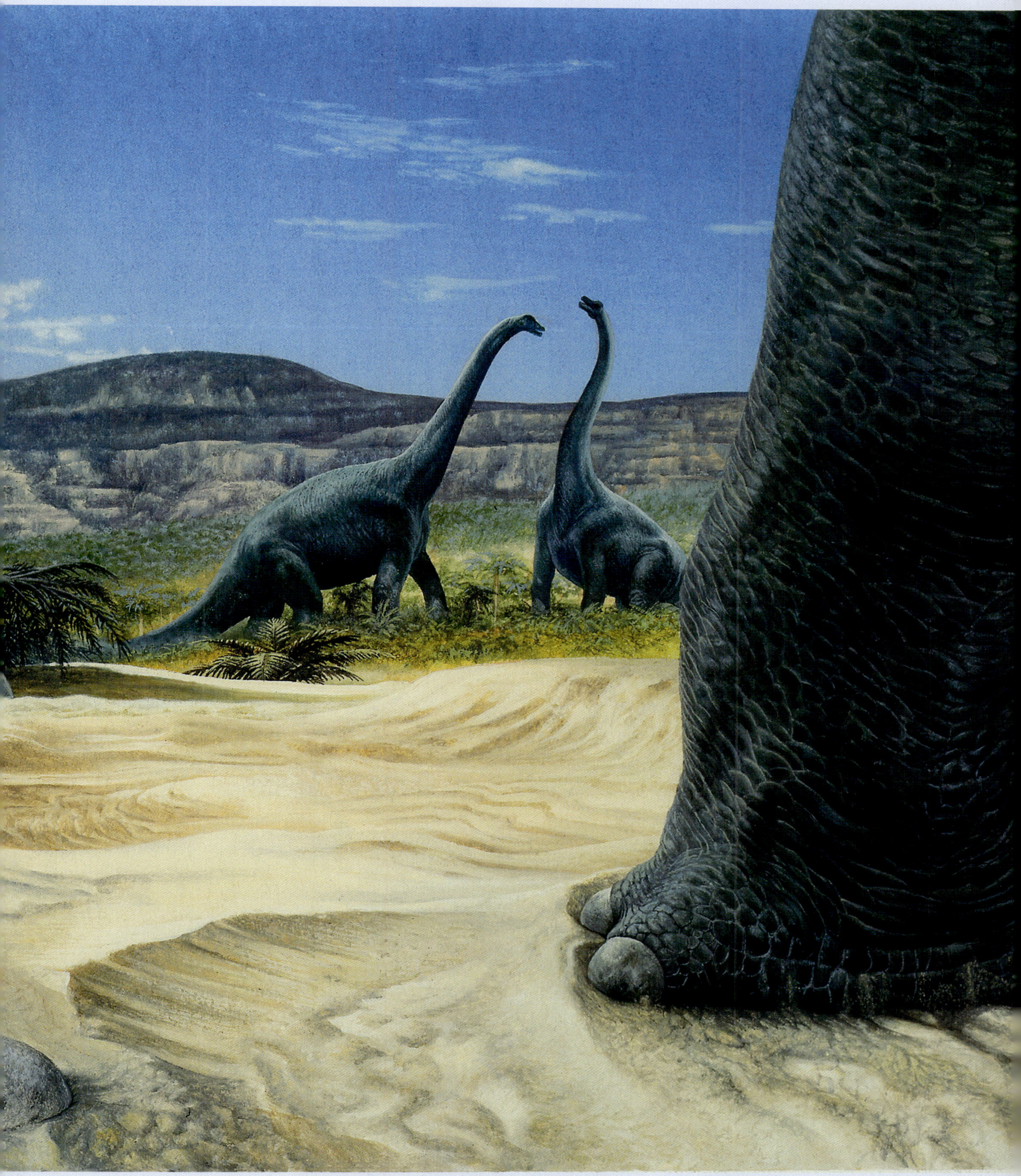

# AMARGASAURUS

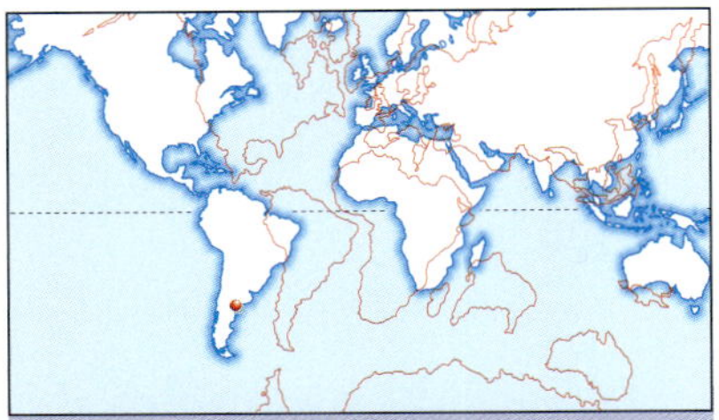

**ÜBERSICHT (DINOSAURIER)**
***Amargasaurus***
**Bedeutung des Namens:** La-Amarga-Reptil
**Periode:** Unterkreide
**Hauptgruppe:** Sauropoda
**Länge:** 10 Meter
**Gewicht:** 5 – 7 Tonnen
**Nahrung:** Pflanzen
**Fossilfundstätten:** In Argentinien

0 · 5 10 15 20 25 30

Das „La-Armaga-Reptil" ist nach dem Tal in Argentinien benannt, in dem erstmals Überreste dieses Sauropoden entdeckt wurden. *Amargasaurus* lebte vor rund 130 – 125 Millionen Jahren, stammte also wie viele argentinische Dinosaurierfossilien aus der Kreidezeit. Der Fund bestand aus einem fast vollständigen Skelett, dem lediglich die Vorderfront des Schädels und der Schwanz fehlten. Das Skelett wurde 1991 von Leonardo Salgado und José Bonaparte benannt. Die allgemeinen Proportionen des *Amargasaurus* sind typisch für die Sauropoden – kleiner Kopf, langer Hals und vermutlich auch ein langer Schwanz, ein runder, massiger Körper und vier säulenartige Beine. Mit seiner Gesamtlänge von nur zehn Metern ist *Amargasaurus* allerdings einer der kleineren Sauropodenvertreter; etwa die gleiche Länge weist der Netzpython, das längste Reptil der Jetztzeit, auf. Die Länge des Halses war der Gesamtlänge des Körpers angemessen, die Vorderbeine waren kürzer als das hintere Paar, und an den Füßen saßen die typischen fünf Zehen, deren erste (die große Zehe) wie bei den meisten Sauropoden eine Kralle trug.

*Amargasaurus* war vermutlich ein Vertreter der *Diplodocus*-Familie. Auffallend an ihm ist eine Reihe doppelter Dornen, die sich fast über die gesamte Wirbelsäule hinzog. Über deren Funktion ist schon ausgiebig diskutiert worden. Dornen dieser Art treten auch bei bestimmten anderen Dinosauriergruppen auf, darunter bei großen Theropoden (Fleischfressern) wie *Spinosaurus*; bei dem Pflanzen fressenden *Iguanodon*-artigen *Ouranosaurus*; bei *Dicraeosaurus*, der ebenfalls zu den Sauropoden gehört und bei einigen prähistorischen Reptilien wie *Dimetrodon* (siehe Seite 160), die keine Dinosaurier waren. Die übliche Erklärung dazu lautet, dass die Dornen einen fleischigen oder hautartigen Lappen oder ein „Segel", im Fall des *Amargasaurus* zwei dieser Gebilde hielten. Denkbar ist, dass die Lappen der Regelung der Körpertemperatur, als optisches Signal oder bei *Amargasaurus* vielleicht zur Einschüchterung und als Schutz vor den massigen, kräftigen Raubdinosauriern gedient haben, die in der Kreidezeit das heutige Südamerika durchstreiften.

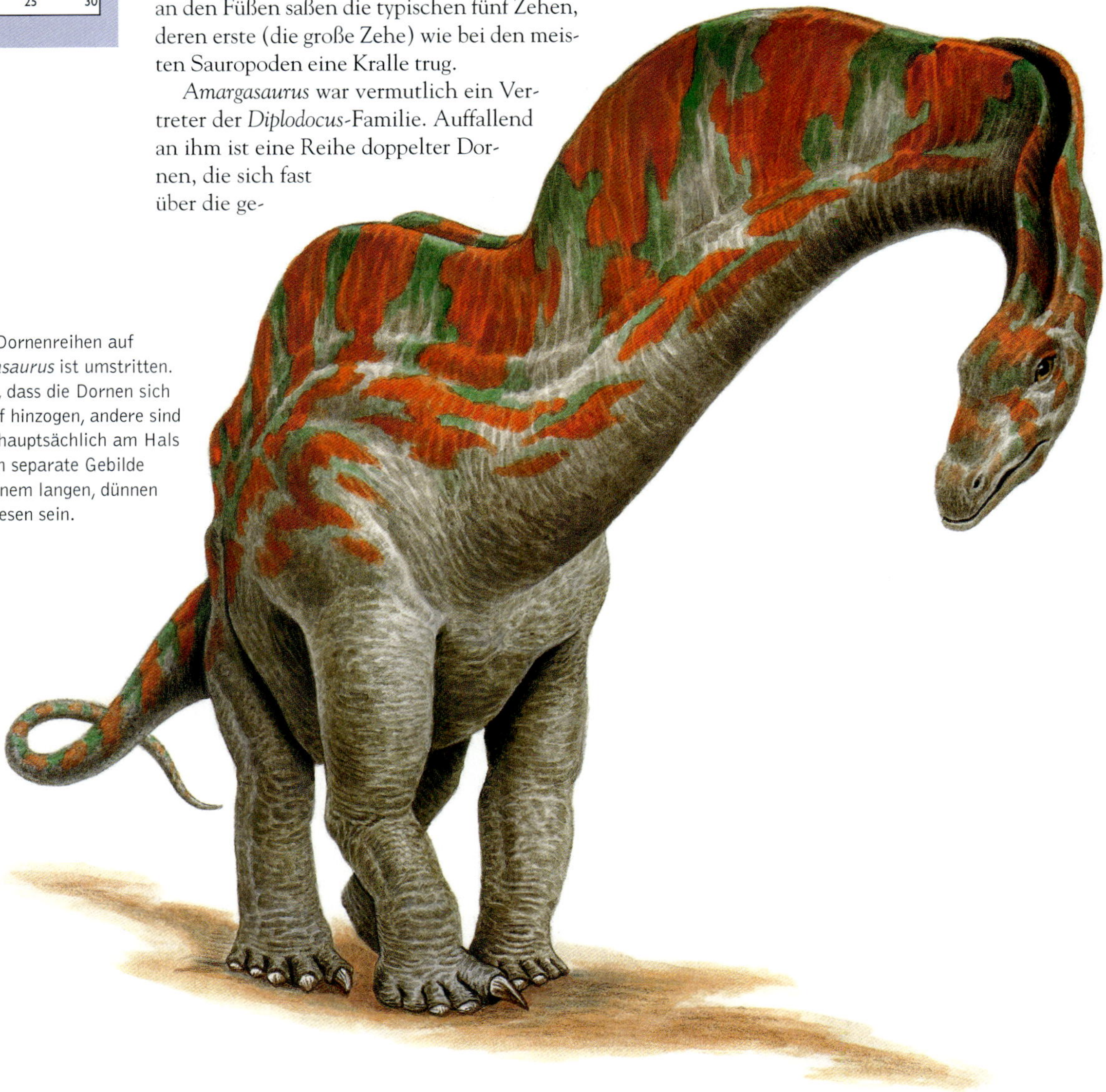

**RECHTS** Die Länge der Dornenreihen auf dem Rücken des *Amargasaurus* ist umstritten. Einige Fachleute meinen, dass die Dornen sich nur über Hals und Rumpf hinzogen, andere sind der Auffassung, dass sie hauptsächlich am Hals saßen. Die Dornen mögen separate Gebilde oder wie ein Segel von einem langen, dünnen Hautlappen bedeckt gewesen sein.

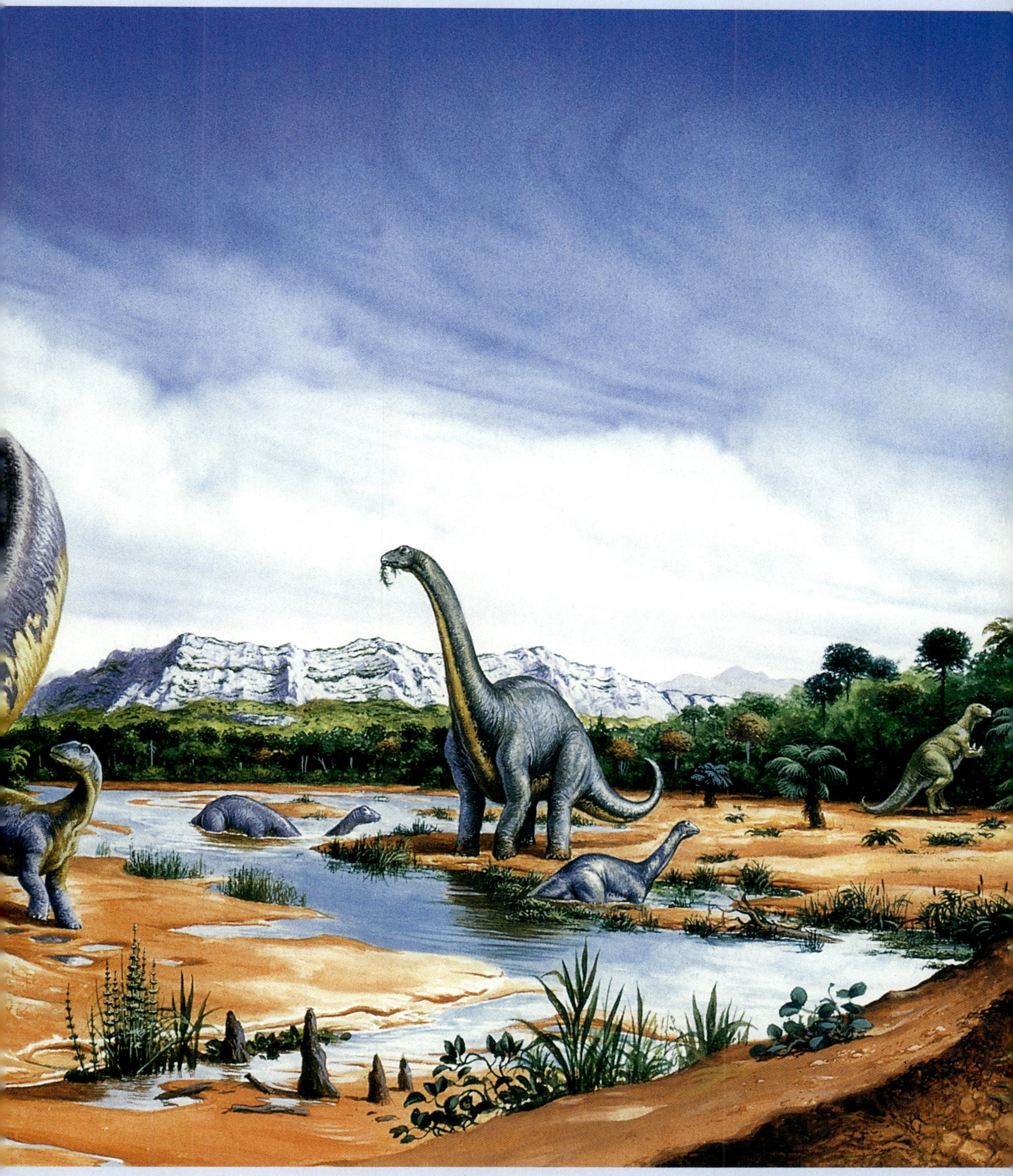

# CHUBUTISAURUS

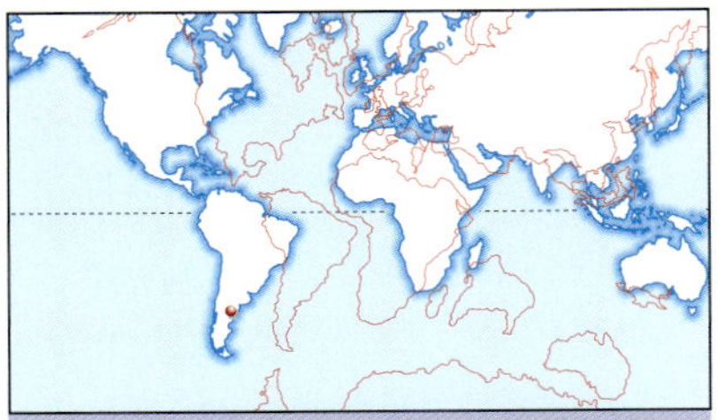

**ÜBERSICHT (DINOSAURIER)**
***Chubutisaurus***
**Bedeutung des Namens:** Chubut-Reptil (nach der Provinz benannt, in der die Fundstätte liegt)
**Periode:** Mittlere Kreidezeit
**Hauptgruppe:** Sauropoda
**Länge:** 24 Meter
**Gewicht:** 20–25 Tonnen
**Nahrung:** Pflanzen
**Fossilfundstätten:** In Argentinien

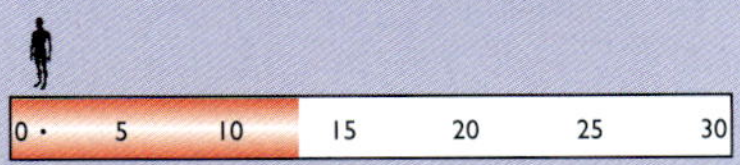


In der Provinz Chubut im Süden Argentiniens sind im Lauf der Jahre viele faszinierende Fossilien entdeckt worden; die Region ist für die Paläontologen nach wie vor interessant. Der nach dieser Provinz benannte *Chubutisaurus* wird zu den großen Pflanzen fressenden Dinosauriern vom Typ des *Brachiosaurus* gestellt.

Nach anderer Auffassung gehört *Chubutisaurus* jedoch zur Familie der Titanosauriden. Viele dieser großen Pflanzenfresser auf den südlichen Landmassen lebten in der Kreidezeit; sie gehörten zu den letzten Sauropoden, die vor dem großen Aussterben sämtlicher Dinosaurier und vieler anderer Reptilientypen vor 65 Millionen Jahren noch existierten. Die Familie wurde 1885 von dem britischen Paläontologen Richard Lykker mit *Titanosaurus* als „Gründungsmitglied" aufgestellt. Sie hat in den letzten Jahren mit der Entdeckung neuerer Mitglieder wie *Saltasaurus*, *Janenschia* und *Argentinosaurus* eine Neubelebung erfahren. In den südlichen Regionen ist man inzwischen auch auf kreidezeitliche Fossilien gestoßen, die möglicherweise von Raubdinosauriern stammen; unter den Funden waren Reste eines *Carnotaurus* – von derselben Fundstelle wie *Chubutisaurus* – sowie Knochen des mächtigen *Giganotosaurus* (siehe Seite 1987).

*Chubutisaurus* wurde 1974 auf der Grundlage zweier unvollständiger Exemplare etwa aus der Zeit vor 110–95 Millionen Jahren benannt. Anhand von Kenntnissen über verwandte Spezies wurden Einzelheiten ergänzt; das Ergebnis ist ein Sauropode, dessen Rücken und Rumpf wahrscheinlich wie bei dem jüngeren *Saltasaurus* einen Buckelpanzer aus Knochenplatten oder Knochenstücken hatten, die in die Haut eingebettet waren. Wie die anderen Sauropoden harkte vermutlich auch *Chubutisaurus* mit seinen kleinen Zähnen Blätter von den Pflanzen in sein Maul und verschluckte die Nahrung, die erst in seinem Muskelmagen mit speziell zu diesem Zweck verschluckten Gastrolithen zermahlen wurde.

**UNTEN** *Chubutisaurus* ist von mehreren Rücken- und Schwanzwirbeln, Knochenteilen der Hinter- und Vorderbeine, Knochen der Vorderfüße und auch Teilen des Beckens bekannt.

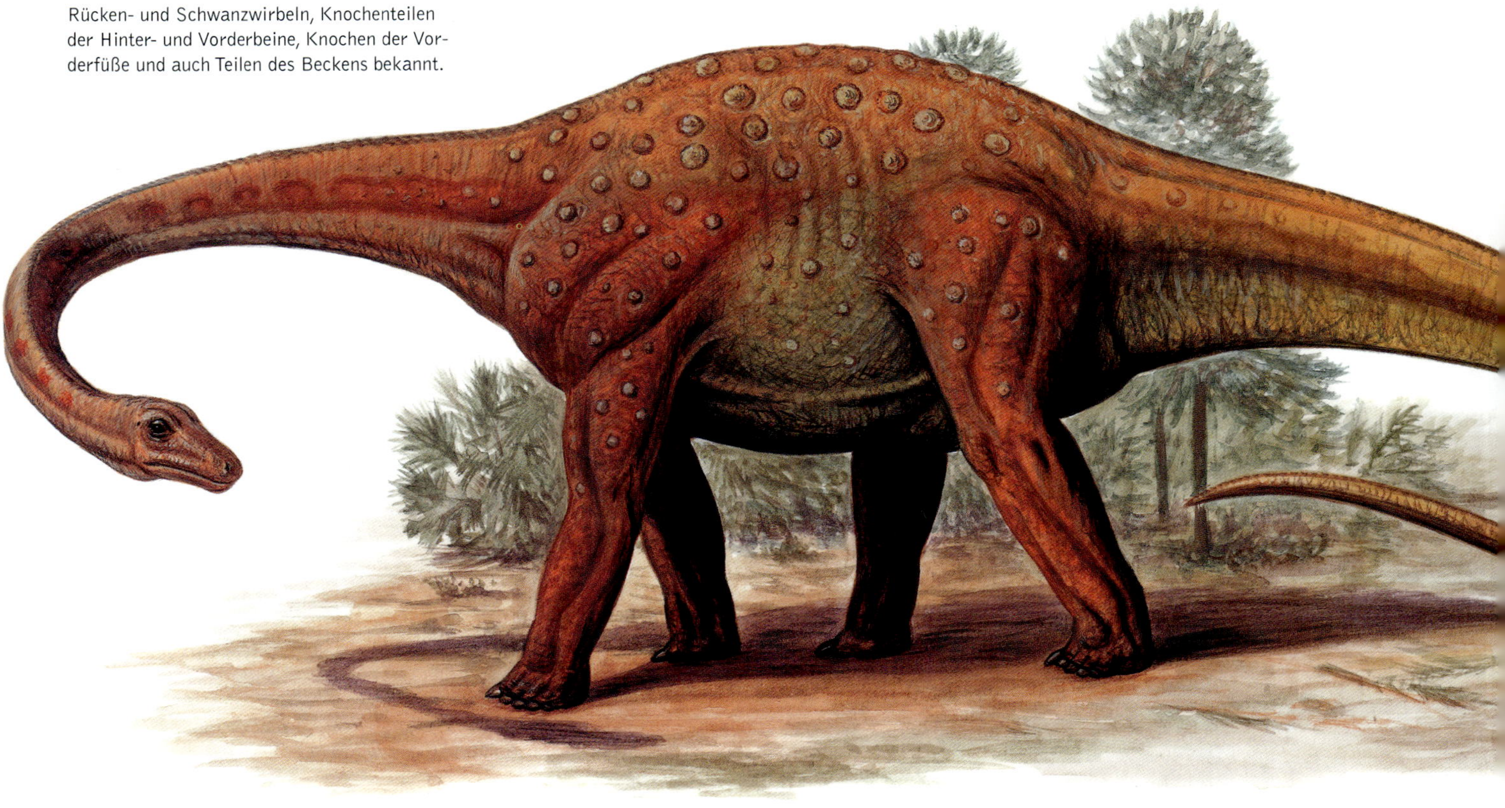

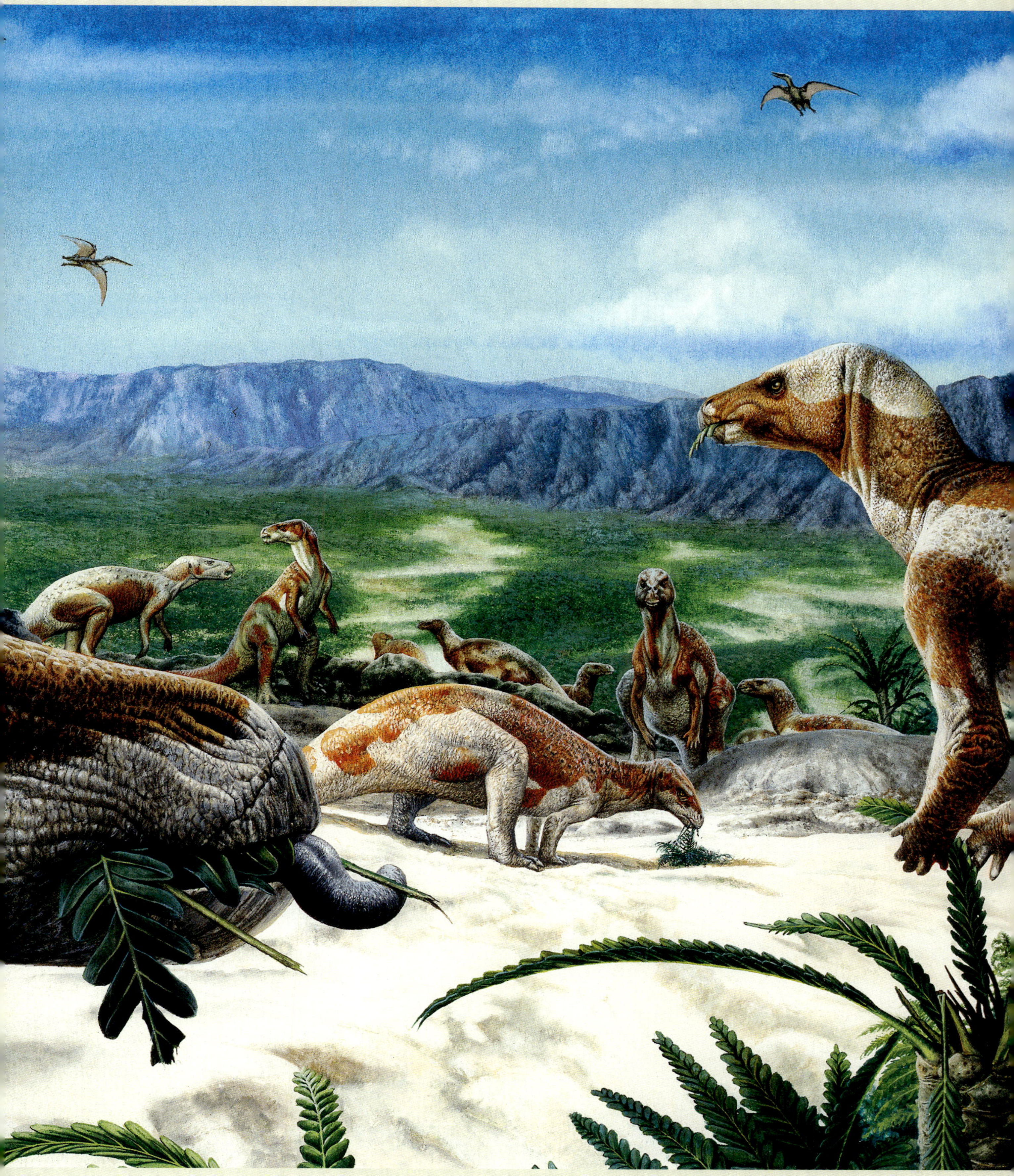

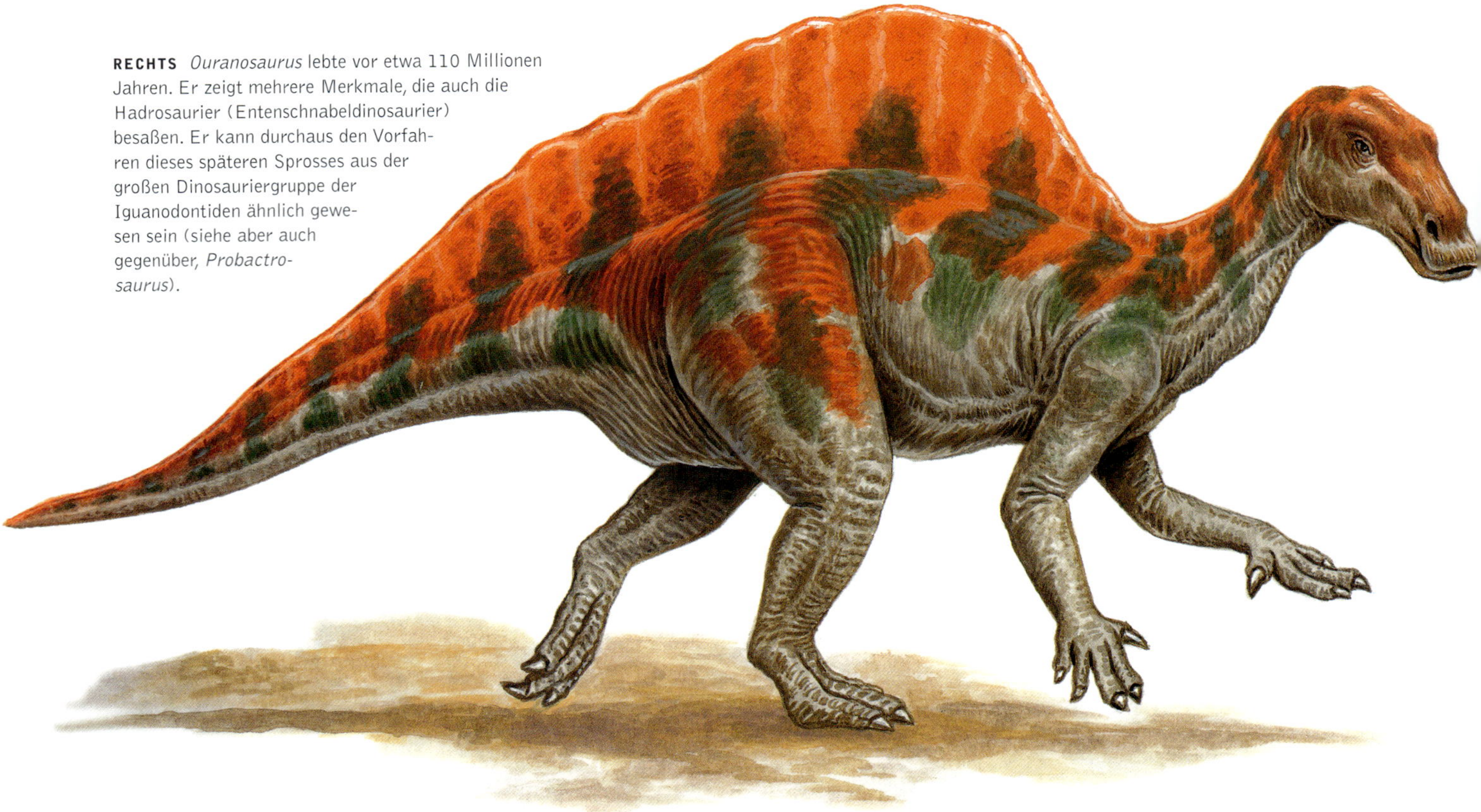

**RECHTS** *Ouranosaurus* lebte vor etwa 110 Millionen Jahren. Er zeigt mehrere Merkmale, die auch die Hadrosaurier (Entenschnabeldinosaurier) besaßen. Er kann durchaus den Vorfahren dieses späteren Sprosses aus der großen Dinosauriergruppe der Iguanodontiden ähnlich gewesen sein (siehe aber auch gegenüber, *Probactrosaurus*).

# OURANOSAURUS

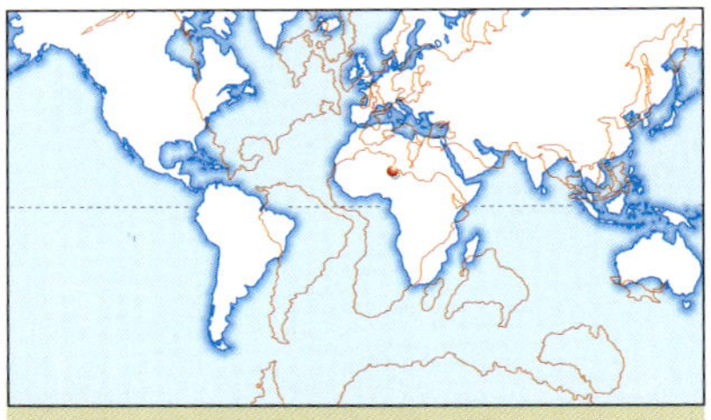

**ÜBERSICHT (DINOSAURIER)**
***Ouranosaurus***
**Bedeutung des Namens:** Stattliches Reptil, stattlicher Waran
**Periode:** Untere und Mittlere Kreide
**Hauptgruppe:** Ornithopoda
**Länge:** 7 Meter
**Gewicht:** 3 – 4 Tonnen
**Nahrung:** Pflanzen
**Fossilfundstätten:** Im Niger

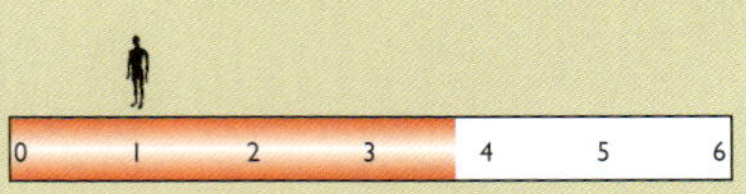


Im Jahr 1966 wurden im nordöstlichen Niger, im Wüstensand der Sahara, die Überreste zweier Exemplare des *Ouranosaurus* gefunden. Zehn Jahre später benannte der französische Paläontologe Philippe Taquet die Fossilien. *Ouranosaurus* ähnelte zwar in vielerlei Hinsicht seinem nahen Verwandten *Iguanodon* (siehe Seite 261) und gehörte auch zur selben Familie, den Iguanodontidae, doch an ihm wurden auch mehrere bemerkenswerte Abweichungen vom Familienschema festgestellt. Am augenfälligsten war das hohe Segel auf dem Rücken. Es wurde nach den langen, riemenartigen Fortsätzen der Rückenwirbel, den Dornfortsätzen, rekonstruiert, die von den Schultern bis fast zum Schwanzende vorhanden waren. Über die Funktion eines solchen Gebildes wurden schon viele Thesen aufgestellt. Das Segel könnte beispielsweise der Temperaturregelung gedient haben, eine Erklärung, die möglicherweise auf für andere „Segelrücken" wie etwa den großen Raubdinosaurier *Spinosaurus* oder den Fleisch fressenden Nicht-Dinosaurier *Dimetrodon* (Erläuterung siehe Seite 106) zutrifft. Einer anderen Theorie zufolge war das Segel auffallend gefärbt und diente *Ouranosaurus* in der Paarungszeit zum Werben um potenzielle Fortpflanzungspartner, so wie heute die Vogelmännchen während der Balz ihr buntes Gefieder vor den Weibchen zur Schau stellen.

*Ouranosaurus* war etwa sieben Meter lang, also etwas kleiner als *Iguanodon*. Seine Gliedmaßen ähnelten denen anderer Iguanodontiden – zwei größere Hinterbeine, die das Gros der Körpermasse trugen, doch auch zwei kräftige vordere Gliedmaßen zur Fortbewegung auf allen vieren, wobei er in gebeugter Haltung ging. *Ouranosaurus* trug auf der Stirn, vor den Augen, einen flachen Höcker. Seine Schnauze war lang und flach und endete vorn in einem verbreiterten zahnlosen „Schnabel", der wie ein Entenschnabel oder die „Schnäbel" der Hadrosaurier (siehe Seite 282, Entenschnabeldinosaurier) aussah. Wie die Fossilien halbaquatisch lebender Krokodile, beispielsweise *Sacrosuchus* (siehe Seite 387), belegen, muss der Lebensraum des *Ouranosaurus*, der heute Sandwüste ist, in der frühen bis mittleren Kreidezeit ein Mosaik aus Flüssen, Sümpfen und trockenerem Land gewesen sein.

# PROBACTROSAURUS

Die Stellung dieses Dinosauriers in der Entwicklungsgeschichte und demzufolge auch in der heutigen wissenschaftlichen Klassifikation ist sehr umstritten. Beginnen wir mit *Bactrosaurus*. Das „Keulenstachelreptil" gehörte zur Gruppe der Hadrosaurier oder Entenschnabeldinosaurier. Diese wird oft als Schwestergruppe der *Iguanodon*-artigen Pflanzenfresser, der Iguanodontiden (siehe nächstes Kapitel), betrachtet. *Bactrosaurus* war etwa sechs Meter lang und wog bis zu zwei Tonnen. Er gehörte zu den Lambeosauriern (siehe Seite 298), einer Untergruppe der Hadrosaurier, und lebte in der mittleren und späten Kreidezeit. Seine Fossilien stammen aus der Mongolei und aus China, sie wurden 1933 benannt.

*Probactrosaurus* lebte zweifellos vor *Bactrosaurus*, in der frühen und mittleren Kreidezeit. Dieser Dinosaurier wird gewöhnlich als Vertreter der Iguanodontiden, nicht als Hadrosaurier betrachtet. Tatsächlich weist er viele Ähnlichkeiten mit *Iguanodon* selbst auf. Seinen Namen erhielt er 1966 von Anatolij K. Roždestvenskij, die ihm zugeordneten Fossilien stammen aus verschiedenen Gegenden, darunter aus Gesteinen der Dashuigou-Formation im chinesischen und auch aus dem mongolischen Teil der Wüste Gobi. Die Funde beinhalten den Großteil eines Skeletts, einen unvollständigen Schädel sowie weitere Bruchstücke anderer Skelette. *Probactrosaurus* könnte trotz seiner Einstufung als Iguanodontide einige gemeinsame Merkmale mit den Hadrosauriern besessen haben. Es wurde auch schon die These aufgestellt, dass er, wenn schon kein direkter Vorfahr der Hadrosaurier, so doch zumindest der Dinosauriertyp war, aus dem diese jüngere Gruppe hervorgegangen sein könnte. Sein Name aber ist insofern irreführend, als kein Beleg dafür existiert, dass *Probactrosaurus* der direkte Vorfahre des *Bactrosaurus* war. Auch lag die historische Landschaft Baktrien (bekannt durch *Camelus bactrianus*, das Zweihöckerige Kamel) am Oxus, dem heutigen Amu-Darja, der auch durch Turkmenistan, Usbekistan und Tadshikistan fließt, war also weit von der Mongolei und von China entfernt.

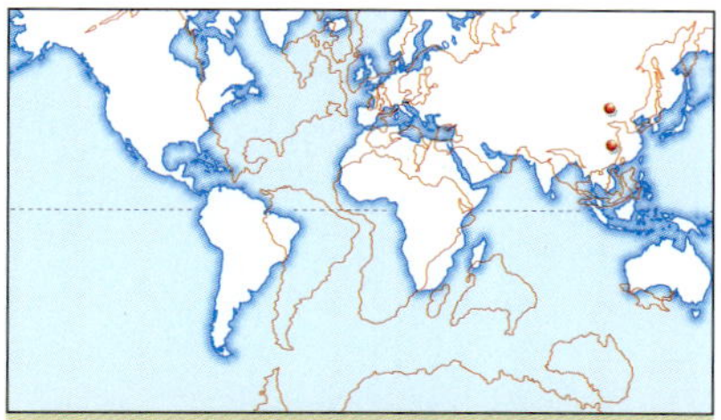

**ÜBERSICHT (DINOSAURIER)**
***Probactrosaurus***
**Bedeutung des Namens:** Vor dem baktrischen Reptil
**Periode:** Frühe und Mittlere Kreide
**Hauptgruppe:** Ornithopoda
**Länge:** 5–6 Meter
**Gewicht:** 1–1,5 Tonnen
**Nahrung:** Pflanzen
**Fossilfundstätten:** In China, in der Mongolei

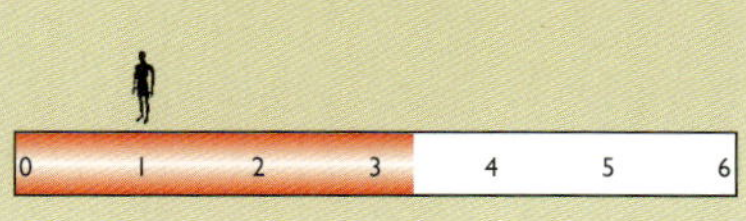


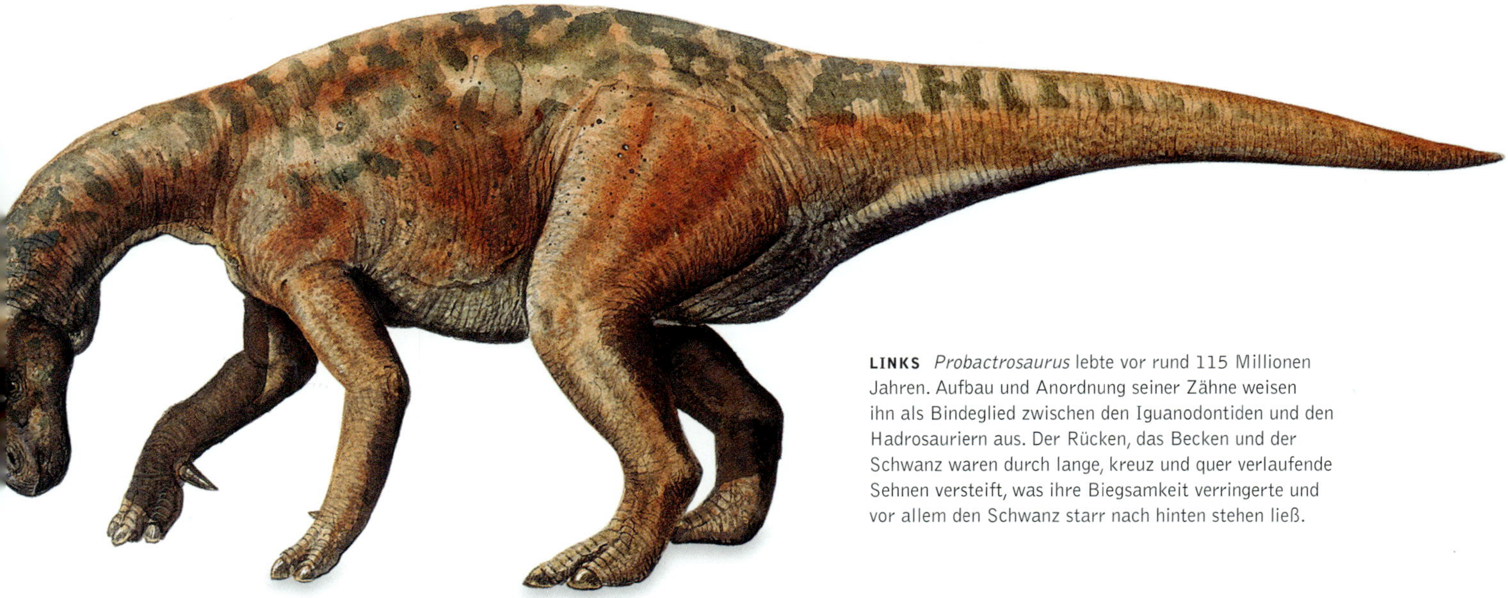

**LINKS** *Probactrosaurus* lebte vor rund 115 Millionen Jahren. Aufbau und Anordnung seiner Zähne weisen ihn als Bindeglied zwischen den Iguanodontiden und den Hadrosauriern aus. Der Rücken, das Becken und der Schwanz waren durch lange, kreuz und quer verlaufende Sehnen versteift, was ihre Biegsamkeit verringerte und vor allem den Schwanz starr nach hinten stehen ließ.

# DRINKER

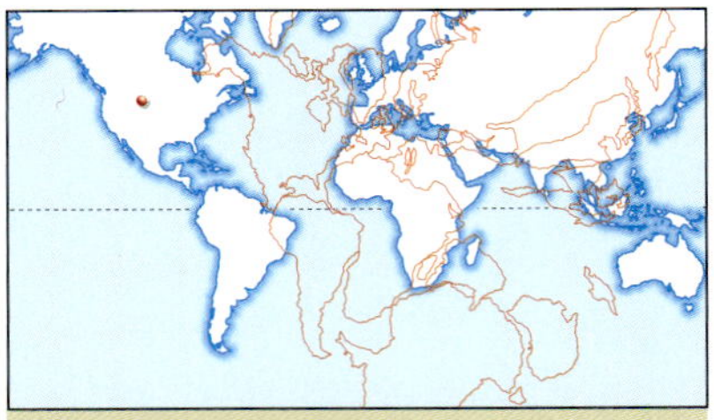

**ÜBERSICHT (DINOSAURIER)**
***Drinker***
**Bedeutung des Namens:**
Drinker (zu Ehren von Edward Drinker Cope)
**Periode:** Oberer Jura
**Hauptgruppe:** Ornithopoda
**Länge:** 2 Meter
**Gewicht:** 10–25 Kilogramm
**Nahrung:** Pflanzen
**Fossilfundstätten:**
In den USA (Wyoming)

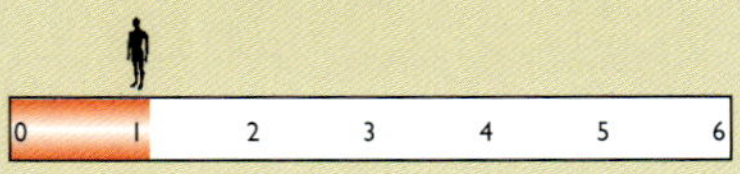


Der seltsame Name dieses Dinosauriers bedeutet nicht, dass es sich hier um ein besonders durstiges Reptil handelt. Mit diesem Namen wird Edward Drinker Cope geehrt. Im Verlauf der „Dinosaurierkriege in Wildwestmanier“ des Fossilienjägers und Paläontologen Cope mit seinem größten Rivalen Othniel Charles Marsh wurde damals eine große Zahl heute weltberühmter Fossilien entdeckt. (An Marsh wird auf ähnliche Weise erinnert – siehe Seite 279, *Othnielia*). Den Namen *Drinker* erhielt der Dinosaurier, um den es hier geht, 1990 von Robert Bakker. Bakker gehört zu den Paläontologen, die das Bild von den Dinosauriern als lahme, wechselwarme Trampel infrage stellten (siehe Seite 153).

Der Dinosaurier *Drinker* war ein kleiner Ornithopode, ein Pflanzenfresser von insgesamt rund zwei Meter Länge. Er lebte im Oberen Jura, vor 155–144 Millionen Jahren. Die Fossilien von vielleicht drei Individuen – einem adulten, einem noch nicht ganz ausgewachsenen und einem jungen Tier – stammen aus dem US-Bundesstaat Wyoming. Zu den Überresten des größeren Tieres gehören Stücke von Schwanzwirbeln, die auf einen biegsamen Schwanz hinweisen, sowie eine Zehe von einer hinteren Gliedmaße und ein Zahn. Von den kleineren Tieren waren mehr Zähne, Teile der Kiefer, die Wirbelkörper der Rückenwirbel sowie Abschnitte der vorderen und hinteren Gliedmaßen, darunter ein vorderes Oberarmbein (Humerus), ein Oberschenkelbein (Femur) und Fußknochen vorhanden.

Begleitfossilien wie Lungenfischzähne und Reste von Sumpfvegetation deuten darauf hin, dass diese kleinen Pflanzenfresser einst in oder nahe bei einem Sumpf lebten oder zumindest starben. Wegen der grundlegenden Ähnlichkeiten zwischen *Drinker* und *Hypsilophodon* (siehe Seite 273), einem sehr gut bekannten kleinen Ornithopoden, hat man *Drinker* in die Familie der Hypsilophodontidae gestellt.

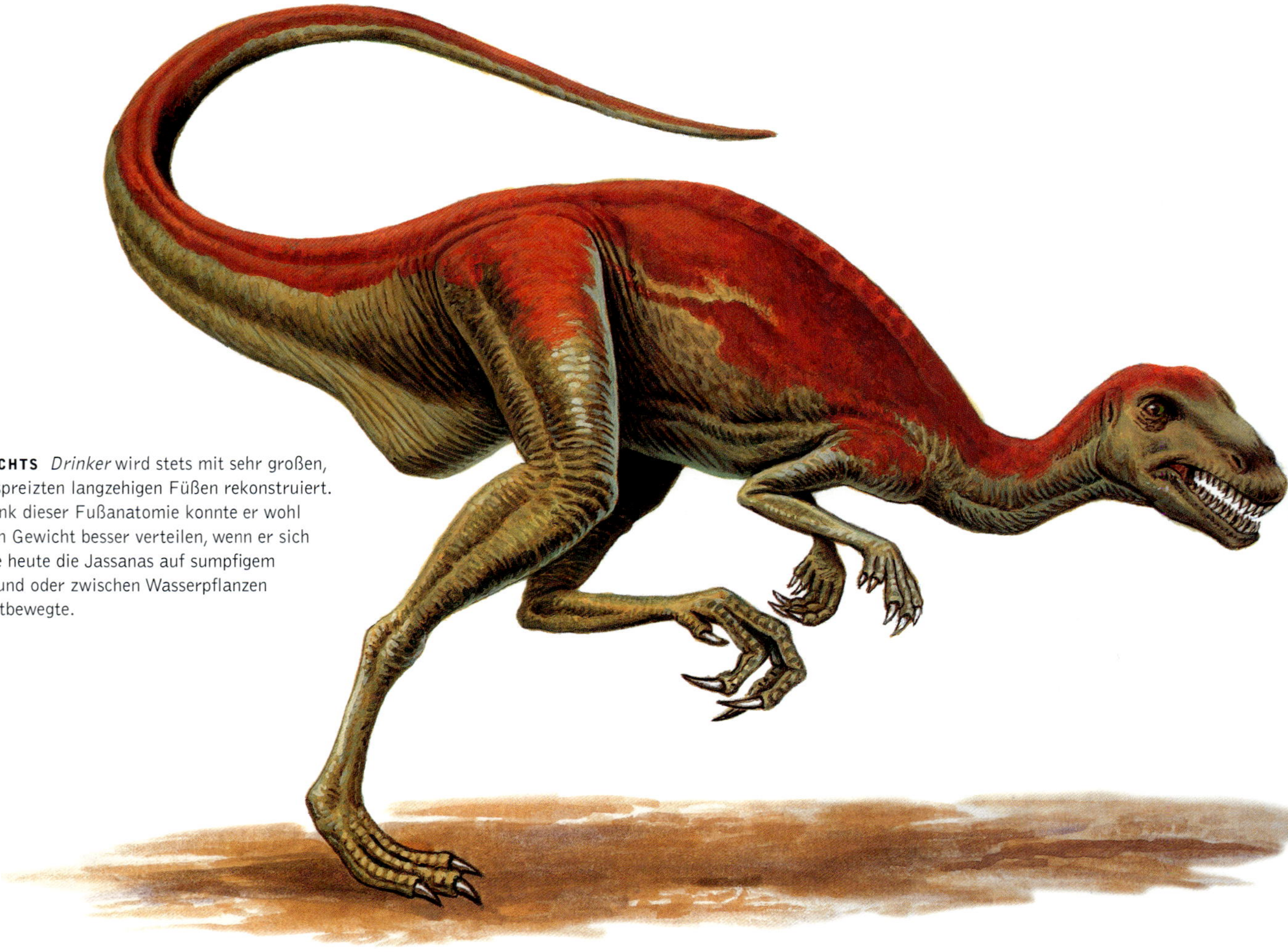

**RECHTS** *Drinker* wird stets mit sehr großen, gespreizten langzehigen Füßen rekonstruiert. Dank dieser Fußanatomie konnte er wohl sein Gewicht besser verteilen, wenn er sich wie heute die Jassanas auf sumpfigem Grund oder zwischen Wasserpflanzen fortbewegte.

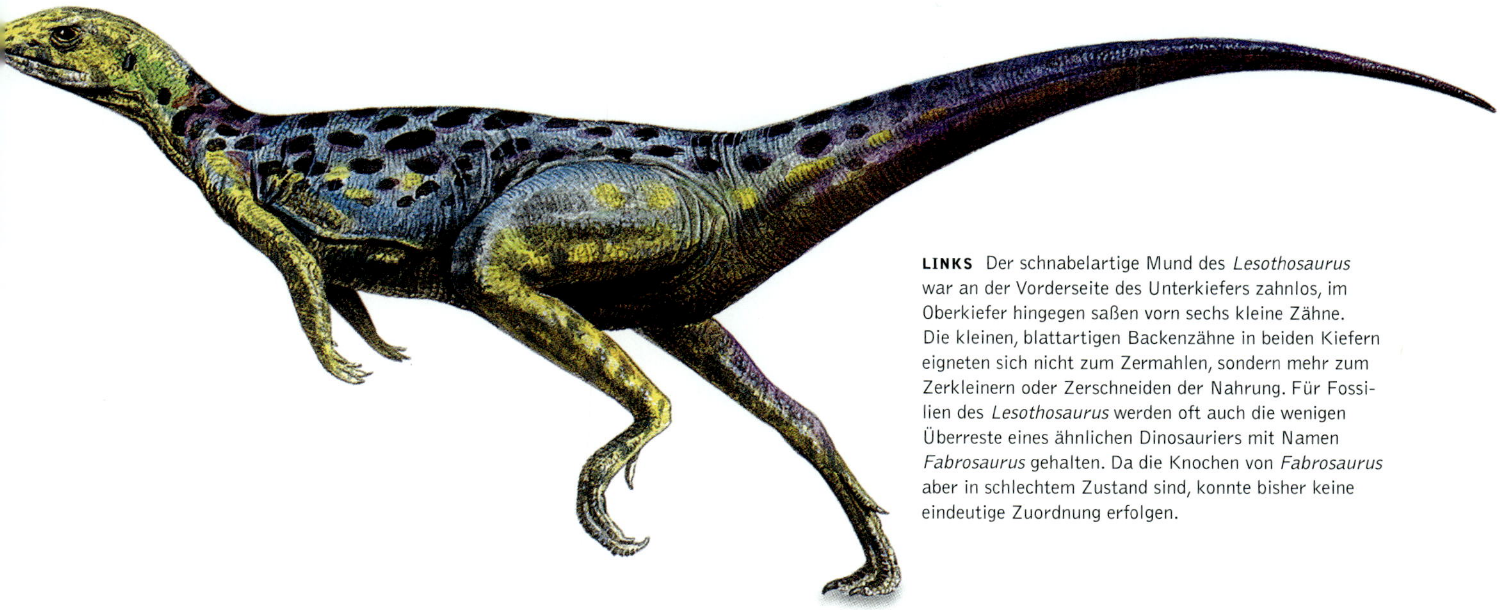

**LINKS** Der schnabelartige Mund des *Lesothosaurus* war an der Vorderseite des Unterkiefers zahnlos, im Oberkiefer hingegen saßen vorn sechs kleine Zähne. Die kleinen, blattartigen Backenzähne in beiden Kiefern eigneten sich nicht zum Zermahlen, sondern mehr zum Zerkleinern oder Zerschneiden der Nahrung. Für Fossilien des *Lesothosaurus* werden oft auch die wenigen Überreste eines ähnlichen Dinosauriers mit Namen *Fabrosaurus* gehalten. Da die Knochen von *Fabrosaurus* aber in schlechtem Zustand sind, konnte bisher keine eindeutige Zuordnung erfolgen.

# *LESOTHOSAURUS (FABROSAURUS)*

*Lesothosaurus* war ein Vertreter der Ornithischier, der Vogelbecken-Dinosaurier, zu denen auch viele andere Pflanzenfresser gehörten. Er galt früher als ein sehr alter Ornithopodentyp innerhalb dieser Gruppe, als einer der ersten Vertreter jener Familie, zu der auch jüngere, größere Typen wie *Iguanodon* (siehe Seite 261), die Hadrosaurier und vielleicht der kleine *Hypsilophodon* (siehe Seite 273) gehörten. Heute ist man der Meinung, dass *Lesothosaurus*, der vor rund 208 bis 200 Millionen Jahren lebte, für einen Ornithopoden zu früh erschien und dass man ihn daher besser als einen „Prä-Ornithopoden" in einer eigenen Gruppe ohne nahe Verwandte beschreibt.

*Lesothosaurus* war vergleichsweise winzig, kaum größer als eine Hauskatze. Er besaß einen leichten Körperbau, sehr kleine Vorderbeine mit jeweils fünf Fingern, einen lang gezogenen Rumpf, die langen, schlanken Hinterbeine eines schnellen Läufers und einen langen, starren, sich allmählich verjüngenden Schwanz. Die Oberschenkel waren kräftig und muskulös, die Unterschenkel lang gezogen, auch die Füße waren sehr lang und endeten in drei Zehen, die das Körpergewicht trugen, und in einer kleineren ersten Zehe ähnlich einer Afterklaue. Der Kopf mit den großen Augen war lang und flach, die schnabelartige Vorderseite des Unterkiefers war hornig und zahnlos. Die kleinen, blattartigen Zähne eigneten sich eher zum Zerkleinern als zum Zermahlen der pflanzlichen Nahrung. *Lesothosaurus* wurde im südafrikanischen Lesotho, in der Nähe von Mafeteng, entdeckt und 1978 von Peter Galton benannt. Die Lage seiner Fossilien sowie einiger Überreste eines *Abrictosaurus* lassen vermuten, dass die winzigen Dinosaurier während einer winterschlafähnlichen Ruhephase umkamen, mit der sie vielleicht die heiße, trockene Jahreszeit überbrückten.

Ein sehr ähnlicher Dinosaurier erhielt 1964 nach nichts weiter als einem von Leonard Ginsburg entdeckten Kieferbruchstück den Namen *Fabrosaurus*; ihn halten manche Fachleute für denselben Typ wie *Lesothosaurus*.

Aus Venezuela stammende Fossilien, die in jüngster Zeit untersucht wurden, hat man vorläufig ebenfalls als *Lesothosaurus* identifiziert.

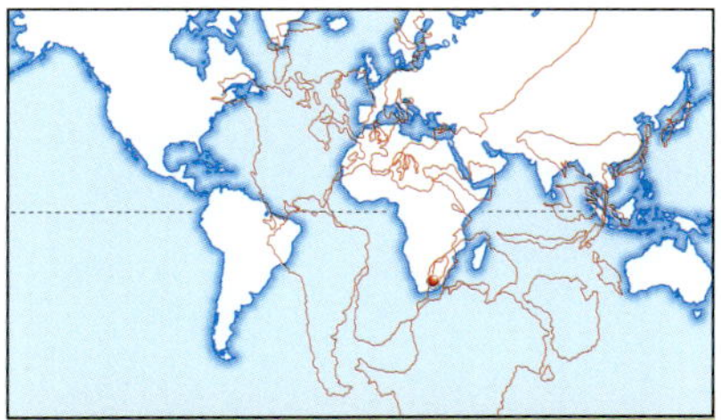

**ÜBERSICHT (DINOSAURIER)**
***Lesothosaurus (= Fabrosaurus?)***
**Bedeutung des Namens:** Lesothoreptil
**Periode:** Obere Trias bis Unterer Jura
**Hauptgruppe:** Ornithopoda
**Länge:** 1 Meter
**Gewicht:** 2 – 3 Kilogramm
**Nahrung:** Pflanzen
**Fossilfundstätten:** Lesotho

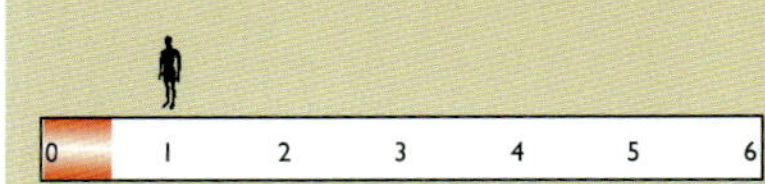

# Verteidigung oder Flucht

*Die Ornithopoden, vor allem die kleineren unter diesen Dinosauriern wie etwa Lesothosaurus und Hypsilophodon, scheinen über nur wenige Mittel zu ihrer Verteidigung verfügt zu haben: Sie besaßen kaum oder überhaupt keine Panzerplatten, auch keine spitzen Hörner oder gar kräftige Füße, mit denen sie abwehrende Tritte hätten austeilen können. Ihre einzige Waffe scheint der lange Daumendorn gewesen zu sein. Vielleicht war ihr Überleben mehr das Ergebnis ihrer wachen Sinne, mit denen sie Gefahren frühzeitig erkannten, und ihrer Gewandtheit, die eine sofortige Flucht ermöglichte.*

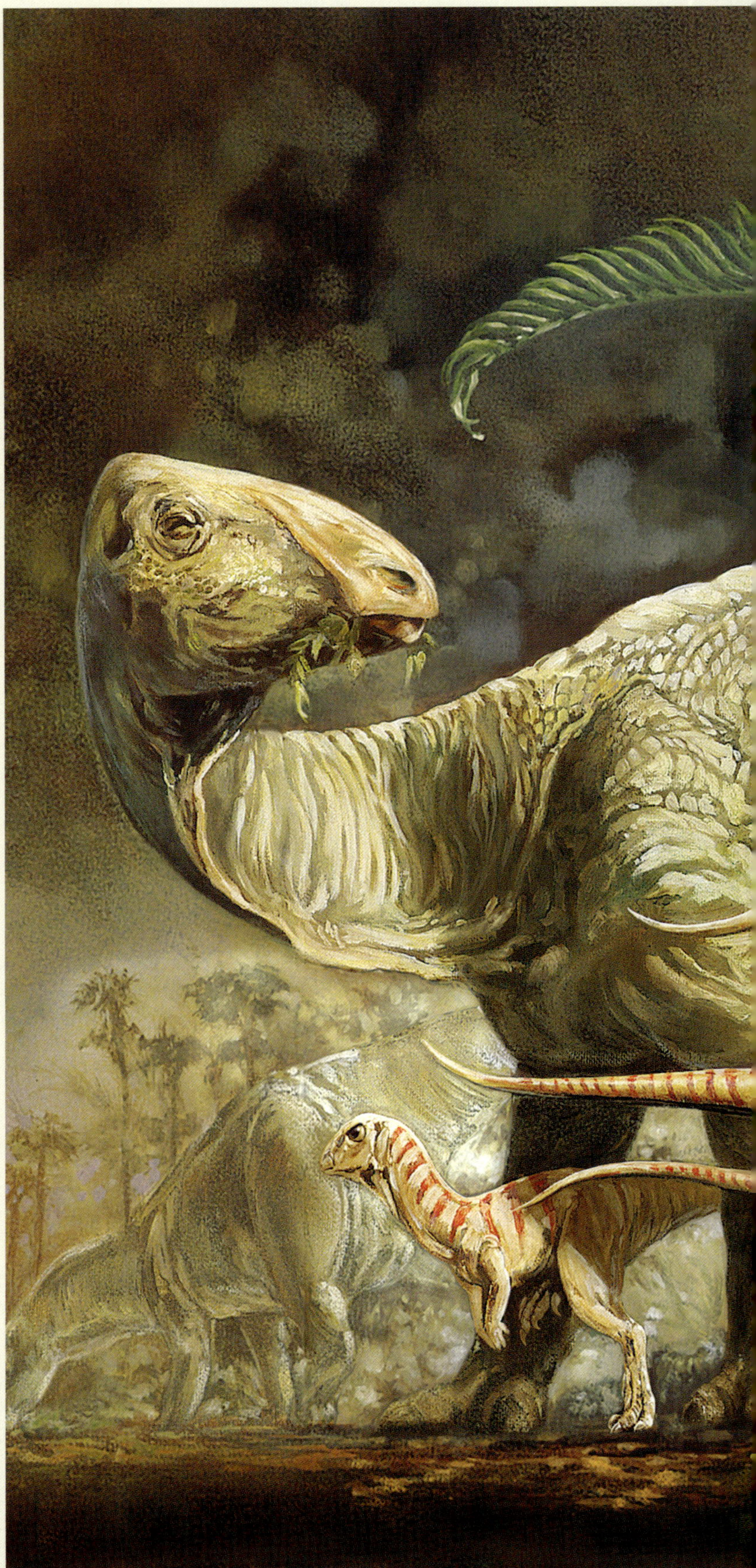

**RECHTS** Zwei Extreme innerhalb der Gruppe der Hypsilophodontiden stellten hinsichtlich ihrer Körpergröße der kleine verwundbare, aber flinke *Hypsilophodon* selbst und der *Tenontosaurus* dar, der vielleicht fünfzigmal schwerer war und seine Körpermasse als Waffe gegen Räuber einsetzen konnte.

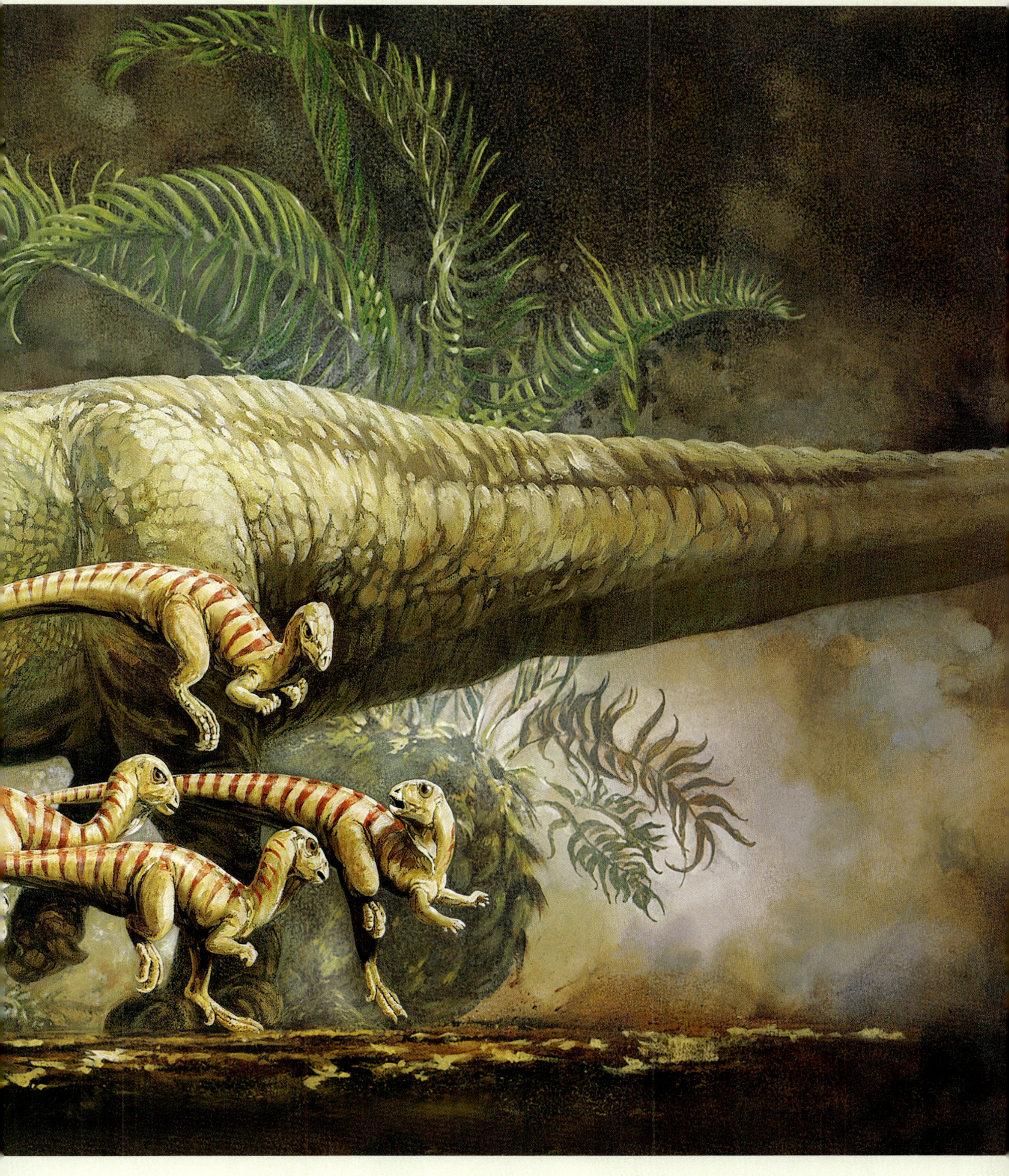

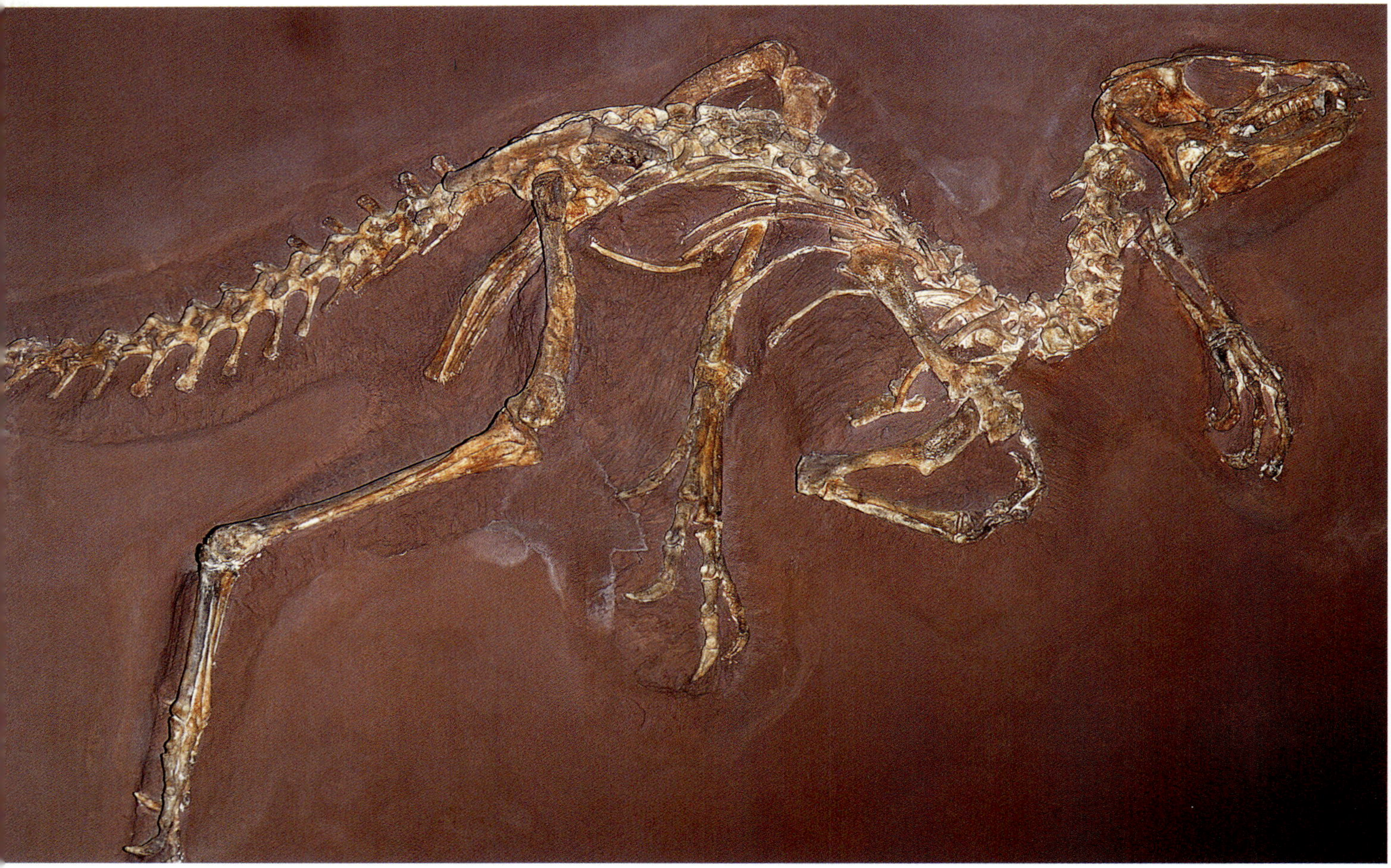

# HETERODONTOSAURUS

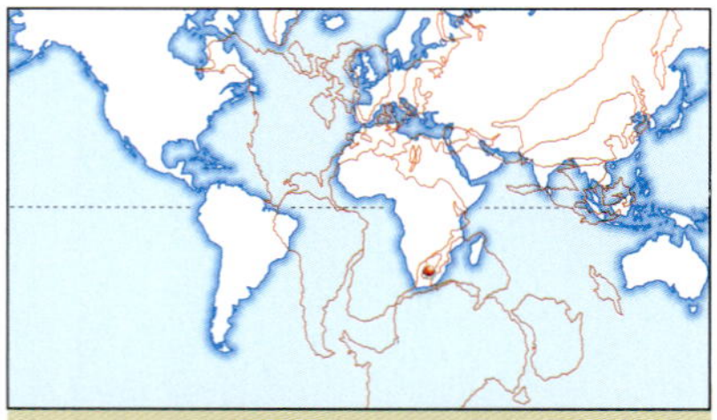

**ÜBERSICHT (DINOSAURIER)**
***Heterodontosaurus***
**Bedeutung des Namens:** Reptil mit unterschiedlichen Zähnen
**Periode:** Unterer Jura
**Hauptgruppe:** Ornithopoda
**Länge:** 1,2 – 1,3 Meter
**Gewicht:** 10 – 20 Kilogramm
**Nahrung:** Pflanzen
**Fossilfundstätten:** Südliches Afrika

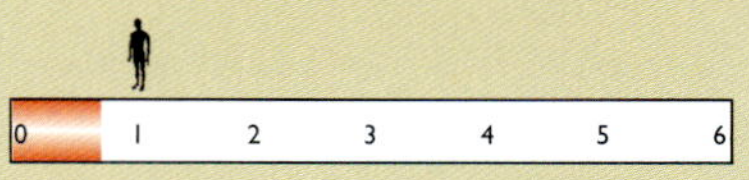


Die langen Zähne, die wir Eck- oder Fangzähne nennen, sind häufig bei Fleischfressern zu finden, doch sie treten heute auch bei verschiedenen Pflanzenfressern auf. So besaß auch der Pflanzen fressende Dinosaurier *Heterodontosaurus* u. a. Eckzähne, weshalb er 1962 von Alfred Crompton und Alan Charig den Namen „Reptil mit unterschiedlichen Zähnen" bekam. *Heterodontosaurus* besaß die Größe eines kleinen Hundes, einen leichten Körperbau und lange Hinterbeine, mit denen er schnell laufen konnte. Sein Kopf war ziemlich hoch, hatte eine kurze Schnauze und große Augen. Die ersten drei Finger an den kleinen, kräftigen Vorderbeinen ließen sich weit nach innen biegen und eigneten sich daher gut zum Greifen. Der Schwanz war lang und schlug wahrscheinlich von einer Seite zur anderen, wenn *Hederodontosaurus* lief – was er wahrscheinlich oft tat, denn im buschbestandenen trockenen Süden Afrikas, wo er im Unteren Jura, vor über 210 – 200 Millionen Jahren lebte, lauerten ständig Gefahren.

Außer den beiden oberen Eckzähnen, die genau in die Lücken am Unterkiefer passten, besaß *Heterodontosaurus* noch zwei andere Arten von Zähnen. An der Vorderseite des Oberkiefers saßen kleine Schneidezähne, mit denen er wahrscheinlich Pflanzenteile gegen den zahnlosen vorderen Teil des Unterkiefers presste und abkniff. Hinter den Eckzähnen saßen hochkronige gefurchte Backenzähne. Dieses Gebiss wich deutlich von dem anderer Dinosaurier und auch anderer Reptilien ab. Bei den meisten lebenden oder ausgestorbenen Reptilien ist hauptsächlich ein Zahntyp vorhanden. Die Zähne können unterschiedlich groß sein, da alte, abgenutzte ausfallen und durch neue ersetzt werden, die dann zwar größer werden, aber die ursprüngliche Form beibehalten. Weshalb andere Reptilien kein Gebiss mit mehreren Zahntypen, dafür aber die Säugetiere ein heterodontes Gebiss entwickelten, ist bislang nicht geklärt.

**OBEN** Bei diesem schönen, fast vollständigen Skelett eines *Heterodontosaurus* ist eine Vordergliedmaße unter den Hals und ein Hinterbein nach oben zum Becken gezogen.

# HYPSILOPHODON

Ein Laie könnte bei oberflächlicher Betrachtung kaum einen Unterschied zwischen *Hypsilophodon* und *Heterodontosaurus*, einem ebenfalls sehr kleinen Pflanzen fressenden Dinosaurier (siehe gegenüber), feststellen. Die beiden Tiere trennt allerdings eine Zeitspanne von mehr als 80 Millionen Jahren, ein ganzer Kontinent und nicht wenige Unterschiede bei den inneren Merkmalen. Thomas Huxley, der bekannte Biologe und Verfechter von Charles Darwins Evolutionstheorie, benannte *Hypsilophodon* 1869. Die ersten Fossilien des Tieres entdeckte man 1849 auf der Insel Wight, der englischen „Dinosaurier-Insel". Sie wurden von Gideon Mantell und Richard Owen untersucht und zunächst für die Überreste eines jungen *Iguanodon* gehalten. Später gelangte Huxley durch weitere Entdeckungen von William Fox zu der Überzeugung, dass es sich bei den Fossilien um ausgewachsene Tiere einer bis dahin unbekannten Dinosaurierart handelt. Huxley stellte die These auf, dass die Tiere in Bäumen gelebt haben könnten wie die heutigen Baumkängurus (was inzwischen widerlegt ist). Heute gibt es zahlreiche Fossilskelette, darunter einige sehr gut erhaltene, die zusammen an einer Stelle gefunden wurden und vielleicht von einer Herde stammen, deren Mitglieder bei einer Überschwemmung ertranken oder auf andere Weise ums Leben kamen.

*Hypsilophodon* wurde nach seinen etwa dreißig hochkronigen, mit Rillen und Furchen versehenen Backenzähnen benannt, mit denen das Tier einst Blätter, Stängel und andere pflanzliche Nahrung zerkleinerte und kaute. Klappten Ober- und Unterkiefer zusammen, glitten die Zähne im Oberkiefer scherend und reibend an der Außenseite der Zähne im Unterkiefer entlang. Das hielt die Zähne in beiden Kiefern scharf. Die Kieferform lässt darauf schließen, dass *Hypsilophodon* möglicherweise Wangentaschen besaß – ein bei Reptilien ungewöhnliches Merkmal –, in denen er beim Kauen die Nahrung behielt. Der lange Schädel endete in einer nur etwa zwölf bis vierzehn Zentimeter kurzen Schnauze, die im Querschnitt fast die Größe einer menschlichen Hand hatte. Die Vorderfüße endeten in fünf Fingern und die Hinterfüße in vier Zehen, von denen drei das Körpergewicht trugen. Möglicherweise waren am Rücken ein oder zwei Reihen flacher Knochenplatten in die Haut eingebettet.

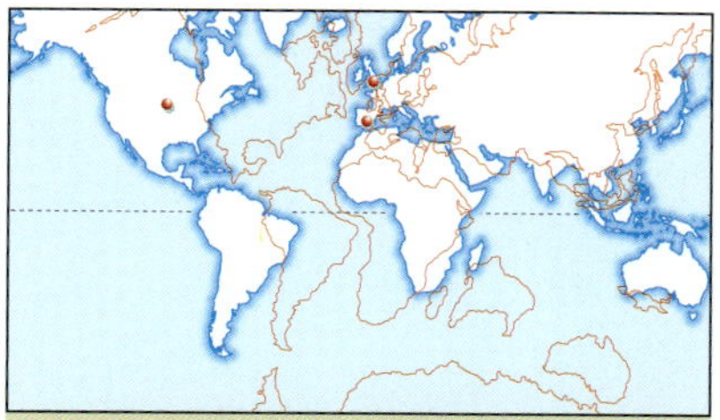

**ÜBERSICHT (DINOSAURIER)**
***Hypsilophodon***
**Bedeutung des Namens:** Hochkroniger Zahn
**Periode:** Unterkreide
**Hauptgruppe:** Ornithopoda
**Länge:** 1,5 – 2,3 Meter
**Gewicht:** 20 – 40 Kilogramm
**Nahrung:** Pflanzen
**Fossilfundstätten:** In England und Spanien, möglicherweise in den USA (South Dakota)

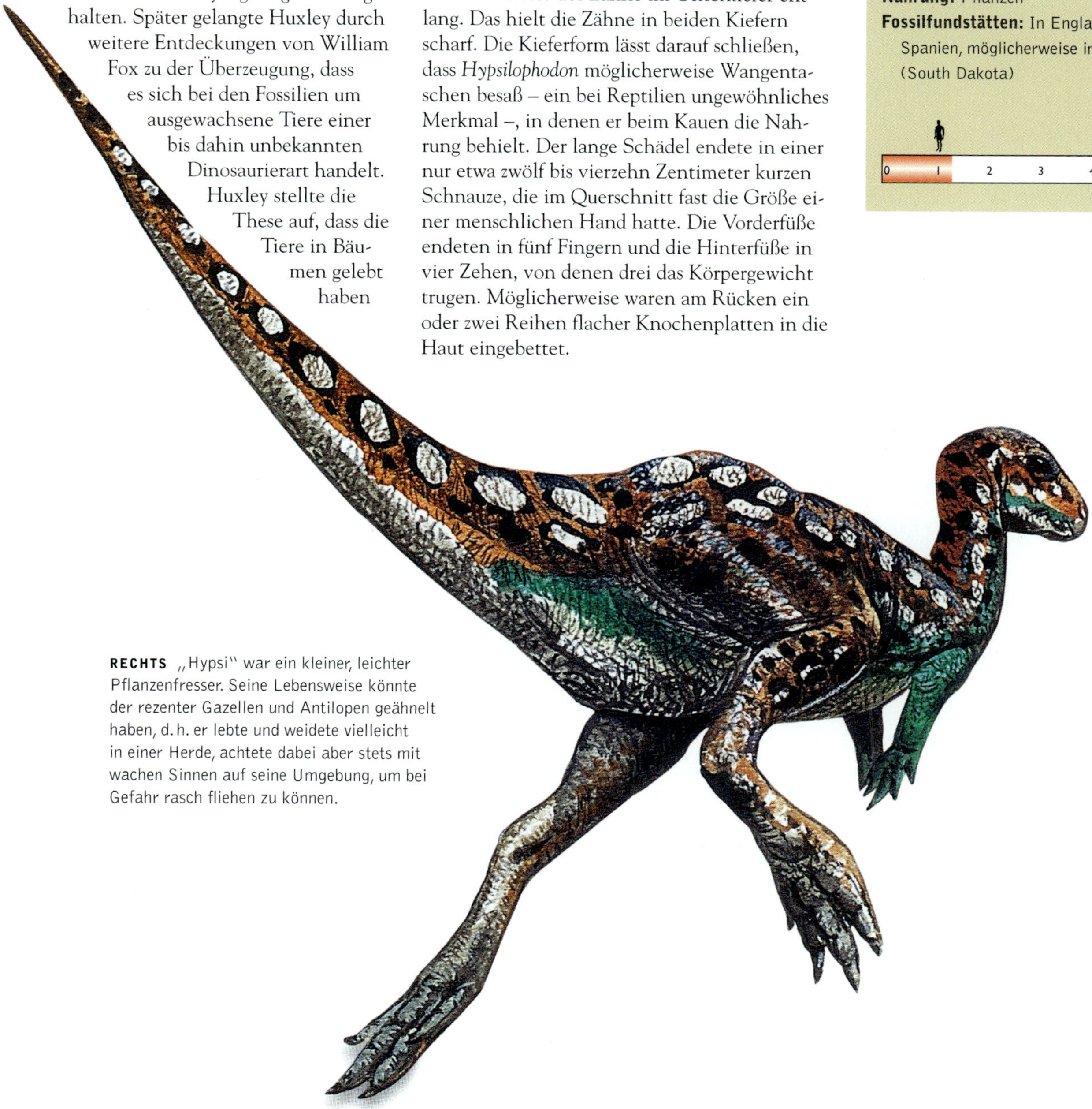

**RECHTS** „Hypsi" war ein kleiner, leichter Pflanzenfresser. Seine Lebensweise könnte der rezenter Gazellen und Antilopen geähnelt haben, d. h. er lebte und weidete vielleicht in einer Herde, achtete dabei aber stets mit wachen Sinnen auf seine Umgebung, um bei Gefahr rasch fliehen zu können.

# THESCELOSAURUS

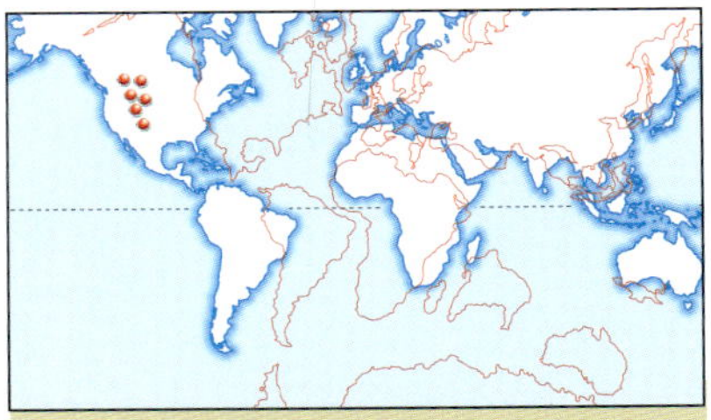

**ÜBERSICHT (DINOSAURIER)**
***Thescelosaurus***
**Bedeutung des Namens:** Wunderbares Reptil
**Periode:** Oberkreide
**Hauptgruppe:** Ornithopoda
**Länge:** 3,5 – 4 Meter
**Gewicht:** 300 Kilogramm
**Nahrung:** Pflanzen
**Fossilfundstätten:** Westliches Nordamerika

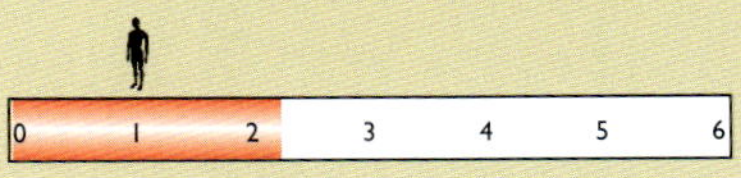


Die Fossilien dieses mittelgroßen Ornithopoden, der in der Oberkreide in Nordamerika lebte, wurden erstmals 1913 von Charles Gilmore untersucht und benannt. Man hatte sie bereits zweiundzwanzig Jahre zuvor gefunden, damals allerdings als bedeutungslos betrachtet und in der Smithsonian Institution in Washington (DC) in einer Kiste abgestellt. Daher rührt auch der Artname *Thescelosaurus neglectus* („neglectus" – vernachlässigt oder unbeachtet). Seitdem sind an verschiedenen Fundorten in den USA (Bundesstaaten Wyoming, Montana, South Dakota und Colorado) sowie in Kanada (Provinzen Alberta und Saskatchewan) weitere Fossilien von ihm ausgegraben worden. Sie zeigen einen gut gebauten Pflanzenfresser mit einem kleinen Kopf, kurzen Vordergliedmaßen, einem kräftigen Körper, langen, starken Hinterextremitäten und einem langen, zum Ende verjüngten Schwanz. *Thescelosaurus* galt früher als Vertreter der Hypsilophodontiden, einer Familie innerhalb der Ornithopodengruppe; einige neuere Untersuchungen haben ihn mit den Iguanodontiden in Verbindung gebracht oder den Schluss nahe gelegt, dass das Tier hinreichend typische Merkmale aufweist um eine eigene Familie, die Familie der Thescelosauridae, zu bilden.

Zu den bemerkenswertesten Funden in der Geschichte der Dinosaurier gehört – wenn sich seine Identität bestätigt – ein *Thescelosaurus*-Skelett, das 1993 in der Nähe von Buffalo (US-Bundesstaat South Dakota) ausgegraben und auf 66 Millionen Jahre datiert wurde. Unter den Überresten befand sich auch etwas, das als Herz des Tieres identifiziert wurde und ein unglaublich seltener Fund ist, da Weichteile wie die Muskeln oder die inneren Organe fast nie erhalten bleiben. Das Individuum wurde nach der Ehefrau des Ranchers und Eigentümers des Landes, von dem der Fund stammte, „Willo" genannt.

Bei der Untersuchung des Herzes mit Hilfe eines Computertomografen wurde festgestellt, dass das Organ aus vier Kammern bestand. Das lässt darauf schließen, dass der Dinosaurier warmblütig war, denn auch die Vögel und Säugetiere der Jetztzeit weisen einen solchen Herztyp auf, die wechselwarmen rezenten Reptilien hingegen nicht. Nach Auffassung einiger Fachleute handelt es sich bei dem Objekt nicht um ein Herz, sondern einfach um ein Gesteinsstück vom Typ einer Eisensteinkonkretion, die zufällig im Innern des fossilierten Dinosaurierkörpers entstanden ist.

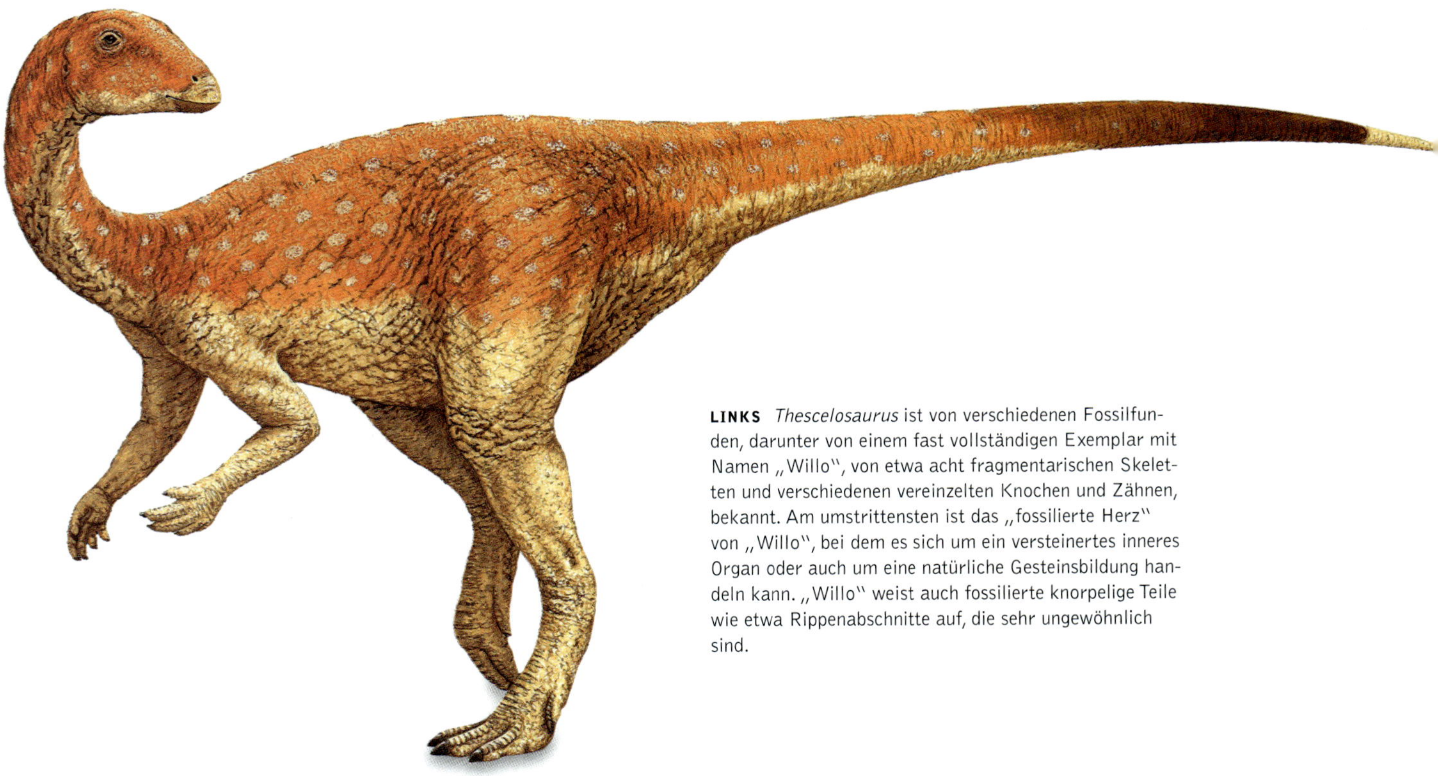

**LINKS** *Thescelosaurus* ist von verschiedenen Fossilfunden, darunter von einem fast vollständigen Exemplar mit Namen „Willo", von etwa acht fragmentarischen Skeletten und verschiedenen vereinzelten Knochen und Zähnen, bekannt. Am umstrittensten ist das „fossilierte Herz" von „Willo", bei dem es sich um ein versteinertes inneres Organ oder auch um eine natürliche Gesteinsbildung handeln kann. „Willo" weist auch fossilierte knorpelige Teile wie etwa Rippenabschnitte auf, die sehr ungewöhnlich sind.

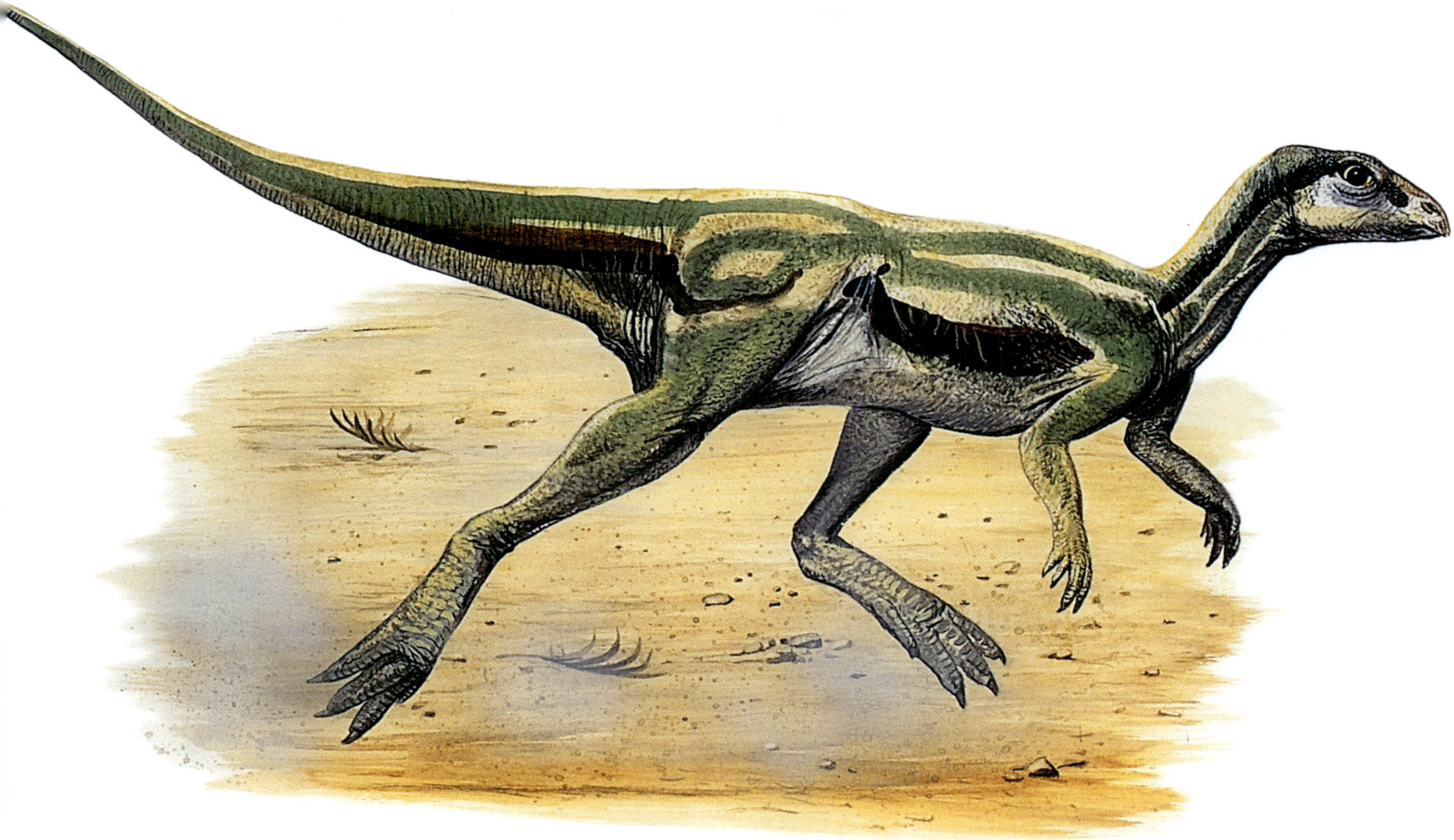

# LEAELLYNASAURA

Der Fund eines fossilierten Schädels in der Dinosaur Cove am Kap Otway in der Nähe von Melbourne hat den wissenschaftlichen Debatten über die Lebensräume und Lebensweise von Dinosauriern ein neues großes Gebiet eröffnet. *Leaellynasaura* wurde 1989 nach der Tochter der Entdecker Patricia Vickers-Rich und Thomas Rich benannt. Bei dem Fund handelte es sich um den Schädel eines kleinen, leicht gebauten Ornithopoden aus der *Hysilophodon*-Familie. Das etwa zwei Meter lange Tier hatte einen Mund mit schnabelartiger Vorderfront und Backenzähnen zum Kauen. Sein Alter wird auf 110 – 105 Millionen Jahre geschätzt. In der Dinosaur Cove wurden inzwischen noch viele andere interessante Entdeckungen gemacht (siehe Seite 15).

Außergewöhnliche Merkmale des Dinosauriers, die das Tier aus seiner Familie herausheben, sind das verhältnismäßig große Hirn und die riesigen Augen. Eine mögliche Antwort auf die Frage, weshalb diese Körperorgane so groß waren, liefert die These, nach der *Leaellynasaura* einst im Innern düsterer Wälder lebte, in deren ständigem Dämmerlicht nur Tiere mit großen Augen gut sehen konnten. Diese Vorstellung hängt mit der Lage des Kontinents Australien zur damaligen Zeit zusammen. Australien lag in der mittleren Kreidezeit weiter südlich als heute, es war Teil eines langsam zerreißenden Superkontinents, der weit in die südliche Polarzone hineinreichte. Das Klima war nicht annähernd so extrem wie in der heutigen Antarktis, jahreszeitlich wohl aber sehr stark schwankend, und es muss eine lange Polarnacht gegeben haben, die dann von ständiger Helligkeit im Sommer ausgeglichen wurde.

Vielleicht waren die großen Augen von *Leaellynasaura* eine Anpassung an die langen dunklen Winter. *Leaellynasaura* könnte die „Haselmaus“ der Gruppe gewesen sein. Dieser Dinosaurier hielt vielleicht Winterschlaf oder fiel bei Minustemperaturen in eine Kältestarre.

**OBEN** *Leaellynasaura* war ein kleiner Pflanzenfresser mit schnabelartig endendem Mund, der sich gut zum Abweiden von Farnen, Cycadeen und vielleicht von Blütenpflanzen (Blumen und Kräutern) eignete. Diese Gewächse breiteten sich damals überall auf der Welt aus und stellten eine neue Art pflanzlicher Nahrung dar.

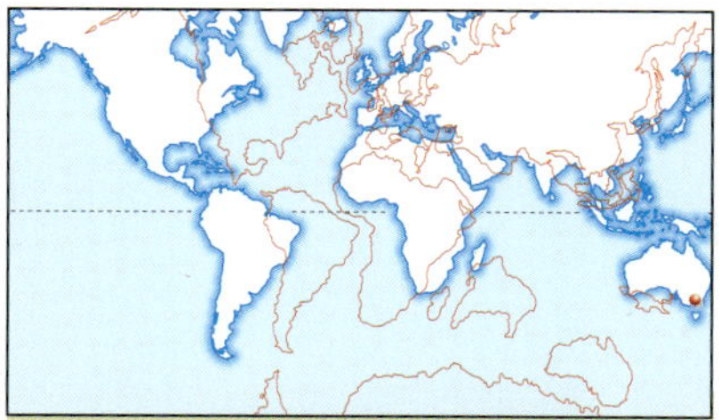

**ÜBERSICHT (DINOSAURIER)**
***Leaellynasaura***
**Bedeutung des Namens:** Leaellynas Reptil
**Periode:** Mittlere Kreidezeit
**Hauptgruppe:** Ornithopoda
**Länge:** 2 – 3 Meter
**Gewicht:** 10 Kilogramm
**Nahrung:** Pflanzen
**Fossilfundstätten:** Australien (Victoria)

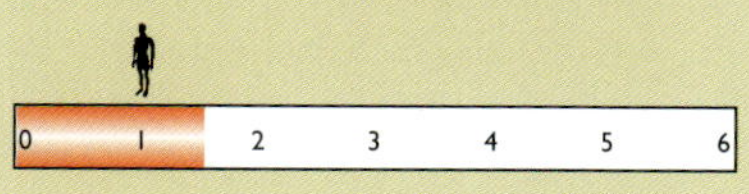

# Dinosaurier in Eis und Schnee?

*Aufgrund der klimatischen Verhältnisse während der mittleren Kreidezeit gab es in den langen, dunklen Wintern in Australien wahrscheinlich auch Schnee. Kleinere Ornithopoden wie Leaellynasaura könnten sich dann irgendeinen Unterschlupf gesucht haben, in dem sie die kalte Jahreszeit zubrachten. Bis heute sind sich die Wissenschaftler nicht einig darüber, ob diese Pflanzenfresser wechselwarme Tiere waren, also durch die niedrige Umgebungstemperatur im Winter zu stark auskühlten um sich bewegen zu können und in eine Kältestarre fielen, oder ob sie normalerweise Warmblüter waren und ihre Körpertemperatur absenkten um Energie zu sparen, wie es noch heute manche Säugetiere tun, wenn sie Winterschlaf halten.*

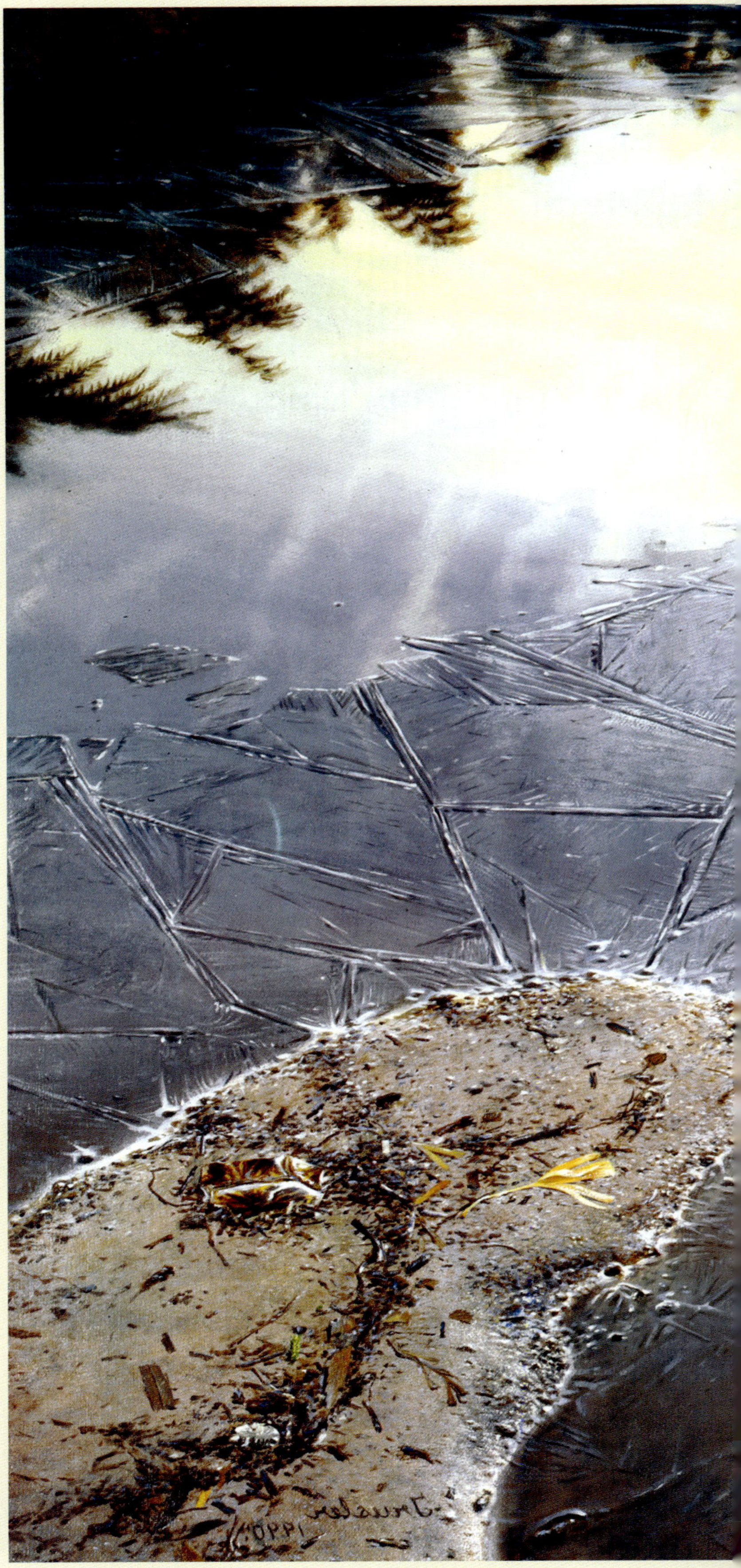

**RECHTS** Dieser ziemlich kleine *Leaellynasaurus* lebte vor etwa 110 Millionen Jahren in einem Teil der Erde, der heute Südaustralien ist. Er ist im Freien von der Kälte überrascht worden und erfriert auf dem vereisten Flussufer. Der Rest seines Clans hat die Tiefen des schützenden Waldes erreicht, wo sich die Tiere auf das Überwintern im dichten Unterholz vorbereiten.

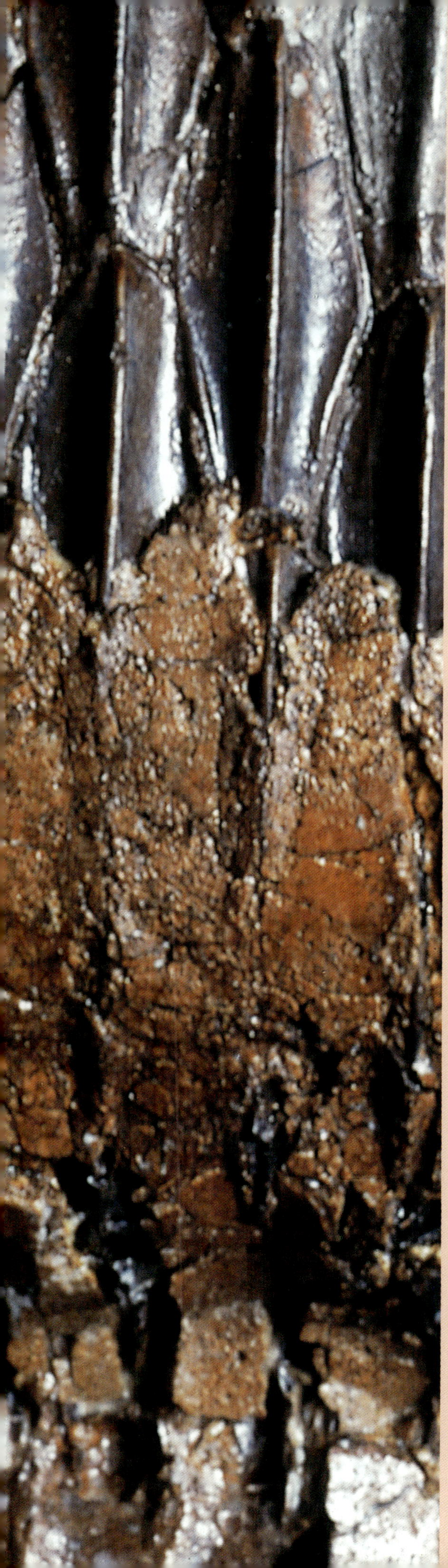

KAPITEL NEUN

# ENTEN-SCHNABEL-DINOSAURIER

*Die Hadrosaurier oder Entenschnabeldinosaurier gehörten zu den letzten großen Dinosauriergruppen, die sich auf der Erde entwickelten. Sie besaßen viele neue Merkmale und waren möglicherweise die lautesten und buntesten Reptilien überhaupt.*

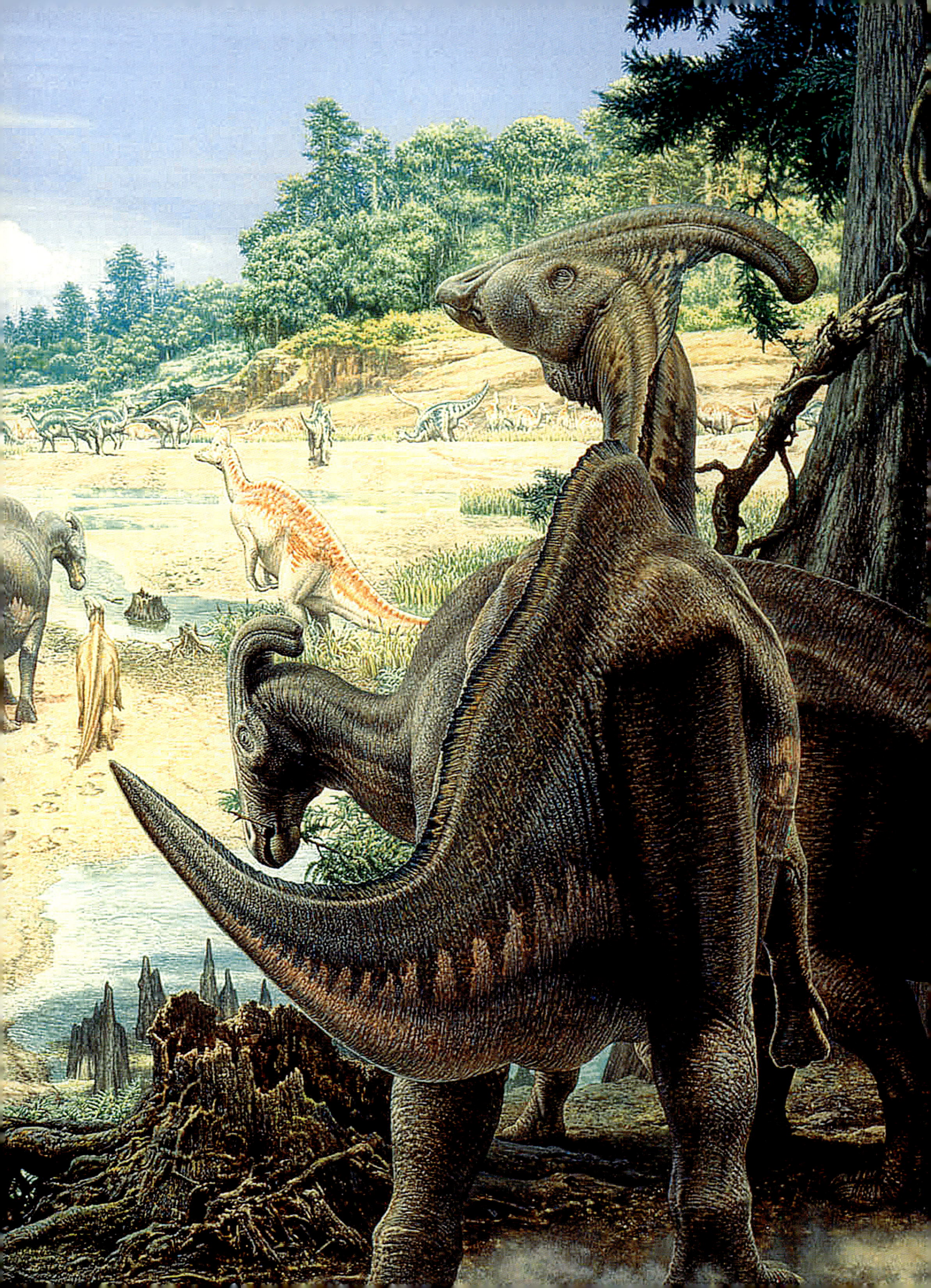

# SPÄTER AUFTRITT

*Die Hadrosaurier entwickelten sich wahrscheinlich vor nicht einmal 100 Millionen Jahren aus Vorfahren, die dem Iguanodon ähnelten. Ihre Blütezeit erlebten sie in der Oberkreide, vor 80 – 65 Millionen Jahren. Die meisten Fossilien von Entenschnabeldinosauriern stammen aus Nordamerika, doch es existieren auch Funde aus Ostasien und von anderen Kontinenten – bisher mit Ausnahme von Afrika und Australien. Aus der Gruppe der Hadrosaurier gingen in kurzer Zeit viele große und verschiedenartige Formen hervor, von denen manche länger als zwölf Meter waren und fünf Tonnen wogen. Die Hadrosaurier unterscheiden sich durch mehrere typische Kennzeichen, nicht zuletzt durch ihre Schnäbel, Zähne, Kopfkämme und ihr Fortpflanzungsverhalten, von anderen Pflanzenfressern ihrer Zeit.*

## DIE SCHNÄBEL

Die Hadrosaurier werden für gewöhnlich auch Entenschnabeldinosaurier oder Entenschnäbel genannt. Diese Namen rühren daher, dass die Vorderfront ihres Mundes wie der Schnabel eines Wasservogels, beispielsweise einer Ente oder Gans, breit, flach und zahnlos war. Früher verstand man die Entenschnabelform als Hinweis darauf, dass die Hadrosaurier einst im Wasser lebten, und auch die hohen Wülste an der Ober- und der Unterseite des Schwanzes deuteten darauf hin, dass der Schwanz ein Flossenband trug oder wie bei einem Krokodil geformt war. Ein Hadrosaurier hätte sich demnach durch Schwanzschläge im Wasser fortbewegt und dabei an den Wasserpflanzen rundum gepickt. Da aber nur wenige andere Körperteile an eine aquatische Lebensweise angepasst scheinen, wird diese Vorstellung heute weitgehend ausgeschlossen. Dennoch hätten die kräftig und massig gebauten Hadrosaurier ohne weiteres durch einen Sumpf oder einen Fluss waten können. Ihre Gliedmaßen waren so gebaut, dass die Tiere auf allen vieren oder auch nur auf ihren beiden Hinterbeinen gehen konnten.

## DIE ZÄHNE

Die Zähne der Hadrosaurier saßen ausschließlich in der Wangenregion, im hinteren Teil der Kiefer. Sie waren in kleinen Dreier- bis Fünferkolonnen angeordnet, die wiederum große Batterien aus fünfzig oder mehr Zähnen bildeten, und diese Batterien saßen so im Ober- und im Unterkiefer, dass die Mahlflächen im entgegengesetzten Winkel zueinander lagen. Schlossen sich die Kiefer, rieben und schabten die Zähne wie Raspeln oder Feilen diagonal aneinander vorbei, so dass die harten Schmelzstrukturen auf den Zähnen selbst die zähesten, faserigsten Pflanzenteile zerkleinern konnten. Manche Hadrosaurier besaßen zur gleichen Zeit mehr als tausend Zähne, und diese wurden wie alle Dinosaurierzähne regelmäßig ersetzt. Bei einigen Hadrosauriern hat man in der Magenregion fossilierte Kiefernnadeln und Zweige gefunden, was darauf hindeutet, dass diese Tiere selbst härtestes Pflanzenmaterial fressen konnten.

## DIE KÄMME

Manche Hadrosaurier hatten einen unauffälligen, flachen reptiltypischen Kopf, doch viele trugen auch Knochenkämme, die vom Schädeldach abstanden. Bei einigen war der Kamm lang und stabartig, bei anderen flacher und abgerundet. Einer früheren Theorie zufolge dienten diese Kämme der Atmung, denn anfangs vermutete man, dass sie am obersten Punkt eine Öffnung für den Luftein- und -austritt gehabt hätten und als eine Art Schnorchel dienten, wenn die Dinosaurier fast vollständig ins Wasser abtauchten. Das stimmte mit den oben erwähnten Theorien über die aquatische Lebensweise überein. Weitere Fossilfunde und Untersuchungen zeigten jedoch, dass die Kämme keine derartige Öffnung besaßen; die Kammern in ihrem Innern bildeten einen Teil der Atemwege der Tiere und waren mit der Nase verbunden. Einer anderen, eher akzeptierten These zufolge funktionierten die Kämme als Vibratoren oder Resonatoren, mit denen die Tiere Schall erzeugten, so wie die heutigen Elefanten durch ihren Rüssel trompeten. Überdies können die Kämme auffällig gefärbt gewesen sein und während der Paarungszeit eine Rolle bei der Partnersuche gespielt haben.

**VORHERGEHENDE SEITE** Dichte Reihen scharfgratiger Backenzähne des *Edmontosaurus*, eines der größten Entenschnabeldinosaurier. Das Tier trug in seinem Maul Hunderte dieser Zähne, die eine außerordentlich kräftige Kauvorrichtung bildeten.

**LINKS** Hier haben sich verschiedene Typen von Hadrosauriern um eine reiche Nahrungsquelle an einem See im Flachland versammelt. Im Vordergrund stehen zwei Tiere der Gattung *Parasaurolophus* mit ihren hohen röhrenartigen Kopfkämmen aus Knochen. Möglicherweise ging es in einer solchen Szene auch etwas laut zu, denn jede Art erzeugte ihre eigenen charakteristischen Laute, schrie, brüllte, trompetete, brummte oder grunzte.

# PROTOHADROS

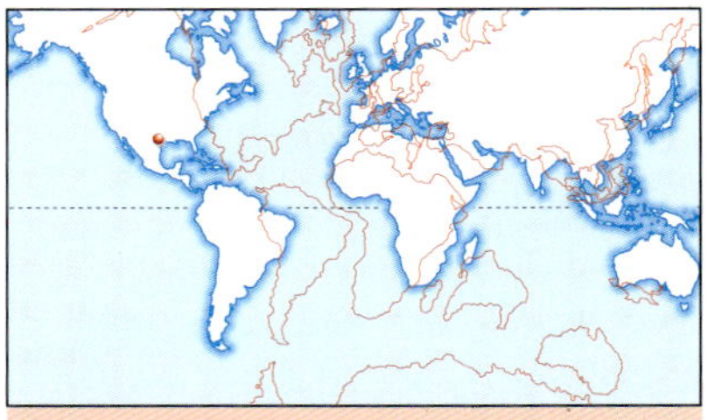

**ÜBERSICHT (DINOSAURIER)**
***Protohadros***
**Bedeutung des Namens:** Zuerst entstandener Hadrosaurus, frühes massiges Reptil
**Periode:** Mittlere Kreidezeit
**Hauptgruppe:** Ornithopoda
**Länge:** 4,5–6 Meter
**Gewicht:** Schätzungsweise 1 Tonne
**Nahrung:** Pflanzen
**Fossilfundstätten:** In den USA (Texas)

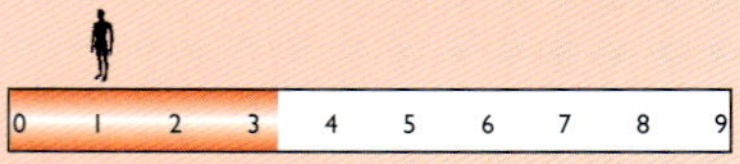


Im Jahr 1994 fand der Hobby-Paläontologe Gary Byrd bei Flower Mound im texanischen Denton County Fossilien eines *Protohadros*. Das Tier wurde 1988 von Jason Head vom Dedman College of Humanities and Sciences in Texas beschrieben und benannt. *Protohadros* lebte vor rund 95 Millionen Jahren, viel früher als die meisten anderen Hadrosaurier. Er ist damit einer der ältesten bekannten Entenschnabeldinosaurier und ein oft genannter Kandidat für die Ahnenreihe der Gruppe (siehe Seite 292, *Bactrosaurus*). Vor der Entdeckung des *Protohadros* galt Asien als Ursprungsgebiet der Hadrosaurier, die wahrscheinlich *Iguanodon*-artige Vorfahren hatten. Inzwischen hat der neue Fund die Aufmerksamkeit auf Nordamerika gelenkt, auch wenn es noch Meinungsverschiedenheiten darüber gibt, wer der erste Hadrosaurier war.

Da der Fossilfund lediglich aus einem unvollständigen Schädel und vielleicht einigen Bruchstücken von Rippen und Fußknochen bestand, ist eine Rekonstruktion dieses Dinosauriers zum größten Teil rein theoretischer Natur. Nach den bisherigen Erkenntnissen wurde *Protohadros* sechs Meter lang und besaß zahlreiche Eigenschaften, die typisch für Hadrosaurier waren. Seine Kiefer waren vermutlich groß und öffneten sich weit, die Schnauze endete vorn in dem typischen zahnlosen „Schnabel", und in den Wangen saßen ganze Batterien von Backenzähnen, die die zähe pflanzliche Nahrung zermalmten. Wie bei späteren Vertretern der Gruppe waren wahrscheinlich auch bei *Protohadros* die Hinterbeine länger als das vordere Paar. Das Tier konnte sich auf allen vieren fortbewegen, vor allem wenn es am Boden wachsende Pflanzen und niedrige Sträucher abweidete, oder auch nur auf den hinteren Gliedmaßen gehen und rennen. An den großen, kräftigen Füßen saßen keine Krallen, sondern Nägel oder hufartige Gebilde. Der Lebensraum des *Protohadros* war in der mittleren Kreidezeit ein flaches Gebiet mit Wäldern und Sümpfen, in dem das feuchtwarme Klima für eine üppige Vegetation sorgte.

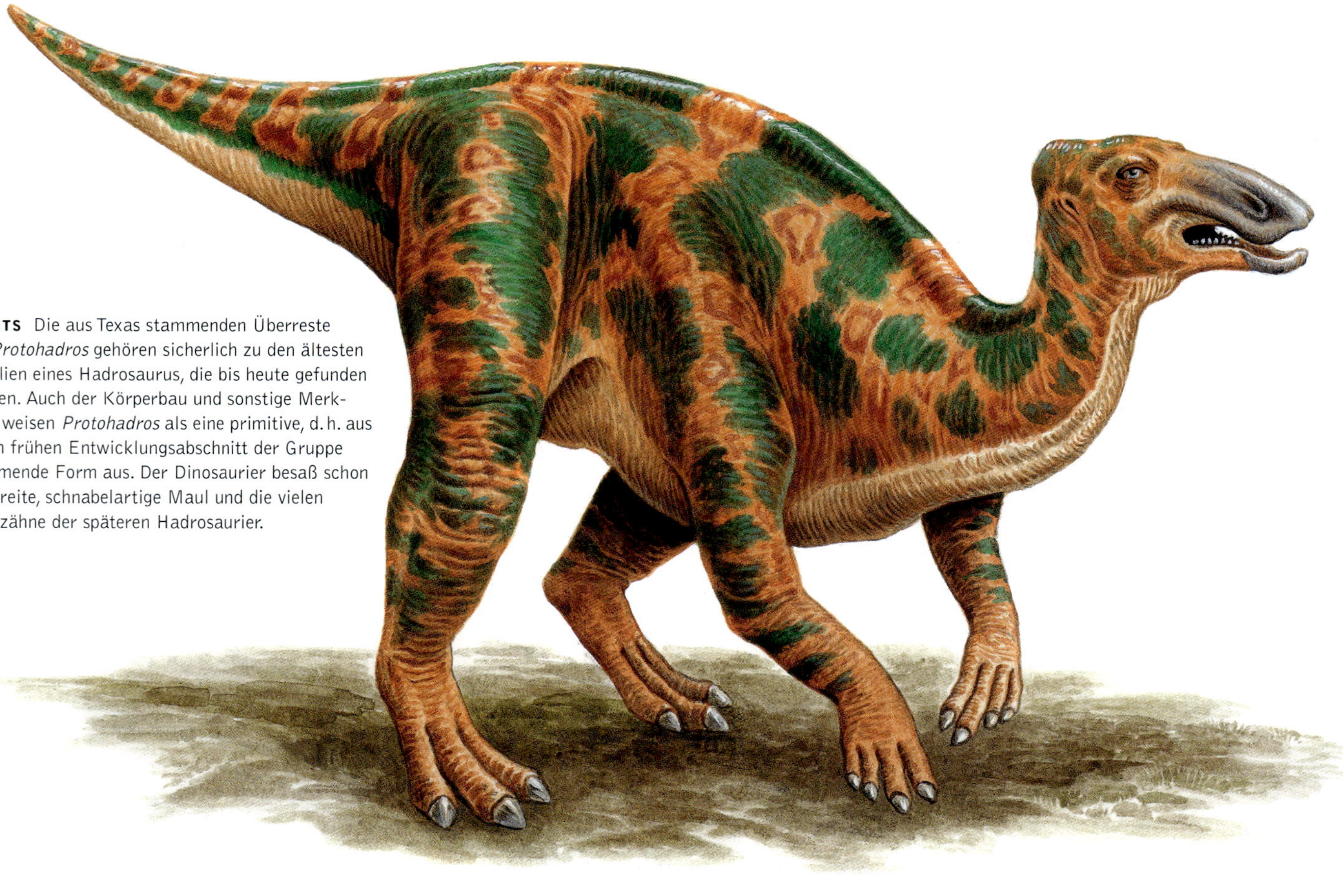

**RECHTS** Die aus Texas stammenden Überreste des *Protohadros* gehören sicherlich zu den ältesten Fossilien eines Hadrosaurus, die bis heute gefunden wurden. Auch der Körperbau und sonstige Merkmale weisen *Protohadros* als eine primitive, d. h. aus einem frühen Entwicklungsabschnitt der Gruppe stammende Form aus. Der Dinosaurier besaß schon das breite, schnabelartige Maul und die vielen Mahlzähne der späteren Hadrosaurier.

**UNTEN** Anhand der Beschreibung von *Hadrosaurus*-Fossilien vor etwa anderthalb Jahrhunderten wurde die Gruppe der Hadrosaurier oder Entenschnabeldinosaurier aufgestellt. Den Fundort Hadonfield, wo man die Überreste kurz vor dem amerikanischen Bürgerkrieg ausgegraben hatte, markiert heute ein Gedenkstein und ein kleiner Park.

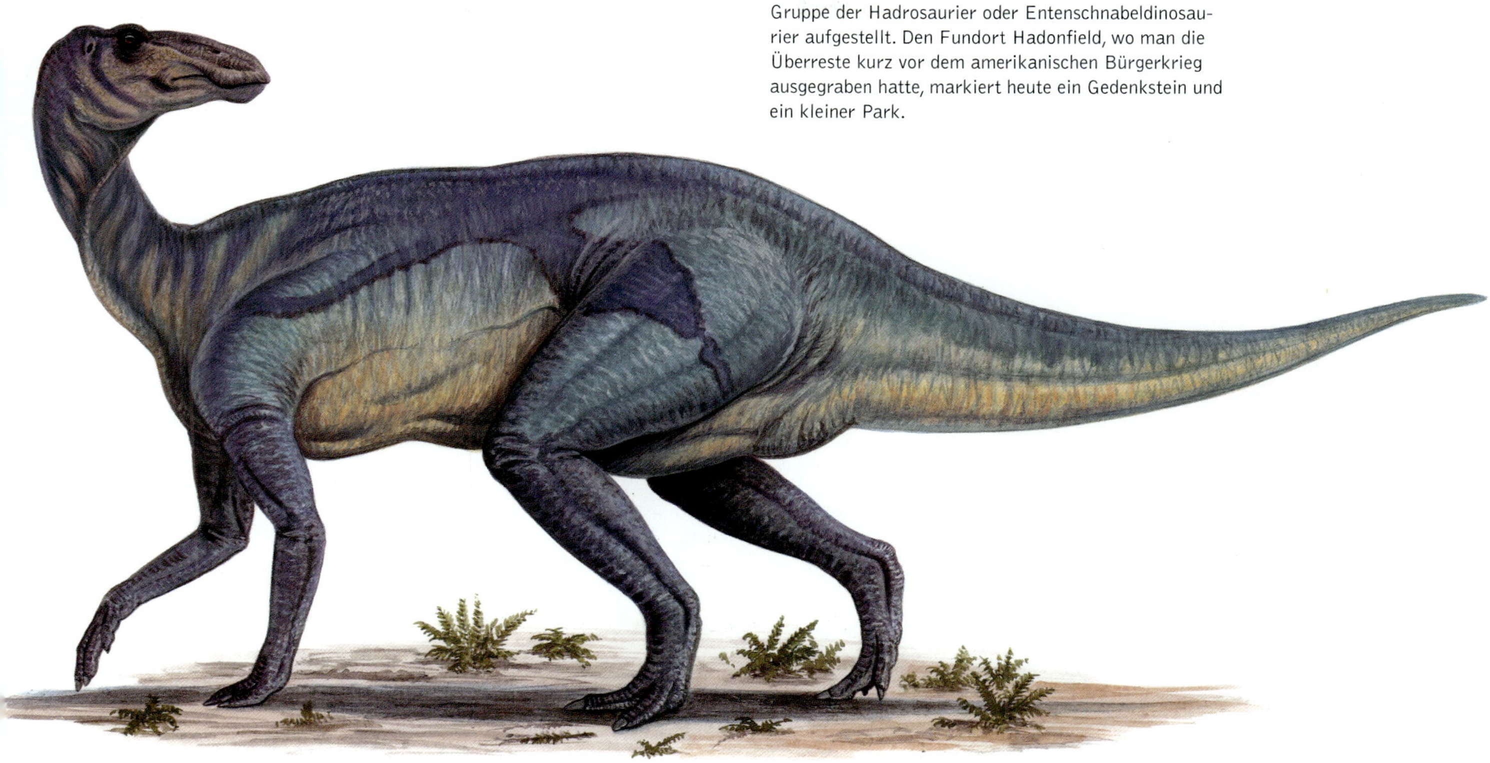

# HADROSAURUS

*Hadrosaurus*, das „massige Reptil“, ist einer von mehreren Dinosauriern, die nicht so sehr wegen ihrer Fossilien, sondern wegen ihres Namens berühmt sind. Wie *Dromaeosaurus* bei den Fleisch fressenden „Raptoren“, so hat auch *Hadrosaurus* seinen Namen einer ganzen Dinosauriergruppe, den Hadrosauriern oder Entenschnabeldinosauriern, gegeben. *Hadrosaurus* selbst hingegen ist kaum und nur von spärlichen, bruchstückhaften Fossilien bekannt. Das liegt daran, dass seine Fossilien zu einem recht frühen Zeitpunkt der wissenschaftlichen Erfassung und Untersuchung von Dinosauriern gefunden wurde. *Hadrosaurus* war sogar einer der ersten nordamerikanischen Dinosaurier, die man wissenschaftlich beschrieb und benannte. Seine Überreste wurden erstmals 1838 in der Nähe von Haddonfield (US-Bundesstaat New Jersey), in einer Mergelgrube auf der Farm eines gewissen John Hopkins entdeckt, doch ohne weitere Untersuchung am Fundort belassen. Erst nach zwanzig Jahren erkannte jemand ihre Bedeutung, und zwar William Parker Foulke, ein Freund von Hopkins, der damals in der Gegend Urlaub machte. Die Knochen wurden 1858 von Joseph Leidy ausgegraben, beschrieben und benannt. Leidy stellte Ähnlichkeiten mit *Iguanodon*, doch auch Unterschiede zwischen diesem und *Hadrosaurus* fest. (*Iguanodon* war ebenfalls ein Ornithopode und einer der ältesten Dinosaurier, die – in diesem Fall in Europa – beschrieben wurden.) 1868 wurde das Skelett des *Hadrosaurus* in der Philadelphia Academy of Science als erstes Dinosaurierskelett in Nordamerika rekonstruiert und ausgestellt.

Der damalige Fossilfund bestand aus Teilen eines Kiefers, einigen Zähnen, Rückenwirbeln und Fragmenten der Gliedmaßen, die wahrscheinlich alle von ein und demselben Tier stammten. Die Reste waren zwar nur bruchstückhaft, doch immer noch zahlreicher als alle seinerzeit bekannten Fossilien von *Iguanodon*. Leidys Beschreibung des *Hadrosaurus* trug auch dazu bei, die Dinosaurier als eigenständige Tiergruppe mit vielen Reptil- und seltsamerweise auch Vogelmerkmalen zu etablieren, wie es Richard Owen 1841 vorgeschlagen hatte. *Hadrosaurus* erreichte vermutlich eine Länge von zehn Metern und ein Gewicht von einigen Tonnen.

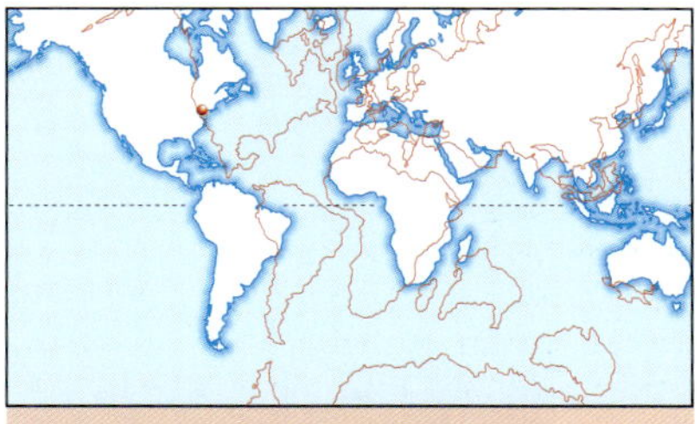

**ÜBERSICHT (DINOSAURIER)**
***Hadrosaurus***
**Bedeutung des Namens:** Massiges Reptil, großes Reptil
**Periode:** Oberkreide
**Hauptgruppe:** Ornithopoda
**Länge:** 7–10 Meter
**Gewicht:** 2–3 Tonnen
**Nahrung:** Pflanzen
**Fossilfundstätten:** In den USA (New Jersey)

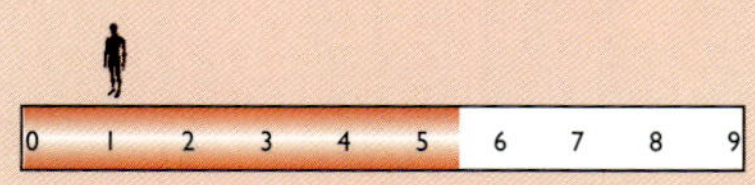

**UNTEN** Zwei ausgewachsene Tiere der Gattung *Maiasaura* in der Brutsaison auf dem Weg zu ihrem traditionellen Eiablageplatz. Die fossilierten Überreste der Nester, die einen Durchmesser von zwei Metern hatten, deuten darauf hin, dass zur Eiablage jedes Jahr ein und derselbe Platz aufgesucht wurde. Verglichen mit ausgewachsenen Tieren hatten die frisch geschlüpften Jungtiere im Verhältnis zu ihrer Körpergröße kürzere Schnauzen und größere Augen, ein Merkmal, das bei jüngeren Tieren häufig vorkommt.

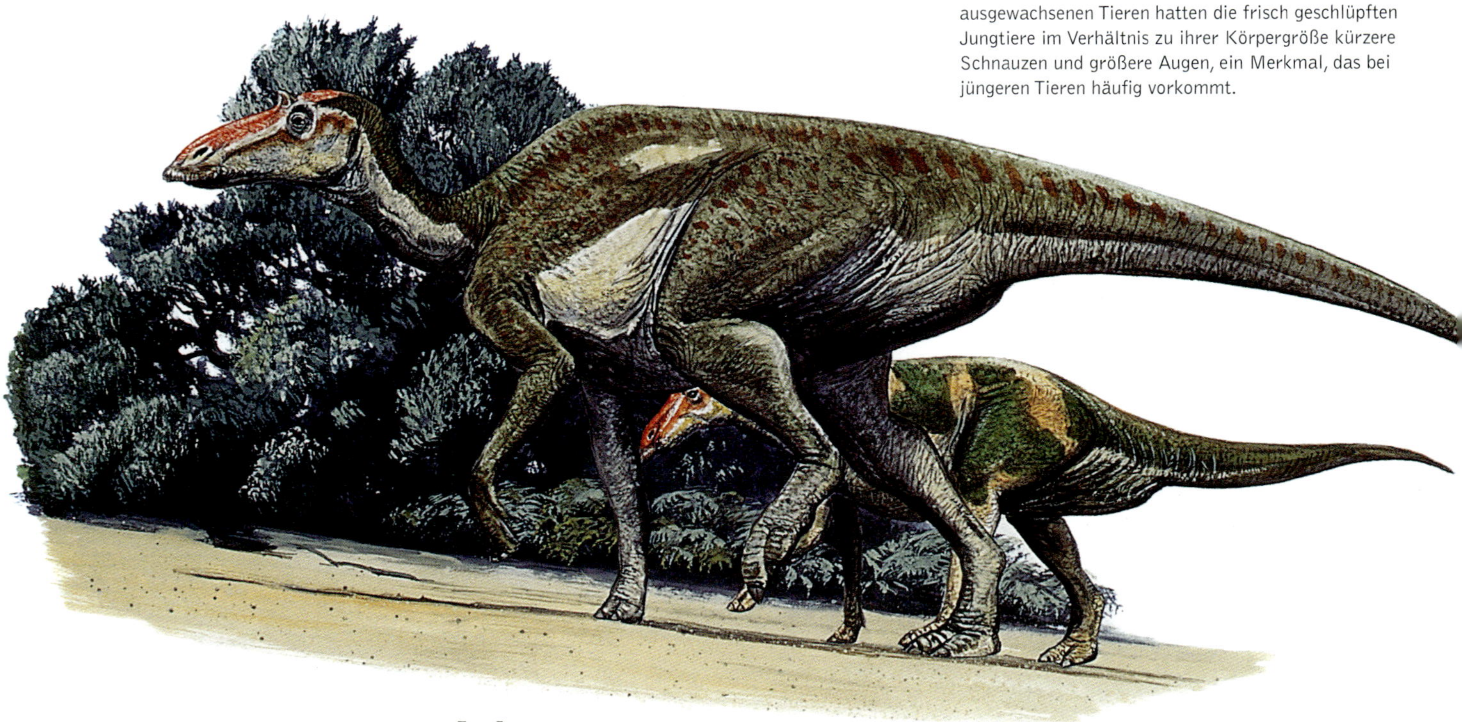

# MAIASAURA

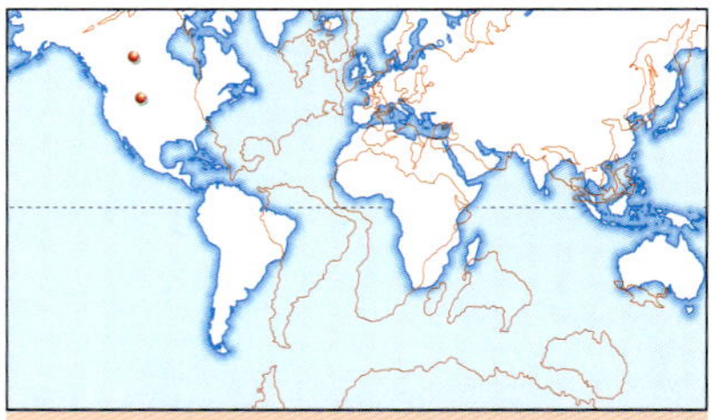

**ÜBERSICHT (DINOSAURIER)**
***Maiasaura***
**Bedeutung des Namens:** Gutes Mutterreptil
**Periode:** Oberkreide
**Hauptgruppe:** Ornithopoda
**Länge:** 9 Meter
**Gewicht:** 3 – 4 Tonnen
**Nahrung:** Pflanzen
**Fossilfundstätten:** In den USA (Montana), in Kanada

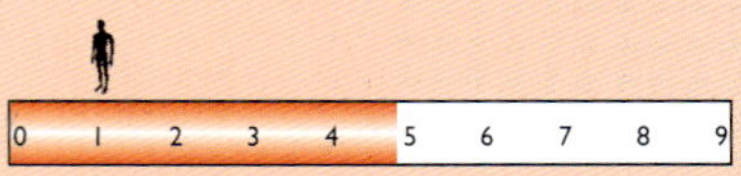


Die lang gehegte Vorstellung von den Dinosauriern als langsame, dumme, roboterartige Automaten wurde in den 1960er Jahren durch die wissenschaftliche Beschäftigung mit dem Fleischfresser *Deinonychus* und in den späten 1970er Jahren durch die Untersuchungen des „Entenschnabels" *Maiasaura* nachhaltig erschüttert. Der neun Meter lange Pflanzenfresser *Maiasaura* wurde 1979 von John Horner und Robert Makela anhand von Fossilien benannt, die bei Bozeman (US-Bundesstaat Montana) von einer gewissen Marion Brandvold und deren Familie gefunden worden waren. Der Hadrosaurier *Maiasaura* hatte einen langen Kopf, der im Profil entfernt einem Pferdekopf ähnelte und über beiden Augen einen wulstigen Kamm trug. Das Maul wies vorn den typischen breiten, zahnlosen Entenschnabel auf, in der Wangenregion standen ganze Reihen von Mahlzähnen, die sich beim Kauen gegenseitig schärften. *Maiasaura* lebte in der Oberkreide, vor rund 78 – 73 Millionen Jahren.

In Montana hat man an einer Stelle bei Bynum, die „Egg Mountain" („Eierberg") genannt wird, Tausende *Maiasaura*-Fossilien gefunden. Darunter befanden sich nicht nur Überreste ausgewachsener Tiere, sondern auch Knochen von Jungtieren, Nester, Eier und frisch geschlüpfte Dinosaurier. Aus diesen Funden hat die menschliche Phantasie ein Bild abgeleitet, nach dem viele *Maiasaura*-Individuen ihre Eier in einer Art Brutkolonie ablegen und hüten, so wie es manche rezente Vogelarten tun. Diese Herden waren möglicherweise viele Tausend Tiere stark. Die Dinosaurier legten nicht nur Nester für ihre Eier an, sondern bewachten oder bebrüteten die Gelege sogar, vielleicht beschützten und fütterten sie ihre Jungen nach dem Schlüpfen auch (siehe Seite 300). An der erwähnten Fundstätte lagen auch Überreste des viel kleineren, leichteren Ornithopoden *Orodromeus* sowie des Räubers *Bambiraptor* und des kleinen, flinken Fleischfressers *Troodon*. Einige Wissenschaftler vertreten die Ansicht, dass einige davon an dieser Stelle ebenfalls ihre Gelege oder Jungtiere versorgten, als ein Vulkanausbruch sie überraschte, die vulkanische Asche alles zudeckte und der Nachwelt diese gewaltige Fossilienmenge hinterließ.

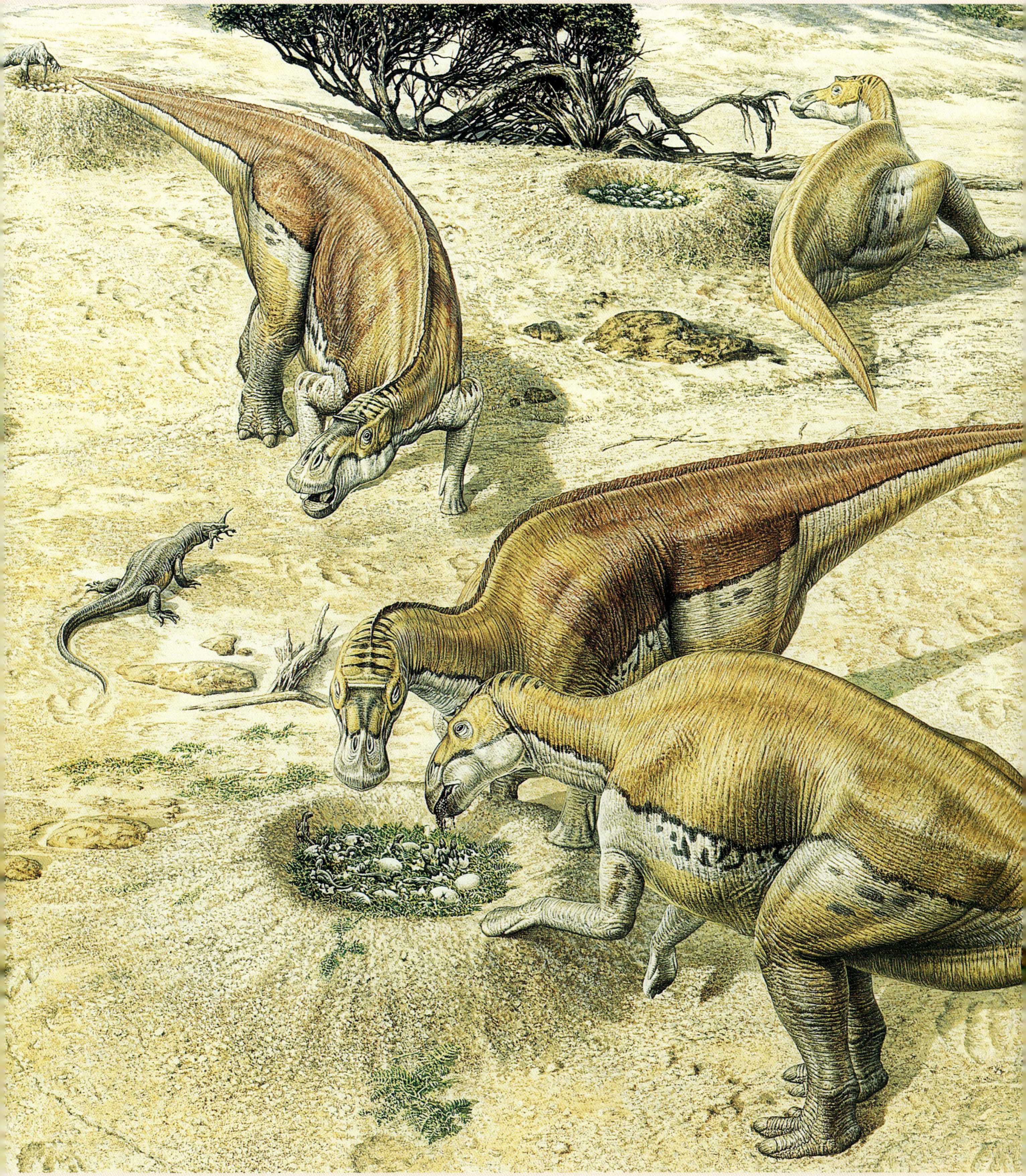

# HYPACROSAURUS

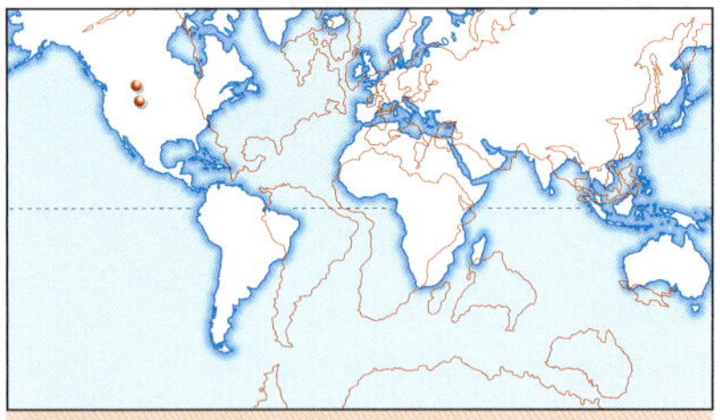

**ÜBERSICHT (DINOSAURIER)**
***Hypacrosaurus***
**Bedeutung des Namens:** Reptil unter dem Gipfel
**Periode:** Oberkreide
**Hauptgruppe:** Ornithopoda
**Länge:** 9 Meter
**Gewicht:** 2 – 3 Tonnen
**Nahrung:** Pflanzen
**Fossilfundstätten:** In den USA (Montana), in Kanada (Alberta)

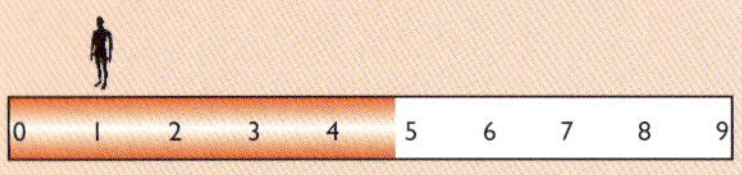


*Hypacrosarus* ähnelte in vielerlei Hinsicht dem *Corythosaurus* (siehe Seite 299). Er war ein typischer Hadrosaurier aus der Zeit der Oberkreide: Er besaß einen gebogenen Hals und einen massigen Körper; lange hintere Gliedmaßen mit jeweils drei kräftigen Zehen an den Füßen, auf denen er ging und rannte; kleinere, doch kräftige Vorderextremitäten mit vier „Fingern" an jeder Hand (die beim vierfüßigen Traben oder Galoppieren das Körpergewicht tragen konnten) und einen langen, schnell sich verjüngenden Schwanz. Die Vorderpartie des Mundes war zahnlos, flach und nach den Seiten verbreitert wie ein Entenschnabel. Die gefurchten, scharfgratigen Zähne bildeten vierzig Reihen oder „Batterien" in den hinteren Kieferregionen, mit denen das Tier selbst härteste Pflanzenteile kräftig kauen und zermahlen konnte. Die meisten Hadrosaurier waren verhältnismäßig großäugig und besaßen wahrscheinlich einen gut ausgeprägten Gesichts- und Geruchssinn, mit denen sie *Albertosaurus*, *Tyrannosaurus* und andere große Räuber rechtzeitig wahrnehmen konnten. An der Oberseite ihrer Wirbelknochen saßen wie bei anderen Hadrosauriern hohe, nach oben weisende Fortsätze, die wie Bänder oder Stacheln aussahen. Diese Fortsätze bildeten auf dem Rücken und der Schwanzoberseite möglicherweise eine lange Wulst.

Der Knochenkamm des *Hypacrosaurus* war nicht so hoch oder schmal wie bei *Corythosaurus*, doch er war hohl. Er enthielt gewundene Luftkanäle, die von den Nasenlöchern vorn an der Schnauze durch den Kamm und dann hinunter in den Kopf und die Kehle führten. (Die Theorien über die Funktion der Kopfkämme bei den Hadrosauriern werden in diesem Kapitel an verschiedenen Stellen aufgeführt.) *Hypacrosaurus* wurde 1913 von dem amerikanischen Dinosaurierexperten und Fossilsucher Barnum Brown benannt. Seine Überreste, darunter Schädel, fragmentarische Skelette von ausgewachsenen und jungen Tieren, sowie Eier mit Embryos stammen größtenteils aus der kanadischen Provinz Alberta und aus dem US-Bundesstaat Montana.

**UNTEN** Den Schädel und das Skelett eines *Hypacrosaurus* kann man im Royal Tyrrell Museum in Drumheller in der kanadischen Provinz Alberta besichtigen.

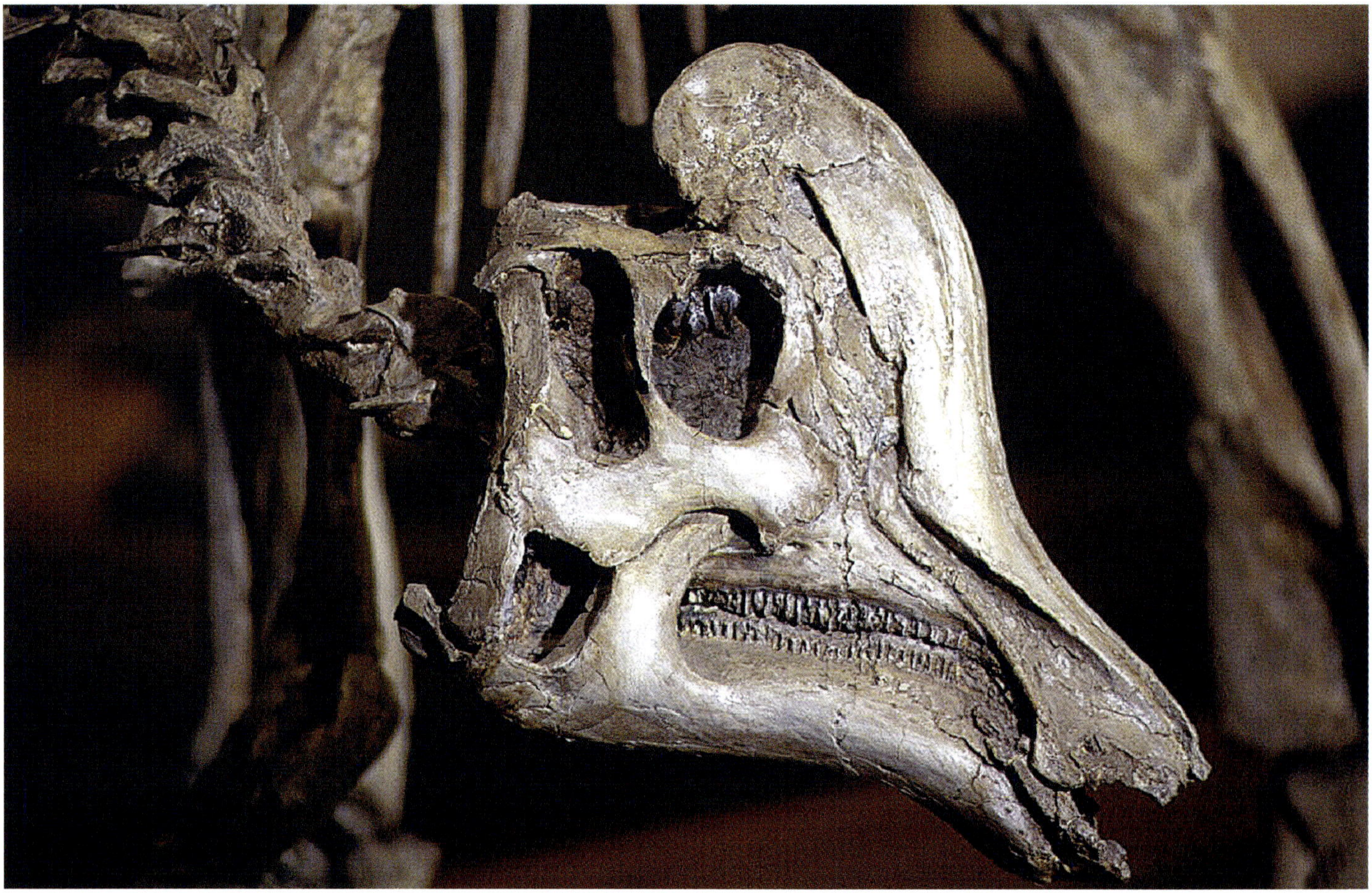

# GRYPOSAURUS (KRITOSAURUS U. A.)

*Gryposaurus*, das „Reptil mit gebogener Nase“, wurde nach der charakteristischen Form der vorderen Schnauze benannt, die wahrscheinlich sehr stark gewölbte Nasenlöcher sowie einen hoch stehenden Vorsprung aufwies und im Profil wie eine Hakennase aussah. Der Kopf des Tieres war lang und schmal. Ansonsten war der rund neun Meter lange und einige Tonnen schwere *Gryposaurus* ein typischer mittelgroßer Hadrosaurier aus der Zeit vor 75 – 70 Millionen Jahren. Der Großteil seiner Schädelreste, die möglicherweise von mehr als zehn Einzeltieren stammen, und andere Knochen sowie Hautabdrücke wurden in der kanadischen Provinz Alberta gefunden. Seinen Namen erhielt *Gryposaurus* 1914 von dem kanadischen Paläontologen Lawrence Lambe, der für seine zahlreichen Entdeckungen von Hadrosaurierfossilien berühmt ist (siehe Seite 298).

Die fossilierten Hautabdrücke zeigen kleine vieleckige Schuppen von nur fünf bis acht Millimeter Durchmesser und mit unterschiedlicher Anzahl gerader Seiten. Diese Schuppen bedeckten wahrscheinlich einen Großteil des Körpers, wobei der Schwanz auch mit verdickten größeren, eher zapfenartigen Platten von mehr als zehn Millimeter Durchmesser bestückt gewesen sein kann, die in Abständen von rund fünfzig bis siebzig Millimetern standen.

Über *Gryposaurus* und mehrere ähnliche Dinosaurier, darunter *Kritosaurus* („prächtiges Reptil“, 1910 benannt), *Trachodon* (1856), *Naashoibitosaurus* (1999) u.a. sowie über die Spezies, die vermutlich zu jeder dieser Gattungen gehören, werden viele Debatten geführt. Schon mehrere Male hat man die Fossilien jedes dieser Dinosaurier einer oder mehreren der anderen Gattungen zugeordnet. Die *Kritosaurus*-Überreste aus Nordamerika beispielsweise, die den Artnamen *Kritosaurus navajovius* („von den Navajo“) tragen und lediglich aus einem unvollständigen, schlecht erhaltenen Schädel bestehen, können vielleicht auch der Gattung *Gryposaurus* zugeordnet werden. Die aus Argentinien stammenden, *Kritosaurus australis* („aus dem Süden“) benannten Fossilien hingegen können auch eine gesonderte Spezies bilden oder stammen vielleicht gar nicht von der Gattung *Kritosaurus*. Diese Dinge bedürfen weiterer Untersuchung und Klärung.

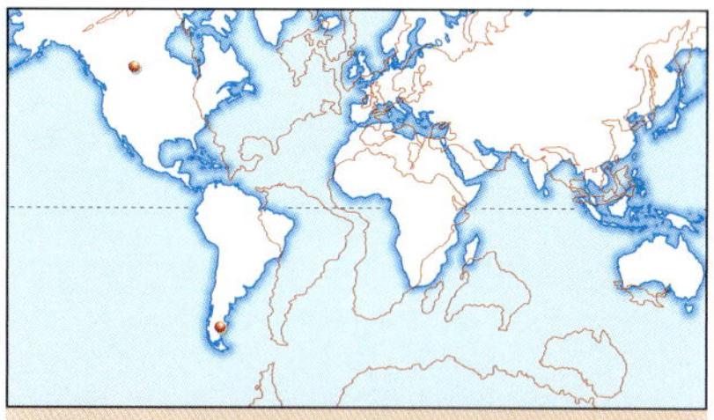

**ÜBERSICHT (DINOSAURIER)**
***Gryposaurus***
**Bedeutung des Namens:** Reptil mit gebogener Nase
**Periode:** Oberkreide
**Hauptgruppe:** Ornithopoda
**Länge:** 9 Meter
**Gewicht:** 2 – 3 Tonnen
**Nahrung:** Pflanzen
**Fossilfundstätten:** In Kanada (Alberta), in Argentinien

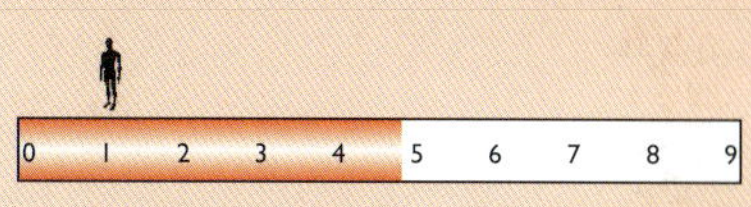


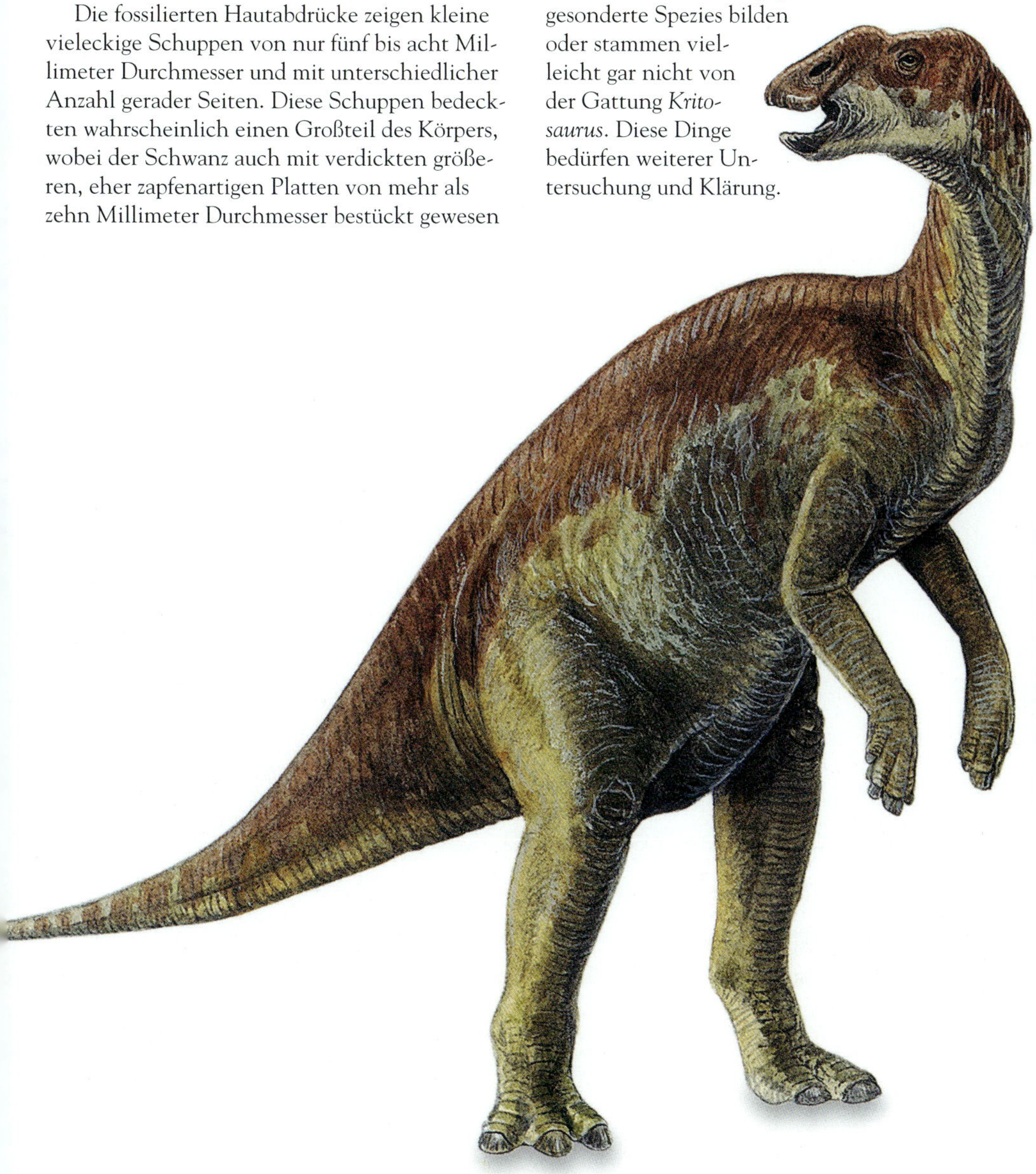

**LINKS** Dank fossilierter Hautabdrücke mit Schuppenmustern konnte die äußere Erscheinung des *Gryposaurus* bis auf die Färbung recht detailliert rekonstruiert werden.

**UNTEN** Dieses Exemplar wurde in Patagonien in Gesteinen der Kreidezeit gefunden und *Kriterosaurus australis* genannt. Der Name könnte sich nach weiteren Untersuchungen allerdings ändern.

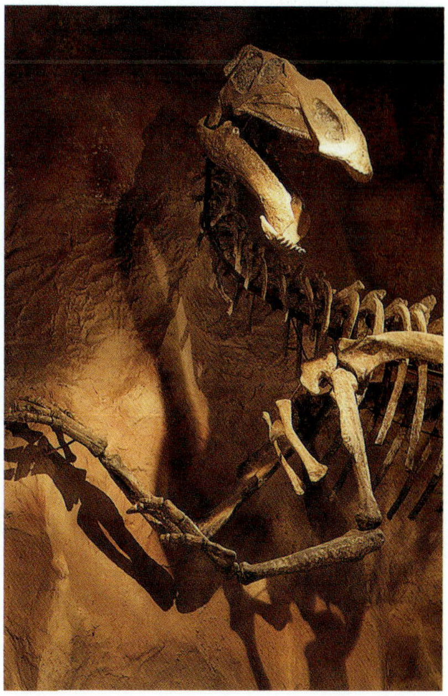

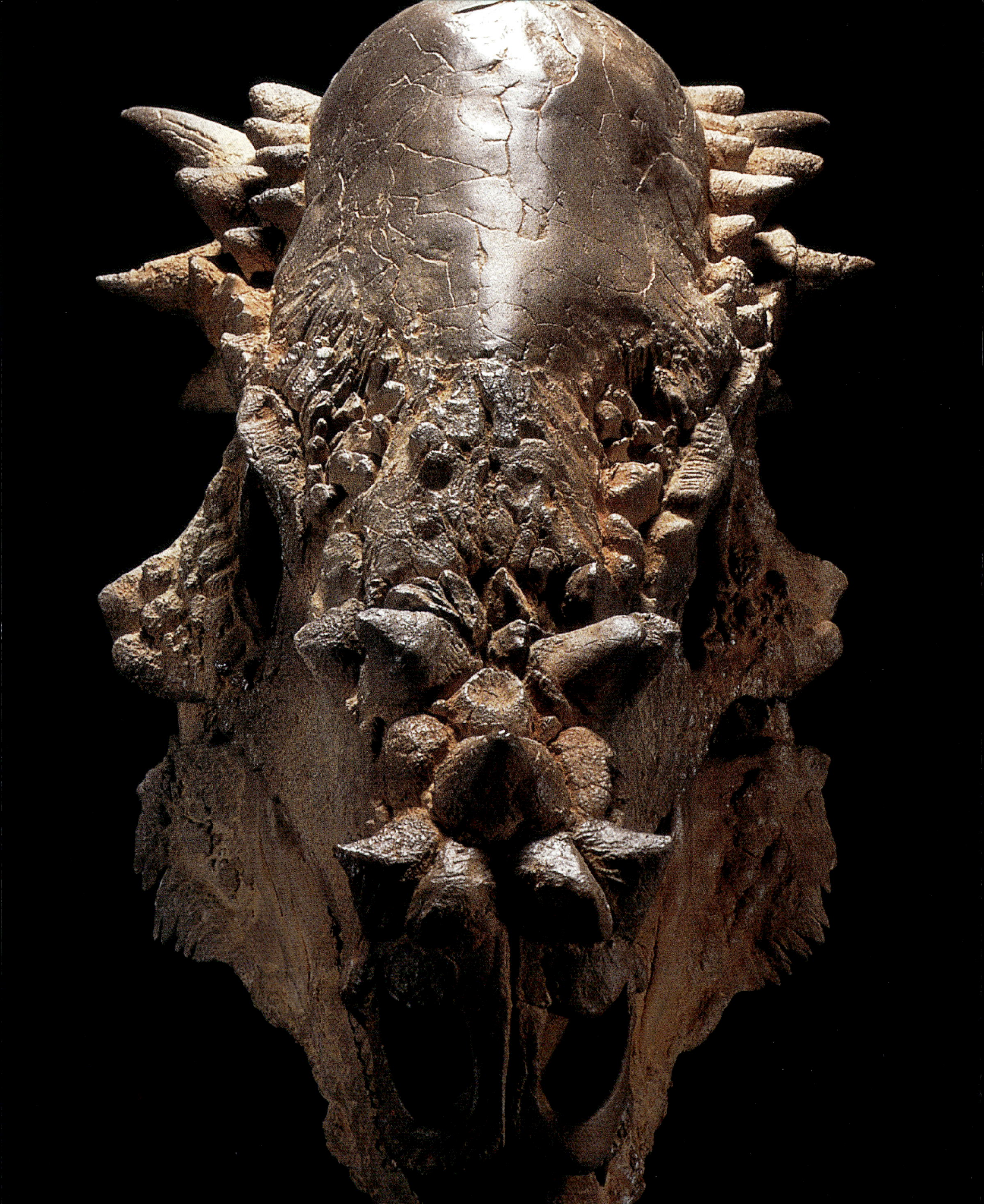

## Kapitel Zehn

# Dickkopf-dinosaurier

*Die Pachycephalosaurier waren „Dickköpfe" mit extrem starken Knochenschichten am Schädeldach.*

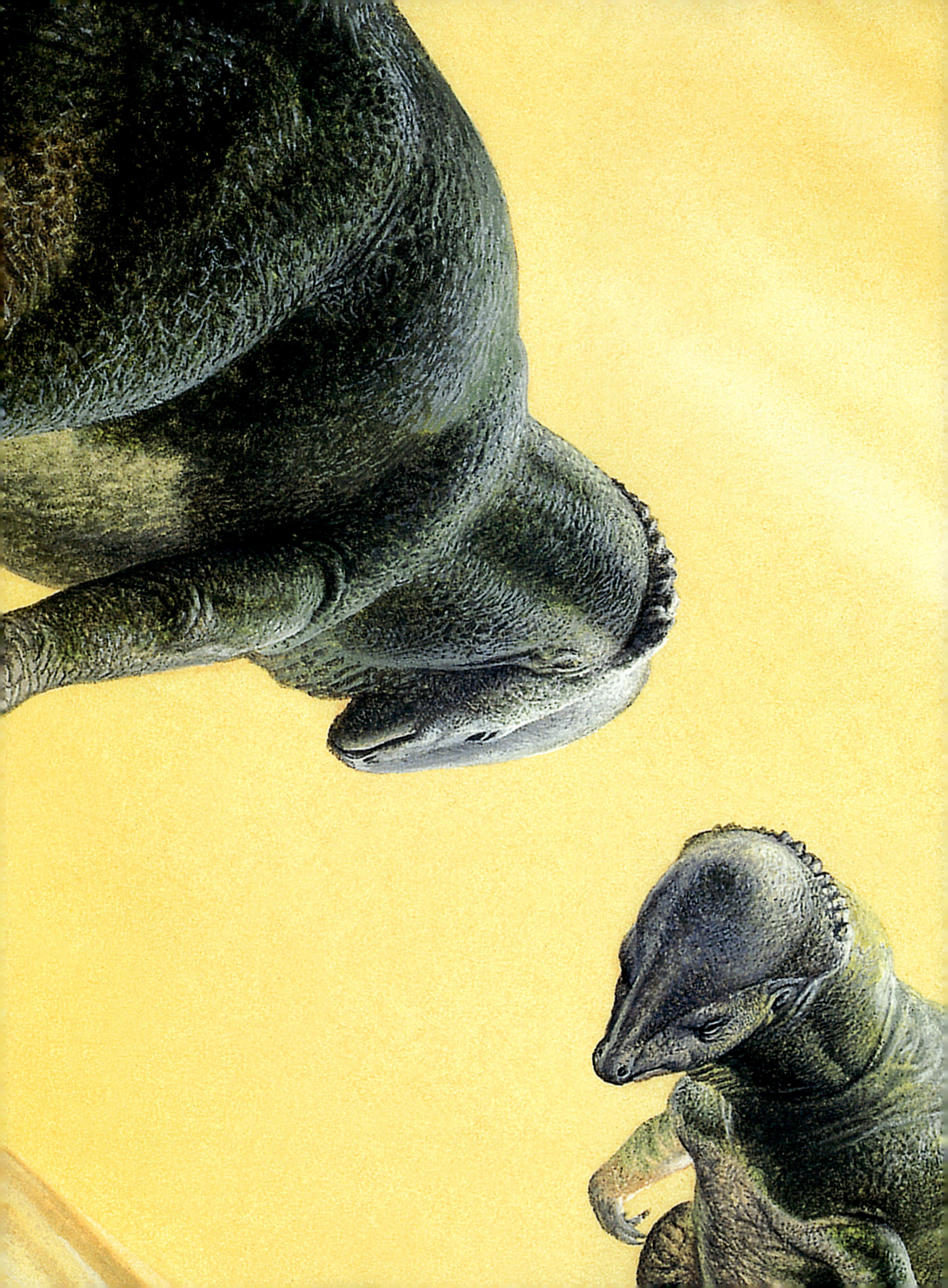

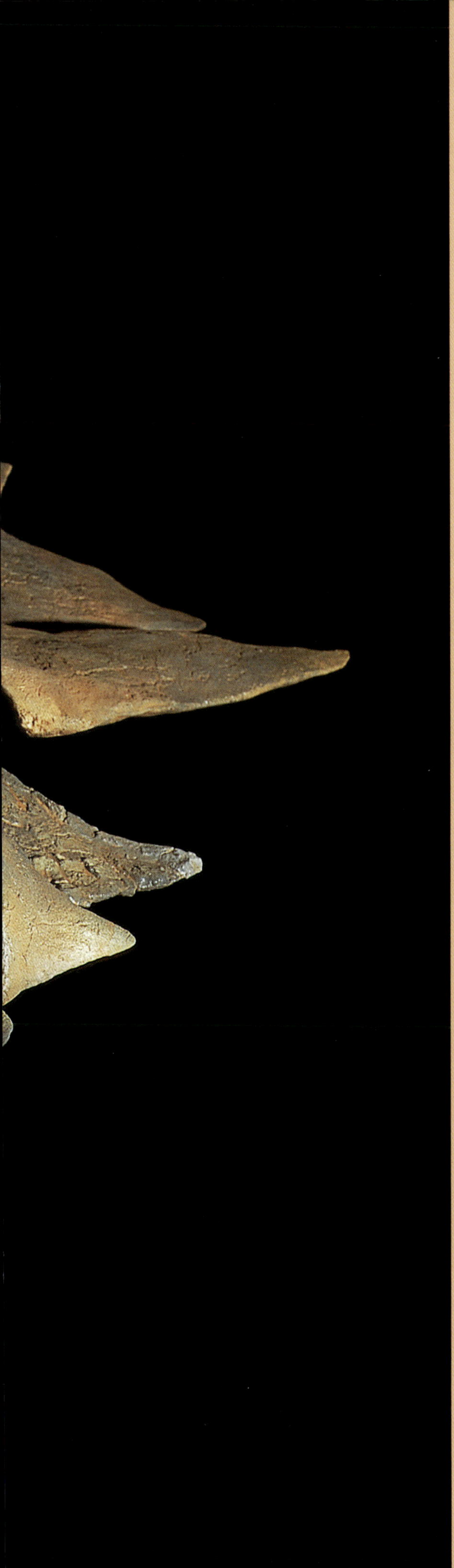

Kapitel Elf

# Panzer-dinosaurier

*Beinamen wie „wandernde Tanks“ oder „Dinosaurier mit Rüstung“ vermitteln eine Vorstellung von der Größe, von der Körpermasse und dem knöchernen Schutzpanzer der vermutlich friedlichen, Pflanzen fressenden Ankylosaurier.*

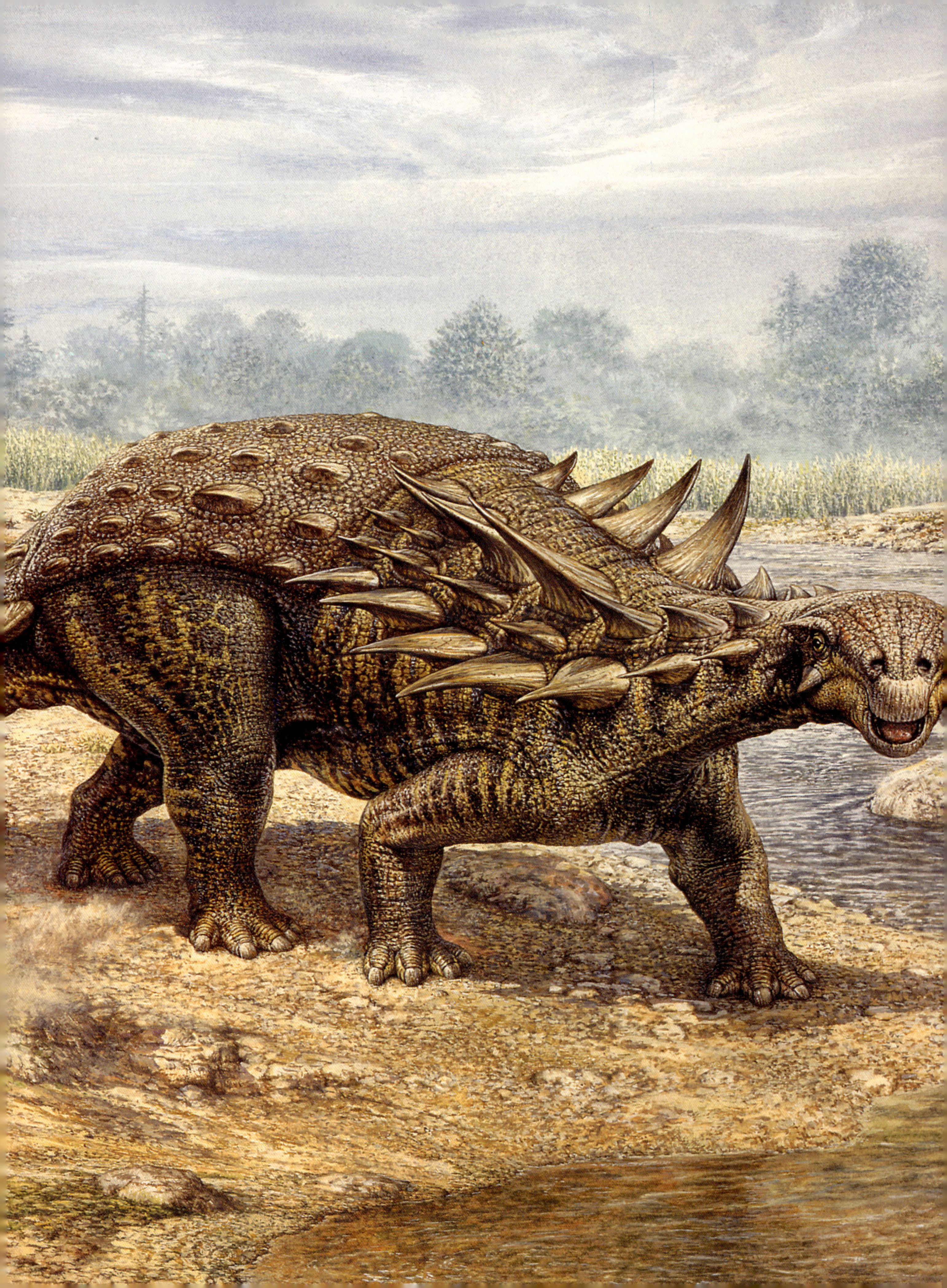

# DICKHÄUTER

***Die Ankylosaurier waren die am besten geschützen Dinosaurier überhaupt. Der Name dieser Gruppe ist von den Platten und anderen Knochenteilen abgeleitet, die über dem Kopf miteinander verbunden oder verwachsen und an Hals, Rücken, Flanken und Schwanz in die Haut eingebettet waren. Als Schutz vor den Krallen und Zähnen der Fleisch fressenden Dinosaurier, der Krokodile und anderer großer Räuber der damaligen Zeit dienten alle nur vorstellbaren Arten von Knochenhindernissen – Buckel, Höcker, Platten, Schilde, Stacheln, Dornen, Schuppen. Die Ankylosaurier stehen zusammen mit den Stegosauriern oder Stacheldinosauriern in einer größeren Dinosauriergruppe, in der Gruppe der Thyreophoren oder Schildträger.***

## UNTERGRUPPEN DER PANZERREPTILIEN

Von den Ankylosauriern gab es zwei große Untergruppen. Der augenfälligste Unterschied zwischen beiden bestand darin, dass bei den Vertretern der älteren Untergruppe, den Nodosauriden, das massive Knochengebilde an der Schwanzspitze fehlte, das für die andere Untergruppe, die Ankylosauriden, typisch war und meistens als „Schwanzkeule" bezeichnet wird. Die Nodosauriden erschienen in Mittleren Jura und sind durch Fossilfunde auf allen nördlichen Kontinenten, möglicherweise auch in Australien und in der Antarktis, bekannt. Einige Vertreter der Nodosauridengruppe existierten noch in der Kreidezeit; sie zeichneten sich durch eine enorme Körpergröße aus. Ein Beispiel dafür ist *Edmontonia* (siehe Seite 324). Die Ankylosauriden breiteten sich während der frühen Kreidezeit aus, hinsichtlich ihrer geografischen und zeitlichen Verbreitung überschnitten sie sich mit mehreren Verwandten aus der Untergruppe der Nodosauriden. In ihren Schnauzen und Köpfe verliefen komplexe gewundene Luftkanäle. Auf den Schultern trugen sie nicht die spitzen Stacheln, die wir von den meisten Nodosauriden kennen. Die Ankylosauriden überdauerten bis spät in die Kreidezeit und lebten hauptsächlich in Nordamerika und Asien. Auch sie erreichten beträchtliche Größen, einige übertrafen darin sogar die Nodosauriden. In manchen Klassifikationen sind weitere Untergruppen angeführt, beispielsweise die Gruppe der Polacanthiden, die nach *Polacanthus* (siehe Seite 327) aufgestellt und benannt wurde.

## JEDE MENGE PANZERUNG

Manche Ankylosaurier verfügten über zwei oder drei Knochenschichten, die bestimmte Teile des Kopfes bedeckten – einander überlagernde Schichten des Schädels selbst und darüber noch eine gesonderte Lage. Die den Körper bedeckenden Knochenteile waren im Allgemeinen nicht mit dem Skelett verbunden. Es handelte sich um Hautverknöcherungen, Teile aus Knochen, die in der dicken, zähen, steifen Lederhaut der Tiere wuchsen und von dieser sehr fest gehalten wurden. Einige dieser Knochenmassen lagen, von der Oberhaut überdeckt, gänzlich im Innern der Haut verborgen. Andere, insbesondere die spitzeren Dornen, besaßen knöcherne Kerne, die zu Lebzeiten von Horn überzogen waren. Sie mussten einst also größer und wahrscheinlich auch schärfer gewesen sein, als sie uns heute erscheinen – der Hornüberzug wurde natürlich schon vor der Fossilierung zersetzt. Natürlich ist es verlockend, die Ankylosaurier mit einer anderen Reptiliengruppe, den Schildkröten, gleichzusetzen, doch die Panzer dieser beiden Gruppen unterschieden sich doch sehr voneinander (siehe Seite 93).

## LANGSAM UND SCHWERFÄLLIG

Der oben beschriebene kräftige Körperschutz machte die Ankylosaurier natürlich ungelenk, massig, schwerfällig und langsam. Als wichtigstes Verteidigungsmittel gegen große Fleischfresser wie beispielsweise die Tyrannosaurier blieb diesen Tieren vermutlich nur, ihren flachen, kurzbeinigen Körper zum Schutz der verwundbareren Unterseite auf den Boden niederzuducken. Da sie mehrere Tonnen wogen, musste es für einen Angreifer außerordentlich schwer sein, den Körper ihres potenziellen Opfers auf den Rücken zu kippen. Andererseits könnte ein Ankylosaurier einen Angriff auch erwidert haben. Die Nodosauriden griffen vielleicht mit ihren langen, spitzen Schulterdornen an, während die Ankylosauriden im Kampf ihre Schwanzkeule als Knochen brechende Waffe schwingen konnten. Die meiste Zeit durchstreiften diese Dinosaurier jedoch die Wälder, vermutlich nicht in Herden, sondern eher als Einzelgänger, und suchten nach weicher pflanzlicher Nahrung (siehe Seiten 322–323).

**VORHERGEHENDE SEITE** *Gastonia* war ein Ankylosaurier aus der frühen Kreidezeit. Seine Fossilien stammen aus Grand County im US-Bundesstaat Utah. Sein stark gepanzerter Körper und die in Gruppen zusammenstehenden Dornen waren sicherlich eine wirksame Verteidigung. Der abgebildete Ankylosaurier ist ein Jungtier, dessen Rücken einem erwachsenen Menschen etwa bis zur Brust gereicht hätte. *Gastonia* war ein Verwandter des *Polacanthus* und wurde 1998 nach dem Paläontologen Robert Gaston benannt.

**LINKS** *Polacanthus* wendet einem Feind seine Vorderseite zu, deren große Hals- und Schulterdornen ausgezeichnete Verteidigungsmittel sind. Wo genau und in welchem Winkel die Dornen am Körper standen, ist unter den Wissenschaftlern umstritten.

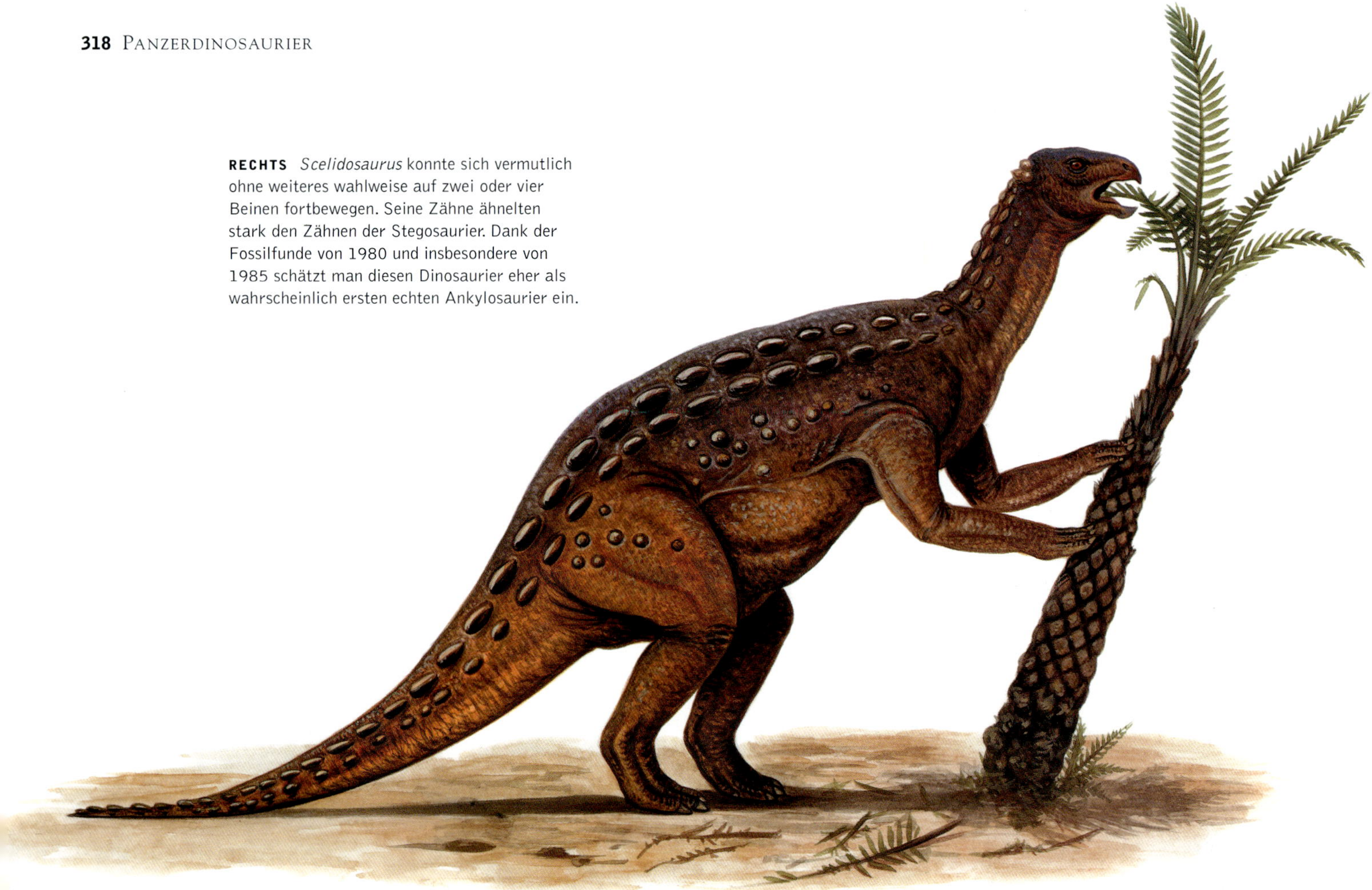

**RECHTS** *Scelidosaurus* konnte sich vermutlich ohne weiteres wahlweise auf zwei oder vier Beinen fortbewegen. Seine Zähne ähnelten stark den Zähnen der Stegosaurier. Dank der Fossilfunde von 1980 und insbesondere von 1985 schätzt man diesen Dinosaurier eher als wahrscheinlich ersten echten Ankylosaurier ein.

# SCELIDOSAURUS

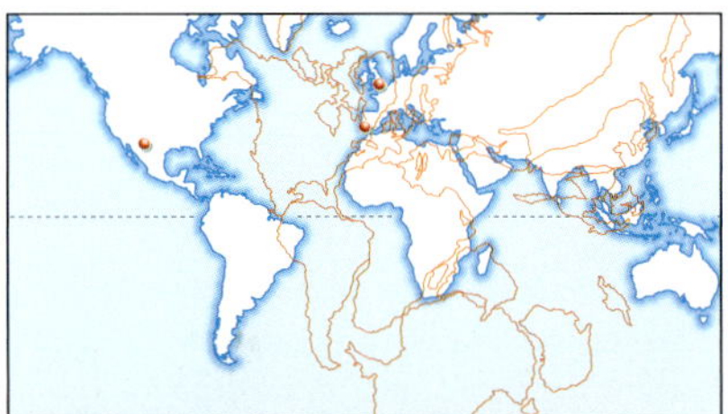

**ÜBERSICHT (DINOSAURIER)**
***Scelidosaurus***
**Bedeutung des Namens:** Gliederreptil
**Periode:** Unterer Jura
**Hauptgruppe:** Scelidosauria
**Länge:** 3 – 4 Meter
**Gewicht:** 200 – 250 Kilogramm
**Nahrung:** Pflanzen
**Fossilfundstätten:** In England, Portugal und den USA (Arizona)

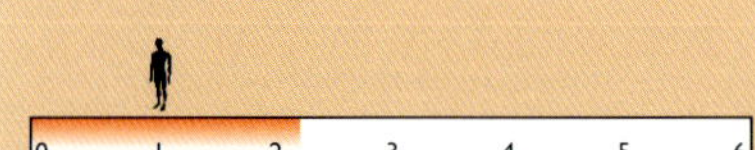


In der Entwicklungsgeschichte der Dinosaurier hatte *Scelidosaurus* möglicherweise eine zentrale Stellung inne; seine Klassifizierung bereitet zweifellos Probleme. Man ordnet ihn als Ornithischier und innerhalb dieser riesigen Gruppe als Thyreophoren oder Schildträger und bei diesen vielleicht als Ankylosaurier ein, doch dann scheiden sich die Geister. Manche Fachleute betrachten das Tier als einen frühen Ankylosauriertypen (weshalb *Scelidosaurus* in diesem Kapitel zu finden ist), bei anderen gilt er als Stegosaurier oder Vorgänger beider Gruppen; wieder andere behaupten, es handele sich um einen gesonderten Typus mit einer eigenen Familie, den Scelidosauriden, zu der vielleicht noch *Scutellosaurus* (siehe gegenüber) und *Emausaurus* gehören. Letzterer wurde 1990 nach Fossilfunden aus Deutschland benannt.

*Scelidosaurus* hatte einen kleinen Kopf, sein Mund war vorn hornig und schnabelartig geformt. Hals, Rumpf und Schwanz waren mit kleinen kieselsteinartigen Schuppen und mit größeren Knochenstücken bedeckt, von denen einige wie flache Kegel oder schmale Dreiecke aussahen. *Scelidosaurus* ging auf allen vieren. Seine hinteren Gliedmaßen waren länger und kräftiger als die vorderen. Alle diese Merkmale entwickelten sich zu einer späteren Zeit des Jura bei den Stegosauriern und prägten sich bei diesen Tieren sehr stark aus; dennoch wies *Scelidosaurus* auch charakteristische Zahn- und Schädelmerkmale auf, die ihn stärker mit den Ankylosauriern verbinden.

Der britische Anatom und Paläontologe Richard Owen benannte *Scelidosaurus* 1868. Owen hatte seit 1859 Fossilien von *Scelidosaurus* untersucht, die hauptsächlich aus unterjurassischen Gesteinen bei Charmouth an der Südküste Englands stammten. 1863 wurde ein ziemlich vollständiges Exemplar ausgegraben. 1985, mehr als ein Jahrhundert später, entdeckten die drei Amateur-Fossiliensucher Simon Barnsley, David Costain und Peter Langham ebenfalls in der Nähe von Charmouth Überreste eines Jungtiers. In der Zeit zwischen diesen beiden Funden stieß man auch im US-Bundesstaat Arizona und in Portugal auf *Scelidosaurus*-Überreste (ein Schädelstück ist auch unter der Bezeichnung *Lusitanosaurus* bekannt). Der Schwanz des *Scelidosaurus* war vermutlich sehr ziemlich starr, denn die entlang der Rückenwirbel liegenden Sehnen waren durch Knochenmineralien verfestigt.

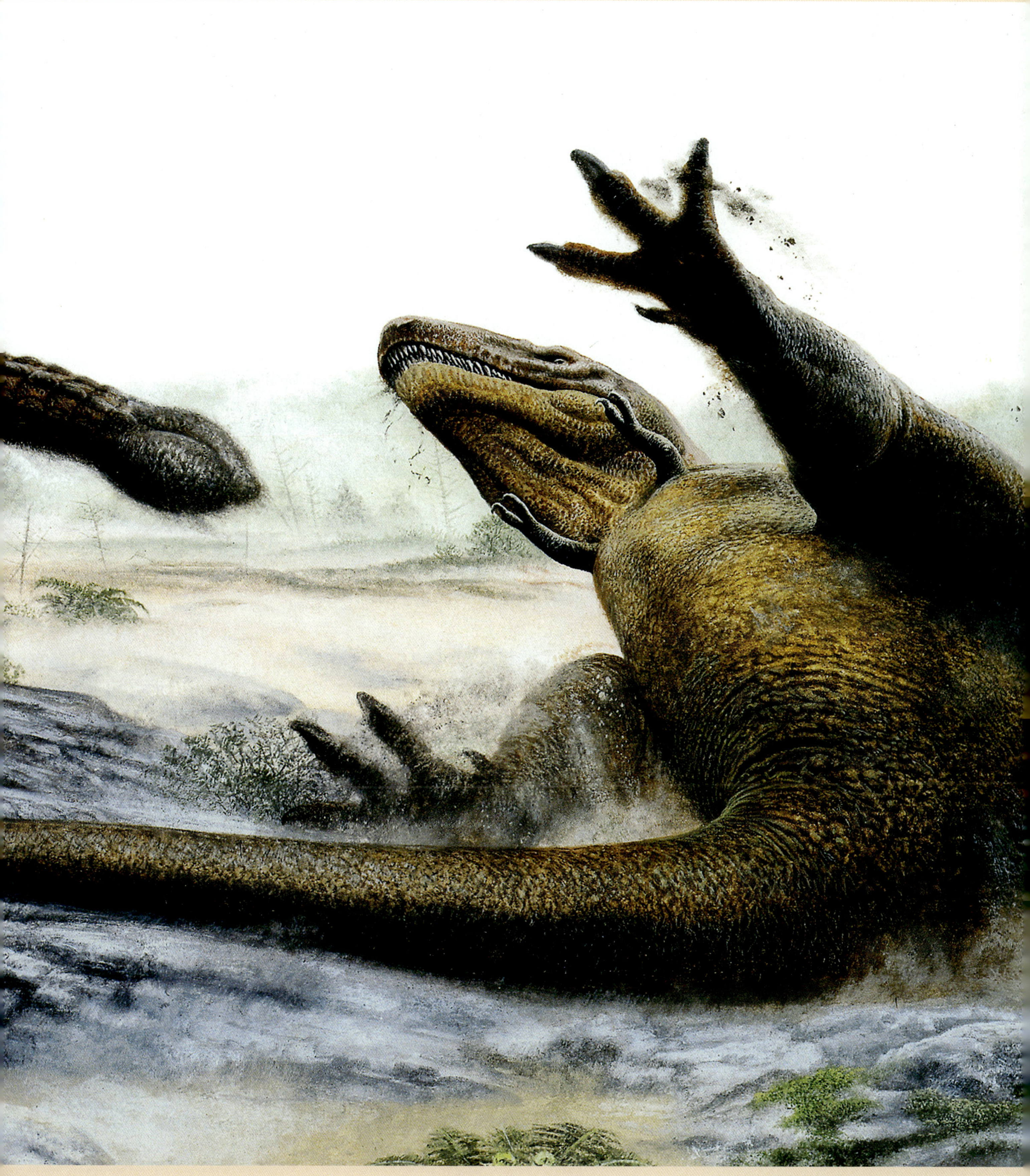

# ANKYLOSAURUS

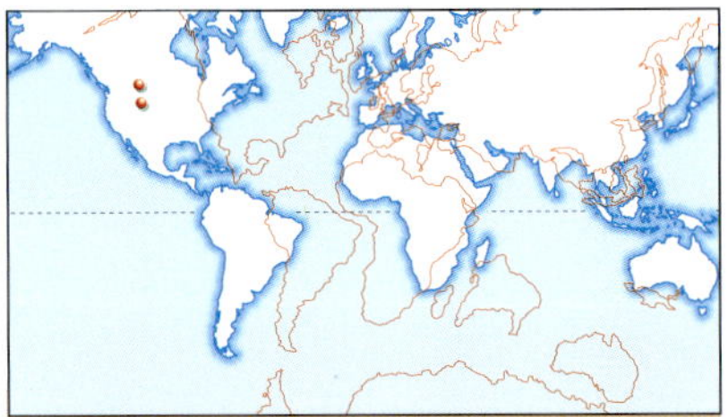

**ÜBERSICHT (DINOSAURIER)**
***Ankylosaurus***
**Bedeutung des Namens:** Starres Reptil
**Periode:** Oberkreide
**Hauptgruppe:** Ankylosauria
**Länge:** 7 – 10 Meter
**Gewicht:** 3 – 4 Tonnen
**Nahrung:** Pflanzen
**Fossilfundstätten:** In den USA (Montana), in Kanada (Alberta)

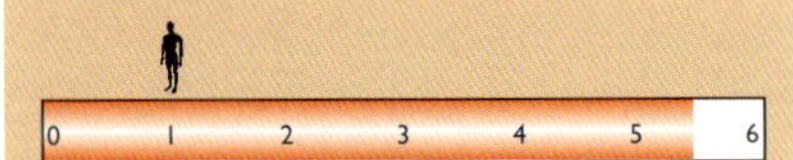


Die große Gruppe der gepanzerten Dinosaurier erhielt den Namen Ankylosaurier nach einem ihrer größten Vertreter. Innerhalb dieser Hauptgruppe existiert die Untergruppe der Ankylosauriden, deren Vertreter mehrere charakteristische Merkmale wie etwa Form und Aufbau des Schädels, die verschlungenen Bahnen der Luftkanäle im Schädelinnern und das große keulen- oder hammerartige Schwanzende aufweisen.

Nach *Ankylosaurus* wurde zwar eine ganze Gruppe aufgestellt und benannt, doch sind von dem Namen gebenden Tier bislang weniger Fossilien vorhanden als von ähnlichen Typen der Gruppe, beispielsweise von *Euoplocephalus*.

Seinen Namen verdankt *Ankylosaurus* dem amerikanischen Paläontologen Barnum Brown, der die Fossilien 1908 untersuchte und dabei die starre Wirbelsäule des Tiere bemerkte. Weitere Überreste wurden inzwischen im US-Bundesstaat Montana und in der kanadischen Provinz Alberta entdeckt. Darunter sind zwei Schädel, Teile einer Vordergliedmaße, verschiedene Wirbel von Hals, Rumpf und Schwanz, stark gebogene Rippen, Hautverknöcherungen, einzelne Zähne und natürlich die berühmte Schwanzkeule.

*Ankylosaurus* war einer der letzten Ankylosaurier und gehörte zu den letzten Dinosauriern überhaupt, denn er lebte vor weniger als 70 Millionen Jahren. Er war nicht nur lang, sondern auch fast zwei Meter breit. Stehend erreichte das Tier lediglich eine Höhe von 1,2 Metern. Seine große Körpermasse wurde von vier kurzen, stämmigen Beinen getragen, deren hinteres Paar etwas länger als das vordere war. Der breite, schwere Kopf wurde von einem kurzen, kräftigen Hals gehalten. Der Schwanz war lang, aber schmal. Die in die Haut eingebetteten Knochenplatten, die beiden Dornenreihen zu beiden Seiten des Körpers, die größeren hornartigen Stacheln am Hals und die hammerartige Schwanzkeule dienten vermutlich der Verteidung. (Die möglichen Zwecke der Schwanzkeule und die Verhaltensmuster der Ankylosaurier werden auf den folgenden Seiten erörtert.) Ein großer, langsamer Pflanzenfresser, der vor weniger als 70 Millionen Jahren in Nordamerika lebte, musste sich gut verteidigen können, denn dort existierten außer ihm auch große Raubdinosaurier wie *Albertosaurus* und *Tyrannosaurus*. Es ist denkbar, dass bei *Ankylosaurus* sogar die Augenlider geschützt waren.

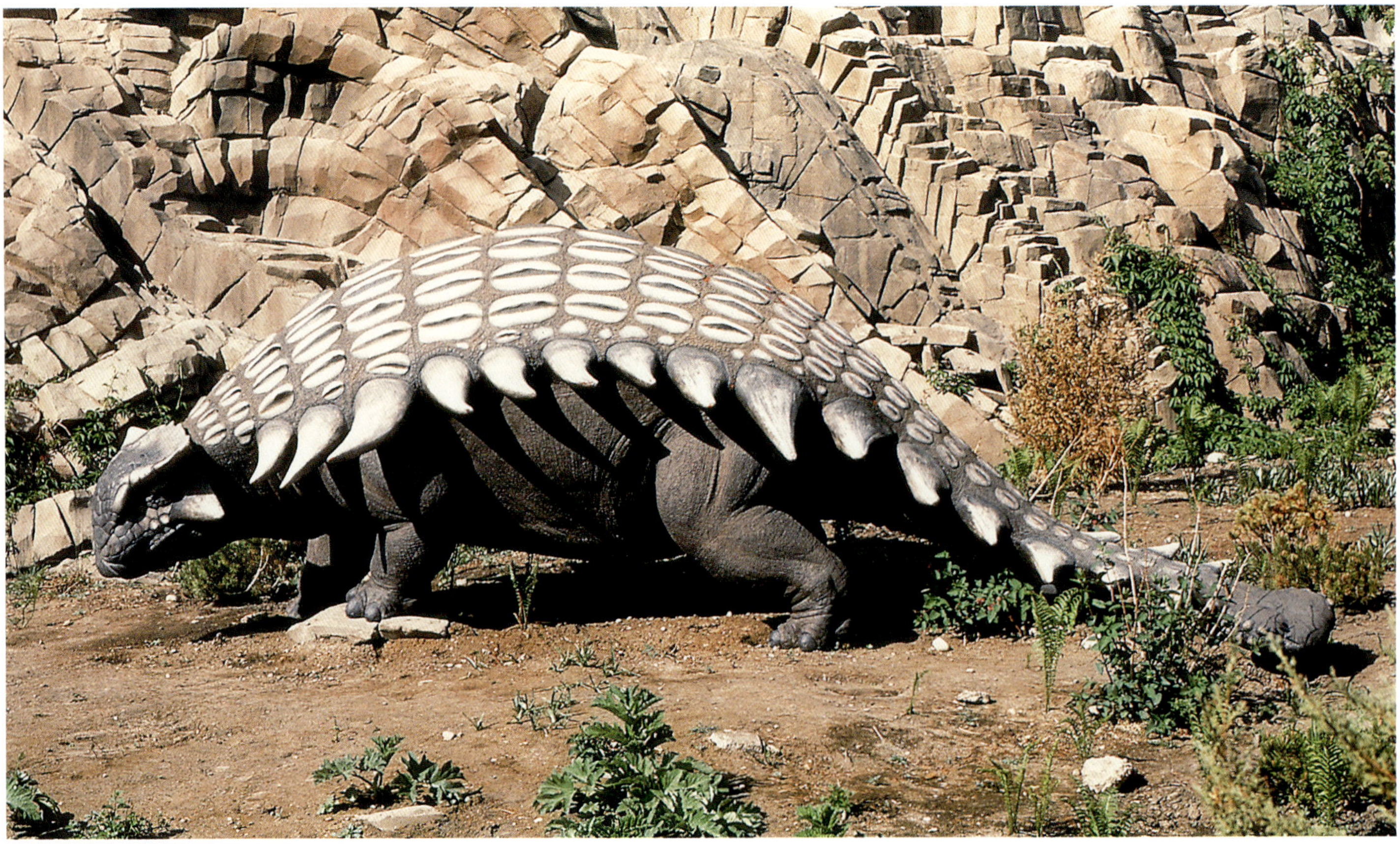

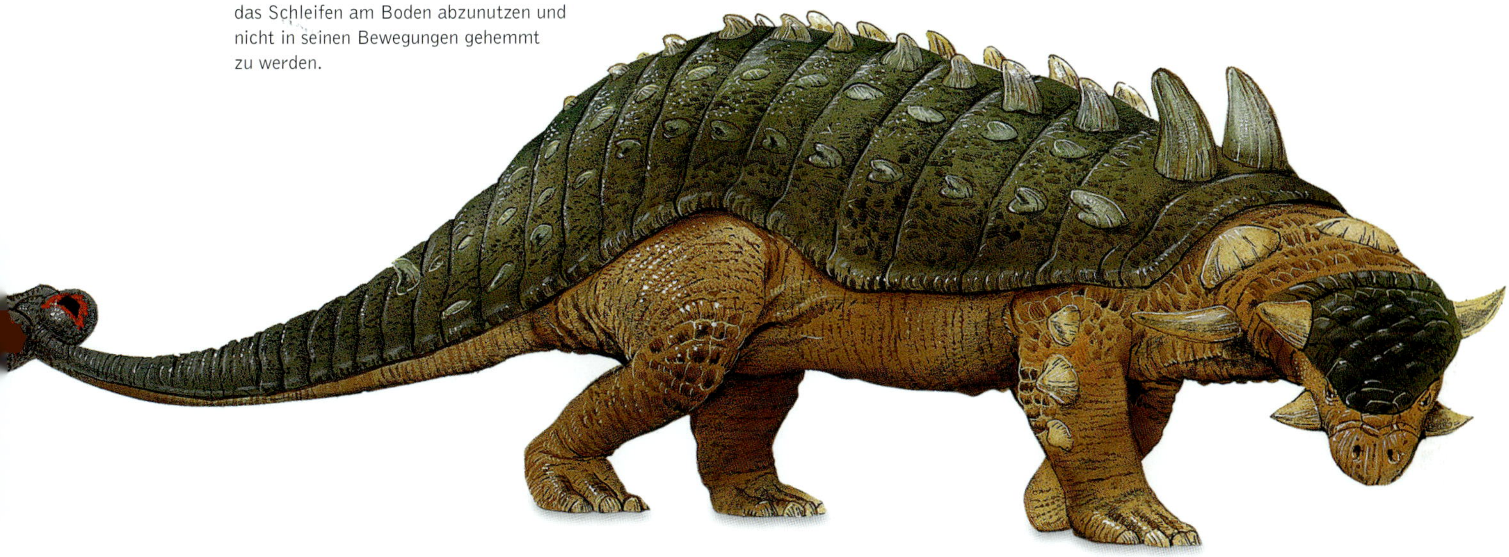

**RECHTS** *Euoplocephalus* trug seine schwere Schwanzkeule möglicherweise leicht angehoben, um sie nicht durch das Schleifen am Boden abzunutzen und nicht in seinen Bewegungen gehemmt zu werden.

# EUOPLOCEPHALUS

Die für einen Ankylosaurier ungewöhnlich zahlreichen Fossilien des *Euoplocephalus* deuten darauf hin, dass diese Gattung zu den individuenreicheren Gruppen gehörte. *Euoplocephalus* lebte in der späten Kreidezeit, vor rund 70 Millionen Jahren, in Nordamerika. Er besaß einen so guten Körperschutz, dass selbst seine Augenlider knöcherne Verstärkungen aufwiesen und wie ein Visier auf- und zuklappten. Über den Schädel verteilt saßen durch Knochen verdickte Schuppen, und hinter dem Schädel wuchsen kleine „Hörner" empor – eines der Merkmale, das die Ankylosauriden von den Nodosauriden unterscheidet. Auf dem Hals saßen flache, auf den Schultern höhere Knochenhöcker, über den Rücken wölbten sich von einer Seite zur anderen quer laufende Bänder mit weiteren Höckern. Die Beine waren stämmig und muskulös, die Füße endeten in jeweils drei kurzen, breiten Zehen mit hufartigen Nägeln. Mit seinem breiten Schnabel weidete *Euoplocephalus* Pflanzen ab. Er besaß wie andere Panzerdinosaurier stiftartige Zähne, die klein und schwach gewesen zu sein scheinen, so dass die Nahrung wohl hauptsächlich im Magen zerkleinert und dann verdaut wurde. Zu beiden Seiten des Schwanzendes saßen zwei riesige Knochenstücke und dahinter ein Paar kleinerer knöcherner Buckel. Da der Schwanz vom Ende bis weit über die halbe Länge starr war, musste die Bewegung an der Basis erfolgen, wenn *Euoplocephalus* zum Schlag gegen die Beine eines Angreifers, beispielsweise eines Tyrannosauriers, ausholte.

Die Fossilien von mehr als vierzig Vertretern der Gattung *Euoplocephalus*, darunter fünfzehn Schädel – mehr als von jedem anderen Ankylosaurier –, wurden in der kanadischen Provinz Alberta und im US-Bundesstaat Montana gefunden. Lawrence Lambe benannte den Dinosaurier 1910. Inzwischen hat man *Scolosaurus* und *Dyoplosaurus* sowie mehrere andere kaum bekannte Ankylosauriden neu als *Euoplocephalus* eingeordnet, da die Ergebnisse erneuter Untersuchungen ihren Status als gesonderte Gattungen nicht rechtfertigten. Gegenwärtig gibt es innerhalb der Gattung nur eine anerkannte Spezies, die ursprünglich so benannte Art *Euoplocephalus tutus*.

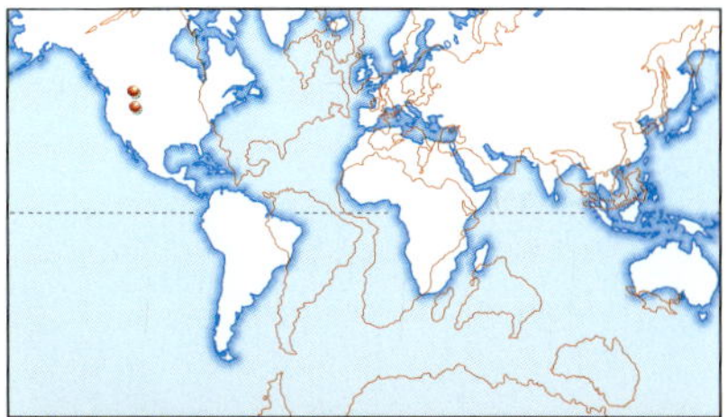

**ÜBERSICHT (DINOSAURIER)**
***Euoplocephalus***
**Bedeutung des Namens:** Gut gepanzerter Kopf
**Periode:** Oberkreide
**Hauptgruppe:** Ankylosauria
**Länge:** 6–7 Meter
**Gewicht:** 2 Tonnen
**Nahrung:** Pflanzen
**Fossilfundstätten:** In Kanada (Alberta), in den USA (Montana)

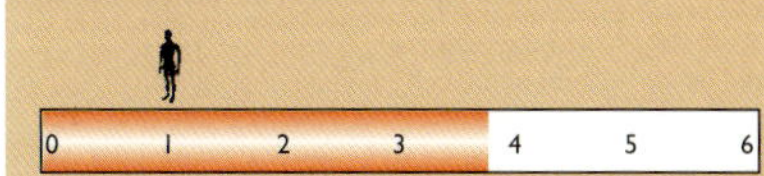

# PINACOSAURUS

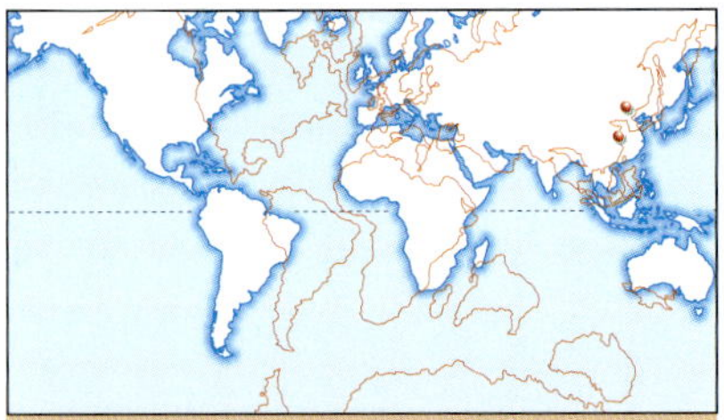

**ÜBERSICHT (DINOSAURIER)**
***Pinacosaurus***
**Bedeutung des Namens:** Tafelreptil
**Periode:** Oberkreide
**Hauptgruppe:** Ankylosauria
**Länge:** 5,5 Meter
**Gewicht:** 1–2 Tonnen
**Nahrung:** Pflanzen
**Fossilfundstätten:** In der Mongolei, in China

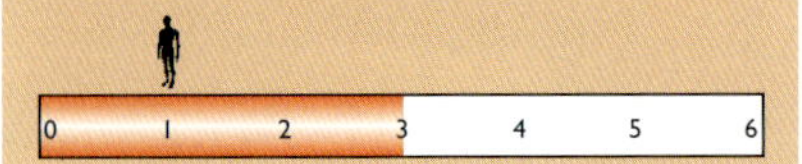


Fossilien dieses Ankylosauriden sind an mehreren Orten in China und in der Mongolei gefunden worden. Es gibt inzwischen Überreste von mehreren Individuen unterschiedlicher Altersstufen und Größen. Seit 1988 hat man aus Knochenschichten zwei große Fossilfunde mit Überresten vieler Vertreter der Gattung *Pinacosaurus* zutage gefördert. Die eine Gruppe enthält Relikte von rund zwölf, die andere von über zwanzig meist jungen Tieren, die die Natur zusammen konserviert hat. Die wissenschaftliche Geschichte von *Pinacosaurus* reicht jedoch bis in die 1920er Jahre zurück. Damals wurden in der Wüste Gobi erstmals Überreste dieser Gattung ausgegraben. Die Expeditionen in die Wüste leitete damals der legendäre Fossiliensucher und Direktor des American Museum of Natural History, Roy Chapman Andrews. Im Verlauf der Gobi-Expeditionen wurden auch viele andere Dinosaurier wie etwa *Protoceratops* und *Oviraptor* samt Eiern sowie der Fleischfresser *Velociraptor* entdeckt. *Pinacosaurus* wurde 1933 von Charles Whitney Gilmore benannt. Der früher als *Syrmosaurus* bekannte Dinosaurier gilt heute als Vertreter der Gattung *Pinacosaurus*.

*Pinacosaurus* besaß zwar einen Körperschutz, war aber wohl nicht so schwer gepanzert wie andere Ankylosaurier. Auf dem Rücken und dem mit einer Keule bewehrten Schwanz saßen knöcherne Spitzen, das vordere Kopfende trug keine Panzerung. Das Rumpfskelett war stämmig, doch nicht besonders massiv, die Beine waren im Vergleich zu den Gliedmaßen anderer Panzerdinosaurier schlank. Die Vorderfüße endeten in fünf, die hinteren in vier Zehen, die stumpfe, an Hufe oder Nägel erinnernde Krallen trugen. Die Entdeckung des Massengrabes vorwiegend junger Vertreter der Gattung *Pinacosaurus* hat einige Fachleuten zu der Auffassung gebracht, Ankylosaurier könnten als Jungtiere in Gruppen gelebt und später, als ausgewachsene Tiere, den Verband verlassen und als Einzelgänger existiert haben (siehe Seite 322).

**UNTEN** Für einen Ankylosaurier war *Pinacosaurus* verhältnismäßig schlank und langbeinig. Er gehörte darüber hinaus zu den kleineren Typen (noch kleiner war *Minmi*). Zu Lebzeiten war er etwa so groß wie ein mittelgroßes Nashorn, trug im Unterschied zu diesem seine wichtigste Verteidigungswaffe aber am Schwanzende und nicht am Kopf.

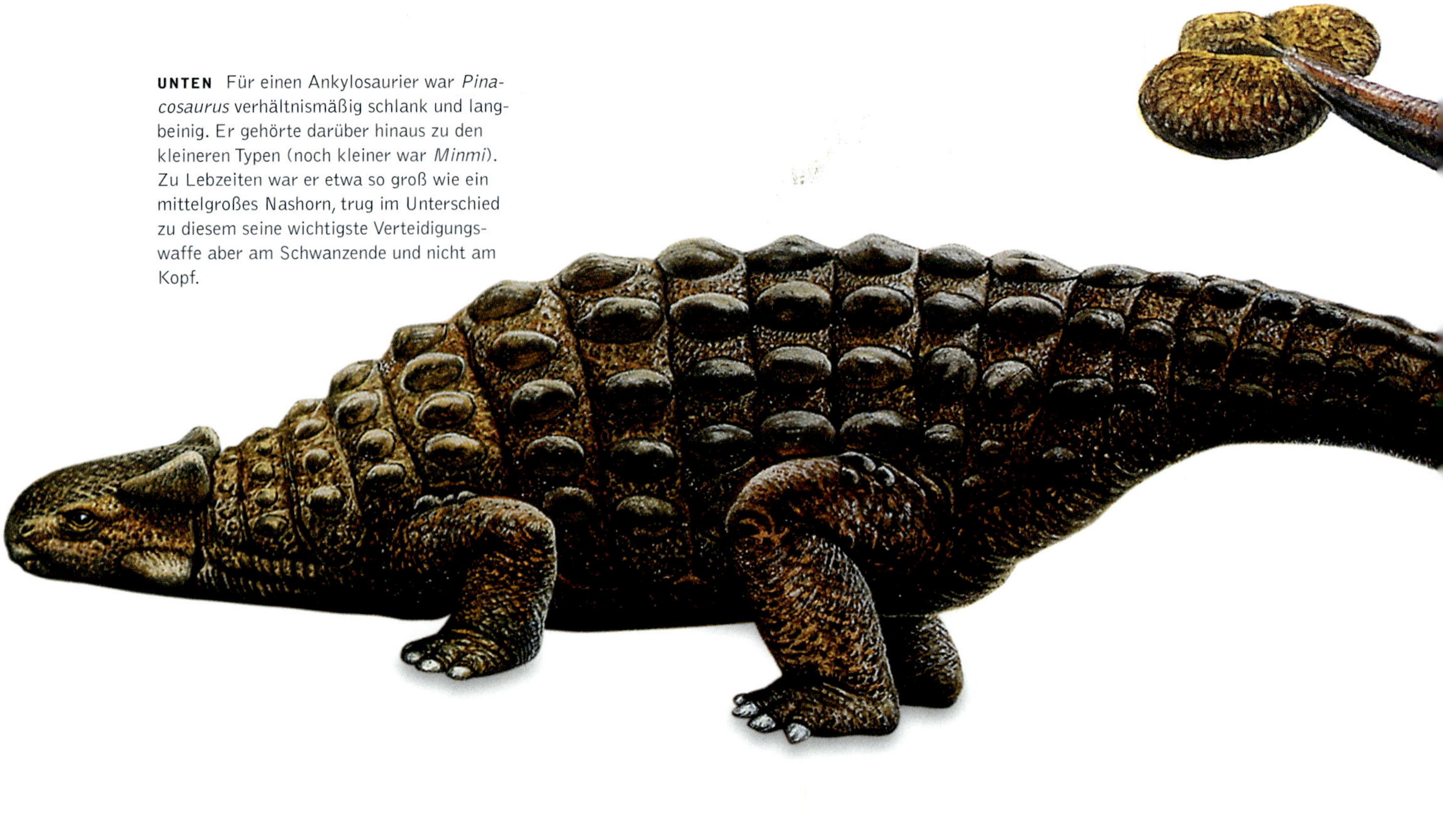

# SAICHANIA

*Saichania* besaß einen breiten, stumpfen Kopf, trug auf Schnauze und Stirn Knochenplatten, an der hinteren oberen Schädelecke ragten Hörner auf, am Hals sowie an den Seiten und auf dem Rücken saßen flache kegelförmige Dornen. Es mag vielleicht schwer zu verstehen sein, weshalb dieses Tier einen Namen trägt, der im Mongolischen „Schöne" bedeutet, doch dieser hängt wohl eher mit dem Erhaltungszustand einiger Fossilien zusammen, deren Details uns faszinierende Einblicke in den allgemeinen Aufbau der Ankylosauriden bieten. Die Ankylosauriden unterscheiden sich von den verwandten Nodosauriden in vielen Punkten, von denen einer der gewundene Verlauf der Atemwege im Innern des Schädels ist. Die Atemwege bei *Saichania* sind noch komplizierter angelegt, was Grund zu Vermutungen gibt, die Tiere hätten so die heiße, trockene Luft der Umgebung anfeuchten und abkühlen können, ehe sie in die Lungen gelangte; auch seien die Atemwege mit einem ungewöhnlichen Geruchssinn oder mit Drüsen verbunden gewesen, die überschüssiges Salz aus dem Körper ausschieden, so wie es bei manchen rezenten Reptilien und Vögeln der Fall ist. *Saichania* mag unter den Ankylosauriern insofern eine ungewöhnliche Erscheinung gewesen sein, als die Bauchseite des Tieres ebenfalls mit Knochenplatten gepanzert war (siehe auch Seite 326, *Minmi*). Die Körperlänge von *Saichania* betrug sieben Meter, was für die Gruppe ein Durchschnittswert ist.

Ein wichtiger *Saichania*-Fund wurde in Chulsan gemacht. Er besteht aus dem Kopf und dem Vorderteil des Körpers in seiner natürlichen Anordnung, d. h. die Teile waren nicht vereinzelt oder durcheinander gebracht wie bei so vielen Fossilfunden von Dinosauriern, sondern lagen so nebeneinander wie zu Lebzeiten des Tieres. Die Überreste wurden 1971 von Mitgliedern einer polnisch-mongolischen Gobi-Expedition ausgegraben und 1977 von der polnischen Paläontologin Teresa Maryańska benannt. Unter den entdeckten Fossilien befanden sich auch zwei fast vollständige Schädel und zahlreiche gesonderte Stücke der Panzerung. (Das Verhalten der Ankylosauriden sowie die Art und Benutzung der Schwanzkeule wird in verschiedenen Beiträgen dieses Kapitels erörtert.)

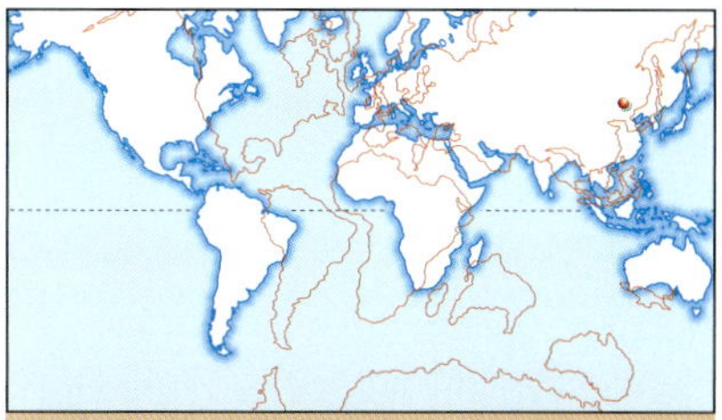

**ÜBERSICHT (DINOSAURIER)**
***Saichania***
**Bedeutung des Namens:** Schöne (aus dem Mongolischen)
**Periode:** Oberkreide
**Hauptgruppe:** Ankylosauria
**Länge:** 7 Meter
**Gewicht:** 2 – 3 Tonnen
**Nahrung:** Pflanzen
**Fossilfundstätten:** In der Mongolei

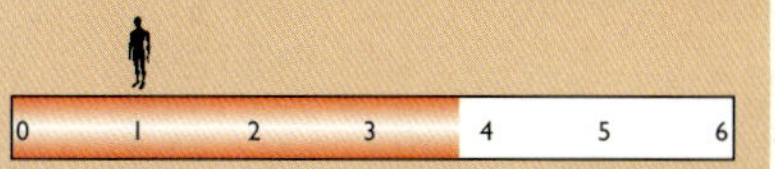


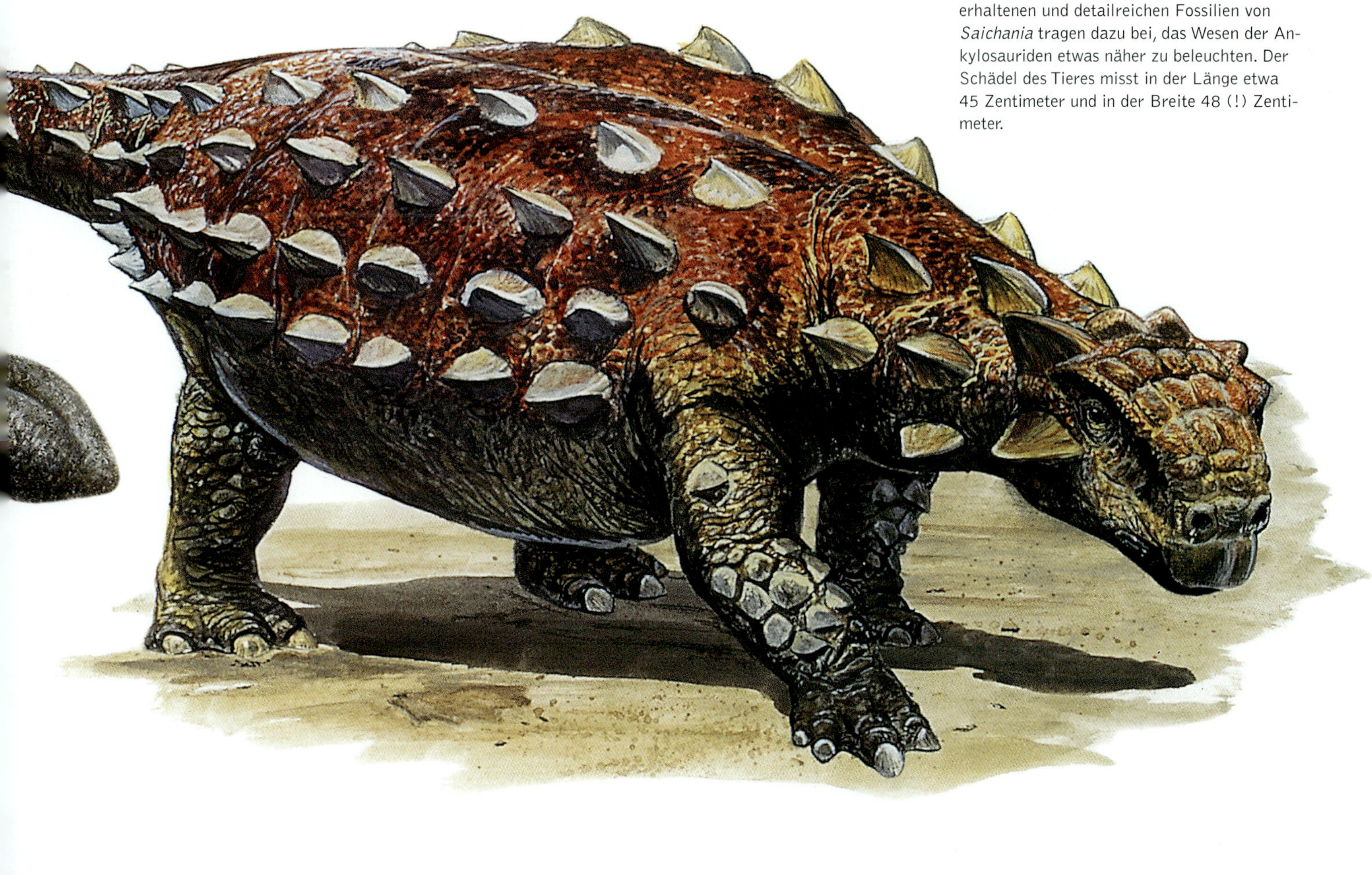

**LINKS** Das Tier mag vielleicht nicht gerade eine Schönheit gewesen sein, doch die gut erhaltenen und detailreichen Fossilien von *Saichania* tragen dazu bei, das Wesen der Ankylosauriden etwas näher zu beleuchten. Der Schädel des Tieres misst in der Länge etwa 45 Zentimeter und in der Breite 48 (!) Zentimeter.

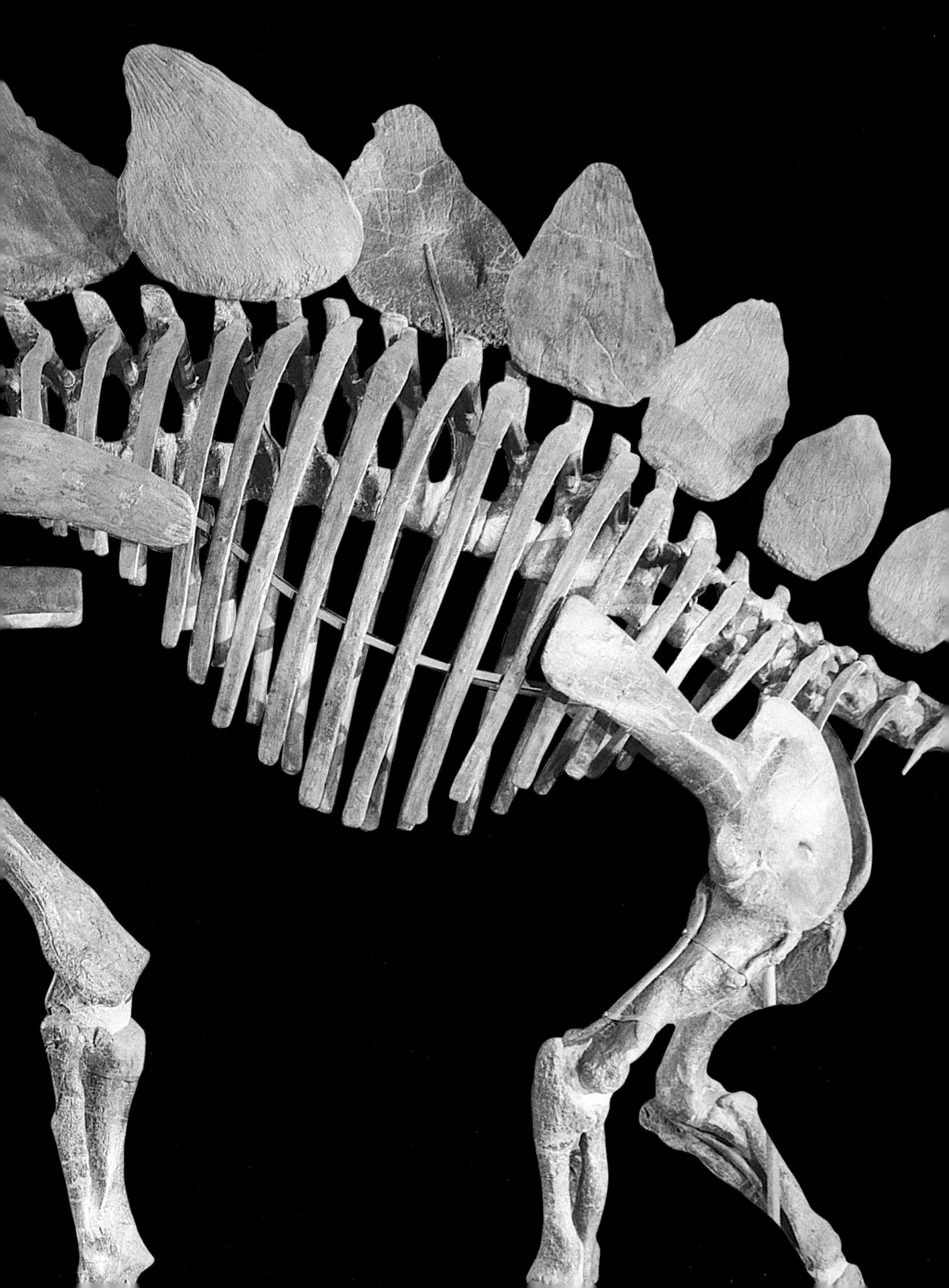

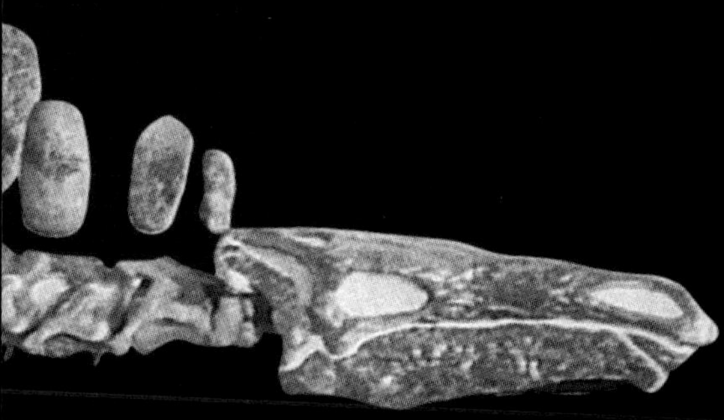

## Kapitel Zwölf

# Stachel-dinosaurier

*Die Stegosaurier sind für ihr kleines Hirn und ihre vermeintliche Dummheit berühmt; sie konnten sich dennoch Dutzende Millionen Jahre lang durchsetzen.*

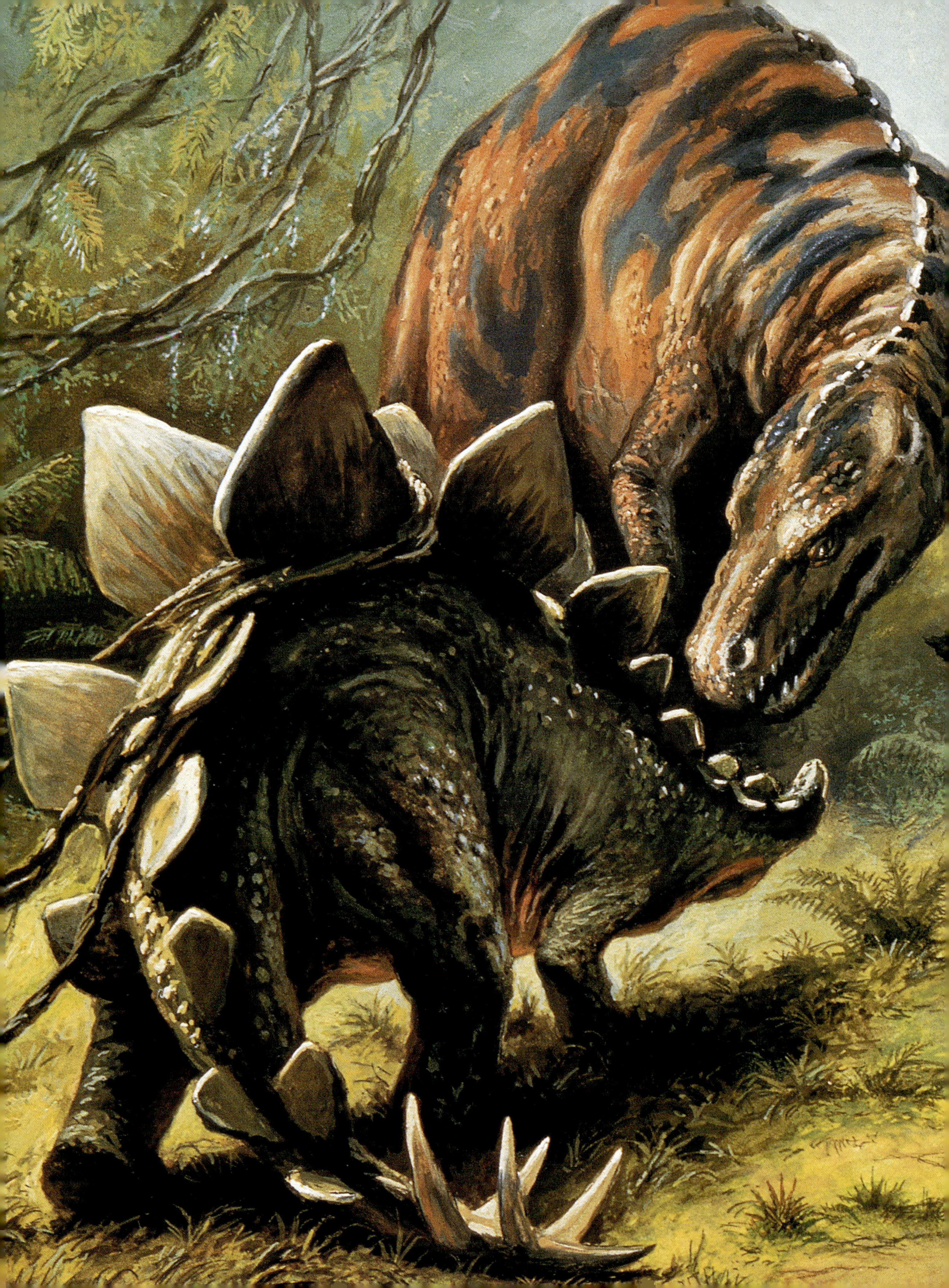

# STACHELN UND PLATTEN

***Die hohen Knochenplatten auf dem Rücken der Stegosaurier sind für die Paläontologen lange Zeit ein Rätsel gewesen. Die höchsten und breitesten Platten besaß Stegosaurus selbst, und jedes dieser Gebilde war dünner als der Arm eines Menschen. Die Platten waren vermutlich vertikal in zwei Reihen und versetzt angeordnet, so dass eine Platte in der einen Reihe sich mit zwei Platten der Reihe daneben überschnitt. Die größeren Platten saßen zwischen Hals und Becken, zur Schwanzspitze hin wurden sie wieder kleiner. Dieses Muster zeigen zumindest die meisten Nachbildungen. Trotz neuerer interessanter Funde (siehe Seite 340, „Spike") stimmen dieser Darstellung nicht alle Fachleute zu. Der Meinungsstreit über Position und Funktion der Platten hält seit den 1870er Jahren an.***

## SCHÜTZENDE PLATTEN

Boten die Platten der Stegosaurier ihren Besitzern körperlichen Schutz? Das ist unwahrscheinlich, da es sich nicht um massive, sondern um wabenartig aufgebaute Gebilde handelte, die viele Hohlräume aufwiesen und verhältnismäßig zerbrechlich waren. Außerdem standen sie wahrscheinlich aufgerichtet und lagen nicht flach am Körper. Dienten sie hauptsächlich der Tarnung inmitten der Bäume und der Umgebung? Auch das scheint ausgeschlossen, denn es mutet seltsam an, dass die Gebilde sich zu derartiger Größe entwickelt haben sollten, wenn ihre wichtigste Funktion darin bestand, ihren Besitzer äußerlich unauffällig zu machen. Allerdings könnte nebenbei auch die Tarnung eine Rolle gespielt haben. Hatten die Platten vielleicht irgendeine optische Funktion? Sie könnten leuchtend bunt gefärbt und gemustert gewesen sein, möglicherweise geschlechts-, alters- und artspezifisch, sodass sie sich bei männlichen und weiblichen, ausgewachsenen und jungen Tieren und selbst bei den einzelnen Spezies, die sich ansonsten stark ähnelten, unterschieden. Auch die Färbung bestimmter Echsen und anderer Reptilien der Jetztzeit ändert sich mit dem Wachstum und der Reife sowie abhängig vom Geschlecht und der Paarungsbereitschaft.

## TEMPERATUR

Eine in breiten Kreisen anerkannte Theorie geht davon aus, dass die Platten bei *Stegosaurus* zur Regelung der Körpertemperatur dienten. Stegosaurier und die meisten anderen Dinosaurier waren vermutlich wechselwarme, oder um einen präziseren Begriff zu verwenden, ektotherme Tiere. Sie nahmen Wärme aus ihrer Umgebung auf, statt sie wie warmblütige Lebewesen – hauptsächlich die Vögel und Säugetiere der Jetztzeit – im Innern ihres Körpers selbst zu produzieren. Wärme war etwas Wichtiges, denn wenn die Körpertemperatur eines Reptils steigt, kann das Tier sich bis zu einem gewissen Grad schneller bewegen, sich besser ernähren und rascher Gefahren ausweichen. Die Platten des *Stegosaurus* funktionierten möglicherweise als umkehrbare Wärmetauscher, ähnlich wie das „Segel" auf dem Rücken von *Spinosaurus*, *Ouranosaurus* und anderen Dinosauriern sowie bei Reptilien wie *Dimetrodon* (alle in diesem Buch).

## WARM UND KALT

Nach der erwähnten Theorie stellte sich *Stegosaurus* bei Sonnenaufgang so auf, dass seine Rückenplatten den wärmenden Strahlen die größtmögliche Fläche boten; die Sonne erwärmte das Blut, das durch die Hohlräume der Platten und von dort wieder in den Körper floss. Auf diese Weise wurde der Dinosaurier natürlich schneller warm, als es ihm ohne seine Platten möglich gewesen wäre. Die versetzte Anordnung der Gebilde scheint zu dieser Vorstellung zu passen, da dank der Lücken auch die Platten der anderen Reihe den Sonnenstrahlen ausgesetzt waren. Erwärmte sich *Stegosaurus* zu stark, konnte er eine schattige Stelle aufsuchen und sich im rechten Winkel zur Windrichtung aufstellen, so dass durch die Brise Körperwärme abgeführt und eine größtmögliche Kühlwirkung erzielt wurde. Die Vorstellung von der Temperaturregelung durch wechselweises Aufheizen und Abkühlen scheint auf *Stegosaurus* mit seinen breiten blattförmigen Platten zu passen. Sie überzeugt allerdings viel weniger bei anderen Stegosauriern, deren eher spitze, dornartige Auswüchse eine viel kleinere Oberfläche besaßen (siehe Seiten 341 und 346).

**VORHERGEHENDE SEITE** An diesem rekonstruierten Skelett eines Stegosauriers ist die winzige Größe des Schädels und die Anordnung der Platten auf dem Rücken zu erkennen; die Platten waren nicht mit dem Skelett verbunden.

**LINKS** Mit einigen seitlichen Schlägen seines Stachelschwanzes kann dieser Stegosaurier seinen Angreifer schwer verwunden. Die Rückenplatten des Pflanzenfressers hatten vermutlich keine Schutzfunktion, denn sie mussten bei ihrem leichten Bau sehr empfindlich sein.

# STEGOSAURUS

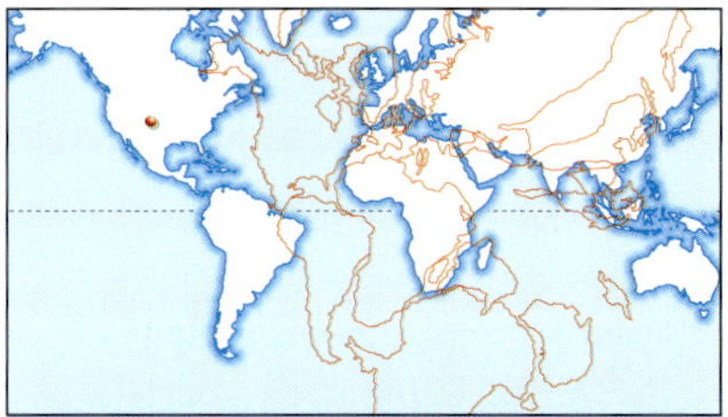

**ÜBERSICHT (DINOSAURIER)**

***Stegosaurus***

**Bedeutung des Namens:** Dachreptil, Dachziegelreptil

**Periode:** Oberer Jura

**Hauptgruppe:** Stegosauridae

**Länge:** 8–9 Meter

**Gewicht:** 2–3 Tonnen

**Nahrung:** Pflanzen

**Fossilfundstätten:** In den USA (Colorado)

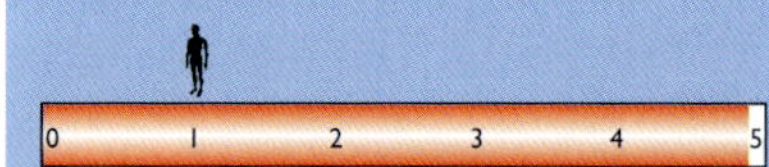


Nach *Stegosaurus* ist eine große Gruppe von Dinoauriern mit unverwechselbarem Aussehen aufgestellt und benannt worden – ihre Vertreter trugen auf dem Rücken hohe Platten und Stacheln. Diese Tiere sind wegen ihres verhältnismäßig kleinen Hirns auch als die „Trottel" unter den Dinosauriern berühmt geworden. Um diese Dinge wird es auch an anderen Stellen in diesem Kapitel gehen. *Stegosaurus* wurde 1877 von Othniel Charles Marsh benannt. Seit dieser Zeit sind von verschiedenen Orten im Westen der USA immer wieder Funde von *Stegosaurus*-Fossilien und von vielen anderen Stellen der Erde Funde von Überresten naher Verwandter dieses Dinosauriers gemeldet worden. 1992 entdeckte man in der Nähe von Canyon City im US-Bundesstaat Colorado (woher auch der erste Fund stammte) ein gut erhaltenes und fast vollständiges *Stegosaurus*-Skelett, das die Anordnung der siebzehn Rückenplatten in größeren Einzelheiten zeigte und später den Namen „Spike" erhielt.

*Stegosaurus* war der größte bekannte Vertreter der Gruppe und mit neun Metern so lang wie ein Elefant mit gerade ausgestrecktem Rüssel und Schwanz. *Stegosaurus* war vielleicht etwas leichter als ein Elefant von heute und besaß vier lange Schwanzstacheln.

*Stegosaurus* lebte während der Blütezeit der Gruppe, im Oberen Jura, vor 150–144 Millionen Jahren. Seine Rückenplatten – dünne Dreiecke, deren obere Spitze 75 Zentimeter über den Rücken hinausragte – besaßen eine riesige Grundfläche. Bei den ersten Nachbildungen lagen die Platten wie Dachziegel auf einem Dach flach auf dem Rücken (daher der Name der Gruppe), bei späteren Versionen standen sie aufgerichtet in zwei Reihen, immer zwei Platten einander gegenüber. Neuere Rekonstruktionen zeigen die Platten um eine halbe Breite gegeneinander versetzt. Hinsichtlich der möglichen Funktion der Knochenplatten hat man schon mindestens zehn Theorien aufgestellt, favorisiert wird die Theorie der Temperaturregelung (siehe Seite 339).

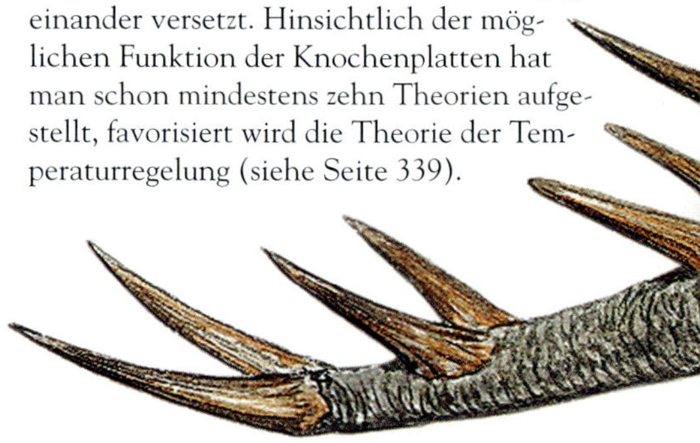

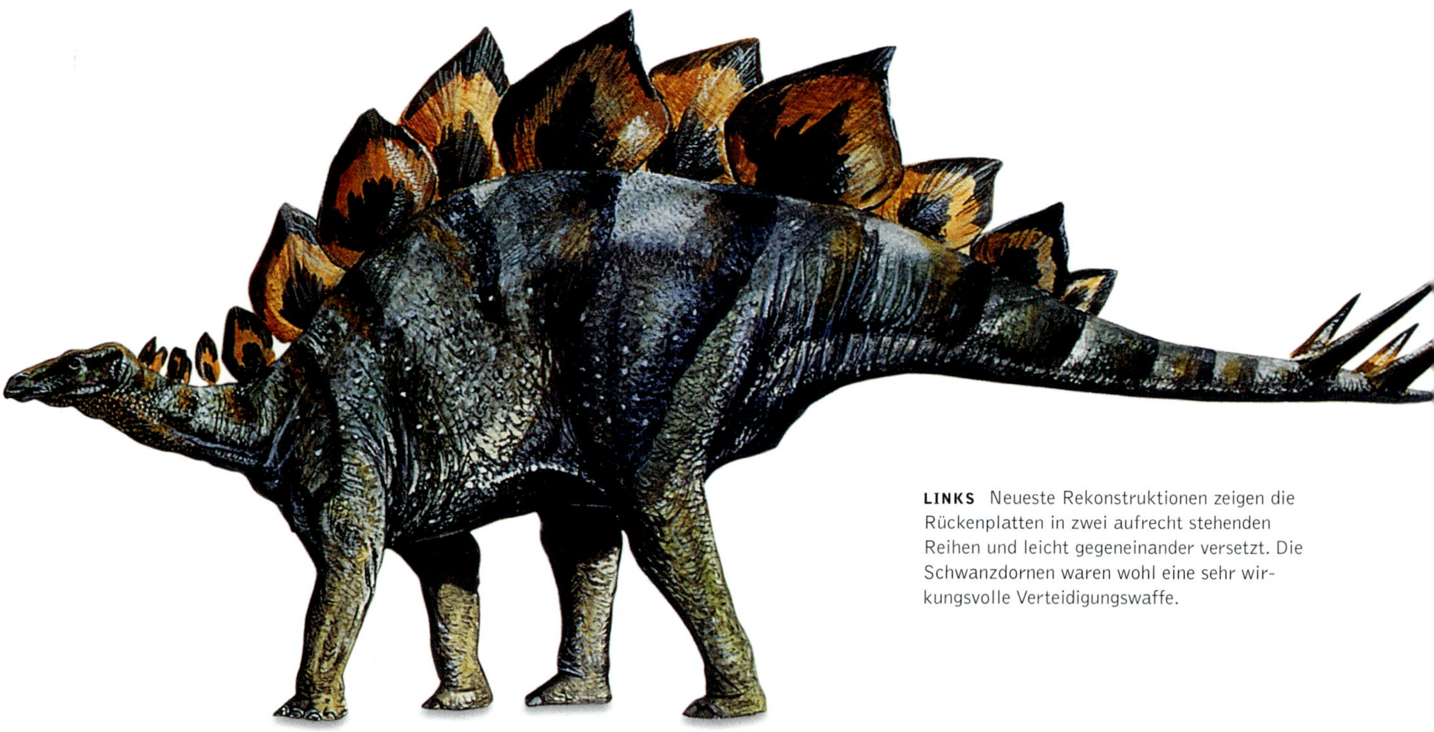

**LINKS** Neueste Rekonstruktionen zeigen die Rückenplatten in zwei aufrecht stehenden Reihen und leicht gegeneinander versetzt. Die Schwanzdornen waren wohl eine sehr wirkungsvolle Verteidigungswaffe.

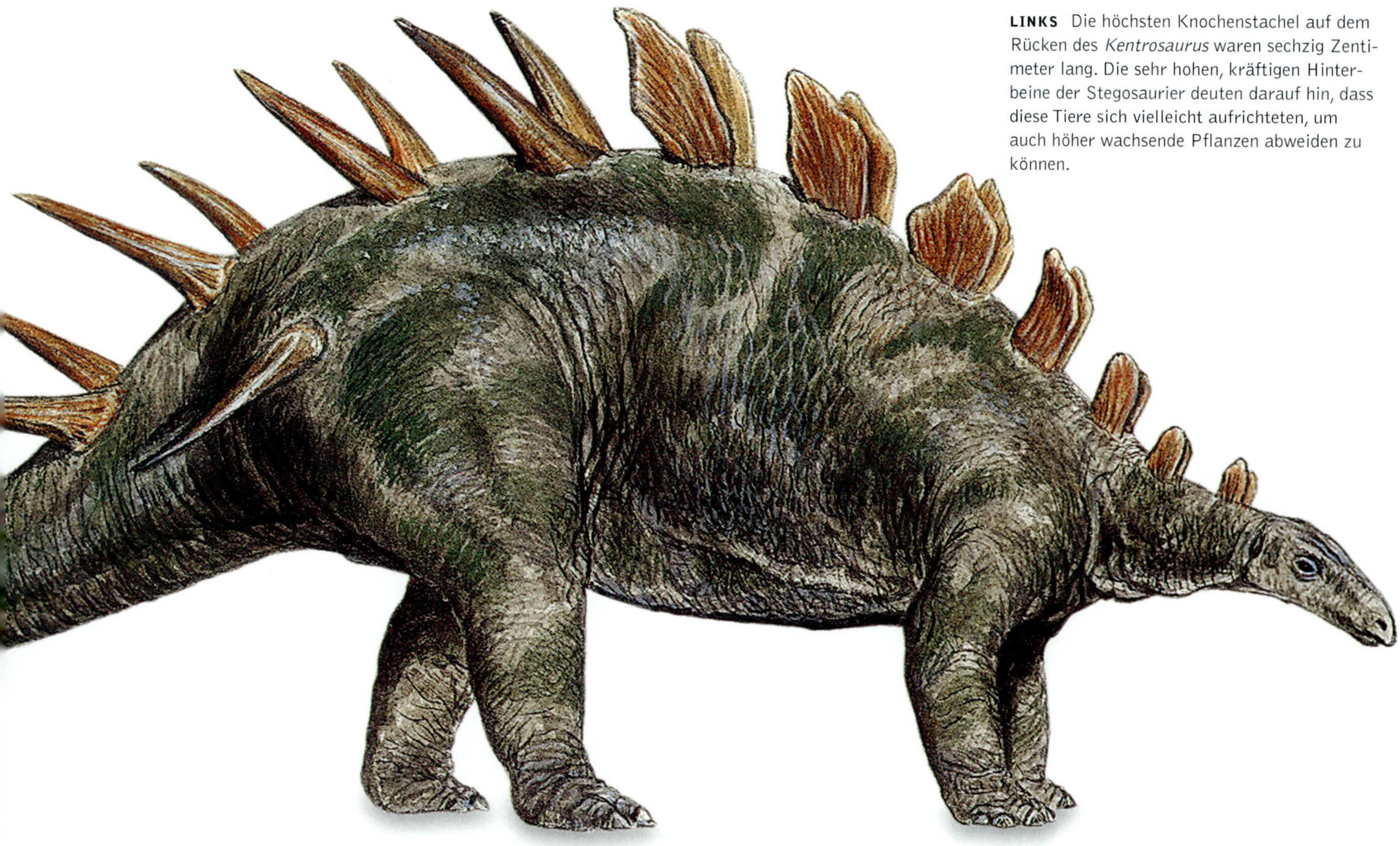

**LINKS** Die höchsten Knochenstachel auf dem Rücken des *Kentrosaurus* waren sechzig Zentimeter lang. Die sehr hohen, kräftigen Hinterbeine der Stegosaurier deuten darauf hin, dass diese Tiere sich vielleicht aufrichteten, um auch höher wachsende Pflanzen abweiden zu können.

# KENTROSAURUS

*Kentrosaurus* wird oft als das afrikanische Pendant des nordamerikanischen *Stegosaurus* betrachtet. Er lebte wie dieser im Oberen Jura, vor rund 155–144 Millionen Jahren. In gewisser Hinsicht ähnelt er jedoch dem *Tuojiangosaurus* aus Ostasien (siehe Seite 343). Die meisten Fossilien des *Kentrosaurus* wurden während der großen Tendaguru-Expeditionen der Jahre 1908–1912 ausgegraben. Diese Expeditionen standen unter deutscher Leitung und führten in die Steinbrüche und Hügel der Region Mtwara des damaligen Deutsch-Ostafrika (später Tanganjika, heute der größere Teil Tansanias). Bei den mühsamen Grabungsarbeiten wurden zahlreiche interessante Entdeckungen gemacht (siehe beispielsweise Seite 232, *Brachiosaurus*). *Kentrosaurus* wurde 1915 von dem deutschen Paläontologen Edwin Hennig benannt. Viele Fossilien des *Kentrosaurus*, die damals im Museum für Naturkunde der Humboldt-Universität Berlin lagerten, hätten uns sicherlich weiteres wertvolles Wissen vermitteln können, doch sie wurden während der Bombenangriffe im Zweiten Weltkrieg zerstört. Zum Glück blieben andere *Kentrosaurus*-Überreste heil, sie liegen noch immer in besagtem Museum.

*Kentrosaurus* besaß die typische Körperform der Stegosauriden: Sein Kopf war klein, darin saß ein winziges Hirn; die vorderen Gliedmaßen waren kürzer als die hinteren; der Rücken wölbte sich steil und fiel leicht zu den langen Hinterbeinen ab, der sich verjüngende Schwanz war länger als der übrige Körper. Vorn am Kopf befand sich ein zahnloser Schnabel, mit dem das Tier Pflanzen abschnitt, die sehr kleinen blattförmigen Zähne waren mit vertikalen Graten versehen. Die Rückenplatten des *Kentrosaurus* waren bei weitem nicht so breit wie die des *Stegosaurus* und wurden vom Hals über den Rücken immer schmaler. Ihre Form wechselte etwa auf halber Körperlänge zu schmaleren Dornen, die sich dann bis zur Schwanzspitze fortsetzten. Dass diese dünnen, spitzen Gebilde die Regelung der Körpertemperatur unterstützt haben sollen, ist schwer vorstellbar.

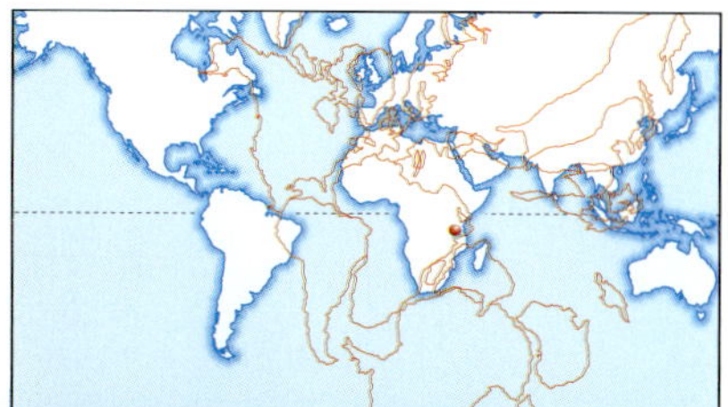

**ÜBERSICHT (DINOSAURIER)**
***Kentrosaurus***
**Bedeutung des Namens:** Bedorntes Reptil, Stachelreptil
**Periode:** Oberer Jura
**Hauptgruppe:** Stegosauridae
**Länge:** 5 Meter
**Gewicht:** 2 Tonnen
**Nahrung:** Pflanzen
**Fossilfundstätten:** In Tansania

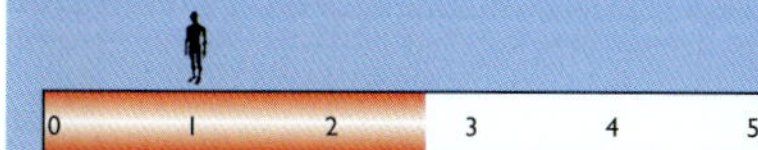

# WUERHOSAURUS

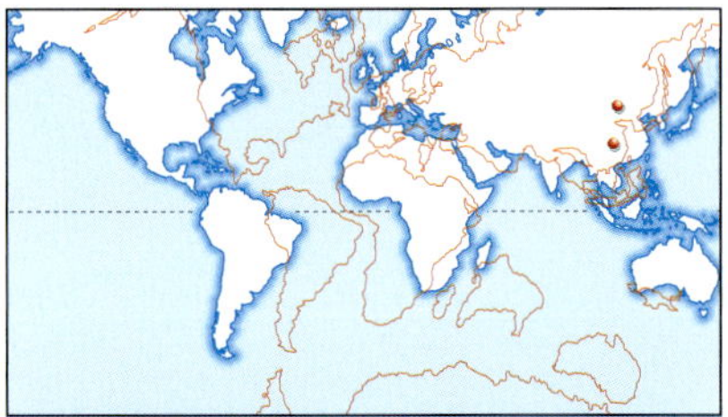

**ÜBERSICHT (DINOSAURIER)**
***Wuerhosaurus***
**Bedeutung des Namens:** Wuerho-Reptil
**Periode:** Unterkreide
**Hauptgruppe:** Stegosauridae
**Länge:** 8 Meter
**Gewicht:** 2 Tonnen
**Nahrung:** Pflanzen
**Fossilfundstätten:** In China, in der Mongolei

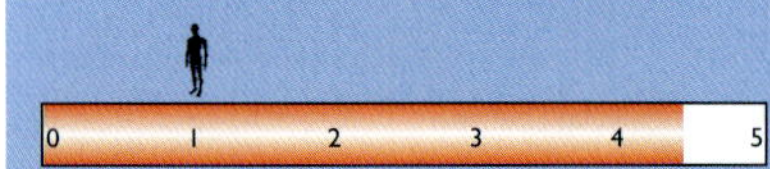


Die Stegosauriden erlebten ihre Blütezeit im Oberen Jura, vor 160–144 Millionen Jahren; einige Vertreter dieser Gruppe existierten nach dieser Zeit. Zu ihnen gehörte auch *Wuerhosaurus*, denn seine Fossilien wurden in rund 140–130 Millionen Jahre alten Gesteinen der frühen Kreidezeit gefunden. Das Tier war fast so groß wie *Stegosaurus*, lebte allerdings nicht in Nordamerika, sondern in Ostasien. Diese beiden Gebiete waren zu verschiedenen erdgeschichtlichen Zeiten (siehe Seite 26) durch Landbrücken miteinander verbunden. Die wichtigsten Fossilien von *Wuerhosaurus*, die vermutlich von verschiedenen Individuen stammen, insgesamt aber nur spärlich sind, stammen aus der chinesischen Region Wuerho, ihren Namen erhielten sie von Dong Zhiming, einem führenden chinesischen Fossilienexperten.

Die Rückenplatten des *Wuerhosaurus* waren vermutlich flacher, weniger zugespitzt oder nicht so ausgeprägt fünfeckig wie bei *Stegosaurus*. Auch der Rumpf des Tieres war wohl kürzer. Zwischen Vorder- und Hinterbeinen gab es einen ähnlichen Längenunterschied wie bei *Stegosaurus*, so dass das Becken doppelt so hoch stand wie die Schultern. So konnte der Kopf ohne Schwierigkeiten und wie von selbst den Boden berühren, was anderen Pflanzen fressenden Dinosauriern nicht so mühelos gelang. Diese mussten sich unter Kraftaufwand und ohne das Gleichgewicht zu verlieren eigens niederbeugen, um die bodennahe Vegetation abweiden zu können. Anderen Theorien zufolge konnten *Wuerhosaurus* und andere Stegosauriden sich dank des gewaltigen, breiten Beckens und der breit stehenden Hinterbeine aufrichten und den kleineren, im Verhältnis leichteren Kopf sowie den vorderen Rumpf auch zu höher wachsenden Pflanzen emporheben. Die eingeschränkte Beweglichkeit der Becken-, Rücken- und Halsgelenke und die kleinen, schwachen Zähne scheinen diesen Gedanken allerdings nicht zu bestätigen.

**RECHTS** Die niedrigeren, oben flacheren, fast rechteckigen Rückenplatten des *Wuerhosaurus* sind unter den Stegosauriern unverwechselbar. Den Platten anderer Stegosaurier ähneln sie allerdings insofern, als sie am Hals beginnen, am Rumpf größer und am Schwanz wieder kleiner werden. Diese Übereinstimmung kann bisher nicht genau erklärt werden.

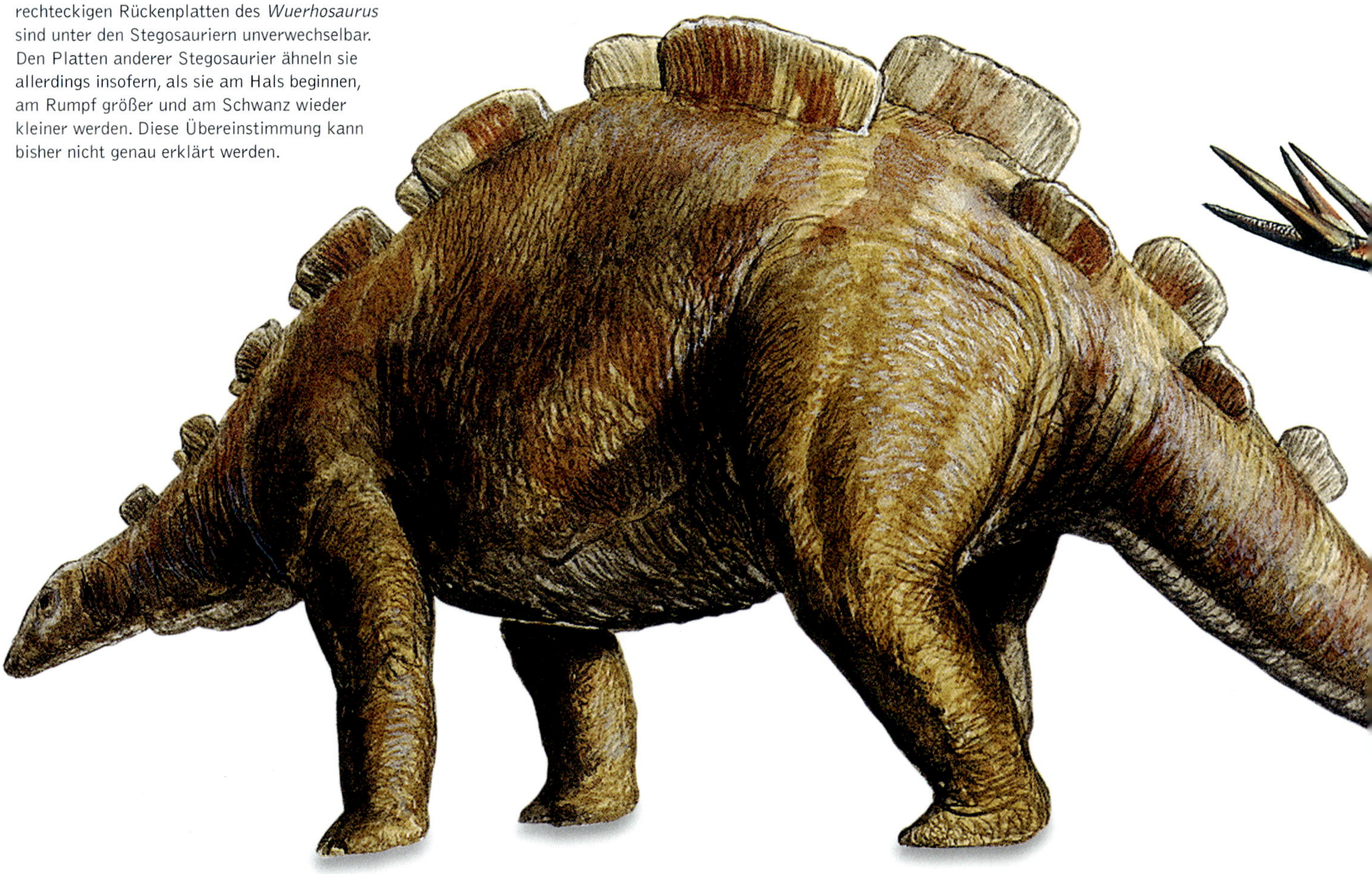

# TUOJIANGOSAURUS

Die Stegosauriden traten wahrscheinlich zuerst in Ostasien, und zwar in der Zeit des Mittleren Jura, auf (siehe Seite 347, *Huayangosaurus*). *Tuojiangosaurus* aus dem Oberen Jura stellt wohl eine Fortsetzung dieses entwicklungsgeschichtlichen Weges in diesem Teil der Erde dar. Das Tier war ein ziemlich großer Stegosauride, seine Länge betrug insgesamt sieben Meter und sein Gewicht wahrscheinlich mehr als eine Tonne. Die großen Knochenplatten, von denen man annimmt, dass sie am Hals, am Rücken und am Schwanz nach oben ragten, lagen bei ihm wie bei vielen Stegosauriden in die Haut eingebettet, waren jedoch nicht fest mit anderen Knochen des Skeletts verbunden. Bei den Überresten mögen zwar viele solcher Platten zum Vorschein kommen, doch sie haben sich im Verlauf der Fossilierung von den verrottenden Weichteilen des Körpers gelöst und sind dann mit anderen Knochen durcheinander geraten. Ihre ursprüngliche Lage und Anordnung ist daher ungewiss.

*Tuojiangosaurus* weist typische Merkmale der Stegosauriden auf – einen kleinen Kopf, einen geneigten Hals, kürzere Vordergliedmaßen, einen gewölbten Rücken und längere Hinterextremitäten. Er besaß rund fünfzehn Paar Rückenplatten. Der Schwanz war nicht ganz so lang gestreckt oder kräftig wie bei *Kentrosaurus*, mit den nach oben stehenden Dornfortsätzen und den beiden Dornpaaren an der Schwanzspitze aber immer noch beeindruckend. Verschiedene andere Stegosauriden trugen ebenfalls vier Schwanzdornen, die demzufolge wohl ein sehr praktisches Merkmal waren und ihren Besitzern vielleicht als Verteidigungswaffen dienten. Der Schwanz war über die gesamte Länge muskulös und konnte mit großer Kraft geschwungen werden. Ein Fossilfund von *Tuojiangosaurus* entpuppte sich als erstes nahezu vollständiges Dinosaurierskelett, das überhaupt in China entdeckt wurde. Das Skelett wurde 1977 von den chinesischen Paläontologen Zhou Shiwu, Dong Zhiming und Zhang-Yang Li benannt.

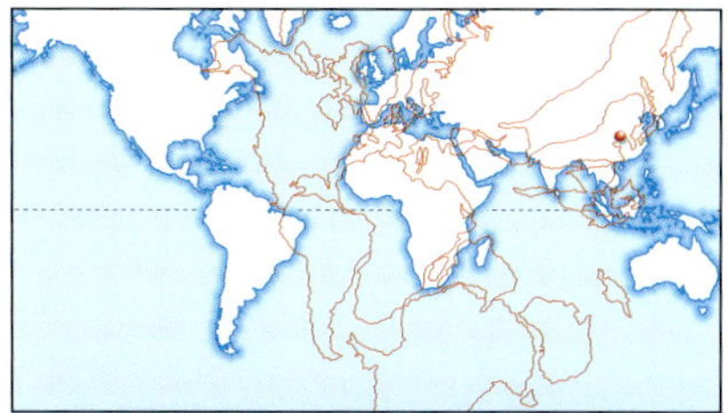

**ÜBERSICHT (DINOSAURIER)**
***Tuojiangosaurus***
**Bedeutung des Namens:** Tuo-Reptil (nach dem Fluss Tuo benannt)
**Periode:** Oberer Jura
**Hauptgruppe:** Stegosauridae
**Länge:** 7 Meter
**Gewicht:** 1–2 Tonnen
**Nahrung:** Pflanzen
**Fossilfundstätten:** In China

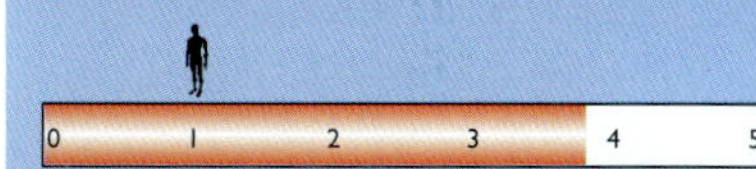


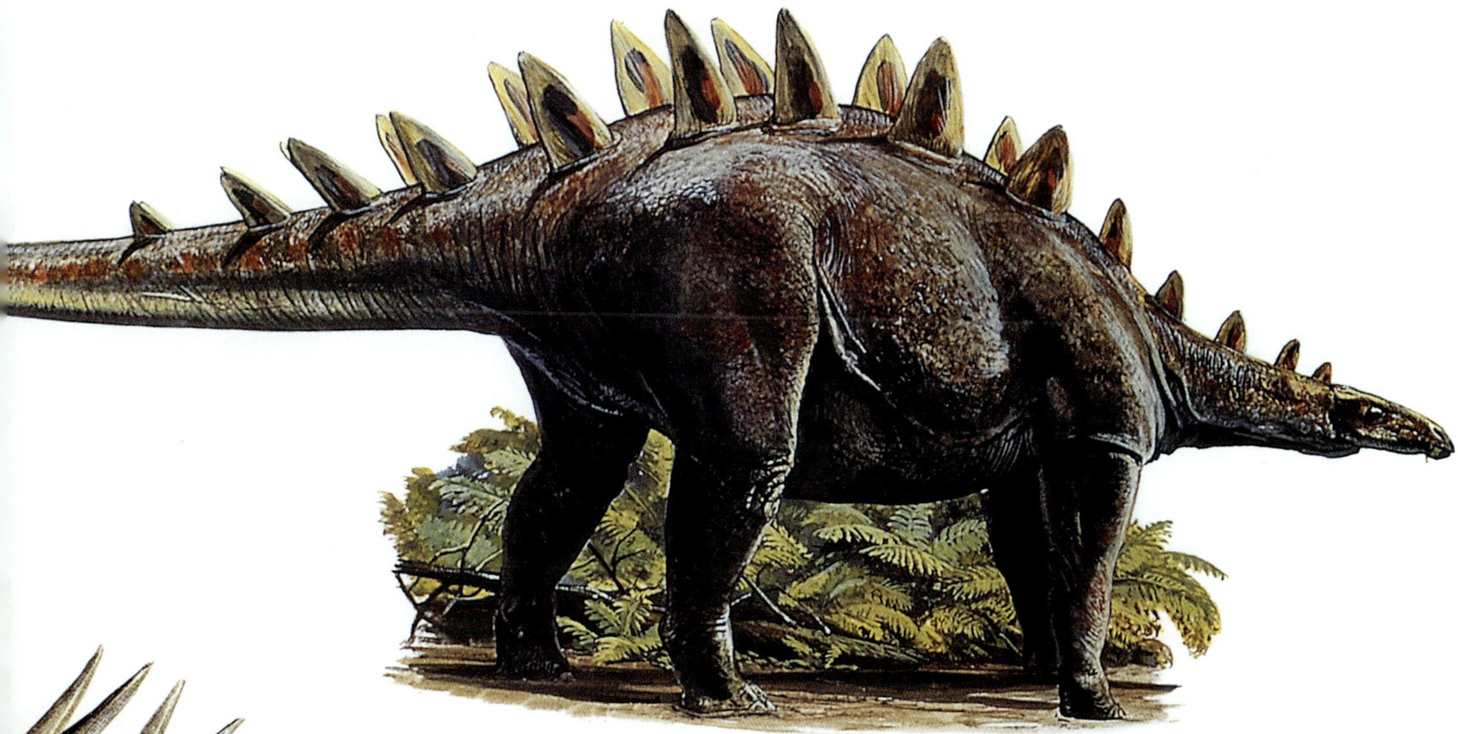

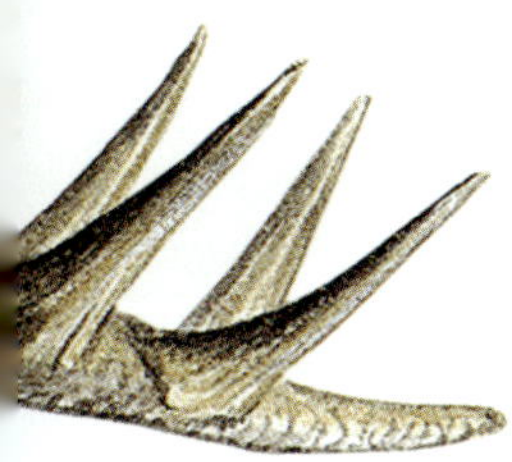

**OBEN** Es mutet unwahrscheinlich an, dass *Tuojiangosaurus* seinen Kopf viel höher als in dieser Rekonstruktion heben konnte.

# Die Ausbreitung der Stegosaurier

*Die ältesten Fossilien von Stacheldinosauriern stammen aus dem Unteren Jura, sie wurden in Ostasien entdeckt. Die Artenvielfalt der Stegosaurier nahm im Verlauf des Jura zu, die Tiere breiteten sich nach Afrika, Europa und Nordamerika aus. Ihre Blütezeit erlebten sie am Ende der Periode, im Oberen Jura. In der Unterkreide war ihre Zahl bereits deutlich reduziert, was vielleicht mit der Konkurrenz durch neue, größere Pflanzenfresser wie etwa die Ornithopoden zusammenhing. Man glaubte zunächst, dass einige Typen, insbesondere Dravidosaurus, dessen Fossilien in Indien gefunden wurden, noch bis in die späte Kreidezeit existierten. Die Identität dieser Überreste ist in jüngster Zeit allerdings infrage gestellt worden. Die Zweifel rühren zum Teil daher, dass der Fund hinsichtlich des Ortes und auch der Zeit so isoliert von den Fossilien anderer Stegosaurier ist.*

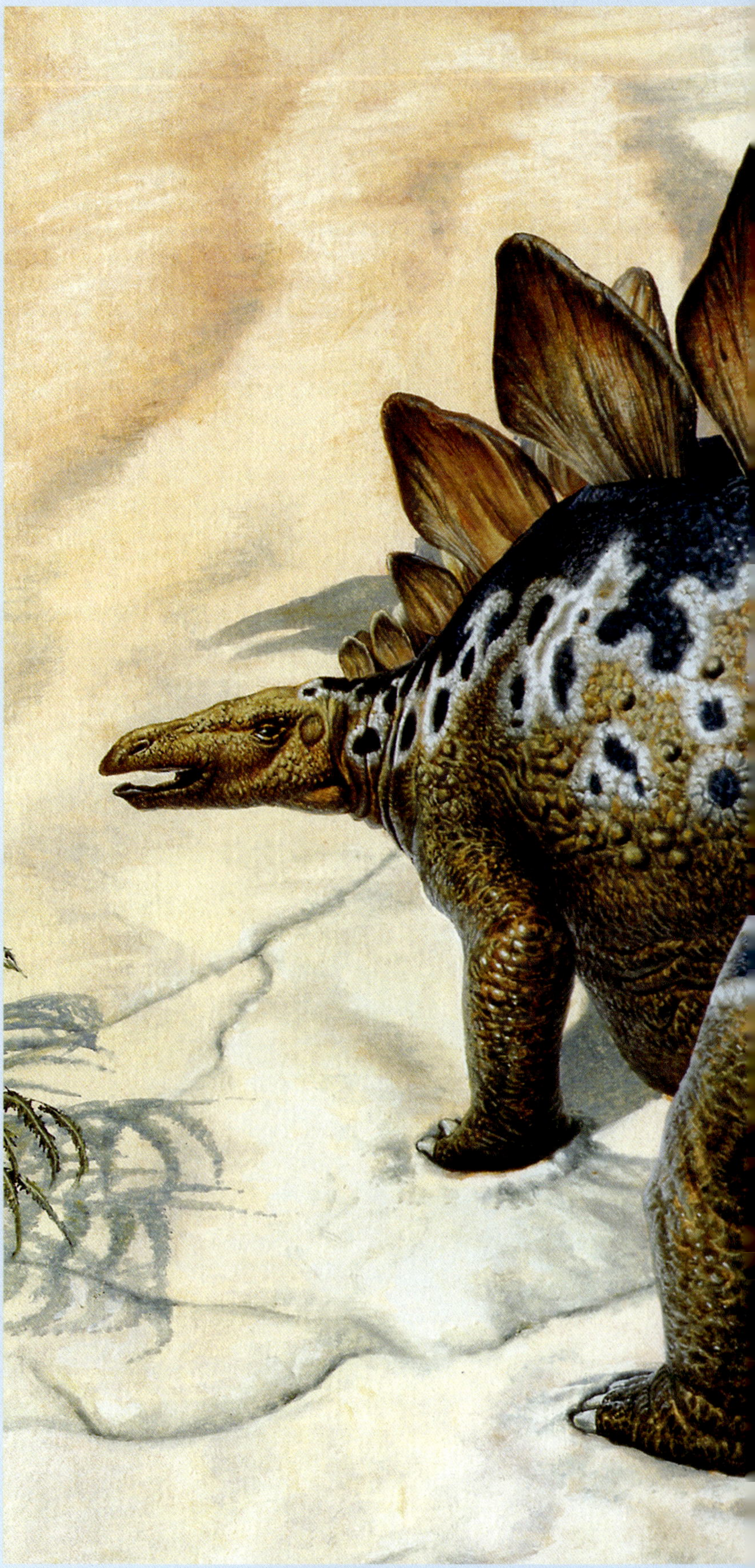

**RECHTS** Diese beiden Stegosaurier – ein adultes und ein juveniles Tier – zeigen zwei bei diesem Dinosauriertypus vermutete Fresshaltungen. Das Jungtier richtet sich an einem Baum auf, um an dessen Laub heranzukommen, während der ausgewachsene Stegosaurier am Boden wohl nach niedrig wachsenden Pflanzen schnuppert.

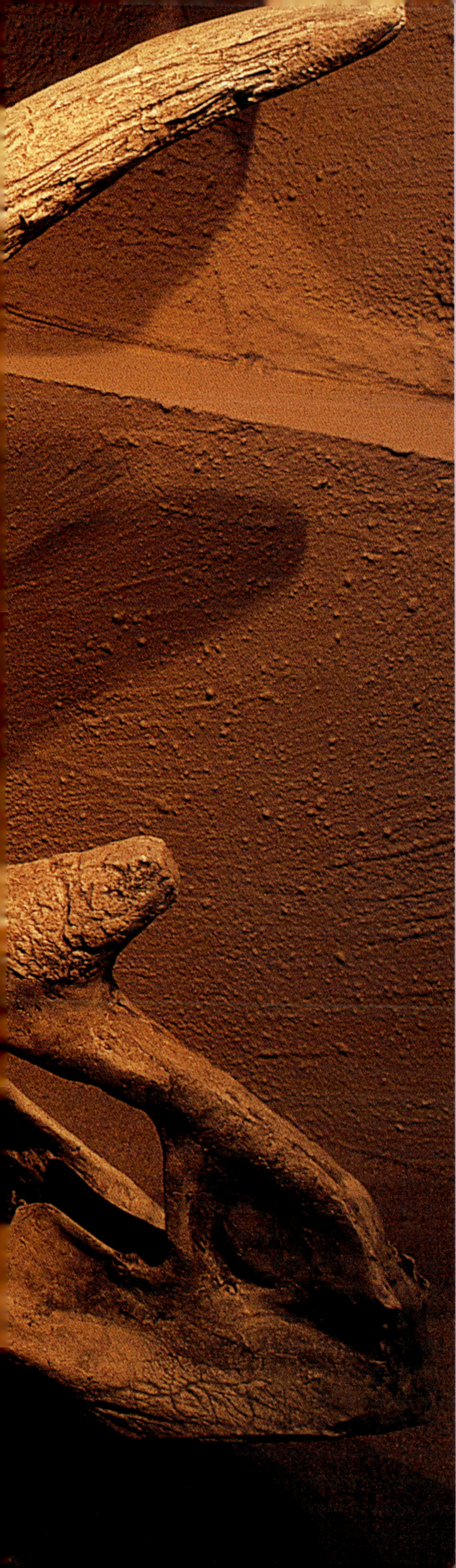

KAPITEL DREIZEHN

# HORN-DINOSAURIER

*Die Ceratopsier, deren Größe zwischen der eines kleinen Schweines bis zur doppelten Länge und Körpermasse des größten Nashorns der Jetztzeit schwankte, waren erfolgreiche und zugleich tragische Neuankömmlinge, weil sie erst am Ende der Dinosaurierzeit erschienen.*

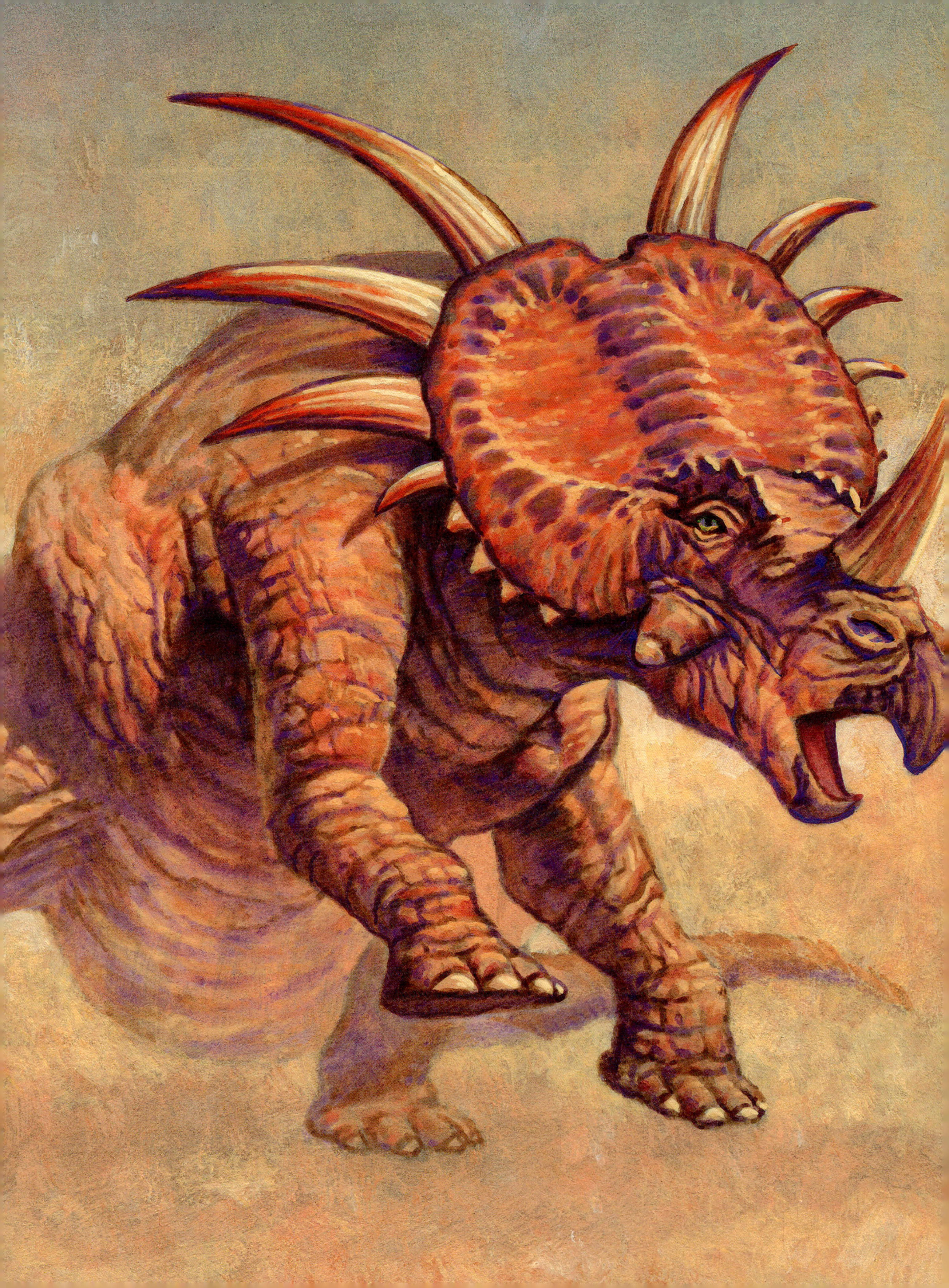

# MONTANOCERATOPS

*Montanoceratops* ist nach dem US-Bundesstaat Montana benannt, wo seine Fossilien gefunden wurden. Bekannt geworden ist er hauptsächlich durch Teile von zwei Skeletten. Seine Überreste wurden von Barnum Brown ausgegraben und 1951 von Charles M. Sternberg benannt. Inzwischen hat man weitere Reste in der kanadischen Provinz Alberta gefunden. *Montanoceratops* lebte gegen Ende der Kreidezeit, vor 72–66 Millionen Jahren. (Einige Überreste, die ursprünglich *Montanoceratops* zugeordnet worden waren, hat man nach nochmaliger Untersuchung als *Leptoceratops*-Fossilien eingestuft.)

*Montanoceratops* weist eine erstaunliche Ähnlichkeit mit *Protoceratops* auf, obwohl er in vielen Merkmalen schon etwas weiter entwickelt war. Er mag allgemein etwas größer gewesen sein, doch die Proportionen seines Kopfes, seines Körpers, der vier untersetzten Beine und des kurzen Schwanzes erinnern alle an *Protoceratops*. So auch der Nackenschild, der am hinteren Teil des Schädeldaches begann und bis über den Hals reichte. Was man anfangs für ein flaches, kegelförmiges Horn auf der Nase des *Montanoceratops* gehalten hatte, wurde später als ein vorstehender Wangenknochen identifiziert, also ähnelten sich schließlich auch die Nasen von *Montanoceratops* und *Protoceratops*. Beide Dinosaurier werden innerhalb der Gruppe der Horndinosaurier den Protoceratopsiden zugeordnet, da sie „altmodische" Merkmale wie beispielsweise die Zähne im oberen Teil des „Schnabels" oder vorn im Oberkiefer sowie die Krallen an den Zehen besitzen. Weiterentwickelte Ceratopsier hatten keine Zähne mehr, und ihre Krallen waren eher huf- oder nagelartig – obgleich das Wort „weiterentwickelt" hier vielleicht irreführt, denn viele dieser Dinosaurier existierten etwa zur gleichen Zeit wie *Montanoceratops*.

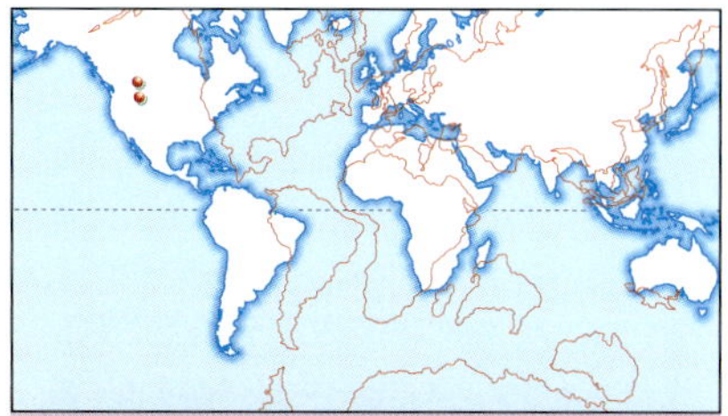

**ÜBERSICHT (DINOSAURIER)**
***Montanoceratops***
**Bedeutung des Namens:** Horngesicht aus Montana
**Periode:** Oberkreide
**Hauptgruppe:** Ceratopsia
**Länge:** 2–3 Meter
**Gewicht:** 400–600 Kilogramm
**Nahrung:** Pflanzen
**Fossilfundstätten:** In den USA (Montana), in Kanada (Alberta)

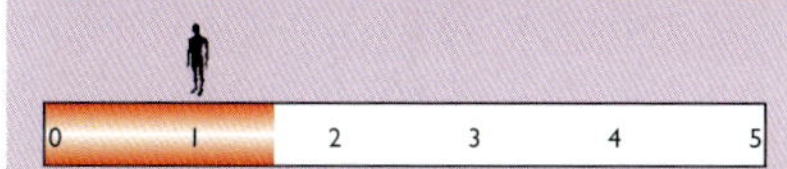


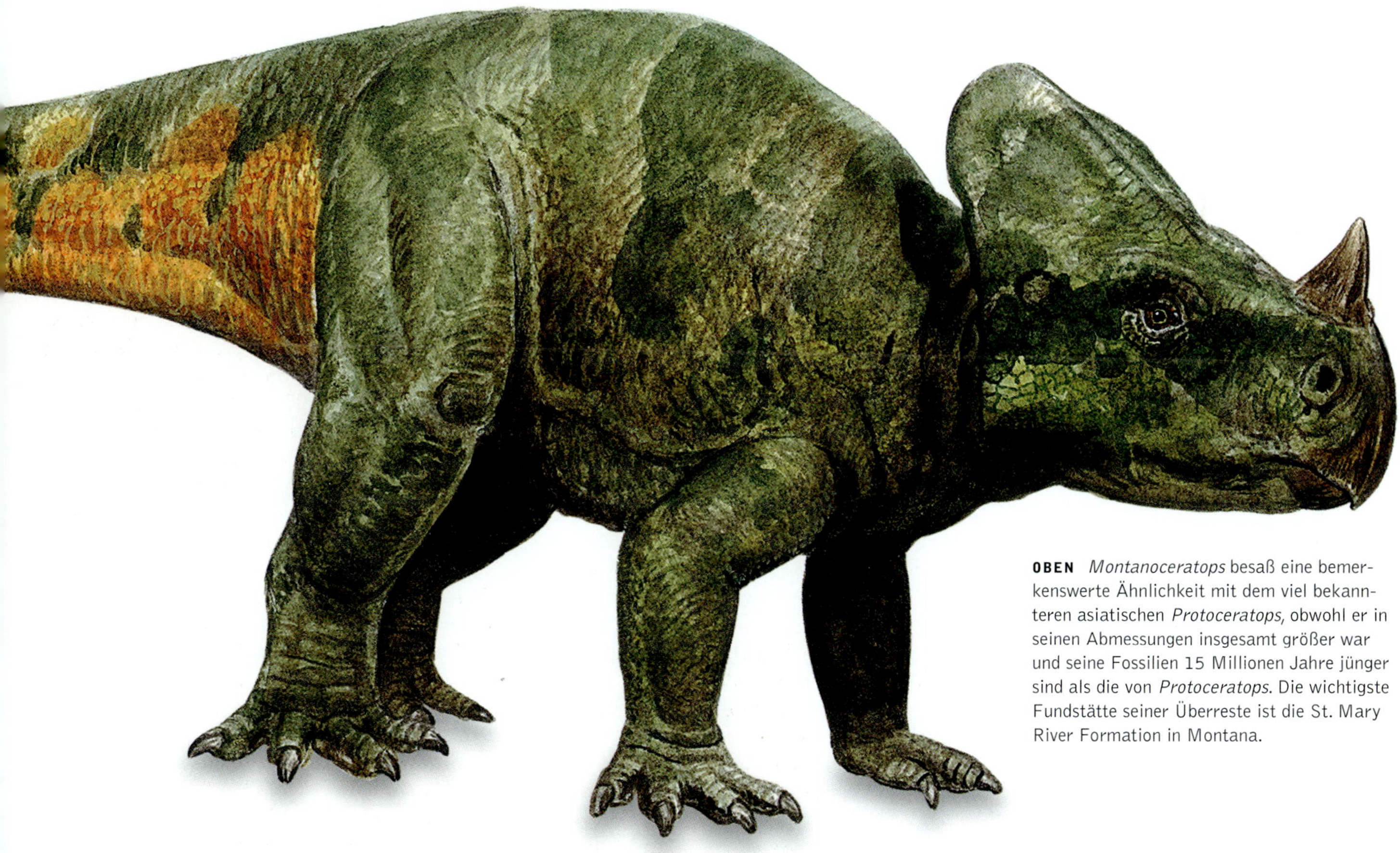

**OBEN** *Montanoceratops* besaß eine bemerkenswerte Ähnlichkeit mit dem viel bekannteren asiatischen *Protoceratops*, obwohl er in seinen Abmessungen insgesamt größer war und seine Fossilien 15 Millionen Jahre jünger sind als die von *Protoceratops*. Die wichtigste Fundstätte seiner Überreste ist die St. Mary River Formation in Montana.

# Wozu der Nackenschild?

*Die Funktion des Nackenschildes der Ceratopsier ist bis heute Gegenstand von Meinungsverschiedenheiten. Bei den meisten Typen – mit Ausnahme von Triceratops – bestand der Schild nicht aus massivem Knochen und wäre deshalb als Schutzschild kaum von Nutzen gewesen. Zu diesem Thema gibt es heute mehrere Theorien. Eine gesagt, dass an der großen Fläche des Schildes die kräftige Kopf- und Kiefermuskulatur verankert war. Eine andere lautet, dass die große Schildfläche ein imposantes optisches Signal erzeugte, insbesondere dann, wenn ihr Besitzer seinen Kopf senkte, so dass der Schild fast senkrecht hochklappte, und wenn der Schild leuchtend gefärbt war.*

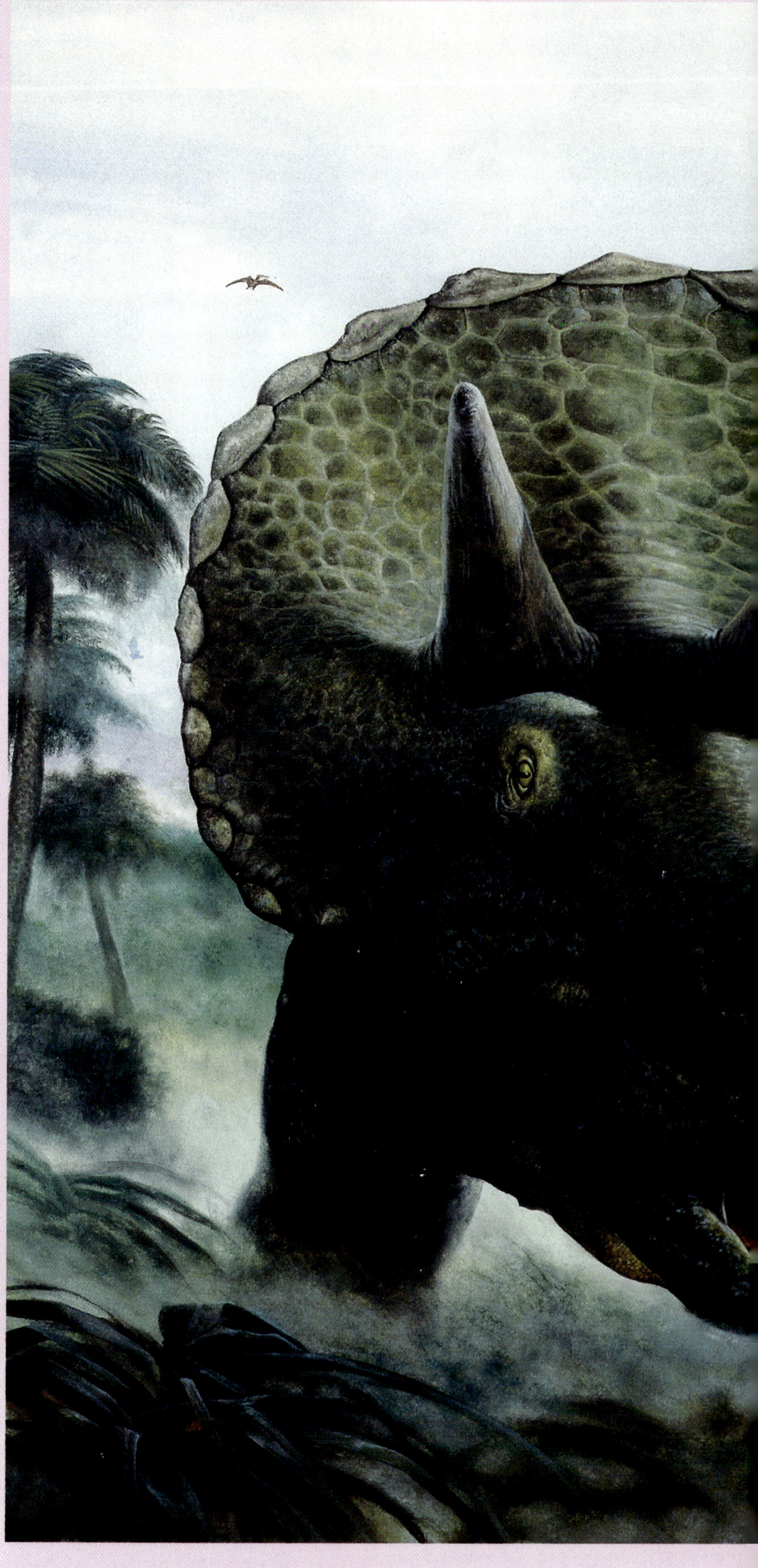

**RECHTS** Der junge *Triceratops* steht wie angewurzelt und weicht keinen Fußbreit von der Stelle; im Hintergrund weidet seine Herde. Bei den Jungtieren scheinen Stirnhörner und Halskrause im Verhältnis zur Gesamtgröße des Körpers kleiner gewesen zu sein als bei den ausgewachsenen Tieren. Der Kopfschmuck vergrößerte sich während des Körperwachstums schneller, so dass er bei dem adulten Tier proportional größer war.

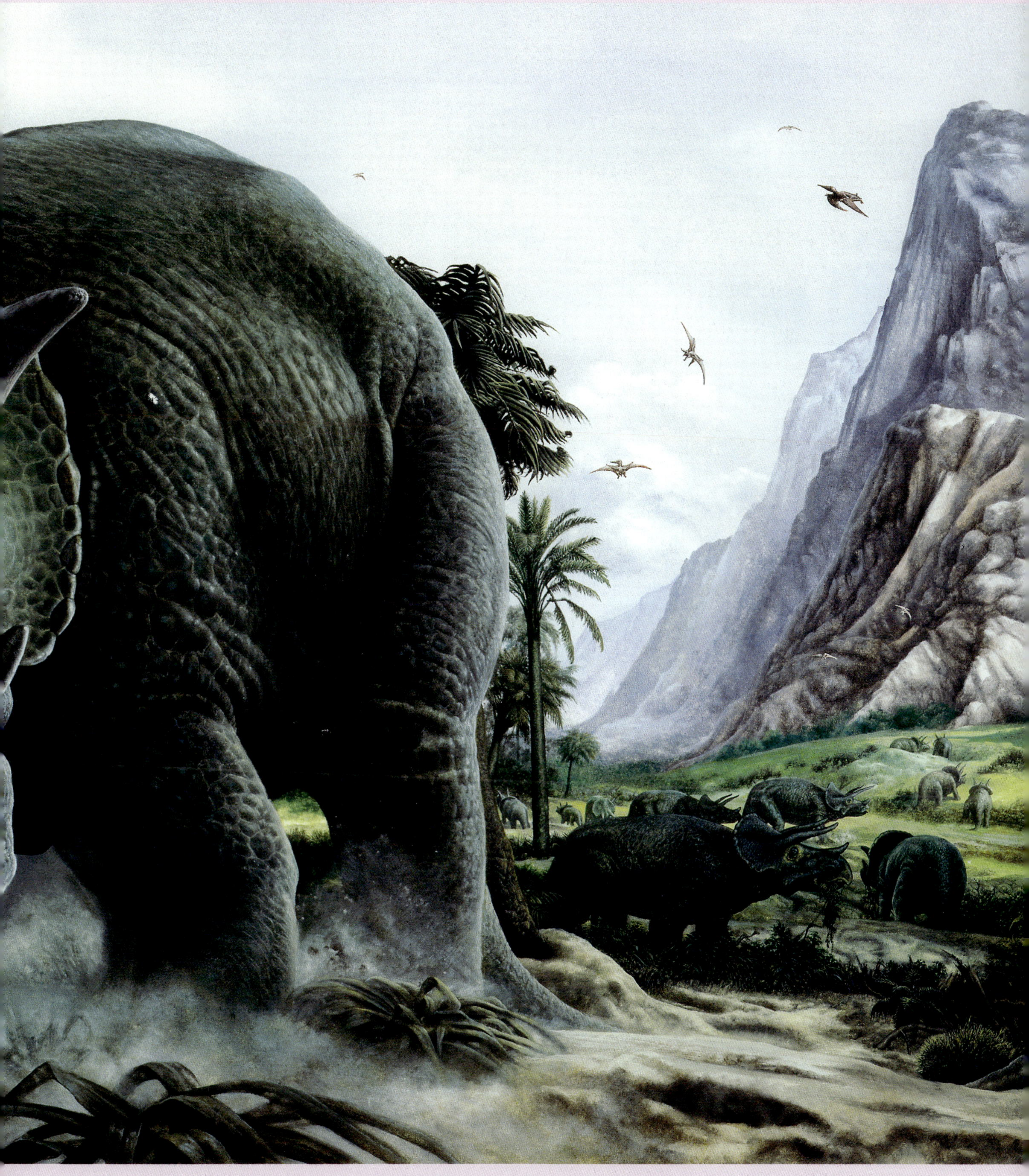

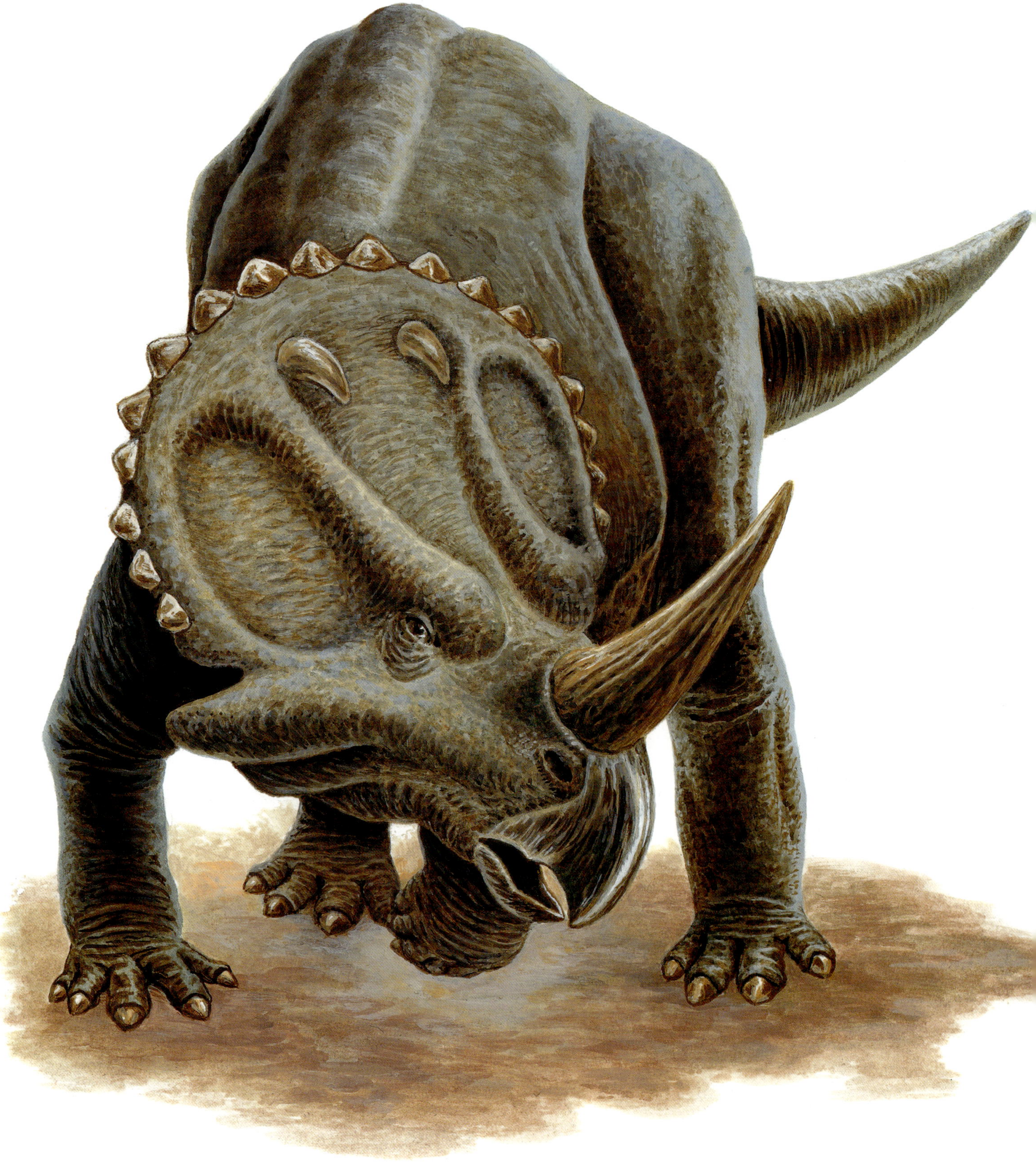

# MONOCLONIUS

*Monoclonius* war vielleicht ein großer Horndinosaurier von über fünf Meter Länge und einigen Tonnen Gewicht, vielleicht verhielt es sich aber auch anders. Als in der zweiten Hälfte des 19. Jahrhunderts in Nordamerika die Überreste riesiger Ceratopsier ausgegraben wurden, gab es unter den Fossilienjägern einen verbissenen Wettlauf darum, wer die meisten Funde vorzuweisen hatte. *Monoclonius* wurde 1876 von Edward Drinker Cope nach einigen Bruchstücken des Nackenschildes, von Knochen und Zähnen benannt, von denen man einige 1855 im US-Bundesstaat Montana, in der Nähe des Judith River, entdeckt hatte. Diese Stücke waren vermutlich die ersten Fossilien von Ceratopsiern, die in Nordamerika beschrieben wurden. Ihre Beschreibung stammt von Joseph Leidy. Der Name *Monoclonius* bezieht sich nicht auf das einzelne Nasenhorn, sondern auf die einzeln stehende Backenzahnreihe im Unter- und im Oberkiefer des Tieres. Cope wollte damit den Unterschied zu der doppelten Zahnreihe verdeutlichen, die man in den Kiefern eines anderen Dinosauriers aus der Zeit vermutete.

*Monoclonius* hat inzwischen Höhen und Tiefen „durchlebt". Einmal galt er als Gattung mit mehr als zehn Spezies, dann wieder ohne Arten, wobei die verschiedenen Formen des *Monoclonius* als Varianten anderer Ceratopsier, in erster Linie von *Centrosaurus* und *Styrosaurus*, angesehen wurden. Sein Nackenschild unterschied sich in Größe und Vollkommenheit von dem anderer Typen – er maß von der Nasenspitze bis zum hinteren Schildrand „nur" 1,8 Meter –, trug in der oberen Hälfte vermutlich aber ein Paar nach unten gebogener Dornen. Auf der Schnauze saß ein Horn, das größer als bei anderen Ceratopsiern war. Der Körper mit dem breiten, kräftigen Hals, den vier gedrungenen Gliedmaßen, die in abgespreizten behuften Zehen endeten, und dem kurzen Schwanz war typisch für einen Horndinosaurier. Mit seinem hakenförmigen Schnabel „erntete" *Monoclonius* Pflanzenteile, diese wurden dann von den zahlreichen Backenzähnen zermahlen.

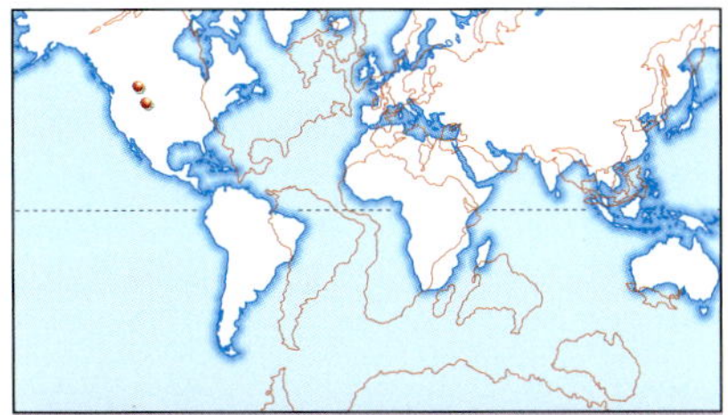

**ÜBERSICHT (DINOSAURIER)**
***Monoclonius***
**Bedeutung des Namens:** Einzelner Stamm oder Stock (oftmals „Einhorn" genannt)
**Periode:** Oberkreide
**Hauptgruppe:** Ceratopsia
**Länge:** 5–6 Meter
**Gewicht:** 2–3 Tonnen
**Nahrung:** Pflanzen
**Fossilfundstätten:** In den USA (Montana), in Kanada (Alberta)

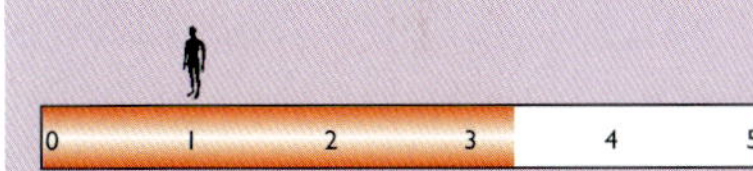


# CENTROSAURUS

Nach diesem Horndinosaurier wurde eine der Untergruppen großer Ceratopsier, die Centrosaurinen, aufgestellt und benannt. Man nennt sie zwar auch oft Dinosaurier mit kurzem Nackenschild, doch *Centrosaurus* selbst besaß einen verhältnismäßig langen, ausladenden Nackenschild. Der Unterschied liegt eher in dem Nasenhorn, das länger als die Brauenhörner war, sowie in der vorderen Gesichtsregion, die im Vergleich zu der anderen Untergruppe, den Chasmosaurinen (siehe Seite 370), ziemlich hoch, schmal und kurzschnäuzig war. *Centrosaurus* war ein mittelgroßer, mehr als sechs Meter langer Ceratopsier. Er wurde 1940 von dem kanadischen Dinosaurierexperten Lawrence Lambe benannt.

Die Brauenhörner des *Centrosaurus* waren kaum mehr als flache, spitz zulaufende Höcker des Schädelknochens, das Nasenhorn hingegen konnte bis zu fünfundsiebzig Zentimeter lang werden. Bei manchen Tieren war es fast gerade, bei anderen schien es nach hinten zu den Augen oder nach vorn über die Schnauze gekrümmt gewesen zu sein. Dennoch bezieht sich der Name *Centrosaurus*, der „gut behorntes Reptil" oder „Reptil mit Spitze" bedeutet, nicht auf dieses Horn. Er kommt vielmehr von einem Paar gebogener „Haken", die etwa in der Mitte des oberen Schildrandes standen; ob sie ohne weiteres sichtbar oder von Haut und Fleisch überzogen waren und sich in den Schildrand einfügten, ist unklar. In Knochenschichten in der kanadischen Provinz Alberta wurden die Überreste zahlreicher Vertreter der Gattung *Centrosaurus* gefunden – Schädel, Bruchstücke von Hörnern, Zähne, Skelettteile und sogar fossilierte Hautabdrücke. Man hat daraus den Schluss gezogen, dass die Tiere, von denen diese Reste stammen, einst eine Herde bildeten, vielleicht gar auf Wanderschaft waren und täglich mehr als hundert Kilometer trotteten (siehe Seiten 364 und 368).

**LINKS** Diese überzeugende Rekonstruktion eines *Monoclonius* zeigt ein einzelnes Nasenhorn, kleinere abwärts gebogene Dornen am Nackenschild und lang ausgezogene Wangenknochen. Alle diese Merkmale können auch von anderen Ceratopsiern stammen. Die hier dargestellte Haltung, in der das Tier den gesenkten Kopf von einer Seite zur anderen schwenkte, um sein langes, spitzes Horn zur Schau zu stellen, diente zur Einschüchterung potenzieller Gegner. Ein solches Verhalten zeigen auch die heutigen Nashörner.

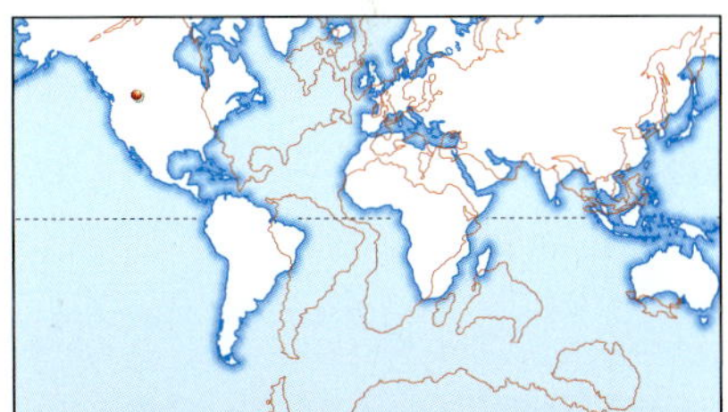

**ÜBERSICHT (DINOSAURIER)**
***Centrosaurus***
**Bedeutung des Namens:** Gut behorntes Reptil, Reptil mit Spitze
**Periode:** Oberkreide
**Hauptgruppe:** Ceratopsia
**Länge:** 6 Meter
**Gewicht:** 3 Tonnen
**Nahrung:** Pflanzen
**Fossilfundstätten:** In Kanada (Alberta)

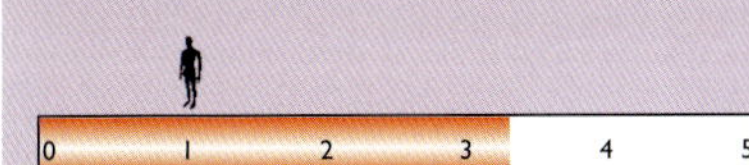

# PACHYRHINOSAURUS

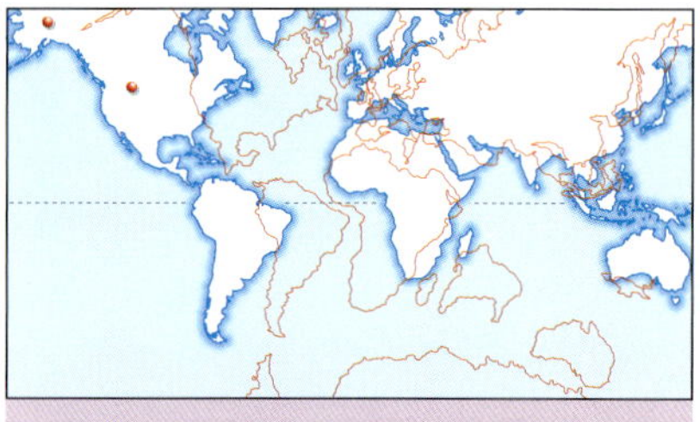

**ÜBERSICHT (DINOSAURIER)**

***Pachyrhinosaurus***

**Bedeutung des Namens:** Dicknasenreptil

**Periode:** Oberkreide

**Hauptgruppe:** Ceratopsia

**Länge:** 5,5 – 7 Meter

**Gewicht:** 3 – 4 Tonnen

**Nahrung:** Pflanzen

**Fossilfundstätten:** In den USA (Alaska), in Kanada (Alberta)

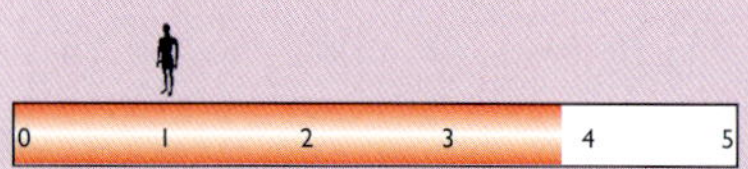


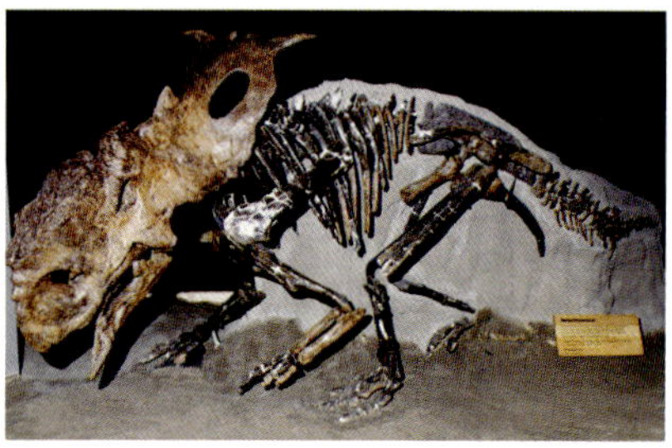

**OBEN** Überreste des *Pachyrhinosaurus* im Royal Turrell Museum in Alberta.

**RECHTS** Diese Nachbildung zeigt die Nase des *Pachyrhinosaurus* lediglich mit einem großen Knochenbuckel, der nicht von einem Horn gekrönt ist.

In der kanadischen Provinz Alberta existiert ein riesiges Knochenbett mit bunt durcheinander gewürfelten Überresten Hunderter Dinosaurier der Gattung *Pachyrhinosaurus* sowie Fossilien von anderen Tieren und auch Pflanzen, die vor über 70 Millionen Jahren in diesem Gebiet heimisch waren. Weitere Funde aus dem Jahr 2002, bei denen weit im Norden, im US-Bundesstaat Alaska, ebenfalls Knochenlagen von *Pachyrhinosaurus* entdeckt wurden, lassen darauf schließen, dass diese Horndinosaurier einst in großen Herden unterwegs waren, im Sommer nach Norden, näher zur Arktis, und zum Überwintern nach Süden, in wärmere Regionen, zogen. Die Jahreszeiten damals unterschieden sich allerdings von den Jahreszeiten heute (siehe Seite 26). *Pachyrhinosaurus* wurde 1950 von Charles M. Sternberg benannt.

*Pachyrhinosaurus* war ein mittelgroßer Horndinosaurier aus der Untergruppe der Centrosaurinen. Er besaß die typischen Merkmale eines Ceratopsiers – einen massigen Körper, Säulenbeine mit hufförmigen Nägeln an den Zehen, einen kurzen, sich rasch verjüngenden Schwanz mit dicker Wurzel und einen kräftigen Hals, der den gewaltigen Kopf tragen konnte.

Der zahnlose, scharf gebogene papageienartige Schnabel an der Vorderseite des Mundes eignete sich sehr gut zum Abstreifen des Laubes von den Bäumen und auch als Verteidigungswaffe. Der Nackenschild war nach oben zurückgebogen und trug am oberen Rand möglicherweise zwei oder mehr Dornen- oder Hörnchenpaare. Das wichtigste, typische Merkmal des *Pachyrhinosaurus* war die „dicke Nase“, der das Tier seinen Namen verdankt. Man vermutet, dass der Ceratopsier auf dem vorderen Teil seiner Nase einen großen knöchernen Höcker oder Buckel trug. Dieses Gebilde könnte als Rammbock gegen Feinde oder – vielleicht während der Paarungszeit – bei Kämpfen mit Rivalen gedient haben, es könnte aber auch der Sockel für ein sehr langes Horn gewesen sein. Eine andere, von einigen Paläontologen favorisierte These lautet, dass die Knochenbuckel bei dem einen Geschlecht, vielleicht bei den Männchen, größer und stärker aufgewölbt, bei dem anderen Geschlecht kleiner und fast konkav (schalenförmig) waren.

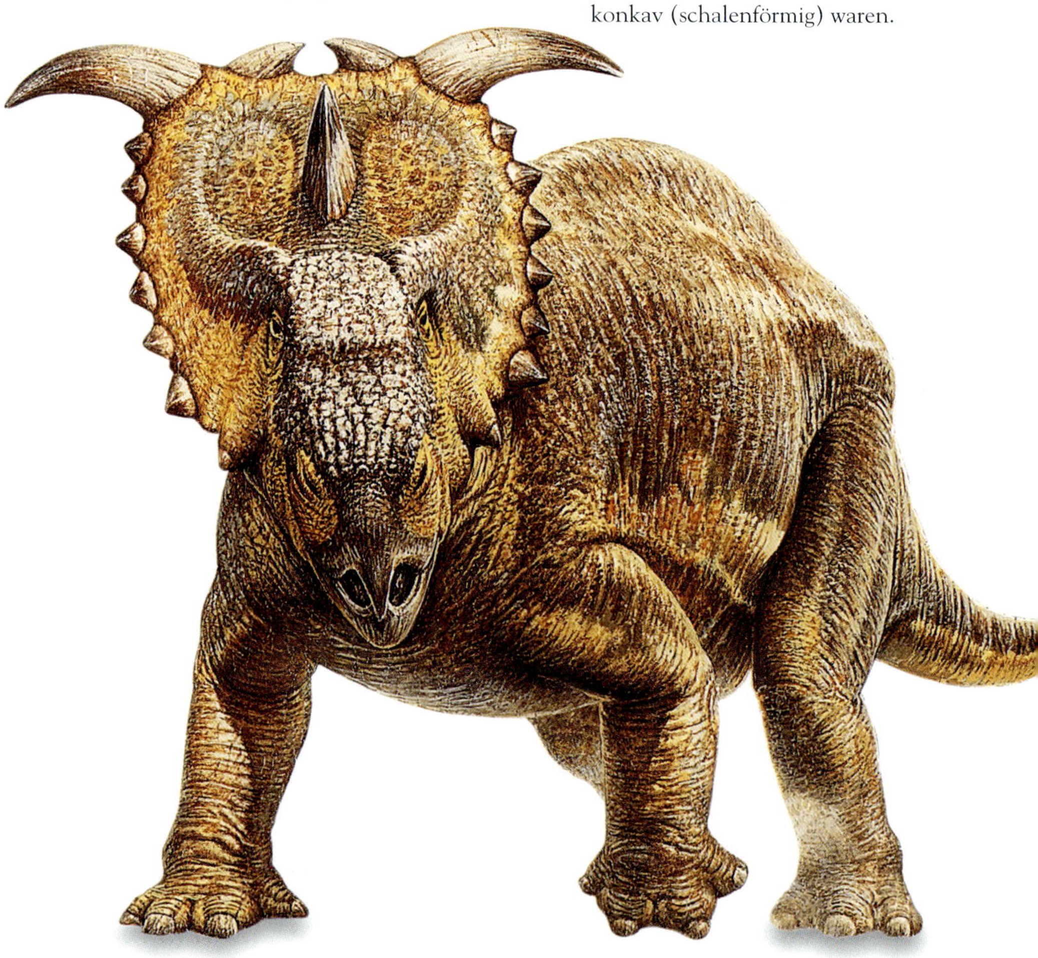

**RECHTS** Der gewaltige Nackenschild des *Pentaceratops* reichte fast über den halben Körper, wenn der Dinosaurier seinen Kopf nach hinten neigte, und er klappte zu einer riesigen fächerartigen Schildfläche hoch, wenn das Tier den Kopf zur Nahrungsaufnahme oder als Drohung senkte, so wie es hier dargestellt ist.

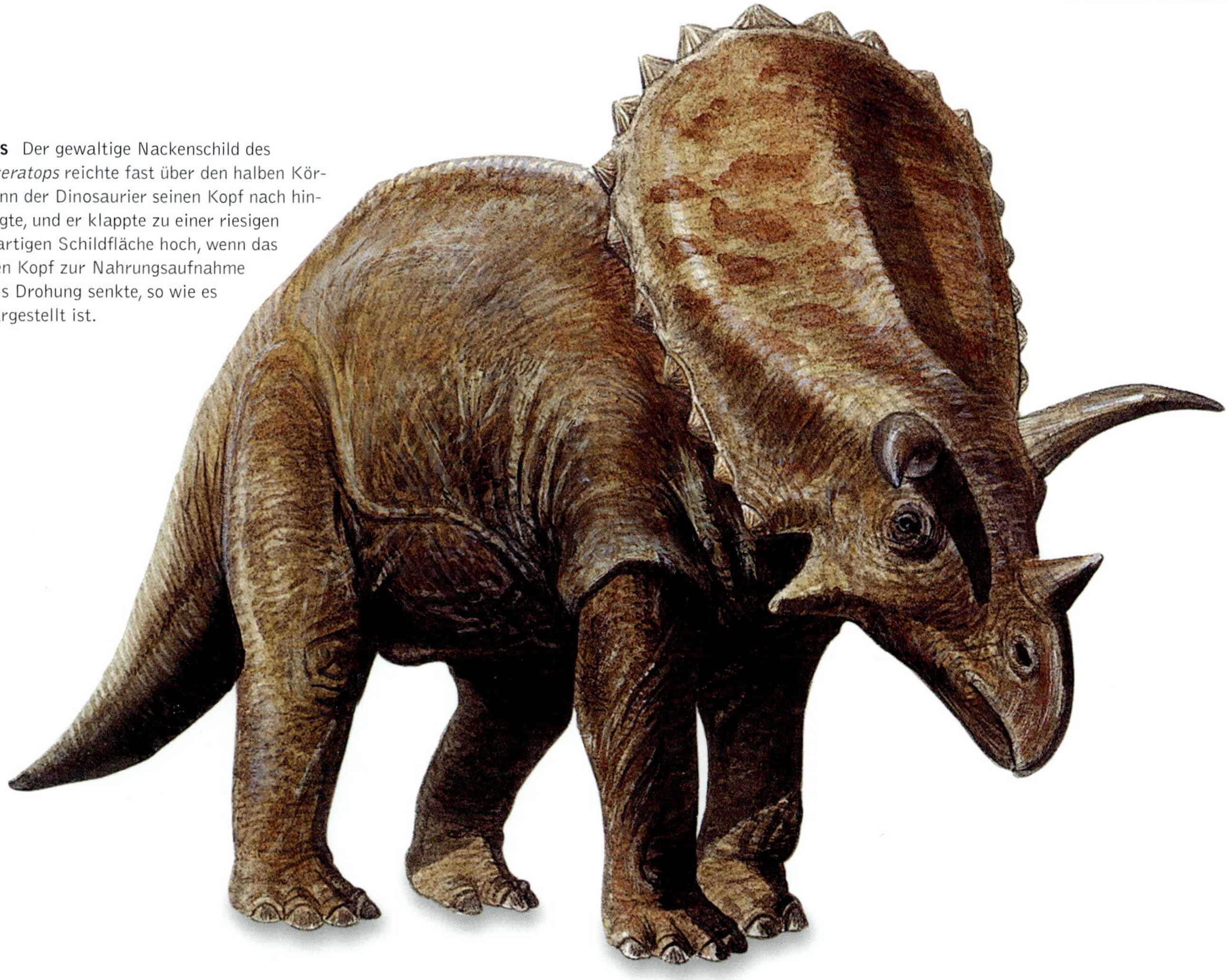

# PENTACERATOPS

Viele Jahre lang hielt der Horndinosaurier *Totosaurus* (siehe Seite 371) den Rekord, den längsten Schädel von allen bekannten Landtieren zu besitzen (siehe auch Seite 396). Die neuere Entdeckung eines riesigen Schädels veranlasste die Wissenschaftler, den Titel nun an *Pentaceratops* zu vergeben. Dem Namen nach könnte man bei diesem Ceratopsier auf Gesicht und Stirn fünf Hörner erwarten, doch davon besitzt das Tier nur drei – ein kurzes Horn auf der Nase und über den Augenbrauen je ein längeres, ganz ähnlich wie bei *Triceratops*. Die beiden anderen Vorsprünge, die Henry Fairfield Osborn für Hörner hielt, als er diesen Dinosaurier 1923 erstmals untersuchte und benannte, sind in Wirklichkeit lang gezogene Spitzen der Wangenknochen, die seitlich unterhalb der Augen schräg nach unten standen. Diese „falschen Hörner" findet man übrigens bei den meisten Ceratopsiern. Immerhin besitzt *Pentaceratops* aber den typischen Nackenschild, der bei ihm lang, breit und geschweift und am äußeren Rand fast rundum mit über zwanzig kleinen Knochendornen, so genannten Epoccipitalen, besetzt war.

Die Fossilien von *Pentaceratops* stammen aus dem US-Bundesstaat New Mexico. Das Tier gehörte zur Untergruppe der Horndinosaurier mit langem Nackenschild, zu den Chasmosaurinen. *Pentaceratops* war ein massiges Urtier, seine Körperform ähnelte entfernt einem Nashorn der Jetztzeit. Er war so lang wie ein Elefant, allerdings schwerer als dieser. Der Schädel war von der Schnauzenspitze bis zum hinteren Schildrand rund drei Meter lang – fast ein Drittel der Gesamtlänge des Tieres. Die Fresswerkzeuge waren typisch für Ceratopsier – am Oberkiefer ein Hakenschnabel, der von dem nur bei Ceratopsiern vorhandenen Schnabelknochen gebildet wurde, und im Unterkiefer der Prädentinknochen, die beide von scharfem Hornmaterial überzogen waren. In der hinteren Kieferregion standen zahlreiche scharfgratige Backenzähne, und dort war auch genügend Raum für die kräftige Kaumuskulatur. Zu den bisher gefundenen *Pentaceratops*-Fossilien gehören acht zum Teil vollständige Schädel und ein Skelett, bei dem verhältnismäßig wenige Knochen fehlen, sowie Skelettfragmente.

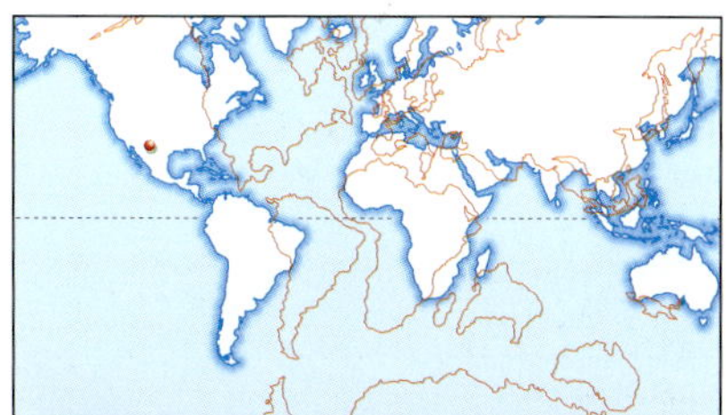

**ÜBERSICHT (DINOSAURIER)**
***Pentaceratops***
**Bedeutung des Namens:** Fünfhorngesicht
**Periode:** Oberkreide
**Hauptgruppe:** Ceratopsia
**Länge:** 8 Meter
**Gewicht:** 7 – 8 Tonnen
**Nahrung:** Pflanzen
**Fossilfundstätten:** In den USA (New Mexico)

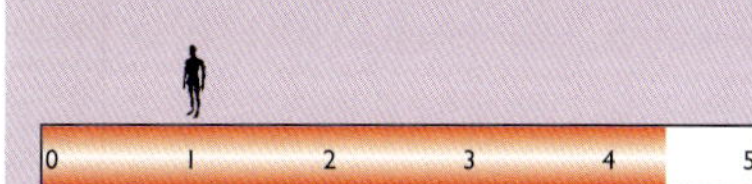

# TRICERATOPS

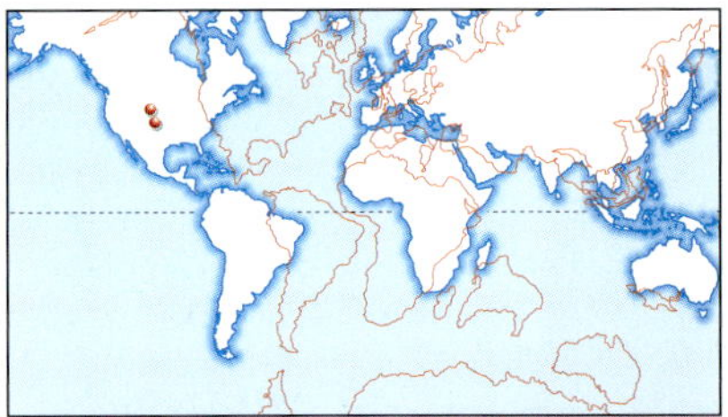

**ÜBERSICHT (DINOSAURIER)**
***Triceratops***
**Bedeutung des Namens:** Dreihorngesicht
**Periode:** Oberkreide
**Hauptgruppe:** Ceratopsia
**Länge:** 9 Meter
**Gewicht:** 5–8 Tonnen
**Nahrung:** Pflanzen
**Fossilfundstätten:** In den USA (Colorado, Wyoming)

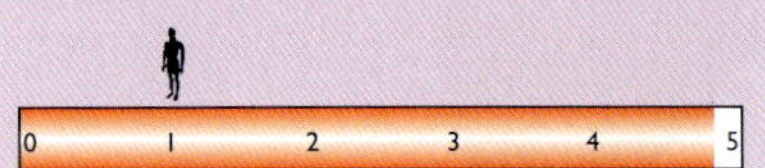


„Dreihorngesicht" zählte zu den größten Ceratopsiern und, nach den zahlreichen Fossilresten zu urteilen, zu den individuenreichsten Ceratopsiergattungen, die in der späten Kreidezeit Nordamerika durchstreiften. Die Fossilien von *Triceratops* werden ebenso wie die seines Todfeindes *Tyrannosaurus* auf ein Alter von 65 Millionen Jahren geschätzt, diese Tiere lebten also ganz am Ende der Kreidezeit. Nach Schätzungen einiger Fachleute hatte *Triceratops* eine Schulterhöhe von drei Metern, eine Gesamtlänge von zehn Metern und ein Gewicht von zehn Tonnen, andere Schätzungen liegen zehn bis zwanzig Prozent unter diesen Werten. *Triceratops* wurde 1889 von Othniel Charles Marsh nach Fossilien benannt, die man in der Nähe von Denver im US-Bundesstaat Colorado gefunden und zunächst für die Überreste einer ausgestorbenen Spezies eines Riesenbüffels gehalten hatte. Im Jahr zuvor hatte John Bell Hatcher mit umfangreichen Ausgrabungen in Niobrara Country im US-Bundesstaat Wyoming begonnen und dabei zahlreiche Fossilexemplare gefunden. Heute sind Teile von weit über fünfzig Individuen bekannt. Einige der zutage geförderten Nackenschilde weisen große Vertiefungen auf, die zu den Zähnen des *Tyrannosaurus* passen. Früher vermutete man, dass die Gattung *Triceratops* aus fünfzehn Spezies bestünde, doch ein großer Teil der Abweichungen kann durchaus geschlechts- oder altersspezifischer Natur sein.

Nach heutigen Auffassungen bestand die Gattung aus einer, zwei oder drei Arten; ein Dinosaurier, der früher als Spezies des *Triceratops* galt, gehört möglicherweise zu einer anderen Gattung, die vorläufig den Namen *Diceratops* erhielt.

Dinosaurier mit großen Hörnern werden in der Regel in Chasmosaurinen (siehe Seite 370), Dinosaurier mit langem Nackenschild, und Centrosaurinen (siehe Seite 363), Dinosaurier mit kurzem Nackenschild, eingeteilt. *Triceratops* scheint eine Mischung aus beiden zu sein, doch man stellt ihn wegen seines kürzeren, massiven Nackenschildes für gewöhnlich zu den Chasmosaurinen. Sein schmaler, stark gekrümmter zahnloser Schnabel konnte einen gewaltigen Druck ausüben, wenn sein Besitzer damit Pflanzenteile abkniff oder auf einen Gegner einhackte und diesem schwere Risswunden beibrachte. Mit seinen Hörnern und dem Nackenschild könnte *Triceratops* Angreifer oder Rivalen eingeschüchtert haben (siehe auch Seite 360).

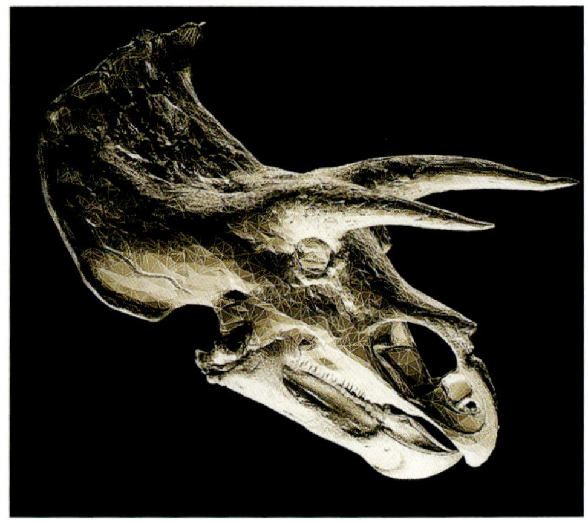

**GANZ RECHTS** Es existieren Dutzende fossiler *Triceratops*-Schädel, an denen der ausladende Nackenschild aus massivem Knochen und die langen Brauenhörner deutlich zu erkennen sind.

**RECHTS** Die Seitenansicht des *Triceratops* macht die Länge der Brauenhörner im Vergleich zu dem Nasenhorn deutlich.

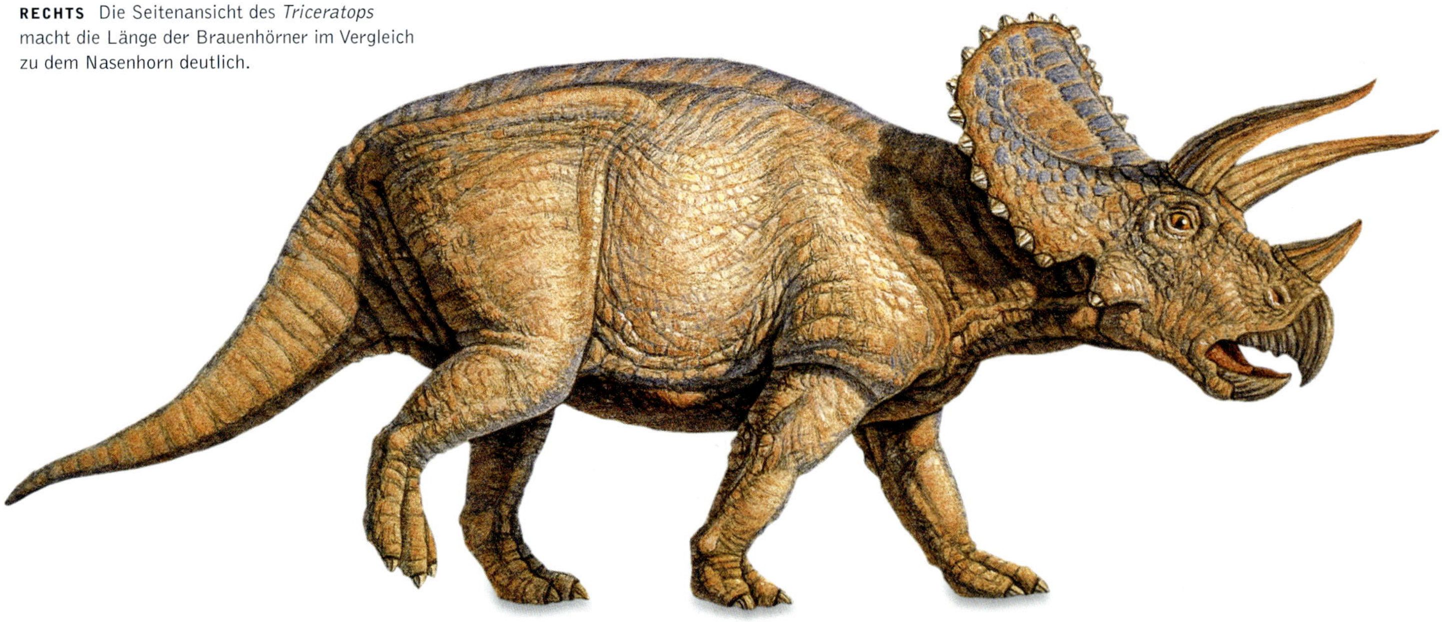

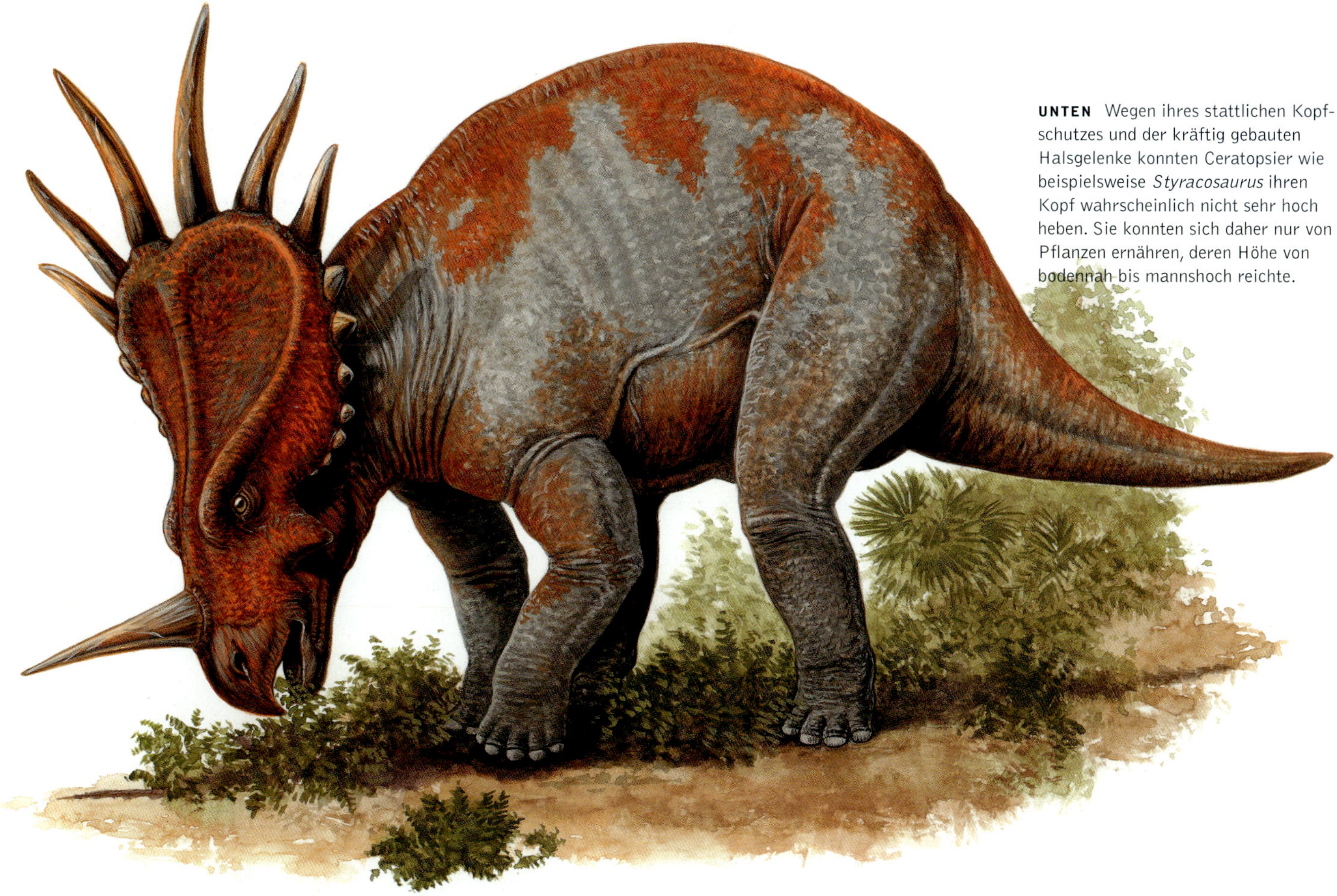

**UNTEN** Wegen ihres stattlichen Kopfschutzes und der kräftig gebauten Halsgelenke konnten Ceratopsier wie beispielsweise *Styracosaurus* ihren Kopf wahrscheinlich nicht sehr hoch heben. Sie konnten sich daher nur von Pflanzen ernähren, deren Höhe von bodennah bis mannshoch reichte.

# Styracosaurus

*Styracosaurus* besaß ein sehr langes, d. h. über sechzig Zentimeter hohes Nasenhorn, noch länger waren die beiden obersten Dornen an seinem Nackenschild. Letztere sind als Knochenkerne erhalten geblieben, die zu Lebzeiten des Tieres wahrscheinlich aber mit einer Hornscheide versehen und deshalb eigentlich noch länger und spitzer waren. Zu beiden Seiten der längsten Dorne standen am oberen Rand des Nackenschildes zwei oder drei weitere, immer kürzer werdende Dornen. Darunter begann eine Reihe kleiner Knochenstummel, die sich am seitlichen Rand bis zu den Augen hinzog und wie eine Bogenkante wirkte. Ähnliche flache Knochenauswüchse zierten auch die Nackenschilde vieler anderer Ceratopsier. Diese und die knöchernen Kerne der Dornen wurden von Auswüchsen der Epoccipitalknochen gebildet, die die Schildkante umrandeten. Am Nackenschild können oben auch noch zwei kleinere Dornen gesessen haben, und zwar an der zentralen Einkerbung des herzförmigen oberen Randes. Leider reichen die Fossilbelege nicht aus, um die Anordnung der Dornen in diesen Einzelheiten zu bestätigen.

Seinen Namen erhielt *Styracosaurus* 1913 von dem kanadischen Fossilienexperten Lawrence Lambe, der auch verschiedene andere Horndinosaurier benannte. *Styracusaurus* lebte gegen Ende des Zeitalters der Dinosaurier, vor 73 – 70 Millionen Jahren. Es gibt zwei ziemlich gut erhaltene Schädel, drei unvollständige Skelette sowie viele ungeordnete Bruchstücke von Knochen und Hörnern, die in Knochenschichten im US-Bundesstaat Arizona gefunden wurden und von denen einige oder auch alle von *Styracosaurus* stammen könnten. Aus den Funden hat man die These abgeleitet, dass *Styracosaurus* wie andere Ceratopsier in Herden umherstreifte und vielleicht jahreszeitlich bedingte Wanderungen zu neuen Nahrungsquellen unternahm. Hinsichtlich seiner Abmessungen war *Styracosaurus* ein mittelgroßer Ceratopsier; seine Körperlänge von der Nase bis zum Schwanz betrug bis zu 5,5 Meter, seine Schulterhöhe etwa 1,8 Meter. Mit seinem Hakenschnabel riss er niedrig wachsende Pflanzenteile ab. Ceratopsier konnten ihren Kopf nicht sehr hoch heben, deshalb kamen hohe Pflanzen als Nahrungsquelle für sie nicht infrage.

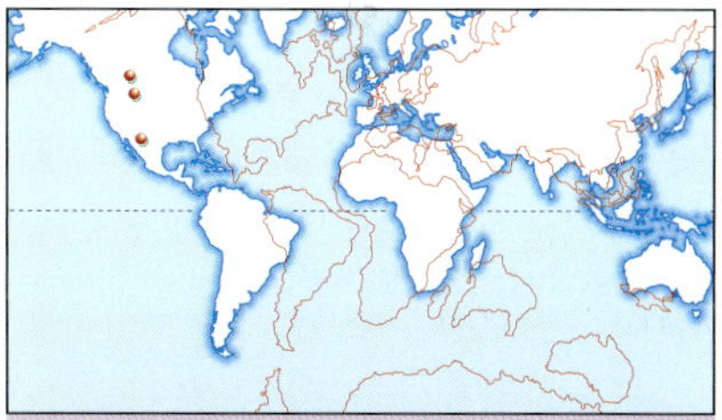

**ÜBERSICHT (DINOSAURIER)**
***Styracosaurus***
**Bedeutung des Namens:** Stachelechse
**Periode:** Oberkreide
**Hauptgruppe:** Ceratopsia
**Länge:** 5 – 5,5 Meter
**Gewicht:** 2 – 3 Tonnen
**Nahrung:** Pflanzen
**Fossilfundstätten:** In den USA (Montana, möglicherweise Arizona), in Kanada (Alberta)

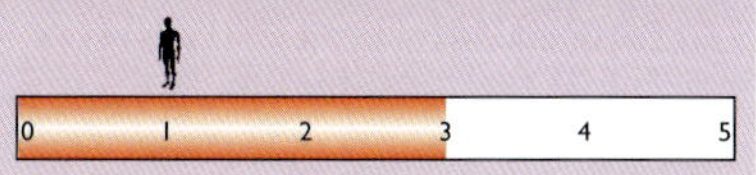

# Zusammen leben und zusammen sterben

*Fossilien von Horndinosauriern werden häufig in Knochenbetten oder Knochenschichten gefunden; an diesen Stellen besteht die Felsmasse mehr aus fossilierten Knochen als aus Gestein. Derartige Fundstätten könnten die Überreste Tausender Tiere enthalten. Wie sind solche Ansammlungen entstanden? Vielleicht versuchten einst große Herden auf ihrer üblichen Wanderung einen Fluss zu durchqueren, wurden dabei von den reißenden Fluten eines jahreszeitlich untypischen Hochwassers mitgerissen und kamen so zu Tode. Einem anderen Erklärungsversuch zufolge stammen die Fossilien von Dinosauriern, die über ein größeres Gebiet verstreut und auch über längere Zeit, vielleicht eine ganze Jahreszeit, dort gelebt hatten und gestorben waren; ihre verwesenden Kadaver oder die bereits von Aasfressern abgenagten Knochen wurden dann von einer plötzlichen Überschwemmung in eine Art Erosionsrinne geschwemmt.*

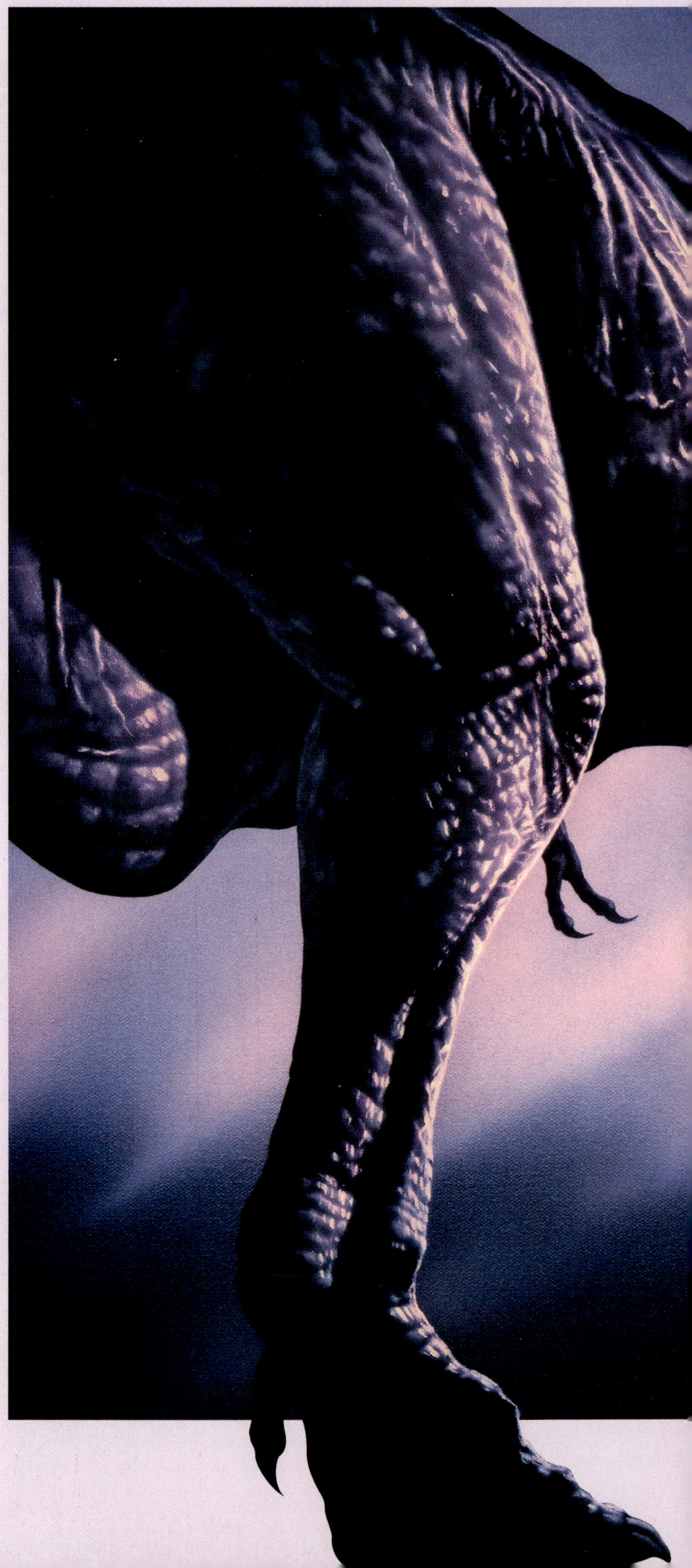

**RECHTS** Ein Tyrannosaurier bedroht im Zwielicht der Dämmerung eine *Styracosaurus*-Herde. Räuberisch lebende Dinosaurier bevorzugten diese Tageszeit um potenzielle Beutetiere anzugreifen. Dass Horndinosaurier in Herden lebten, ist durch verschiedene Quellen belegt, so u. a. auch durch große Fossilienansammlungen in so genannten Knochenbetten und durch fossilierte Bewegungsspuren.

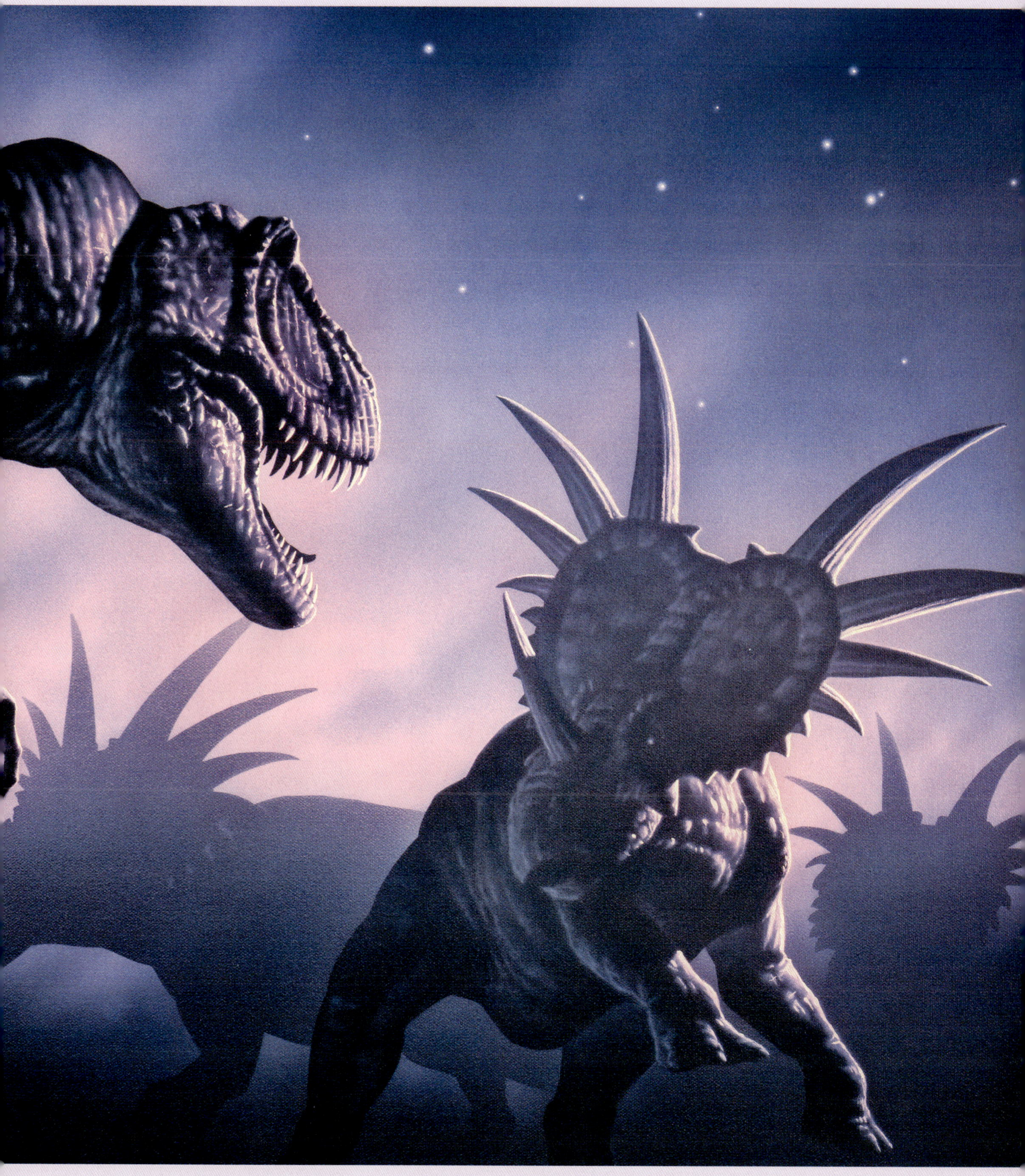

# Chasmosaurus

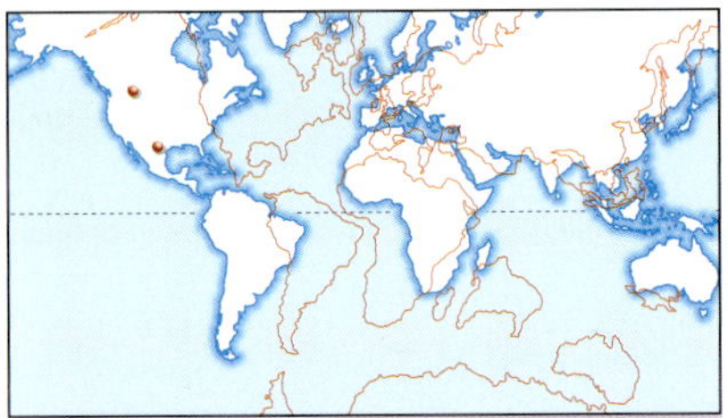

**ÜBERSICHT (DINOSAURIER)**

***Chasmosaurus***

**Bedeutung des Namens:** Abgrund-, Schlucht- oder Klammreptil

**Periode:** Oberkreide

**Hauptgruppe:** Ceratopsia

**Länge:** 5 – 6 Meter

**Gewicht:** 2 – 3 Tonnen

**Nahrung:** Pflanzen

**Fossilfundstätten:** Von Kanada (Alberta) bis in die USA (Texas)

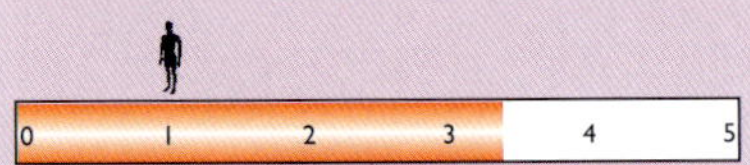


Die Chasmosaurinen waren eine Untergruppe der Horndinosaurier oder Ceratopsier. Sie unterschieden sich von der zweiten Untergruppe, den Centrosaurinen, dadurch, dass ihre Brauenhörner länger als ihr Nasenhorn waren, dass sie längere Schädel und Schnauzen und allgemein längere Nackenschilde besaßen. *Chasmosaurus* war ein mittelgroßer Vertreter der Chasmosaurinen. Er wurde bis zu sechs Meter lang, was etwa der Länge – von der Schnauzenspitze bis zum Schwanzende gemessen – des größten rezenten Nashorns, des Breitmaulnashorns, entsprach. Die Knochenteile des Nackenschildes waren auf die Scheitelbeinstrebe in der Mitte und zwei schmale kantige Bögen reduziert, die den oberen und die seitlichen Ränder bildeten und eine große Aussparung auf beiden Seiten des Schildes umrahmten. Die Aussparungen oder Fenster waren bei *Chasmosaurus* größer als bei fast allen anderen Ceratopsiern; ihnen verdankt die Gattung ihren Namen. Zu Lebzeiten des *Chasmosaurus* waren die Öffnungen wahrscheinlich von einer dünnen Schicht aus Muskeln und Bindegewebe ausgefüllt und mit Haut überzogen. Der Nackenschild war demzufolge kein besonders stabiles Gebilde, und so diente er wohl auch nicht als Schutz, sondern als optisches Signal, das zum Imponierverhalten der Tiere gehörte (siehe Seite 360).

Mit seiner Körpergröße und seinen Proportionen war *Chasmosaurus* ein recht typischer Horndinosaurier; auch sein zahnloser Papageienschnabel an der Schnauzenspitze, die massiven Säulenbeine und der ziemlich kleine, spitz zulaufende Schwanz wiesen ihn als Ceratopsier aus. *Chasmosaurus* lebte vor über 75 – 70 Millionen Jahren. Die zahlreichen Fossilien aus verschiedenen Teilen Nordamerikas – von Alberta bis Texas – deuten darauf hin, dass die Gattung sehr individuenreich und weit verbreitet gewesen zu sein scheint. Der Name *Chasmosaurus* wurde 1914 von Lawrence Lambe geprägt.

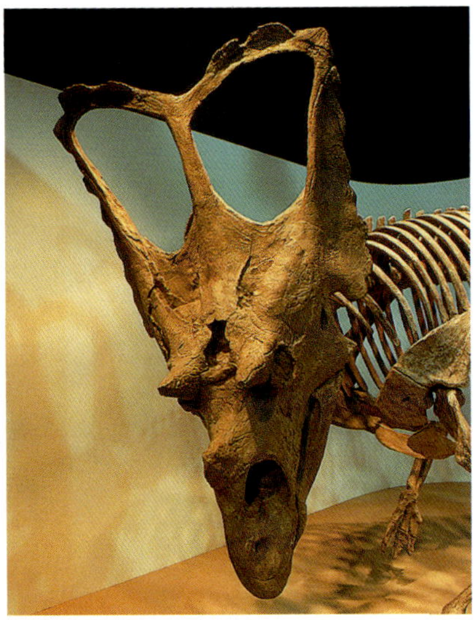

**LINKS** Bei diesem *Chasmosaurus*-Schädel aus dem Royal Turrell Museum in der kanadischen Provinz Alberta sind deutlich die riesigen Fenster zu erkennen, die den Nackenschild zwar leicht, dafür aber auch zerbrechlich machten.

**RECHTS** Bei dieser Nachbildung wird *Chasmosaurus* mit verhältnismäßig langen, spitzen Gesichtshörnern gezeigt. Die Hornsubstanz, mit der die knöchernen Auswüchse ursprünglich überzogen waren, bleibt bei der Fossilierung nur selten erhalten; deshalb lässt sich die einstige Länge der Gesichtshörner nur anhand der Knochenkerne abschätzen.

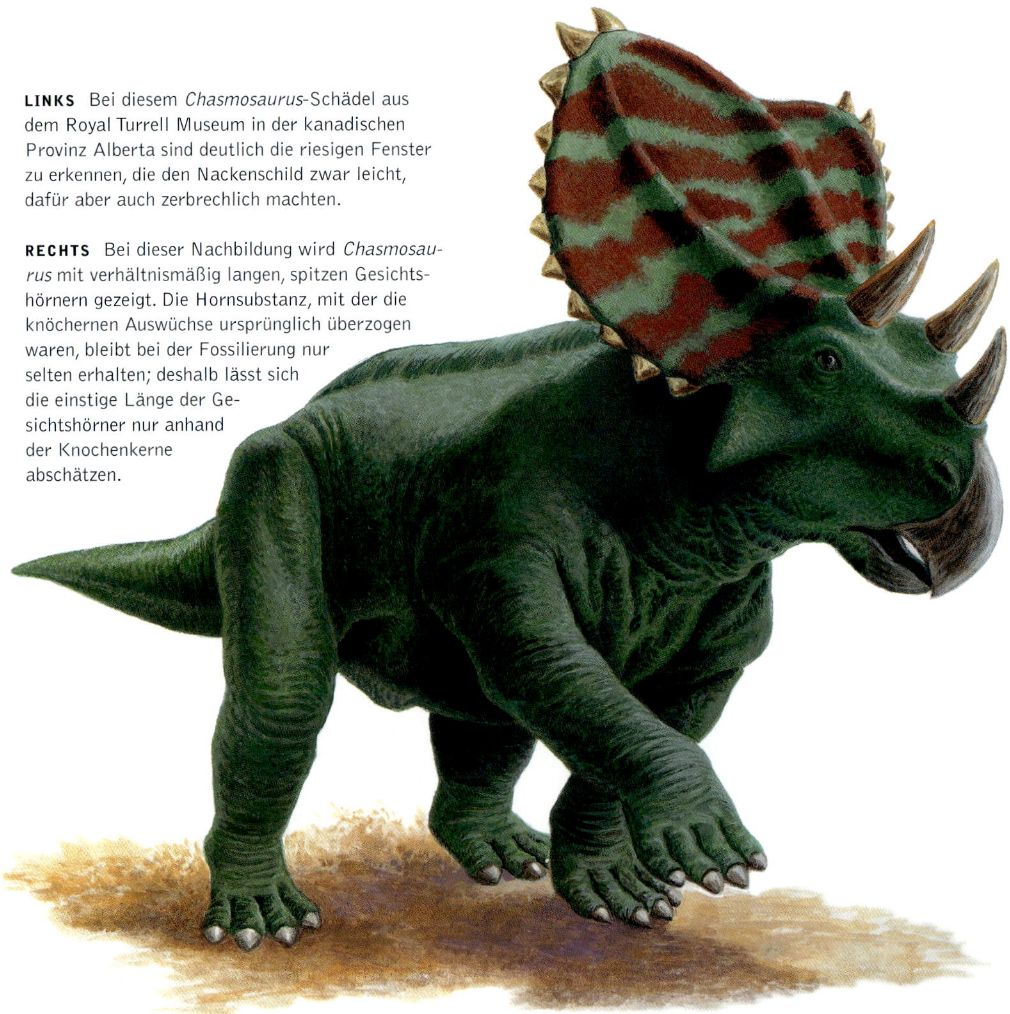

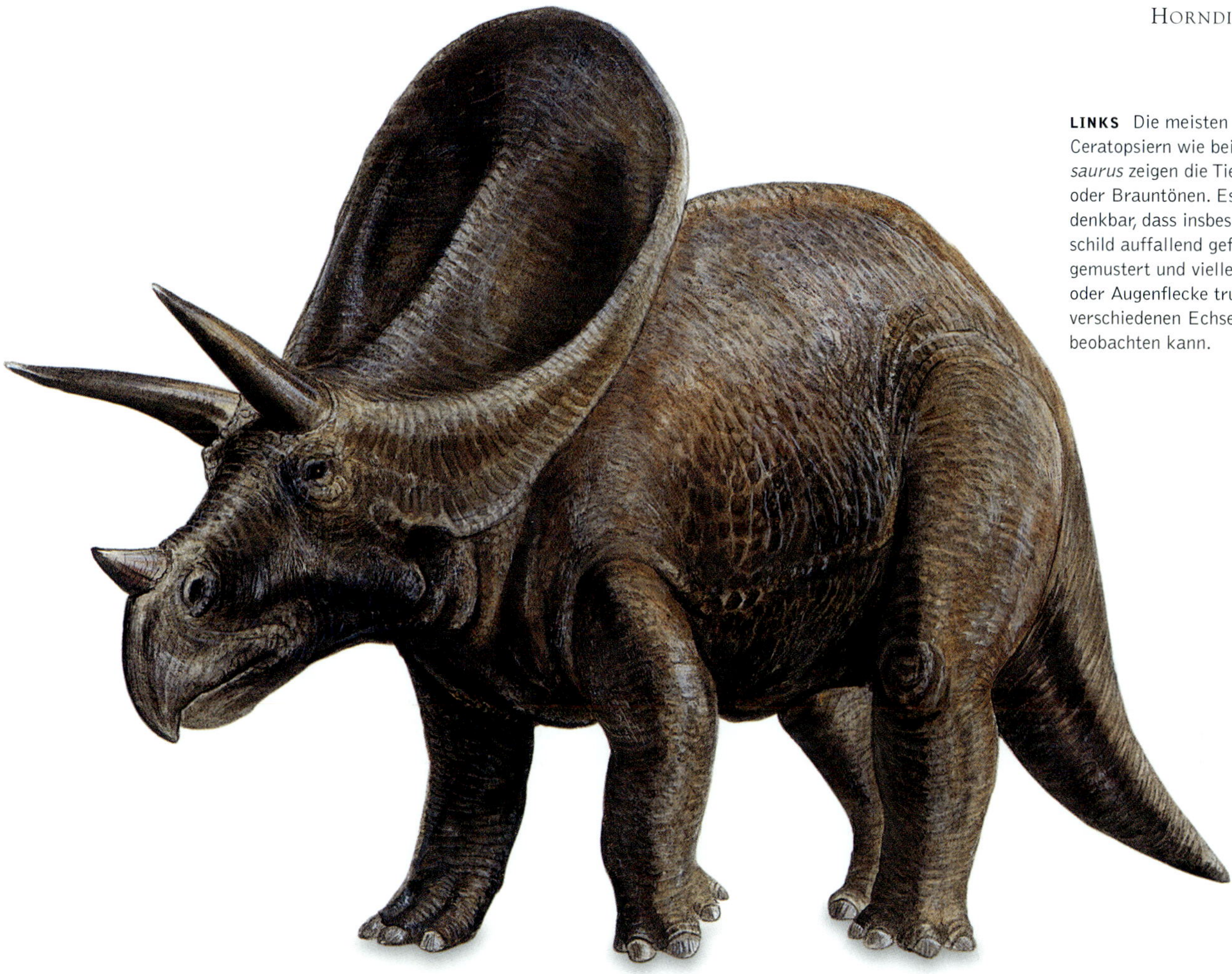

**LINKS** Die meisten Nachbildungen von Ceratopsiern wie beispielsweise *Torosaurus* zeigen die Tiere in tristen Grün- oder Brauntönen. Es ist aber durchaus denkbar, dass insbesondere der Nackenschild auffallend gefärbt und lebhaft gemustert und vielleicht sogar Streifen oder Augenflecke trug, wie man es bei verschiedenen Echsen der Jetztzeit beobachten kann.

# TOROSAURUS

Der Name dieses Dinosauriers wird häufig fälschlicherweise mit „Stierreptil" übersetzt, doch dann müsste er *Taurosaurus* lauten; in Wirklichkeit bedeutet *Torosaurus* „durchlöchertes Reptil". *Torosaurus* wog sieben oder acht Tonnen und hatte eine Beckenhöhe von vielleicht zwei Metern; damit konnte er *Triceratops* hinsichtlich der Größe durchaus Konkurrenz machen. Von *Torosaurus* heißt es auch oft, er habe den längsten Schädel von allen Landtieren besessen. Bei der Rekonstruktion eines unvollständigen Schädels ist man, gemessen von der Schnauze bis zum hinteren Schildrand, auf eine Länge von 2,8 Metern gekommen. Ein jüngerer Fund von *Pentaceratops*-Fossilien stellt diesen Rekord allerdings infrage. Eine Zeit lang ging man davon aus, dass die Gattung *Torosaurus* mehr als fünfundzwanzig Spezies umfasst, doch sind viele der festgestellten Unterschiede wahrscheinlich ein Ergebnis natürlicher Veränderung innerhalb nur einer Art.

Der Nackenschild von *Torosaurus* bestand wie bei *Chasmosaurus* größtenteils aus Haut und Bindegewebe. Der inliegende Knochen war auf dünne Streben reduziert, von denen eine in der Mitte und die übrigen an den Rändern lagen. Dieser Aufbau muss, verglichen mit dem massiven Knochenschild beispielsweise des *Triceratops*, eine deutliche Gewichtsverringerung bedeutet, den Schild als Schutz für Nacken und Schultern aber unbrauchbar gemacht haben. Das legt den Schluss nahe, dass das Gebilde hauptsächlich dem Imponierverhalten seines Besitzers diente (siehe Seite 360). *Torosaurus* trug wie andere Chasmosaurinen zwei große Brauenhörner und auf der Schnauze ein kleineres höckerartiges Horn. Der Mund endete vorn in einem zahnlosen Schnabel, in der Wangenregion befanden sich zwei Reihen kräftiger Backenzähne, die Kiefer wurden von mächtigen Kaumuskeln bewegt. *Torosaurus* besaß wie andere Ceratopsier einen dicken Hals, einen schweren Körper, stämmige elefantenartige Gliedmaßen und einen verhältnismäßig kurzen Schwanz. Aus Begleitfossilien wissen wir, dass das Tier vor über 70 Millionen Jahren Küstenebenen bewohnte, insbesondere jene, die an der heutigen mexikanischen Küste liegen.

Die zuerst untersuchten *Torosaurus*-Fossilien wurden von John Bell Hatcher entdeckt und 1891 von Othniel Charles Marsh benannt.

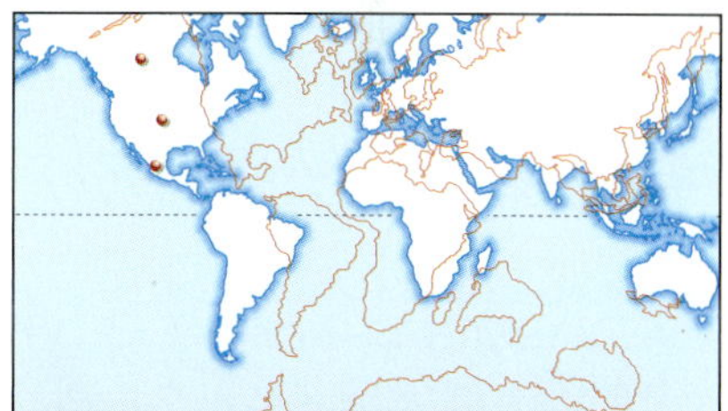

**ÜBERSICHT (DINOSAURIER)**
***Torosaurus***
**Bedeutung des Namens:** Durchlöchertes Reptil
**Periode:** Oberkreide
**Hauptgruppe:** Ceratopsia
**Länge:** 6 – 8 Meter
**Gewicht:** 7 – 8 Tonnen
**Nahrung:** Pflanzen
**Fossilfundstätten:** In Kanada, in den USA, in Mexiko

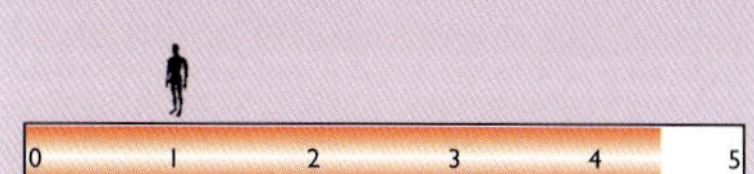

# ANCHICERATOPS

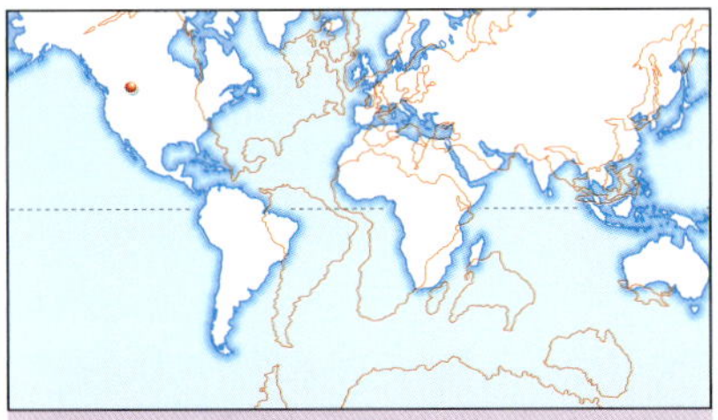

**ÜBERSICHT (DINOSAURIER)**
***Anchiceratops***
**Bedeutung des Namens:** Fast-Horngesicht
**Periode:** Oberkreide
**Hauptgruppe:** Ceratopsia
**Länge:** 4,5 – 6 Meter
**Gewicht:** 2 – 3 Tonnen
**Nahrung:** Pflanzen
**Fossilfundstätten:** In Kanada (Alberta)

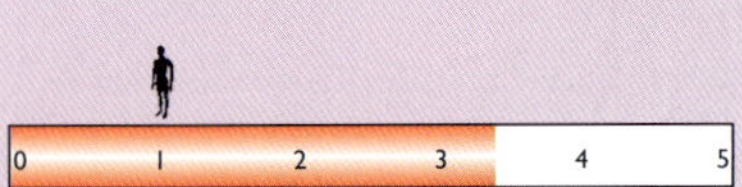


*Anchiceratops* ähnelte in vielerlei Hinsicht, beispielsweise hinsichtlich der Größe und der Proportionen seines Körpers, *Chasmosaurus* (siehe Seite 370). Wie bei den meisten Ceratopsiern mit langem Nackenschild lagen die hauptsächlichen Unterschiede in der Größe des Nackenschildes mit den dazugehörigen Knochenhöckern und -dornen sowie in den Proportionen der Gesichtshörner. *Anchiceratops* trug sehr lange Brauenhörner und ein viel kürzeres Nasenhorn, das wahrscheinlich schräg nach vorn, in Richtung der schnabelartigen Vorderseite des Mundes, wuchs. Die Knochenstruktur des Nackenschildes wies Aussparungen oder Fenster auf, die allerdings nicht so groß wie bei *Chasmosaurus* waren. Auf dem hinteren Rand des Schildes saßen wahrscheinlich drei Paar kurzer Dornen, die aus lang gestreckten Epoccipitalknochen bestanden; dicht unter diesen Dornen können an der mittleren Knochenstrebe zwei weitere flache, wie Napfschnecken geformte Knochenauswüchse gesessen haben.

Im Jahr 1914 wurden mehrere von Barnum Brown beschriebene Ceratopsier benannt; darunter war auch *Anchiceratops*. Sein Name widerspiegelt die Ähnlichkeit des Tieres mit anderen Langhorn-Dinosauriern wie beispielsweise *Monoclonius*, *Centrosaurus* oder *Triceratops*. Fossilienexperten der damaligen Zeit vertraten die Ansicht, dass bei diesen Dinosauriern eine Veränderung des Nackenschilds und des Nasenhorns hinsichtlich Größe und Komplexität zu beobachten sei, die eine zeitliche Entwicklungsreihe mit dem großen *Triceratops* als Endglied bilde. Heute wissen wir jedoch, dass viele dieser Dinosaurier nicht in aufeinander folgenden Zeiträumen, sondern nebeneinander existierten. Das Alter der Fossilien von *Anchiceratops* wird auf 73 – 70 Millionen Jahre geschätzt. Die Überreste stammen größtenteils aus der kanadischen Provinz Alberta; zu ihnen gehören sechs Schädel unterschiedlichen Vollständigkeitsgrades, Brauenhörner und der Großteil eines Skeletts.

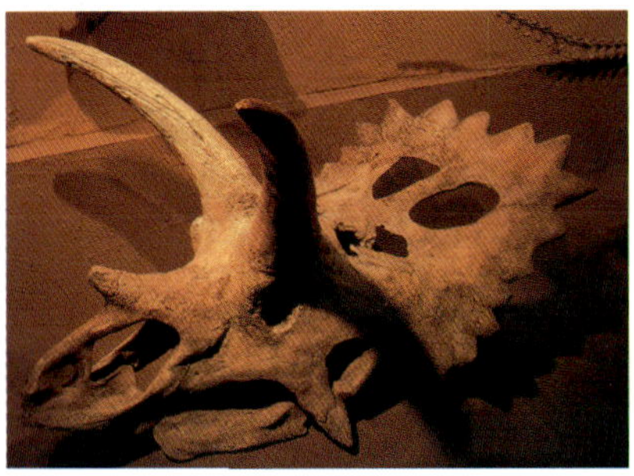

**OBEN** Der fossilierte *Anchiceratops*-Schädel weist ziemlich kleine Fenster in der Knochenfläche des Nackenschildes auf.

**RECHTS** *Anchiceratops* hatte etwa die Körpergröße eines heutigen Nashorns. Sein spitzer Schnabel muss selbst mit zäher pflanzlicher Nahrung zurechtgekommen sein.

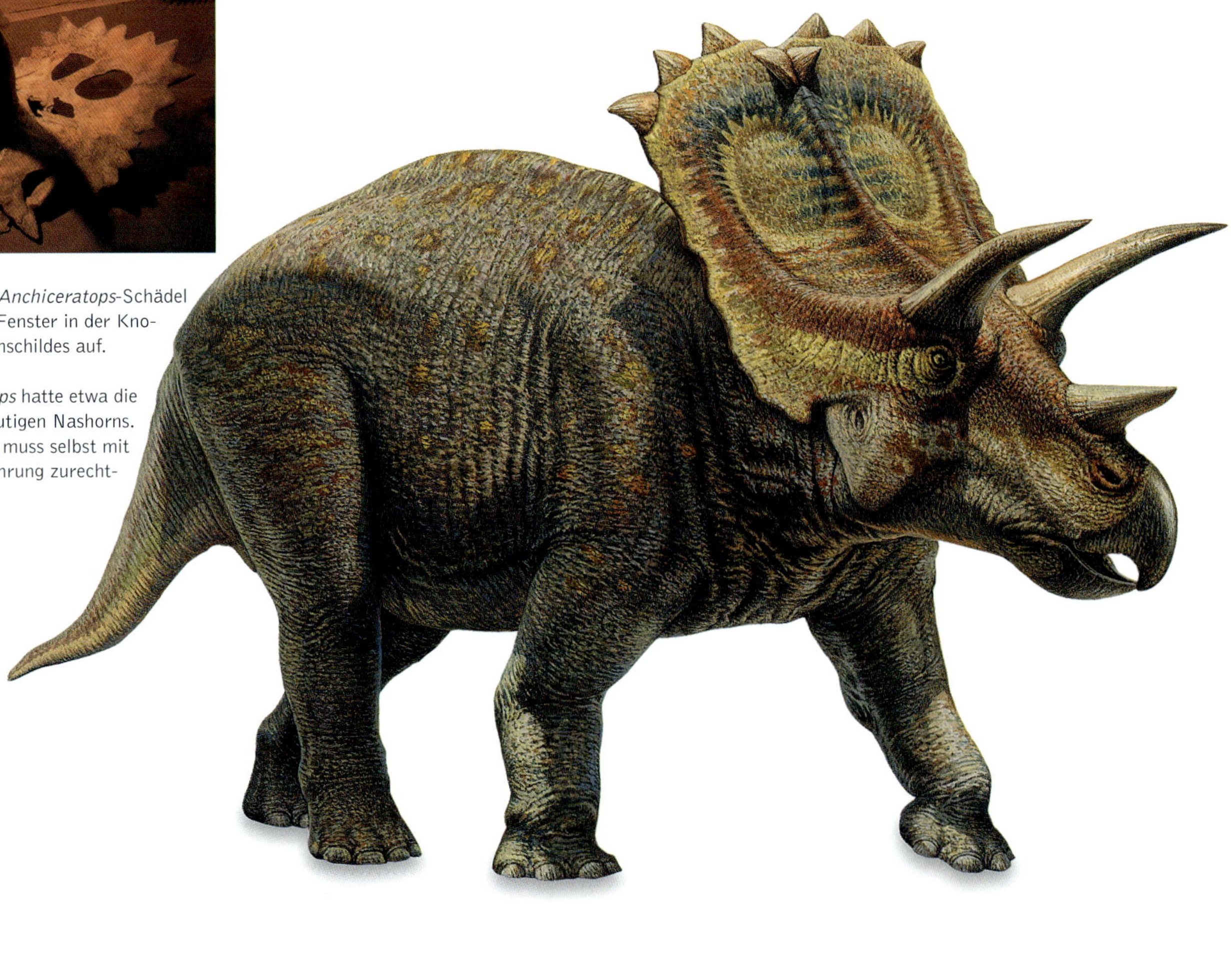

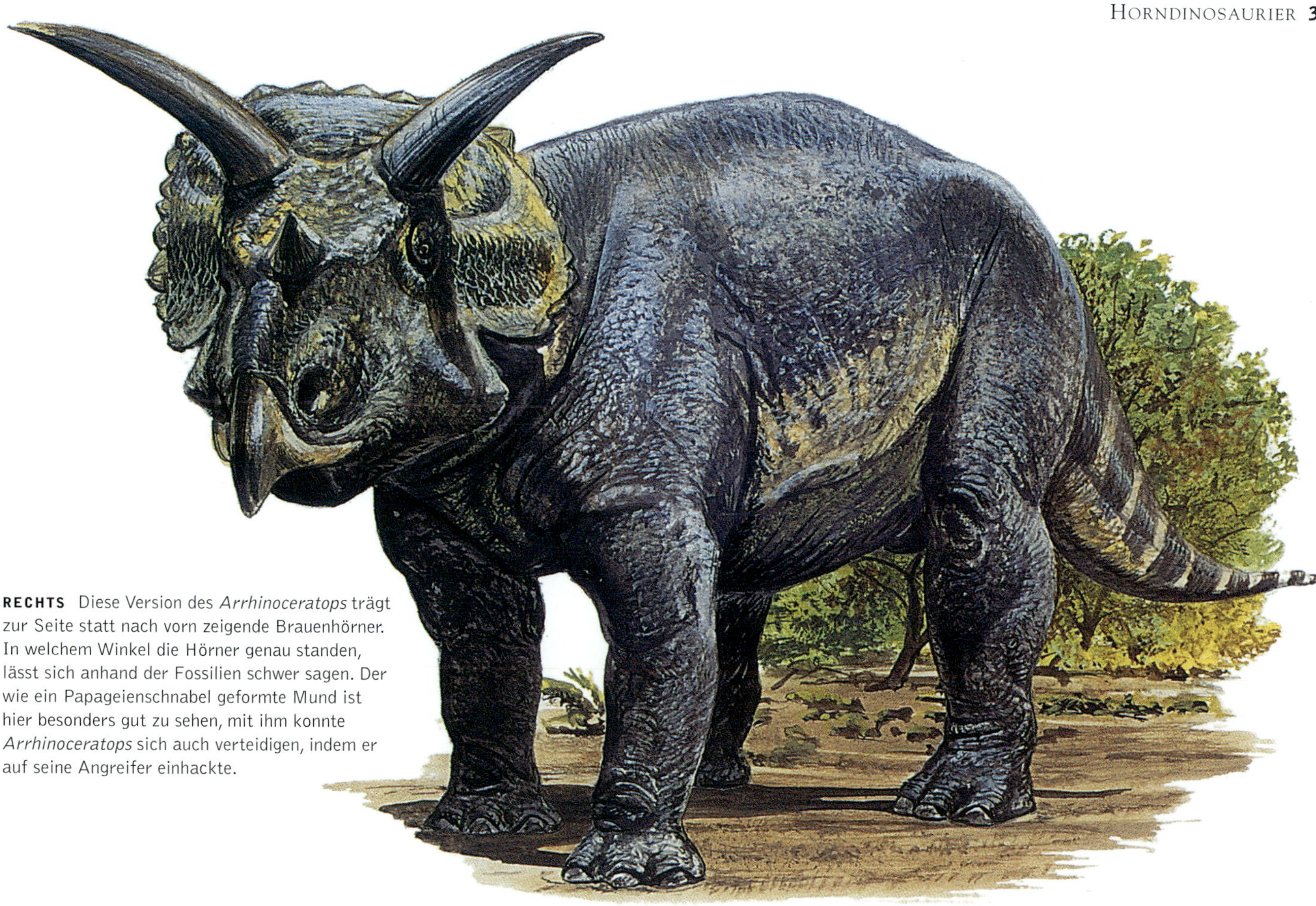

**RECHTS** Diese Version des *Arrhinoceratops* trägt zur Seite statt nach vorn zeigende Brauenhörner. In welchem Winkel die Hörner genau standen, lässt sich anhand der Fossilien schwer sagen. Der wie ein Papageienschnabel geformte Mund ist hier besonders gut zu sehen, mit ihm konnte *Arrhinoceratops* sich auch verteidigen, indem er auf seine Angreifer einhackte.

# ARRHINOCERATOPS

Der Name dieses Dinosauriers wurde 1925 von William Parks anhand von Fossilien geprägt, die man zwei Jahre zuvor in der Region des Red Deer River in der kanadischen Provinz Alberta entdeckt hatte. Die Überreste haben etwa das gleiche Alter und kommen von derselben Fundstätte wie die Knochen von *Anchiceratops* (siehe gegenüber). Das heißt, dass beide Tiere wahrscheinlich zur gleichen Zeit lebten. *Arrhinoceratops* ist allerdings nur von einem Schädelfund bekannt. Parks war bei der Benennung davon ausgegangen, dass das Tier über den Augenbrauen je ein langes, spitzes Horn trug, dass der Knochenhöcker auf der Nase des *Arrhinoceratops* aber kein echtes Horn war. Das Horn hätte als gesondertes Knochenstück existieren müssen, wurde aber nicht gefunden, und deshalb gab Parks dem Tier einen Namen, der „Gesicht ohne Nasenhorn" bedeutet. Heute ist man der Meinung, dass *Arrhinoceratops* doch ein Nasenhorn besaß, so dass der Name inzwischen höchst unpassend erscheint.

Der Nackenschild von *Arrhinoceratops* ähnelte in Größe und Proportionen dem von *Triceratops*, wies allerdings seitliche Fenster auf, während der Schild des *Triceratops* aus massivem Knochen bestand. Der Schildrand ist von flachen, runden Epoccipitalknochen gesäumt, die wie eine zierende Bogenkante wirken und bei vielen Ceratopsiern zu sehen sind. Der zahnlose Hakenschnabel an der Vorderseite des Mundes eignete sich ausgezeichnet zum Abschneiden und „Ernten" zäher pflanzlicher Nahrung, die von ganzen Reihen großer Backenzähne zermahlen und während des Kauens in den fleischigen Wangentaschen des Mundes behalten wurde. Von *Arrhinoceratops* sind bislang zwar keine weiteren Fossilien gefunden worden, doch man nimmt wohl zu Recht an, dass das Tier anderen Ceratopsiern ähnelte, die in der späten Kreidezeit im westlichen Nordamerika lebten. Diese stellten im Großen und Ganzen eine Gruppe mit vergleichsweise geringer Fortentwicklung dar, wie die vielen Tausend Fossilien von Hunderten Fundstätten belegen. Diese Überreste zeigen, dass die Horndinosaurier verhältnismäßig „konservativ" waren, d.h. dass diese Gruppe ihre ursprüngliche Grundform trotz ihrer langen Geschichte nicht bedeutend verändert hat (siehe Seite 10 f).

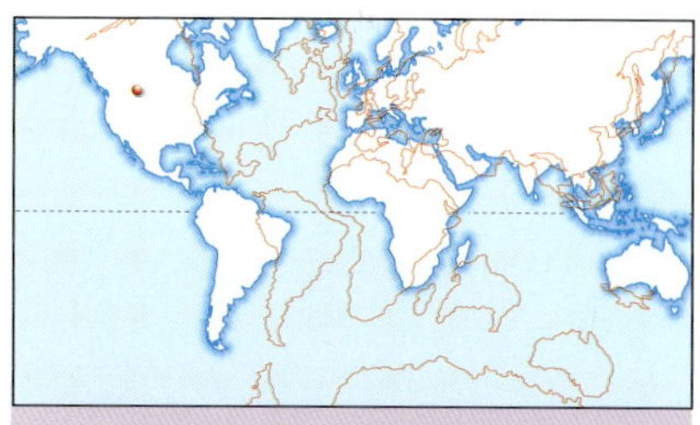

**ÜBERSICHT (DINOSAURIER)**
***Arrhinoceratops***
**Bedeutung des Namens:** Gesicht ohne Nasenhorn
**Periode:** Oberkreide
**Hauptgruppe:** Ceratopsia
**Länge:** 6 Meter
**Gewicht:** 3,5 Tonnen
**Nahrung:** Pflanzen
**Fossilfundstätten:** In Kanada (Alberta)

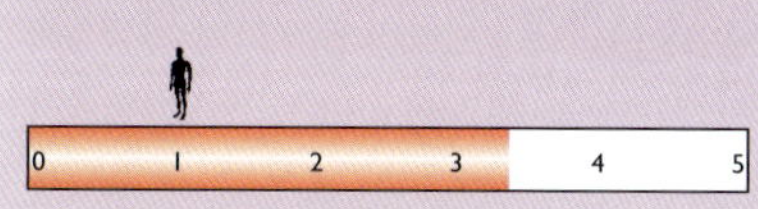

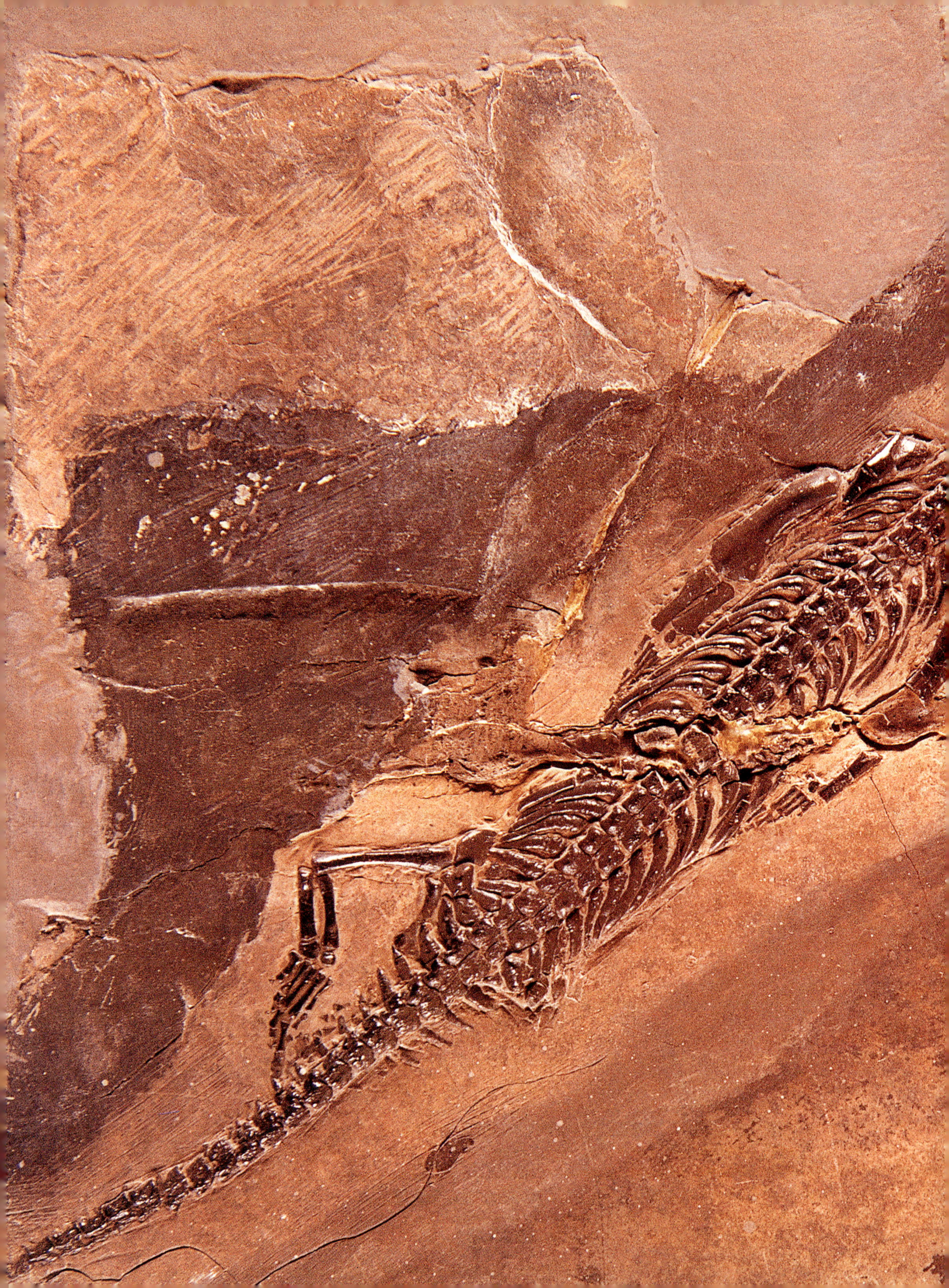

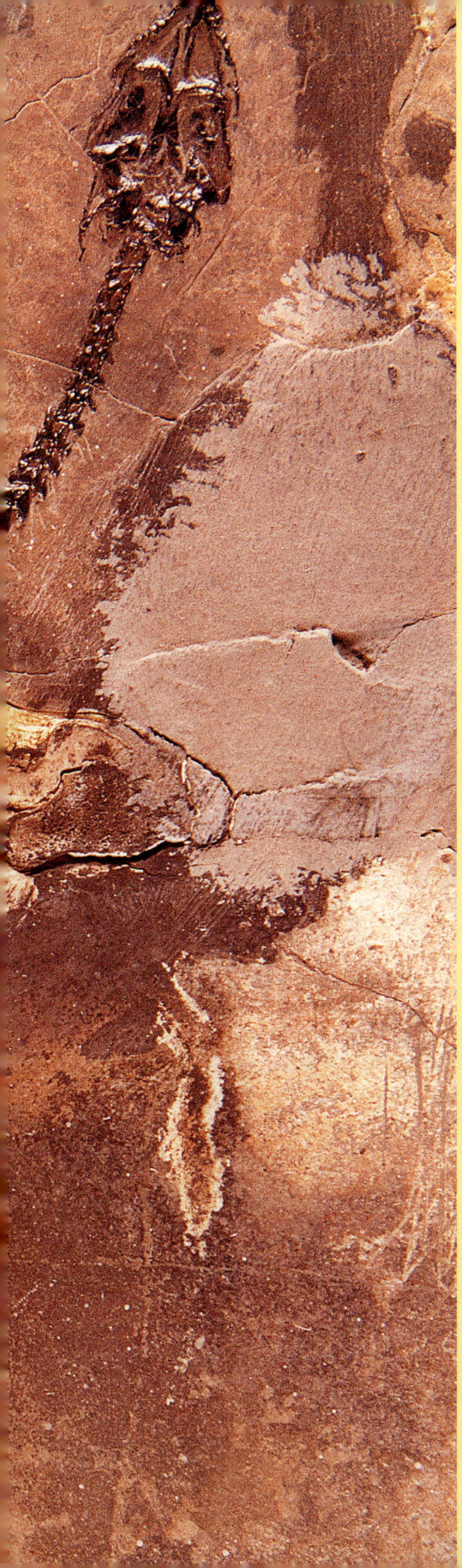

KAPITEL VIERZEHN

# ANDERE LEBEWESEN IM ZEITALTER DER DINOSAURIER

*Die Dinosaurier waren während des Mesozoikums die Beherrscher des Festlandes, doch sie besaßen auch Verwandte, die keine Dinosaurier waren. Diese „Cousins“ teilten die Welt mit ihnen – sie beherrschten die Lüfte und die Meere. In der Zeit, da auf der Erde die Reptilien dominierten, erschienen auch die ersten Säugetiere und Vögel.*

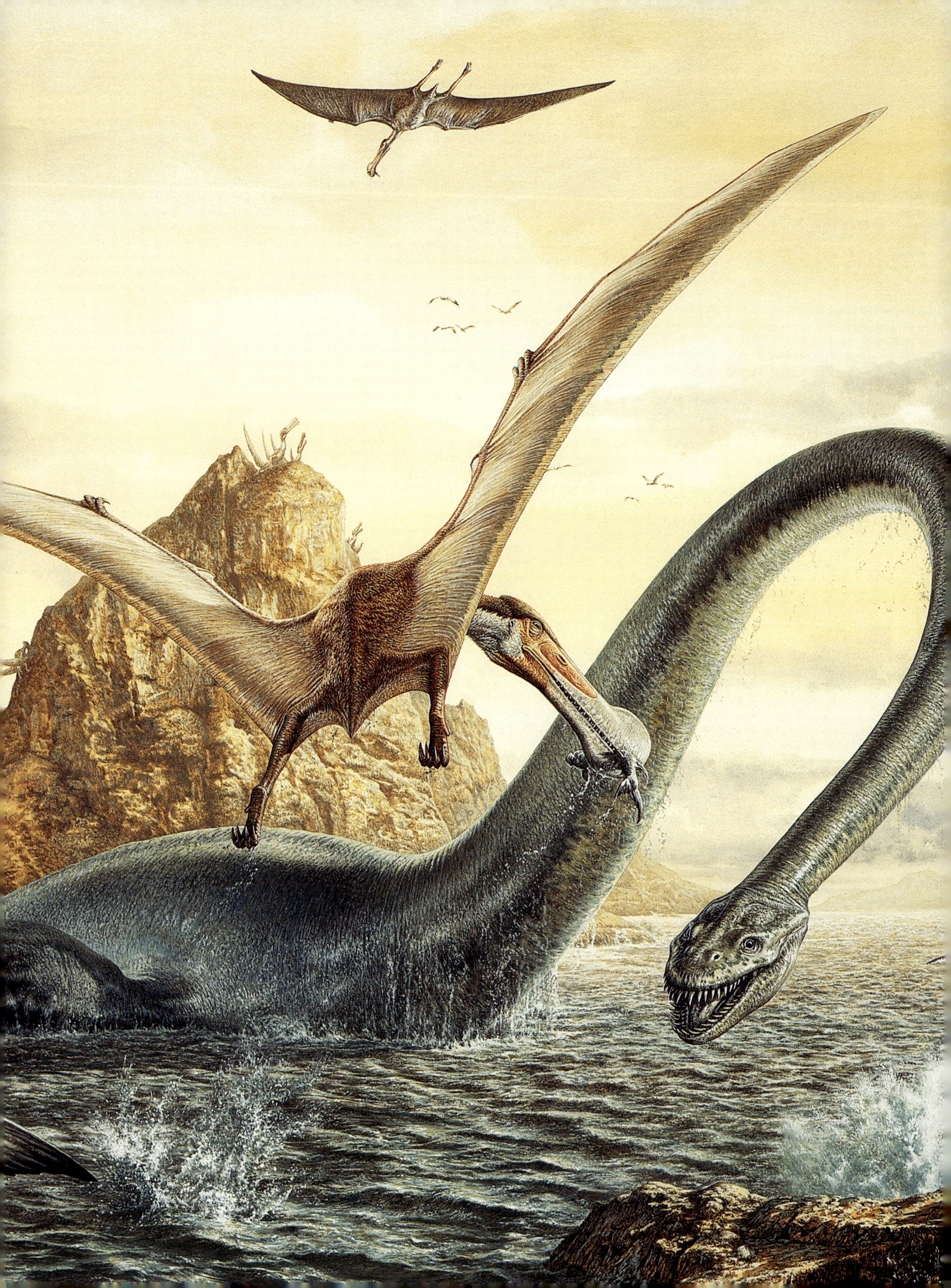

# TIERE ÜBERALL

***Das Mesozoikum (vor 250–65 Millionen Jahren) wird so oft das Zeitalter der Dinosaurier genannt, dass man dabei mitunter die anderen damals existierenden Tiere ganz übersieht. Dennoch lebten die gesamte lange Zeit hindurch auch unzählige andere Reptilien auf dem Land, in den Meeren und Lüften, gab es noch andere Wirbeltiere wie beispielsweise Fische und Amphibien. Noch weniger wird in der Regel an die Scharen der wirbellosen Tiere gedacht, die in nahezu allen Ecken und Winkeln zu Hause waren – Insekten, Spinnen, Würmer und Schnecken auf dem Festland und die endlose Vielfalt der Krebstiere, Mollusken, Seesterne, Korallen und Quallen in ihren aquatischen Lebensräumen.***

## SÄUGETIERE UND VÖGEL

Die beiden großen Tiergruppen, die zu Beginn des Zeitalters der Dinosaurier noch nicht existierten, waren die Säugetiere und die Vögel. Die Säugetiere erschienen schon sehr bald, in der Oberen Trias, blieben das gesamte Zeitalter hindurch allerdings klein und unscheinbar. Vom Oberen Jura, also etwa von der Mitte des Mesozoikums an, flatterten Vögel wie *Archaeopteryx* durch die Lüfte. Sie hatten sich wahrscheinlich aus kleinen Fleisch fressenden Dinosauriern entwickelt, die wir Maniraptoren nennen.

## AUSSERGEWÖHNLICHE „REPTILIEN"

Zu den außergewöhnlichsten mesozoischen Tieren gehörten die Pterosaurier. Man nennt sie mitunter auch Pterodaktylen, doch *Pterodactylus* war nur eine von Dutzenden Gattungen, und so wird für die gesamte Gruppe der „Flugsaurier" der Name Pterosaurier verwendet. Die Pterosaurier gelten als eine gleichwertige Gruppe neben den Dinosauria – den Dinosauriern – und den Crocodylia – den Krokodilen und Alligatoren. Alle drei, Pterosaurier, Dinosaurier und Krokodilier, stellt man in die Obergruppe der Archosaurier oder „Herrscherreptilien". Wie die genauen Verwandtschaftsverhältnisse der Pterosaurier auch beschaffen sein mögen, die Tiere besaßen eine einzigartige Anatomie, wie es Ähnliches weder zuvor noch danach gegeben hat.

## FLIEGER IM HAARKLEID

Aus Fossilfunden wissen wir, dass manche Pterosaurier eine Schuppenhaut, andere hingegen ein Fell oder ein Haarkleid trugen. Die meisten waren gewandte Flieger, und das Leben in der Luft erforderte, dass sie warmblütig waren. Die Pterosaurier existierten zur gleichen Zeit wie die Dinosaurier. Sie hatten sich in der Trias wahrscheinlich aus kleinen bodenlebenden Reptilien entwickelt, erlebten im Jura und in der Kreidezeit ihre Blütezeit und verschwanden dann während des Massenaussterbens. Die frühen Pterosaurier nennen wir Rhamphorhynchoiden. Sie besaßen lange Schwänze, ihre schnabelartigen Münder waren mit vielen Zähnen besetzt. Die späteren Flugsaurier werden als Pterodaktyloiden bezeichnet. Die meisten dieser Tiere waren kurzschwänzig und hatten zahnlose Schnäbel. Manche Pterodactyloiden trugen seltsame knöcherne Kopfkämme. Einige später erschienene Typen erreichten eine gigantische Größe und entwickelten sich zu den größten fliegenden Tieren aller Zeiten.

## FINGERFLÜGEL

Der Körper der Pterosaurier zeigte eine perfekte Anpassung an das Fliegen. Er war kompakt und leicht und mit hohlen Knochen sowie einer kräftigen Brustmuskulatur zum Bewegen der Flügel ausgestattet. Die kräftigen Füße endeten in fünf bekrallten Zehen; manche Pterosaurier konnten rennen oder hüpfen, andere schliefen vielleicht kopfüber im Ruhehang wie die Fledermäuse. Der Aufbau ihrer Flügel unterschied sich von dem der Vögel, er ähnelte oberflächlich vielleicht eher dem eines Fledermausflügels. Die Pterosaurierflügel bestanden aus einer sehr dünnen, dehnbaren Flugmembran, die zum Teil von den Armknochen, in erster Linie aber von den übermäßig lang gestreckten Knochen des vierten Fingers ausgespannt wurden. (Den Flügel einer Fledermaus halten vier – der zweite bis fünfte – Finger.) Die ersten drei Finger bildeten kurze Klauen an der Vorderkante des Flügels. Die Pterosaurier waren aber weder die Vorfahren der Vögel oder Fledermäuse noch stammten sie von Vögeln oder Fledermäusen ab. Während die Einen die Lüfte eroberten, gingen andere Reptiliengruppen des Mesozoikums einen gänzlich anderen Weg: Aus ihren Gliedmaßen wurden Schwimmflossen, denn sie eroberten das Wasser für sich und entwickelten in diesem Milieu eine rein aquatische Lebensweise (siehe Seiten 382–383).

**VORHERGEHENDE SEITE** Sedimentgesteine lagerten sich in der Regel in Schichten ab, die vom Gewicht späterer Ablagerungen allmählich zusammengepresst wurden. Von der Masse der Schichten wurden auch Tierkadaver oder andere Überreste wie dieses Meeresreptil der Gattung *Pachypleurosaurus* förmlich platt gedrückt.

**LINKS** Der Pterosaurier *Criorhynchus* hat im Sturzflug einen Fisch erbeutet, auf den es auch der langhalsige Plesiosaurier (Meeresreptil) *Elasmosaurus* abgesehen hatte. *Criorhynchus* lebte in der frühen Kreidezeit. Seine Flügelspannweite war mit fünf Metern deutlich größer als bei irgendeinem rezenten Vogel.

# RHAMPHORHYNCHUS

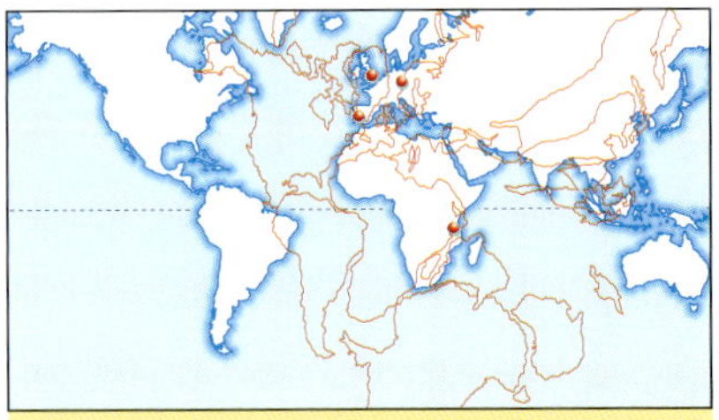

**ÜBERSICHT (PTERIOSAURIER)**

***Rhamphorhynchus***

**Bedeutung des Namens:** Schnabelschnauze

**Periode:** Mittlerer bis Oberer Jura

**Hauptgruppe:** Pterosauria (Rhamphorhynchoidae)

**Flügelspannweite:** Bis 1,8 Meter

**Gewicht:** Bis 5 Kilogramm

**Nahrung:** Fische, Kalmare u. ä. Meerestiere

**Fossilfundstätten:** In England, in Deutschland, möglicherweise in Ostafrika und Portugal

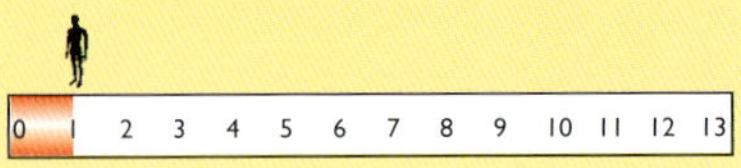


*Rhamphorhynchus* ist einer der bekannteren Pterosaurier, von ihm wurden zahlreiche Fossilien in der Umgebung von Solnhofen, in der Gegend um Oxford, vielleicht auch in Ostafrika und Portugal gefunden. Nach ihm wurde eine der beiden Hauptgruppen der Pterosaurier, die Gruppe der Rhamphorhynchoiden, benannt. Diese Pterosaurier lebten größtenteils in der Trias und im Jura. Sie besaßen im Gegensatz zu den kurzschwänzigen Pterodaktyloiden lange Schwänze. Über einen Zeitraum von mehr als 30 Millionen Jahren erschienen verschiedene *Rhamphorhynchus*-Spezies unterschiedlicher Größe und verschwanden wieder. Die größeren Arten tauchten in der Regel später, gegen Ende des Jura, auf. Der Schädel eines solchen Tieres war bis zu zwanzig Zentimeter lang, der Rumpf mit dem langen, starren Schwanz, an dessen Spitze ein rautenförmiges Ruder saß, maß nochmals einen Meter. Die kleinsten Vertreter der Gattung besaßen daumengroße Schädel, ihre Flügel spannten sich nur vierzig Zentimeter weit. Zu den Merkmalen, die die Anpassung an das Fliegen verdeutlichen, gehörten beispielsweise die vielen langen Röhrenknochen, deren Wände fast papierdünn waren.

Der durchaus passende Name dieses Pterosauriers bedeutet „Schnabelschnauze". An den Schnabelseiten des *Rhamphorhynchus* standen schmale, spitze Zähne schräg nach vorn heraus; diese Anordnung und Form eignete sich ausgezeichnet zum Aufspießen und Festhalten zappelnder Fische. *Rhamphorhynchus* fing seine Nahrung wahrscheinlich in den flachen Salzlagunen, die im Oberen Jura in seinem Lebensraum mehr als reichlich vorhanden waren, indem er seinen Schnabel einfach durch das Oberflächenwasser streifen ließ. Berührte ein Fisch den empfindlichen Schnabel, schnappte dieser sofort zu, und dann riss der Pterosaurier seine Beute wahrscheinlich mit einem Ruck seines Kopfes aus dem Wasser heraus.

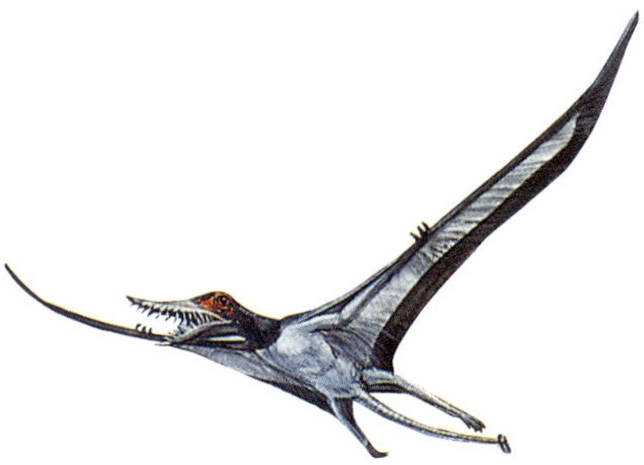

**OBEN** *Rhamphorhynchus* zog seinen langen Schwanz als eine Kombination aus Ruder und Stabilisator hinter sich her.

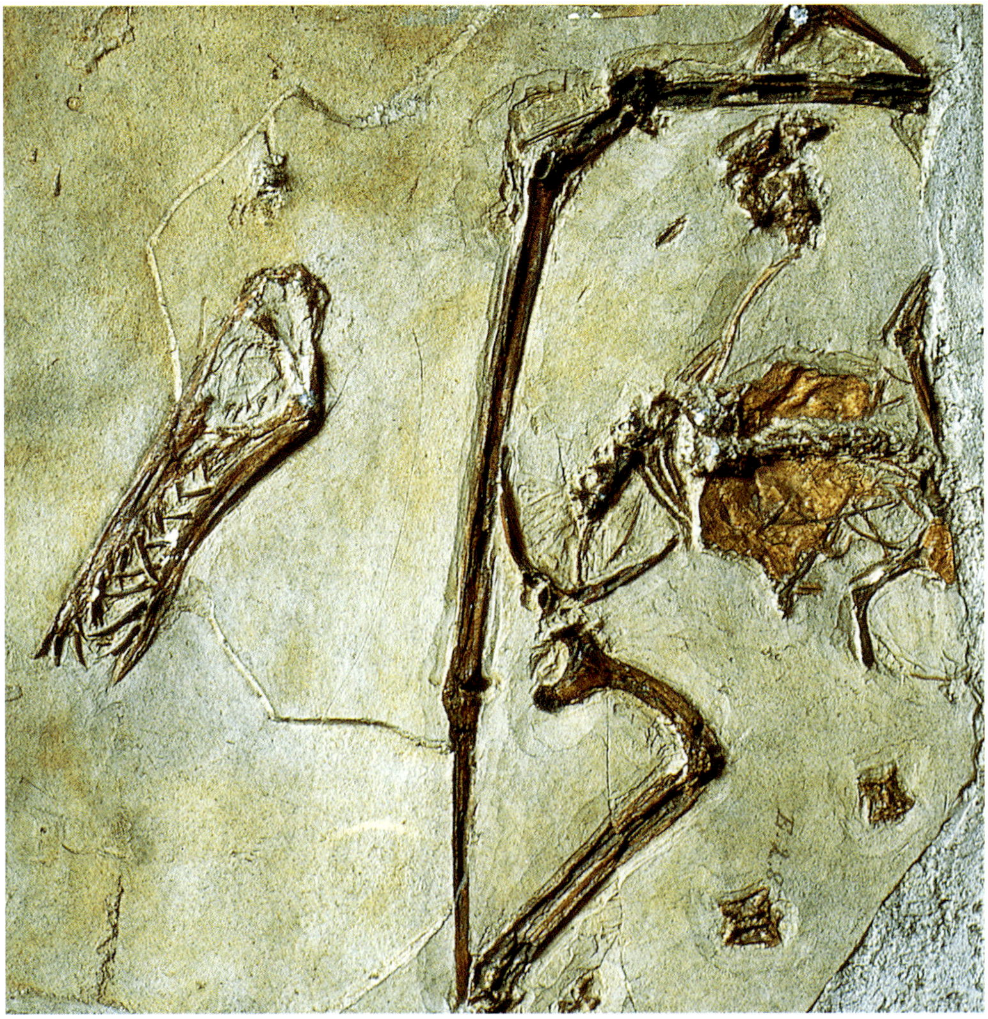

**RECHTS** Ein in vielen Einzelheiten erhaltenes *Rhamphorhynchus*-Fossil aus dem feinkörnigen Kalkstein von Solnhofen. In den Steinbrüchen von Solnhofen wurden auch Fossilien des Vogels *Archaeopteryx* sowie mehrerer Dinosaurierarten gefunden. Links ist der Schädel mit den charakteristischen schräg stehenden Zähnen zu sehen.

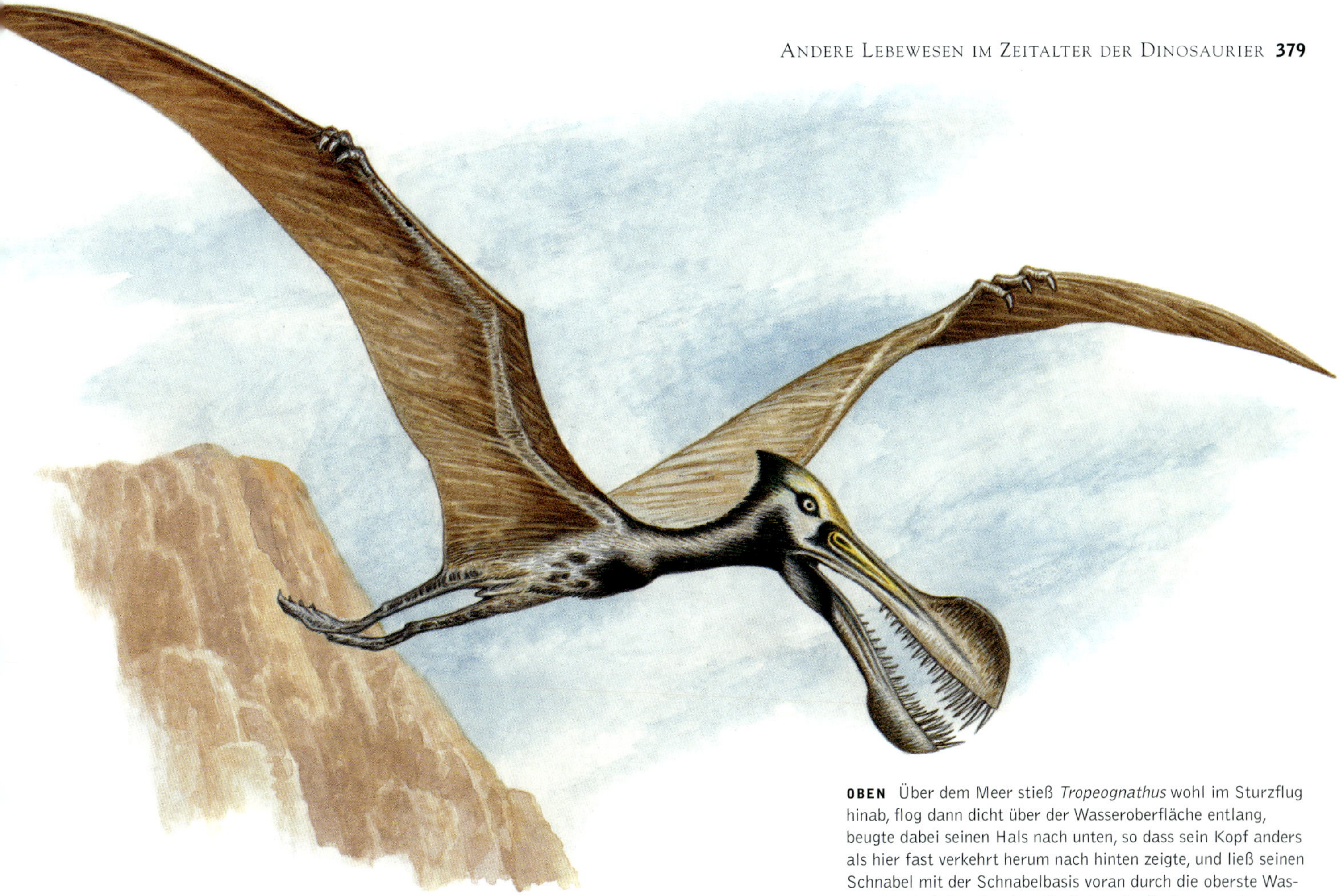

**OBEN** Über dem Meer stieß *Tropeognathus* wohl im Sturzflug hinab, flog dann dicht über der Wasseroberfläche entlang, beugte dabei seinen Hals nach unten, so dass sein Kopf anders als hier fast verkehrt herum nach hinten zeigte, und ließ seinen Schnabel mit der Schnabelbasis voran durch die oberste Wasserschicht gleiten. In einer ähnlichen Kopfhaltung suchen auch die heutigen Flamingos ihre Nahrung im Wasser.

# TROPEOGNATHUS

*Tropeognathus* war ein Pterosaurier der frühen bis mittleren Kreidezeit. Seine Überreste wurden in den erstaunlich fossilreichen Gesteinen der Santana-Formation im Nordosten Brasiliens entdeckt. Von *Tropeognathus* gibt es nur spärliche Funde, und so hat man seinen Körper, wie in solchen Fällen üblich, größtenteils mit Fossilbelegen ähnlicher, aber besser erforschter Pterosaurier von anderen Fundorten „aufgefüllt". Einer dieser Fossilienspender ist *Criorhynchus* („Widderschnauze", siehe Seite 376, 377), dessen Überreste hauptsächlich aus der Gegend um Cambridge stammen und von Richard Owen untersucht und benannt wurden. Derselbe Owen prägte auch den Namen Dinosauria. *Criorhynchus* lebte vor rund 130 – 110 Millionen Jahren, während es für die Relikte von *Tropeognathus* eine präzisere Altersangabe – 115 Millionen Jahre – gibt.

*Tropeognathus* war ein ziemlich großes Reptil mit einer Flügelspannweite von sechs Metern. Sein Name bedeutet „Kielkiefer" und bezieht sich auf die Kämme an seinem sehr schmalen Schnabel. Diese saßen mittig am vorderen Ende, fast an der Spitze des Ober- und des Unterschnabels. Sie waren halbmondförmig und sehr schmal und hatten beide etwa die gleiche Größe und Form. *Tropeognathus* zeigte am Hinterkopf, genau über dem Genick, Ansätze eines kleinen Kammes. Die Kammgröße ist bei den wenigen Individuen, die von *Tropeognathus* gefunden wurden, unterschiedlich. Möglicherweise hing sie vom Geschlecht ab. Vielleicht hatten die Kämme außerdem oder ausschließlich eine hydrodynamische Funktion und waren etwas Ähnliches wie der Kiel einer Jacht. Es ist anzunehmen, dass die Kämme den Schnabel stabilisierten und plötzliche Seitenbewegungen verhinderten, wenn *Tropeognathus* dicht über der Wasserfläche flog und auf der Suche nach Nahrung seinen Schnabel durch das Wasser zog.

Im Oberkiefer des *Tropeognathus* saßen gleichmäßig verteilt rund sechsundzwanzig schmale, spitze Zähne, im Unterkiefer waren es etwa zweiundzwanzig. Möglicherweise existierte eine zweite Art dieser Gattung, die sich durch eher dreieckige Schnabelkämme auszeichnete.

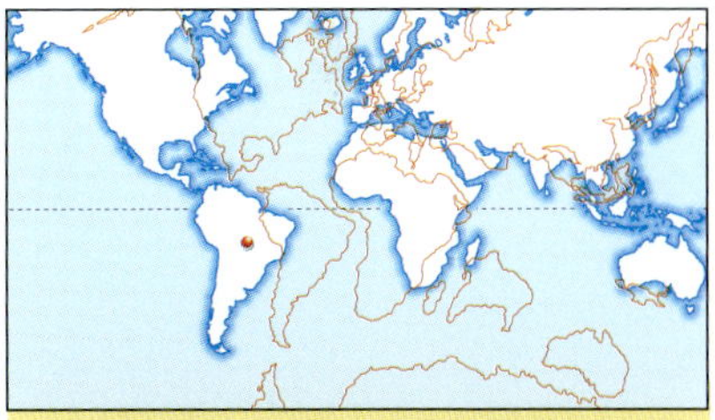

**ÜBERSICHT (PTEROSAURIER)**

***Tropeognathus***

**Bedeutung des Namens:** Kielkiefer

**Periode:** Untere bis Mittlere Kreide

**Hauptgruppe:** Pterosauria (Pterodactyloidea)

**Flügelspannweite:** 6 Meter

**Gewicht:** 12 – 14 Kilogramm

**Nahrung:** An der Meeresoberfläche schwimmende Beute, Fische oder Kalmare

**Fossilfundstätten:** In Südamerika

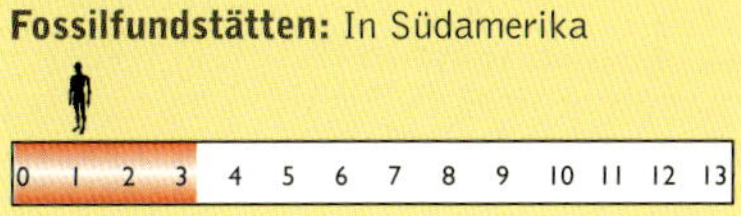

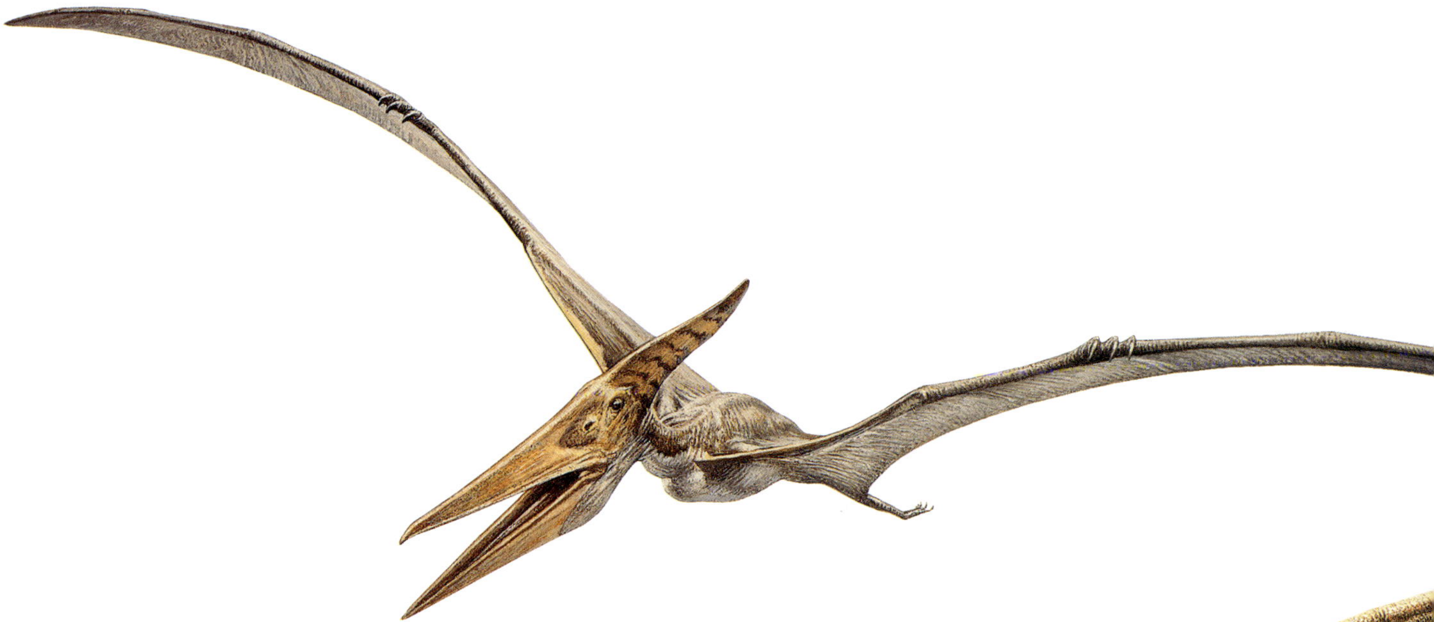

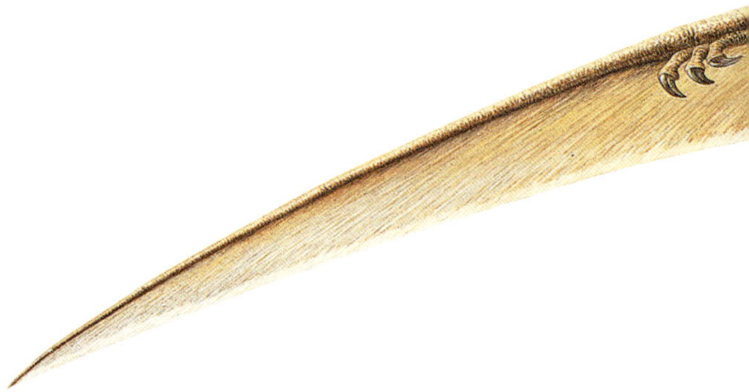

# PTERANODON

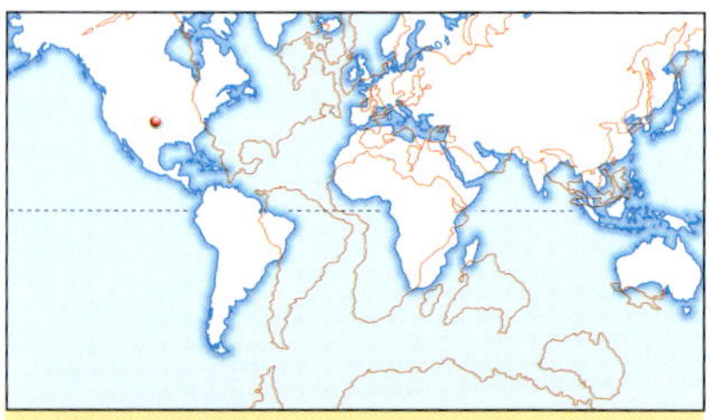

**ÜBERSICHT (PTEROSAURIER)**

***Pteranodon***

**Bedeutung des Namens:** Zahnloser Flügel, unbezahnter Flieger

**Periode:** Oberkreide

**Hauptgruppe:** Pterosauria (Pterodactyloidea)

**Flügelspannweite:** 9 Meter

**Gewicht:** 18 Kilogramm

**Nahrung:** An der Meeresoberfläche schwimmende Beute, Fische oder Kalmare

**Fossilfundstätten:** In den USA

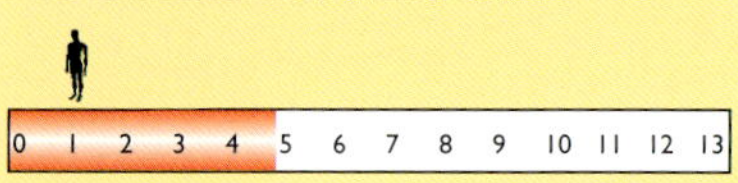


*Pteranodon* ist der Gattungsname für mehrere Spezies großer, langschnäbliger Pterosaurier mit Kopfkämmen, die in der späten Kreidezeit existierten. Die Fossilien dieser Tiere stammen größtenteils aus dem mittleren Westen und Südwesten der USA. Die ersten Exemplare wurden 1876 von Othniel Charles Marsh benannt, der auch zahlreiche Dinosaurierfossilien entdeckt hat. Die Vertreter der größeren Spezies waren massige Urtiere mit Flügeln, die sich von einer Flügelspitze zur anderen fast zehn Meter weit spannten. Der Unterkiefer war 1,2 Meter lang. Der schmale, schnabelartige Mund war zahnlos. Der ganze Pterosaurier war fein gebaut, besaß daher ein geringes Gewicht und konnte sich in der Luft flink bewegen. Seine Fluggeschwindigkeit wird meistens auf vierzig bis fünfzig Stundenkilometer geschätzt.

Die verschiedenen Spezies der Gattung *Pteranodon* unterschieden sich nicht nur durch ihre Größe, sondern auch durch die Form ihrer Kopfkämme voneinander. Die Kämme waren ausnahmslos schmal und ragten vom Schädeldach schräg nach hinten auf; manche sahen im Profil wie ein umgekehrtes „P" aus, andere ähnelten mehr einem spitzen Hexenhut. Aerodynamische Untersuchungen deuten darauf hin, dass ein solcher Kamm einen Ausgleich zu dem langen Schnabel bildete. Vielleicht diente der Kamm auch als Ruder, mit dem *Pteranodon* seinen Körper während des Fluges stabil hielt und steuerte. Denkbar ist auch, dass der Kamm als Zeichen der Geschlechtsreife und der Paarungsbereitschaft auffallend gefärbt war, so wie die Schnäbel der rezenten Tukane oder Papageitaucher. Der Rest seines Körpers wies *Pteranodon* als einen ziemlich unverkennbaren Pterosaurier vom Typ der Pterodactylen aus, auch wenn das Tier sehr groß war, einen kurzen, kräftigen Hals und einen kompakten Rumpf besaß, seine Beine zurückgebildet waren und der Schwanz fast fehlte. *Pteranodon* lebte vermutlich an Küsten und fand seine Nahrung im Meer.

**OBEN** Der Kopfkamm dieses *Pteranodon* ist auffällig gemustert. Das Muster war vielleicht arttypisch und diente während der Paarungszeit zur Erkennung potenzieller Fortpflanzungspartner. Der lange, spitze Kamm gehörte zur Spezies *Pteranodon ingens*. Er war bei manchen Tieren schwach S-förmig gebogen, bei anderen gerade.

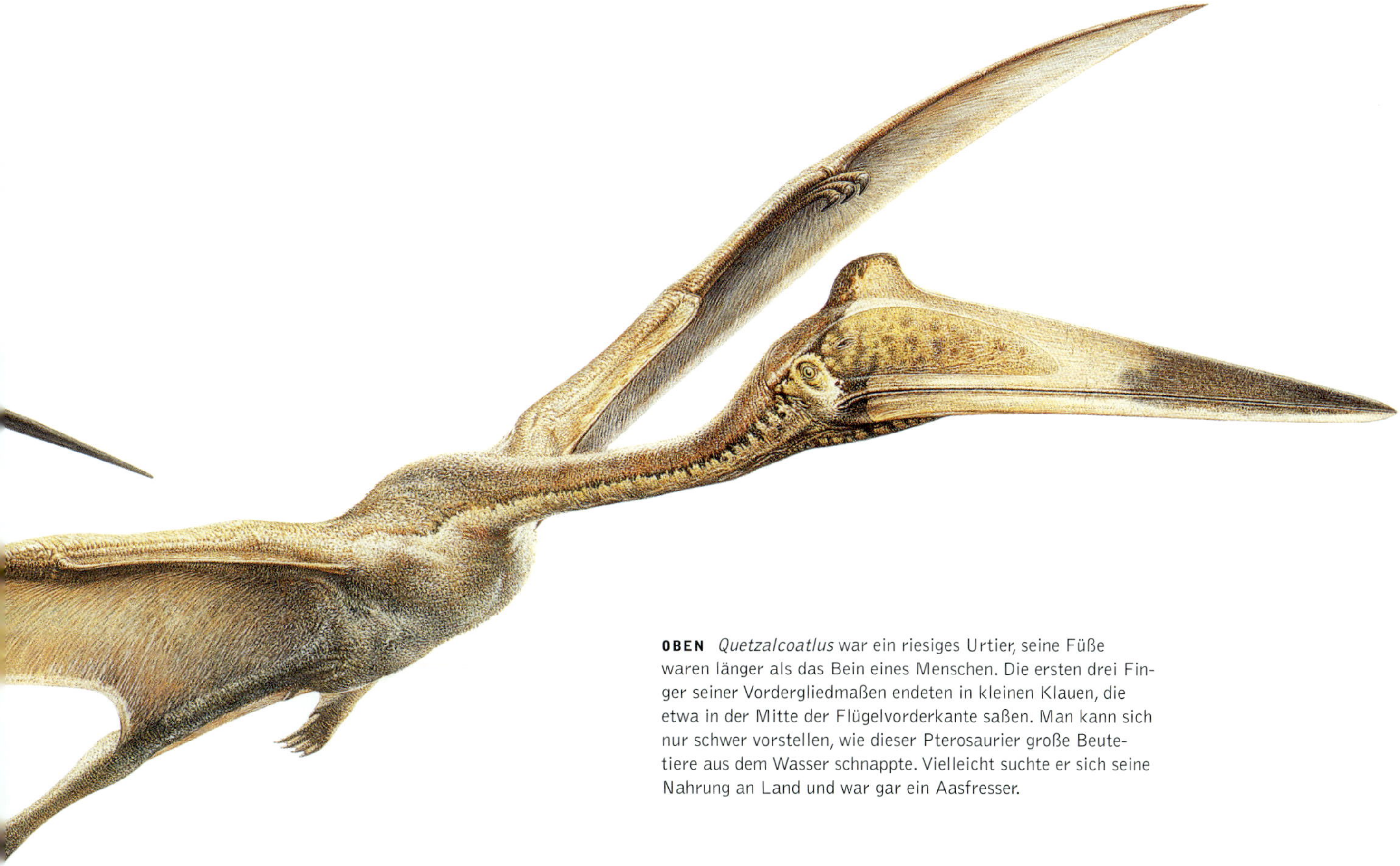

**OBEN** *Quetzalcoatlus* war ein riesiges Urtier, seine Füße waren länger als das Bein eines Menschen. Die ersten drei Finger seiner Vordergliedmaßen endeten in kleinen Klauen, die etwa in der Mitte der Flügelvorderkante saßen. Man kann sich nur schwer vorstellen, wie dieser Pterosaurier große Beutetiere aus dem Wasser schnappte. Vielleicht suchte er sich seine Nahrung an Land und war gar ein Aasfresser.

# Quetzalcoatlus

Dieser riesige Flugsaurier ist von Fossilbruchstücken bekannt, die man im Grenzgebiet zwischen dem Nordosten Mexikos und dem südlichen Texas gefunden hat. Von ihm ist weder ein komplettes noch ein unvollständiges Skelett vorhanden, dafür aber Knochenabschnitte von einem Flügel, Schädelteile und andere Reste, die auf seine gewaltige Größe hindeuten. *Quetzalcoatlus* war eines der größten bekannten flugfähigen Tiere, die jemals auf der Erde gelebt haben. Seine Flügelspannweite betrug mindestens zwölf, möglicherweise sogar vierzehn oder mehr Meter, die Schätzwerte für sein Gewicht liegen zwischen siebzig Kilogramm, was etwa dem Gewicht eines erwachsenen Menschen entspricht, und mehr als hundert Kilogramm. Allein der Hals war drei Meter lang, und der Kopf mit dem langen, schmalen zahnlosen Schnabel und dem hinten abstehenden kurzen Knochenkamm erreichte eine Länge von zwei Metern.

*Quetzalcoatlus* war ein Pterosaurier vom Typ eines Pterodactyloiden (siehe Seite 377). Er wurde 1975 nach Quetzalcoatl, dem gefiederten Schlangengott der Azteken und anderer mexikanischer Völker, benannt. Es ist nicht sicher, ob *Quetzalcoatlus* Federn besaß – er kann, wie viele Pterosaurier, auch behaart gewesen sein. Er lebte am Ende des Zeitalters der Dinosaurier, vor rund 70 – 65 Millionen Jahren und kann durchaus über den letzten nordamerikanischen Dinosauriern wie beispielsweise *Tyrannosaurus* und *Triceratops*, durch die Lüfte geflogen sein. Andere Fossilien, die man bei den Überresten von *Quetzalcoatlus* gefunden hat, lassen darauf schließen, dass das Tier in ziemlich flachen Landschaften mit mäandernden Flüssen, mit Ebenen und Sümpfen gelebt hat oder zumindest dort gestorben ist. Es gibt eine Theorie, nach der es sich bei *Quetzalcoatlus* um einen riesigen Aasfresser handelte, obgleich dieser mehr als viermal größer als jeder Aas fressende Vogel der Jetztzeit, beispielsweise der Kondor oder der Geier, war. Vielleicht ist *Quetzalcoatlus* einst im Sturzflug auf Dinosaurierkadaver niedergestoßen und hat mit seinem langen, schlanken Schnabel darin herumgestochert, um sich mit den hornbesetzten Kieferrändern Fleischstücke herauszuschneiden.

In den letzten Jahren hat man Fossilien noch größerer Pterosaurier wie *Arambourgiana* entdeckt, die eine übermäßig große Flügelspannweite von fünfzehn Metern gehabt haben könnten.

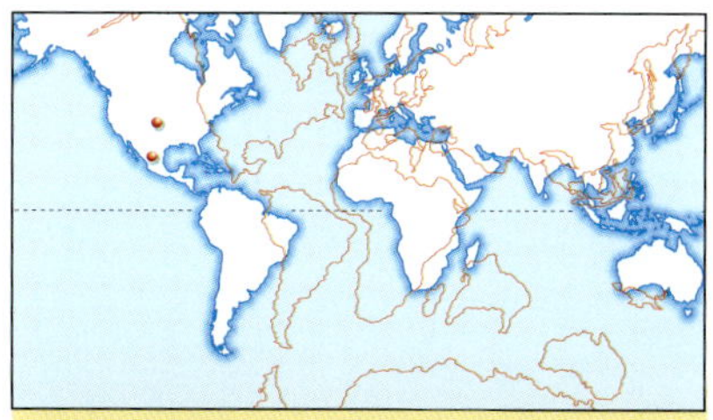

**ÜBERSICHT (PTEROSAURIER)**
***Quetzalcoatlus***
**Bedeutung des Namens:** Nach Quetzalcoatl, dem mexikanischen gefiederten Schlangengott, benannt
**Periode:** Oberkreide
**Hauptgruppe:** Pterosaurier (Pterodactyloidae)
**Flügelspannweite:** 12 – 14 Meter
**Gewicht:** 70 – 100 Kilogramm
**Nahrung:** Aas oder Fische und Schalentiere
**Fossilfundstätten:** In den USA (Texas), in Mexiko

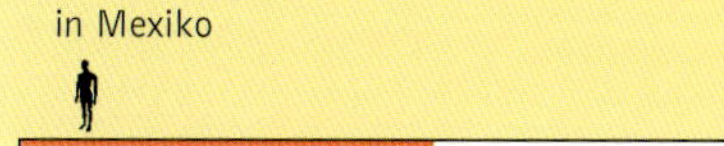

# Reptilien der Seen und Meere

*Die Reptilien erlangten dank bestimmter Entwicklungen – der wasserfesten Schale ihrer Eier, der Schuppenhaut u.a. Merkmale – die Unabhängigkeit vom Wasser, die ihre amphibisch lebenden Vorfahren nie erreicht hatten. Später tauchten nahezu gleichzeitig verschiedene Typen wieder in die Seen und Ozeane ab; ihre Beine passten sich dem neuen Lebensraum an und verwandelten sich in Flossen. Während des Zeitalters der Dinosaurier kehrten mindestens zwanzig große Reptiliengruppen zu einer aquatischen Lebensweise zurück. Von ihnen existieren heute nur noch wenige, darunter die Schildkröten und einige Krokodiliertypen.*

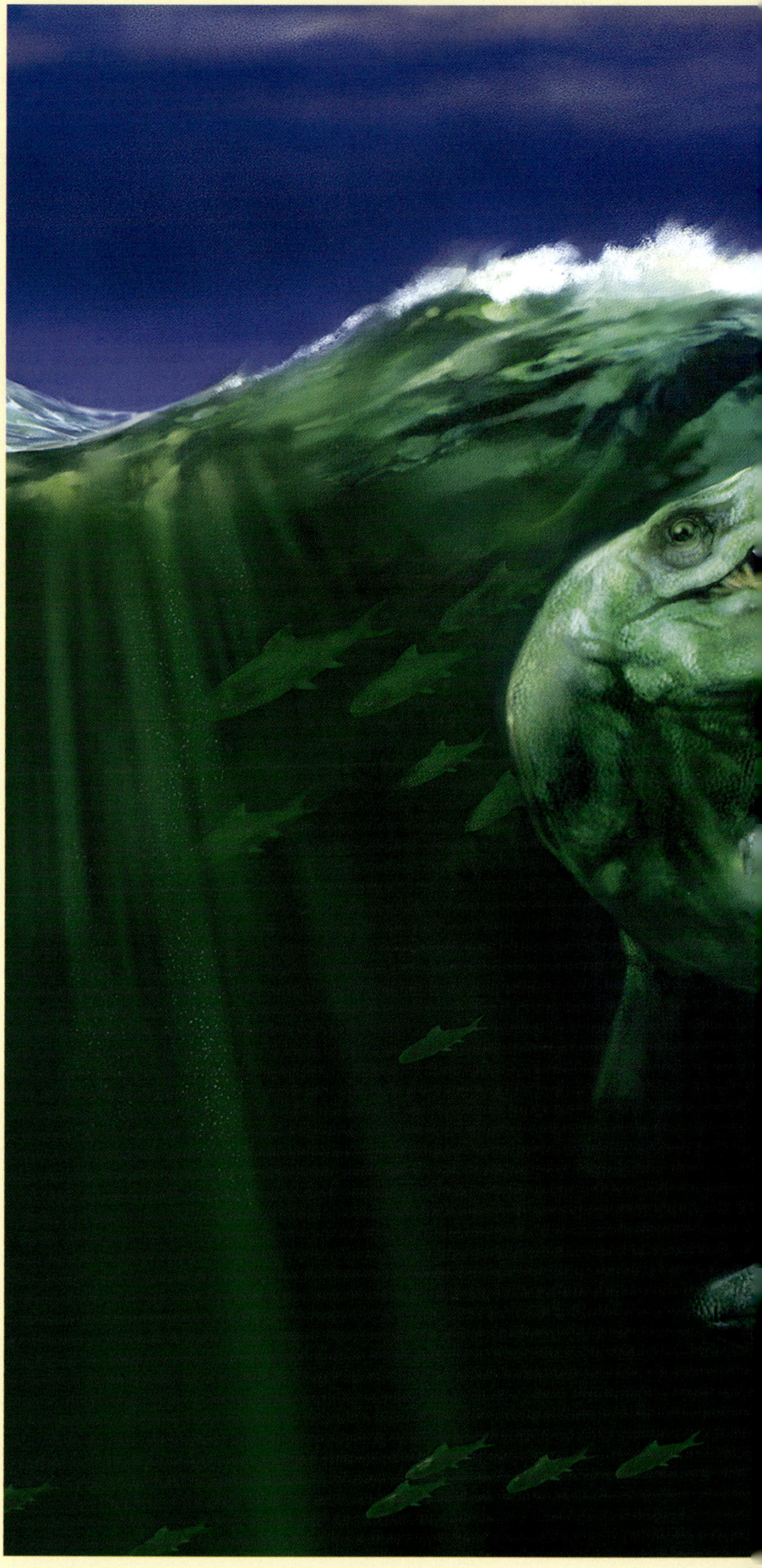

**RECHTS** Die Mosasaurier waren riesige langzähnige, kräftig gebaute Räuber aus der Oberkreide. Trotz ihrer Größe und Stärke überlebten sie das Massenaussterben am Ende dieser Periode nicht. Manche Mosasaurier waren doppelt so lang und fünfmal so schwer wie der größte Raubfisch der Jetztzeit, der Weißhai.

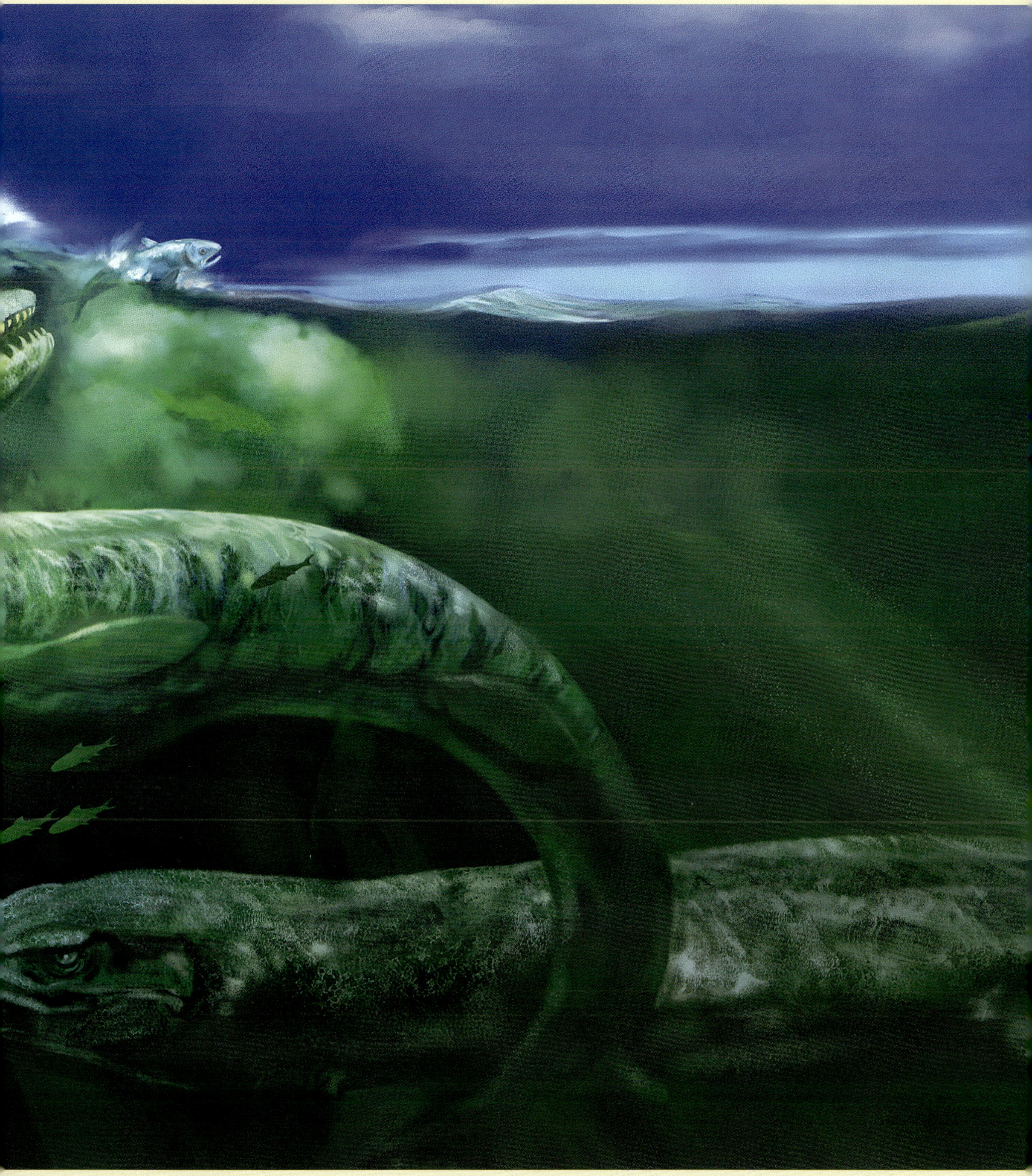

# NOTHOSAURUS

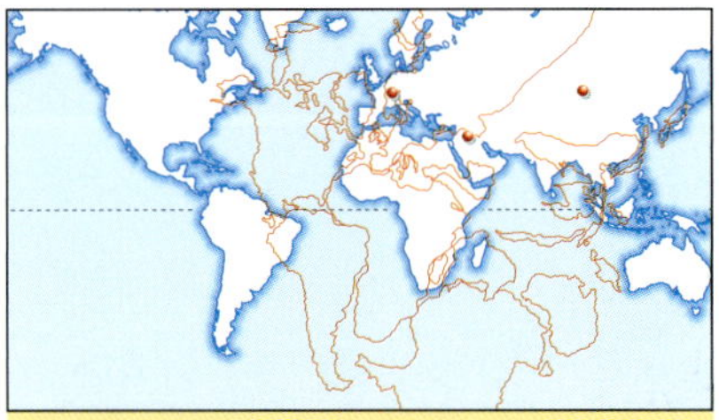

**ÜBERSICHT (REPTILIEN)**

***Nothosaurus***

**Bedeutung des Namens:** Falsches Reptil

**Periode:** Trias

**Hauptgruppe:** Nothosauria

**Länge:** Bis 3 Meter

**Gewicht:** Bis 250 Kilogramm

**Nahrung:** Fische und ähnliche Meerestiere

**Fossilfundstätten:** In Europa, im Nahen Osten, in Asien

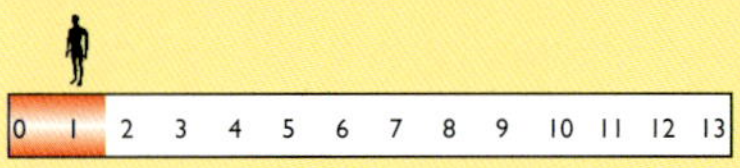


Die Nothosaurier zählen zu den ersten Reptiliengruppen, die das Leben im Meer aufnahmen. Das geschah in der Trias, vor über 240 Millionen Jahren und noch vor dem Erscheinen der Dinosaurier. Die gesamte Gruppe der Nothosaurier war am Ende der Trias gerade ausgestorben, als die Dinosaurier die Herrschaft über das Festland übernahmen.

Die Nothosaurier waren lange, schlanke Tiere mit langem, schmalem Schädel und Hals, langen, spitzen Zähnen, die im Kiefer hauptsächlich vorn, an der Schnauzenspitze, saßen. Ihr schlanker Körper endete in einem langen, biegsamen Schwanz, und ihre Gliedmaßen waren teilweise zu Flossen umgebildet. Die Nothosaurier behielten allerdings auch einige Körpermerkmale, die noch vom Leben auf dem Festland stammten – ihre Extremitäten waren nicht gänzlich flossenartig wie bei den späteren Ichthyosauriern, sondern besaßen fünf Zehen, die wahrscheinlich durch Schwimmhäute miteinander verbunden waren.

*Nothosaurus* war eine recht typische Gattung unter den Nothosauriern; die Vertreter der meisten Spezies waren rund einen Meter, eine Spezies sogar bis zu drei Meter lang. Verschiedene Fossilien von ihm wurden an Fundstätten quer durch Europa sowie im Nahen Osten und in Asien entdeckt. In Israel hat man vor kurzem auch Überreste einer kleineren „Zwergspezies“ von *Nothosaurus* gefunden. Die langen Zähne und Kiefer des pfeilartigen Kopfes lassen auf einen Fischfresser schließen, der mit den Beinen rudernd umherschwamm, seine Bewegung vielleicht durch seitliches Ausschlagen mit dem Schwanz beschleunigte und den langen Hals nach Beute schnellen ließ. War ein Fisch zwischen die spitzen Zähne geraten, die bei geschlossenen Kiefern eine Art Käfig bildeten, gab es kein Entrinnen mehr, und die Beute wurde unzerkaut verschluckt. Auch die Gliedmaßen deuten darauf hin, dass *Nothosaurus* sich, wenn auch nicht schnell, so doch im Watschelgang, an Land fortbewegen konnte. Denkbar ist, dass er sich wie die heutigen Robben verhielt, im Meer seine Nahrung wie beispielsweise Fische und Kalmare fing und zu Ruhepausen sowie vielleicht zur Fortpflanzung an Land ging.

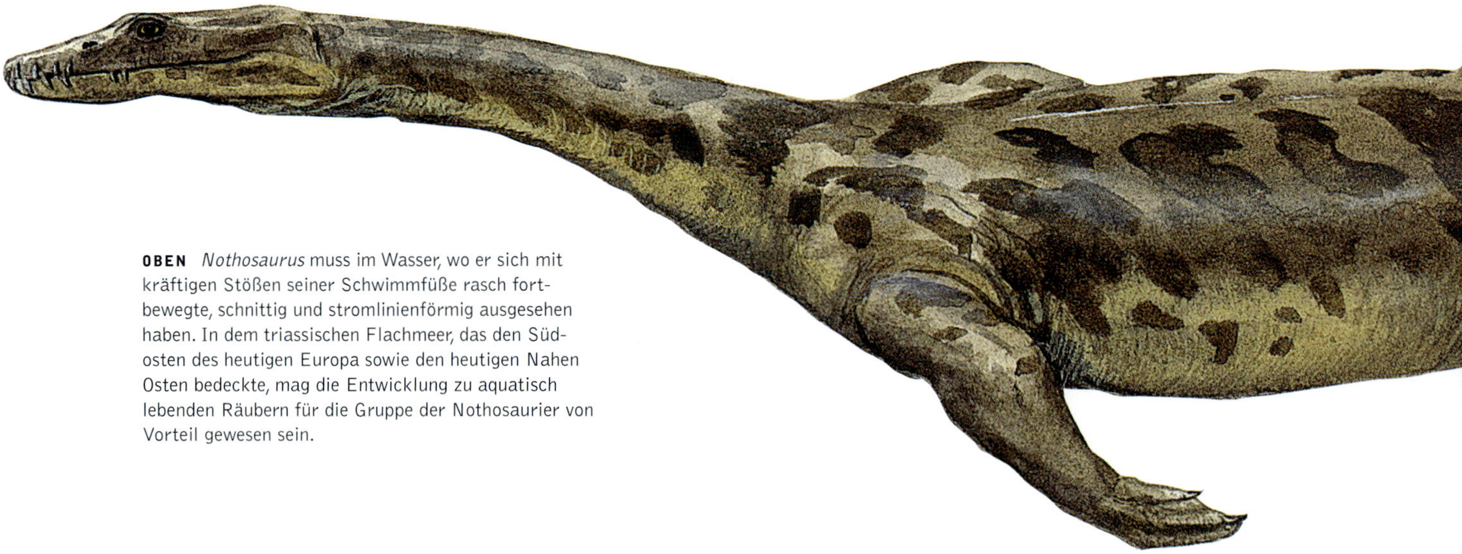

**OBEN** *Nothosaurus* muss im Wasser, wo er sich mit kräftigen Stößen seiner Schwimmfüße rasch fortbewegte, schnittig und stromlinienförmig ausgesehen haben. In dem triassischen Flachmeer, das den Südosten des heutigen Europa sowie den heutigen Nahen Osten bedeckte, mag die Entwicklung zu aquatisch lebenden Räubern für die Gruppe der Nothosaurier von Vorteil gewesen sein.

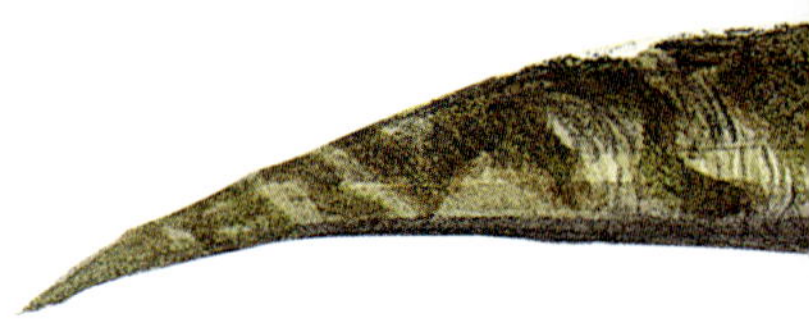

# PLACODUS

Die Placodonten gehörten wie die Nothosaurier (siehe gegenüber) zu den ersten Reptilien, die den Lebensraum Wasser für sich entdeckten. Die Gruppe überdauerte, ebenfalls wie die Nothosaurier, nur eine erdgeschichtliche Periode, die Trias. Auf den ersten Blick ähnelt *Placodus*, der über zwei Meter lang war, einem riesigen Wassermolch oder vielleicht auch einem Krokodil. Die Placodonten stellten jedoch eine gesonderte Reptiliengruppe dar. Ihr Name bezieht sich auf die abgeflachten, breiten Zähne in der hinteren Region des Ober- und des Unterkiefers, die sich zum Zermahlen von Schalentieren und anderer harter Nahrung eigneten. Ähnliche Zähne finden wir bei einigen rezenten Haifischen, beispielsweise bei den Hornhaien. Bei *Placodus* saßen selbst am Gaumen verhärtete zahnartige Platten. Die Zähne an der Vorderseite der Kiefer waren eher stiftartig und standen schräg nach vorn. Sie dienten möglicherweise als Hebel zum Abtrennen der an Steinen festsitzenden Muscheln, vielleicht holte *Placodus* mit ihrer Hilfe auch Schalentiere aus dem schlammigen Meeresboden und zwischen den Wasserpflanzen hervor.

*Placodus* bewegte sich schwimmend fort, indem er wie die Krokodile mit dem Schwanz von einer Seite zur anderen ruderte. Auf der Schwanzoberseite kann ein flaches Flossenband gesessen haben, das dem Tier einen zusätzlichen Antrieb verschaffte. Das Steuern und Beschleunigen im Wasser bewerkstelligte *Placodus* wahrscheinlich durch Stöße mit seinen Schwimmfüßen. An Land konnte er sich vermutlich recht gut fortbewegen, auch wenn seine Beine vom Körper seitlich abgespreizt waren, wie es bei den meisten Nicht-Dinosauriern unter den Reptilien der Fall war. Man nimmt an, dass *Placodus* in flachen Küstengewässern und Sümpfen lebte, denn dieses Milieu war für ein Lebewesen, das sich sowohl auf dem Festland als auch im Wasser fortbewegen konnte, günstiger als für ein Tier, das nur einem dieser Lebensräume angepasst war. Der Körper des *Placodus* war vielleicht teilweise mit kleinen Buckeln und Platten gepanzert. Bei einigen späteren Placodonten wie *Placochelys* und *Henodus* waren diese Platten stark vergrößert und ähnelten dem Panzer der Schildkröten.

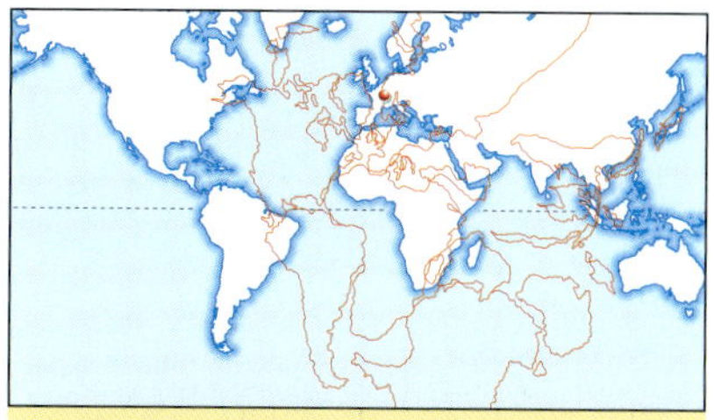

**ÜBERSICHT (REPTILIEN)**
***Placodus***
**Bedeutung des Namens:** Flacher Plattenzahn, abgeflachter Zahn
**Periode:** Untere und Mittlere Trias
**Hauptgruppe:** Placodontia
**Länge:** 2 Meter
**Gewicht:** 100 Kilogramm
**Nahrung:** Schalentiere
**Fossilfundstätten:** In Europa

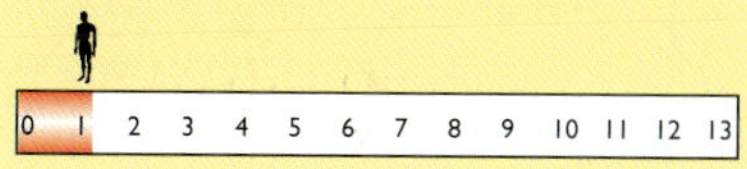


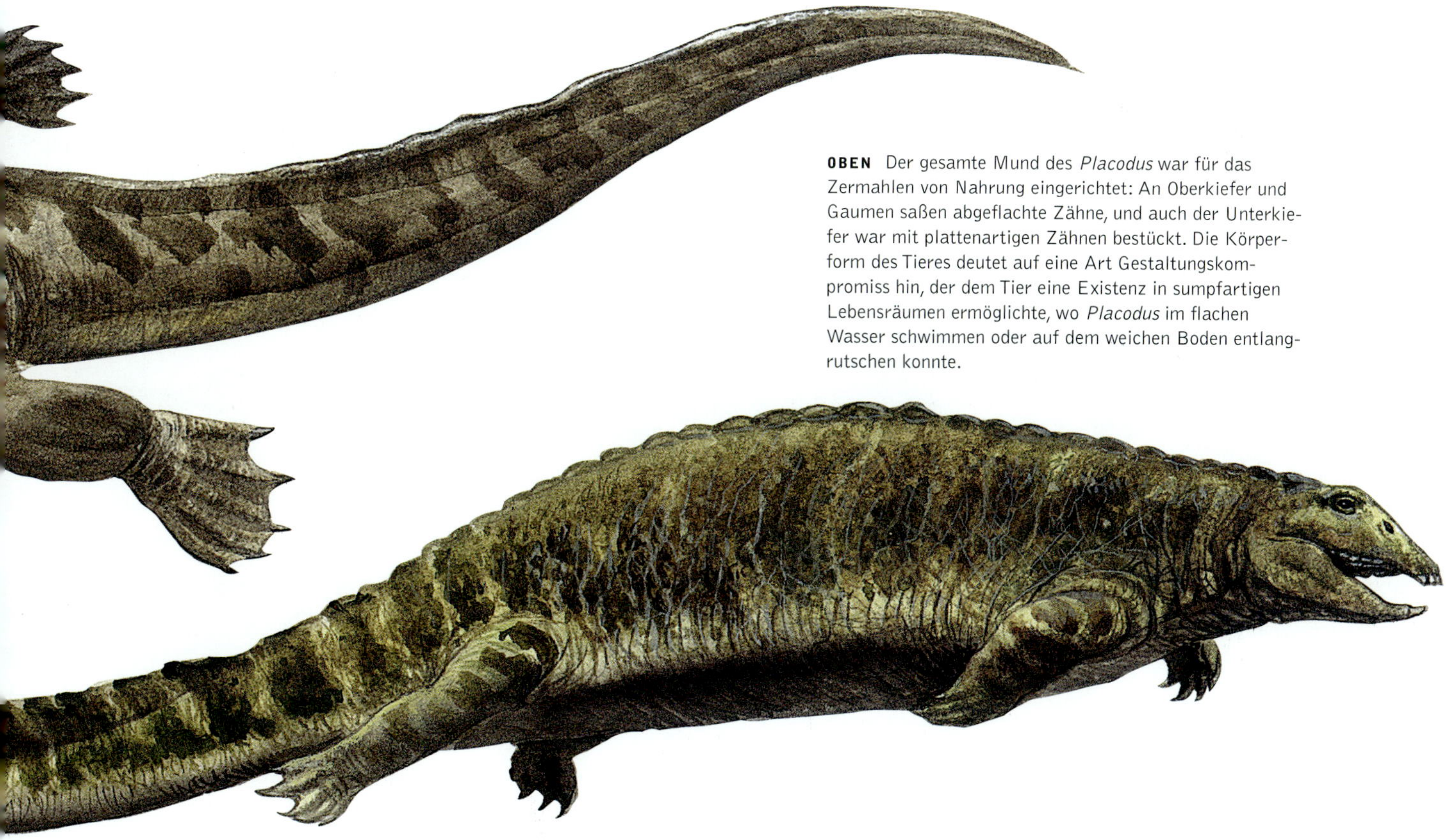

**OBEN** Der gesamte Mund des *Placodus* war für das Zermahlen von Nahrung eingerichtet: An Oberkiefer und Gaumen saßen abgeflachte Zähne, und auch der Unterkiefer war mit plattenartigen Zähnen bestückt. Die Körperform des Tieres deutet auf eine Art Gestaltungskompromiss hin, der dem Tier eine Existenz in sumpfartigen Lebensräumen ermöglichte, wo *Placodus* im flachen Wasser schwimmen oder auf dem weichen Boden entlangrutschen konnte.

# METRIORHYNCHUS

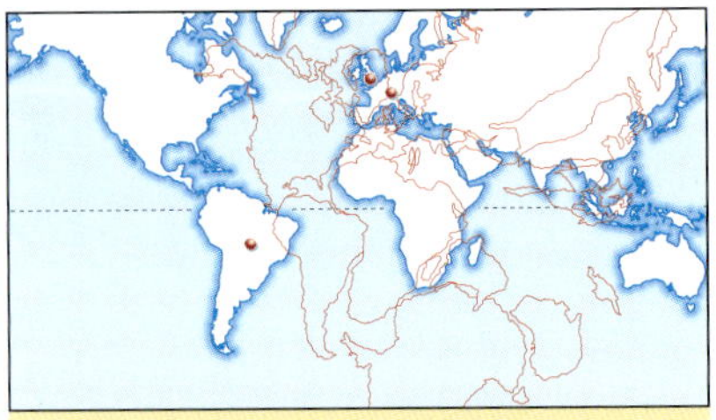

**ÜBERSICHT (REPTILIEN)**

***Metriorhynchus***

**Bedeutung des Namens:** Mittelgroße Schnauze, mittelgroße Nase

**Periode:** Oberer Jura

**Hauptgruppe:** Crocodilia

**Länge:** 3 Meter

**Gewicht:** 200 Kilogramm

**Nahrung:** Fische und ähnliche Meerestiere

**Fossilfundstätten:** In Südamerika und Europa

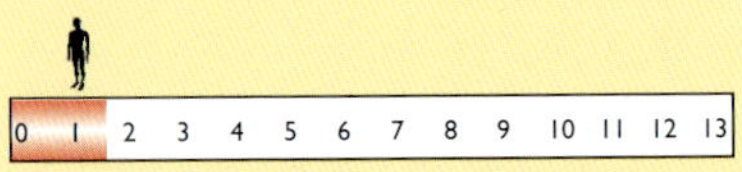


Heute existiert nur noch ein Krokodil, das sich üblicherweise ins Meer wagt – das Leistenkrokodil des Indopazifischen Ozeans. Es ist gleichzeitig das größte lebende Reptil. Mit nur dreiundzwanzig Spezies gehören die Krokodilier heute zu den kleinsten Reptilgruppen, doch sie haben eine lange, wechselvolle Geschichte aufzuweisen, die etwa zur gleichen Zeit wie die Geschichte der Dinosaurier – in der Trias, vor über 200 Millionen Jahren – begann. Manche lebten auf dem trockenen Festland, andere in Flüssen und Süßwassersümpfen wie ihre Nachfahren von heute.

*Metriorhynchus* gehörte zu jenen Krokodilen aus der Dinosaurierzeit, die am stärksten an das Leben im Meer angepasst waren. Die Fundstätten von *Metriorhynchus*-Fossilien liegen weit voneinander entfernt in Südamerika und Europa – in Chile, in Frankreich und England. Das Tier war zwar nur halb so groß wie das rezente Leistenkrokodil, dafür aber besser an das Schwimmen und das Fischefangen angepasst. Mit seiner langen, schmalen Schnauze und den in Reihen stehenden kleinen, doch sehr spitzen Zähnen ähnelte es einem Krokodilier der Jetztzeit, dem Gavial vom indischen Subkontinent. Der hintere Schädelteil, an dem sich die Augen und die Ohren befanden, war breit und kastenartig, der Hals kurz und dick. Die vorderen Gliedmaßen konnten als Steuerruder und auch als Tragflächen für das Auf- und Abtauchen benutzt werden. Die Hintergliedmaßen mit den längeren Füßen können als Antriebs- und Steuerorgan gedient haben. Der Schwanz erweiterte sich am Ende vermutlich zu einer Flosse mit fleischigem Ober- und Unterlappen, und die Wirbelsäule knickte ähnlich wie beim Schwanz mancher Haifische zum unteren Lappen ab. *Metriorhynchus* besaß wahrscheinlich keine großen schützenden Knochenplatten, die typisch für viele andere Krokodilier nicht nur seiner Zeit waren; er verließ sich beim Fischefangen und auf der Flucht vor Feinden auf seine Schnelligkeit und Wendigkeit im Wasser.

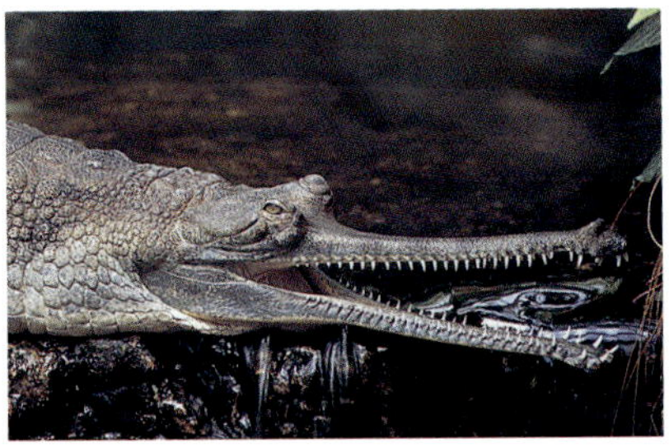

**LINKS** Der rezente Gavial hat eine lange, schmale Schnauze, die mit kleinen, aber scharfen Zähnen bestückt ist.

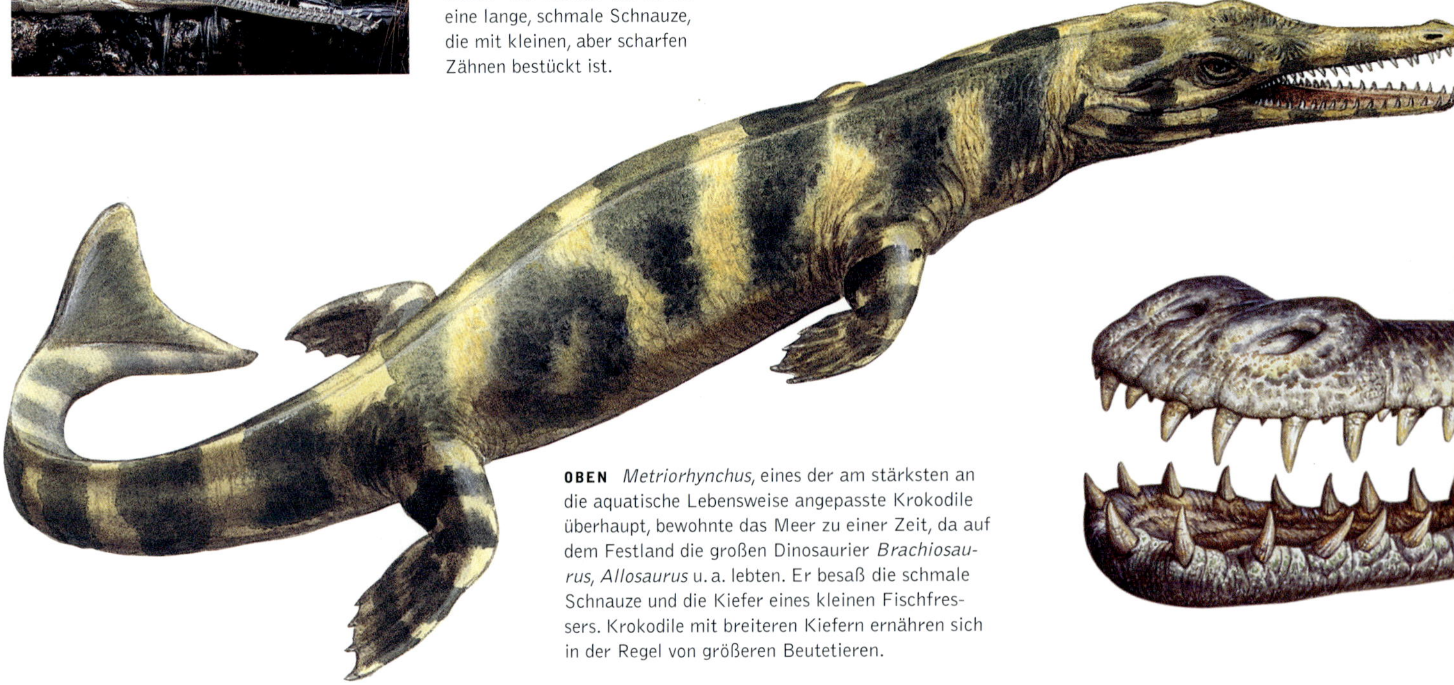

**OBEN** *Metriorhynchus*, eines der am stärksten an die aquatische Lebensweise angepasste Krokodile überhaupt, bewohnte das Meer zu einer Zeit, da auf dem Festland die großen Dinosaurier *Brachiosaurus*, *Allosaurus* u. a. lebten. Er besaß die schmale Schnauze und die Kiefer eines kleinen Fischfressers. Krokodile mit breiteren Kiefern ernähren sich in der Regel von größeren Beutetieren.

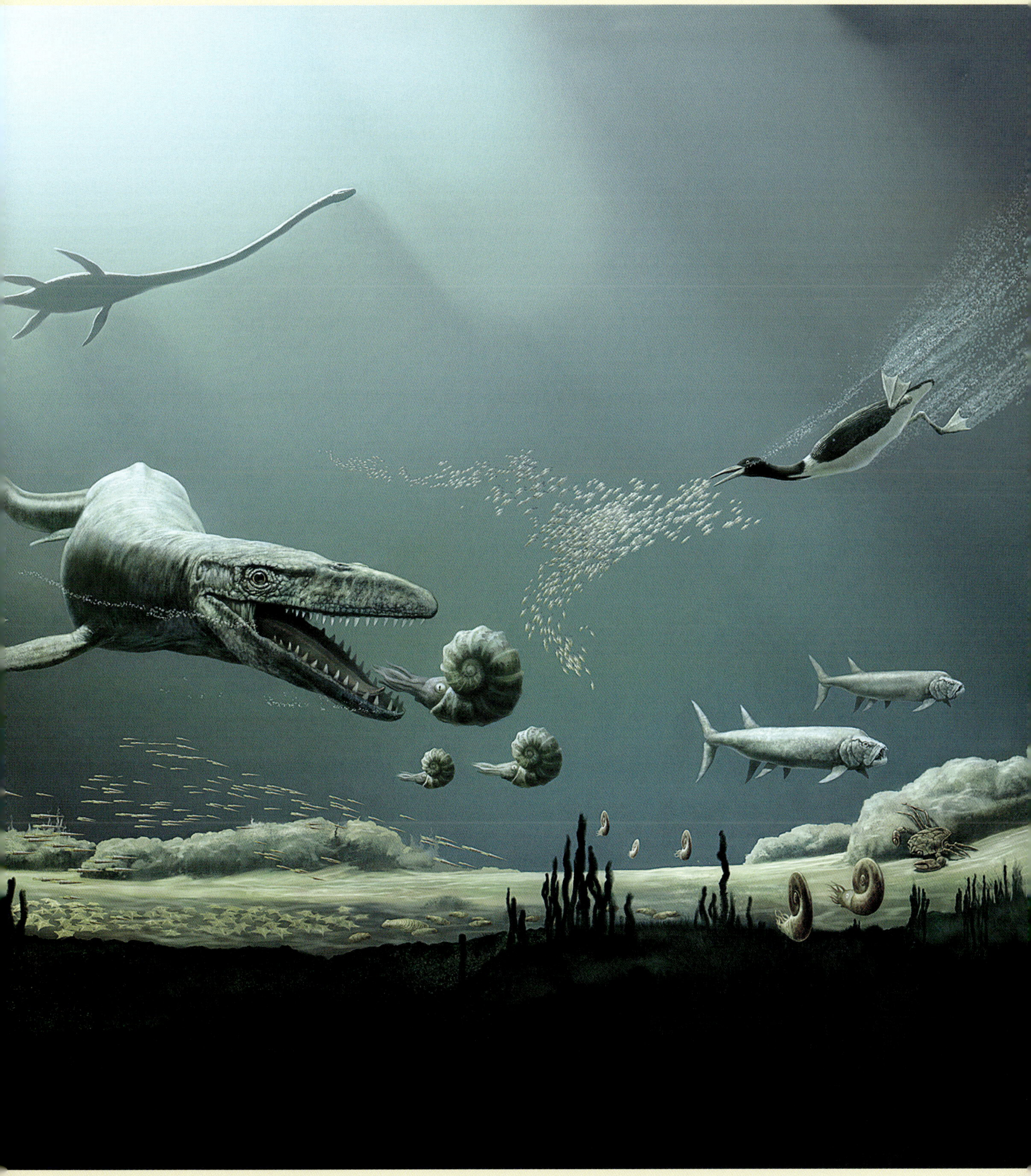

# OPHTHALMOSAURUS

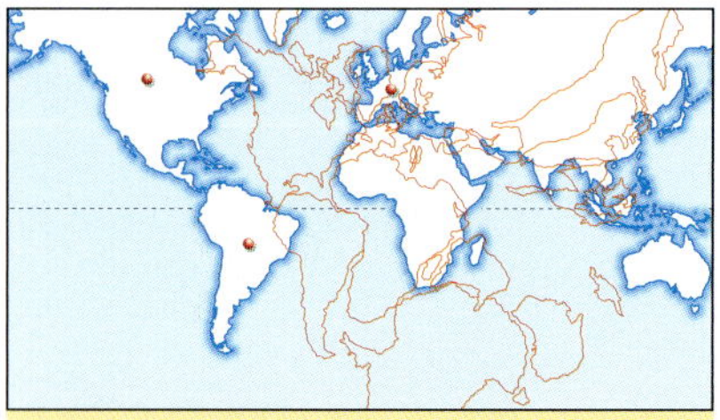

**ÜBERSICHT (REPTILIEN)**
***Ophthalmosaurus***
**Bedeutung des Namens:** Augenreptil
**Periode:** Oberer Jura
**Hauptgruppe:** Ichthyosauria
**Länge:** 3–5 Meter
**Gewicht:** 500 Kilogramm
**Nahrung:** Kalmare, Fische
**Fossilfundstätten:** In Nord- und Südamerika, in Europa

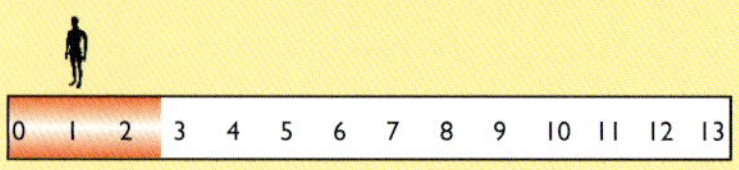


Die größten Augen in der heutigen Tierwelt besitzen die Riesenkalmare, ihre Sehorgane sind fast fußballgroß. Unter den prähistorischen Lebewesen und zweifellos unter den Wirbeltieren überhaupt hielten hinsichtlich der Augengröße die Ichthyosaurier den Rekord. Die Augäpfel des *Ophthalmosaurus* hatten einen Durchmesser von fast zehn Zentimetern – so groß ist etwa die Faust eines erwachsenen Menschen. (Die Augen des *Temnodontosaurus*, eines anderen jurassischen Ichthyosauriers, waren doppelt so groß.) Überreste von *Ophthalmosaurus* wurden an mehreren Fossilfundstätten, vor allem in Argentinien, entdeckt. Bei einigen Funden aus Argentinien scheint es sich um Fossilien von Tieren unterschiedlichen Alters zu handeln, die die unterschiedlichen Wachstums- und Entwicklungsphasen vom jüngsten bis zum ausgewachsenen Tier belegen. Fossilien anderer Ichthyosaurier, insbesondere aber von *Ichthyosaurus* selbst, zeigen, dass diese Reptilien nicht aus Eiern schlüpften, sondern als kleine, aber schon voll ausgebildete lebende Wesen den Mutterleib verließen. Im Unterschied zu den meisten anderen Meeresreptilien in diesem Kapitel scheinen die Ichthyosaurier so stark an das Leben im Wasser angepasst gewesen zu sein, dass sie gar nicht an Land gehen konnten, um dort Eier abzulegen.

Seine riesigen Sehorgane besaß *Ophthalmosaurus* wahrscheinlich aus demselben Grund wie der Riesenkalmar – um im dunklen Ozean Beutetiere jagen zu können. Die vorstehenden Augäpfel waren von einem Knochenring (Sklerotikalring) eingefasst, der das Auge hielt und schützte. Dieses Skelettmerkmal findet man auch bei manchen Dinoauriern. Zusammen mit den Überresten von *Ophthalmosaurus* wurden Begleitfossilien wie Fischschuppen, die flachen Spiralgehäuse von Ammoniten und die Innengehäuse von Belemniten im Gestein gefunden. Ammoniten und Belemniten sind prähistorische Verwandte der heutigen Kalmare und Kraken (siehe Seite 49). Alle diese Lebewesen könnte einst *Ophthalmosaurus* nach rascher Verfolgung und mit plötzlichem Zuschnappen seiner langen, schmalen Schnabelschnauze voller Zähne erbeutet haben.

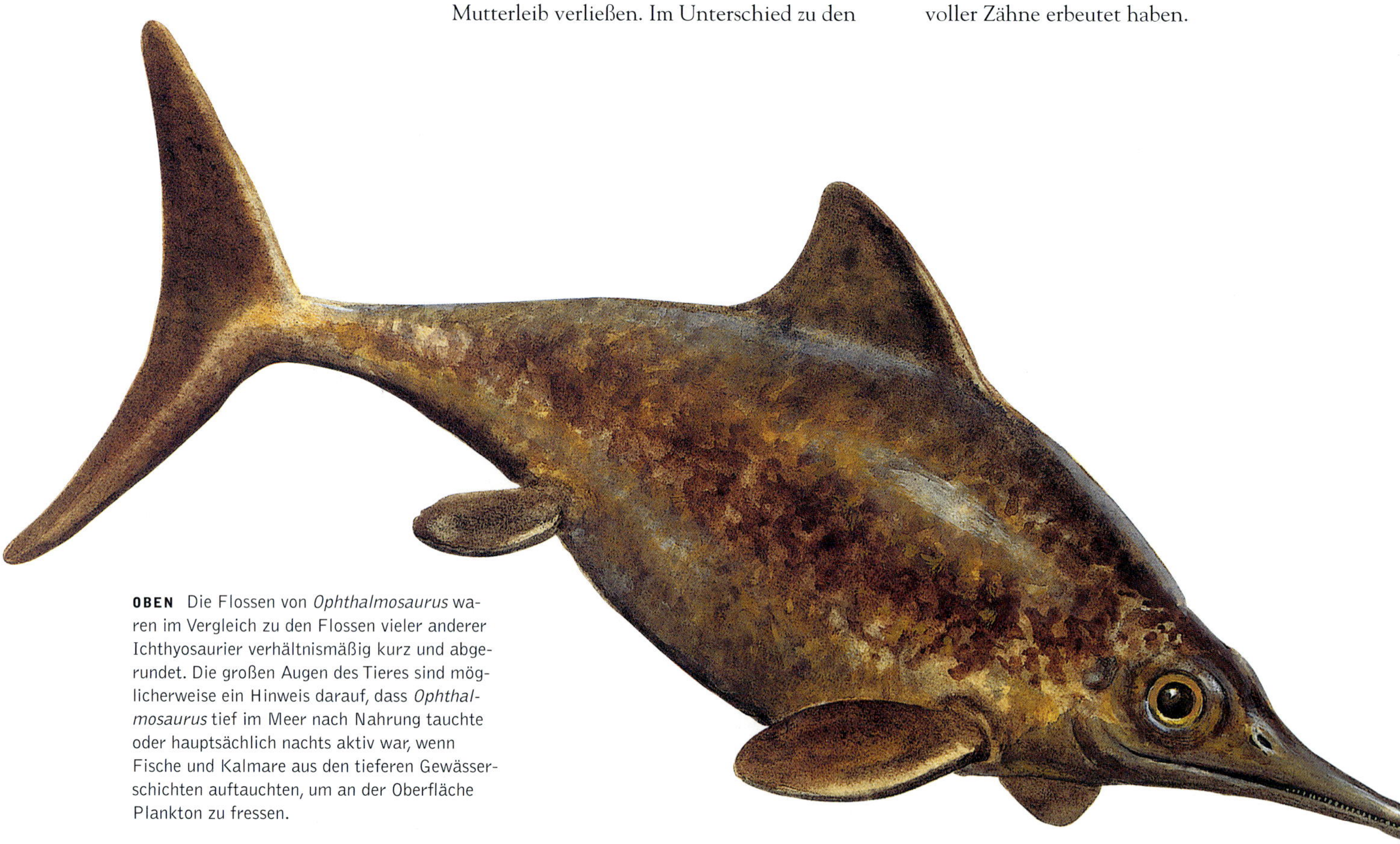

**OBEN** Die Flossen von *Ophthalmosaurus* waren im Vergleich zu den Flossen vieler anderer Ichthyosaurier verhältnismäßig kurz und abgerundet. Die großen Augen des Tieres sind möglicherweise ein Hinweis darauf, dass *Ophthalmosaurus* tief im Meer nach Nahrung tauchte oder hauptsächlich nachts aktiv war, wenn Fische und Kalmare aus den tieferen Gewässerschichten auftauchten, um an der Oberfläche Plankton zu fressen.

# PLESIOSAURUS

Die Plesiosaurier waren eine große, erfolgreiche Gruppe von Meeresreptilien, die fast während des gesamten Zeitalters der Dinosaurier existierte. Es gab mehrere Untergruppen, darunter die kurzhalsigen Pliosaurier wie beispielsweise *Kronosaurus* und *Liopleuron* (siehe Seiten 395 und 396). Die Gruppe wurde nach *Plesiosaurus* aufgestellt und benannt. Seinen Namen, der „Fast-Reptil" bedeutet, erhielt *Plesiosaurus*, weil sein Schädel und sein Rückgrat im Großen und Ganzen reptiltypisch, die Schultern, das Becken und die flossenartigen Gliedmaßen hingegen für ein Reptil ungewöhnlich waren. Den Namen prägten 1821, zwanzig Jahre bevor es den Begriff „Dinosaurier" gab, Henry de la Beche und William Conybeare für versteinerte Überreste, die aus den fossilreichen jurassischen Gesteinen bei Lyme Regis in der südenglischen Grafschaft Dorset stammten. In dieser Gegend sammelte der (eigentlich die) erste bekannte professionelle Fossilsucher(in) Mary Anning schöne, interessante Fossilexemplare, die sie dank des in Mode gekommenen Interesses an der Naturgeschichte als Liebhaberstücke verkaufen konnte.

*Plesiosaurus* hatte einen ziemlich kleinen Kopf, einen langen Hals, einen rundlichen Körper, vier wie Paddel geformte Gliedmaßen und einen kurzen Schwanz, der sich stufenlos verjüngte. Die Knochen des Becken- und des Schultergürtels sowie der Brust- und Bauchbereich waren kräftig verstärkt und durch stabile Gelenke verbunden, die von sehr starken Muskeln bewegt worden sein müssen. Die oberen Extremitätenknochen in der Flossenbasis waren kurz und kräftig, den Großteil der Flossenfläche bildeten die lang gestreckten Zehenknochen. Früher nahm man an, die Plesiosaurier hätten beim Schwimmen ihre Flossen wie die Ruder eines Bootes vor- und zurückbewegt. Inzwischen vermutet man, dass sie ihre Flossen wohl eher wie Vogelflügel auf- und abbewegten. Auf ähnlich Weise – flatternd statt rudernd – bewegen sich die heutigen Meeresschildkröten und Pinguine im Wasser.

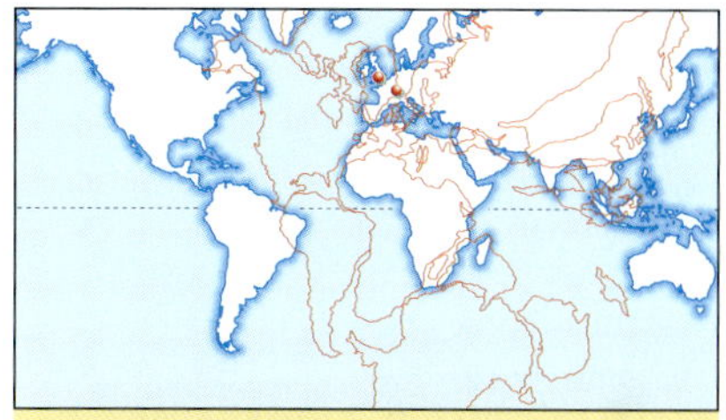

**ÜBERSICHT (REPTILIEN)**
***Plesiosaurus***
**Bedeutung des Namens:** Fast-Reptil
**Periode:** Unterer Jura
**Hauptgruppe:** Plesiosauria (Plesiosauridae)
**Länge:** Bis 2,5 Meter
**Gewicht:** 150 Kilogramm
**Nahrung:** Fische und ähnliche Beute aus dem Meer
**Fossilfundstätten:** Hauptsächlich in Europa (besonders in England), auch auf fast allen anderen Kontinenten

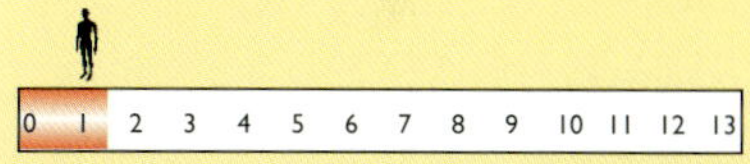


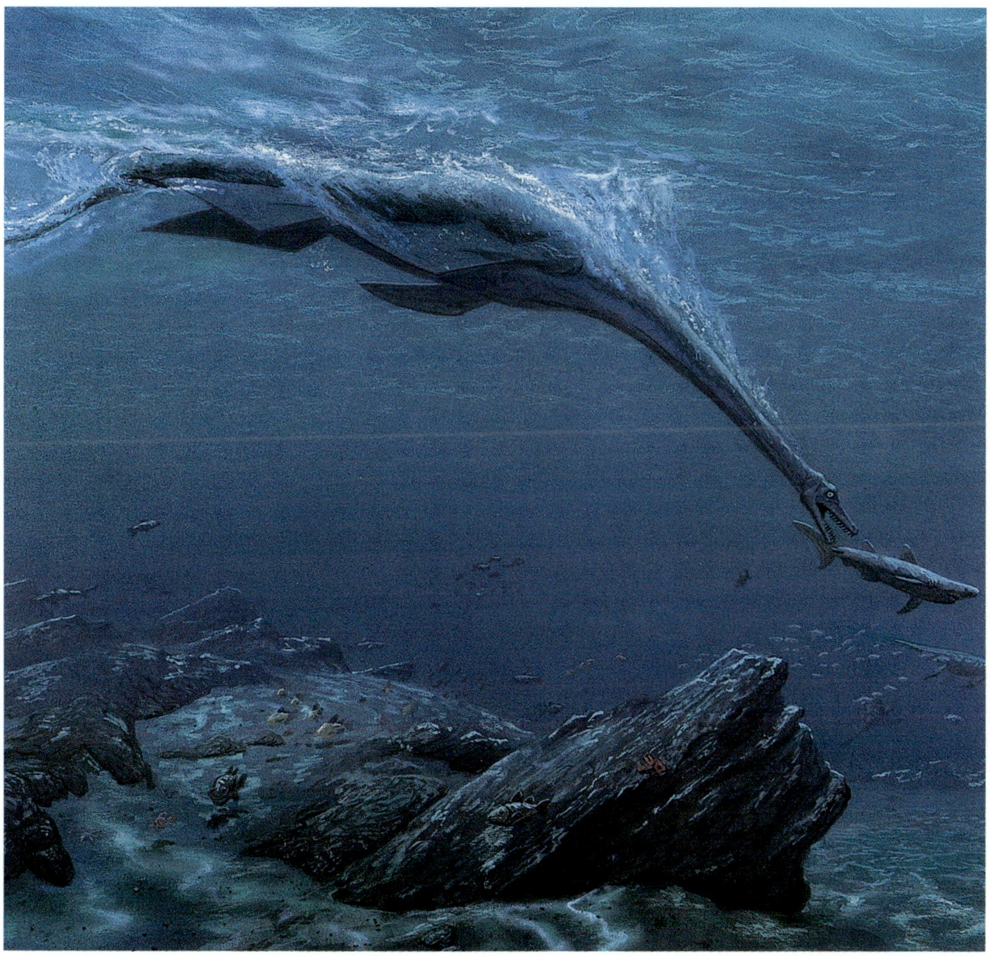

**LINKS** Ein *Plesiosaurus* lässt seinen langen Hals nach unten schnellen, um sich eine Fischmahlzeit zu beschaffen.

**UNTEN** Die langen Finger und Zehen des *Plesiosaurus* sind bei diesem wunderbar vollständigen Fossilexemplar teilweise in den Paddeln verborgen.

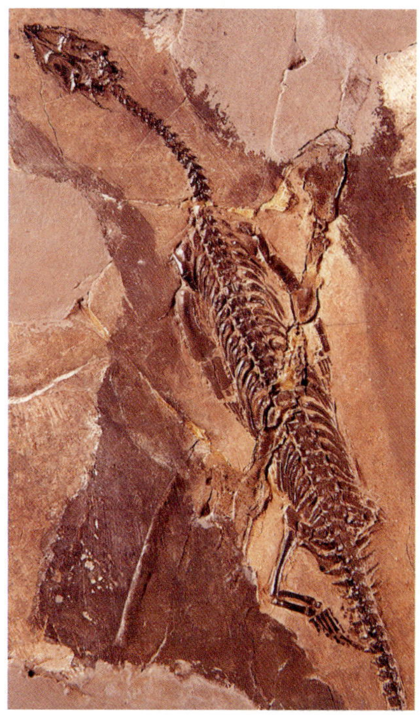

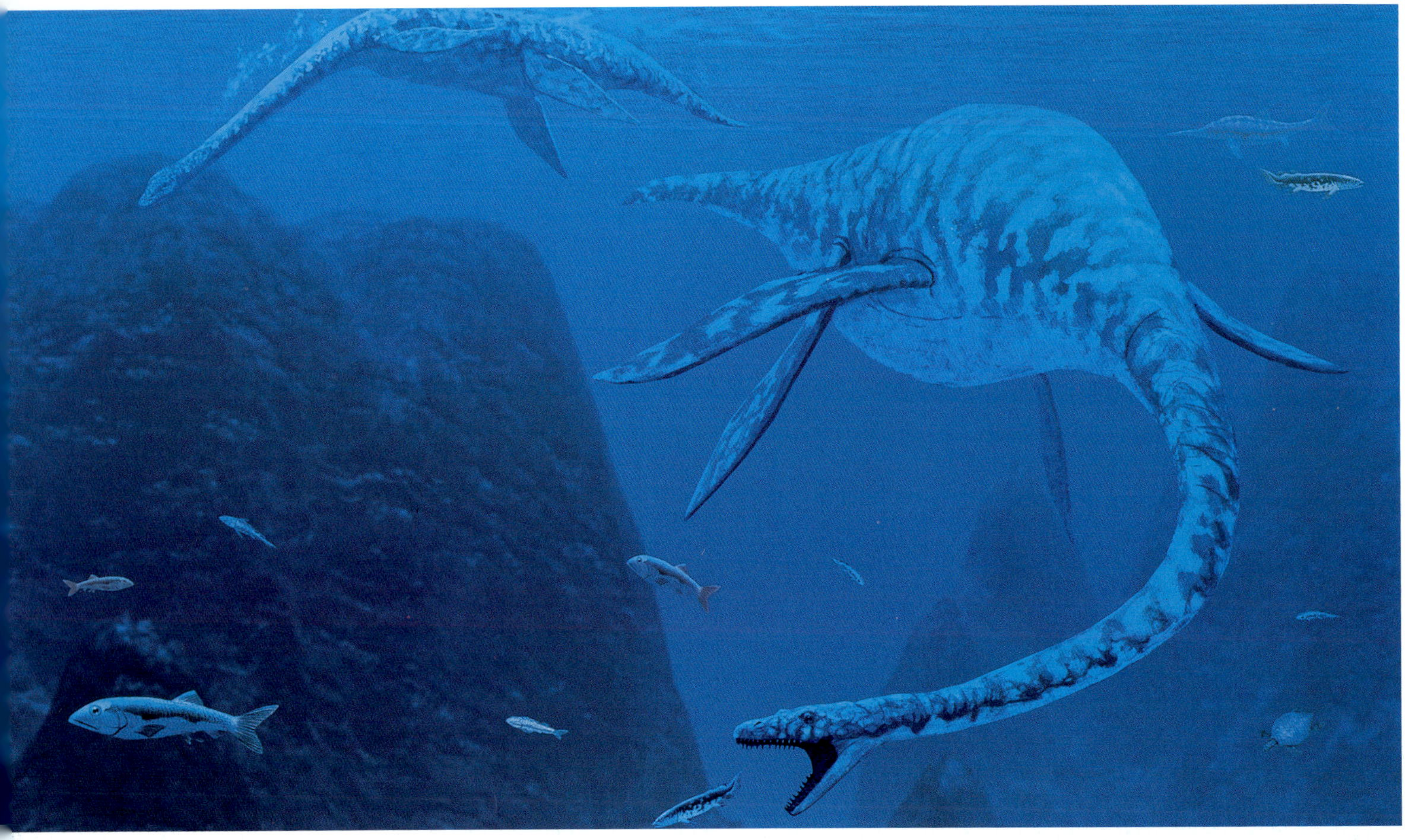

# Elasmosaurus

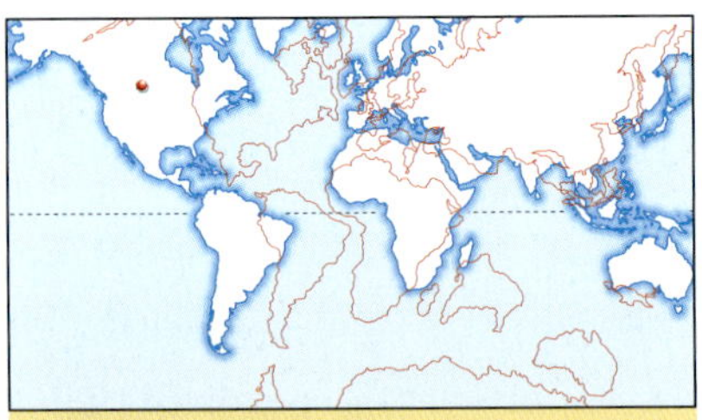

**ÜBERSICHT (REPTILIEN)**

***Elasmosaurus***

**Bedeutung des Namens:** Plattenreptil

**Periode:** Oberkreide

**Hauptgruppe:** Plesiosauria (Plesiosauridae)

**Länge:** 13–14 Meter

**Gewicht:** 2 Tonnen

**Nahrung:** Fische und ähnliche Tiere

**Fossilfundstätten:** In Nordamerika

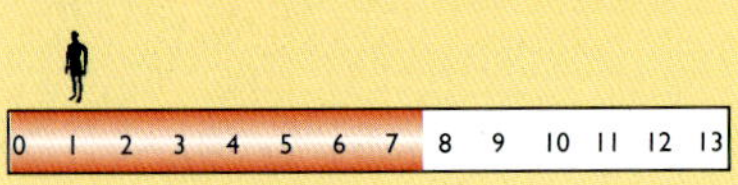


Überreste von *Elasmosaurus* wurden in Nordamerika, die Fossilien naher Verwandter dieses Tieres in Japan und anderswo in Ostasien ausgegraben. Die Fundstätten waren gegen Ende der Dinosaurierzeit alle Teil desselben Meeresbodens oder zumindest ein und desselben Systems miteinander verbundener Meere. *Elasmosaurus* war ein langhalsiger Plesiosaurier (siehe Seite 393, *Plesiosaurus*). Seine Gesamtlänge betrug vierzehn Meter, davon entfielen etwa sechs Meter auf den Hals. Einen längeren Hals hatte kein anderer Vertreter der Gruppe aufzuweisen. *Elasmosaurus* gehörte außerdem zu den letzten Plesiosauriern; die gesamte Gruppe verschwand zusammen mit den Dinosauriern bei dem Massenaussterben am Ende der Kreidezeit.

*Elasmosaurus* besaß einen vergleichsweise winzigen Kopf; wie er damit ausreichend Nahrung für seinen massigen Körper erbeutete, war lange Zeit ein Rätsel. Früher nahm man an, dass das Tier sich an der Meeresoberfläche treiben ließ oder umherschwamm und dabei seinen Kopf mehrere Meter aus dem Wasser ragen ließ, um nach Fischen oder anderer Nahrung in der Nähe der Wasseroberfläche Ausschau zu halten. Dann ließ er wohl seinen Hals niederschnellen und schnappte sein Opfer, indem er es mit seinen langen Vorderzähnen aufspießte oder die Beute mit seinem Maul einschloss, dessen Zähne wie Käfigstangen ein Entkommen des gefangenen Tieres verhinderten. Da bei *Elasmosaurus* die Augen aber an der Schädeloberseite saßen, muss das Beobachten des Wassers aus der Höhe schwierig gewesen sein. Einer anderen Theorie zufolge schwamm *Elasmosaurus* langsam auf Fischschwärme zu, ließ dann plötzlich seinen Hals in irgendeine Richtung schnellen und packte dann alles, was ihm vor das Maul kam. Uneins sind sich die Wissenschaftler bei der Frage, ob der Hals des *Elasmosaurus* biegsam war oder nicht. Fossilierte Reste des Mageninhalts von Plesiosauriern zeigen im Allgemeinen, dass diese Tiere sich von Fischen, Weichtieren wie Kalmaren und Ammoniten sowie von anderen kleinen Meerestieren ernährten.

**OBEN** *Elasmosaurus* besaß rund zweiundsiebzig Halswirbel. Das sind mehr als irgendein anderes Tier aufzuweisen hat. (Säugetiere, darunter auch die Menschen, haben nur sieben.)

# KRONOSAURUS

Dieses Meeresreptil aus der frühen Kreidezeit war ein Pliosaurier, d. h. es war ein Vertreter der Plesiosauriergruppe, gehörte aber in die Untergruppe Pliosauridae, die sich von den anderen Plesiosauriern durch einen viel kürzeren, dickeren Hals unterschieden. Die Pliosaurier waren schwerer gebaut, besaßen eine ausgeprägtere Stromlinienform, waren schneller und wilder als andere Plesiosaurier. Mit ihren massiven Kiefern und den in Reihen stehenden, bis zu fünfundzwanzig Zentimeter langen, spitzen Vorderzähnen konnten sie größere Beutetiere fangen. Der riesige Kopf, der größtenteils aus dem Maul bestand, war mit großen Augen und einem Paar erhöht sitzender Nasenlöcher versehen. Mit diesen Nasenlöchern konnte *Kronosaurus* wie andere Plesiosaurier auch Gerüche im Wasser wahrnehmen. Die Pliosaurier schwammen mit allen vier Gliedmaßen, die sich zu langen, breiten, kräftigen Flossen entwickelt hatten und von denen an jeder „Ecke" des lang gestreckten Körpes eine saß. Der Schwanz war kurz und verjüngte sich zum Ende hin wie bei anderen Plesiosauriern; er diente möglicherweise nur als Steuerorgan. *Kronosaurus* zählte zu den größten Pliosauriern. Fossilien von ihm wurden erstmals 1889 im australischen Bundesstaat Queensland gefunden, dessen Gebiet vor über 120 Millionen Jahren von einem Flachmeer bedeckt war. Seinen Namen erhielt *Kronosaurus* 1924 von Heber Longman. Anfangs ging man davon aus, dass das Tier insgesamt bis zu dreizehn Metern lang werden konnte, doch die Ergebnisse neuerer Untersuchungen seines fossilierten Schädels und anderer Teile sowie Vergleiche mit anderen Pliosauriern deuten darauf hin, dass *Kronosaurus* in Wirklichkeit wohl nur neun bis zehn Meter lang war. Unter den Begleitfunden waren Überreste zahlreicher Fische und verschiedener Mollusken. Einige der fossilierten Gehäuse weisen Abdrücke auf, die *Kronosaurus* mit seinen abgerundeten, zum Zermalmen hartschaliger Beutetiere geeigneten Zähnen hinterlassen haben könnte.

**UNTEN** Paddelte *Kronosaurus* mit den beiden einander gegenüberliegenden Flossen in entgegengesetzter Richtung, konnte er sich auf der Stelle drehen.

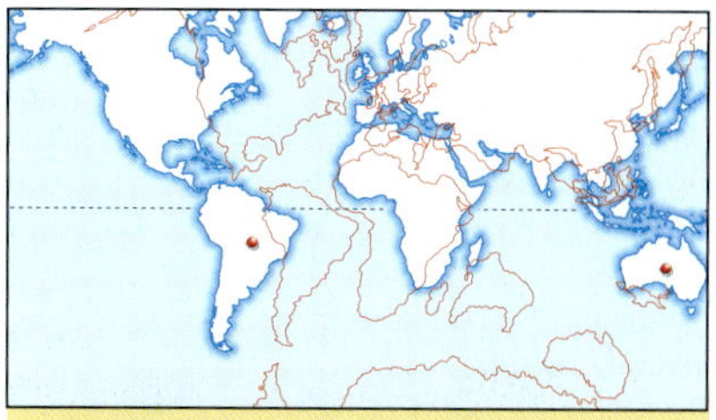

**ÜBERSICHT (REPTILIEN)**
***Kronosaurus***
**Bedeutung des Namens:** Zeitreptil
**Periode:** Unterkreide
**Hauptgruppe:** Plesiosauria (Plesiosauridae)
**Länge:** 9–10 Meter
**Gewicht:** 10–20 Tonnen
**Nahrung:** Große Meerestiere
**Fossilfundstätten:** In Australien und Südamerika

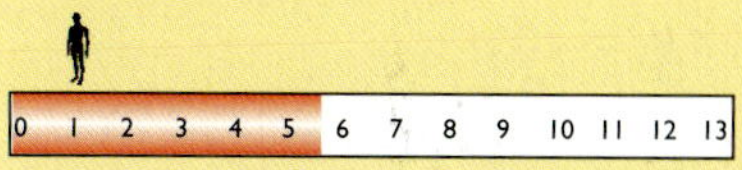


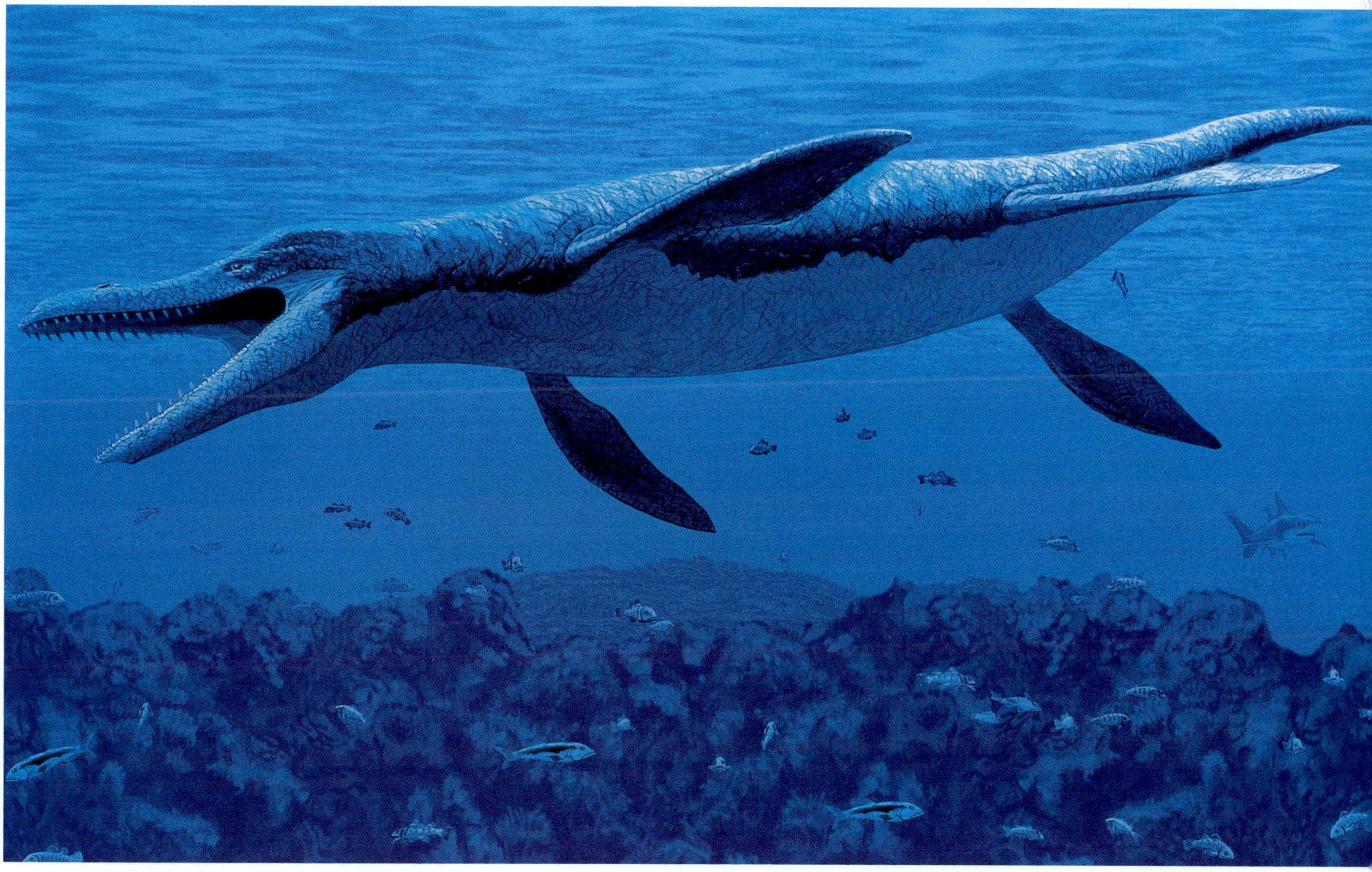

# LIOPLEURODON

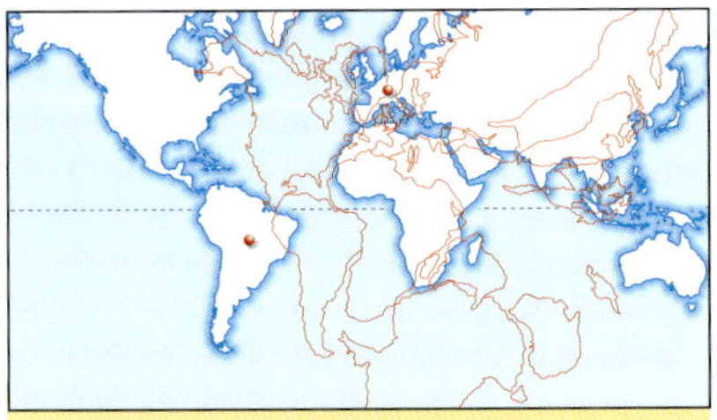

**ÜBERSICHT (REPTILIEN)**

***Liopleurodon***

**Bedeutung des Namens:** Glattseitiger Zahn

**Periode:** Oberer Jura

**Hauptgruppe:** Plesiosauridae (Pliosauridae)

**Länge:** 15 – 20 Meter

**Gewicht:** 30 – 50 Tonnen

**Nahrung:** Große Meerestiere

**Fossilfundstätten:** In Europa, möglicherweise in Südamerika

0 1 2 3 4 5 6 7 8 9 10 11 12 13

Stellt man sich die größten Räuber der Dinosaurierzeit vor, kommen einem für gewöhnlich *Tyrannosaurus* und der noch größere *Giganotosaurus* in den Sinn. Diese Riesen konnten sich allerdings nicht mit *Liopleurodon* vergleichen, der wie die Dinosaurier ein Reptil war, aber im offenen Meer lebte. *Liopleurodon* gehörte zu den Pliosauriern oder kurzhalsigen Plesiosauriern wie *Kronosaurus* (siehe vorhergehende Seite), war vermutlich aber riesiger als dieser. Der höchste geschätzte Wert für die Körperlänge des *Liopleuron* liegt bei fünfundzwanzig Metern, für das Gewicht bei einhundert Tonnen; das bedeutet, dass dieses Tier eines der größten Lebewesen war, die je auf der Erde existiert haben, und mit den größten Sauropoden und selbst mit dem größten rezenten Wal konkurrieren konnte. Seine wirkliche Größe lag aber vielleicht nur bei rund der Hälfte des Schätzwertes. Dann wäre *Liopleurodon* nur etwas kleiner als das Tier gewesen, das man oft den größten Jäger der Welt nennt und von dem wir mit Sicherheit wissen, dass es tatsächlich existiert – der rezente Pottwal. Dieser Wal kann über fünfzig Tonnen schwer und gut über sechzig Jahre alt werden.

Fossilien von *Liopleurodon* wurden an verschiedenen Fundstätten in Frankreich, Deutschland, England, Osteuropa und möglicherweise in Chile ausgegraben. Zu den Funden gehören Schädelteile, Kiefer, Zähne und Skelettknochen. Sie sind seit über einem Jahrhundert bekannt, denn *Liopleurodon* wurde 1873 von dem französischen Fossilienexperten Henri Sauvage benannt. Eine Entdeckung im Jahr 1991 brachte ein noch viel größeres Exemplar zutage, dessen Schädel allein bereits drei Meter lang war. Der Mund und die Kiefer waren so riesig und so kräftig, dass ihr Besitzer sich nicht wie die großen Wale oder andere Tiere, die ihre Nahrung aus dem Wasser seihen, mit dem Einfangen Unmengen kleiner Beutetiere abmühen musste, sondern wahrscheinlich auch mit gelegentlich auftauchenden einzelnen großen Beutetieren, beispielsweise mit Plesiosauriern, Ichthyosauriern oder anderen aquatisch lebenden Reptilien, fertig wurde.

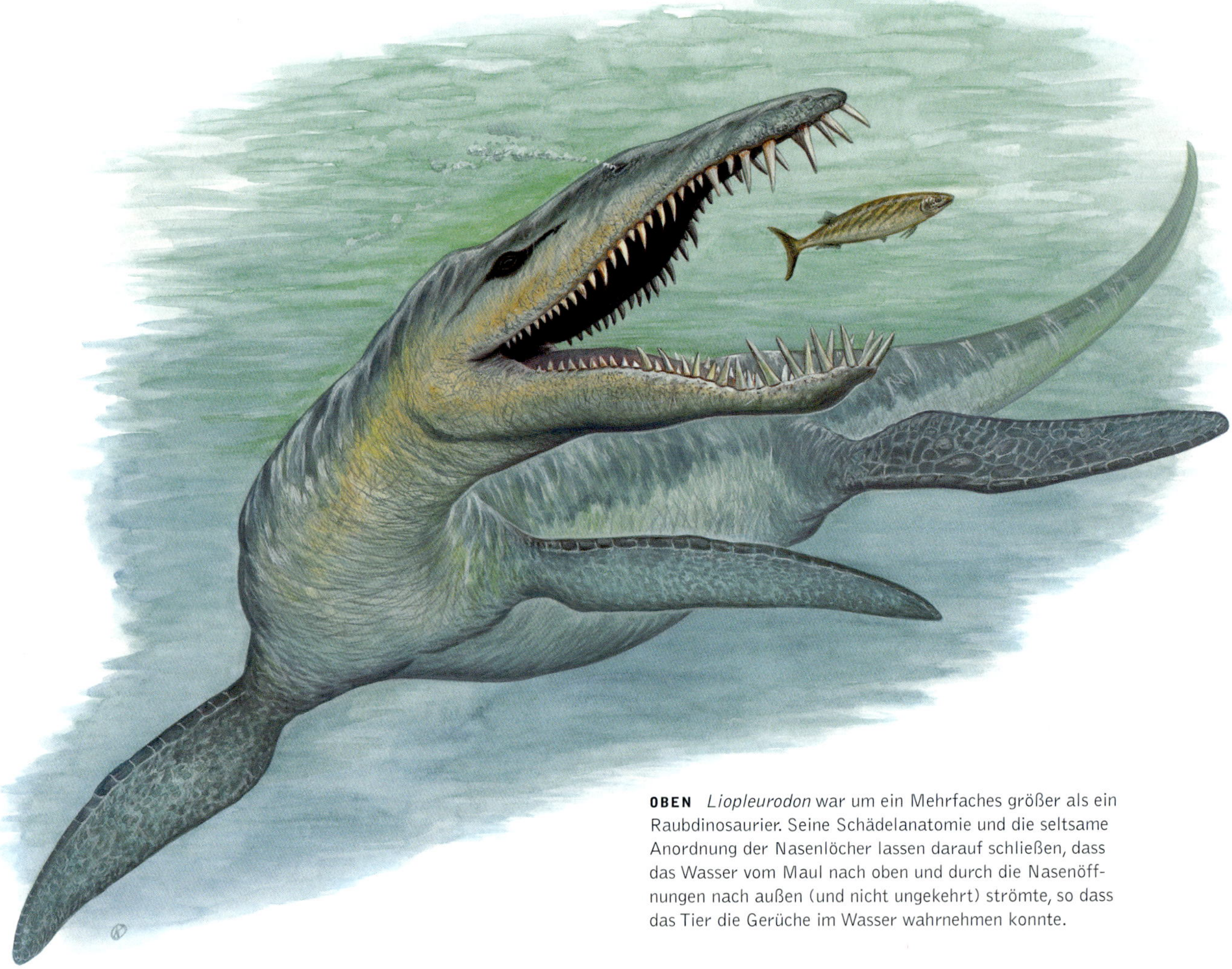

**OBEN** *Liopleurodon* war um ein Mehrfaches größer als ein Raubdinosaurier. Seine Schädelanatomie und die seltsame Anordnung der Nasenlöcher lassen darauf schließen, dass das Wasser vom Maul nach oben und durch die Nasenöffnungen nach außen (und nicht ungekehrt) strömte, so dass das Tier die Gerüche im Wasser wahrnehmen konnte.

# Mosasaurus

In den 1770er Jahren wurden auf dem Gebiet der heutigen Niederlande, in einer Kreidegrube in der Nähe der Maas, rätselhafte gewaltige Kiefer- und Zahnfossilien ausgegraben. Rund dreißig Jahre später stellte der französische Biologe Georges Cuvier, damals einer der weltweit führenden Fachleute auf dem Gebiet der Fauna, die Ähnlichkeit der Fossilien mit den Kiefern und Zähnen heutiger Echsen fest und gab den Überresten den Namen *Mosasaurus* – „Maas-Reptil". Cuvier glaubte, dass die Fossilien von Tieren stammten, die wie jedes andere Lebewesen von Gott geschaffen und bei einer großen Überschwemmung, vielleicht gar während der Sintflut umgekommen waren. So beurteilten die meisten Wissenschaftler der damaligen Zeit all jene Relikte, die wir heute dokumentierte fossile Funde nennen. Es dauerte noch viele Jahre, bis Richard Owen den Namen Dinosauria prägte oder Charles Darwin seine Evolutionstheorie entwickelte (siehe Seite 10).

In einer Hinsicht hatte Cuvier allerdings Recht: *Mosasaurus* gilt als alter, doch naher Verwandter der heutigen Warane. Die Mosasaurier, im Meer lebende Urtiere, erschienen in der späten Kreidezeit; sie hatten sich wahrscheinlich aus kleinen vierbeinigen Räubern entwickelt, die halbaquatisch in Sümpfen und an Meeresküsten lebten. Die Mosasaurier wurden außerordentlich groß – einige sogar über fünfzehn Meter lang. Ihr Kopf verjüngte sich über den Hals zum Körper, der lang und schlank wie bei einem Aal war. Die vier Gliedmaßen waren zu Flossen umgebildet und dienten als Steuerorgane. Der Hauptantrieb für die Fortbewegung im Wasser kam von dem sehr langen, biegsamen, muskulösen Schwanz, der seitlich abgeflacht und am Ende flossenartig war. Als die Ichthyosaurier langsam verschwanden, konnten Mosasaurier und Pliosaurier wie *Kronosaurus* und *Liopleurodon* als größte räuberische Reptilien der Kreidemeere miteinander wetteifern. Einer der gewaltigsten Mosasaurier – *Tylosaurus* – ist durch Fossilfunde aus dem US-Bundesstaat Kansas bekannt. Dort sind inzwischen so viele Überreste von Mosasauriern gefunden worden, dass Kansas als das „World Center" für diese Gruppe berühmt ist.

**UNTEN** Nicht nur die riesigen Kiefer des *Mosasaurus* waren mit spitzen Zähnen bestückt, sondern auch der knöcherne Gaumen.

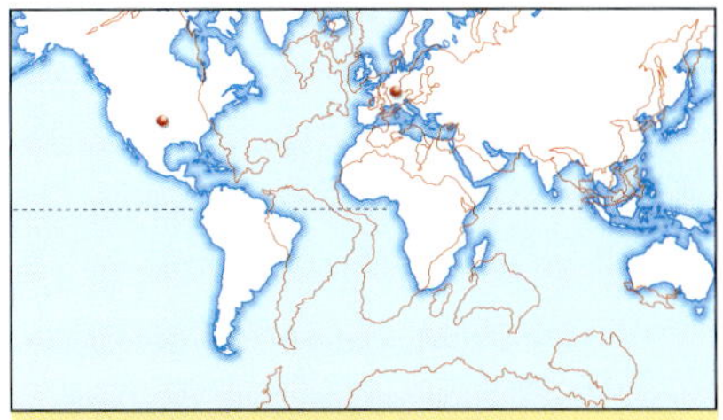

**ÜBERSICHT (REPTILIEN)**
***Mosasaurus***
**Bedeutung des Namens:** Maas-Reptil (nach dem Fundort benannt)
**Periode:** Oberkreide
**Hauptgruppe:** Mosasauria
**Länge:** 10 Meter
**Gewicht:** 5 Tonnen
**Nahrung:** Meerestiere
**Fossilfundstätten:** In den USA (Kansas), in Europa

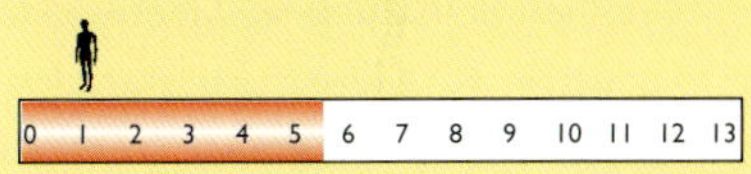


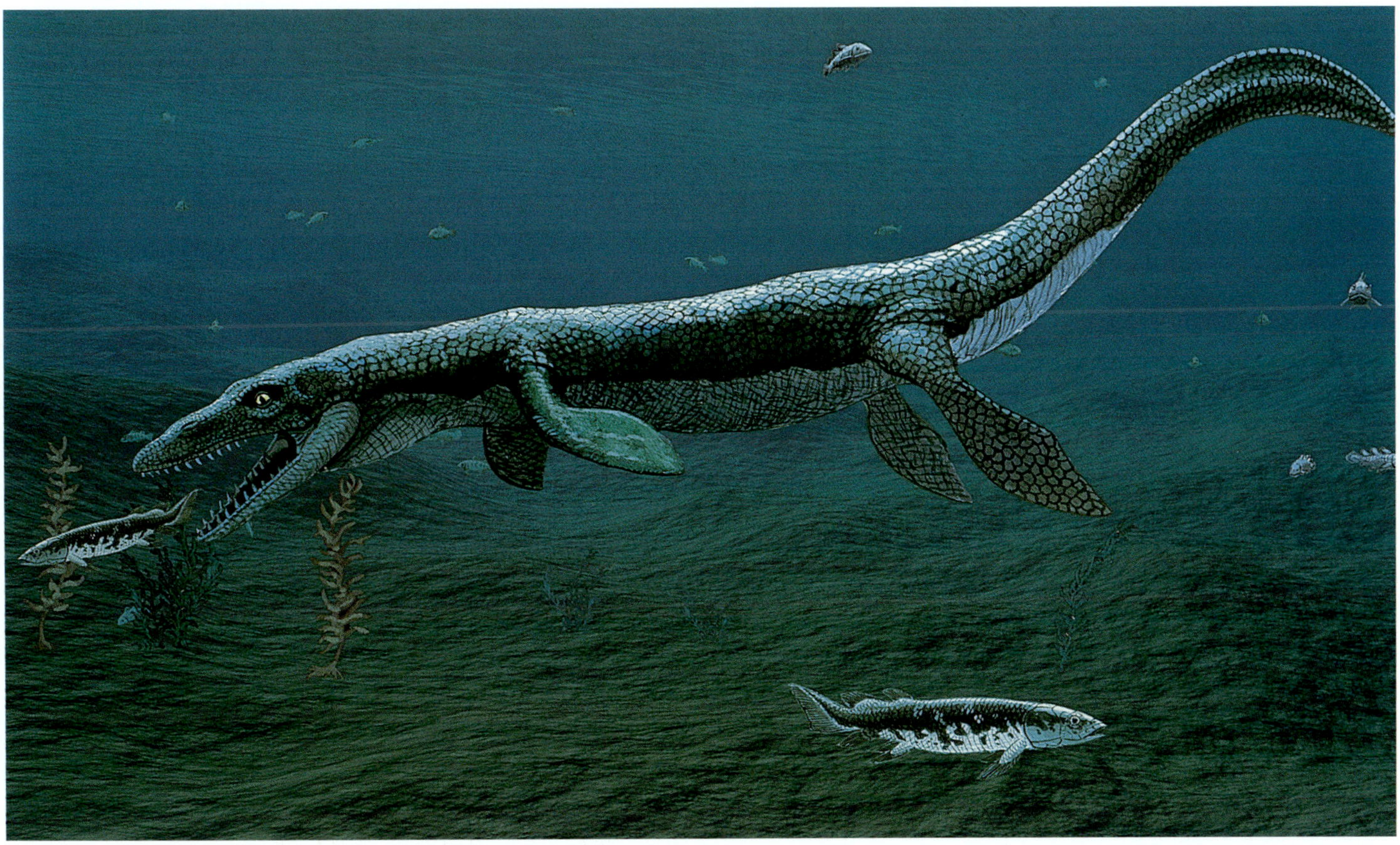

# Der Himmel und die Meere der Kreidezeit

*An verschiedenen Fossilfundstätten lässt sich an der Zusammensetzung der Sedimente aus der mittleren Kreidezeit und anhand der verschiedenartigen Überreste kleiner Schalentiere und anderer Meereslebewesen ablesen, dass die betreffenden Gebiete einst von warmen Flachmeeren bedeckt waren oder in Küstennähe lagen. Unter den Fossilien, die man bisher dort zutage gefördert hat, befinden sich Reste von Meeresreptilien wie Plesiosauriern und Mosasauriern und auch von Pterosauriern, die vor langer Zeit vielleicht bei der Jagd auf das Wasser stürzten, sich dann nicht wieder in die Luft erheben konnten und in den konservierenden Schlamm am Meeresboden sanken. Die mittlere Kreidezeit war eine Periode der Mannigfaltigkeit bei den großen Reptilien und deren Verwandten.*

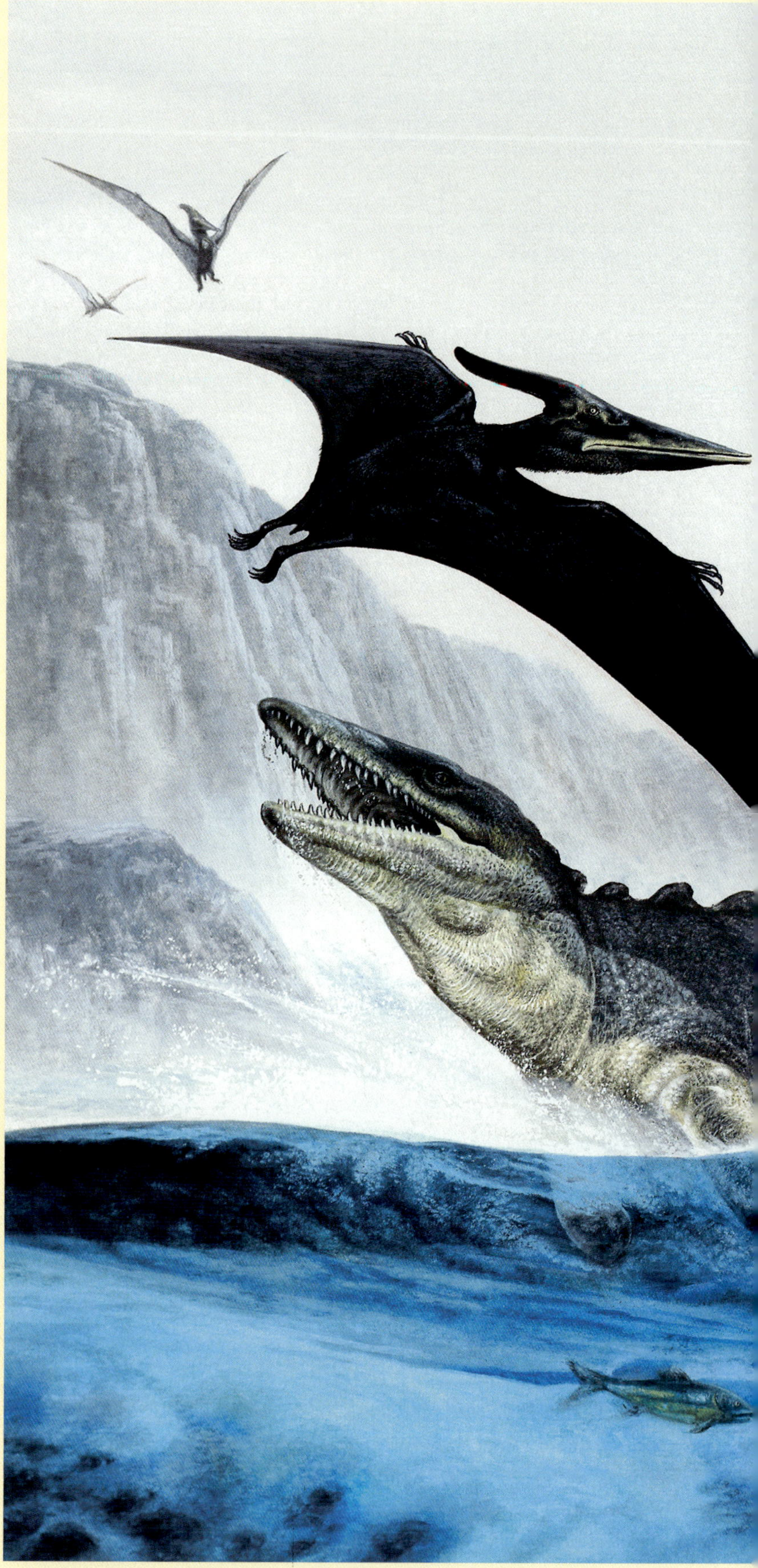

**RECHTS** In steiler Kurve und mit kräftigen Flügelschlägen versucht der Pterosaurier *Pteranodon* den Zähnen und Kiefern eines Mosasauriers zu entkommen, der gerade aus dem Meer emporschießt. Rechts beugen drei Elasmosaurier ihre erstaunlich langen Hälse über die Wellen, denn sie sind auf der Suche nach kleinen Fischen und anderen Beutetieren, die dicht unter der Wasseroberfläche schwimmen. Neuere Theorien zweifeln allerdings an, dass *Elasmosaurus* auf diese Art gejagt hat; sie gehen davon aus, dass er zur Nahrungssuche ganz ins Wasser abtauchte.

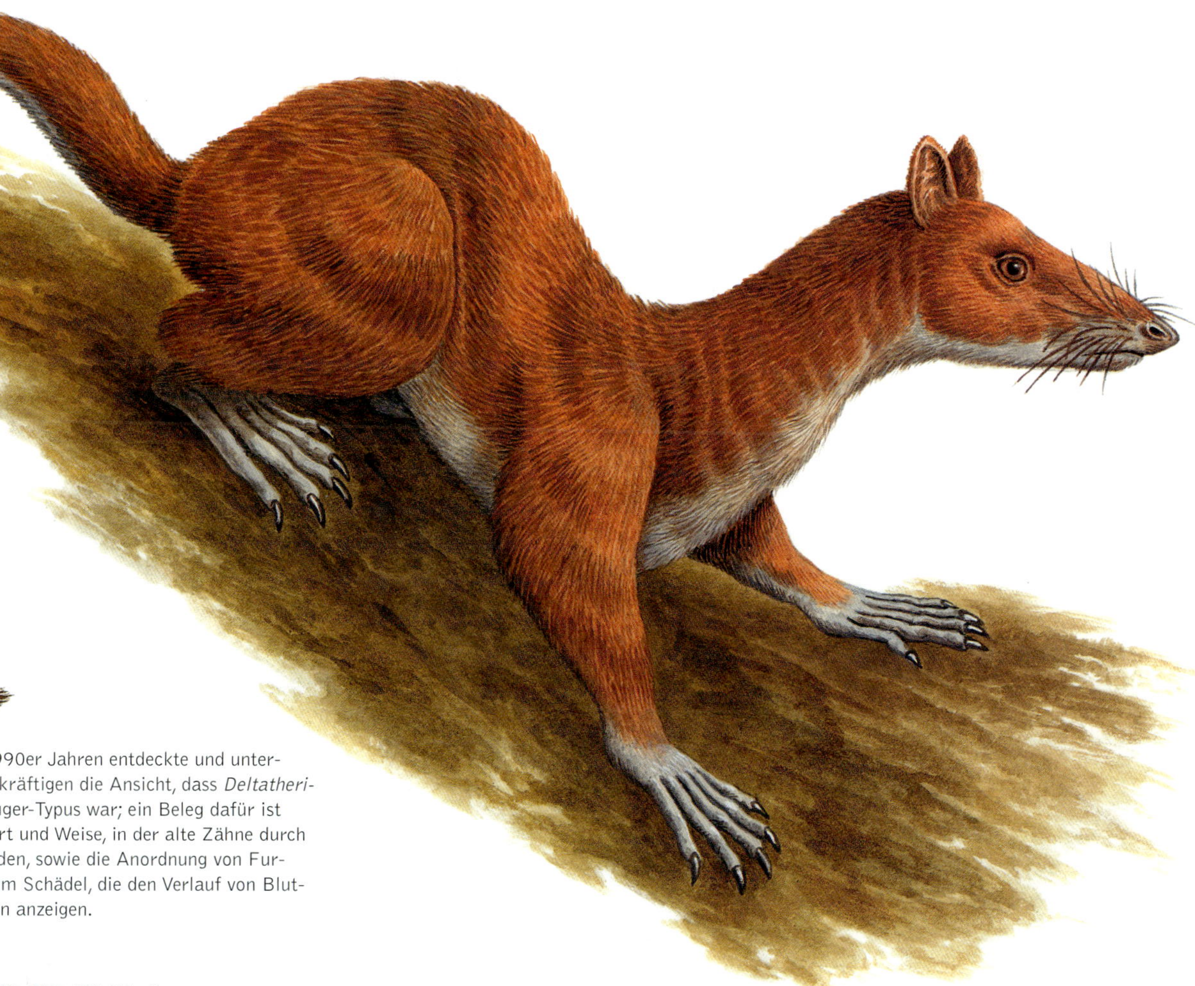

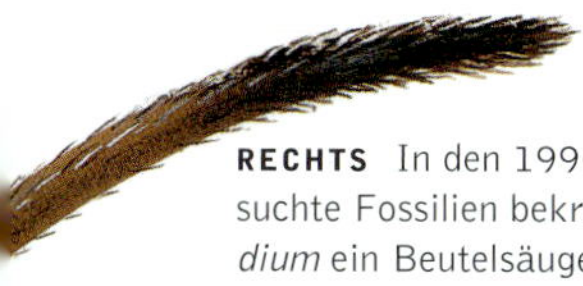

**RECHTS** In den 1990er Jahren entdeckte und untersuchte Fossilien bekräftigen die Ansicht, dass *Deltatheridium* ein Beutelsäuger-Typus war; ein Beleg dafür ist insbesondere die Art und Weise, in der alte Zähne durch neuere ersetzt wurden, sowie die Anordnung von Furchen und Löchern im Schädel, die den Verlauf von Blutgefäßen und Nerven anzeigen.

# DELTATHERIDIUM

Dieses Säugetier lebte vor 80 Millionen Jahren in der Mongolei, also etwa zur gleichen Zeit und im gleichen Gebiet wie *Zalambdalestes* (siehe gegenüber). Es war kleiner – seine Länge betrug einschließlich des Schwanzes etwas über fünfzehn Zentimeter –, unterschied sich jedoch in vielerlei Hinsicht von *Zalambdalestes*. *Deltatheridium* gehörte zu den vielen Säugetieren, die gegen Ende des Zeitalters der Dinosaurier existierten und die ein Beleg dafür waren, welche Vielfalt und Verbreitung über verschiedene Regionen der Erde die Mammalia in den vorangegangenen 130 Millionen Jahren erreicht hatten.

*Deltatheridium* wird in seiner allgemeinen Erscheinung üblicherweise mit dem rezenten Opossum oder vielleicht mit dem Wiesel verglichen, das etwas längere Beine besitzt. Sein Schädel war lang und die Schnauze verhältnismäßig hoch, was dem Kopf ein langnasiges Aussehen verlieh. Der Schwanz war ebenfall ziemlich lang. Die Zähne wiesen die bei Säugetieren übliche Anordnung auf – vorn scharfe Schneidezähne, dann ein langer, spitzer Eckzahn links und rechts in beiden Kiefern, dahinter niedrigere, breitere vordere Backenzähne und in der Wangenregion Backenzähne zum Zermahlen der Nahrung. Die Backenzähne zeigen in der Draufsicht kein abgerundetes Rechteck, sondern eine Dreiecksform. Dieser Form verdankt das Säugetier seinen Namen, denn „Delta" bedeutet so viel wie dreieckige Form. (Viele kleine frühe Säugetiere sind nach ihrer Zahnform benannt – siehe auch gegenüber.) Die Zähne von *Deltatheridium* waren so angeordnet, dass die Backenzähne des Ober- und des Unterkiefers aneinander vorbei glitten und ineinander griffen, statt mit ihren Mahlflächen aufeinander zu stoßen. Das erhöhte die Kraft, mit der die Zähne die Nahrung zerkleinerten; diese Anordnung ist auch bei der schon lange ausgestorbenen Gruppe der Creodonten zu sehen, die räuberisch lebende, d. h. Fleisch fressende Säugetiere waren. Man betrachtet die Creodonten als Plazentatiere, doch sie besaßen auch einige Schädel- und Skelettmerkmale, die stärker denen der Beutelsäuger ähnelten. *Deltatheridium* machte vermutlich Jagd auf Insekten und sehr junge Reptilien; mit seinen kräftigen Kiefern könnte er sich auch von Aas ernährt haben.

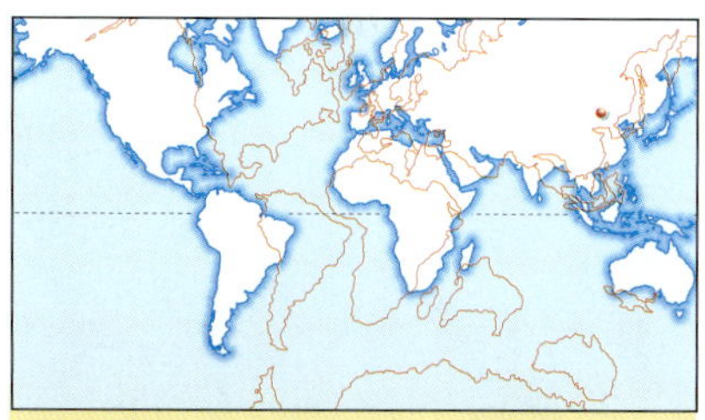

**ÜBERSICHT (SÄUGETIERE)**

***Deltatheridium***

**Bedeutung des Namens:** Dreiecks- oder Delta-Urtier

**Periode:** Oberkreide

**Hauptgruppe:** Mammalia

**Länge:** 15 Zentimeter

**Gewicht:** 80 Gramm

**Nahrung:** Insekten

**Fossilfundstätten:** In der Mongolei

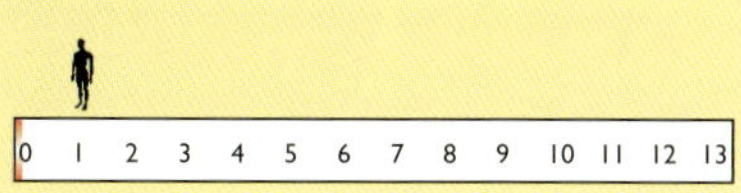

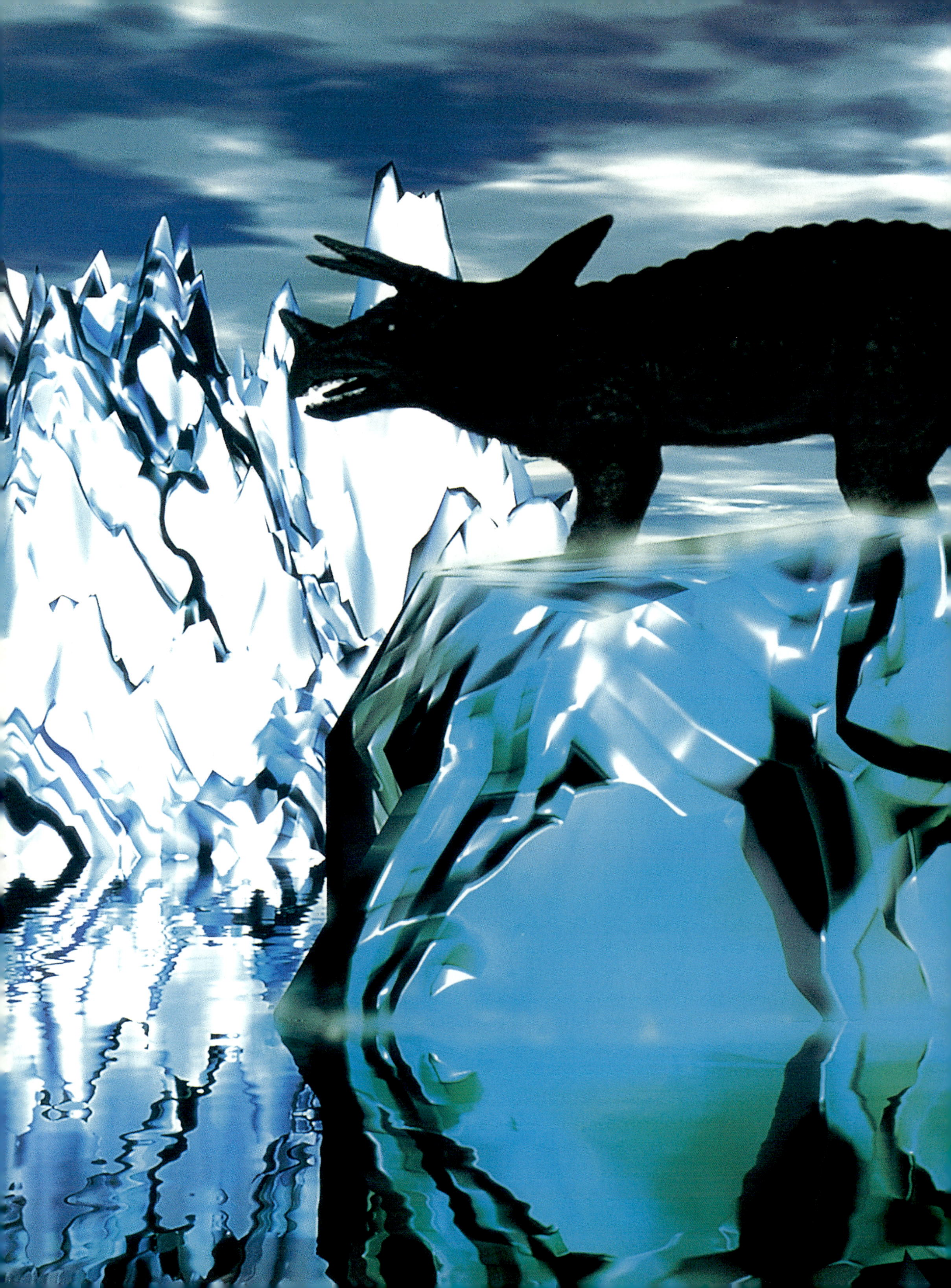

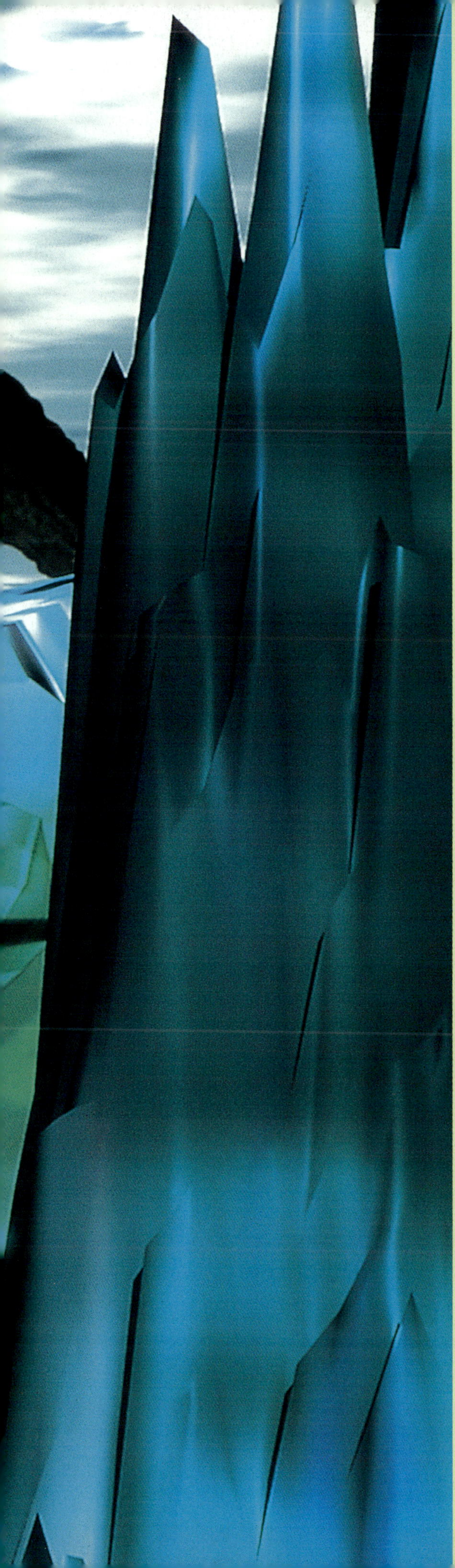

## Kapitel Fünfzehn

# Nach den Dinosauriern

*Das Zeitalter der Dinosaurier ging vor 65 Millionen Jahren mit einem der großen Massenaussterben, die immer wieder auftraten und verheerende Auswirkungen auf die Lebewelt der Erde hatten, abrupt zu Ende. Zwei große Tiergruppen – die Vögel und die Säugetiere – überlebten dieses Ereignis und entfalteten sich auch bald danach zu voller Blüte.*

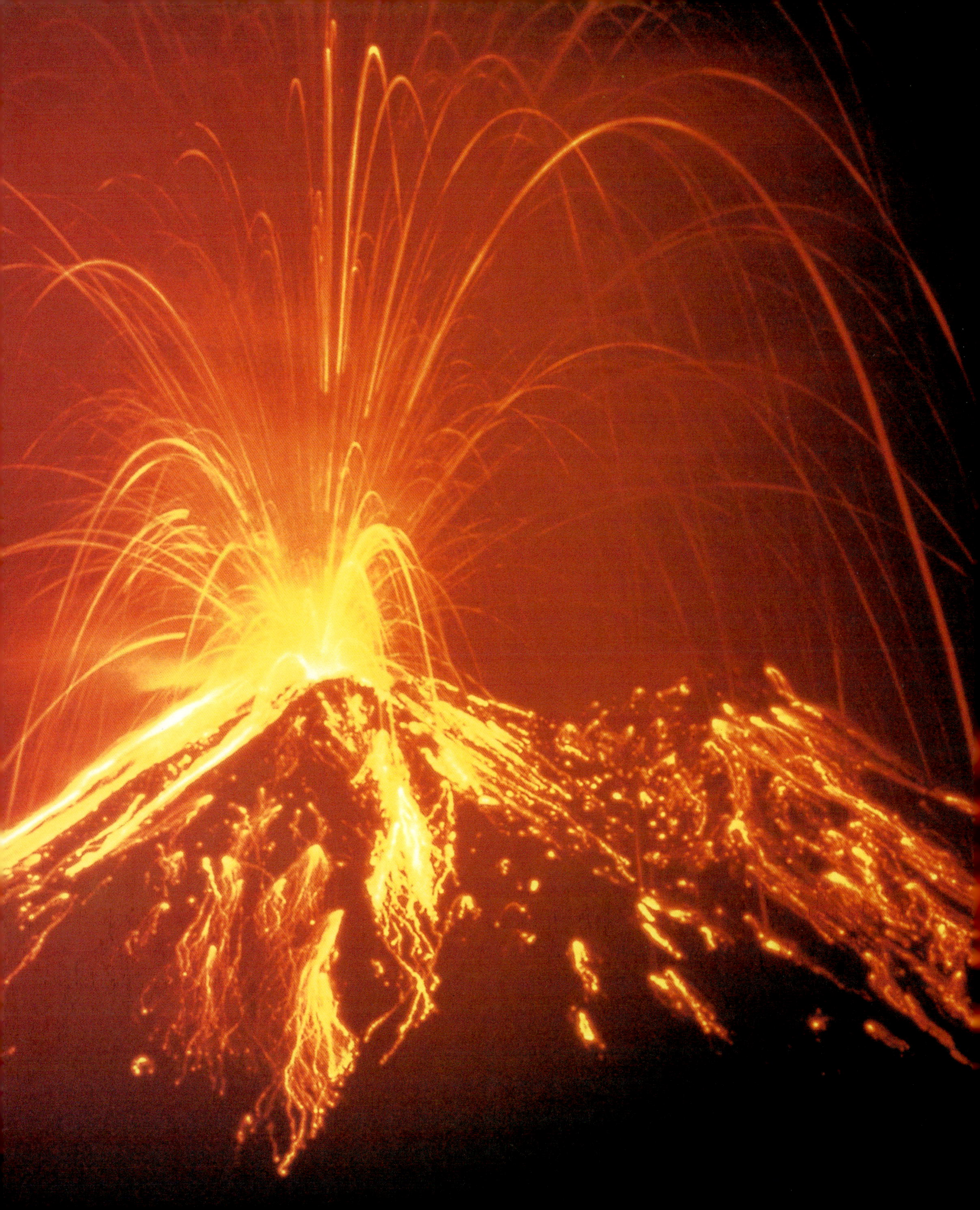

# MASSENAUSSTERBEN

***Es mag wie ein sonderbarer Zufall anmuten, dass der Übergang von einer Periode zur nächsten – von der Kreidezeit zum Tertiär vor 65 Millionen Jahren – von einer der größten Katastrophen gekennzeichnet war, die die Welt je erlebt hat. Dieses Zusammentreffen ist jedoch einfach der üblichen wissenschaftlichen Verfahrensweise geschuldet, geologische Perioden anhand plötzlicher Veränderungen in den Gesteinen und den darin enthaltenen Fossilien zu definieren. Den von einem Massenaussterben begleitete Übergang, um den es hier geht, nennt man K/T-Schnitt. Erscheinungen wie dieses Massensterben waren allerdings nicht neu. In der Vorgeschichte gab es mindestens ein Dutzend davon. Das größte Massensterben vor 250 Millionen Jahren beispielsweise, also 185 Millionen Jahre vor dem Umbruch von der Kreide zum Tertiär, bezeichnet das Ende des Perms und den Beginn der Trias. Untersuchungen von Fossilbelegen deuten darauf hin, dass am Ende des Perms vielleicht neunzehn von zwanzig lebenden Spezies bei einem so genannten „großen Sterben“ verschwanden. Diese massive Erschütterung der Lebewelt kündigte den Beginn einer neuen Ära – des Mesozoikums oder Erdmittelalters – an, das auch Zeitalter der Dinosaurier genannt wird. Der K/T-Schnitt beendete diese Ära und damit auch die Herrschaft der Dinosaurier. Er markiert den Beginn des Känozoikums oder der Erdneuzeit, und um dieses Erdzeitalter soll es im Folgenden gehen.***

## OPFER DES AUSSTERBENS

Die Dinosaurier haben einen solch herausragenden Ruf, dass Berichte über ihren Untergang die Informationen über alle anderen Lebewesen, die zur gleichen Zeit verschwanden, meist in eine Nebenrolle drängen. Von dem großen Aussterben waren viele Reptilien und ähnliche Geschöpfe – nicht nur die Dinosaurier, sondern auch die Pterosaurier in der Luft und die Mosasaurier, die Plesiosaurier u. a. in den Meeren betroffen. Es starben auch viele Formen mariner Mollusken und andere Meerestiere, ebenso verschiedene Pflanzen, vor allem Meeresalgen, aus. Am stärksten scheinen die größeren Landtiere unter der Katastrophe gelitten zu haben, denn danach existierte von den terrestrischen Lebewesen, die größer als ein Labradorhund waren, keines mehr. Insgesamt kamen zwei Drittel aller Familien der Lebewelt um. Seltsamerweise waren einige Reptilgruppen wie beispielsweise die Krokodile nur teilweise betroffen. Viele Typen, die in Sümpfen und Süßgewässern existierten, überlebten, während die Meereskrokodile ausgelöscht wurden. Andere Reptilien, die das Massenaussterben überstanden, darunter die Schildkröten, Echsen und Schlangen, teilen noch heute die Erde mit uns.

## SCHON IM SCHWINDEN BEGRIFFEN?

Der K/T-Schnitt kann sich über einige Tage, mehrere Monate oder auch Hunderte von Jahren hingezogen haben. Beim Blick in eine so ferne Vergangenheit ist es unmöglich, die Zeitdauer genau festzustellen. Auch gibt es unterschiedliche Meinungen darüber, ob die Dinosaurier nicht bereits vor dem Faunenschnitt vor 65 Millionen Jahren im Schwinden begriffen gewesen waren. Manche Studien deuten darauf hin, dass bereits rund 20 Millionen Jahre zuvor ein Rückgang ihrer Gesamtzahl und ihrer Vielgestaltigkeit eingesetzt hatte, obgleich diese Verringerung eher regionalen als globalen Charakter trug. Außerdem hatten sich während dieser Zeit einige große Dinosauriergruppen, beispielsweise die Hadrosaurier, die Ceratopsier, die großen Fleisch fressenden Tyrannosaurier und die Straußdinosaurier, entfaltet.

## SIND DIE DINOSAURIER AUSGESTORBEN?

Gelegentlich wird behauptet, die Fossilien irgendeines Dinosauriers seien jünger als 65 Millionen Jahre. In vielen Fällen stellt sich dann heraus, dass man die Überreste falsch identifiziert hat oder dass es sich um Dinosaurierfossilien handelt, die durch Wind und Wetter aus älterem, d. h. aus der Zeit vor dem großen Aussterben stammendem Gestein herausgewaschen und später in jüngeres Gestein eingeschlossen worden sind. Die übergroße Mehrzahl der Fossilbelege deutet auf ein totales Massenaussterben der Dinosaurier hin; wo die Ursachen für dieses Aussterbens liegen, wird unter den Paläontologen noch immer heftig diskutiert (siehe folgende Seiten). In gewissem Sinn kann man allerdings sagen, dass die Dinosaurier weiterleben, wenn auch stark verändert und mit Federn und Flügeln – als Vögel.

**VORHERGEHENDE SEITE** Auch der Ceratopsier *Torosaurus*, einer der letzten Dinosaurier, überlebte den plötzlichen Klimawechsel gegen Ende der Kreidezeit nicht. Der Wechsel könnte durch mehrere Faktoren hervorgerufen worden sein, beispielsweise durch den Aufschlag eines Asteroiden oder Meteoriten auf der Erde, durch massenhafte Vulkanausbrüche oder veränderte Witterungsverhältnisse aufgrund der Kontinentaldrift.

**LINKS** Der Ausbruch eines einzelnen Vulkans ist ein sehr eindrucksvolles Naturereignis. Eine Erklärung für das Massenaussterben am Ende der Kreidezeit lautet, dass damals eine Vielzahl solcher Eruptionen stattfand, die die Erdatmosphäre mit erstickendem Rauch und alles zudeckendem Ascheregen vergifteten.

## THEORIEN ZUM K/T-SCHNITT

Der aussichtsreichste Bewerber um den Titel „Dinosaurier-Tod" ist gegenwärtig der Aufschlag eines Asteroiden (Meteoriten) auf der Erde. Der Asteroidentheorie zufolge erschien vor 65 Millionen Jahren ein riesiger Gesteinsbrocken von vielleicht zehn Kilometer Durchmesser aus dem Weltraum, kreuzte zufällig den Weg der Erde und stürzte mit einer Geschwindigkeit von über zwanzigtausend Stundenkilometern auf unseren Planeten nieder. Die gewaltige Erschütterung am Ort des Aufschlags ließ alles, was sich dort befand – Boden, Wasser, Tiere, Pflanzen, selbst unter der Erdoberfläche lagerndes Gestein und schließlich den Asteroiden selbst – verdampfen. Dadurch wurden riesige Mengen Staub, Gesteinsstücke und Erde in die Atmosphäre geschleudert, die sich mit dem Wind um den ganzen Globus verbreiteten. Ein Teil dieses Materials war so heiß, dass es beim Niederfallen auf die Erde auf nahezu jedem Kontinent verheerende Brände aufflammen ließ. Der aufsteigende Rauch verdeckte die Sonne tage-, wochen- und sogar jahrelang. In der kalten Düsternis des „Asteroidenwinters" vergingen die Pflanzen, die Folge war, dass die Pflanzenfresser und nach ihnen die Fleischfresser verhungerten. Den aquatisch lebenden Tieren bot das Wasser einen gewissen Schutz vor der Katastrophe.

## HINWEISE

Es gibt mehrere Anzeichen, die die Asteroidentheorie stützen. Bestimmte Gesteine, die aus der bewussten Zeit stammen, weisen eine dünne Schicht auf, die außergewöhnlich viel Iridium enthält. Dieses Metall kommt auf und in der Erde im Allgemeinen selten, in kosmischen Gesteinen dagegen häufig vor. Vielleicht sind damals Teile des Asteroiden verdampft, wurden vom Wind davongetrieben und setzten sich ab, als die erwähnten Gesteine entstanden. Ein weiterer Hinweis ist ein gewaltiger senkenartiger Krater von über zweihundert Kilometern Durchmesser vor der Küste der mexikanischen Halbinsel Yucatán, der heute vom Schlick des Meeresbodens bedeckt ist. Diese Chicxulub-Krater genannte Senke könnte der Ort sein, an dem der Asteroid einst aufschlug. Die Kollision könnte auch Tsunamis (Seebebenwellen) ausgelöst haben, die weite Gebiete überfluteten; ein Regen heißer Trümmerteile könnte zu verheerenden Bränden geführt haben; schließlich muss die Erdkruste, die schalenartige äußere Gesteinsschicht unseres Planeten, die Stoßwellen mehrfach reflektiert haben. Diese seismischen Reaktionen könnten bereits unter Spannung stehende Teile der Erdkruste an den Rand der Belastbarkeit gebracht und so massenhafte Vulkanausbrüche und sich selbst fortsetzende Erdbebenketten bewirkt haben. Vor allem in Indien, aber auch in vielen anderen Gebieten der Erde vorkommende Schichten aus komprimierter Asche und Ruß stammen aus der Zeit vor 65 Millionen Jahren.

## KONTINENTE UND KLIMA

Aus der Asteroidentheorie ergeben sich viele Folgen. Einige davon könnten auch ohne extraterrestrischen Anstoß durch den Asteroiden selbst in einem relativ kurzen Zeitraum eingetreten sein. Am Ende der Kreidezeit drifteten die Kontinente um den Erdball, in manchen Gebieten stiegen Gebirge empor, während in anderen Grabensysteme entstanden; Meeresspiegel, Wind- und Meeresströmungen veränderten sich rapide. Solche Naturereignisse können einen ungewöhnlich raschen Klimawechsel zusammen mit massenhaften Vulkanausbrüchen verursacht haben. Die bei den Eruptionen in die Atmosphäre gelangten giftigen Gase und Aschemengen könnten das Ende der großen Landtiere durch Erfrieren und/oder Ersticken bewirkt haben; sie könnten die Ozonschicht der Atmosphäre verdünnt haben, die die Erdoberfläche vor schädlichen Sonnenstrahlen schützt; sie könnten zu saurem Regen geführt haben, der die Pflanzen verbrannte und zerfraß. (Von zwei dieser Naturerscheinungen sind wir heute betroffen.) Der Dekhan, eine riesige Hochfläche in Zentralindien, wurde vor etwa 65 Millionen Jahren durch Ergüsse flüssiger vulkanischer Lava gebildet. Dieses Hochplateau wird heute als Beleg für eine massenhafte vulkanische Tätigkeit angeführt, die einst einen raschen Klimawechsel auslöste.

## KRANKHEIT UND KONKURRENZ

Mit dem Verschwinden der Dinosaurier beschäftigen sich auch weniger komplizierte Theorien. Diese gehen davon aus, dass sich einst epidemisch auftretende Krankheiten über die Erde ausbreiteten, die manche Tiergruppen mehr, andere weniger heimsuchten; dass kleine Säugetiere sich allmählich durchsetzten, weil sie die Eier der Dinosaurier fraßen; dass für die Dinosaurier ein genetischer Stillstand eintrat oder diese Tiere in eine evolutionäre Sackgasse geraten waren, da sie sich zu stark modifizierten Formen entwickelt hatten, die sich nicht mehr ohne weiteres den raschen Veränderungen der Umweltbedingungen anpassen konnten; oder dass es damals im Weltraum einen Ausbruch tödlicher Strahlung, vielleicht von der Sonne oder einem in der „Nähe" explodierenden Stern (Supernova), gab. Diesen Theorien wird vonseiten der Wissenschaft allerdings nur wenig ernsthafte Unterstützung zuteil.

**RECHTS** Die Oberfläche unseres Planeten ist durch Kollisionen mit Meteoriten schon seit langem wie mit Pockennarben übersät. Die Einschläge hinterließen Krater, die über Jahrtausende hinweg von Wind und Wetter erodiert und wieder aufgefüllt wurden. Der hier abgebildete Wolfe-Creek-Krater in Western Australia ist bereits über eine Million Jahre alt – die Erosion geht in diesem Wüstengebiet nur sehr langsam vonstatten. Der Krater hat einen Durchmesser von fast einem Kilometer. Die Kollision am Ende der Kreidezeit könnte einen zweihundertmal breiteren Krater hinterlassen haben, der heute vom Schlamm des Meeresbodens bedeckt ist.

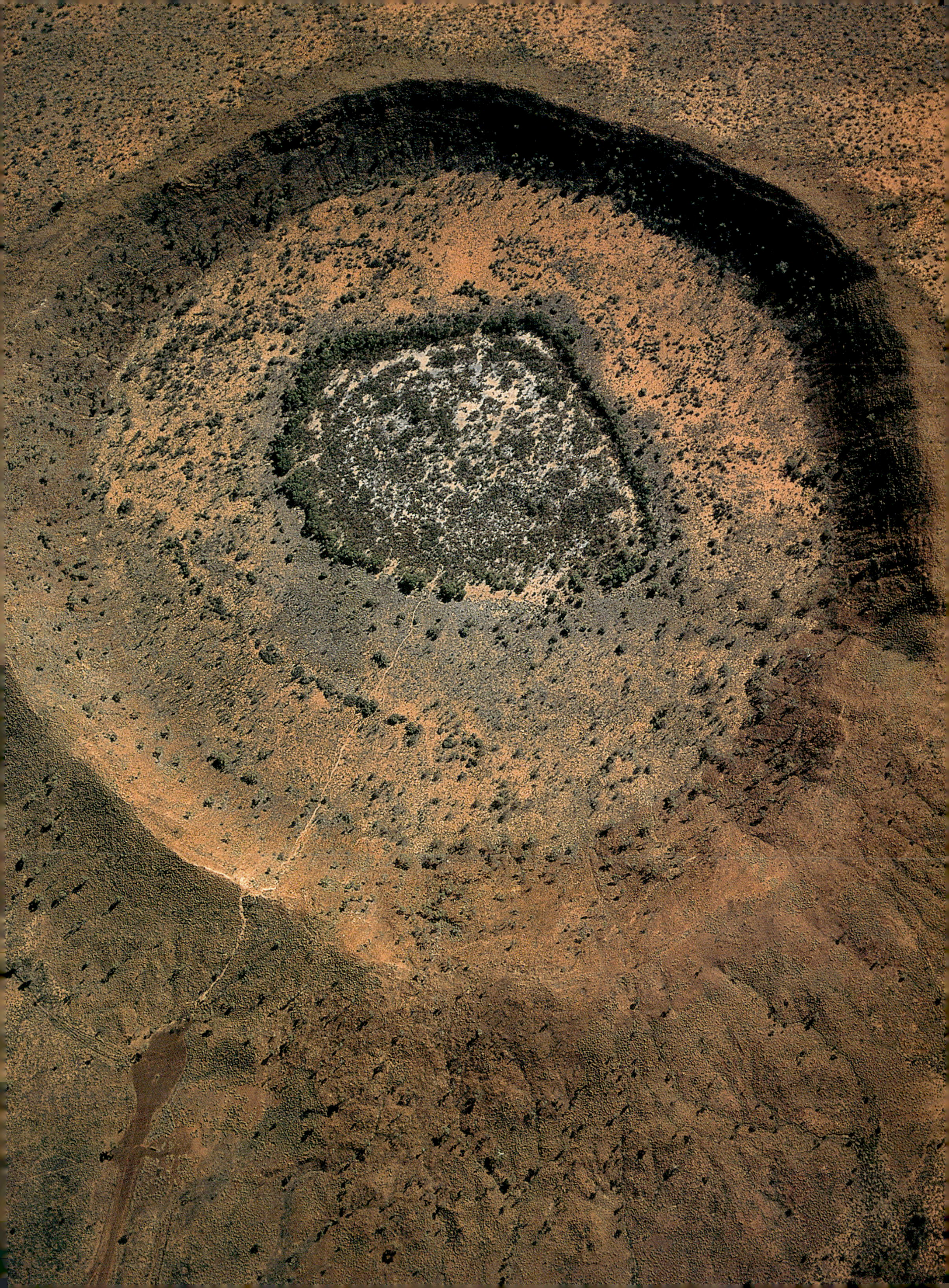

# GASTORNIS (DIATRYMA)

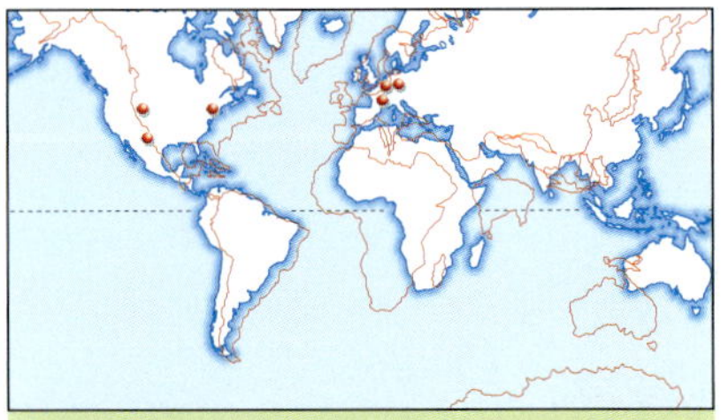

**ÜBERSICHT (TIERE)**
***Gastornis***
**Bedeutung des Namens:** Magenvogel
**Periode:** Tertiär
**Hauptgruppe:** Aves
**Länge:** 1,8–2 Meter
**Gewicht:** 100–120 Kilogramm
**Nahrung:** Beutetiere unterschiedlicher Größe, Aas
**Fossilfundstätten:** In den USA (Wyoming, New Jersey, New Mexico), in Deutschland, Frankreich und Belgien

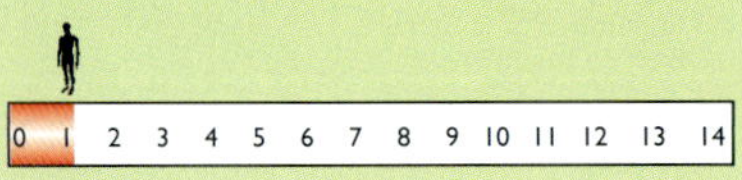


*Gastornis*, den man oft auch mit seinem früheren Namen *Diatryma* bezeichnet, hat unter den rezenten Vögeln kein eindeutiges Pendant und keinen Verwandten. Er ist vielleicht ein Spross oder Verwandter der Anseriformes (Wasservögel), zu denen heute Enten, Gänse und Schwäne gehören, oder vielleicht der Gruiformes (Kranichvögel), also beispielsweise der Kraniche, Rallen oder Trappen. Das massiv gebaute Tier war im Stand so groß und wog fast zweimal so viel wie ein erwachsener Mensch der heutigen Zeit. Seine kleinen Flügel eigneten sich nicht zum Fliegen, doch mit seinen kräftigen, sehr muskulösen Beinen konnte *Gastornis* wohl schnell und ausdauernd laufen. Seine Füße endeten in vier langen Zehen, von denen eine kleiner war und nach hinten zeigte und die alle große Krallen trugen. Mit diesen Füßen konnte *Gastornis* wahrscheinlich fast jedes Landlebewesen seiner Zeit zu Tode treten. Sein Kopf war so groß wie der Kopf eines Pferdes der Jetztzeit; die Hälfte davon nahm der stabil gebaute riesige Schnabel ein, der hoch und seitlich abgeflacht war und Knochen so leicht wie ein Mensch heute Erdnüsse knacken konnte. Fachleute haben die Theorie aufgestellt, dass in einer Landschaft ohne räuberische Dinosaurier oder andere sehr große Reptilien bestimmte Vogelgruppen aufkamen, die nach einer raschen Entwicklung so ausgestattet waren, dass sie die Rolle der großen landlebenden Räuber übernehmen konnten, ehe manche Säugetiere sich ebenfalls den Erfordernissen des Jagens anpassten. (Zu den vermuteten Verhaltensmustern von *Gastornis* siehe gegenüber, *Phorusrhacus*).

Fossilien von *Gastornis* sind an verschiedenen Orten in den US-Bundesstaaten New Mexico, Wyoming und New Jersey sowie in Deutschland, Frankreich und Belgien gefunden worden. Die ältesten Überreste stammen aus der Zeit vor etwa 55 Millionen Jahren, also aus dem Paläozän. Die erste Spezies wurde 1876 von Edward Drinker Cope nach Fossilfunden aus New Mexico *Diatryma gigantea* genannt. In neuerer Zeit hat man für das Tier den Namen *Gastornis* akzeptiert.

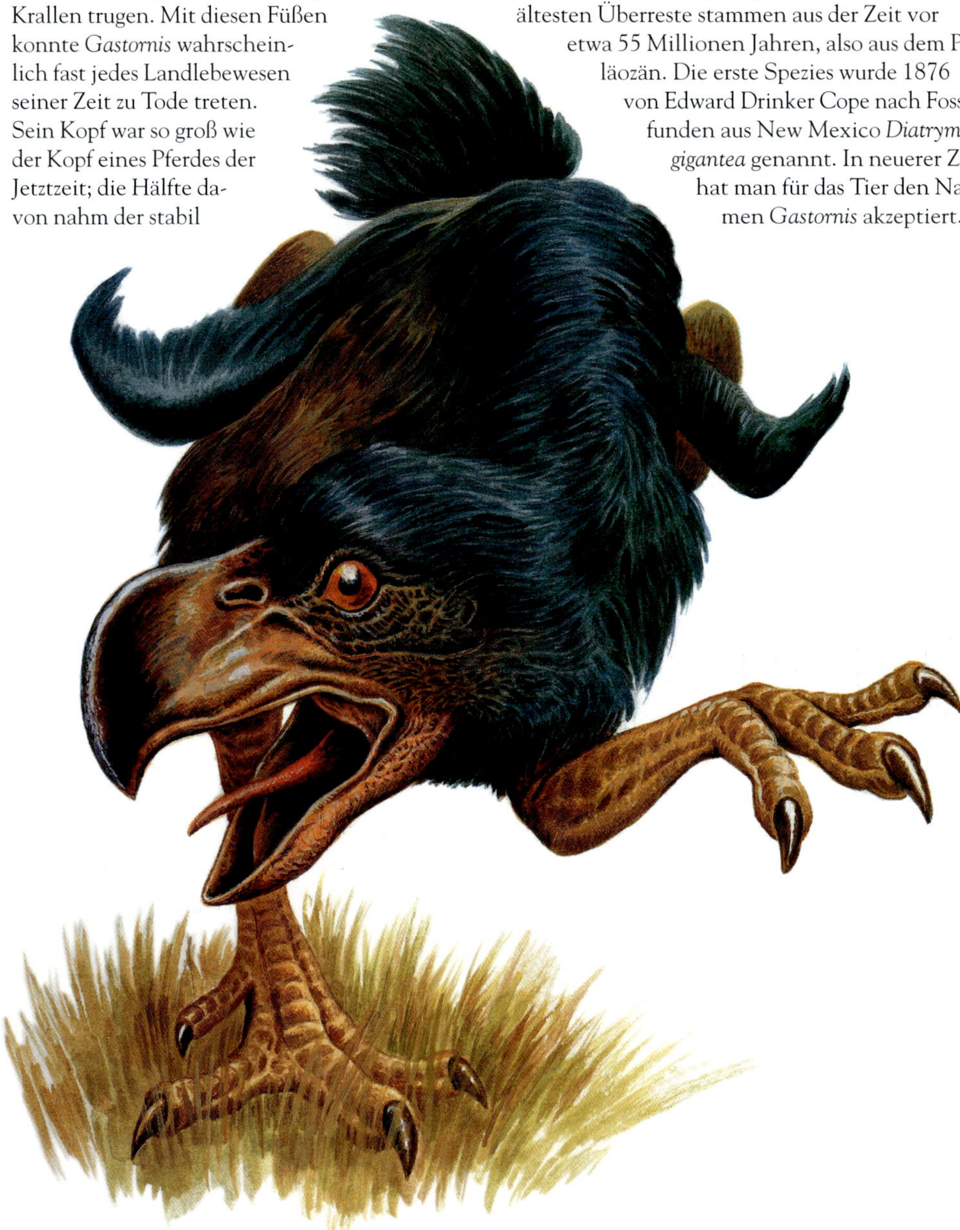

**RECHTS** Dieser riesige *Gastornis* legt seine lächerlich kleinen Flügel nach hinten und beugt seinen Kopf zum Angriff nach vorn. Der massive Schnabel konnte mit Leichtigkeit Knorpel zerschneiden und Knochen zerbrechen. Manche Fachleute halten es für denkbar, dass der Vogel damit auch Nüsse knackte und überhaupt ein Allesfresser war.

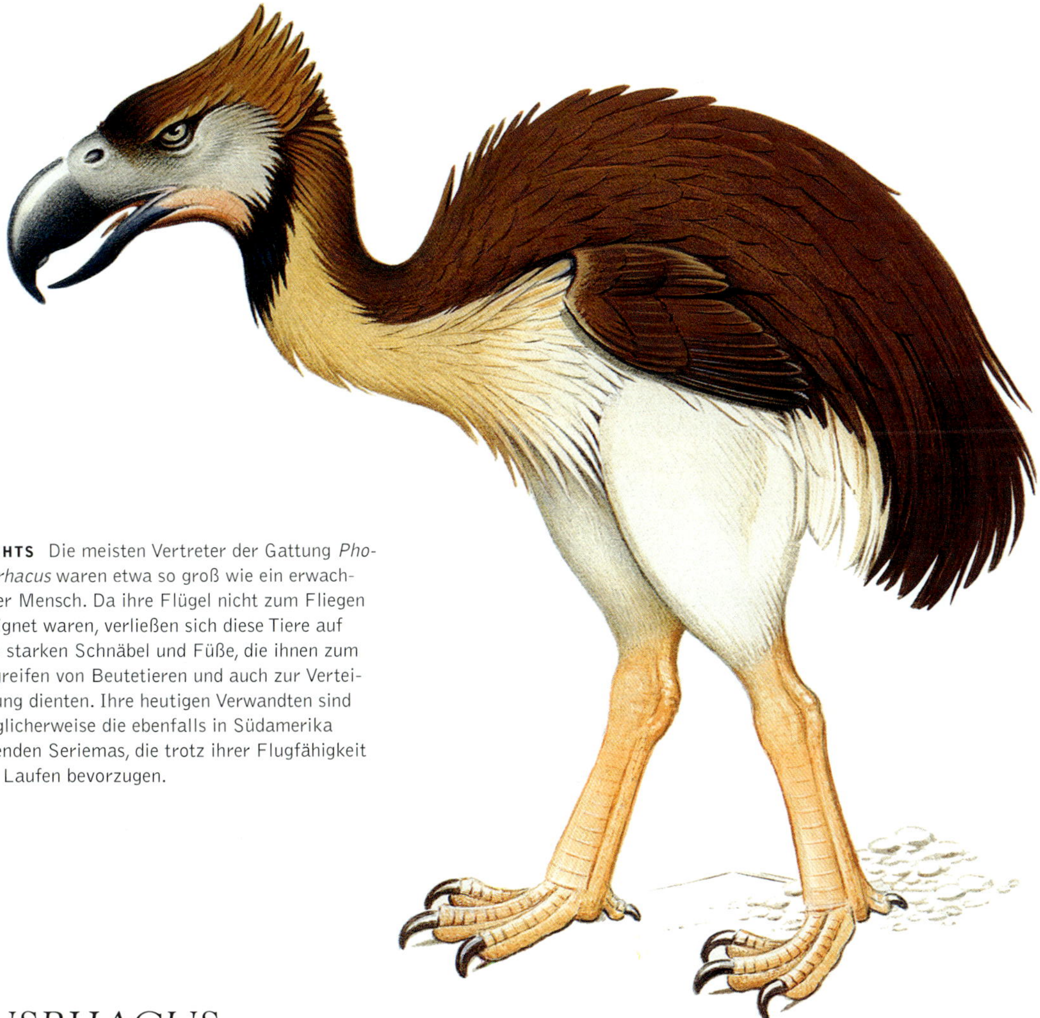

**RECHTS** Die meisten Vertreter der Gattung *Phorusrhacus* waren etwa so groß wie ein erwachsener Mensch. Da ihre Flügel nicht zum Fliegen geeignet waren, verließen sich diese Tiere auf ihre starken Schnäbel und Füße, die ihnen zum Angreifen von Beutetieren und auch zur Verteidigung dienten. Ihre heutigen Verwandten sind möglicherweise die ebenfalls in Südamerika lebenden Seriemas, die trotz ihrer Flugfähigkeit das Laufen bevorzugen.

# PHORUSRHACUS

Die Phorusrhaciden – „schreckliche Kraniche" – waren riesige, kräftige flugunfähige Vögel, die in der zweiten Hälfte des Tertiärs in Südamerika lebten. Dieser Kontinent war über einen großen Zeitraum des Tertiärs von anderen Landmassen getrennt, er driftete erst irgendwann in den letzten Jahrmillionen näher an Nordamerika heran und war schließlich über eine Landbrücke mit diesem Erdteil verbunden (siehe Seite 27). Die Tier- und Pflanzenwelt Südamerikas entwickelte sich isoliert von der Fauna und Flora anderer Kontinente, und so erschienen zahlreiche seltsame Geschöpfe, die nirgendwo sonst auf der Erde nahe Verwandte oder entwicklungsgeschichtliche Pendants besaßen. Äußerlich ähnelten die Phorusrhaciden anderen großen Land bewohnenden Vögeln wie beispielsweise *Gastornis* (siehe gegenüber), die räuberisch lebten und schon lange ausgestorben sind. *Gastornis* existierte allerdings Millionen Jahre früher und auf ganz anderen Kontinenten.

Dennoch wiesen die Verhaltensmuster beider Vogelgattungen vielleicht Ähnlichkeiten auf. Beide waren starke Räuber, die auf ihren kräftigen, sehr muskulösen Beinen umherschritten oder auch rannten. Mit ihren stabilen, kräftigen Hakenschnäbeln fingen sie kleinere Lebewesen wie etwa Säugetiere oder Vögel, schnitten oder rissen sie Fleischstücke aus größeren Beutetieren heraus, die sie vermutlich mit einem ihrer starken, scharfkralligen Füße festhielten. Denkbar ist auch, dass sie Teile von Kadavern abtrennten und darin nach Knochen suchten, die sie aufbrechen konnten. Dabei setzten sie ihre Schnäbel fast auf die gleiche Weise ein wie die heute lebenden Hyänen beim Stöbern nach Aas. In Südamerika gab es damals – falls überhaupt – nur wenige große Raubsäugetiere, die mit ihnen konkurrieren konnten.

*Phorusrhacus* erschien zu Beginn des Miozän, vor 25 Millionen Jahren. Der Vogel erreichte eine Standhöhe von etwa 1,8 Meter. In der Folgezeit tauchten ähnliche Vertreter der Gruppe auf und verschwanden wieder. Zu den letzten und größten gehörte *Titanis*, der im Stand über 2,5 Meter groß war und an den beiden Zehen seiner Füße Krallen trug. Seitdem hat es auch noch größere Vögel gegeben, darunter die über drei Meter hohen Moas in Neuseeland, die allerdings keine so wilden Räuber wie die „schrecklichen Kraniche" waren.

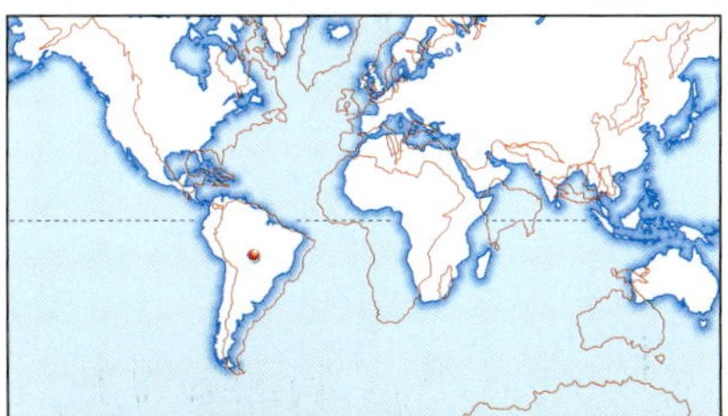

**ÜBERSICHT (TIERE)**
***Phorusrhacus***
**Bedeutung des Namens:** Schrecklicher Kranich
**Periode:** Tertiär
**Hauptgruppe:** Aves
**Länge:** 1,5 – 2,5 Meter
**Gewicht:** Bis 140 Kilogramm
**Nahrung:** Beutetiere, Aas
**Fossilfundstätten:** In Südamerika

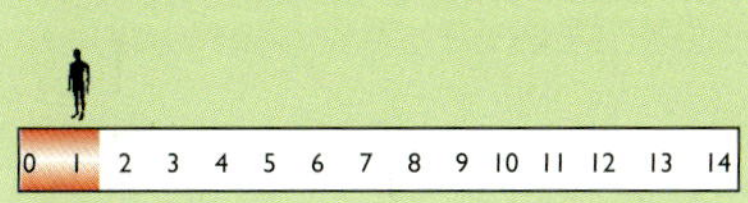

# PLESIADAPIS

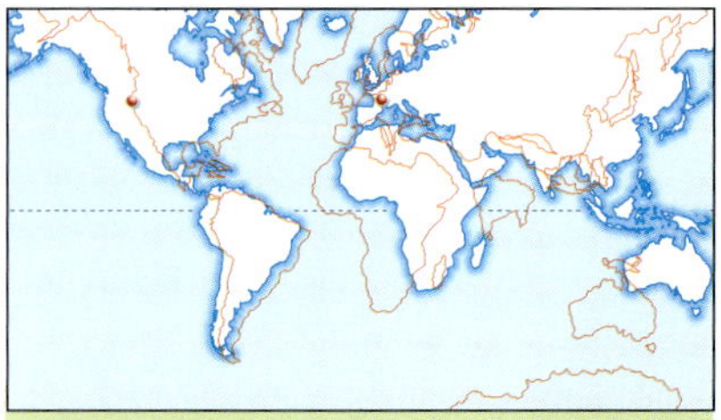

**ÜBERSICHT (TIERE)**

***Plesiadapis***

**Bedeutung des Namens:** Fast-Adapis (ein weiteres Säugetier des Tertiärs)

**Periode:** Tertiär (Abteilungen Paläozän–Eozän)

**Hauptgruppe:** Mammalia (wahrscheinlich Primates)

**Länge:** Kopf und Rumpf 80 Zentimeter, Schwanz 50 Zentimeter

**Gewicht:** 10 Kilogramm

**Nahrung:** Unklar (siehe Text)

**Fossilfundstätten:** In Frankreich, in Nordamerika (Rocky Mountains)

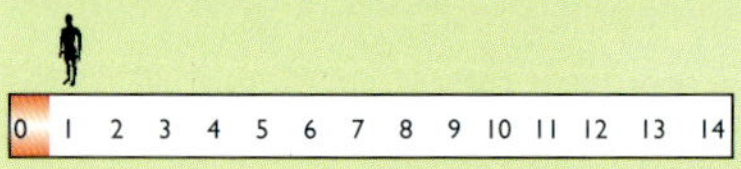


Zur Säugetiergruppe der Primaten gehören die Lemuren, die Galagos, die Affen und die Menschen. Ob *Plesiadapis* einer der ältesten Primaten oder ein sehr naher Verwandter dieser Herrentiere war, ist unklar. Auf den ersten Blick ähnelt er den auf Bäumen lebenden Lemuren der Insel Madagaskar. Er hatte etwa die Größe eines sehr großen Eichhörnchens der Jetztzeit, besaß vier kräftige, bewegliche Gliedmaßen, deren lange, bekrallte Zehen fest zugriffen, wenn sich *Plesiadapis* wie vermutet auf den Ästen und an den Stämmen der Bäume fortbewegte. Er besaß einen langen, biegsamen Schwanz, der möglicherweise buschig behaart war und wohl als Steuerorgan diente, wenn *Plesiadapis* hoch oben von Ast zu Ast lief und sprang. Gesicht und Zähne des *Plesiadapis* sahen ähnlich wie bei den heutigen Mäusen, Ratten oder anderen rezenten Nagetieren aus. Die Schnauze des *Plesiadapis* war schmal, im Ober- und im Unterkiefer saßen vorn lange Nagezähne, dann folgte eine Lücke, in der die echten Primaten einen Eckzahn tragen, und in der Wangenregion befanden sich breite Backenzähne zum Zermahlen der Nahrung. Über die Ernährungsweise von *Plesiadapis* gibt es viele verschiedene Ansichten, nach denen das Tier entweder hauptsächlich Insekten und andere kleine Tiere; Früchte und Samen; Laub; Pflanzensaft und Larven aus der Rinde der Bäume oder eine Mischung aus allem fraß.

Viele Fossilien von *Plesiadapis* wurden im Nordwesten Frankreichs gefunden, doch auch an Fundstätten im US-Bundesstaat Colorado sowie in anderen Gegenden in den nordamerikanischen Rocky Mountains und in der Umgebung des Gebirges hat man Überreste entdeckt. Die meisten Funde stammen aus der Zeit vor 60–50 Millionen Jahren; manche scheinen allerdings erst 35 Millionen Jahre alt zu sein. *Plesiadapis* wird oft mit dem rezenten Katta *(Lemur catta)* verglichen. Der Lemur ist zwar kleiner, hält sich aber gelegentlich ebenfalls in Bäumen auf, bewegt sich auch am Boden fort und ernährt sich von vielerlei Pflanzen.

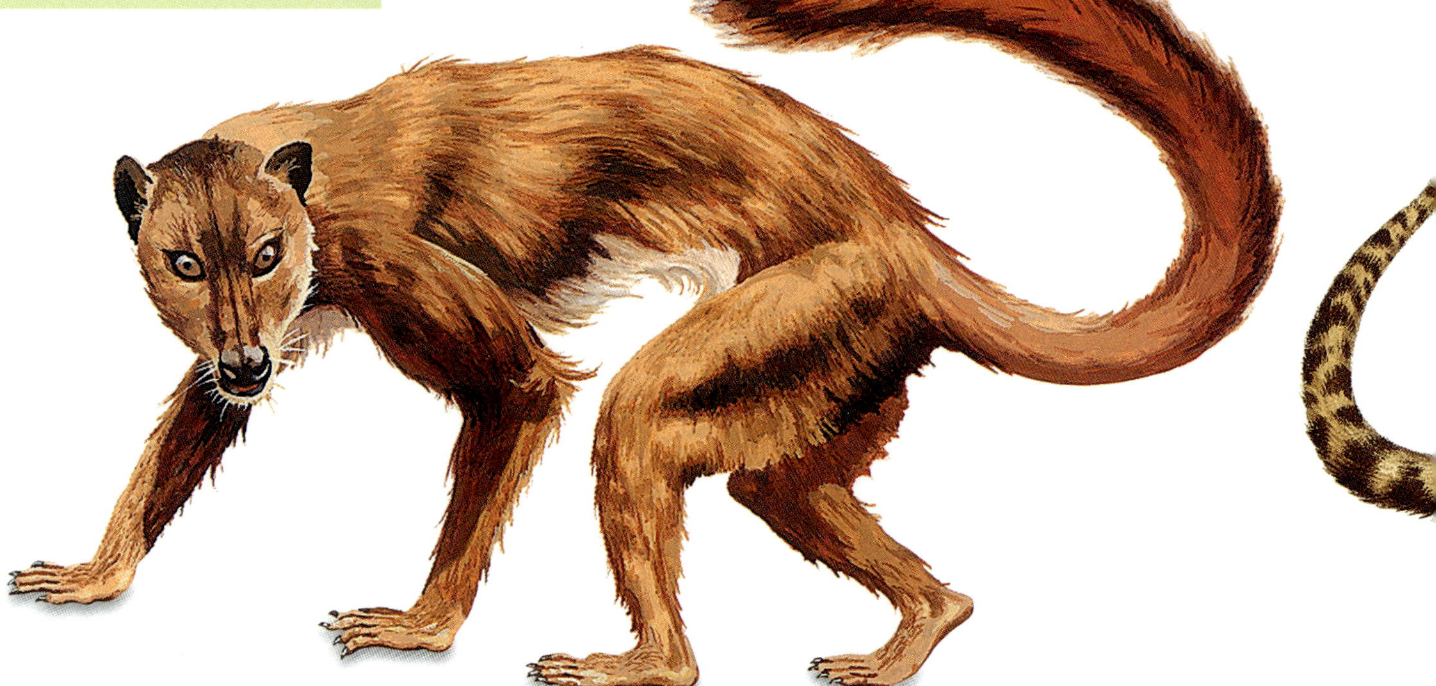

**OBEN** *Plesiadapis*, an dessen Nachbildung die kräftigen Zehen und der buschige Schwanz auffallen, schien gut an das Leben sowohl in Bäumen als auch am Boden angepasst gewesen zu sein. Sein Schwanz diente ihm sicherlich als Steuerorgan, wenn er von Ast zu Ast flitzte oder sprang.

# ANDREWSARCHUS

Die bislang gefundenen fossilen Überreste dieses beeindruckenden Urtieres bestehen aus kaum mehr als dem Schädel des *Andrewsarchus*. Dieser ist fast fünfundachtzig Zentimeter lang und deutet darauf hin, dass sein Besitzer ein Riesentier war, dessen Kopf und Rumpf zusammen über sechs Meter maßen. Stimmt diese Annahme, muss *Andrewsarchus* das größte Fleisch fressende Säugetier gewesen sein, das je auf der Erde gelebt hat. Seine spitzen Vorderzähne, insbesondere die Eckzähne, waren gewaltig; *Andrewsarchus* konnte sie in seine Beute bohren und mit ihnen Fleisch von erlegten Tieren abreißen. Seine Backenzähne waren so geformt, dass sie die Nahrung sowohl zerschneiden als auch zermahlen konnten. Trotz der Merkmale, die an heutige Fleischfresser wie Katzen, Hunde und, vielleicht passender, an Bären und Hyänen erinnern, war *Andrewsarchus* kein Vertreter der Fleisch fressenden Säugetiere (Carnivora). Seine näheren Verwandten waren in Wirklichkeit Hirsche, Pferde und Rinder. *Andrewsarchus* war ein Huftier – er besaß nicht die echten Krallen einer Katze oder eines Hundes, sondern nägelartige Hufe, die wie Krallen geformt waren. Er gehörte zur Untergruppe der Mesonychidae (oder Acreodi), die zu den ältesten großen Raubsäugetieren zählen. Man geht davon aus, dass er im späten Eozän, vor etwa 45–40 Millionen Jahren, lebte. Die Mesonychiden breiteten sich nach dem Aussterben der Dinosaurier aus und erlebten in den folgenden Jahrmillionen ihre Blütezeit, starben vor 35 Millionen Jahren im Zusammenhang mit dem Auftauchen einer neueren Gruppe großer Raubsäugetiere, der Creodonten, aber allmählich aus.

Die wenigen Überreste von *Andrewsarchus* wurden 1923 während einer amerikanischen Expedition von Fossiliensuchern in der Mongolei gefunden. Das Unternehmen, bei dem man auch Fossilien vieler Dinosaurier entdeckte, wurde vom damaligen Direktor des American Museum of Natural History Roy Chapman Andrews geleitet. Ihm zu Ehren erhielt der Fleischfresser, um den es hier geht, den Namen *Andrewsarchus*.

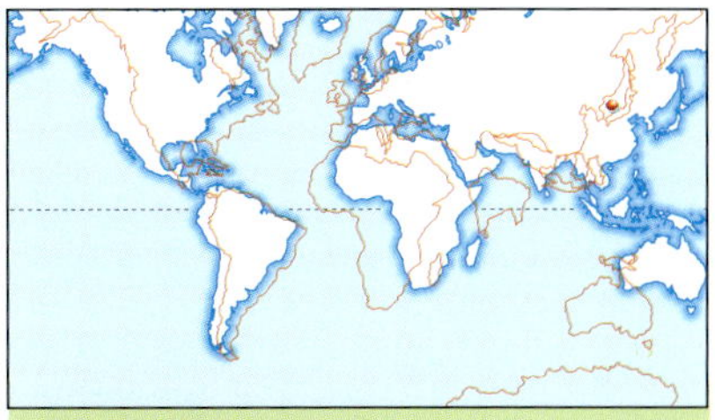

**ÜBERSICHT (TIERE)**

***Andrewsarchus***

**Bedeutung des Namens:** Andrews' Fleischfresser

**Periode:** Tertiär (spätes Eozän)

**Hauptgruppe:** Mammalia (Ungulata)

**Länge:** Kopf und Rumpf möglicherweise etwa 6 Meter

**Gewicht:** 500–800 Kilogramm

**Nahrung:** Fleisch, Aas, vielleicht verschiedenartige tierische und pflanzliche Nahrung

**Fossilfundstätten:** In der Mongolei

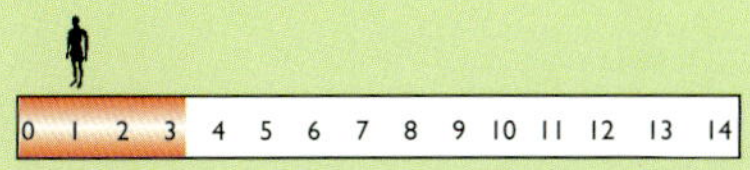


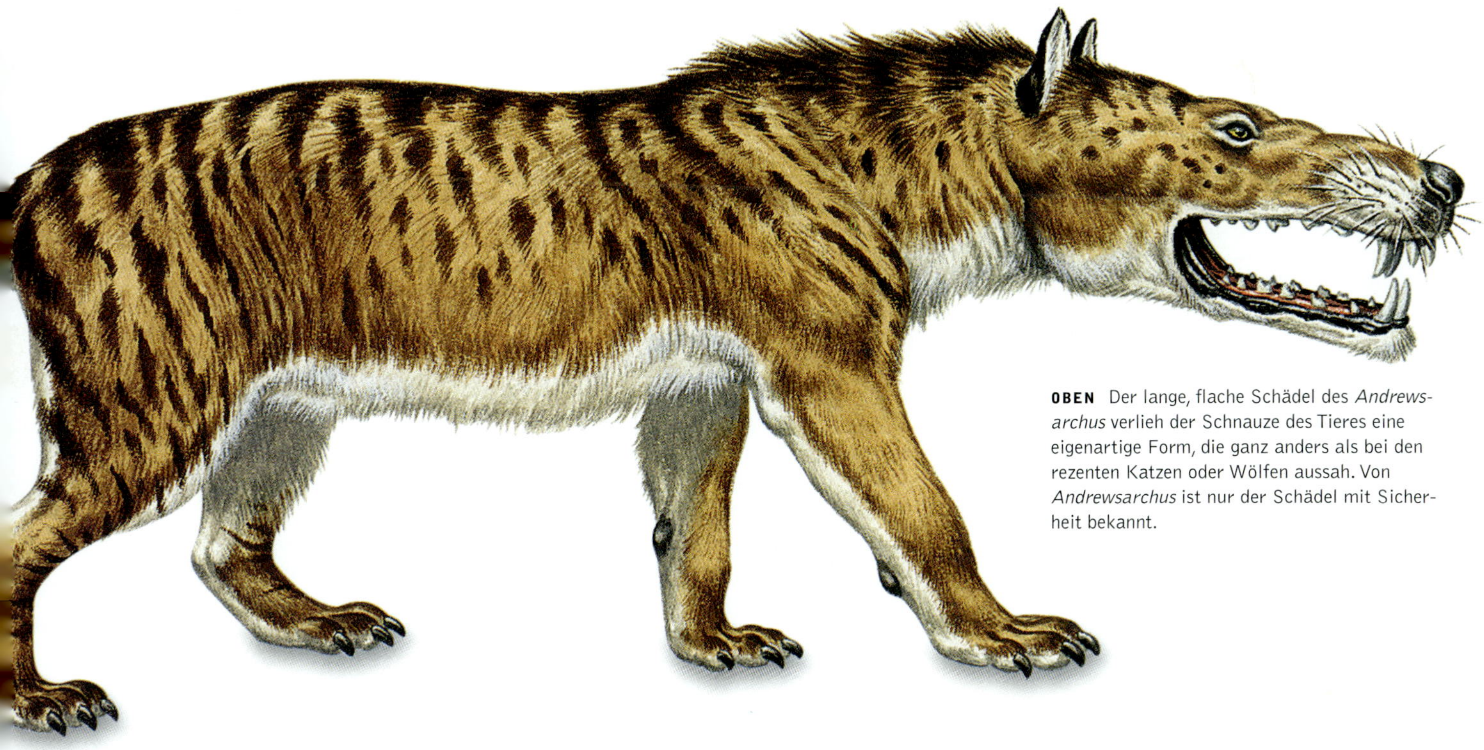

**OBEN** Der lange, flache Schädel des *Andrewsarchus* verlieh der Schnauze des Tieres eine eigenartige Form, die ganz anders als bei den rezenten Katzen oder Wölfen aussah. Von *Andrewsarchus* ist nur der Schädel mit Sicherheit bekannt.

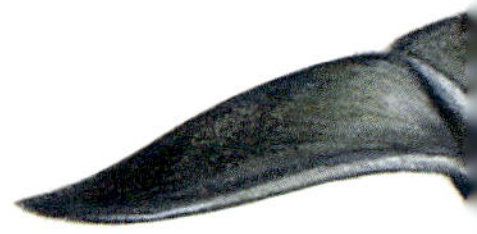

**RECHTS** Auf den ersten Blick ließe sich *Icaronycteris* von einer kleinen Insekten fressenden Fledermaus der Jetztzeit nur schwer unterscheiden. Das offene Maul des *Icaronycteris* soll andeuten, dass das Tier gerade sehr hohe Signaltöne im Ultraschallbereich ausstößt. Das Echo der Ultraschallsignale wird von den großen Ohren des Tieres aufgefangen, und die Analyse der Echos zeigt *Icaronycteris* Position und Größe naher Objekte an.

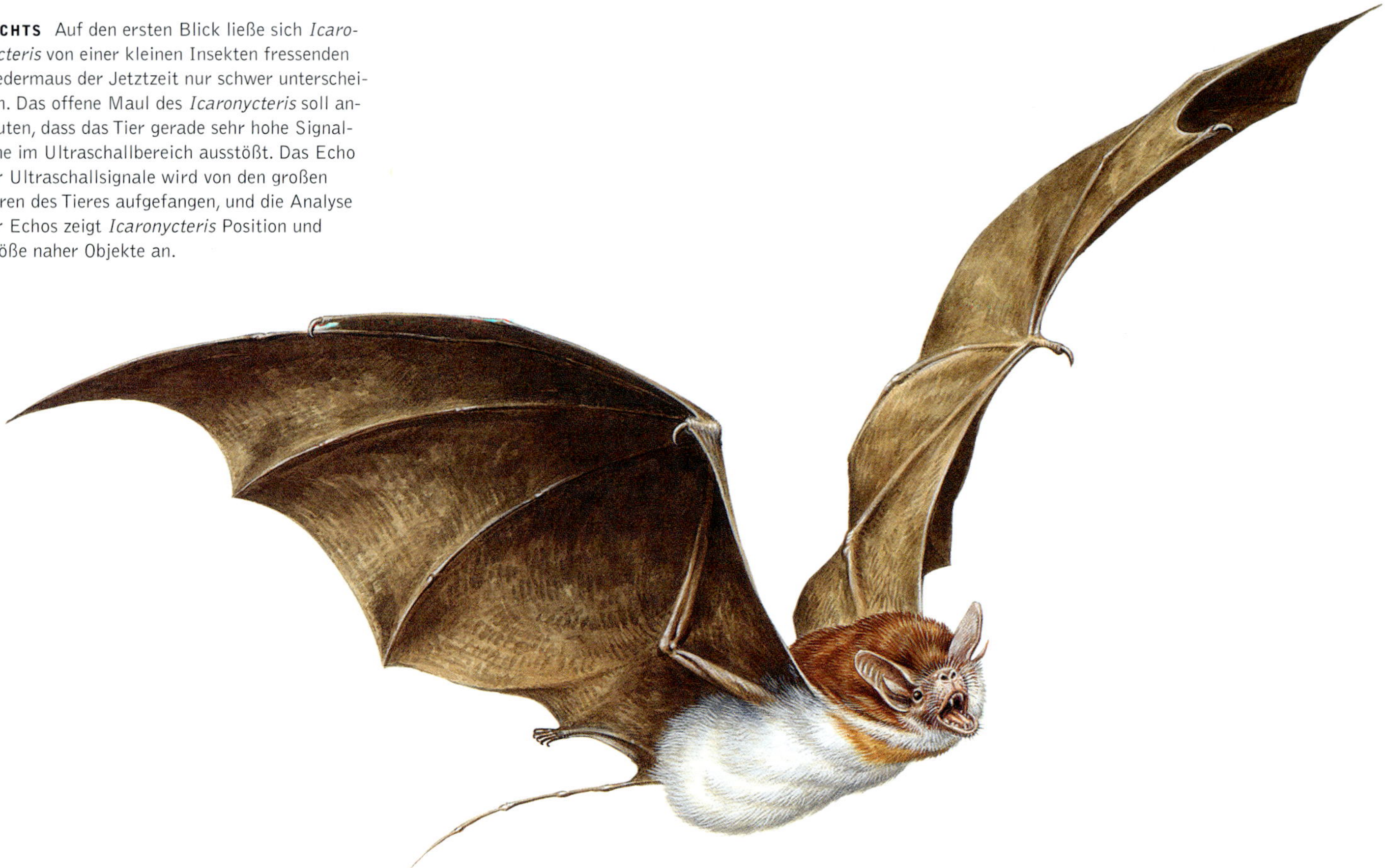

# ICARONYCTERIS

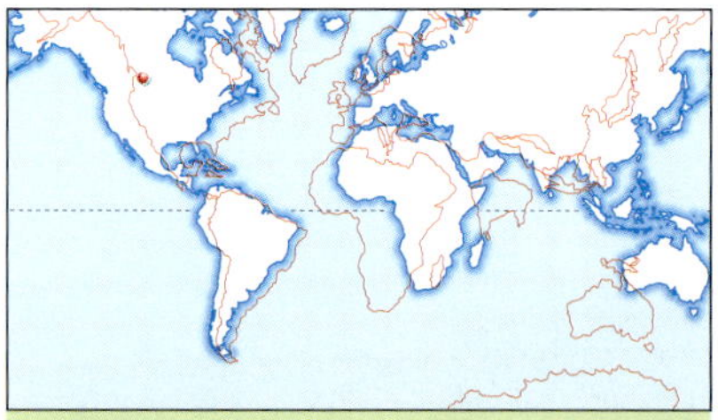

**ÜBERSICHT (TIERE)**
***Icaronycteris***
**Bedeutung des Namens:** Nachtflügel des Ikarus
**Periode:** Tertiär
**Hauptgruppe:** Mammalia (Chiroptera)
**Länge:** Flügelspannweite 38 Zentimeter
**Gewicht:** 100 Gramm
**Nahrung:** Insekten, ähnliches Kleingetier
**Fossilfundstätten:** In Nordamerika

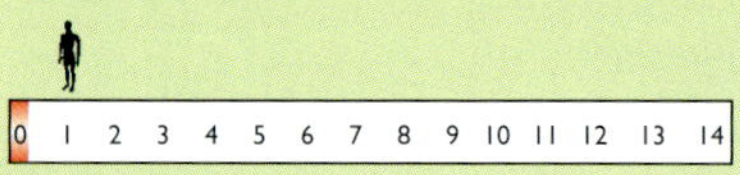


Zu den am stärksten spezialisierten Vertretern der Säugetiere gehören die Fledermäuse. Sie zählen auch zu den ältesten großen Säugetiergruppen, die nach dem Verschwinden der Dinosaurier erschienen. *Icaronycteris* huschte im frühen Eozän, vor mehr als 50 Millionen Jahren, durch das Dunkel, um fast wie die heutigen Fledermäuse Jagd auf Nachtfalter und andere kleine Fluginsekten zu machen. Seine hoch entwickelten Vordergliedmaßen dienten als Flügel, deren sehr dünne, dehnbare Flughaut sich zwischen den sehr lang gestreckten Fingerknochen spannte. Winzige Ohrknöchelchen, die als Fossilien von ähnlichen frühen Fledermäusen erhalten sind, zeigen, dass *Icaronycteris* wahrscheinlich quiekende oder schnalzende Ultraschallsignale aussandte, um nach dem Prinzip der Echoortung oder des Sonars in den dunklen Nachtstunden Beutetiere in der Luft aufzuspüren und zu fangen. Die mit spitzen Klauen versehenen Füße wiesen spezialisierte Knöchelgelenke auf; sie ließen sich nach hinten drehen, wenn das Tier sich im Ruhehang (kopfunter hängend) an einem Halt festklammerte. Die meisten dieser Merkmale treten auch bei anderen Fledermäusen des Eozäns (vor 53 – 33 Millionen Jahren) auf, darunter bei *Palaeochiropteryx*, *Archaeonycteris* und *Hassianycteris*.

Die genannten Merkmale finden sich noch heute bei den Fledermäusen, doch *Icaronycteris* besaß auch ältere Eigenschaften, die er von seinen spitzmausartigen Insekten fressenden Vorfahren geerbt hatte. Er trug noch eine Kralle am zweiten Finger, die bei den Fledermäusen später verschwand; übrig geblieben ist heute nur die Kralle am ersten Finger, dem „Daumen". *Icaronycteris* besaß mehr Zähne als die Insekten fressenden Fledermäuse der Jetztzeit. Seine Flügel waren vergleichsweise kurz und breit. Der Schwanz war lang und nicht mit dem hintersten Teil der Flughaut verbunden. Der Rumpf einer rezenten Fledermaus ist kompakt und starr, der von *Icaronycteris* war länger und biegsam. Fossilien von Fledermäusen findet man genau wie die Überreste von Vögeln im Großen und Ganzen selten, da die Knochen dieser Tiere dünn und zerbrechlich waren. Eine interessante Neuentdeckung ist die „Mahenge-Fledermaus", die nach ihrem Fundort in der zentraltansanischen Region Singida benannt wurde.

# PARACERATHERIUM

*Paraceratherium* ist das größte bekannte Landsäugetier aller Zeiten. Es lebte hauptsächlich im Oligozän, vor rund 30 Millionen Jahren. Überreste von diesem riesigen Urtier wurden an verschiedenen Orten in Osteuropa und in Asien, darunter auch in China und im pakistanischen Teil Belutschistans, gefunden. Fossilien, die früher unter der Bezeichnung *Baluchitherium* oder *Indricotherium* bekannt waren, zählt man heute meistens zur Gattung *Paraceratherium*, obwohl die Untergruppe, zu der das Tier gehört, als Indricotheren oder Hyracodontiden bezeichnet wird. *Paraceratherium* ähnelte zwar einem großen, massigen Pferd und trug auch kein Nasenhorn, war aber trotzdem ein Vertreter der Gruppe der Nashörner oder Rhinozerosse. Heute zählen die Nashörner, von denen es nur noch fünf Spezies – drei in Asien und zwei in Afrika – gibt, zu den am stärksten bedrohten Säugetierfamilien. In vorgeschichtlicher Zeit hingegen existierten viele weit verbreitete Arten, darunter auch schnelle Tiere von der Größe eines Ponys (siehe auch Seite 422, *Coelodonta*). Die ersten Fossilien von *Paraceratherium* wurden 1910 von dem englischen Paläontologen Clive Forster-Cooper in Belutschistan gefunden.

Es hat den Anschein, dass die männlichen Vertreter von *Paraceratherium* größer als die weiblichen waren und schwerere Schädel mit stärker ausgeprägtem kuppelförmigem Dach besaßen. Diese Form spielte vielleicht in der Paarungszeit bei Kopfkämpfen zwischen Rivalen eine Rolle. Der Schädel eines großen Männchens maß in der Länge 1,3 Meter, und da das Tier seinen Hals lang ausstrecken konnte, reichte es bis zu Blättern und anderen Pflanzenteilen heran, die in acht Meter Höhe wuchsen. Damit übertraf *Paraceratherium* die Giraffe, die heute das Lebewesen mit der größten Scheitelhöhe ist, um zwei Meter. Die weiblichen Tiere maßen einen oder zwei Meter weniger. Die Vorderzähne des *Paraceratherium* waren ungewöhnlich: Im Oberkiefer saß ein Paar nach unten und im Unterkiefer ein Paar nach vorn zeigender großer Eckzähne. Der Schädelbau im Nasenbereich lässt darauf schließen, dass das Tier sehr bewegliche Lippen besaß, die vielleicht zu einem kurzen, aber biegsamen Rüssel – ähnlich dem Rüssel der rezenten Tapire – zum Abweiden von Pflanzen verlängert waren.

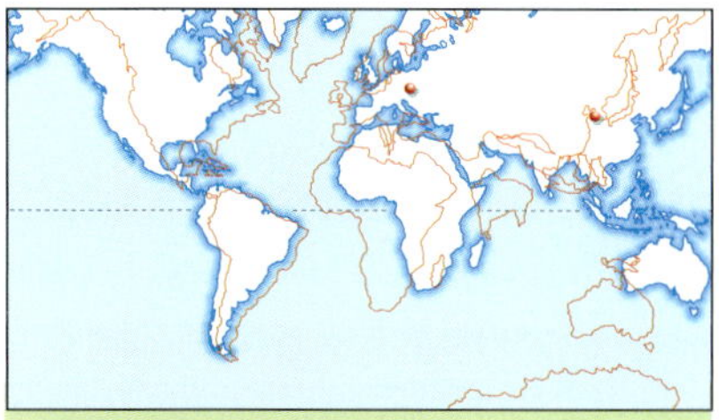

**ÜBERSICHT (TIERE)**
***Paraceratherium***
**Bedeutung des Namens:** Abweichendes Horntier
**Periode:** Tertiär
**Hauptgruppe:** Mammalia (Ungulata)
**Größe:** Kopf und Körper 9 Meter
**Gewicht:** Bis 20 Tonnen
**Nahrung:** Laub, Knospen, Triebe, Zweige
**Fossilfundstätten:** In Asien und Osteuropa

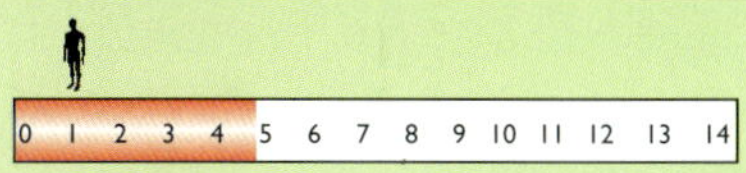


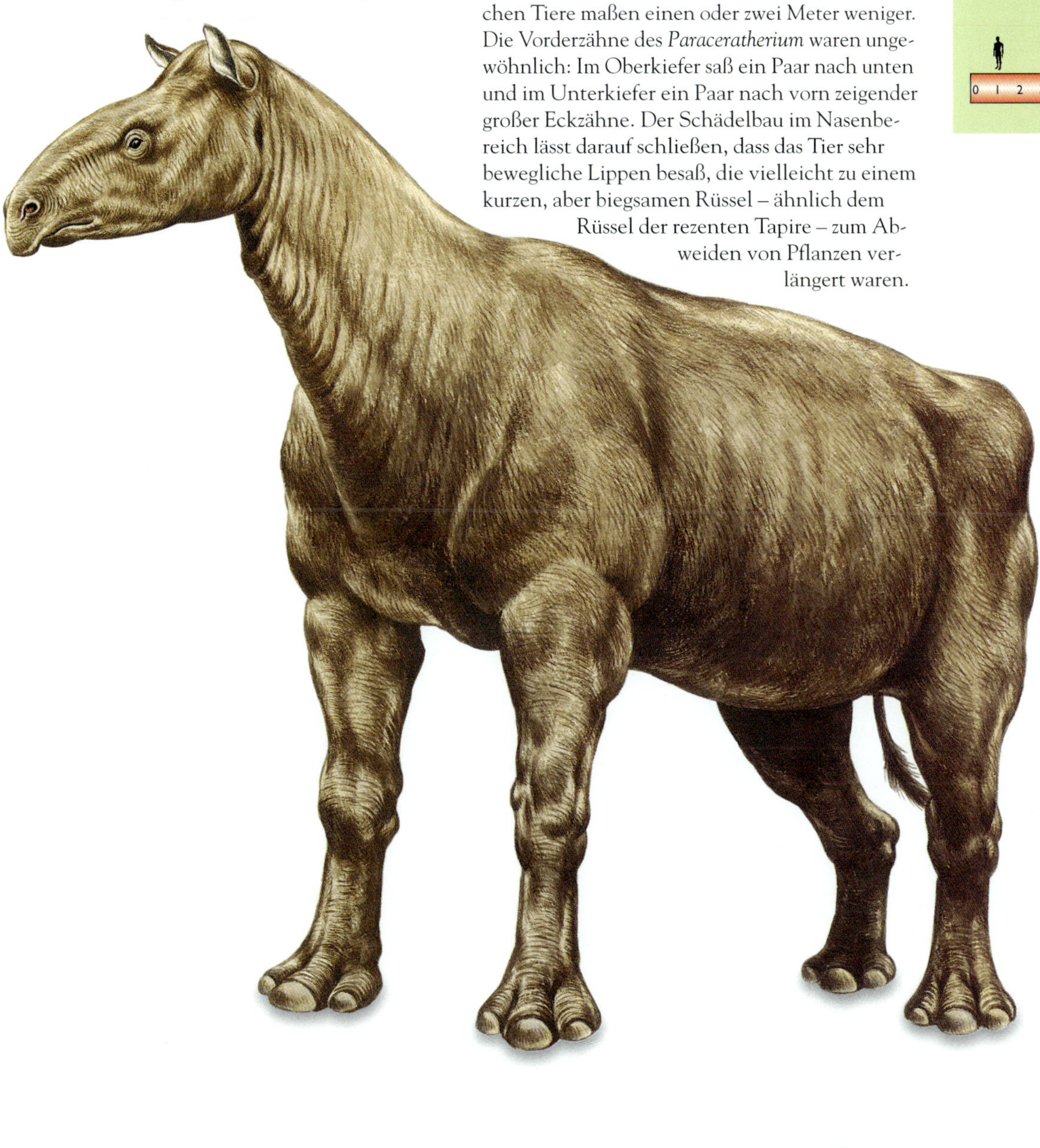

**LINKS** *Paraceratherium* war ein in jeder Dimension gewaltiges Tier; seine Schulterhöhe entsprach der Scheitelhöhe einer Giraffe von heute. Es gehörte wahrscheinlich zur entwicklungsgeschichtlich ersten Untergruppe der Nashörner, die man Hyracodontiden oder „rennende Nashörner“ nennt.

# ZWISCHENEISZEIT

*In den vergangenen zwei Jahrmillionen traten weltweit in langsamem Zyklus Temperaturschwankungen auf, wechselten Eiszeiten (Glaziale) und Warmzeiten (Interglaziale) einander ab. Die Eiszeiten gingen mit Vergletscherungen einer mehr oder weniger großen Festlandfläche einher. Die härteste dieser Glazialzeiten ließ die nördlichen Kontinente zur Hälfte unter einem Eismantel verschwinden. Jedesmal erwärmte sich das Klima wieder für die Dauer einer Warmzeit oder Zwischeneiszeit, der Eismantel und die Gletscher wichen zurück, Pflanzen und Tiere breiteten sich wieder nach Norden aus. Als die Kälte zurückkam, starben manche Spezies aus, weil sie sich nicht auf die Veränderung einstellen konnten.*

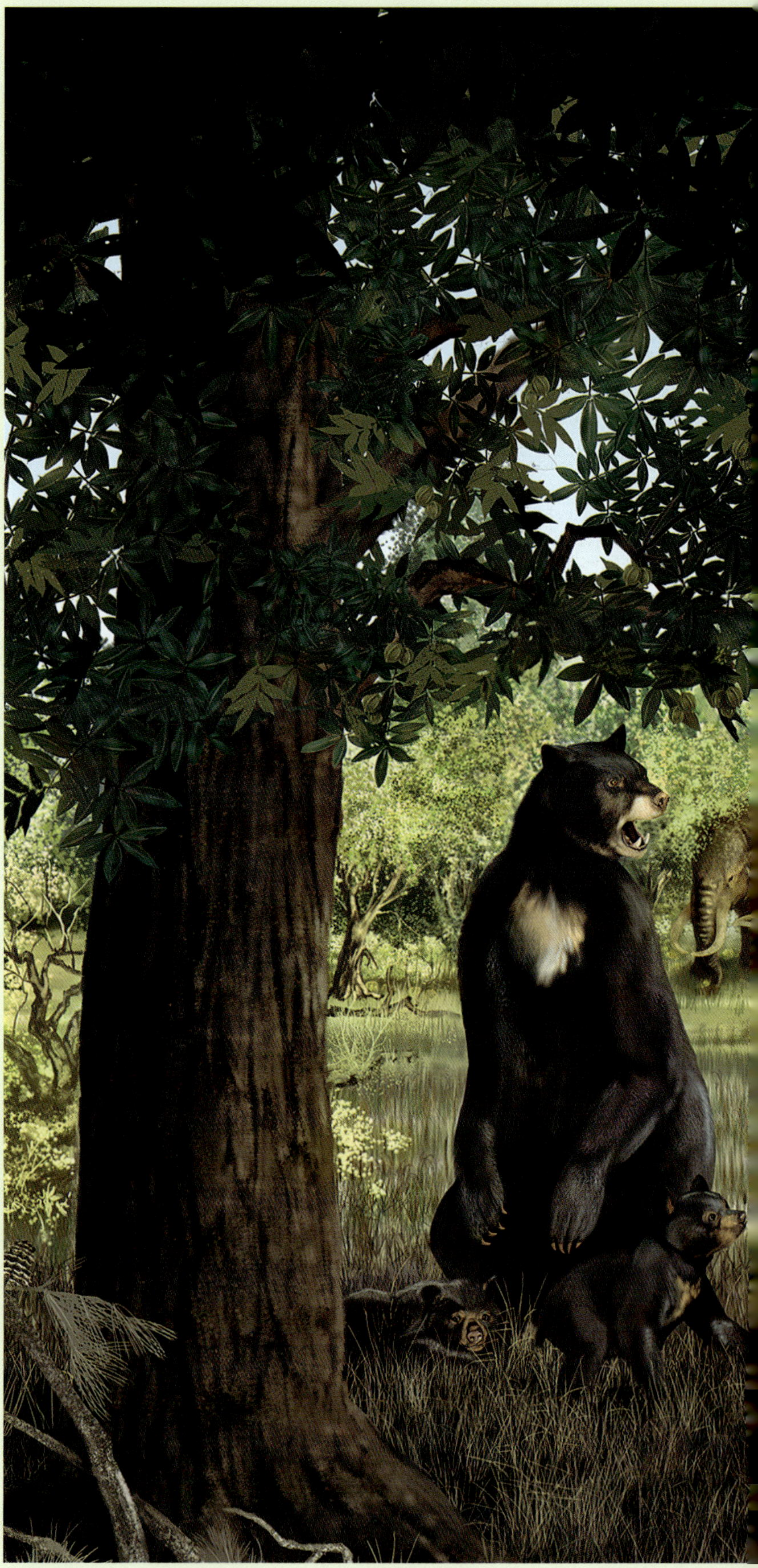

**RECHTS** Die Abbildung zeigt von Laub- und Nadelwald gesäumtes Grasland, wie es während der Zwischeneiszeiten in den vergangenen rund 250 000 Jahren ausgesehen haben könnte. Eine Höhlenbärin richtet sich zum Schutz ihrer Jungen drohend auf und brummt die Säbelzahnkatzen am jenseitigen Wiesenrand an, während eine kleine Mammutherde auf den Gehölzrand zusteuert und ein prähistorischer Fuchs einer Gruppe truthahnähnlicher Vögel nachspürt.

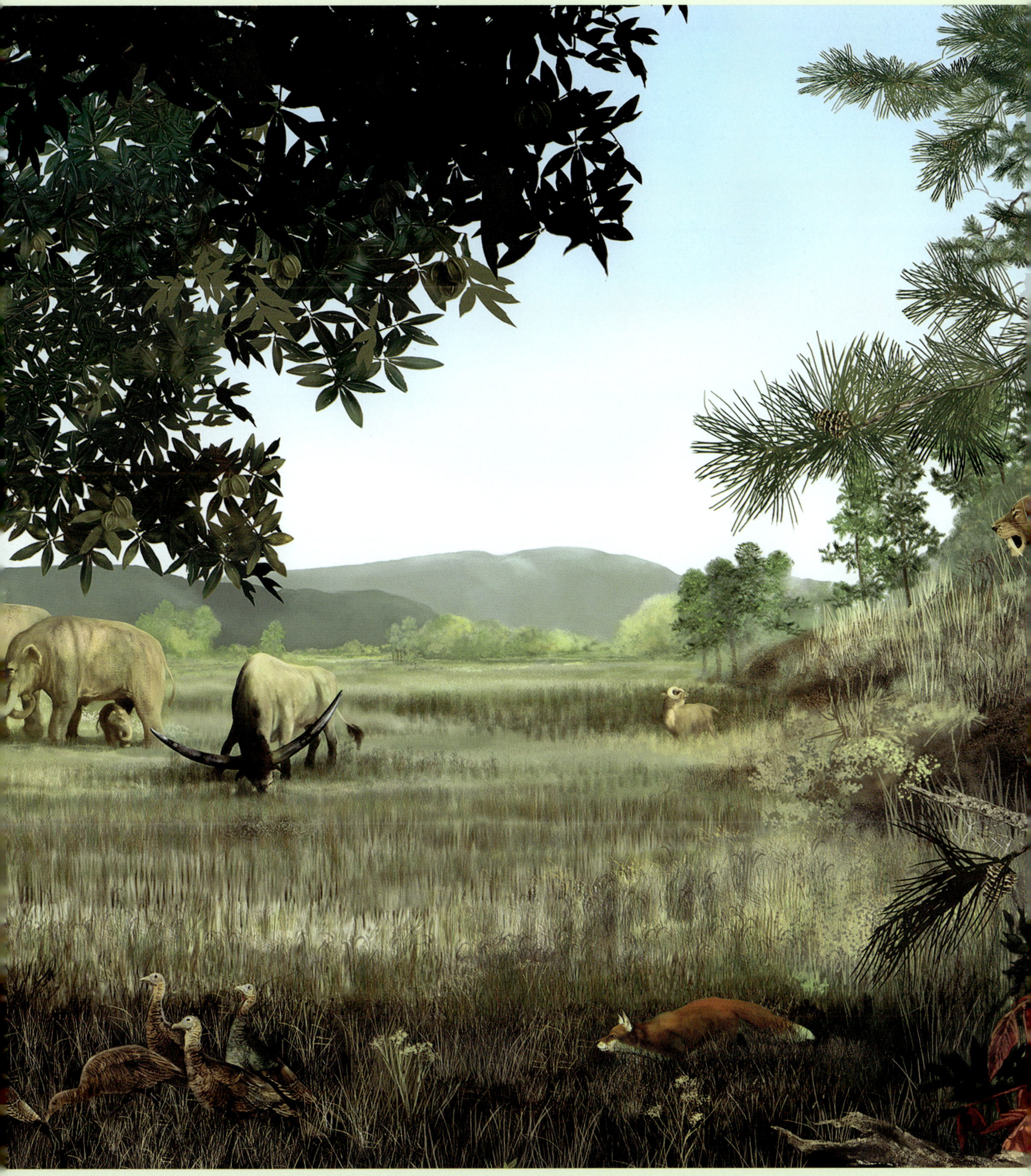

# Coelodonta

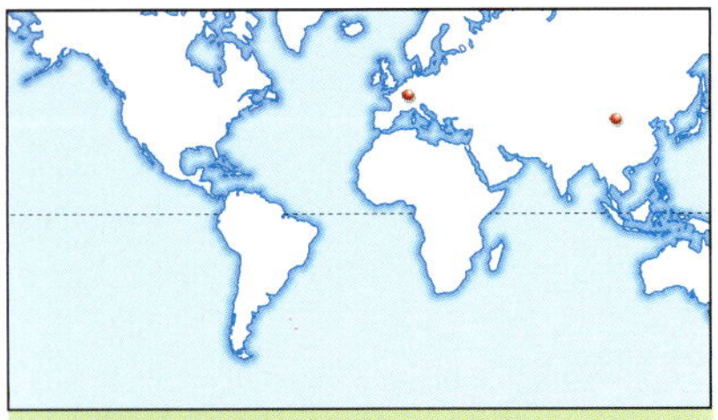

**ÜBERSICHT (TIERE)**
***Coelodonta***
**Bedeutung des Namens:** Höhlenzahn
**Periode:** Quartär
**Hauptgruppe:** Mammalia (Ungulata)
**Größe:** 3,5 Meter
**Gewicht:** Bis 2 Tonnen
**Nahrung:** Gräser und andere bodennahe Pflanzen
**Fossilfundstätten:** In Europa und Asien

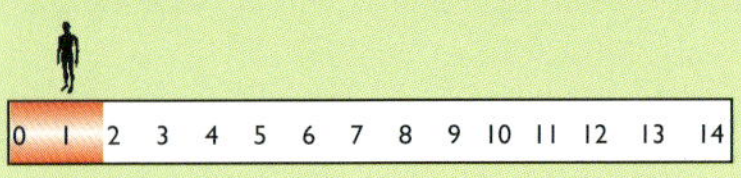


*Coelodonta*, das gewöhnlich Wollnashorn genannt wird, gehörte tatsächlich zur Gruppe der Nashörner und war auch sehr stark behaart. Das Tier hatte zwei lange Nasenhörner, buckelartig erhöhte Schultern, einen kräftigen Rumpf, vier stämmige Gliedmaßen, einen kurzen, dünnen Schwanz und langes, dunkles Zottelhaar. All diese Einzelheiten sind belegt, denn *Coelodonta* ist nicht nur von fossilierten Knochen und Zähnen bekannt, sondern im Eis des Hohen Nordens in Asien – speziell in Sibirien – und in Europa vollständig erhalten geblieben. Man erkennt das Tier auch in den nicht weniger als 30 000 Jahre alten Höhlenmalereien und –zeichnungen der Urmenschen wieder. Einige dieser Bilder scheinen Wollnashörner darzustellen, die mit Speeren und anderen Waffen gejagt werden.

*Coelodonta* war so groß wie die größeren rezenten Nashörner, seine Schulterhöhe betrug jedoch bis zu 2,2 Meter. Das Tier lebte im Pleistozän, vor rund 500 000 Jahren und starb wahrscheinlich während der letzten großen Eiszeit (siehe vorhergehende Seite), vielleicht erst vor 10 000 Jahren, aus. Das vordere Nasenhorn war länger als das hintere, und bei manchen Individuen – wahrscheinlich bei älteren männlichen Tieren – erreichte es eine Länge von fast zwei Metern. Es war im Unterschied zu dem Horn der rezenten Rhinozerosse seitlich abgeflacht, hatte also keinen nahezu runden Querschnitt, sondern sah wie eine dicke, gebogene Schwertklinge aus. Man nimmt an, dass *Coelodonta* mit seiner „Nasenklinge" den Schnee beiseite fegte und die Vegetation darunter freilegte, und dass er damit vielleicht sogar in den halb gefrorenen Boden eindrang, um niedrig wachsende Pflanzen auszugraben. Darüber hinaus war das Horn wie bei den Rhinozerossen der Jetztzeit ein sichtbares Symbol der Geschlechtsreife und der Kraft, mit dem *Coelodonta* Feinde abschreckte und Fortpflanzungspartner anlockte.

**RECHTS** Das Haarkleid des Wollnashorns ist von gefrorenen Kadavern und uralten Höhlenmalereien bekannt. Das Fell hatte wahrscheinlich eine dunkelbraune oder graue Farbe. Der Schulterbuckel war bei den einzelnen Tieren unterschiedlich stark ausgeprägt. Bei diesem Buckel handelte es sich um ein Fettdepot, das sich bei wohl genährten Individuen bildete und dann in Zeiten der Nahrungsknappheit aufgebraucht wurde.

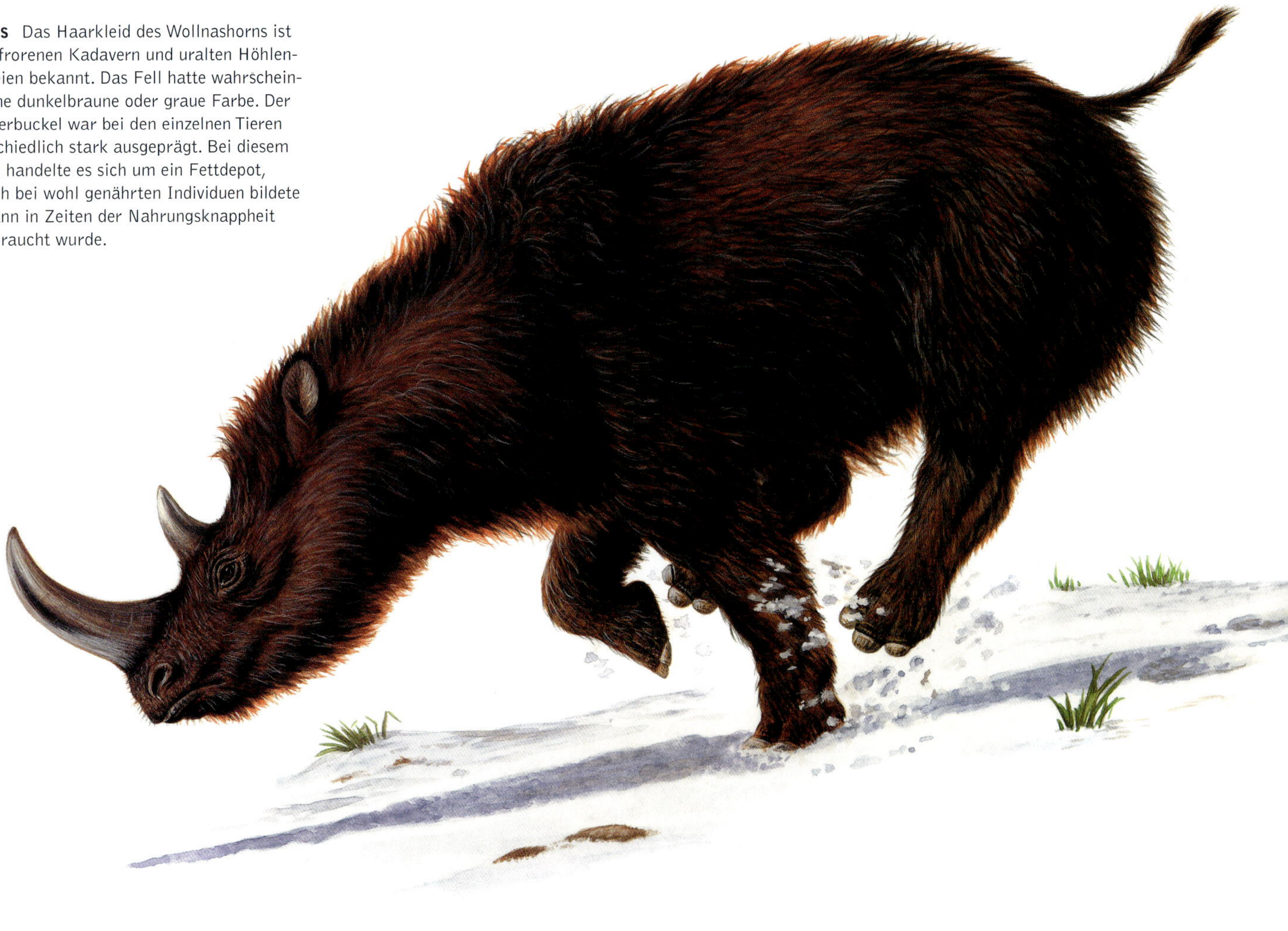

# DEINOTHERIUM

Von den Elefanten existieren heute zwar nur noch drei Spezies, doch die Gruppe der Rüsseltiere, die Proboscidea, hat eine lange und wechselvolle Vorgeschichte, in deren Verlauf es zahlreiche Untergruppen und Dutzende Spezies gab. Die ältesten Formen der Proboscidea aus der Zeit vor über 55 Millionen Jahren waren etwa schweinsgroß, ihre Entwicklung tendierte aber schon bald zu größeren Tieren mit Säulenbeinen, deren Nase und Oberlippe zusammenwuchsen und sich zu dem charakteristischen biegsamen Rüssel verlängerten. Einige Typen blieben ohne Stoßzähne, hatten kürzere Beine und lebten wahrscheinlich wie die heutigen Flusspferde (siehe auch nächste Seite, *Mammuthus*).

Die Gattung *Deinotherium* war eine der größten und langlebigsten Rüsseltiergruppen. Sie trat erstmals im Miozän, vor über 20 Millionen Jahren, in Afrika auf. Später verbreitete sich die Gattung nach Europa und Asien, wobei es nur geringe entwicklungsgeschichtliche Veränderungen gab. Ein typischer Vertreter der Gattung *Deinotherium* war etwas größer als die rezenten Elefanten, auch sein Rüssel war vermutlich kürzer und dicker als bei einem Elefanten von heute. Sein typischstes Merkmal stellten die Stoßzähne dar, die nicht wie bei den meisten anderen Proboscidea im Oberkiefer, sondern vorn im Unterkiefer standen. Sie wuchsen nach unten und waren nach hinten gekrümmt, durchstießen also die Haut der Kinnregion. Wie das Tier seine seltsamen Stoßzähne benutzte, ist umstritten. Vielleicht grub es damit im Boden nach unterirdischen Pflanzenteilen, zog sich Äste nach unten, um an das Laub heranzukommen oder streifte weiche Rinde von den Baumstämmen. Fossilien von *Deinotherium* wurden an mehreren afrikanischen Fundstätten entdeckt, wo man auch auf Überreste von Hominiden, prähistorischen Verwandten des heutigen Menschen, stieß.

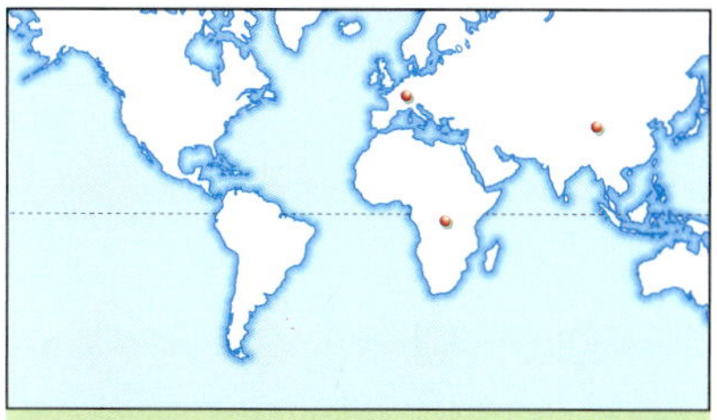

**ÜBERSICHT (TIERE)**
***Deinotherium***
**Bedeutung des Namens:** Schreckliches Urtier
**Periode:** Quartär
**Hauptgruppe:** Mammalia (Proboscidea)
**Größe:** Schulterhöhe bis 4 Meter, Kopf-Rumpf-Länge 7–8 Meter
**Gewicht:** 5 Tonnen oder mehr
**Nahrung:** Pflanzliche Materie
**Fossilfundstätten:** In Afrika, Europa und Asien

0 1 2 3 4 5 6 7 8 9 10 11 12 13 14

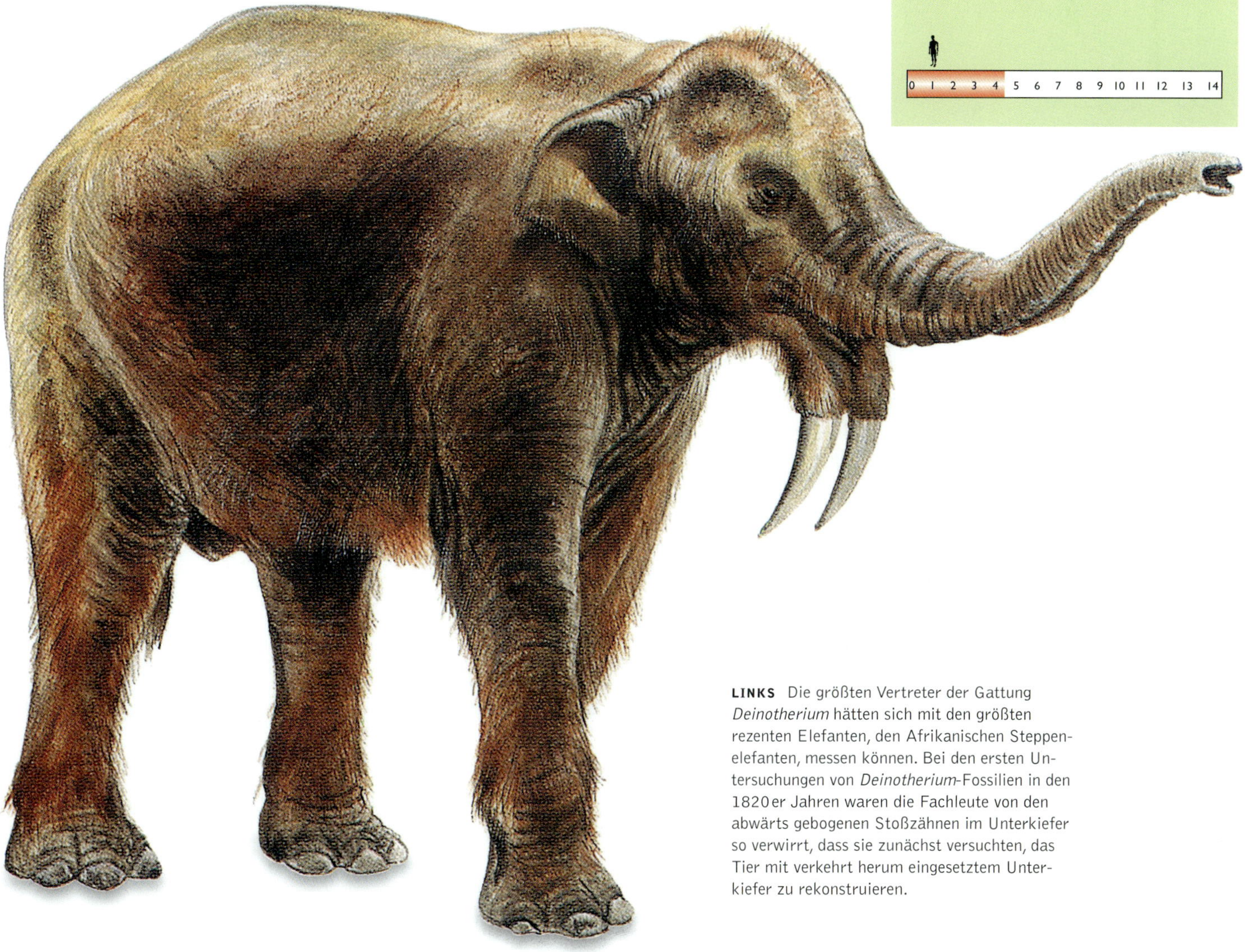

**LINKS** Die größten Vertreter der Gattung *Deinotherium* hätten sich mit den größten rezenten Elefanten, den Afrikanischen Steppenelefanten, messen können. Bei den ersten Untersuchungen von *Deinotherium*-Fossilien in den 1820er Jahren waren die Fachleute von den abwärts gebogenen Stoßzähnen im Unterkiefer so verwirrt, dass sie zunächst versuchten, das Tier mit verkehrt herum eingesetztem Unterkiefer zu rekonstruieren.

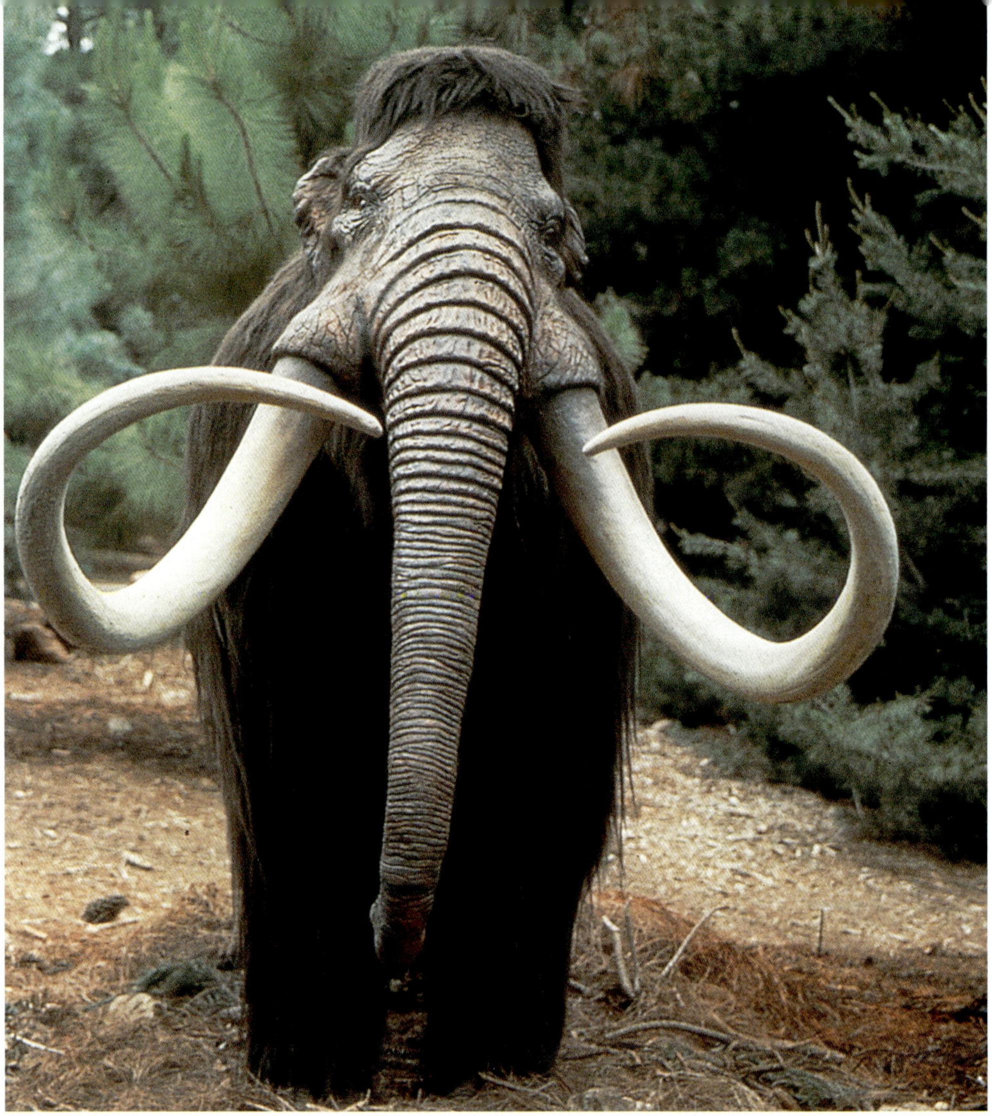

**RECHTS** Auge in Auge mit dem größten Landlebewesen der letzten Eiszeit – so haben vielleicht die Menschen vor fünfhundert Generationen das Mammut gesehen.

**UNTEN** Die harte, gefurchte Oberfläche eines Mammut-Backenzahns konnte selbst harte, zähe Pflanzenteile zermahlen. Die Mahlfläche eines solchen Backenzahnes war etwa so groß wie die Schuhsohle eines erwachsenen Menschen.

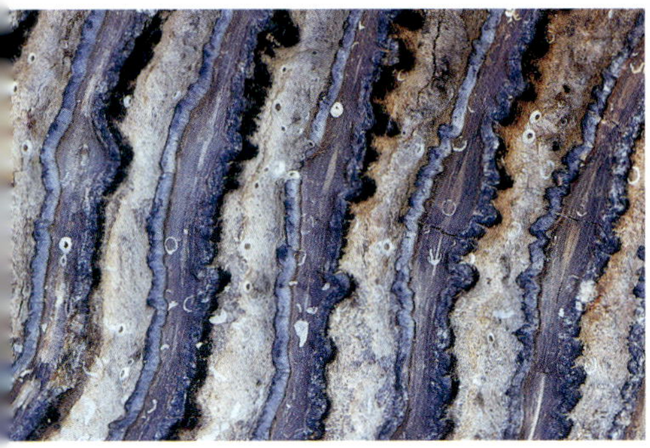

# MAMMUTHUS (MAMMUT)

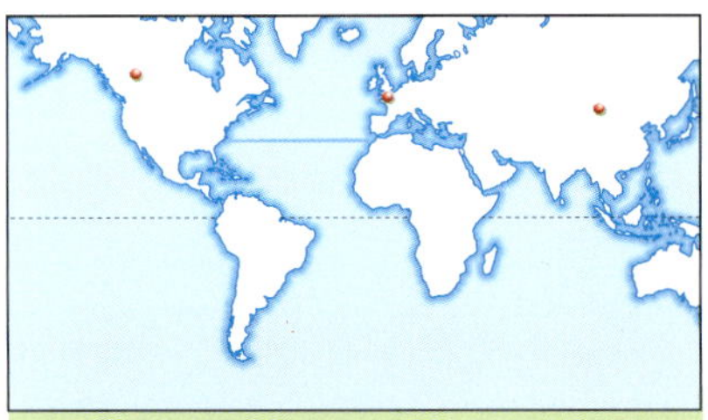

**ÜBERSICHT (TIERE)**
***Mammuthus***
**Bedeutung des Namens:** Erstgeborenes Mammut
**Periode:** Quartär
**Hauptgruppe:** Mammalia (Proboscidea)
**Höhe:** Schulterhöhe 3 Meter
**Gewicht:** 5 – 8 Tonnen
**Nahrung:** Gräser und andere Pflanzen
**Fossilfundstätten:** In Europa, Asien und Nordamerika

0 1 2 3 4 5 6 7 8 9 10 11 12 13 14

*Mammuthus* war eine Gattung riesiger Rüsseltiere, zu der immerhin acht Spezies gehörten. Ihre Vertreter waren in der Mehrzahl groß bis sehr groß und besaßen lange gebogene Stoßzähne. Wir kennen sie durch Fossilien, Subfossilien, tief gefrorene Tierkörper aus dem Dauerfrostboden des Hohen Nordens und durch Höhlenmalereien der Eiszeitmenschen. Verschiedene anatomische und genetische Vergleiche – die DNS des Mammuts wurde in den 1990er Jahren untersucht – zeigen, dass die Mammuts, verglichen mit viel entfernteren „Cousins" wie *Deinotherium* (siehe vorhergehende Seite) sehr nahe Verwandte der rezenten Elefanten waren.

Das eiszeitliche Kältesteppenmammut *Mammuthus primigenius* existierte noch vor weniger als 10 000 Jahren, und vor nur 4000 Jahren kann es auf der Wrangel-Insel vor der Nordküste Sibiriens auch noch einige kleinere Formen gegeben haben. Das Kältesteppenmammut war auf allen nördlichen Kontinenten anzutreffen. Es hatte Buckelschultern, eine ausgeprägt kuppelartige Erhöhung auf dem Kopf und einen sehr kurzen Schwanz. Es war zwar nicht das größte, dafür aber das Mammut mit dem dichtesten Haarkleid; im Dauerfrostboden gefundene Exemplare belegen, dass die Zotteln ihrer Felle 90 (!) Zentimeter lang waren. Sie waren dunkel, fast schwarz. Die rote Fellfarbe, die frühere Nachbildungen zeigen, war durch das Eindringen chemischer Verbindungen aus dem Boden und aus Gesteinen in die Tierkadaver entstanden.

Der im weiteren Sinne ebenfalls als Mammut bezeichnete Steppenelefant *Mammuthus trogontherii* trug ein kürzeres Fell und war mit einer Schulterhöhe von 4,6 Metern und einem Gewicht von über zehn Tonnen eines der größten Mammute. Das amerikanische Mammut *Mammuthus columbi* war etwas kleiner, unbehaart und lebte nur in Nordamerika. Der Vorfahr aller dieser Formen kann der Südelefant *Mammuthus meridionalis* gewesen sein.

# MEGALOCEROS

*Megaloceros*, auch unter der Bezeichnung Riesenhirsch bekannt, gehörte wie die rezenten Elche zur Gruppe der Cervidae oder Hirsche. Er war allerdings kein echter Elch, obwohl er diesem an Größe gleichkam, sondern näher verwandt mit dem Europäischen Damhirsch. Auf Überreste von *Megaloceros* stieß man an vielen Orten überall in Europa und Asien – von Irland bis China. Viele frühe Funde stammen aus Irland, darunter auch aus einem Moor bei Dublin, wo man Teile von fast hundert Tieren zutage förderte. Der Wortteil „-ceros" des wissenschaftlichen Namens bedeutet zwar „Horn", doch das Geweih der Cervidae unterscheidet sich deutlich vom Gehörn solcher Säugetiere wie Rinder und Antilopen. Während die Hörner bei männlichen wie weiblichen Horntieren fortwährend wachsen, wird das nur von Männchen getragene Geweih jedes Jahr abgeworfen und wächst immer wieder nach. (Eine Ausnahme bilden die rezenten Rentiere, bei denen beide Geschlechter ein Geweih ausbilden.)

Für die jährlich wiederkehrende Bildung eines neuen Geweihes musste ein *Megaloceros* seine Nahrungsquellen über die Maßen stark abweiden, um ausreichend Nährstoffe für den Aufbau neuer großer, ausladender Geweihschaufeln aufzunehmen. Bei manchen Tieren spannte sich das Geweih über 3,5 Meter und wog fünfzig Kilogramm. *Megaloceros* existierte vor 500 000 Jahren und starb vor weniger als 10 000 Jahren aus. Winzige Abnutzungsspuren an fossilierten Fundstücken belegen, dass die Geweihe nicht nur zur Schau gestellt wurden, sondern wie heute bei den brünstigen Hirschen auch als Waffe dienten. Einer populären Vorstellung zufolge wurde das Geweih der Riesenhirsche im Lauf der Entwicklung so groß und so schwer, dass *Megaloceros* seinen Kopf nicht mehr heben konnte. Wahrscheinlicher ist aber, dass die Bejagung durch den Eiszeitmenschen und vielleicht der Klimawechsel das Aussterben des gewaltigen Tieres beschleunigt haben. In Höhlenzeichnungen ist *Megaloceros* braun und mit hellerer Brust dargestellt.

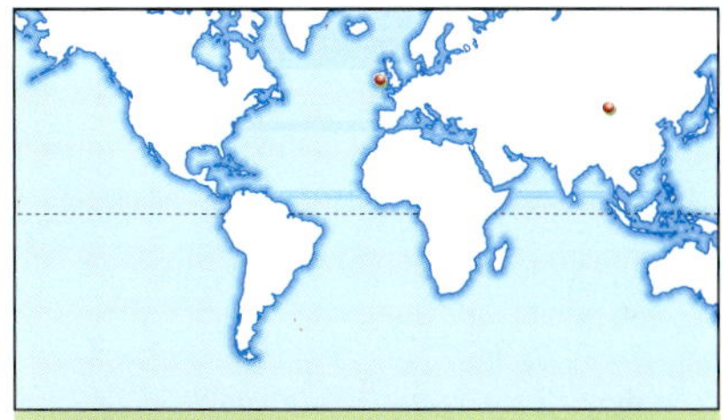

**ÜBERSICHT (TIERE)**
***Megaloceros***
**Bedeutung des Namens:** Riesengroßes Horn (Geweih), Riesenhorn
**Periode:** Quartär
**Hauptgruppe:** Mammalia (Ungulata)
**Größe:** Kopf und Rumpf 2,5 Meter, Schulterhöhe 2 Meter
**Gewicht:** 400 – 500 Kilogramm
**Nahrung:** Gräser, Blätter
**Fossilfundstätten:** In Europa (vor allem in Irland), in Asien (hauptsächlich im Norden)

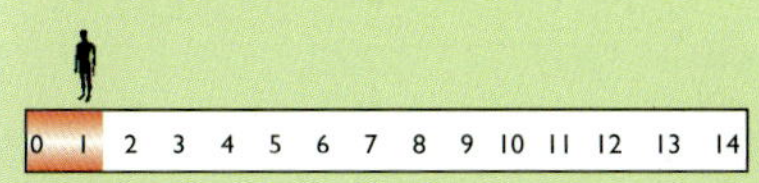


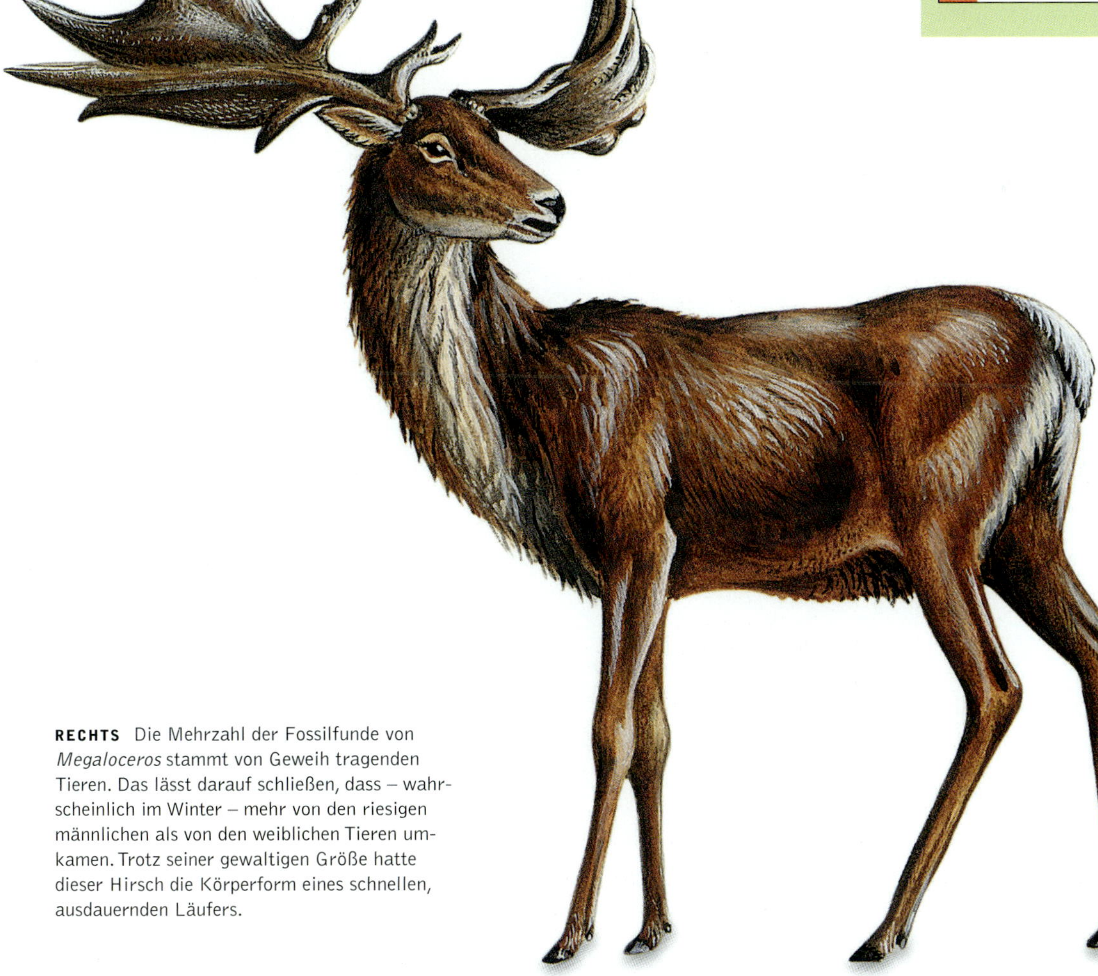

**RECHTS** Die Mehrzahl der Fossilfunde von *Megaloceros* stammt von Geweih tragenden Tieren. Das lässt darauf schließen, dass – wahrscheinlich im Winter – mehr von den riesigen männlichen als von den weiblichen Tieren umkamen. Trotz seiner gewaltigen Größe hatte dieser Hirsch die Körperform eines schnellen, ausdauernden Läufers.

# Ursus spelaeus (Höhlenbär)

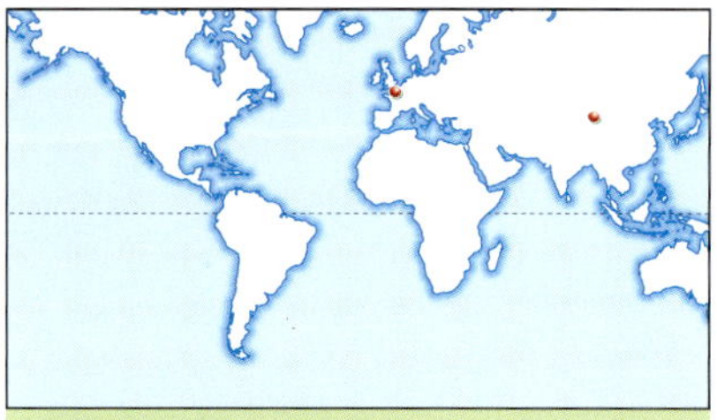

**ÜBERSICHT (TIERE)**

***Ursus spelaeus***

**Bedeutung des Namens:** Höhlenbär

**Periode:** Quartär

**Hauptgruppe:** Mammalia (Carnivora)

**Länge:** Bis 3 Meter

**Gewicht:** Bis 500 Kilogramm

**Nahrung:** Hauptsächlich pflanzliche Nahrung, vielleicht kleine Beutetiere und Aas

**Fossilfundstätten:** In Europa und Asien

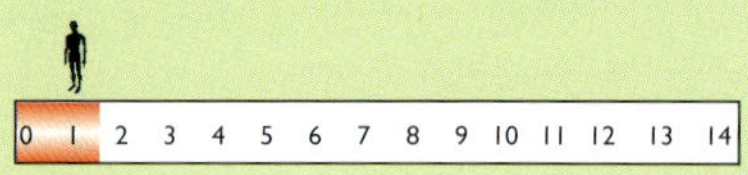


Die Ursidae sind Großbären, die Gattung *Ursus* umfasst die Hälfte der acht rezenten Bärenspezies – die Eisbären, die Braunbären, die Amerikanischen und die Asiatischen Schwarzbären. *Ursus spelaeus* war der riesige Höhlenbär der Eiszeit, der noch bis vor einigen tausend Jahren existierte. Mit seiner Körpergröße ähnelte er dem rezenten Grizzlybären, einer Unterart des Braunbären, er besaß allerdings eine längere, markantere Schnauze. Sein Fell war lang und zottig, seine Gliedmaßen sehr muskulös und kräftig, und die Füße endeten in fünf Zehen mit langen gebogenen Krallen. Abbildungen von *Ursus spelaeus* kennen wir aus alten Höhlenzeichnungen, seine Knochen und Zähne wurden vor allem von den Neandertalern für Schnitzereien, als Schmuckgegenstände wie etwa Halsketten und für rituelle Handlungen verwendet (siehe Seite 432).

*Ursus spelaeus* verdankt seinen Namen der Tatsache, dass viele seiner Überreste in Höhlen, insbesondere in Höhlen der Alpen, entdeckt wurden. Die Funde umfassen Knochen und Zähne, Subfossilien (noch nicht vollständig versteinerte Materie) und mumifizierte Fetzen von Haut und anderen Weichteilen. Die übrigen für Höhlenbärfossilien bekannten Fundstätten liegen über ganz Europa und Asien, von Spanien und Großbritannien im Westen bis nach Russland im Osten, verstreut. In einigen Höhlen, so beispielsweise in der Drachenhöhle in Österreich, liegen Fossilien vieler Tausender Individuen. Die Bären der heutigen Zeit leben auch in der kalten Jahreszeit als Einzelgänger. Um die extremen Winter zu ihrer Zeit zu überleben, passten die eiszeitlichen Höhlenbären ihr Sozialverhalten möglicherweise den Gegebenheiten an und fanden sich in Gruppen zum Winterschlaf an geschützten Orten ein; in der Drachenhöhle scheinen sie allerdings von einem Wassereinbruch oder einer ähnlichen Katastrophe überrascht worden zu sein. Bei der Suche nach einer schützenden Unterkunft können Höhlenbären und Eiszeitmenschen sehr wohl in Konflikt miteinander geraten sein, doch der Bär war vermutlich fast ausschließlich Pflanzenfresser.

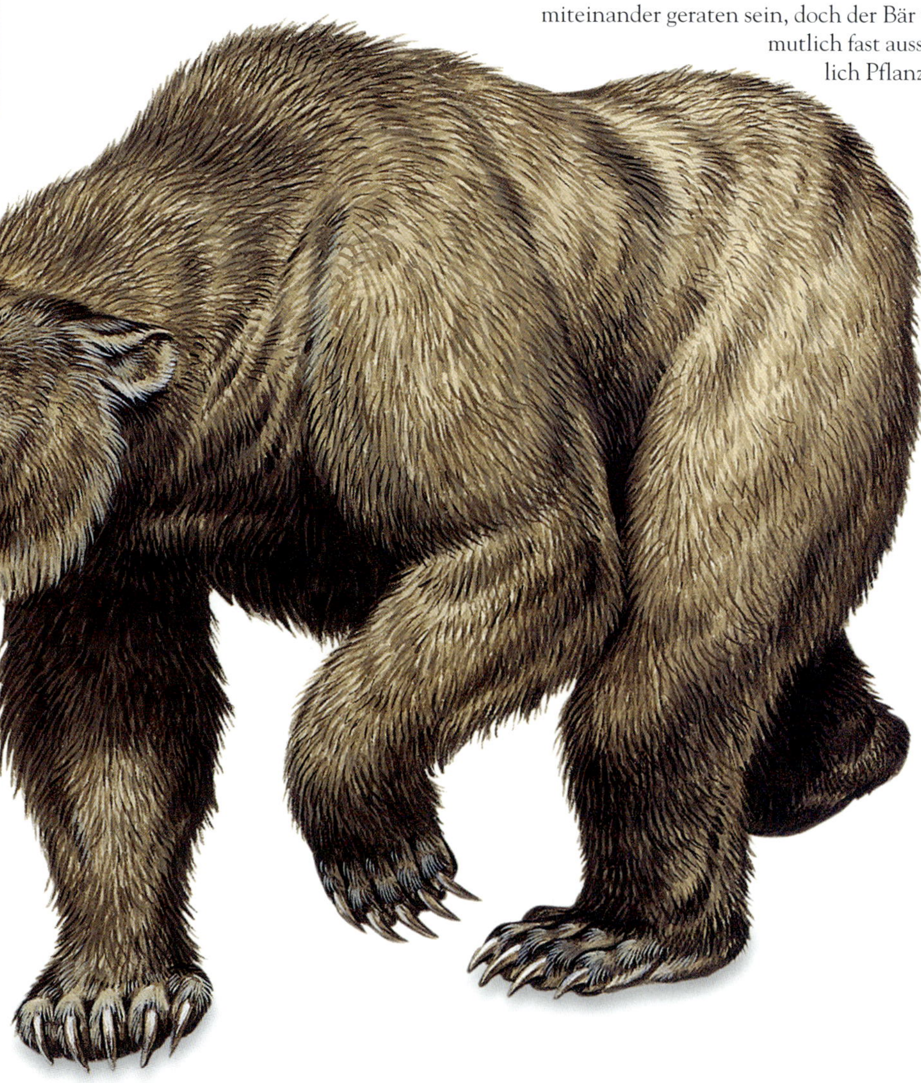

**RECHTS** Höhlenbären und Eiszeitmenschen standen sich vielleicht manches Mal Auge in Auge gegenüber, wenn sie sich auf der Suche nach einem Schutz vor den bitterkalten eiszeitlichen Wintern begegneten. Auf seinen Hinterbeinen stehend war *Ursus spelaeus* über drei Meter hoch, also etwa so groß wie der rezente Grizzlybär.

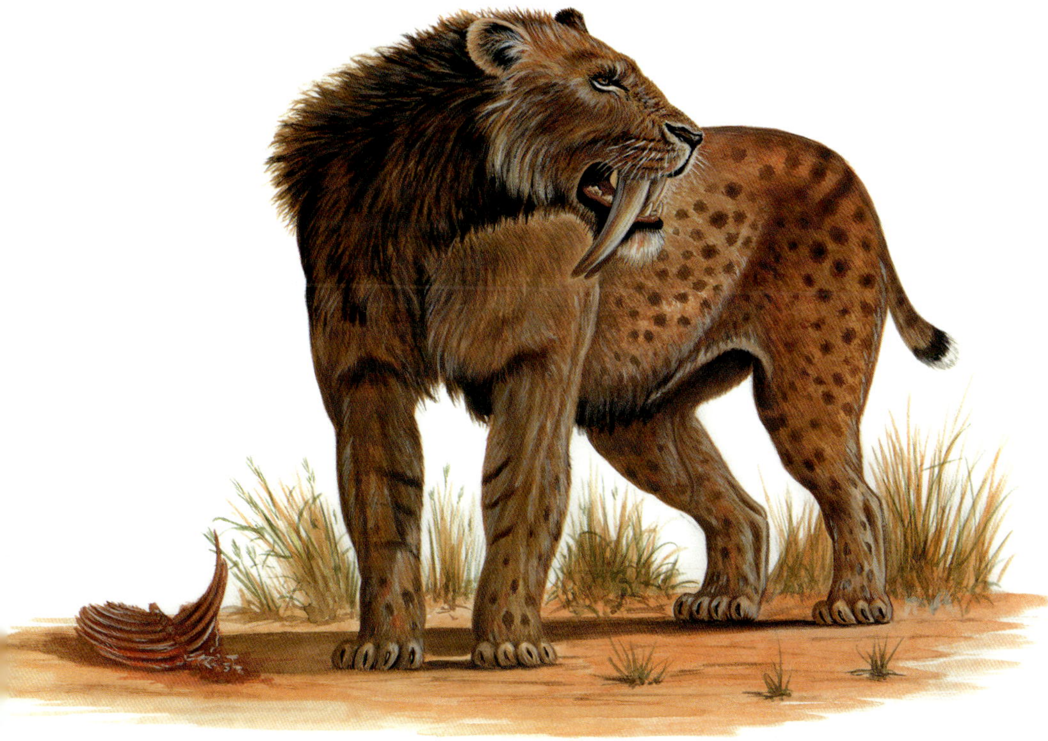

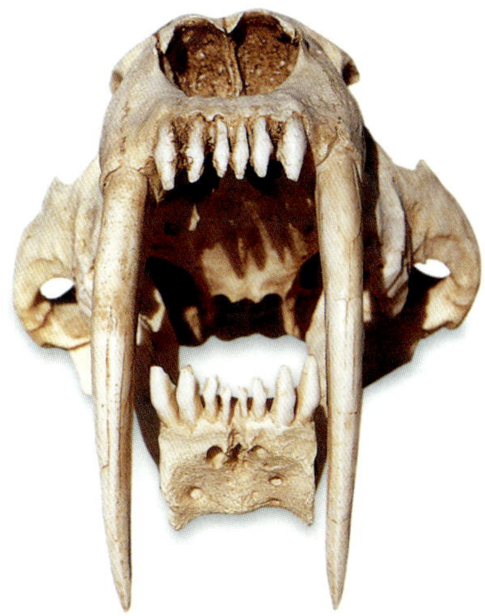

**OBEN** An „Smileys" Maul stachen deutlich die beiden massiven Eckzähne hervor, die länger als die Hand eines Menschen waren, von vorn jedoch schmal und dolchartig aussahen. Die Eckzähne im Unterkiefer waren klein oder gar nicht, die Backenzähne in nur geringer Anzahl vorhanden.

**LINKS** Der Säbelzahn„tiger" *Smilodon* war nur geringfügig kleiner als die großen Tiger der heutigen Zeit. Sein Skelett war für einen katzenartigen Fleischfresser verhältnismäßig kräftig und stabil gebaut.

# SMILODON (SÄBELZAHNKATZE)

Der wahrscheinlich bekannteste Vertreter der Säbelzahnkatzen ist *Smilodon*. Die größten Exemplare hatten etwa die Größe der rezenten Löwen. Mitunter nennt man *Smilodon* auch Säbelzahntiger. Die Tiger gehören zwar zur Familie der Katzen, sind allerdings deren entferntere Verwandte. Von der Gattung *Smilodon* kennen wir mehrere Spezies, darunter *Smilodon fatalis/californicus*, von der Tausende Individuen im ehemaligen Asphaltsee La Brea im Stadtgebiet von Los Angeles im US-Bundesstaat Kalifornien fossiliert wurden. Sie gerieten einst zusammen mit Wölfen und anderen Raubtieren in die zäh-klebrigen Lachen eines natürlichen Asphaltvorkommens, als sie sich an der Stelle vermutlich an den Mastodonten (ausgestorbene Rüsseltiere) und anderen großen Pflanzenfressern gütlich tun wollten, die bereits in die Falle getappt waren. Der etwas größere *Smilodon populator/neogaeus* lebte in Südamerika. Er entwickelte sich wahrscheinlich dort, nachdem seine Vorfahren nach der einige Millionen Jahre zurückliegenden Verbindung Nord- und Südamerikas durch die zentralamerikanische Landbrücke aus dem Norden eingewandert waren. Weitere Typen von Säbelzahnkatzen sind aus Europa, Asien und Afrika bekannt.

*Smilodon* war eine besonders an Schultern und Vordergliedmaßen kräftig gebaute, sehr muskulöse Katze. Ihre „Säbel" waren die spitzen oberen Eckzähne, die eine Länge von fünfundzwanzig Zentimetern erreichten. Ihre hinteren Kanten wiesen eine sägeartige Zähnung auf. Von vorn erschienen sie schmal-dolchartig und ziemlich zerbrechlich. Einen kräftigen Biss auf einen harten Knochen hätten sie wohl kaum heil überstanden. Wahrscheinlicher ist, dass das Tier sein Maul sehr weit (120 °) aufriss und mit seinen Säbelzähnen Haut und Fleisch von Beutetieren anstach, aufschlitzte und zerschnitt, dem Opfer Wunden zufügte, an denen es verblutete. Von dem toten Tier konnte *Smilodon* dann Fleischstücke abbeißen und verschlingen, ohne Gefahr zu laufen, dass die riesigen Zähne durch heftige Bewegungen der Beute beschädigt würden. *Smilodon* machte wahrscheinlich Jagd auf Bisons, Kamele, Pferde und Riesenfaultiere.

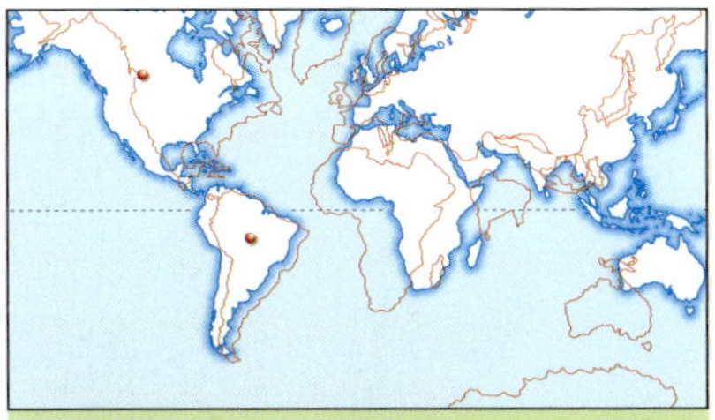

**ÜBERSICHT (TIERE)**
***Smilodon***
**Bedeutung des Namens:** Messerzahn
**Periode:** Quartär
**Hauptgruppe:** Mammalia (Carnivora)
**Länge:** Bis 3 Meter
**Gewicht:** 200 Kilogramm
**Nahrung:** Fleisch
**Fossilfundstätten:** In Nord- und Südamerika

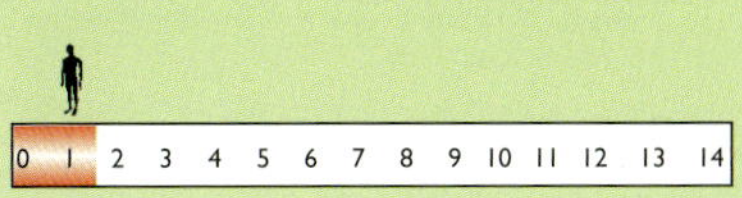

# *FRÜHE HOMINIDEN*

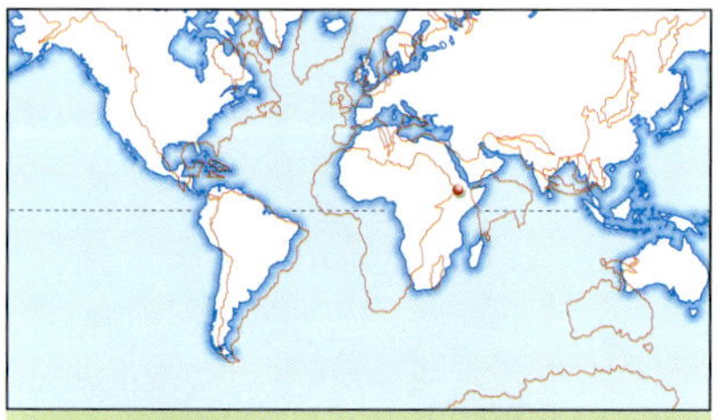

**ÜBERSICHT (HOMINIDEN)**

***Ardipithecus***

**Bedeutung des Namens:** Bodenaffe, Wurzelaffe
**Periode:** Tertiär (Pliozän)
**Hauptgruppe:** Mammalia (Primates)
**Größe:** Standhöhe 1 Meter
**Gewicht:** 40 Kilogramm
**Nahrung:** Vielleicht Mischkost, meistens jedoch pflanzlich
**Fossilfundstätten:** In Äthiopien

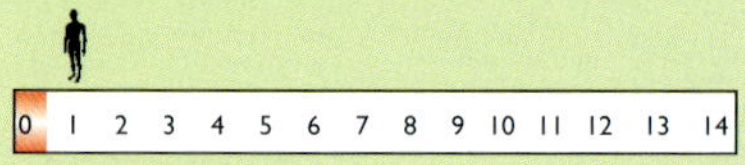


Die Wissenschaft von unserer Herkunft und insbesondere davon, wo und wie unsere fernen Vorfahren lebten, hat nicht nur etwas ganz besonders Faszinierendes, sondern sorgt auch für sehr viele Diskussionen. Zur Säugetiergruppe der Primaten gehören Lemuren, Galagos, Affen und Hominiden. Zur Gruppe der Hominiden zählt man für gewöhnlich nur eine rezente Spezies – den *Homo sapiens*, also uns selbst – sowie verschiedene Vorfahren und Verwandte aus Seitenlinien, die bis zu dem gemeinsamen (aber nicht zu den Hominiden gestellten) Urahn zurückreichen, aus dem wir und unsere nächsten lebenden Verwandten, die Schimpansen, hervorgegangen sind. Dieser gemeinsame Vorfahr lebte mit großer Gewissheit in Afrika, und das vermutlich vor mindestens fünf Millionen Jahren.

Vor einem Jahrhundert noch erschien die Vorstellung, dass die Menschen sich über Zwischenformen aus affenartigen Vorfahren entwickelt haben, entweder lächerlich oder ketzerisch. Heute ist uns durch Fossilien eine Vielzahl dieser Bindeglieder, nämlich ausgestorbene Hominiden, bekannt. Die frühen Typen stammen sämtlich aus Afrika. Einer der ältesten war *Ardipithecus*, seine Überreste aus der äthiopischen Region Middle Awash sind fast 4,5 Millionen Jahre alt. Das schimpansenartige Geschöpf bewegte sich wohl schon in halb aufrechter Haltung, doch sein Hirnvolumen betrug vermutlich nur 400 – 500 Kubikzentimeter; das des heutigen Menschen liegt schon näher bei 1500. In einigen Klassifikationen gilt *Ardipithecus* als eine Spezies des *Australopithecus* (siehe gegenüber). Noch älter als *Ardipithecus* ist *Orrorin*, dessen sechs Millionen Jahre alte Überreste im Jahr 2000 in den Tugen Hills von Kenia entdeckt wurden. Ein noch neuerer Fund stammt von dem noch älteren *Sahelanthropus* aus dem Tschad. Diese Fossilien wurden 2002 ausgegraben, ihr Alter liegt bei fast sieben Millionen Jahren. Die genannten Lebewesen werden unterschiedlich als sehr frühe Hominiden, als Vertreter der Schimpansengruppe oder im Fall des *Sahelanthropus* als nahe Verwandte der Gorillas eingeordnet, und Diskussionen über die Funde wird es sicherlich auch weiterhin geben.

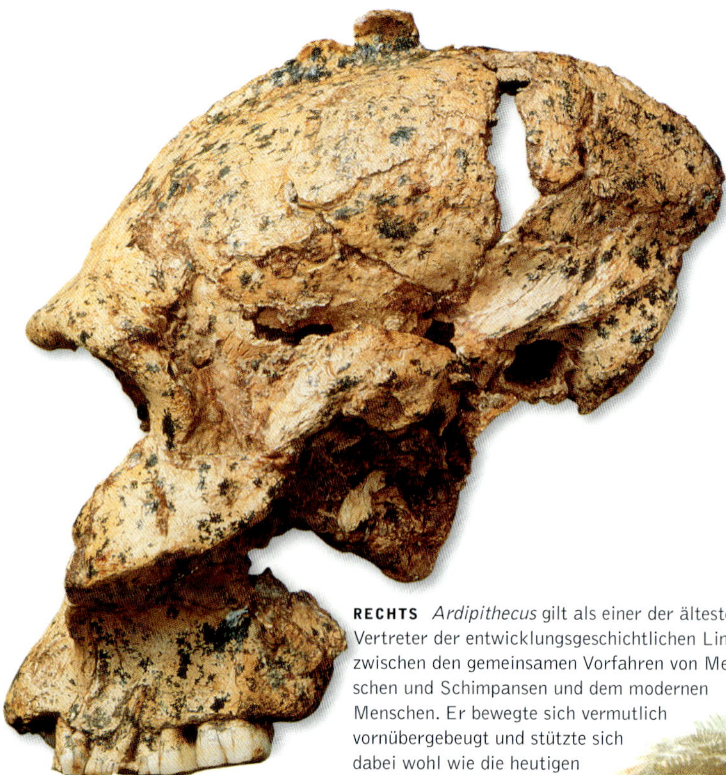

**LINKS** Dieser „robuste" Hominidenschädel, der gewöhnlich *Paranthropus* (siehe gegenüber) zugeordnet wird, zeigt große Backenzähne und einen Sagittalkamm – das knöcherne Gebilde (hier zum Teil abgebrochen) auf der Mittellinie des Kopfes, an dem einst kräftige Kiefermuskeln verankert waren.

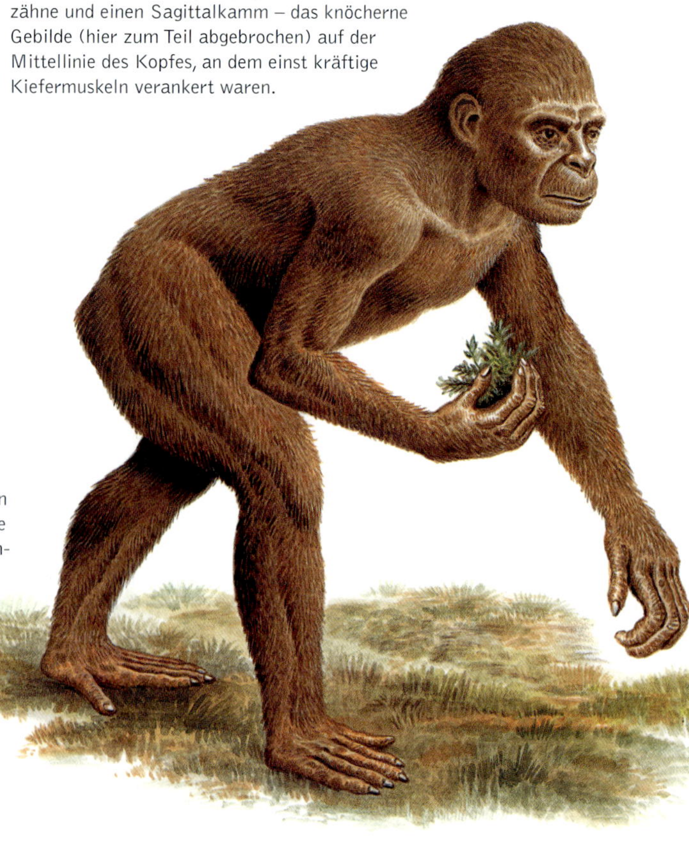

**RECHTS** *Ardipithecus* gilt als einer der ältesten Vertreter der entwicklungsgeschichtlichen Linie zwischen den gemeinsamen Vorfahren von Menschen und Schimpansen und dem modernen Menschen. Er bewegte sich vermutlich vornübergebeugt und stützte sich dabei wohl wie die heutigen Schimpansen auf seine Fingerknöchel. Schimpansen benutzen Werkzeuge wie etwa Steine zum Öffnen hartschaliger Früchte; möglicherweise tat das auch dieser frühe Hominide.

# AUSTRALOPITHECUS

Fossile Hominiden sorgen stets für reichlich Debatten und wissenschaftlichen Meinungsstreit (siehe auch gegenüber). So führen manche Fachleute mehr als zehn Spezies der Gattung *Australopithecus* auf, andere beschränken sich auf drei Arten. Eines der wichtigsten Fundexemplare ist AL 288-1, besser bekannt unter dem Namen „Lucy". Ihr zu etwa zwei Fünfteln erhaltenes Skelett wurde 1974 in Äthiopien, in der Nähe des Hadar in der Afarsenke, entdeckt und 1978 von Donald Johanson und Tim White *Australopithecus afarensis* benannt. Diese Hominidenform lebte vor rund vier Millionen Jahren und starb vor weniger als drei Millionen Jahren aus. Ihre Vertreter konnten zwar schlecht und recht aufgerichtet gehen, ähnelten jedoch ihren Vorfahren, den Affen, in vielerlei Hinsicht, beispielsweise mit der fliehenden Stirn, der vorstehenden Nase und dem ebenfalls vorstehenden Mund, dem weniger eckigen Kinn und den schimpansenartigen Zähnen. Manche Experten behaupten inzwischen, dass „Lucy" in Wirklichkeit ein männlicher *Australopithecus afarensis* sei und gaben ihm den Namen „Luzifer". Auch die Fähigkeit dieser Hominidenform zum aufrechten Gehen ist in neuerer Zeit in Zweifel gezogen worden.

*Australopithecus afarensis* ist mit einer gewissen Wahrscheinlichkeit ein Bindeglied zwischen früheren Hominiden und späteren Typen – eines jener Geschöpfe, die sich zu den heutigen Menschen entwickelt haben. Eine andere Spezies – *Australopithecus africanus* – lebte vor drei Millionen Jahren im südlichen Afrika und starb vor zwei Millionen Jahren aus. Sie wurde 1925 von dem südafrikanischen Paläontologen Raymond Dart anhand des fossilierten Schädels eines jungen, vielleicht drei bis sechs Jahre alten Vertreters benannt, der nach dem Ort seiner Entdeckung auch als „Kind aus Taung" bekannt ist. Zu der Gattung *Australopithecus* zählte man früher außerdem „robuste" Typen – größere, stärkere, schwerer gebaute Spezies wie *Australopithecus robustus* und *A. boisei* (früher *Zinjanthropus*). Sie besaßen sehr starke Kiefer und große Zähne, die die Nahrung gründlich zerkleinern konnten. Sie lebten größtenteils zwischen zweieinhalb und einer Million Jahren vor der Jetztzeit. Diese robusten Arten stellt man heute allerdings zu der Gattung *Paranthropus*.

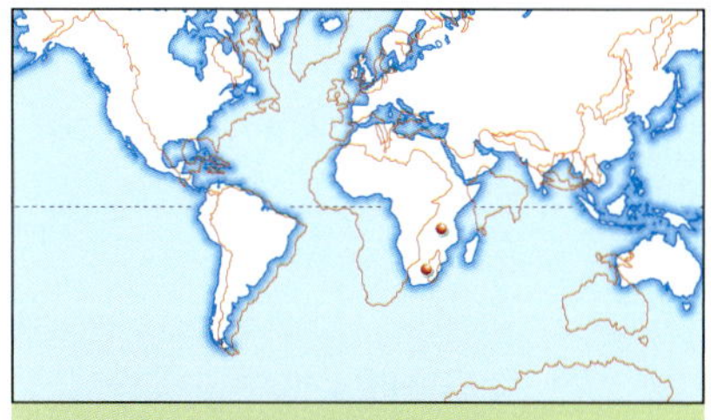

**ÜBERSICHT (HOMINIDEN)**
***Australopithecus afarensis***
**Bedeutung des Namens:** Südlicher Menschenaffe von Afar
**Periode:** Tertiär (Pliozän)
**Hauptgruppe:** Mammalia (Primates)
**Größe:** Standhöhe 1 Meter
**Gewicht:** 40 Kilogramm
**Nahrung:** Wahrscheinlich vor allem pflanzliche Materie
**Fossilfundstätten:** In Afrika, hauptsächlich in Ost- und Südafrika

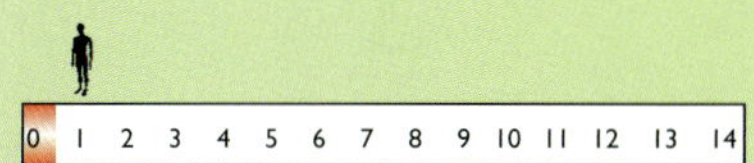


**UNTEN** Ein Exemplar eines *Australopithecus africanus* aus dem berühmten Höhlenfundort Sterkfontein in Südafrika. Der niedrige Hirnschädel, die ausgeprägten Überaugenwülste und der vorstehende Oberkiefer stellen sämtlich primitive Merkmale dar.

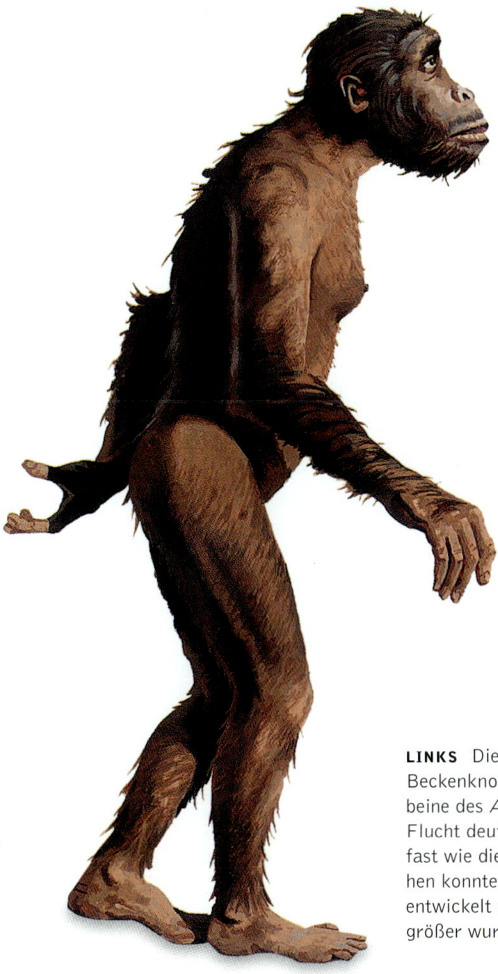

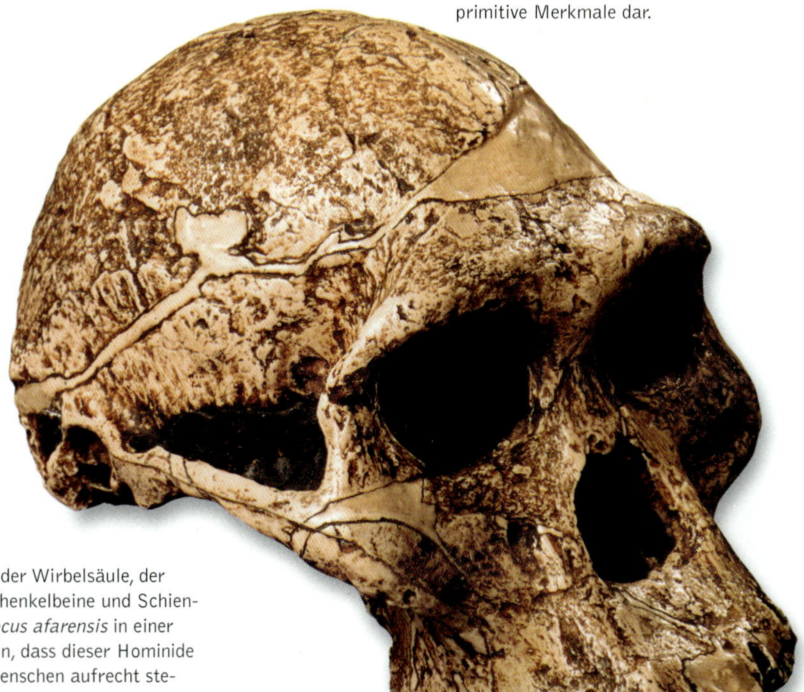

**LINKS** Die Anordnung der Wirbelsäule, der Beckenknochen, Oberschenkelbeine und Schienbeine des *Australopithecus afarensis* in einer Flucht deuten darauf hin, dass dieser Hominide fast wie die heutigen Menschen aufrecht stehen konnte. Der aufrechte Gang scheint bereits entwickelt gewesen zu sein, bevor das Hirn größer wurde.

# FRÜHE SPEZIES DES HOMO

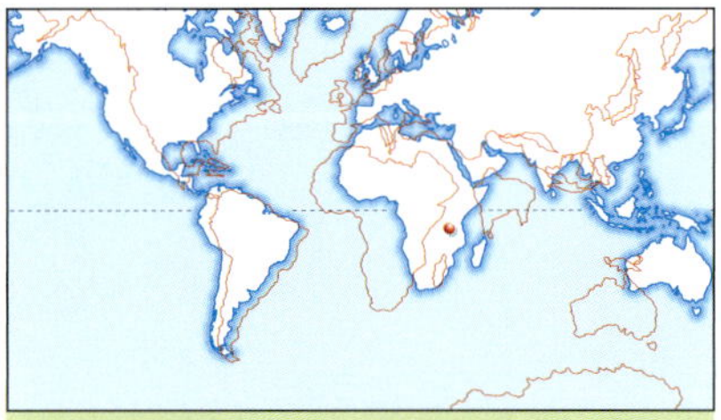

**ÜBERSICHT (HOMINIDEN)**

***Homo (Australopithecus) habilis***

**Bedeutung des Namens:** Geschickter Mensch

**Periode:** Tertiär

**Hauptgruppe:** Mammalia (Primates)

**Höhe:** Bis 1,3 Meter

**Gewicht:** 30 – 40 Kilogramm

**Nahrung:** Mischkost, darunter vielleicht Fleisch erlegter Tiere

**Fossilfundstätten:** In Ostafrika

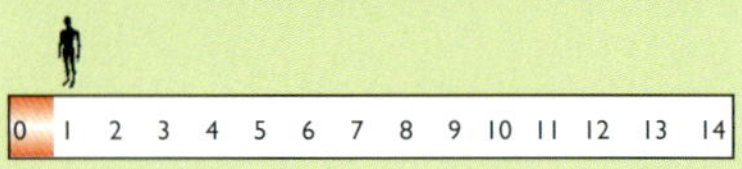


Zu unserer eigenen Gattung *Homo* gehören auch unsere nächsten Verwandten (siehe auch Seite 428, zur Entwicklungsgeschichte des Menschen). Manche Klassifikationen führen acht oder mehr *Homo*-Spezies an, andere nur drei oder vier. Eine der frühesten Arten ist *Homo habilis*, der „geschickte Mensch", der seinen Namen dem Umstand verdankt, dass man bei seinen Überresten einfache, in Olduvantechnik hergestellte Steinwerkzeuge gefunden hat. Die bisher gefundenen Fossilien des *Homo habilis* stammen aus Ostafrika, speziell aus der Olduvai-Schlucht in Tansania, und sind rund zweieinhalb bis anderthalb Millionen Jahre alt. Die Spezies wurde 1964 von Louis Leaky, John Napier und Phillip Tobias benannt. Rekonstruktionen zeigen einen „Affenmenschen" mit einer Mischung aus affenartigen und menschlichen Merkmalen, wie ihn sich viele Menschen heute vorstellen; er konnte aufrecht gehen, war aber mit einer Standhöhe von vielleicht 1,3 Metern ziemlich klein.

Manche Fachleute betrachten *Homo habilis* als eine Spezies des *Australopithecus* oder als eine Kombination von Fossilien zweier oder mehr Arten. Eine dieser Arten ist *Homo rudolfensis*, 1986 nach dem Schädel „1470" benannt, der 1972 von einem Team unter Leitung von Richard Leakey (dem Sohn von Louis Leakey) entdeckt worden war. Wie die Fundorte vieler anderer Hominidenfossilien liegen auch die des *Homo rudolfensis* über das Ostafrikanische Grabensystem verteilt. Die Überreste stammen aus der Zeit vor rund zweieinhalb Millionen bis knapp zwei Millionen Jahren. Das Hirnvolumen des *Homo rudolfensis* betrug schätzungsweise 750 Kubikzentimeter, also etwa die Hälfte unseres Hirnvolumens, und war etwa vergleichbar mit dem des *Homo habilis*, das bei 650 Kubikzentimetern lag. Weitere vorgeschlagene, aber sehr umstrittene Spezies sind *Homo ergaster* (vor 1,9 bis 1,2 Millionen Jahren, ebenfalls in Ostafrika); *Homo antecessor* (vor 800 000 Jahren, hauptsächlich in Spanien); *Homo heidelbergensis* (vor 600 000 bis vielleicht vor 100 000 Jahren oder länger, hauptsächlich in Europa, der mögliche Vorfahre der Neandertaler) und *Homo erectus*.

**UNTEN** Dieser Schädel eines *Homo (Australopithecus) habilis* aus der Olduvai-Schlucht in Tansania ist 1,6 Millionen Jahre alt. Die Habilinen werden oft als die ersten Hominiden bezeichnet, die ständig Steinwerkzeuge herstellten und benutzten.

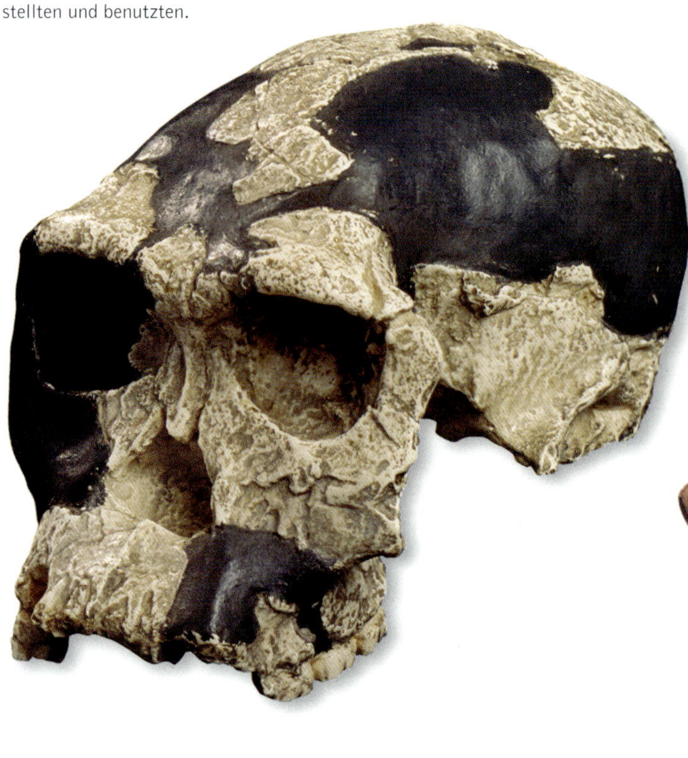

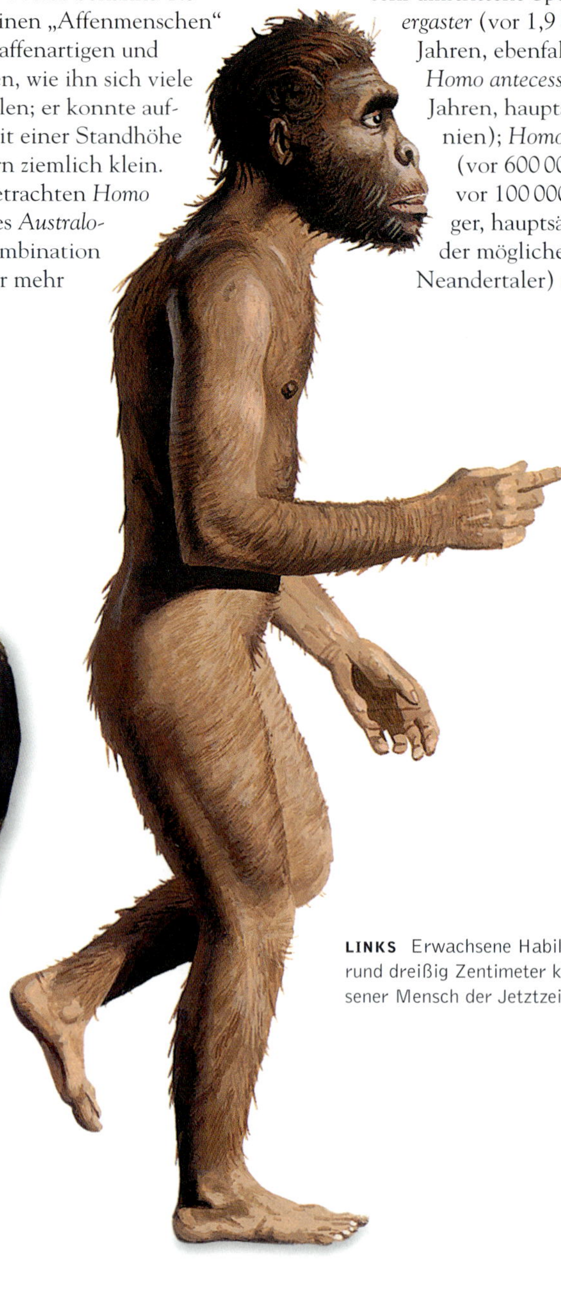

**LINKS** Erwachsene Habilinen waren im Stehen rund dreißig Zentimeter kürzer als ein erwachsener Mensch der Jetztzeit.

# HOMO ERECTUS

Man geht im Allgemeinen davon aus, dass *Homo erectus* vor fast zwei Millionen Jahren erschien und vor etwa 500 000 Jahren verschwand, dass er zunächst in Afrika lebte und sich dann allmählich über fast alle Teile der Alten Welt ausbreitete. Eine der ersten Entdeckungen seiner Überreste wurde von Eugène Dubois auf der indonesischen Insel Java gemacht. Dubois fand 1891 den Teil eines Schädels und nannte diesen *Pithecanthropus erectus*. Der Name wurde damals von angesehenen Paläontologen rundweg abgelehnt. In den 1920er Jahren grub man im chinesischen Zhoukoudian weitere Fossilien aus und gab ihnen den Namen „Pekingmensch". Diese und viele andere Funde wurden in den 1960er Jahren neu als *Homo erectus* klassifiziert, und die Spezies galt dann bei einigen Fachleuten als unser direkter Vorfahre. Nach einer neueren Tendenz wird *Homo erectus* als ein Artenmosaik interpretiert, zu dem man frühe Fossilien aus Afrika wie etwa *Homo ergaster* sowie spätere aus Europa, beispielsweise *Homo heidelbergensis* (siehe gegenüber und auch Seite 428) rechnet.

Eines der am wenigsten unvollständigen frühen afrikanischen Exemplare ist der „Junge aus Turkana", auch „Junge aus Nariokotome" (Exemplar KNM-ER 15000) genannt, aus Kenia. Der in die Zeit vor 1,6 Millionen Jahren datierte Fund zeigt, dass *Homo erectus* stark gebaut, doch schlank war und, wie der Artname schon sagt, aufrecht ging; im Stehen hatte er etwa die gleiche Größe wie viele Menschen der Jetztzeit. Der „Junge" war zehn bis zwölf Jahre alt, als er starb. Viele der Überreste von *Homo erectus* wurden zusammen mit Werkzeugen – Faustkeilen, Hacksteinen, Schabern – aus Stein, Holz, Knochen, Geweihen und anderen Materialien gefunden. Diese Beispiele der so genannten Acheuléen-Industrie wurden mit der Zeit immer weiter verfeinert. Vielfach entdeckte man an den Fundorten von Fossilien des *Homo erechtus*, insbesondere bei den späteren Funden in Europa und Asien, auch Reste von Feuerstellen.

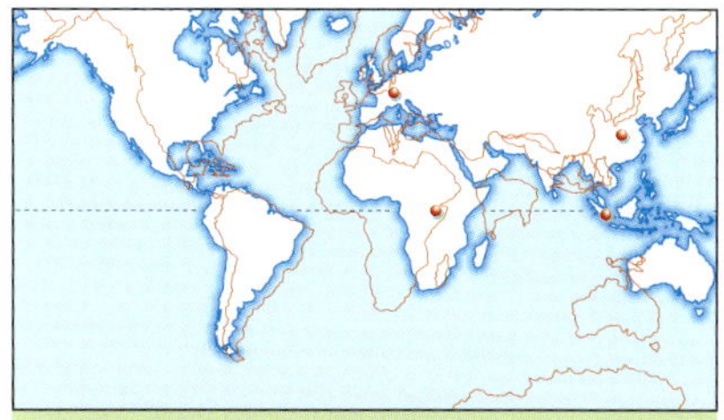

**ÜBERSICHT (HOMINIDEN)**

***Homo erectus/ergaster***

**Bedeutung des Namens:** Aufrechter Mensch/Arbeits- oder Werkmensch

**Periode:** Tertiär

**Hauptgruppe:** Mammalia (Primates)

**Höhe:** Bis 1,8 Meter

**Gewicht:** 60 – 80 Kilogramm

**Nahrung:** Mischkost, darunter vielleicht Fleisch erlegter Tiere

**Fossilfundstätten:** In Afrika (möglicherweise Homo ergaster), in Europa und Asien

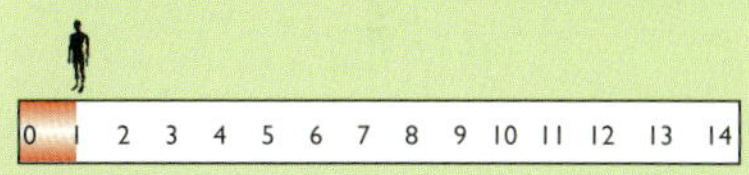


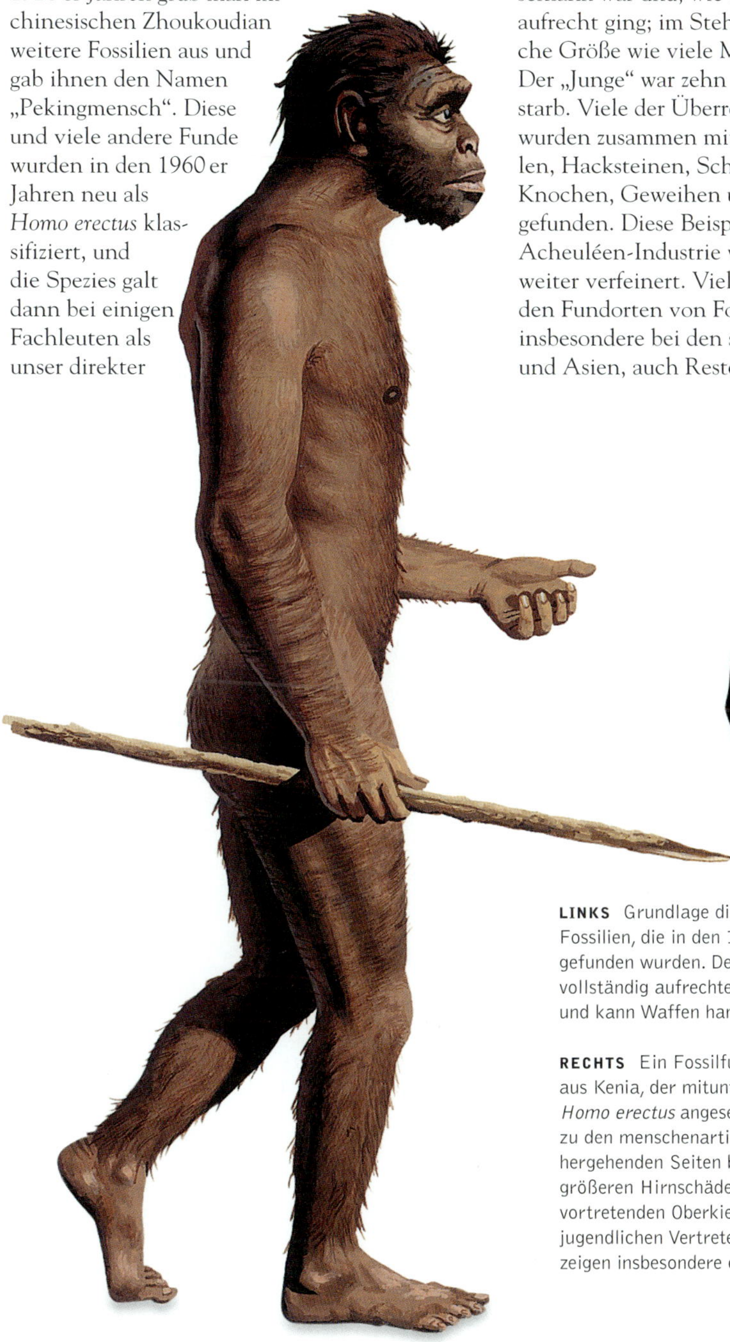

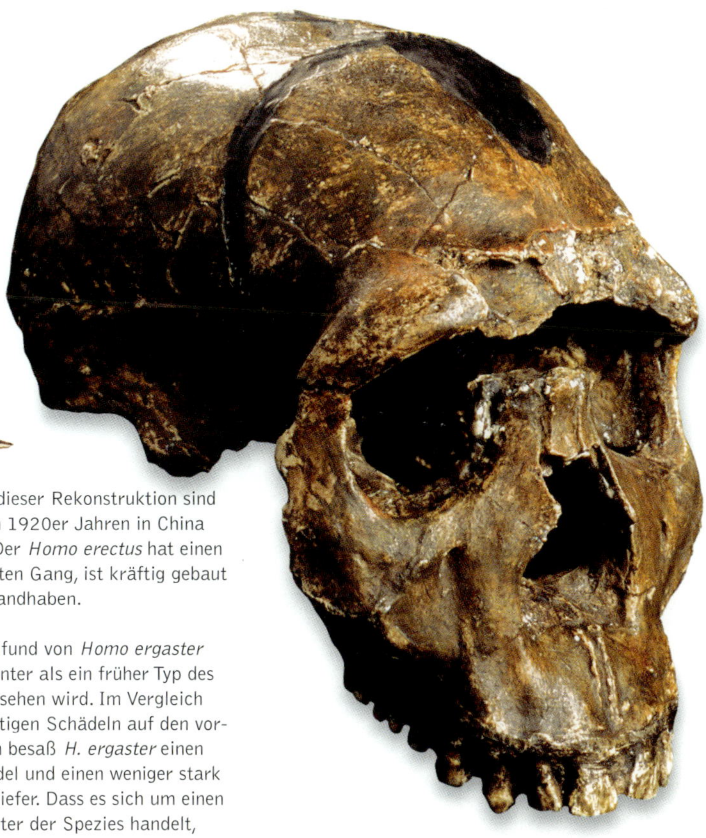

**LINKS** Grundlage dieser Rekonstruktion sind Fossilien, die in den 1920er Jahren in China gefunden wurden. Der *Homo erectus* hat einen vollständig aufrechten Gang, ist kräftig gebaut und kann Waffen handhaben.

**RECHTS** Ein Fossilfund von *Homo ergaster* aus Kenia, der mitunter als ein früher Typ des *Homo erectus* angesehen wird. Im Vergleich zu den menschenartigen Schädeln auf den vorhergehenden Seiten besaß *H. ergaster* einen größeren Hirnschädel und einen weniger stark vortretenden Oberkiefer. Dass es sich um einen jugendlichen Vertreter der Spezies handelt, zeigen insbesondere die Zähne.

# Homo neanderthalensis

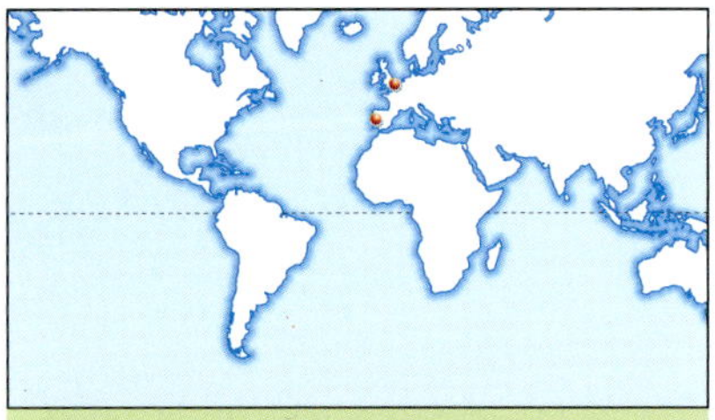

**ÜBERSICHT (HOMINIDEN)**

***Homo neanderthalensis***

**Bedeutung des Namens:** Neandertaler

**Periode:** Quartär

**Hauptgruppe:** Mammalia (Primates)

**Größe:** Höhe bis 1,7 Meter

**Gewicht:** 70 – 90 Kilogramm

**Nahrung:** Mischkost, darunter vielleicht Fleisch erlegter Tiere

**Fossilfundstätten:** In Deutschland und Portugal

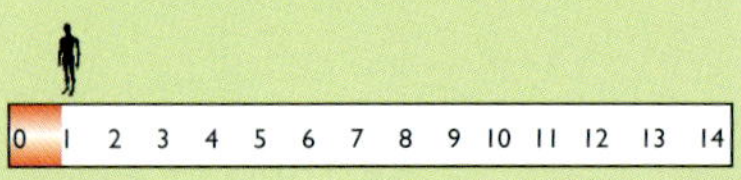


Die ersten der Wissenschaft bekannt gewordenen Fossilien des Neandertalers wurden von Steinbrucharbeitern 1856 in einer Höhle im Neanderthal bei Düsseldorf entdeckt. (Das ohnehin stumme -h- taucht heute nur noch im wissenschaftlichen Namen des Neandertalers auf, wird in der heutigen Schreibweise aber weggelassen.) Viele weitere Entdeckungen ließen erkennen, dass die Neandertaler kräftig gebaut waren und ihr Hirnvolumen von mehr als 1700 Kubikzentimeter unserem Schädelinhalt gleichkam oder diesen sogar übertraf. Das typische Neandertalergesicht zeigte eine niedrige, fliehende Stirn, vorstehende Knochenwülste über den Augen, vortretende Kiefer und ein fliehendes Kinn. Der Rumpf war lang und hatte einen zylinderförmigen Brustkasten, die Gliedmaßen waren verhältnismäßig kurz, aber sehr muskulös. Die untersetzten Proportionen hängen mit der Anpassung an das kalte Klima zusammen, denn eine solche Körperform gibt weniger Wärme an die Umgebung ab. Viele Jahre nach der Entdeckung der ersten Neandertaler-Fossilien galt *Homo neanderthalensis* als eiszeitlicher Höhlenbewohner. Das traf jedoch nur zum Teil zu. Die möglicherweise von *Homo heidelbergensis* abstammenden Neandertaler erschienen vor 200 000 Jahren, sie lebten in Europa und Westasien. Man betrachtet sie mitunter noch immer als hirnlose Wesen ohne Sprache oder Kultur, die vornübergebeugt durch die Gegend schlurften. Dennoch überlebten sie mehrere Eiszeiten, insbesondere in Europa, und benutzten immer kompliziertere Beile, Speere, Schaber und andere Werkzeuge und Waffen, die typisch für das Moustérien sind. Sie machten wahrscheinlich Jagd auf große Tiere wie das Kältesteppenmammut; sie verfügten vielleicht auch über eine gesprochene Sprache; sie hielten sicherlich Zeremonien ab und bestatteten ihre Toten nach bestimmten kultischen Bräuchen (was sie den heutigen Menschen sehr ähnlich macht und von allen anderen bekannten Tieren völlig unterscheidet). Vor 28 000 Jahren scheinen die Neandertaler jedoch verschwunden zu sein. Vielleicht erlosch ihre Art durch das Auftreten der neuesten Spezies des *Homo – Homo sapiens* –, die sich rasch ausbreitete. Einige Fossilien wie beispielsweise das in Zentralportugal gefundene „Kind von Lagar Velho“ sollen sowohl Merkmale des Neandertalers als auch des modernen Menschen aufweisen, was auf eine Vermischung beider Spezies hindeuten könnte.

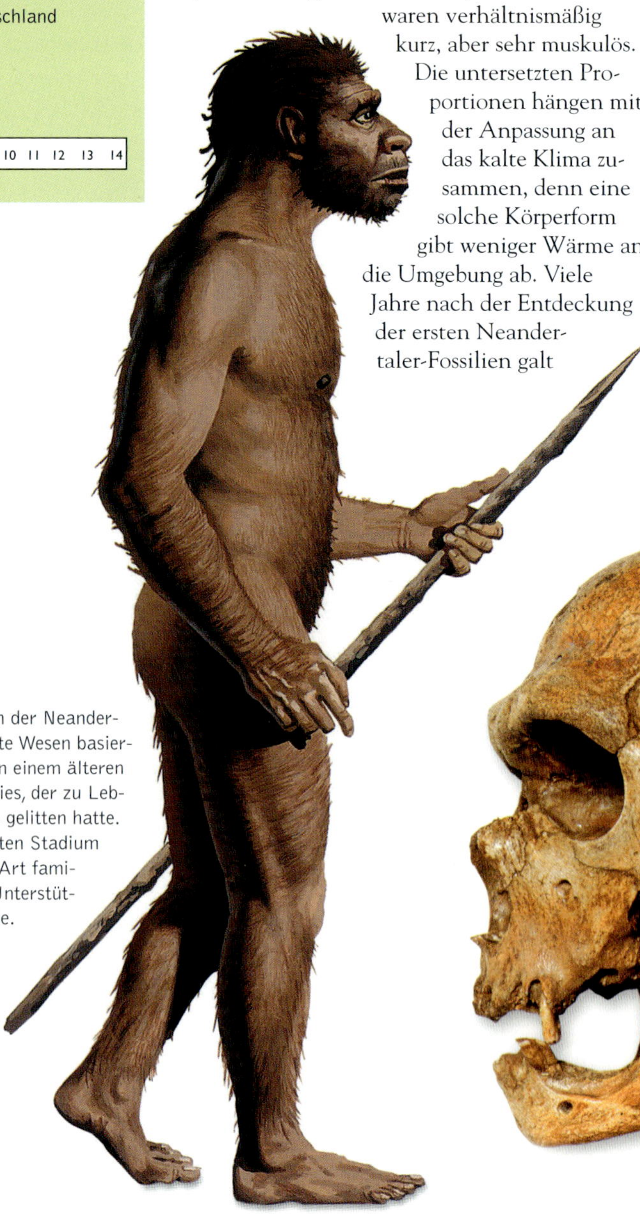

**RECHTS** Ältere Nachbildungen der Neandertaler als gebeugte, missgebildete Wesen basierten auf einem Knochenfund von einem älteren männlichen Vertreter der Spezies, der zu Lebzeiten unter schwerer Arthritis gelitten hatte. Dass dieser bis zu dem bewussten Stadium überlebte, zeigt, dass ihm eine Art familiärer oder sonstiger sozialer Unterstützung und Fürsorge zuteil wurde.

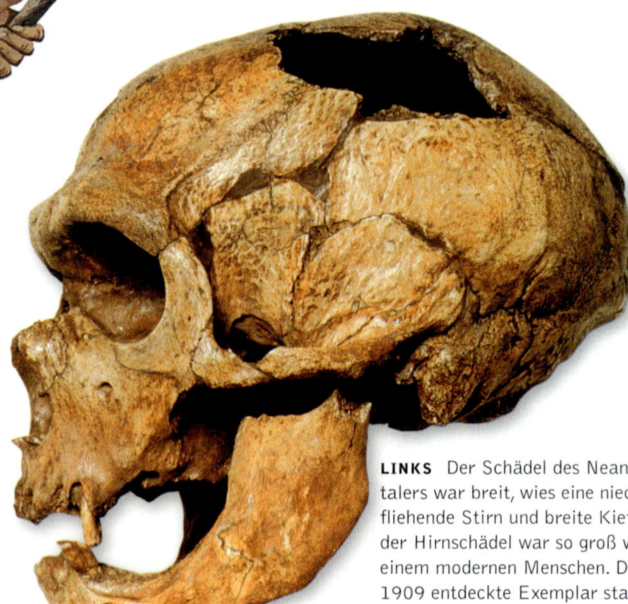

**LINKS** Der Schädel des Neandertalers war breit, wies eine niedrige, fliehende Stirn und breite Kiefer auf; der Hirnschädel war so groß wie bei einem modernen Menschen. Dieses 1909 entdeckte Exemplar stammt aus dem berühmten französischen Höhlenfundort La-Chapelle-aux-Saints.

# HOMO SAPIENS

Von den vielen Hominidenarten, die in den vergangenen Jahrmillionen existierten (siehe Seite 428, zur Entwicklungsgeschichte des Menschen), gibt es nur noch eine Spezies. Eine der wissenschaftlichen Theorien über unsere Abstammung ist die Theorie der „multiregionalen Entwicklung". Sie geht davon aus, dass unsere direkten Vorfahren die Vertreter der Spezies *Homo erectus* waren. Sie breiteten sich über viele Teile der Welt aus und entwickelten sich durch Vermischung mit anderen, regionalen Arten allmählich zu verschiedenen geografischen und ethnischen Gruppen des *Homo sapiens*, die heute rund um den Globus vorzufinden sind. Das „Monogenese-Modell" wiederum baut darauf auf, dass anatomisch moderne menschliche Wesen erstmals in der Zeit vor 200 000 bis 100 000 Jahren in Ost- oder Südafrika erschienen. Bestätigt wird dieses Modell durch Funde von Überresten solcher Wesen und auch durch die Analyse des genetischen Materials heutiger Menschen; die meisten heutigen Paläontologen unterstützen diese Ansicht.

Vor 100 000 Jahren breiteten sich die modernen Menschen in Richtung Norden nach Europa und in Richtung Osten nach Asien aus. Auf dem Weg über das Festland oder vielleicht in primitiven Booten an den Küsten entlang besiedelten sie neue Regionen, passten sich dem jeweiligen Klima und den lokalen Bedingungen an, und so entstanden die verschiedenen Gruppen, die wir heute kennen. Unklar ist, ob sie Vertretern der mit ihnen verwandten Spezies *Homo erectus* begegneten und dann deren Stelle einnahmen oder sich mit ihnen vermischten. Diese modernen Menschen langten vor frühestens 40 000 Jahren in Südostasien und Australien an. Nord- und Südamerika waren vor rund 15 000 Jahren besiedelt; neuere Funde deuten darauf hin, dass die Menschen bereits vor 35 000 Jahren von Nordostasien über die Beringstraße – damals eine Landbrücke – nach Amerika einwanderten. Vor 40 000 Jahren gab es in der Verfeinerung der Werkzeuge, des Körperschmucks, der Zeremonien, der Riten und der Kunst der so genannten Cro-Magnon-Menschen regelrechte Quantensprünge. Dies war die Zeit der sehr jungen Fossilien: Von diesem Punkt an tritt an die Stelle der Paläontologie allmählich die Archäologie, wird aus der Vorgeschichte Geschichte.

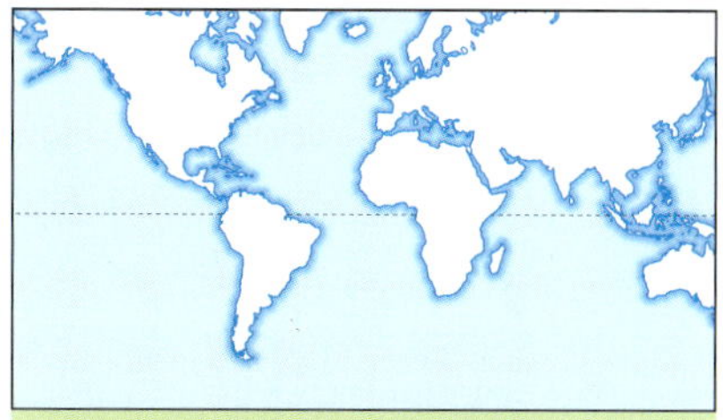

**ÜBERSICHT (HOMINIDEN)**

***Homo sapiens***

**Bedeutung des Namens:** Vernunftbegabter Mensch

**Periode:** Quartär

**Hauptgruppe:** Mammalia (Primates)

**Größe:** Höhe bis 1,8 Meter

**Gewicht:** 50 – 80 Kilogramm

**Nahrung:** Mischkost, darunter Fleisch erlegter Tiere

**Fossilfundstätten:** Weltweit

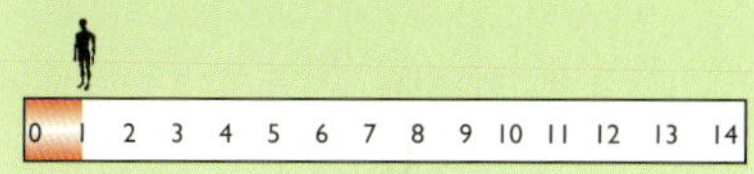


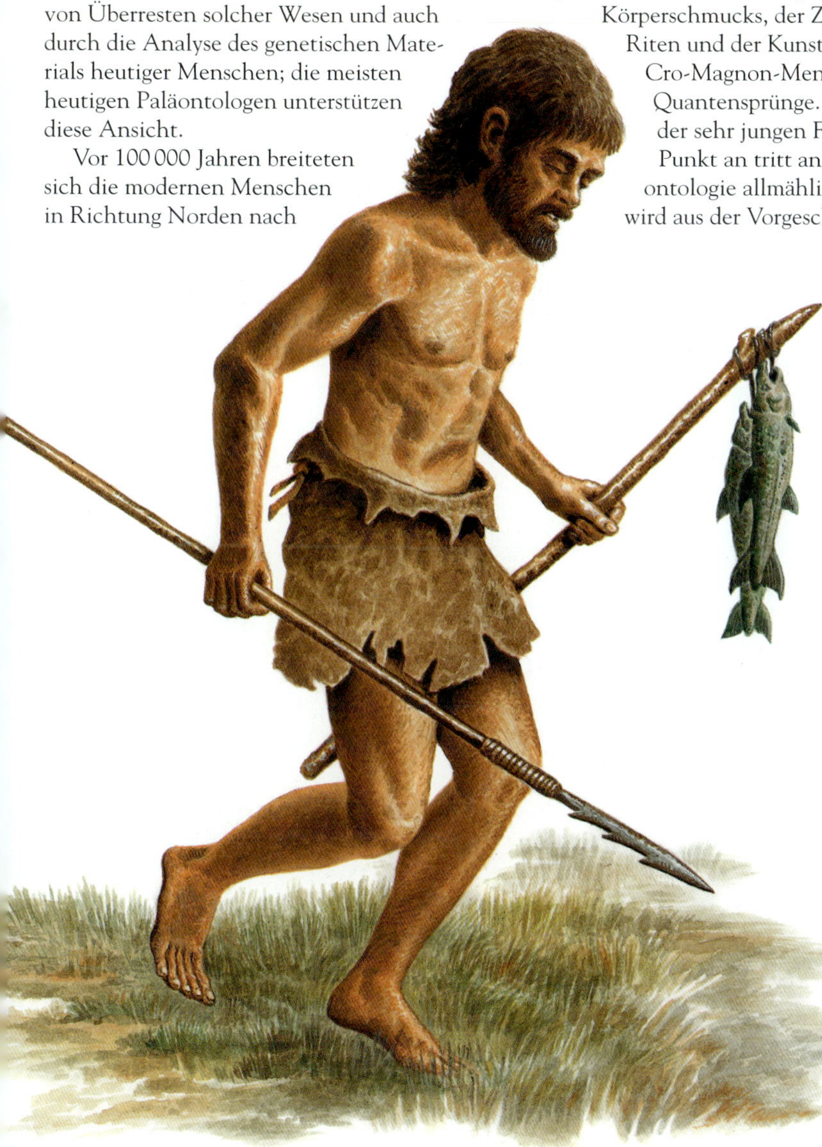

**LINKS** Die Menschen vor rund 100 000 Jahren und danach waren mit den heutigen Menschen anatomisch fast identisch. Ergebnisse genetischer Untersuchungen deuten darauf hin, dass sie einst aus einer ziemlich kleinen Gruppe in Afrika hervorgingen und sich dann weltweit ausbreiteten, wobei es in Europa bedeutende Phasen früher kultureller Entwicklung gab.

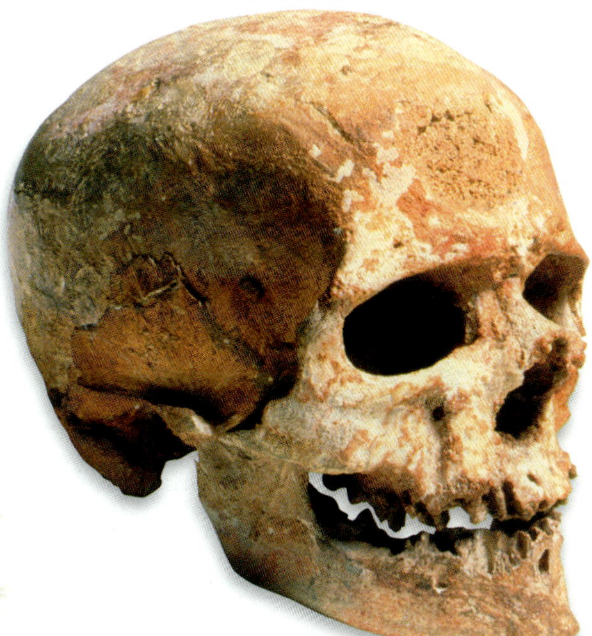

**UNTEN** Verglichen mit dem Schädel eines Neandertalers (gegenüber) hat der des modernen Menschen eine höhere, stärker gewölbte Stirn und kleinere Kiefer.

# EINE NACHBEMERKUNG ZUR EVOLUTION

*Die Entwicklung unserer Spezies Homo sapiens hat mehr und schnellere Veränderungen hervorgerufen, als die Welt je zuvor erlebt hat. Industriegebiete, geplünderte Bodenschätze, eine explosionsartig anwachsende Bevölkerung, aus dem Boden schießende Städte, die Verschmutzung von Boden, Wasser und Luft, die globale Erwärmung und die Reduktion der Ozonschicht gehen mit einem erschreckend raschen Verlust von Natur in all ihren Formen – Urwälder und andere unberührte Gebiete, Pflanzen und Tiere – einher. An der Dauer der Prähistorie gemessen geschieht all das in weniger als einem Augenblick. Welches Erbe werden wir als die Fossilien der Zukunft wohl hinterlassen, falls wir überhaupt ein Erbe hinterlassen?*

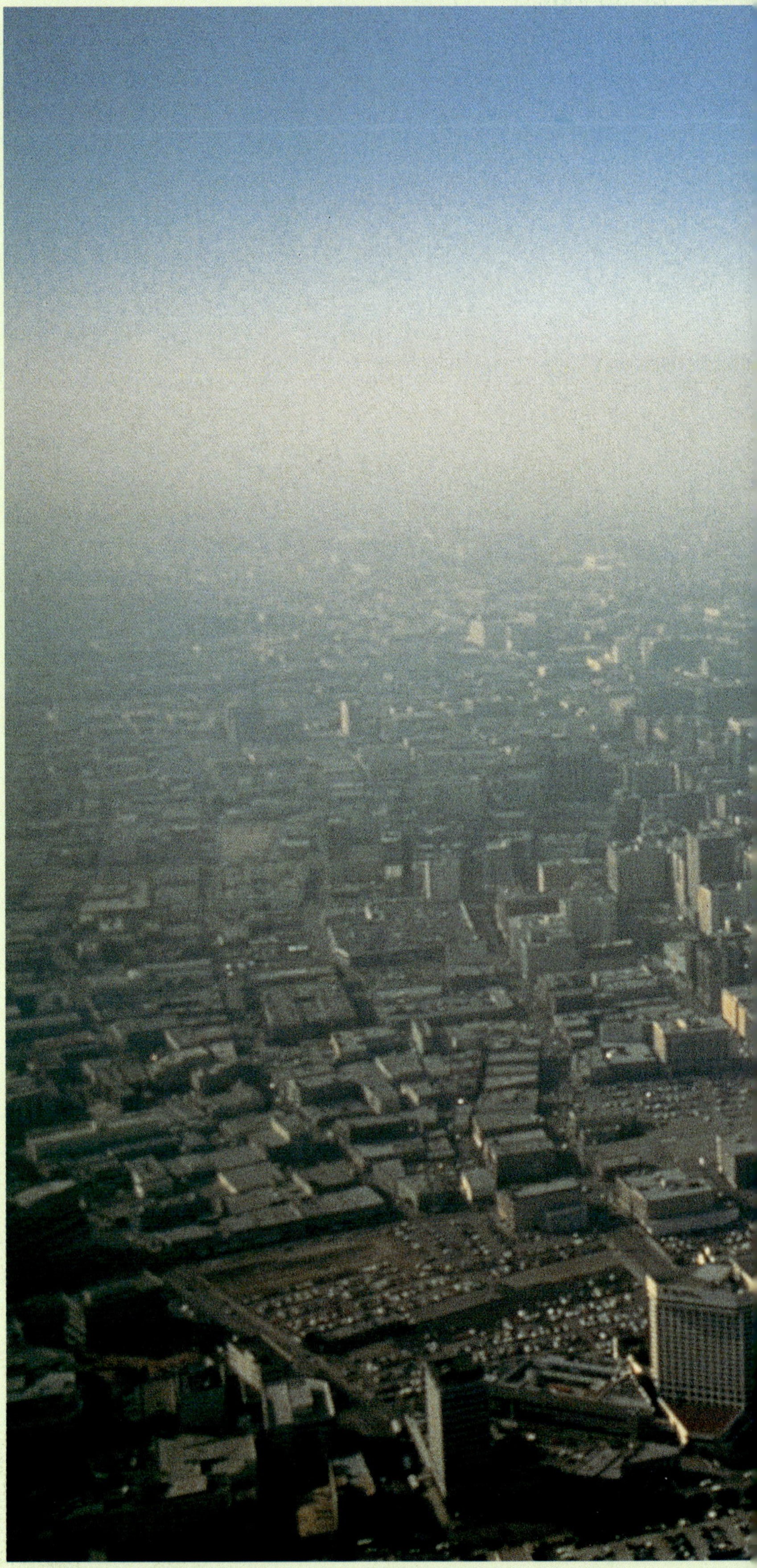

**RECHTS** Unkontrolliert wachsendes Stadtgebiet, so weit das Auge in Los Angeles reicht – was an einem dunstigen Tag, da Luftschadstoffe die Sicht trüben, nicht sehr weit ist. Wie wird diese Gegend in einer Million oder nur in tausend Jahren aussehen? Die Menschen können das gegenwärtige Tempo des Bevölkerungswachstums und der industriellen Entwicklung nicht beibehalten. Unser Planet hat dafür nicht genug Platz und Rohstoffe.

# Bildnachweis

Erläuterung der Abkürzungen
o = oben, u = unten, r = rechts, l = links, M = Mitte

**American Museum of Natural History**
Seite 44, 208, 336

**Ardea**
8, 9, 12 (o), 12 (u), 15, 17, 18, 21 (u), 22, 34, 50, 51, 53, 64, 84, 90 (r), 106 (l), 106 (r), 110 (o), 113, 114, 121 (u), 140, 148, 152 (o l), 152 (l), 155 (u), 170, 173, 186 (l), 196 (l), 202 (l), 205 (r), 212, 218, 223, 227, 272, 279, 282, 289 (r), 303 (r), 304, 311 (l), 314, 350, 354, 355 (l), 355 (r), 370 (l), 372 (l), 374, 393 (r), 424 (l)

**Richard Burgess**
24–25, 26, 27, 436, 437, 438 und sämtliche zu den Übersichtstafeln gehörenden Karten

**Karen Carr**
61 (o), 61 (u), 150, 153, 159, 179, 185, 270, 382, 390, 420

**Dinosaur Isle**
36 (r), 43 (l), 49

**Pamela J. W. Gore**
Georgia Perimeter College
82 (o)

**Steve Kirk**
118, 120, 121 (o), 133, 139, 160, 164, 191, 196 (r), 217, 247, 248, 252, 273, 275, 288, 291, 309, 310, 335, 340, 343, 356, 373, 378

**Marshall Cavendish Archive**
104, 174, 205 (l), 220, 228, 264, 306, 308, 330, 334, 344, 360, 398

**Marshall Editions**
*Colin Newman* 60 (o), 60 (u), 65 (o), 66 (o), 66 (u), 68; *Steve Kirk* 80, 81, 82, 86, 87, 93, 101, 102, 103, 107, 126, 127, 129, 132, 137, 144, 145, 146, 149, 158, 184, 192, 204, 215, 223, 225, 236, 237, 244, 255, 263, 267, 269, 280, 290, 292, 293, 296, 298, 299, 303 (l), 320, 321, 328, 341, 342, 358, 359, 365, 371, 384, 385, 386, 389, 392; *Malcolm Ellis* 411; *Andrew Wheatcroft* 412, 429 (l), 430 (r), 431 (l), 432 (l), *Graham Allen* 413, 414, 415, 416, 419, 426; *Steve Holden* 423; *Andrew Robinson* 425

**Monash Science Centre**
*Peter Trusler* 210, 276

**Oxford Scientific Films Ltd**
5 (u), 122, 130, 134, 152, 165, 168, 176, 190, 206, 214, 243, 250, 274, 319, 325, 333

**Royal Tyrrell Museum**
162, 294, 302, 364 (l)

**Science Photo Library**
2, 10, 11 (o), 13 (o), 13 (u), 14, 15 (u), 16, 19 (o), 19 (u), 23 (l), 23 (r), 25, 30, 32, 35, 37, 40, 41, 42, 43 (r), 48 (l), 48 (r), 54, 55, 56, 62, 65 (u), 69, 70, 72, 74, 75 (o), 75 (u), 76, 80, 87, 99 (l), 112, 142, 160 (l), 180, 186 (r), 240, 256, 322, 332, 338, 366 (o), 366 (u), 378, 386 (l), 393 (l), 394, 395, 397, 404, 406, 409, 424 (r), 427 (r), 428 (l), 429 (r), 430 (l), 431 (r), 432 (r), 433 (r), 434

**John Sibbick**
5 (o), 6, 20, 21, 25, 25, 36 (l), 38, 46, 78, 78, 88, 92, 94, 109, 110 (u), 116, 128, 156, 172, 182, 213, 226, 253, 258, 261, 262, 284, 300, 316, 327, 364 (r), 372 (r), 376, 380, 381, 387, 388

**Joe Tucciarone**
155 (o), 166, 169, 188, 194, 197, 200, 202 (r), 232, 281, 297, 352, 357, 368

**Wildlife Art Ltd**
*Ken Oliver* 52, 67, 83, 85, 98, 100, 108, 111, 178, 198, 216, 222, 231, 233, 234, 235, 238, 239, 242, 245, 254, 287, 289, 311, 313, 318, 347, 367, 396, 401, 418, 422, 427 (l); *Philip Hood* 58 (l), 90, 96, 97, 119, 124, 125, 136, 138, 147, 159, 161, 163, 187, 193, 199, 207, 230, 246, 249, 260, 266, 268, 278, 286, 312, 326, 329, 346, 348, 362, 370, 379, 400, 403, 410, 417, 428 (r), 433 (l), 440, 441, 442, 443, 444, 445; *Myke Taylor* 91, 99 (r), 203, 349, 402; *Wayne Ford* 177, 224

# Danksagung

Steve Parker dankt anerkennend Jane Parker für die Unterstützung seiner Forschungsarbeit, Dr. Paul Barrett vom Londoner Natural History Museum für seine wertvollen Ergänzungen und seine kritischen Anmerkungen zum Text, Peter Coates für seine Informationen über Süßwasserreptilien und John Rush für die „Erweckung" der Dinosaurier zum Leben.

Der Verlag dankt dem Paläontologen Dr. Thomas Holtz, Direktor des Earth, Time & Life Program an der University of Maryland, College Park, für seine Unterstützung; Sarah Whittley von Wildlife Art Ltd für das Organisieren der Herstellung vieler wundervoller Illustrationen für dieses Buch; und Richard Burgess für sämtliche Karten und für die Zeitskala der Vorgeschichte auf den Seiten 24–25.

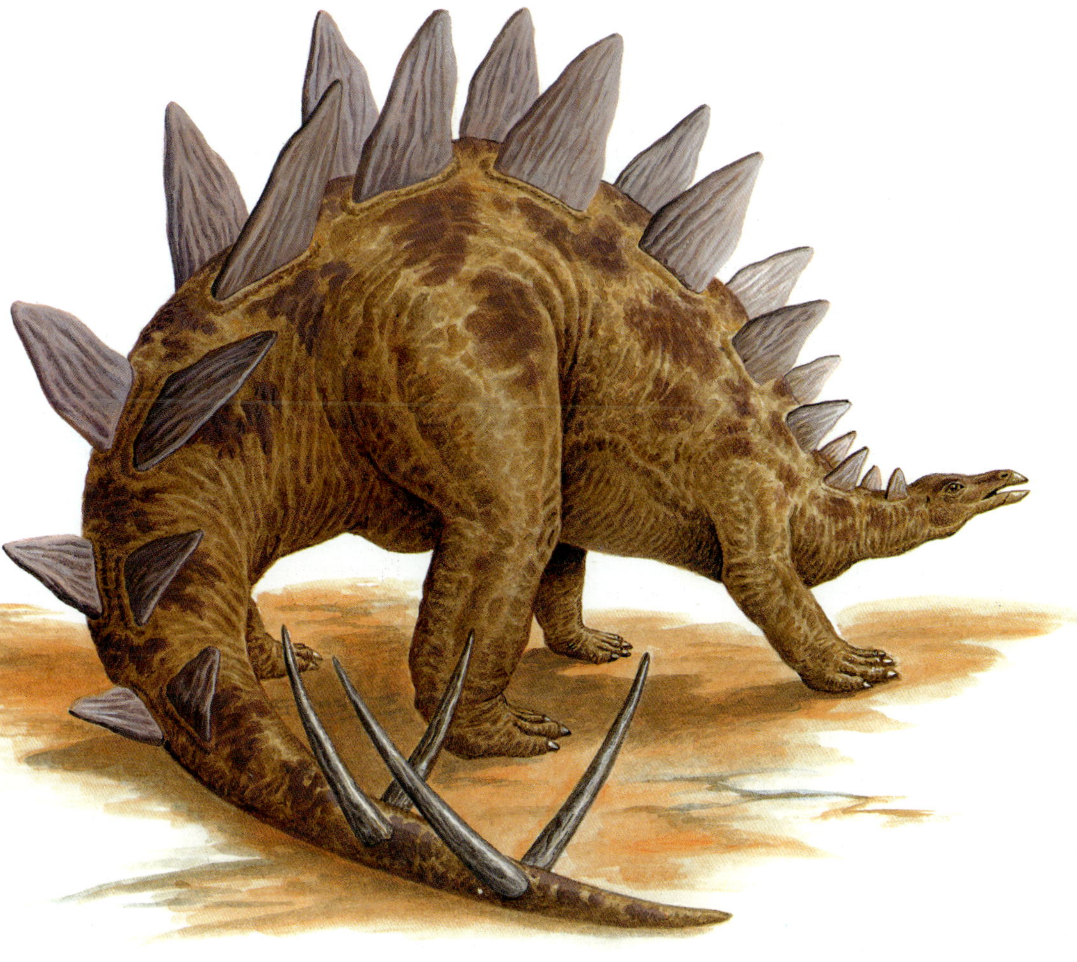

# REGISTER

*Kursiv* gesetzte Seitenzahlen beziehen sich auf Bildunterschriften.

**Halbfett** gesetzte Seitenzahlen verweisen auf Haupteinträge.

## A



## B



## C



## D



## E

# P



# Q



# R



# S



# T



# U



# V



# W



# X



# Y



# Z

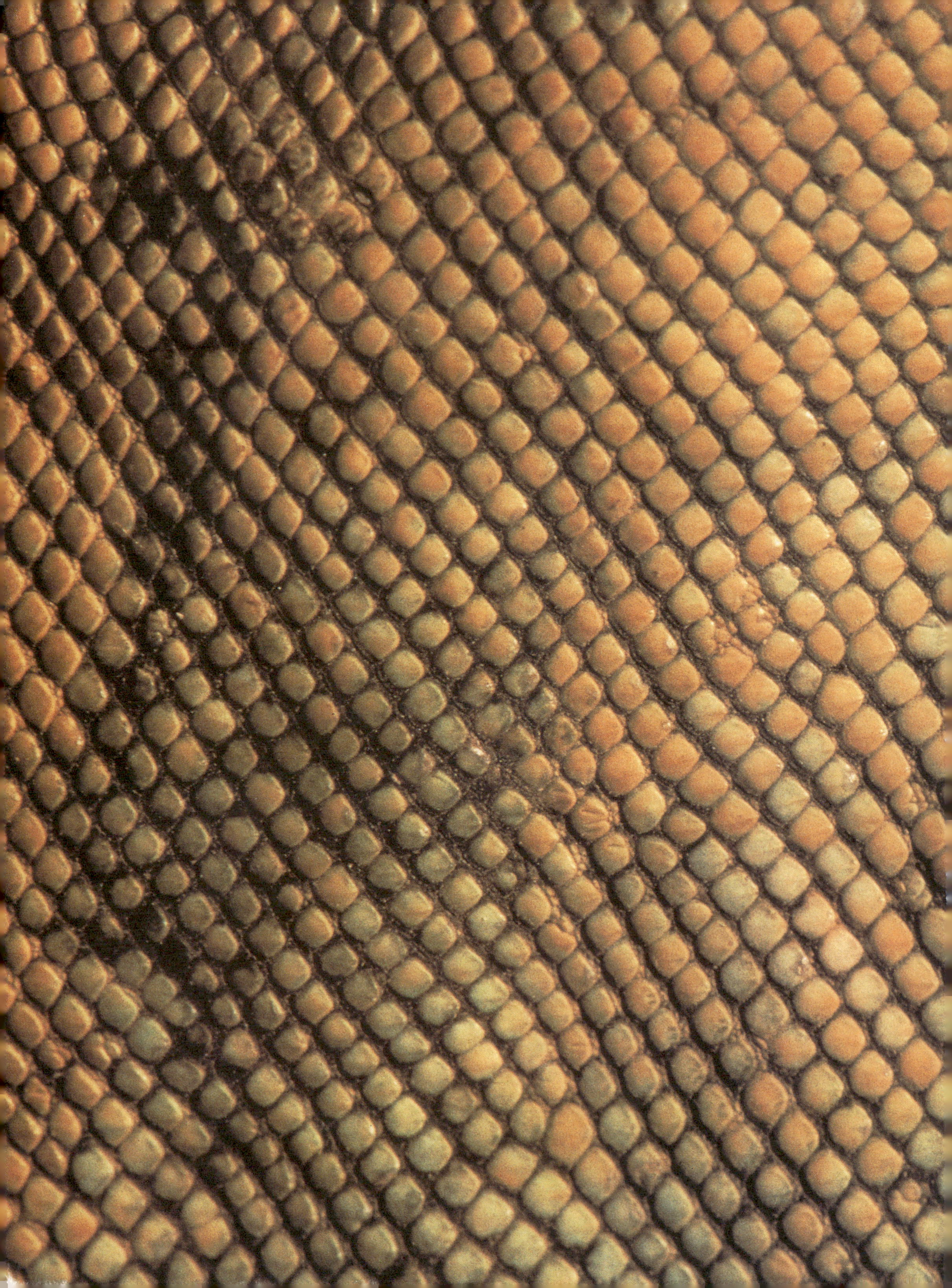